ADULT DEVELOPMENT

LINDA SMOLAK

Kenyon College

Prentice Hall, Englewood Cliffs, New Jersey 07632

Library of Congress Cataloging-in-Publication Data

Smolak, Linda,
    Adult development / Linda Smolak.
        p.   cm.
    Includes bibliographical references and index.
    ISBN 0-13-009044-1
    1. Adulthood--Psychological aspects. 2. Aging--Psychological
aspects. 3. Adulthood--Physiological aspects. 4. Aging-
-Physiological aspects. 5. Aging--Social aspects. I. Title.
BF724.5.S66 1993
155.6--dc20   92-6214
                                                                CIP

To Jim,
who provides much of the social support
for my adult development

Acquisitions editor: Carol Wada and Susan Brennan
Editorial/production supervision and
    interior design: Serena Hoffman
Cover design: Ben Santora
Prepress buyer: Kelly Behr
Manufacturing buyer: Mary Ann Gloriande
Copy editor: Jeannine Ciliotta

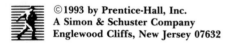

©1993 by Prentice-Hall, Inc.
A Simon & Schuster Company
Englewood Cliffs, New Jersey 07632

Printed in the United States of America
10 9 8 7 6 5 4 3 2 1

ISBN 0-13-009044-1

PRENTICE-HALL INTERNATIONAL (UK) LIMITED, *London*
PRENTICE-HALL OF AUSTRALIA PTY. LIMITED, *Sydney*
PRENTICE-HALL CANADA INC., *Toronto*
PRENTICE-HALL HISPANOAMERICANA, S.A., *Mexico*
PRENTICE-HALL OF INDIA PRIVATE LIMITED, *New Delhi*
PRENTICE-HALL OF JAPAN, INC., *Tokyo*
SIMON & SCHUSTER ASIA PTE. LTD., *Singapore*
EDITORA PRENTICE-HALL DO BRASIL, LTDA., *Rio de Janeiro*

Contents

PART II: YOUNG ADULTHOOD

4   PHYSICAL AND COGNITIVE DEVELOPMENT   72

5   PERSONALITY   103

6   FAMILY AND SOCIAL RELATIONSHIPS   132

7   WORK   173

PART III: MIDDLE AGE

PART IV: OLD AGE

Preface

When I graduated from Temple University in 1980, their developmental program was one of the few truly life-span programs in the country. Indeed, people still thought that all the action was in child or adolescent development. Although there was some slight interest in the elderly, the really neglected groups were young and middle-aged adults. There just did not seem to be much going on.

Now, of course, everyone has heard of the mid-life crisis. People routinely wonder why the divorce rate is so high. Dual-career couples wonder whether their work and marriage can survive having a child. And we all wonder whether physical decline is inevitable. There are just a few examples of the burgeoning interest in all phases of adulthood. It has become clear that development can and does continue throughout the life span as adults face new challenges and opportunities.

Adult development is a rapidly growing field of research and theory, and because it is still a young field, there are many unanswered questions. Throughout this book, you may often be frustrated by our ability to describe situations but not explain them. You may also be frustrated by our inability to solve many of the problems that are presented. But I hope you will also be invigorated by the positive accomplishments and outcomes of the study of adult development. Furthermore, I hope you will take the unanswered questions as a challenge for future research you might develop.

As a teacher and student of both child and adult development, I am particularly impressed with the individual differences among adults. It is clear that both genetics and environment contribute to these differences. We must consider environment as broadly as possible, to include not only a person's immediate environment but also broader social forces. You will see that cohort, sex, race, and socioeconomic status all constrain or facilitate development in various ways. Similarly, the decisions people make about marriage, career, children, and life style all have short-term and long-term implications. Individuality embedded within commonality will be, I hope, a source of unending hypotheses for you.

Writing a book of this length takes time. My editors at Prentice Hall have been unrelentingly supportive and patient. I especially wish to thank Susan Brennan and Carol Wada for their pushes when I stalled. My colleagues in the Psychology Department at Kenyon College have been similarly supportive. I extend special thanks to Michael Levine, Art Lecesse, and Sarah Murnen, who not only offered support but provided assistance in gathering material and discussing ideas. Thanks also to John and Amy Macionis for their advice and aid.

I want to thank the following reviewers for their insightful analyses of the rough manuscript: Fredda Blanchard-Fields, Louisiana State University; Victoria J. Molfese, Southern Illinois University at Carbondale; Eugene Thomas, University of Connecticut; Harvey Lesser, Rutgers University; Steven W. Cornelius, Cornell University; Charles W. Johnson, University of Evansville; Mark Byrd, University of Kansas; Janet W. Johnson, University of Maryland; Denise R. Barnes Nacost, University of Carolina at Chapel Hill; and Evan G. DeRenzo, Marymount University.

The students in my adult development classes over the past decade have forced me to clarify my thinking and presentation. Their questions formed much of the organization of this book. I appreciate their help.

Finally, my family, as always, was always supportive. My children—Marlyce, Jesse, and Meghan—kept me going with their praise for how much I'd already completed. They also helped with the index. My husband, Jim, led me to numerous articles in economics that have been important in several of the chapters. For his assistance and his constant support, I am especially grateful.

Linda Smolak

1 Issues and Models of Adult Development

An actress in her forties recently appeared on a late-night talk show. She had dressed in the style of a popular rock star, who she claimed was her new hero. The talk show host asked the actress if she wasn't a bit old for adoring fan behavior.

Within a few weeks of that interview, an item appeared in gossip columns quoting the teenage daughter of another well-known actress. The daughter said she was often embarrassed by her mother's appearance (which included revealing clothing and unusual hairstyles). She also said that she often tried to curb her mother's spending habits. In reporting these statements, most of the columnists commented on the irony of a teenager being embarrassed by her mother's trendy, sexy appearance and extravagance.

These anecdotes are an appropriate beginning to a text on adult development because they demonstrate our belief in *age roles* (Neugarten, Moore, & Lowe, 1965/1968). We expect that people of different ages will behave differently in terms of how they look, how they spend their free time, how they think (their attitudes and values), and how they speak. It is acceptable for a 14-year-old to dress like a rock star. After all, a 14-year-old *should* be experimenting with styles, values, and attitudes. We expect adolescents to assume the identity of others, including public personalities. But by 40, a person should be less susceptible to such influences. Forty-year-olds should know who they are. Indeed, if they don't, we use the term "midlife crisis" to explain what we see as their inconsistent and somewhat juvenile behavior.

Age roles, like sex roles, are learned behaviors. Society defines *age norms,* which express what behaviors are considered typical (or normative) for normal people of different ages. These norms are indicative of shared cultural values. Most members of a society can define various age groups and describe age-appropriate behavior, but they are not usually aware of

1

the impact of these expectations on their own daily lives (Neugarten et al., 1965/1968). These norms are also evident in certain *age-graded* events. These events tend to occur at about the same time for most members of a society. Some of these events are biological (like puberty), but many others are "socially programmed . . . associated with specific social expectations, changing roles and task requirements, and altering patterns of privileges and responsibilities" (Hetherington & Baltes, 1988, p. 10). Such events are thought to influence development (Baltes, 1987; Hetherington & Baltes, 1988). Examples include starting school, graduation, and retirement.

Since age norms are socially defined, age roles vary from culture to culture. In Bali, for example, postmenopausal women are expected to be less modest in their dress and language than younger women (Bart, 1971). In Samoa, the elderly are given the best housing and can behave as they wish with no fear of punishment. Younger Samoan men regularly seek out older men for advice and counsel (Cowgill, 1972, cited in Wallace & Wallace, 1985). Such practices and attitudes are markedly inconsistent with American values.

Cultural differences may sometimes contribute to animosity between groups. Ed Magnuson (1990), for example, referred to age roles in explaining tension between black residents and Korean shopkeepers in New York City:

> The most common black complaint is that Korean merchants treat them rudely. Some shopkeepers concede that the complaints are often valid but cite cultural conflicts. Black youngsters think nothing of saying "Hey, man!" to store owners accustomed to being treated deferentially in their homeland. Koreans, who highly respect their elders, do not joke back. (Magnuson, 1990, p. 22)

Every society pressures people of various ages into appropriate behavior. Some of the pressure is quite formal, as in mandatory retirement ages. Other pressure is more informal, as in the familiar rebuke "act your age," or in the expectations of what activities people of different ages will enjoy. In other words, *socialization,* the process by which we acquire socially defined roles and behaviors, continues throughout adulthood. But there are differences between the socialization of children and that of adults (Tischler, Whitten & Hunter, 1983). First, adults are far more aware of their own socialization than children are; in fact, they may actively participate in their own socialization by choosing to go to school or to change careers. Second, adult socialization often involves *resocialization*—exposure to roles, attitudes, and values that conflict with those acquired earlier. Think, for example, of the changes in attitudes toward women in the workforce or the reorientation a full-time homemaker may go through after a divorce.

The purpose of this book is to describe how people's roles change throughout adulthood. We also describe how individual characteristics—physiological, social, emotional, intellectual, and motivational—change. But description alone is inadequate; we also offer explanations for what changes and what does not. Some of the explanations focus on external factors, others on internal ones. Most, however, suggest a combination of internal and external forces working in conjunction to produce either stability or change. Indeed, internal and external factors are not mutually exclusive. For example, certain personal characteristics might lead an individual to choose a particular environment, which in turn leads to a particular developmental path (Scarr & McCartney, 1983).

Before we look at various developmental phenomena during different periods of adulthood, it is important to place adult development theory and research within a context. Professional interest in adult development is fairly recent, but it is not unrelated to other areas of psychology. Thus, we begin by looking at the historical and philosophical development of the field and then turn to research methodology issues. Only then will we be ready to examine adult development in detail.

SCIENTIFIC INTEREST IN AGING

The existence of age roles indicates that we have always known development continues throughout life. Yet scientific interest in adult development is a relatively recent phenomenon; the National Institute on Aging in the United States was not founded until 1974. This does not mean, however, that there was no interest in adulthood and aging prior to the 1970s; people have long been fascinated by aging.

A Historical Overview

Historically, there has always been great interest in reversing the aging process. In the Greek myth of Aurora and Tithonus, Aurora wished for eternal life for her husband, Tithonus, and Zeus granted her wish. But Aurora neglected to ask for eternal youth for Tithonus, so he suffered all the physical and psychological declines of aging, but could not die (Hamilton, 1942). In a similar vein, the Spaniard Ponce de León, searching for the fountain of youth, instead discovered Florida in 1513. Sir Francis Bacon (1561–1626) argued that the study of aging would help to uncover its causes. He personally believed that poor hygiene was the major reason for aging. Sir Francis Galton (1822–1911), a cousin of Charles Darwin, also studied aging. By observing over nine thousand people aged 5 to 80, he demonstrated many age-related changes in such characteristics as grip strength, hearing, and vision (Birren & Clayton, 1975).

Modern scientific interest in aging began in the 1920s. In psychology, G. Stanley Hall's (1922) *Senescence, the Second Half of Life* was a landmark contribution. He first reported the now widely documented finding that the elderly do not fear death as much as young people do (see Chapter 17). During the same period, the Russian Ivan Pavlov, discoverer of classical conditioning, reported age-related changes in ease of training people to form associations by means of classical conditioning (Birren & Clayton, 1975).

Despite this interest, research and theorizing on adulthood and aging made very slow progress. This was at least partially because of Freud's suggestion that personality was basically formed by about age 5 (Gould, 1972; Labouvie, 1982). Indeed, when Roger Gould presented his theory of adult personality development in 1972, he lamented the lack of scientific interest in adult development. Of course, several important works had already been published, notably Erik Erikson's (1963) theory of life-span development, Bernice Neugarten's (1964; 1966) research on personality development, and K. Warner Schaie's (1970) work on intellectual changes. It was, in fact, during the 1960s and 1970s that interest in adult development began to grow dramatically (Birren & Clayton, 1975). But scientists were not the only people with an increasing interest in adult development. Demographic changes have increased the percentage of our population that is elderly, necessitating a greater understanding of adult development.

The Graying of America

Increased longevity, lower fertility, and the coming of age of the "baby boomers" have combined to produce an effect popularly known as the *graying of America.* Simply put, this means that the percentage of the American population that is elderly is growing more rapidly than other age groups (see Figure 1–1). In 1980, people 65 years and older constituted 11 percent of the American population. In raw numbers, this translates to about 25 million elderly Americans. By 2030, about 59 million Americans will be at least 65 years old. If fertility rates continue at their current level, with the average American woman giving birth to two children, the elderly will make up about 19 percent of the American population in 2030. Of course, if

FIGURE 1-1:   Projected Proportion of Persons Aged 65 and Over in the U.S. Population, 1980–2050.

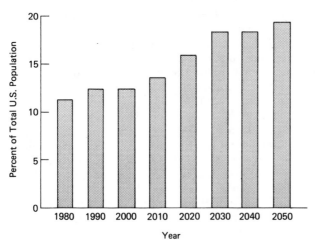

Source: Based on data from Bouvier, L. (1980). America's baby boom: The fateful bulge. *Population Bulletin, 35,* 29.

women start having more children, the percentage of the population that is elderly will be smaller, but actual numbers of elderly will still be more than double what they were in 1980 (Bouvier, 1980).

Longevity: A person born in the United States in 1900 could expect to live to be 47.3 years old (World Almanac, 1981). In 1988, an American newborn had a life expectancy of 74.8 years old (*Statistical Abstract,* 1990). In general, women can expect to live longer than men, and white life expectancy is longer than black (see Table 1–1). There is also evidence that people of higher social classes have historically outlived poorer people (Friedlander, Schellekens, Ben-Moshe, & Keyser, 1985; Pamuk, 1985).

Improved medical care and a better understanding of what causes disease are probably the major factors in the increased life expectancy of Americans. We are now more likely to survive heart attacks and accidents. For example, the rate of death from heart diseases in 1960 was about 286 per 100,000 Americans over 15 years old. By 1988, this figure had dropped to 167 per 100,000 (U.S. Department of Commerce, 1990). At the same time, we have learned more about how to prevent such diseases; we now know, for example, the risks of cigarette smoking and we have substantially altered our lifestyles to avoid them.

Vaccinations against many killer diseases, such as smallpox, whooping cough, and polio, have also contributed to increased life expectancy by dramatically improving the chances of surviving beyond childhood. This raises an important point about life expectancy figures. The higher the death rate in childhood, the lower life expectancy will be. Thus, a life expectancy of 47 years old in 1900 does not mean that no one lived to be 50 or 60. There have always been old people. What is new is the number of Americans who are living to be old. In colonial America, for example, only about 2 percent of the population was 65 or older (Spencer, 1985) compared to about 11 percent in 1980.

TABLE 1–1: Expectation of Life in Years by Sex and Race

		WHITE		BLACK	
Age in 1986	Total	Male	Female	Male	Female
Newborn	74.8	72.0	78.8	65.2	73.5
1	74.6	71.7	78.4	65.5	73.7
10	65.8	62.9	69.6	56.8	65.0
20	56.2	53.4	59.9	47.3	55.3
40	37.4	34.9	40.5	30.3	36.6
60	20.4	18.2	22.6	16.1	20.3
80	8.1	6.9	8.8	6.8	8.5

Expectation of life in years means number of years a person of this age can expect to live. Thus, 80-year-old white women, on the average, can expect to live another 8.8 years, to almost 89 years.

Source: Adapted from *U.S. Statistical Abstract, 1990,* p. 74. Washington, D.C.: Government Printing Office.

Greater numbers and increased longevity have not only contributed to the growing interest in aging; as more and more people live to be older, age roles may change. The result may be that 40-year-olds in the 1990s may behave differently from 40-year-olds in the 1930s. More middle-aged women, for example, are returning to the workforce after their children are grown, partly because they have so much time ahead of them. Such differences are known as *cohort effects*. In certain types of research designs, these can be mistaken for age differences (see Chapter 2).

Longevity may also affect the norms defining stages of life. As more and more people live to be 80 or 90, 60 may no longer seem "old." In addition, differences in life expectancy from culture to culture (see Table 1–2) may make it difficult to attach universally applicable ages to stages of adult development. In societies where people live fewer years, the age markers for middle and old age may differ from our own.

Increased longevity also carries social implications. As the number of elderly increases, we will need to provide more medical care, housing, and financial support to older Americans. Consider, for example, the impact of providing care for victims of Alzheimer's disease. Recent estimates indicate that the prevalence rate of Alzheimer's in community dwelling samples aged 65 to 74 is about 3 percent. But for those aged 75 to 84, the prevalence rate is 18.7; and for those 85 and older, the rate may be 47.2 percent (Evans et al., 1989) (see Chapter 12). If population projections are correct, the number of very old people (over 80) will increase to about 21 million by the year 2040, compared to about 5 million in 1970 (Bouvier, 1980). This huge growth in the elderly population is partially due to the maturation of the baby boomers.

TABLE 1–2:   Life Expectancy at Birth (in Years) for Males and Females in Various Countries

Country	Years Reported	Male	Female
Uruguay	1985–90	67.8	74.4
Vietnam	1988	59.4	63.8
Swaziland	1985–90	53.7	57.3
Phillipines	1988	61.8	65.5
Sweden	1987	74.2	80.2
Jordan	1986	65.0	68.8
Hungary	1987	65.7	73.7
Egypt	1986	59.0	62.1
Costa Rica	1985–90	72.4	77.0
China	1988	68.1	71.0
Bangladesh	1988	51.3	50.6
Afghanistan	1987	40.6	41.6
USSR	1987	65.1	73.8

Source: Based on data from Daume, D. (1990). *Britannica Book of the Year*, pp. 754–755. Chicago, IL: Encyclopaedia Britannica.

The Baby Boomers: Following World War II, and especially between 1950 and 1962, an unusually high number of children were born in the United States. This demographic phenomenon is commonly referred to as the *baby boom.* At every point in their lives, these baby boomers have had a major impact on American society. In the 1950s and 1960s, for example, the educational system was strained by too many children and too few schools and teachers. The baby boomers are now middle-aged, creating a large demand for housing and jobs (Bouvier, 1980).

The impact of the baby boom on the number of elderly in the United States will begin to be felt by 2010. A large percentage of these people will live to be quite old, which will raise numerous social policy issues. In fact, it is partially in response to the aging of the baby boom that Congress raised the eligibility age for Social Security (see Chapter 16). Some policymakers have suggested that without careful planning, the burden on young workers for providing Social Security and other services to aged baby boomers may be excessive (Bouvier, 1980).

To find out what services these elderly people will need, as well as their potential contributions to society, we need to better understand adult development and functioning. We need to know, for example, when memory and intellectual functioning start to decline (if they do), and we also need to know what factors in earlier adult development affect functioning in old age. The need for such information has spurred the growth of adult development as a field of study and helped to define the central issues.

THE GOALS OF LIFE-SPAN DEVELOPMENTAL PSYCHOLOGY

During the last three or four decades, the study of development has been extended beyond childhood and adolescence into adulthood, in a new field often called *life-span developmental psychology.* In some cases, the extension simply involves applying concepts from child and adolescent work. Other theorists and researchers have offered new propositions about the nature of development to better suit the needs of a truly life-span approach (Hetherington & Baltes, 1988). Some of these new propositions are summarized in Table 1–3.

Describing Change

Development as Change: One goal of life-span developmental psychology is to describe the constancy and change in behavior that is related to age. Notice there is no claim here that age actually causes the changes. We cannot even make this claim when discussing biological changes, because different people show varying rates of physiological change. The age range for menopause, for example, is from about 45 to 55 and is influenced by factors ranging from genetics to weight to cigarette smoking (see Chapter 8). In fact, Paul Baltes and Sherry Willis (1977) have argued that age may not be the best way to conceptualize or monitor time-related change. They

TABLE 1-3:   Summary of Family of Theoretical Propositions Characteristic of Life-Span Developmental Psychology

Concepts	Propositions
Life-span development	Ontogenetic development is a life-long process. No age period holds primacy in regulating the nature of development. During development and at all stages of the life-span, both continuous (cumulative) and discontinuous (innovative) processes are at work.
Development as gain/loss	The process of development in any given class of behavior is complex, and not a simple movement toward efficacy such as incremental growth. Rather, throughout life development is always constituted by the joint occurrence of gain (growth) and loss (decline).
Multidirectionality	The direction of change varies by categories of behavior. In addition, during the same developmental periods, some systems of behavior show increases, whereas others evince decreases in level of functioning.
Plasticity	Much intra-individual plasticity (within-person modifiability) is found in psychological development. Depending on the life conditions and experiences by a given individual, his or her developmental course can take many forms.
Historical embeddedness	Ontogenetic development can also vary substantially in accordance with historical-cultural conditions. How ontogenetic (age-related) development proceeds is markedly influenced by the kind of sociocultural conditions existing in a given historical period, and by how these evolve over time.
Contextualism as paradigm	Any particular course of individual development can be understood as the outcome of the interactions (dialectics) among three systems of developmental influences: age-graded, history-graded, and nonnormative. These systems also show interindividual differentiation in conjunction with biological and social structure.
Field of development as multidisciplinary	Psychological development needs to be seen in the interdisciplinary context provided by other disciplines (e.g., anthropology, biology, sociology) concerned with human development. The openness of the life-span perspective to interdisciplinary posture implies that a "purist" psychological view offers but a partial representation of behavioral development from conception to death.

Source: Hetherington, E. M., & Baltes, P. B. (1988). Child psychology and life-span development. In E. Hetherington, R. Lerner, & M. Perlmutter (eds.). *Child development in a life-span perspective,* p. 4. Hillsdale, NJ: Erlbaum.

As more people live to old age, the political agenda in this country will have to reflect their needs for services.

point out, for example, that there is often a decline in intellectual functioning within the two years preceding death, independently of the person's age.

It is also important to note that change need not be "positive"—that is, growth or progression oriented—in order to be considered development (Hetherington & Baltes, 1988). A definition that precluded looking at decline would tend to make it seem that the childhood and adolescent years were more "important" than the adult years. This perspective is inconsistent with the life-span approach, which argues that all stages of life are equally important (Hetherington & Baltes, 1988). Furthermore, the exclusive focus on positive change overlooks the losses of efficiency that often accompany even childhood growth. There is, for example, some loss in perceptual (visual) accuracy as conceptual developmental occurs in young children (Baltes, 1987).

Life-span developmentalists argue that development is often a *gain-loss process*. A loss in one area may be accompanied by a gain in another. So, for example, the elderly often experience losses in reserve capacity for "peak" intellectual functioning. They can, and apparently do, compensate for this by being selective about the intellectual tasks they tackle (Baltes, 1987). They may focus on tasks most important for daily living. These tasks will include habit patterns that require little "processing space" and hence help to utilize the available capacity most efficiently. Should the situation change, the elderly person could switch focus and excel in another area. The point here is that while there may be general losses, the elderly often are more efficient than young adults (and therefore experience a "gain") in certain specific tasks.

The other reason it would be inappropriate to focus only on growth is that development seems to be both *multidimensional and multidirectional* (Baltes, 1987; Hetherington & Baltes, 1988). We cannot just talk about changes in intelligence, because different types of intelligence have different developmental paths (see Chapters 8 and 13). Similarly, some areas of personality seem to change while others are fairly consistent across adulthood (see Chapters 9 and 14).

Adults surely can change. This is particularly evident after an unusual and demanding event such as a divorce or a sudden job loss. There is, then, plasticity in development (Hetherington & Baltes, 1988); it is not fixed by early events. Rather, previous development increases the probability that later development will move in certain directions. Having a baby as a teenager may set a woman on a path of poverty, depression, and unsatisfying marital relationships. However, such a path can be reversed by job training, appropriate day care, and social support (Hetherington & Baltes, 1988).

In describing adult behavior, the primary focus is typically on *intraindividual* change, changes within the individual (Baltes & Goulet, 1970; Baltes & Willis, 1977; Labouvie, 1982). How does a person's memory, personality, or intellectual functioning change? Does memory get poorer? Does the person become more self-centered? Ideally, we would hope there is some consistency in such changes across individuals. Indeed, this is what theorists who propose universally applicable stages of adult development assume. Table 1–4 presents the stage theories of Erik Erikson, Daniel Levinson, K. Warner Schaie, Roger Gould, and Robert Havighurst.

Examinations of intra-individual development include consideration of how modifiable a behavior (or a loss) is, as well as the circumstances under which the modification might occur (Baltes, 1987). This modifiability is sometimes called *plasticity* and refers to the potential people have to develop or behave in different ways. It is clearly the case that a behavior may look consistent (or even rigid) because of the consistency of the environmental demands. On the other hand, studies show that changes in nursing home staff behavior may alter the level of dependency exhibited by elderly clients (Baltes & Baltes, 1982).

Since we are interested in the factors that influence development, we also look at *interindividual* differences and similarities (Baltes, 1987). This focus prevents us from overgeneralizing research findings. For example, Carol Gilligan (1982a and b) has argued that early life-span developmental psychologists erred in overlooking the differences between male and female development. Furthermore, if we assume that the environment, including non-normative events, is a major force in development, then it follows that as people age, they become increasingly distinctive individuals.

Indeed, different choices (career, marital partner, and so on) may well have resulted in a different outcome for an individual (Baltes & Baltes, 1982; Hetherington & Baltes, 1988). A college education, for example, may facilitate personal development (Rest & Thoma, 1985). College-educated people tend to marry later; they also have fewer children than their peers.

1st class - Erikson?

TABLE 1-4:   Models of Development

Erikson's Psychosocial Crises (The first four stages are childhood stages)

Age	Crisis	Description
Adolescence	Identity versus Role Confusion	Establishing sense of self which links past, present, and future. Sense of self as unique yet having a place in society.
Young adult	Intimacy versus Isolation	A love relationship that allows sharing work, play, and daily living. Based on trust and mutuality.
Middle adult	Generativity versus Stagnation	Passing on skills, knowledge, and values to the next generation. This may be at work or in the family.
Maturity	Ego integrity versus Despair	A sense that you did the best you could with your life. No regrets. Trust in oneself and humanity.

Levinson's Model of Adult Male Development

	Age	Description
Early adulthood	17–21	*Early adult transition.* Begin to form initial definition of self as an adult and to make choices that will lead to initial place in adult world.
	22–28	*Entering the adult world.* Exploration of adult-life options; creation of stable life structure.
	28–33	*Age 30 transition.* Transition into "realities" of adult life. Recognition that one needs to work on one's flaws and imperfections now.
	33–40	*Settling down.* Establishment of niche in society. Planning and attaining major goals. Contributing to society. Now an "adult."
Middle adulthood	40–45	*Midlife transition.* Transition from early to middle adulthood. Questioning of values, accomplishments.
	45–50	*Entering middle life.* Issues are similar to 22–28 but with a broadened perspective.
	50–55	*Age 50 transition.* Modification of life style based on midlife transition.
	55–60	*Culmination of middle adulthood.* Building middle life structure again.
	60–65	*Late Adult Transition.*
	65–80	*Late Adulthood.*
	80+	*Late, Late Adulthood.* Process of aging overshadows process of growth.

TABLE 1-4:   (continued)

Schaie's Model of Adult Cognitive Development

Stage Name and Age	Description
Acquisitive (Childhood)	Development of basic cognitive structures (as described, for example, by Piaget). Learning for the sake of learning.
Achieving (Young adult)	Cognitive behavior becomes more goal oriented toward achievement and independence.
Responsible (Middle adult)	Integration of personal goals with family responsibilities in solving real-life problems.
Executive (Middle adult)	Not universal. Involves dealing with complex organizational hierarchies before making a decision.
Reintegrative (Old age)	Increased selectivity in choosing problems to be solved. Problem must have meaning to the individual's own life to be of interest, though some older adults will be interested in more cosmic questions in the interest of gaining wisdom.

Gould's Seven Developmental Stages of Adult Life

Stage	Age	Development(s)
1.	16–18	*Desire to escape parental control.*
2.	18–22	*Leaving the family:* peer group orientation.
3.	22–28	*Developing independence:* commitment to a career and to children.
4.	29–34	*Questioning self:* role confusion; marriage and career vulnerable to dissatisfaction.
5.	35–43	*Urgency to attain life's goals:* awareness of time limitation; realignment of life goals.
6.	43–53	*Settling down:* acceptance of one's life.
7.	53–60	*More tolerance:* acceptance of past; less negativism.

Havighurst's Developmental Tasks

Young adulthood: (18–30)
1. Courting and selecting a mate for marriage.
2. Learning to adjust to, and living harmoniously with, a marriage partner.
3. Beginning a family and assimilating the new role of parent.
4. Rearing children and meeting their individual needs.
5. Learning to manage a home and assuming household responsibilities.
6. Embarking on a career and/or continuing one's education.
7. Assuming some type of civic responsibility.
8. Searching for a congenial social group.

Middle age: (30–55)
1. Helping teenage children to become responsible and happy adults.
2. Achieving adult social and civic responsibility.
3. Reaching and maintaining satisfactory performance in one's occupation.
4. Developing adult leisure-time activities.

TABLE 1–4:   (continued)

Havighurst's Developmental Tasks

5. Relating oneself to one's spouse as a person.
6. Accepting and adjusting to the physiological changes of middle age.
7. Adjusting to aging parents.

Retirement years: (55+)

1. Adjusting to declining physical strength and health.
2. Adjusting to retirement and reduced income.
3. Adjusting to death of a spouse.
4. Establishing an explicit affiliation with one's age group.
5. Adopting and adapting social roles in a flexible way.
6. Establishing satisfactory physical living arrangements.

Sources: Erikson, E. (1963). *Childhood and society.* New York: Norton.   Levinson, D. (1978). *The seasons of a man's life.* New York: Knopf.   Schaie, K. W. (1977/78). Toward a stage theory of adult cognitive development. *Journal of Aging and Human Development, 8,* 129–138.   Gould, R. (1972). The phases of adult life: A study in developmental psychology. *American Journal of Psychiatry, 129,* 521–531.   Havighurst, R. (1972). *Developmental tasks and education.* New York: McKay.

This, in conjunction with higher earning power, is likely to result in a higher standard of living for college graduates. The effects of college attendance do not end in young adulthood. Delaying childbearing means delaying nest emptying. In other words, college graduates will be older when their children leave home. This could affect the onset of their midlife transition. College attendance may even affect adjustment to old age. Better-educated people tend to live longer and be healthier. It is very clear that career choice affects adjustment to retirement (see Chapter 16). So a choice early in life may influence the nature of changes throughout adulthood.

Stability and Continuity in Adulthood: Many behaviors and characteristics seem to be at least somewhat stable throughout adulthood (see, for example, Chapters 9 and 14). Indeed, Continuity Theory (Atchley, 1989) posits that continuity is the norm and usually the most adaptive coping mechanism available:

> . . . in making adaptive choices, middle-aged and older adults attempt to preserve and maintain existing internal and external structures and . . . they prefer to accomplish this objective by using continuity. . . . Continuity Theory views both internal and external continuity as robust adaptive strategies that are supported by both individual preference and social sanctions. . . . (Atchley, 1989, p. 183)

Why would continuity be adaptive? Because it enables people to know what to expect in various situations. They do not have to expend as much time and energy (and cognitive processing space) trying to generate multiple hypotheses about what will happen and how they should react in various situations (Atchley, 1989). Continuity allows us to plan for the future

(McCrae & Costa, 1982). Previous experience probably also increases our confidence that we can handle tasks and crises. Continuity also allows us to build an identity (Atchley, 1989).

Continuity does not mean *no* change (Atchley, 1989). Rather, continuity is the framework that guides the nature of change. Personality characteristics might be displayed in different ways at different times. There may be job changes. A particular skill may be highly developed at one time and less evident at another. But the personality characteristic, level of responsibility needed for work to be satisfying, and willingness to learn a new task may all be the same. Hence, change is incorporated within continuity.

So continuity may be adaptive and still allow for some change. Nonetheless, students often wonder what the study of development has to gain from examining or considering continuity. Here are several advantages.

First, of course, life-span developmentalists want to describe behaviors—whether they decline, improve, or remain stable. The fact that some will be stable while others change underscores the value of the assumption of multidirectionality and multidimensionality in development.

A second approach would be to try to explain consistency. Consider, for example, the apparent consistency of several personality characteristics (McCrae & Costa, 1982). It could be that genetic or evolutionary factors determine personality (Buss & Plomin, 1984; Rothbart & Derryberry, 1981). Perhaps environmental consistency only gives the appearance of stability (Thomas & Chess, 1980). Or, there may be an interaction of genetics and environment (Scarr & McCartney, 1983). Genetic predispositions may lead a person to make choices within the environment that maintain those predispositions. A person who is introverted might choose a job that requires little social interaction or might marry someone who is willing to make and maintain social contacts for them as a couple. This person could easily continue to be introverted while living a happy, satisfying life. There would be little need to change.

It is important to consider the role of environment, either alone or in interaction with genetics, in seeking explanations of consistency. Otherwise, we may end up ascribing greater importance to childhood than to other periods of development because we will assume that the roots of adult behavior lie in childhood.

Yet another approach might be to treat the stable characteristic as an independent variable (McCrae & Costa, 1982). An *independent variable* is a factor that is believed to influence behavior. Ideally, an independent variable is controlled by the investigator. So, for example, a researcher might vary the rewards a nursing home patient receives for autonomous behavior (Baltes & Baltes, 1982). In this case, the rewards serve as an independent variable. Increased rewards should lead to more autonomous behavior. But developmental researchers often use more descriptive variables—such as age, gender, and social class—as independent variables.

It is in this sense that personality could serve as an independent variable. Investigators could examine the effect of personality on coping with major life transitions such as marriage, nest-emptying, retirement, and widowhood (Costa & McCrae, 1982). Indeed, research that has taken this approach has often found personality to be a better predictor of adjustment than age or components of the transition itself, such as the decline in social contacts with retirement (Neugarten, Havighurst & Tobin, 1965/1968).

So stability may be as interesting as change. In either case, describing a behavior across the adult years is not sufficient. The course of adult development itself needs to be explained.

Explaining Adult Development

A *theory* is a set of statements and principles that attempts to explain a phenomenon. To be useful, a theory must explain existing data. It should also generate additional questions for research and be able to accommodate the results of that research. Some psychologists (Baltes & Willis, 1977) also expect that the theory will suggest ways to intervene to change behavior.

Theories tend to deal with a specific behavioral realm (such as personality or intelligence) or a transition (such as midlife or adjustment to retirement). Some theories, in fact, are fairly narrowly focused (see Table 1-4).

The purposes of theory imply that a theory must be written down before all the relevant data are available. Otherwise, we would not know how to proceed. Thus, theories cannot be rooted solely in data. They also include general assumptions about the nature and course of development. These assumptions can be summarized in *models* which try to describe general influences on development. These models of life-span development guide the selection of some of the variables to be considered in theories.

MODELS OF ADULT DEVELOPMENT

Traditional Models

Traditionally, three models of aging dominated theory and research: stability, irreversible decrement, and decrement with compensation. They were intended to describe normal, as opposed to pathological, aging. In other words, either stability or decrement was assumed to be the developmental trajectory during adulthood; growth was not postulated.

The fundamental assumption of the *stability model* is that people develop until maturity, which typically occurs in adolescence or young adulthood, and then plateau. Behavior is stable after this point. The theories of Sigmund Freud and Jean Piaget are examples of this model. The only questions to be answered by adult development research within such a model have to do with the attainment of stability. One might ask, for example, whether the age of maturity varies from generation to generation or cross-culturally. In a sense, the stability model prevented research in adult development because it focused on childhood as the "paramount" period of development.

The second traditional model of aging is *irreversible decrement.* Aging is assumed to be marked by a relentless and irreversible decline in function. Researchers working from this model are interested in identifying the magnitude, timing, and causes of the decline. This model has tended to dominate both professional and lay approaches to adult development (Baltes & Willis, 1982). But it has several serious problems. First, it assumes that change of development moves in only one direction—down. Research has shown that this is not true. Second, what looks like irreversible decline may actually be a deficient environment. For example, elderly people often score more poorly than young adults on both IQ and Piagetian measures of intelligence. But with minimal training (less training than it would take to learn the skills), the elderly show dramatic improvements (Baltes & Willis, 1982; Hornblum & Overton, 1976). This suggests that in their daily lives the elderly do not have the opportunity to use and practice these skills, but given that opportunity, they are able to "revive" skills which they always really possessed.

Imagine for the moment that a researcher did introduce change in the environment and still found that the elderly performed less well on an IQ test than young adults did. Would this be evidence of irreversible decline? Not necessarily. Differences between older and younger adults involve more than simply the number of years they have lived. Younger adults are likely to be better educated. They may have taken more tests throughout their lives and therefore be more comfortable in a test situation. Differences in life experiences may contribute to IQ performance differences. These *cohort effects,* attributable to differences in the sociohistorical period during which development occurred, actually seem to play a greater role in younger versus older adults' IQ performance than age itself (Schaie, 1979; Schaie & Hertzog, 1983).

Finally, there is the *decrement with compensation* model. This model also assumes that there is functional decline associated with aging, so many of the criticisms of the irreversible decrement model also apply here. However, there is one important difference between the two; the decrement with compensation model, unlike the irreversible model, suggests that the environment can compensate for the losses. Researchers using the compensation model are at least interested in environmental effects on functioning that the irreversible model ignores, though neither model assumes that the declines can actually be reversed. In the compensation model the elderly may use cues, such as lists, to help compensate for memory loss. Or they may learn to read lips to overcome mild hearing loss. Glasses or hearing aids can also help overcome sensory declines. In such cases, the decline is real but does not have the same impact on day-to-day functioning as it would without compensation.

Baltes's Model of Life-Span Development

Paul Baltes has offered a trifactor model of aging. He suggests at least three types of influences on adult development and, in fact, on development throughout the life span: age-graded, history-graded, and nonnormative influences (Baltes, 1987; Hetherington & Baltes, 1988).

Age-graded influences: Age-graded influences are experiences or events that tend to occur at approximately the same chronological age within a particular culture (Hetherington & Baltes, 1988). Some examples were provided earlier. Traditionally, age-graded influences have been seen as the most important factor in explaining development (Baltes, 1987).

History-graded influences: Like age-graded influences, history-graded influences may be biological or environmental. The difference is that these influences are associated with historical time rather than chronological age (Baltes, 1987). History-graded influences refer to the broader biocultural context in which development occurs. Some are specific, time-delineated events, such as a war or the Great Depression. Others are more gradual trends, such as the change in attitudes toward women's roles in the United States during the past three decades. Schaie (1970) called these *cohort effects.* Although history-graded influences have received little empirical attention in life-span developmental psychology, when they have been investigated, they have proved to be powerful forces. As we noted earlier, they are often more helpful in explaining behavior than chronological age (Elder et al., 1988; Schaie & Parham, 1976).

Nonnormative influences: Age-graded events are normative in that they are expected to happen to each individual at a particular point in time. In other words, they reflect what the "average" person goes through during various points in development. There are numerous advantages to events being predictable and "on time" (Neugarten, 1979). For example, there is a natural support group formed by one's peers. Those who become a parent for the first time during their twenties have friends (and perhaps siblings) who are also first-time parents. They can exchange both instrumental and emotional support.

Not all events are predictable, however, and some are unique to the individual. These nonnormative events, which can be biological or environmental, may have a major impact upon development (Baltes, 1987). Examples might include surviving a natural disaster, early widowhood, or infertility.

It is important to recognize that nonnormative influences are not static, one-time events; rather, they can have long-term, multiple implications (Hetherington & Baltes, 1988). Indeed, the "crises" that most alter individual development are those whose effects emerge over time. Think, for example, of divorce; this event often involves changes in family roles (with children, in-laws, and others), economic status, work status, and living arrangements. Many people find their attitudes and life styles permanently altered by a divorce (see, for example, Wallerstein & Blakeslee, 1989). Events that have more temporary effects, such as an acute physical illness, do not always have long-term implications for development, and the person may return to "pre-crisis" functioning and life style (Hetherington & Baltes, 1988).

We could make similar statements about age-graded and history-graded influences. These are not static elements (Baltes, 1987); instead, they allow for various probabilities that lead to choices that lead to other probabilities, and so on. At any point in this chain, a different choice could lead to a different outcome (Hetherington & Baltes, 1988). Furthermore, the types of influences interact. Elder (Elder et al., 1988), for example, reported that the effects of the Great Depression (a history-graded influence) varied depending on stage of adolescence (early versus late).

Imagine you could find a group of people who were the same age, had lived through the same historical events, and had never suffered any substantial nonnormative events. Would you expect them all to have the same coping mechanisms, personality, level of intellectual functioning, interests and values, and attitudes toward work, gender roles, and political issues? You might think they should be very similar. Given your past experience, however, you know they would not be.

There would indeed be differences, because there are interindividual differences within each of the three broad categories of influences. Not everyone experiences age-graded events the same way. The meaning of puberty for boys and girls is an example (Stattin & Magnuson, 1990). Income level seems to influence at least the rate of health decline and thereby living conditions and adjustment in old age. We expect, then, that factors such as gender, race, and socioeconomic group mediate the effects of age-graded, history-graded, and nonnormative influences. Indeed, such factors may even affect the nature and type of influences we experience (Baltes, 1987). American women, for example, are less likely than men to see military action during a war, but men from lower socioeconomic classes are more likely than those from the middle and upper classes to fight. This causes a differential likelihood of traumatic psychological and physical damage (nonnormative events).

Baltes's trifactor model of aging presents a complex picture of "an active organized individual and an active, organized environment" interacting to create that person's developmental trajectory (Hetherington & Baltes, 1988, p. 11). Going a step further, we can divide the environment into various contexts—the family, the community, and the subculture. The individual, of course, must function within all these levels, and both the contextual levels and the individual are constantly changing. Furthermore, the contextual levels interact with and influence one another. Think, for example, of the interaction between family and work demands and their effects on a young working mother. Thus, to understand development, we must understand the changing individual, the changing contexts, and their interactions (Hetherington & Baltes, 1988).

This organismic-contextualist approach is not unusual in life-span developmental psychology, though not all theorists view it as the most appropriate model. Like others, this approach is based on a set of assumptions about the nature and course of human functioning and development. These assumptions are summarized in several different world views.

WORLD VIEWS

World views are even more general in scope than models and theories. They represent untestable assumptions that are translated into specific tenets for theories. The theories are then used to generate testable research hypotheses. These empirical tests form the basis of scientific knowledge. So although scientific knowledge seems to consist of observable, testable

Issues and Models of Adult Development **19**

information, underlying it is a core of untested assumptions. This is one reason why we should be cautious in accepting scientific evidence.

The assumptions underlying the various theories of adult development concern issues such as the basic nature of human beings, change, and causality (Overton, 1985; Overton & Reese, 1973; Reese & Overton, 1970). These assumptions are interrelated. A theorist who makes a particular assumption about human nature is likely to make a compatible assumption about the nature of change. This is why we can group the assumptions together into world views. In life-span developmental psychology, there are at least three world views: mechanistic, organismic, and dialectic. The mechanistic and organismic world views, which dominate the field, are summarized in Table 1–5.

TABLE 1–5: Comparison of Organismic and Mechanistic Scientific Research Programs

Level of Program	Organismic	Mechanistic
I. Hard Core (Ontological assumptions)		
A. World models	1. Organization of nature. 2. Activity. 3. Change (dialectic). 4. Accidental factors *moderate* organization, activity, and change.	1. Uniformity of nature. 2. Stability. 3. Fixity. 4. Accidental factors *cause* organization, activity, and change.
B. Human models	*Active Organism* 1. Inherent organization of psychological functions. 2. Inherent activity. 3. Organizational changes are qualitative.	*Responsive Organism* 1. Uniformity. Apparent organization reduced to accidental causes. 2. Stability. Apparent activity reduced to accidental causes. 3. Changes are quantitative.
C. Epistemology	*Constructivism— Rationalism.* Knower actively constructs the known.	*Realism—Empiricism.* Knower comes to reflect or acquire a copy of reality (the known).
II. Positive Heuristic (Methodological assumptions)	1. *Holism.* Understanding in context of the organic whole. 2. *Structure—Function Analysis.*	1. *Elementarism.* Understanding through reduction to elements. 2. *Antecedent— Consequent Analysis.*

TABLE 1-5: (continued)

Level of Program	Organismic	Mechanistic
	a. Establishing the organization of a system explains behavior (formal explanation). b. Establishing contingent factors explains rate of behavior (contingent explanation).	a. Establishing contingent factors explains behavior (contingent explanation).
	3. *Necessary Change* a. Establishing the order of organizational change explains development (formal explanation). b. Contingent factors explains rate of development (contingent explanation).	3. *Accidental Change* a. Establishing the contingent factors explains development (contingent explanation).
	4. *Discontinuity— Continuity of Change.* Emergent systematic properties and levels of organization.	4. *Strict Continuity of Change.* Strict additivity.
III. Family of Theories	*Contemporary Structuralists.* Piaget, Werner, Chomsky, Kohlberg, Pascual-Leone. *Ego development theories.* Erikson, Sullivan. *Gestalt theories. Humanistic theories.* Rychlak. *Ecological perspective theories.* Bronfenbrenner, Wapner, and Kaplan.	*Behaviorist and neo-behavioristic theories. Conditioning theories. Observational learning theories. Mediational learning theories. Information processing theories.* Skinner, Bijou, Baer, Berlyne, Spiker, Bandura, Gewirtz, H. Kendler, J. J. Gibson.

Source: Overton, W. (1985). Scientific methodologies and the competence-moderator-performance issue. In E. Neimark, R. DeLisi, & J. Newman (eds.). *Moderators of competence*, pp. 28, 29. Hillsdale, NJ: Erlbaum.

The Mechanistic World View

In many ways, the computer adage "garbage in, garbage out" serves as a metaphor for the mechanistic model. Mechanists view humans as similar to computers. We are passive recipients of environmental input. We respond to, rather than shape, our environment.

Another feature of computers is that increasingly complex input results in increasingly complex output capabilities. However, the complexity can be achieved only through a series of small steps, one building upon the other. Similar statements could be made about human beings. Changes in behavior are seen as *continuous* and *quantitative*, not abrupt changes in the underlying basis of behavior. Development is an additive process. Since a complex behavior is composed of a series of simple behaviors, we analyze the simple behaviors in order to understand the complex ones. This approach of reducing a complex behavior to its component parts for analysis is known as *reductionism.*

Since development is a simple accumulation of experiences, it has no fixed endpoint or goal. Mechanistic theorists do not define a final state of maturity. This, in turn, means that there are no stages to go through to reach maturity. Because there is no inherent goal to development, mechanists see no need to ascribe inherent tendencies to human beings. They do not discuss, for example, anything like self-actualizing tendencies. Indeed, in the philosophical tradition of John Locke, they conceptualize human beings as blank slates passively waiting for the environment to write on them. B. F. Skinner, whose theories are based on a mechanistic world view, once drew an analogy between humans and a mound of clay waiting to be shaped (Skinner, 1971).

If there are no innate tendencies guiding human development, what does account for changes in behavior? Mechanists use an *antecedent-consequent* definition of causality. The antecedent is some event in the environment that triggers or controls the consequent behavior in the person. In its simplest form, this view is represented by S-R (Stimulus-Response) theory in psychology. The classic frustration-aggression hypothesis, which proposed that frustration leads to aggression, is an example of S-R theory (Dollard et al., 1939).

Because no particular antecedents will have to occur for every person, in some sense the development path is accidental. The explanation for change lies not in underlying psychological structures that *must* change with development; rather, it lies in antecedent-consequent relations. The crucial point here is that human beings are passive and bring little or nothing to the developmental process. Mechanistic theorists would therefore never study inherent predispositions or needs as an explanation for individual differences. Because they look for explanations in the environment, their world view influences the type of data theorists collect.

The Organismic World View

The organismic world view is virtually diametrically opposed to the merchanistic. As its name implies, the total organism is the basic metaphor of this world view. Human beings are viewed as *active*, as influencing the environment as well as their own development. Motivation for behavior and change comes from *within* rather than exclusively from without. Indeed, the environment exists only psychologically for the individual in his or her construction of it. In other words, the effect of the environment is filtered through the individual's understanding and interpretation of it.

Among the inherent characteristics of humans is a particular form of maturity. Development does have an endpoint within the organismic model, and this endpoint represents maturity. Of course, the definition of maturity varies from theorist to theorist.

Organismic psychologists argue that this developmental goal is *qualitatively* different from earlier forms of behavior. In other words, there is not simply a continuous building up of experience; rather, experience is periodically reinterpreted and reorganized. New concepts, skills, and understandings emerge with these successive reorganizations. Behavior does not simply become more complex; it becomes different. So organismic theorists argue that development is *discontinuous,* that there are shifts that signal whole new modes of thought or personality functioning. Each shift represents a different *stage* of development.

Since there are qualitative shifts in behavior, a complex behavior cannot be reduced to its simpler components. The simple elements are organized in such a way as to create a unique behavior. We can borrow an example from the physical sciences. Water, a liquid, is composed of two gases, hydrogen and oxygen. If you simply examined the component parts, you would be completely misled as to the properties of water. Organismic theorists argue that the same is true of complex behavior. They take a *holistic* approach; they look at the entire behavior rather than its parts.

This does not mean that the component parts—that is, earlier experience—have no role in present functioning. In Erikson's theory, for example, the resolution of each crisis influences subsequent development. He predicts that someone who resolves the identity crisis on the side of isolation will be incapable of establishing an intimate relationship in young adulthood (Erikson, 1968). But intimacy will also require some reworking of identity and will place new demands on identity. Therefore, development is both quantitative and qualitative.

How does a person move from one stage to the next? Organismic theorists use a *structure-function analysis* to explain development. A *structure* is an organized general pattern that guides behavior in a particular realm. Think of it as being like the framework of a house, which limits and defines the basic form of the house, yet allows for different uses for specific rooms and different decorating schemes. It can even be dramatically altered, thereby changing the shape of the house. Similarly, personality structures allow people to behave in a relatively consistent manner, yet they have the flexibility to allow people to cope with a variety of situations. And they too can be altered as biological and environmental demands require. Thus, in Erikson's theory, changing biological needs and sociocultural demands lead to different crises to be resolved at each stage of development. Similar statements could be made about cognitive structures.

In the organismic model, then, individuals are the primary determinant of development. The way they organize experience guides their behavior. The organization is limited by innate tendencies that move them toward a particular form of maturity. Organismic theorists and researchers focus on identifying these forms of organization and their impact on behavior. This, of course, is precisely the opposite of the mechanistic approach.

The different assumptions of these models lead to different questions for research as well as different interpretations of human behavior. These are clearly the traditional and dominant models in developmental psychology, but both have been challenged by dialectic psychology.

The Dialectic World View

Klaus Riegel (1976; 1977) has argued that both the mechanistic and organismic approaches are inadequate. In his opinion, the organismic world view overrates the role of the organism in development, while the mechanists overemphasize the contribution of the environment. What is needed, he claims, is a greater appreciation of the *interaction* between the person and the environment. The individual is indeed influenced by the environment. But the environment is also shaped by the individual. The two are *reciprocal* in their influence. They are in *transaction* with one another, with neither dominating the other. This belief is a core principle of the dialectic approach.

Riegel draws an analogy between dialogue and development. In a dialogue, participants take turns in determining the path of the conversation. Yet each participant's turn depends on the previous statement of the other person. Because of this mutual influence, the conversation is in a constant state of change. Furthermore, the course of the discussion is affected by the culture and historical period within which it occurs. Just think, for example, of the number of conversations you have had about television shows, nuclear war, or the national debt. Would you have had these conversations in 1920? Would you talk about these issues if you were a member of a New Guinea tribal society?

This example introduces several other components of the dialectic world view. For one thing, the dialectic model emphasizes change. At first glance, this may not seem like a novel approach. After all, the study of development is supposedly focused on change. But according to Riegel, developmental psychologists have not really tried to explain how change occurs. Instead, they have concentrated on describing what a person is like when he or she is in a state of balance or equilibrium. For example, Piaget's theory outlines differences in cognitive functioning at four stages of development. He did give an explanation of why people change, but did not fully describe the transition from one stage to the next. He was not very clear about how cognitive structures actually undergo their transformations. In Riegel's opinion, this is because Piaget, like most developmentalists, focused on balance rather than change. Given that change is the core process in development, the emphasis seems misguided. Dialecticians have shifted the emphasis and consider change to be their primary concern.

How does change occur? Riegel (1976) proposed four dimensions that guide human behavior:

1. *Inner-biological:* These are internal physiological events, such as illness or death, as well as the physical maturation that leads us to leave our parents and form our own families.

2. *Individual-psychological:* These include psychological processes such as memory, values, attitudes, and coping styles.

3. *Cultural-sociological:* Social forces, including laws and traditions about marriage, childbearing, and work, are included in this dimension.

4. *Outer-physical:* This dimension covers physical events that are out of our control, such as drought, tornadoes, or other natural disasters.

When any two of these dimensions are out of synchrony, a crisis is triggered. A crisis may also be caused by asynchrony within a dimension. For example, the coping mechanisms of the individual-psychological dimension are usually inadequate when a terminal illness, part of the inner-biological dimension, is discovered (Riegel, 1976). These crises require people to change themselves or the environment in order to achieve synchrony. The synchrony, however, will probably be shortlived. Asynchrony, and thus change and development, is the rule.

Notice that the four dimensions include both internal and external factors. Again, this represents dialecticians' emphasis on interaction. They want to include sociohistorical as well as biological influences on behavior. This is an important point in studying adult behavior, for as we have already noted, the environment influences both intra-individual and interindividual differences. Indeed, animal research indicates that the environment can influence not only behavior, but the actual physical composition of the brain (Rosenzweig, 1984). Environmental influences, of course, are not limited to the present environment. As Baltes (1987), Schaie (1970) and others have noted, they also include the person's individual history and experiences within a particular culture and within a particular time.

Environmental influences are not the whole story. Biological changes in the brain, resistance to disease, reproductive functioning, and other physiological mechanisms clearly influence adult development. Riegel argues that in order to understand development, we must therefore consider all these factors. This viewpoint has gained considerable popularity among life-span developmental psychologists.

Early descriptions of world views (Overton & Reese, 1973; Reese & Overton, 1970) focused on the organismic and mechanistic perspectives. Indeed, even in a more recent article, Overton (1985) suggested that these are the two principal perspectives and that the dialectic world view is not really distinct from the organismic.

World views, then, shape models of aging, which in turn influence specific theories. The theories are used to generate research questions. A particular theory will only raise certain types of questions that reflect not only the specific theory but also the more general world view. Schaie, for example, reflects the organismic world view's emphasis on qualitative shifts by examining different cognitive structures at various stages of development. A mechanistic theorist would not postulate such stages and hence would not even look for qualitatively different structures.

Appropriate research questions do not guarantee valid findings. The research must also be designed to successfully isolate influences on behavior and development. The next chapter describes some of the issues faced by researchers in adult development.

SUMMARY

This chapter introduces the assumptions, principles, and models underlying the study of adult development. The issues raised here will recur throughout the text.

Age roles and age norms are indicators that we should expect differences between adults and children. Yet for many years there was little interest in adult development. Now there has been an enormous increase in interest, due to demographic factors (the "graying of America") and to a shift in our perspective on when and how development occurs.

Earlier developmental psychologists had focused on childhood as the primary period of development; more recent theorists have adopted a life-span perspective. This is marked by several principles:

1. No one age period is dominant in its control of the other.
2. Development is multidirectional and multidimensional.
3. There is a dynamic interplay between loss and gain at all stages of development.
4. There is plasticity in development.

Although we tend to emphasize changes in behavior, it is clear that some characteristics are quite stable across adulthood. This can be positive because it adds predictability to behavior. It is important not only to describe these behaviors but to consider circumstances which might interrupt stability. Furthermore, it is important to understand how stable characteristics might influence other behaviors and their development.

Traditionally, models of aging focused on decrement. There was little recognition of growth as a possibility. More recent models do not assume that growth ceases after adolescence. Instead, they emphasize the influences on development. Baltes's model, for example, describes age-graded, history-graded, and nonnormative influences.

At a more general level, world views underlie scientific theories. Developmental psychology reflects three major world views: (1) the organismic view stresses qualitative structural shifts in an organism actively engaged with the environment; (2) the mechanistic view assumes people are passive and are shaped by the environment; (3) the dialectic view focuses on change as most basic in development. The assumptions of these world views are untestable; rather, they are a part (often a hidden part) of the assumptions we bring to our theories and research.

2 Research Methods in the Study of Adult Development

Most of the information in this text will be based on scientific theory or on research. Data will come primarily from psychology, but there will also be references to economics, sociology, medicine, biology, anthropology, and other fields. There are similarities in how research is conducted in all these fields. All, for example, use the *scientific method,* which focuses on publicly observable phenomena. This means that data refer to events or structures that could be observed by many people, although they may need special equipment (such as an electron microscope) or training (in running blood tests, for example) in order to make the observations. Intuition, visions, and other more private or personal forms of data are not considered scientific.

In other eras, people routinely turned to priests, prophets, monarchs, and other individuals believed to have special powers in order to find answers to questions about human behavior and the human condition. In modern America, we tend to rely quite heavily on science for answers to these questions. We generally prefer science to philosophy, religion, and literature for "real" answers. Even advertisements refer to studies by doctors, medical centers, the American Cancer Society, the Heart Association, and other groups to try to sell products ranging from sunscreen to breakfast cereal to health insurance.

The scientific method does provide a powerful tool for understanding a wide variety of phenomena. However, this does not mean that science is infallible; nor does it mean that scientific evidence should be accepted uncritically. Questions can be raised about measures, participants, and the general design of the study. The purpose of this chapter is to introduce research methods commonly used in studying adult development to help you more effectively evaluate the research presented in this book. Bear in mind the relationship between theory and research noted in Chapter 1. Data are not "pure"; they are influenced by philosophical assumptions and theoretical models.

RESEARCH DESIGNS

Research designs are the general strategies used in collecting data. The design a researcher chooses depends on what question he or she is trying to answer. The choice of design is also influenced by pragmatic issues such as time, money, and the availability of participants. In adult development research, we can categorize the commonly used strategies into two broad categories: traditional designs and sequential designs.

Traditional Designs

The most frequently used designs in developmental psychology are the *cross-sectional* and *longitudinal*. The third type of traditional design is the *time lag*.

Descriptions of Traditional Designs: In a *cross-sectional study,* the performance of two or more different-aged groups of people is compared. For example, you might compare the sexual behavior of a group of 20-year-olds to that of groups of 40-, 60-, and 80-year-olds. Each participant would be tested or surveyed once. All the participants would be tested at about the same time, usually within a few weeks of one another. After testing everyone, you would calculate the mean or average score of each group. In this example, you might calculate the mean number of times per week each group had intercourse. You would then compare these averages to see if there were any statistically significant differences among the four age groups. In other words, you would mathematically evaluate whether the group differences were larger than would be expected just by chance.

In a *longitudinal study,* you start with a group of same-aged people, people who are all from the same birth cohort. You would then test these people at several different ages. If you selected people born in 1945, you might measure their sexual behavior at 20, then at 40, again at 60, and finally at 80. Longitudinal studies can last a very long time. The Oakland Growth Study began in the 1920s, as did Terman's study of genius. The Oakland study followed children from birth into adulthood. Terman's study began when the children were in elementary school. In the 1970s, information concerning the adult achievements of these about-to-retire gifted people were presented (Sears & Barbee, 1977). Two other well-known longitudinal studies which will be frequently cited are the Duke Longitudinal Study (begun in the 1950s) and the Baltimore Longitudinal Study of Aging (begun in 1958).

In the third type of traditional design, *the time lag study,* researchers are more interested in cultural change than in personal development. They might compare the sexual behavior of 20-year-olds in 1960 to the sexual behavior of 20-year-olds in 1980. This would allow them to see whether the sexual behavior of 20-year-olds changed historically.

The traditional designs are summarized in Table 2–1.

Advantages of Each Design: There are several reasons for the great popularity of the cross-sectional design. First, it does not usually take very long to complete a cross-sectional study. Indeed, in some of these studies,

TABLE 2-1: **Traditional Research Designs in Developmental Psychology**

Design	Description	Example
Cross-sectional	Tests people from several different age groups at one point in time. Age groups are then compared. It is more accurate to consider these comparisons of cohort groups than of age groups.	Testing the effects of a training program on 20- vs. 40- vs. 60- vs. 80-year-olds.
Longitudinal	Testing the same group of people at several different times. This design allows researchers to examine intra-individual change.	Testing the effects of a training program over several years. Participants are tested first when they are 65, then again at 70, and again at 75 and 80.
Time-lag	Testing a particular age group at one point in time and then testing a comparable age group at another point in time. The two groups are then compared to observe changes in cultural/group norms or attitudes.	Measuring attitudes about sex in 20-year-olds in 1970. Then attitudes about sex are measured in 20-year-olds in 1990.

data collection can be completed in a matter of days. Compare this to the Oakland Growth Study or Terman's study of genius, which are still going on after more than 50 years. The speed with which a cross-sectional study can be completed also means that such studies are relatively inexpensive. Furthermore, the measures used in these studies do not become outdated while the study is in progress.

Another advantage of cross-sectional research is that people are more likely to agree to participate in such studies than in longitudinal research. They simply require less of a time commitment. This is a concern in psychology, because we want our research findings to have *external validity*— that is, to apply to the broadest group of people possible. We would not be very interested in the results of a study if they described only the specific participants and could not be generalized to many (if not all) people. In order to achieve this generalizability, we must have a *sample* of participants that is representative of the *broader population* to whom we wish to generalize our results. Yet we know that only certain people agree to participate in psychology experiments. For example, young and middle-aged women are more likely to agree to participate than same-aged men. Similarly, whites are more likely to participate than African-Americans (Todd, Davis & Cafferty, 1983/1984). Medical research is often limited to those who seek medical help.

The problem of obtaining a representative sample exists in all research. This problem is greater, however, in longitudinal research. Furthermore, the initial selectivity of the longitudinal sample may be exacerbated by selective attrition. *Attrition* refers to people dropping out of a longitudinal study. This is so normal that researchers routinely try to start with a large enough sample to absorb a certain amount of subject loss. It is possible that the loss will be random. In other words, there will be no systematic differences between the subjects who are lost and those who continue. This type of loss would not present a serious threat to external validity.

But what if the attrition is selective? What if there are important differences between those who drop out and those who don't? Research suggests that there are some differences. First, as might be expected, some of those who do not continue have died or are too ill to participate. These people typically had lower intellectual and personality functioning than those who continued (Cooney, Schaie & Willis, 1988; Norris, 1985). So as time goes on, a longitudinal sample becomes positively biased. In other words, the participants are psychologically and physically healthier than we would expect in a representative sample of people that age.

Not everyone drops out for health reasons; some just lose interest. These people are more similar to the continuing participants than those who drop out for health reasons (Cooney et al., 1988; Norris, 1985). Indeed, especially among middle-aged (as compared to elderly) participants, there may be no meaningful differences between those who stay in the study and those who voluntarily leave. This limits the impact of attrition somewhat.

Given the problems with longitudinal designs, you might wonder why we ever use them. In fact, as you will see, longitudinal studies are actually preferred over cross-sectional ones because cross-sectional data cannot provide definitive information on two issues of paramount concern to developmentalists. First, cross-sectional studies do not allow us to examine individual differences in development. Since each participant is seen only once, we cannot draw any conclusions about the path of that person's development. We cannot, for example, divide each age group into various categories of sexual activity and then say that people in category 1 at age 20 will still be in that category at ages 40 and 60. We also cannot say what might cause a person to change categories or continue in one category throughout adulthood. In order to examine such individual differences in rate and style of development, we need longitudinal data. Longitudinal data allow us to compare a person's behavior to his or her own earlier behavior, thus enabling us to describe the individual's path of development.

Similarly, cross-sectional research cannot document developmental change. Let's say that in your cross-sectional study of sexual behavior, you found a steady age-related decline. Twenty-year-olds were more sexually active than 40-year-olds, who were more active than 60-year-olds, who were more active than 80-year-olds. Can you say that as people get older they become less sexually active? Schaie (1973) argues that this would be a premature interpretation. It is equally possible that cohort factors influenced the outcome of the study. For example, the older adults may have more conservative attitudes about sexuality. These attitudes may have been lifelong for these people, so that if you had tested them when they were 20, they may still have been less sexually active than the 20-year-olds of 1980. Cohort and age are synonymous in a cross-sectional study. People of different ages are also of different cohorts. This means that it is impossible to tell whether the group differences are attributable to age, to cohort, or to some combination of the two. In a cross-sectional study, you would not be able to ascertain whether there was a decline due perhaps to biological changes, or just differences due to changing cultural mores.

This is not a problem in a longitudinal study. Since all participants are from the same cohort, any changes observed cannot be attributed to growing up during different sociohistorical periods. Does this mean that the changes are due to the aging process? Not necessarily.

Imagine that you are doing a longitudinal study that measured attitudes toward minority groups. Let's say that you first assessed these attitudes in 1940, when your subjects were 20 years old. You found that 75 percent of the participants' attitudes could be categorized as at least mildly racist. By the time you retest the same people in 1980, when they are 60 years old, this figure has dropped to 40 percent. Would you interpret this to mean that people become more tolerant as they age? That certainly is one plausible interpretation. But it is also possible that you are seeing *time of measurement* effects. This means that the cultural standards (or setting or other environmental influences) existing at the time are the major determinant of the difference. In this example, changes in American society's attitudes toward racial segregation and discrimination between 1940 and 1980 may have contributed to the observed decrease in racism among your subjects.

You could, of course, examine the effects of time of measurement by doing a time lag study. That is, you could compare the attitudes of 20-year-olds in 1940 to those of 20-year-olds in 1980. But you still would not know how age might affect these attitudes as people grow older. Furthermore, keep in mind that the people who are 20 in 1940 are from a different cohort than those who are 20 in 1980. Hence, it is possible that any differences between the two groups are due to cohort, time of measurement, or both.

To sum up, Schaie (1973) has argued that at least three broad categories of factors influence development: age, cohort, and time of measurement. (Note the similarity of these to Baltes's age-graded, history-graded, and nonnormative influences.) Part of the goal of life-span research is to determine which of these factors influences a particular developmental phenomenon. Unfortunately, the traditional research designs consistently present us with a dilemma. In each of them there are two potential explanations for group differences. Only one of the three factors can clearly be eliminated as the "cause" of group differences or change; the other two factors are *confounded*—that is, their effects cannot be separated. So in the longitudinal design, age and time of measurement are inseparable; in the cross-sectional design, cohort and age are confounded; and in the time-lag design, cohort and time of measurement co-occur (see Table 2–2).

This confounding does not make the designs useless. There are many situations in which a researcher's assumptions or information from earlier research allows the use of a traditional design. Let's say, for example, that you are interested in memory functioning, which you believe shows an irreversible decline with age. You are interested in charting that decline. You also think that early nutrition and education might affect the rate of de-

TABLE 2-2: Considerations in Selecting a Research Design

Design	Variables Confounded	Use
Cross-sectional	Age and cohort	Under the stability model, can assume that group differences are due to cohort. Also useful for making immediate social policy decisions.
Longitudinal	Age and time of measurement	Only one cohort is being examined, so the behavior must be unrelated to cohort. With stability model, assume that changes are due to time of measurement. With irreversible decrement, assume that changes are due to age (since environment cannot affect this decrement).
Time-lag	Cohort and time of measurement	With the stability model, there would be no cohort effect, so any differences could be attributed to time of measurement. Only looking at one age.
Cohort-sequential	Time of measurement	Must assume no cultural impact on the behavior. Useful with irreversible decrement model when cohort and age effects are expected.
Time-sequential	Cohort	Used to assess the effect of cultural change on different age groups using the decrement with compensation model. Allows separation of age and time of measurement effects.
Cross-sequential	Age	Since age cannot be a factor, used with stability model to separate effects of time of measurement and cohort.

cline. Both nutrition and education vary from cohort to cohort, so you want to be certain to be able to separate out cohort. In other words, you cannot afford to confound age and cohort. Thus, you cannot use a cross-sectional design. Remember, though, that you think the decline is irreversible. There can be nothing in the immediate environment that affects memory functioning, so time of measurement should not be an issue. Therefore, you could use a longitudinal design. This would allow you to examine individual differences in memory decline as a function of education and early nutrition without confounding cohort and age.

There will be cases when the traditional designs are inadequate. What if you wanted to be able to examine the impact of both age and cohort on memory? What if, for example, you wanted to see if the memory declines of people born in the 1940s (after vaccinations became routine) were slower than those of the cohort born in the 1910s? A simple longitudinal study would not suffice; you would need to use a more complex design. Schaie's *sequential* designs, which allow us to separate two of the three factors within one study, might be useful.

Sequential Designs

Description: The three sequential designs are the cohort-sequential, cross-sequential, and time-sequential. Each sequential study involves doing two or more traditionally designed studies. Table 2–3 summarizes these designs.

The *cohort-sequential* study involves monitoring two or more cohorts longitudinally. This allows you to separate the effects of cohort and age. You could see, for example, if the rate and overall amount of memory decline were the same for people born in 1920, 1940, and 1960. This would let you evaluate whether the improved nutrition, health care, and education of the later generations affected memory decline. If it did, you would expect differences between the cohorts in terms of memory. For example, you might find that the 60-year-olds born in 1920 had suffered a steeper decline (compared to when they were 30, 40, and 50) than did 60-year-olds born in 1940 and 1960. This would be evidence of a cohort effect. If the three groups of 60-year-olds were comparable in amount and rate of decline experienced, you would conclude that there is no significant cohort effect. Note that you might find evidence of both cohort and age effects because there might be an age-related decline in all three cohorts, but the magnitude of the decline might vary. You could statistically estimate the impact of both cohort and age.

Note that each of these groups of 60-year-olds would be tested at different points in time. The 1920 cohort would be 60 in 1980, whereas the 1940 and 1960 cohorts would not reach this age until 2000 and 2020, respectively. If there are differences among the three groups' abilities, you could not say whether the differences were due to cohort or time of measurement. In order for this design to be useful, a researcher must be able to assume

TABLE 2-3: Summary of the Sequential Designs Used in Developmental Psychology

Design	Description	Example
Cohort-sequential	Two or more longitudinal samples from two different cohorts	Measuring people born in 1910 when they were 60 and again at 70. Measuring people born in 1920 when they were 60 and again at 70.
Cross-sequential	Two or more time-lag studies	Testing 40- vs. 50- vs. 60-year-olds in 1980. Testing 40- vs. 50- vs. 60- vs. 70-year-olds in 1990. The 50–70-year-olds in 1990 would be follow-up data on the 1980 sample.
Time-sequential	Two or more cross-sectional studies	Looking at the attitudes of 20- and 40-year-olds in 1960 and looking at the attitudes of new groups of 20- and 40-year-olds in 1980. There are no longitudinal data in this design.

Source: Schaie, K. W., & Hertzog, C. (1982). Longitudinal methods. In B. Wolman (ed.), *Handbook of developmental psychology*, pp. 91–115. Englewood Cliffs, NJ: Prentice Hall.

that only cohort and age are important determinants of the behavior under investigation. Time of measurement must be assumed to be irrelevant.

In the *time-sequential* design, two or more cross-sectional studies are performed. This design permits us to separate time of measurement effects from age. Let's say that data collected in 1940 comparing 60-year-olds to 80-year-olds indicated that between 60 and 80 years, there is a decline in interest in current events. This could indicate that as people age they withdraw from society, an age effect. On the other hand, it could be that in 1940 news was available only from newspapers, radio, and newsreels (shown at movie theaters). Since vision, hearing, and ambulatory abilities might all decline between age 60 and age 80, perhaps news became less accessible to the elderly. You could test this hypothesis by repeating the study in 1980, when hearing and visual aids were more advanced (and available) and television brought the news into the home. If the decline was comparable in the 1940 and 1980 studies, you would argue that time of measurement had no effect and that age was a more important determinant.

The problem in this design is that the people who were 60 in 1940 were from a different cohort than those who were 60 in 1960. In order for the time-sequential design to be useful, the researcher must be able to assume that cohort is not a relevant factor in the behavior being studied. This is a difficult assumption to make, since cohort has been demonstrated to be relevant to a wide variety of personality and cognitive characteristics as well as to attitudes (Schaie & Parham, 1976; Schaie & Hertzog, 1983).

Finally, two or more time-lag studies make up the *cross-sequential* design. In these studies, the researcher is interested in examining the effects of time of measurement versus cohort. Since age cannot be examined in this type of study, the researcher must be able to assume stability in the behavior of interest. Only sociohistorical influences could account for individual differences in behavior (although these sociohistorical influences can affect physical development and functioning, which in turn affect behavior). So, for example, a researcher interested in altruism might assume that this is a stable characteristic in an individual. But it certainly could vary from cohort to cohort; it could be that when people moved from place to place less frequently, they were more willing to help those who lived near them. Altruism might also be affected by time of measurement. During times of national crisis, such as World War II, people might be more willing to help each other because they are "all in it together."

Advantages and Disadvantages: Baltes (1968) suggested that a model giving equal emphasis to three factors was not very useful if you could never consider more than two of them simultaneously. He argued that time of measurement was typically less important than cohort or age in developmental issues and suggested that researchers really only needed to choose between a design that was basically multiple longitudinal studies (as in the cohort sequential) or one that was multiple cross-sectional studies (as in the time-sequential design). Schaie agrees that this is probably a more practical approach, although time of measurement should not be completely omitted from consideration in all circumstances (Baltes & Schaie, 1976; Schaie & Baltes, 1975).

The sequential designs are generally preferable to the traditional designs because they allow us to examine two, rather than just one, influences on development. Furthermore, research has indicated that longitudinal and cross-sectional designs do lose important information (Schaie, 1982). Yet the sequential designs are rarely used in adult development research, mostly because they take considerably longer to perform than the traditional designs. They carry all the disadvantages of the longitudinal study in terms of time, money, personnel loss, and measurements becoming outdated. Furthermore, they require a larger number of subjects than the traditional designs. This makes them even more costly and more difficult to perform.

Whenever they are adequate, then, the traditional designs are preferable. However, as we have seen, sometimes only a sequential design can provide the answer. Then the researcher must decide which sequential design is most appropriate. Some considerations in making this selection were noted in Table 2–2.

Selection may apply to how the data are collected. However, it may also apply only to a particular data analysis. It is possible to collect enough data to do all three types of sequential analysis (see, for example, Schaie, 1979 or Schaie & Hertzog, 1983). When all three types of data are available, researchers can compare the outcomes of the three analyses and draw conclusions about the impact of age, cohort, and time of measurement on the behavior being studied. But these conclusions can only be interpretations; it is impossible empirically to consider all three factors simultaneously.

Finally, it is important to emphasize that age, cohort, and time of measurement are broad descriptive categories (Baltes, 1968). They do not constitute explanations of the behavior. Explanations rely on more detailed theory and measures.

TYPES OF VALIDITY

In evaluating any piece of research, three types of validity must be considered: internal, external, and ecological.

Internal Validity

Much research is designed to try to uncover cause and effect relationships. We try to discover what factors cause, or at least influence, a particular developmental phenomenon. Internal validity tests the validity of the relationship we are proposing to explain cause and effect. The question is whether the factor we claim causes the effect actually is the cause. Could some other variable in the research design have also influenced the result?

We have already seen several examples of such variables in the discussion of traditional research designs. When two potentially "causal" factors co-vary, it becomes impossible to determine which is responsible for the observed changes. Think, for example, of the covariation (or confounding) of age and cohort in a cross-sectional design.

Demand characteristics of an experiment can also threaten internal validity. These are features of the experimental setting that might unintentionally influence behavior. They include experimenter expectations, subject expectations, and setting cues. Subjects, for example, sometimes figure out what they think experimenters want them to do and then do it. This is called the *social desirability effect*. Sometimes experimenters unwittingly reward certain behaviors and thereby increase the likelihood of getting the results they expected. This is why many experiments use a double-blind procedure in which neither the researcher nor the subject knows how a particular participant is expected to perform.

In order to have strong internal validity, it is important to control potential confounding variables. This can be done in a number of ways. In an experiment, you could use a control group. Another approach is to limit the range of characteristics of the subjects. For example, age and cohort are not confounded in a longitudinal design because only one cohort is used. Similarly, research with the elderly using only healthy people can eliminate health status as a determinant. Unfortunately, this solution threatens external validity.

External Validity

External validity refers to the validity of extending the research findings beyond the study itself. Will other people be affected the same way as the participants? Will the tested intervention work in other settings? These are the types of questions addressed in evaluating external validity.

Both subject selectivity and, in longitudinal designs, attrition can work to limit the representativeness of a sample. Furthermore, in our efforts to ensure internal validity, we may opt to use only certain types of subjects. Hence, there is often a tradeoff between internal and external validity.

Typically, researchers have tried to select subjects on the basis of characteristics that still ensured widespread generalizability. The assumption of minimal gender and race differences underlies many of these decisions. In other words, it has frequently been assumed that knowing about the development of white, middle-class, American men provided information about "normal human development" that could be generalized to blacks, women, Hispanics, the working class, and other cultures. Levinson, Gould, Kohlberg, the Baltimore Longitudinal Study of Aging, and numerous other studies collected data only about men. As we will see throughout this text, a substantial portion of adult development theory—which is assumed to have near-universal applicability—is built on data collected about men.

Carol Gilligan (1982a) has been particularly influential in alerting psychologists to the pitfalls of such an approach. Women's development is not identical to men's. Socialization, career opportunities, reproductive capabilities and roles, and a myriad of other factors combine to ensure that there will be substantive differences. Similar statements could be made about race, social class, and other cultures. You may be thinking that women are a unique case because of the biological differences between the genders. However, it is broadly agreed that socialization is also a powerful influence in many realms of development. If this is true, then race, social class, and cultural background will be important factors to consider. As we will see later in the text, we have little information to evaluate in which realms and to what extent these factors are operative. In the meantime, it is probably wise to be cautious about generalizing the results of studies using only white men to other populations.

Ecological Validity

James Birren and Sherry Willis (1977) have argued that developmental theories ought not only to describe and explain development, but also to suggest how this information could be used. In other words, they expect developmental research and theory ultimately to have practical implications. It is not enough to know that memory declines. It is not even enough to know why it declines. We also need to know whether those declines affect daily living, and if they do, how their negative effects might be mediated.

In order to make such practical suggestions, we need research that looks at real-life behavior in real-life situations. If all we know about memory is that the elderly are less adept at recalling word lists in reverse order, we won't be able to delineate the effects of memory decline on daily living. Nor can we make suggestions to alleviate decline. Controlled laboratory studies do have considerable value. For example, they ensure that younger and older adults are performing identical tasks. They provide the basic research that will describe and explain the behaviors most in need of and amenable to intervention. But, to answer the core questions of intervention, we need data that have greater *ecological validity*.

The more a study approximates the setting in which a behavior normally occurs, the more ecologically valid the research is. We might see, for example, whether the elderly are less able than young adults to remember what they are supposed to pick up at the supermarket or the steps in operating the company's new computer. Or we might look at older adults' ability to generate and use memory cues such as lists or word associations.

The importance of ecological validity extends beyond the usefulness of a study for designing interventions. Ecological validity may actually affect the behavioral description we generate from a study. For example, the elderly may perform better on realistic tasks than on artificial laboratory tasks. They may be more motivated when they can see a reason for remembering something, such as a grocery list, than when asked to remember a list of nonsense syllables. Indeed, several theorists have suggested that cognitive development during adulthood involves shifts toward greater selectivity (in attention and interests) and practicality (Labouvie-Vief & Schell, 1982; Schaie, 1977/78; see also Chapter 13). Thus, research using artificial tasks may indicate a functional decline that does not exist in day-to-day living situations.

If human beings functioned independently of their environment, ecological validity would not be an important issue. But, as we have seen repeatedly, the context of behavior *is* important. Unfortunately, only a few developmental theorists have taken both the individual and the environment into account in their theories (Birren et al., 1980). Robert Havighurst's (1972) developmental tasks, listed in Table 1–4, provide one example. Havighurst considered physical, psychological, and cultural factors in delineating the issues that face adults. Schaie's trifactor model and Baltes's trifactor model also include both individual and cultural factors. Many developmentalists believe that such models, coupled with ecologically valid research, show the future direction of life-span developmental psychology.

STATISTICAL EVIDENCE

In this text, we will not ordinarily examine statistical evidence from a particular study in great detail. Nonetheless, the research-based statements made throughout are based on statistical evidence. Researchers examine their data using the principles of *probability*. Statistical tests are designed to ascertain whether an observed difference (between groups) or an observed relationship (between two or more variables) is stronger than would be expected by chance. In other words, we expect that a certain level of difference or relationship would occur even if there really is no difference or relationship, due to random or measurement error. To argue that we have discovered a relationship or difference, we want to be sure it is larger than this random error possibility. Typically, scientists accept any finding that has a 5 percent or less probability of occurring even if there is no difference or relationship as evidence of a difference or relationship. When this happens, we say the finding is *statistically significant*.

This probably seems like a fairly conservative approach. After all, you may often decide to do things with much lower odds. For example, if you are very ill and there is a drug that has a 60 percent chance of helping but a 30 percent of making you worse, you might take it. When scientists adopt this fairly conservative approach, it means they are lessening the chances of saying there is a group difference (between adults of different ages, for example) when there is not. This is known as minimizing the chance of a *Type I error*. The downside of this approach is that it also lessens the scientist's likelihood of saying there is a relationship even when there really is. The approach increases the possibility that scientists will overlook a real difference or relationship in the data because it is not quite strong enough to emerge at this 5 percent level. This is called a *Type II error*.

Scientists decrease the chances of a Type II error by increasing the *power* of the statistical test. This is often done by using a large sample. Because of the way statistical tests are designed, it is easier to detect a difference or relationship with a large sample size. A much smaller difference will show up as statistically significant with a larger group of participants.

Think about the implications of the connections among the size of the relationship, the size of the sample, and statistical significance. In a sufficiently large sample, a very small relationship can be significant. For example, a *correlation*, which describes the linear relationship between two variables, can range from −1.00 to 0 to 1.00. We would usually think of a correlation in the .30–.70 range as "moderately" strong. Stattin and Magnuson (1990) reported a correlation of .09 as statistically significant because they had 425 subjects. Yet a correlation of this magnitude (.09) is so small as to be almost meaningless. It does not identify a relationship strong enough to be particularly helpful in designing an intervention or in explaining a behavior. Similarly, with a large enough sample, an IQ difference or change of a few points can be statistically significant (see Schaie & Hertzog, 1983). So small a change would have virtually no impact on daily functioning. It is important, then, to try to assess the size of an effect, not just its statistical significance. We will see that not every age-related change is important for job, family, psychological, or physical effectiveness.

RESEARCH ETHICS

The American Psychological Association has established a code of ethics for research involving human subjects (American Psychological Association, 1973). It establishes some appropriate limits as to what types of research are possible. It also serves to remind us of the humanity of the research participants.

The APA code requires that all participants give *informed consent.* This means that the potential subject is informed of the risks, benefits, procedures, and time commitment involved in participation. There may sometimes need to be some deception in order to avoid social desirability effects. But such deception should be used only when there is no alternative and the research question is sufficiently important to justify it. Similarly, risks, both psychological and physical, should be minimized. Universities and research institutes have panels to evaluate both the safety and the ethics of research proposals. Indeed, federal funding is contingent upon the presence and effectiveness of Human Subjects Review Panels.

There are circumstances under which informed consent is difficult to obtain. In the case of adult development research, problems are most likely to arise when diseases (such as Alzheimer's) or their treatment (such as psychotropic drugs) render a person incapable of making a decision. When this happens, someone else who is legally responsible for that adult must give permission for participation. This may be a family member or a staff member in a nursing home. Researchers must be extremely vigilant in these situations to protect and respect the rights of the ill person.

The APA code also guarantees *confidentiality.* This means that the results of a particular individual's participation will not be available to anyone without that individual's permission. The researcher must take measures such as not putting names on tests to be certain that others do not accidentally associate a particular score or result with a specific person. It also means that individual results are not automatically given to family members, personal physicians, nursing home staff, and so on.

The APA code covers two other areas worth mentioning. First, researchers may not do things that guarantee that the hypotheses will be confirmed. One may not withhold findings, for example. Samples and measures must be selected to permit various answers to the research questions to be discovered.

Second, the code considers treatment of animal subjects. We will not refer to very much animal research in this book. However, especially in the areas of illness and physical functioning, there is considerable animal research. The APA requires that the animals be properly maintained. It also requires any pain the animal suffers be minimal and unavoidable. Pain for animals, then, is similar to the use of deception with humans. Indeed, universities have Animal Research Review Panels as well as Human Subjects Boards. Such panels must review research in order to obtain federal funding.

SUMMARY

Science is a powerful tool for describing and understanding human behavior and development. But like any other tool, science is imperfect. This chapter presents basic information about the scientific method as it is applied in life-span developmental research and highlights some of the potential pitfalls of this endeavor.

Several basic research designs are commonly used in adult development research. The three traditional designs are the cross-sectional, the longitudinal, and time-lag studies. In each, two of the three basic variables of age, time of measurement, and cohort are confounded. This limits their usefulness for answering cause and effect questions. Schaie and Baltes have suggested that we use sequential designs instead: the cohort sequential, cross-sequential, and time sequential. Although these designs do a better job of not confounding the basic variables, they still cannot separate all three. It is always the case that the researcher must decide which to sacrifice. Furthermore, the sequential designs are costly and time-consuming. Researchers must evaluate both pragmatic and theoretical considerations in deciding which design is most appropriate.

Scientists typically evaluate data using statistical techniques that rely on probability theory. Statistically significant findings are those which are unlikely to occur just by random error. These are the findings emphasized by researchers. It is important to recognize, however, that many factors, including sample size, influence the likelihood of obtaining statistical significance. Therefore, one should not assume that statistical significance is synonymous with significance for daily living. Finally, there are ethical considerations in research. These considerations can and should limit the types of research attempted with both humans and animals.

3 Transition to Adulthood

Not too long ago, when talking to a male student in my office, I chastised him for referring to the women students as "girls" although he never referred to the male students as "boys." "That usage," I said, "reinforces the stereotype of females as being childlike. How would you like it if I called you a boy?" "I wouldn't like that," he said. "But," he continued, "I don't feel comfortable calling the girls women. I don't even call the guys men. I call them guys. I wish there was a word like guys that applied to girls. We're not really men and women. We're more like guys and something."

This student is not alone in his confusion; many of my colleagues call college students boys and girls. Many others, including me, refer to them as men and women. This language difficulty underscores the transitional nature of the college years (18 to 22). College students certainly aren't children. They aren't teenagers. Yet they often don't quite seem like adults.

Research concerning the personality, moral, interpersonal, and cognitive development of college students also indicates that these are transitional years. But before we explore this research, let's consider again what an adult is and try to justify the conclusion that college students are not yet adults.

CRITERIA FOR ADULTHOOD

In the United States, there is no single "rite of passage" clearly marking the transition from minor status to adulthood. Even legal age of adulthood varies, depending on the situation. You are an "adult" driver at 18, when you can also vote. However, you cannot legally drink alcohol until you are 21. On the other hand, the early teenage years (the exact age varies among states) mark the age of consent for sexual activity. Thus, adult status will need to be at least partially defined in terms of more individual characteristics.

We cannot rely on biological maturity as the major or sole indicator of adult status. In the United States, the average age for first menstrual period is just under 13 years. Girls will achieve reproductive maturity (be able to conceive children) within about a year of menarche. Boys' physical maturity is a bit slower. However, they too will typically achieve reproductive maturity during their middle teens. Therefore, we need to turn to psychosocial markers to define adult status.

Boyd McCandless and Richard Coop (1979) suggest three criteria for defining adulthood. First, there is economic independence. Adults support themselves financially. This doesn't just mean that they have a job; many college students have jobs. It doesn't even mean that they make enough money to support themselves, for some college students do. Rather, it means that the money they make is their sole source of support. It buys food, shelter, medical care, and so on. While some college students do this, most are still somewhat dependent on their parents. Even if they are paying some or all of their own tuition, they are often "riders" on their parents' medical or automobile insurance.

The second criterion is readiness to marry and raise children. Some college students are married and have children, but most have not yet begun their own families. This is also indicated by average age at first marriage, which was 25.5 for men and 23 for women in 1985. College students may be settling into more "serious" relationships than they had in high school, but they are not ready to jump into marriage.

Finally, there is the question of decision making. We've already argued that college students are not ready to make the decision to marry. Their lack of decisiveness about careers is one reason they are not yet self-supporting. Many of them are still exploring religious, political, and sex-role ideologies. Even the moral framework used to make some decisions is still evolving.

Looking at these criteria, it is clear that the original point still holds. College students are not children. They are closer to economic independence, establishing a family, and making major decisions than children are. Yet they are not doing these things. One possible reason they are not quite ready to be adults is that they are not yet certain of who they are—that is, they have not resolved their identity crises. In addition, both moral and cognitive development are still proceeding. These issues are the focus, then, of personal development during the college years.

PERSONAL DEVELOPMENT ISSUES

Economic independence, marriage, and adult decision making all require establishing oneself as a separate entity from one's parents and establishing one's own identity. While there are numerous ideas about how this is done, we can point to at least two processes that are fundamental: separation-individuation and identity formation.

Separation-Individuation

Definitions: Individuation is a lifelong intrapsychic process involving increased responsibility for the self. *Separation* involves a decrease in dependence on family, especially parents. At the very least, we can divide dependency into emotional and instrumental dependency. *Emotional dependency* refers to reliance on others for nurturance, emotional support, affection, and, to some extent, self-bolstering. *Instrumental dependency* refers to turning to others for aid with tasks or such needs as financial assistance or car repair. Clearly, we never become completely independent in either realm. Indeed, a recent study indicated that of eight types of separation, emotional detachment from parents was *least* important to college students (Moore, 1987).

We can be more specific about the types of independence being sought during this transition. Moore (1987) used factor analysis to identify eight self-reported dimensions of parent-adolescent separation in a college sample. In order from most to least important, these were: self-governance, graduation from high school and college, starting a family, financial independence, disengagement (psychologically and physically moving away from parents), school affiliation, separate residence, and emotional detachment.

Hoffman (1984, pp. 171–72) derived four types of separation from the theoretical literature:

1. *Functional independence:* The ability to manage and direct one's practical and personal affairs without the aid of mother or father
2. *Attitudinal independence:* The image of oneself as being unique from one's mother and father, having one's own set of beliefs, values, and attitudes
3. *Emotional independence:* Freedom from an excessive need for approval, closeness, togetherness, and emotional support from parents
4. *Conflictual independence:* Freedom from excessive guilt, anxiety, mistrust, responsibility, inhibition, resentment, and anger in relation to parents

Research indicates that separation in these areas does increase during the college years. Furthermore, higher levels of separation seem to be associated with better adjustment (Hoffman, 1984; Lapsley et al., 1989; Moore, 1987). Low conflictual dependence seems particularly important, and attitudinal independence appears to be less so (Hoffman, 1984; Lapsley et al., 1989). The relationship between separation and adjustment is probably curvilinear rather than linear. In other words, it is likely that both too much and too little separation are related to poor adjustment in college students.

It is interesting to note that society may not have the same expectations of men and women in terms of level of independence achieved (Gilligan, 1982b). There is some evidence that women are expected to and do maintain closer ties to their parents, especially in emotional areas (Broverman et al., 1972; Lapsley et al., 1989). Furthermore, greater separation is apparently needed for healthy male adjustment than for healthy female adjustment (Lapsley et al., 1989).

In any case, complete detachment from family is not desirable (except, perhaps, in the case of extreme family pathology). The importance of some continued attachment is underscored in Harold Grotevant's (Grotevant & Cooper, 1985) definition of *individuation*. He suggests that the individuation process has two components. The first is individuality, which is reflected in separateness (distinctiveness of self) and self-assertiveness. The second component is connectedness, which is indicated by mutuality (sensitivity to others) and permeability (openness to others).

Process: The dynamics of this distancing process are captured in David Ausubel's (Ausubel, Montemayor & Svajian, 1977) model of *desatellization*. As children, we are dependent on our parents for physical, social, and psychological support. We "agree" to behave as they wish, and they "agree" to support us. We are, in a sense, "satellites" of our parents. This is beneficial because it facilitates socialization of the child (because the child wants to please the parents) while providing the child with a "safe" environment in which to grow.

As a child enters adolescence, however, dependence on parents begins to break down. Peers become increasingly important (P. Newman, 1982). Status among peers is based on actual performance, not on being a member of the "family." Furthermore, children are increasingly able to function independently of parents. They can eat, dress, and work with little or no help from parents. The parents expect children to become increasingly independent. This increased independence permits the children to have more diversified experiences. All these factors require that adolescents begin to establish their own identity, which in turn necessitates desatellization from the family.

Desatellization involves three processes. First, there is *resatellization*, which involves transferring emotional dependence from the parents to other people (peers or other adults). This is a gradual process that does not require a complete break from the family. Indeed, it is clear that both adolescents and college students maintain close emotional ties with their parents and consult them concerning major life decisions (Hunter, 1985; Lapsley et al., 1989; Moore, 1987; P. Newman, 1982; Sullivan & Sullivan, 1980). However, peers do become increasingly important as consultants for personal problems and decisions (Hunter, 1985; Newman, 1982). Resatellization may be viewed as a stepping stone to the autonomous decision making that marks adult functioning.

The next step is *attempting to earn status.* The young people are no longer simply trying to please those upon whom they are dependent. Rather, they are trying to be accepted for themselves, for their own ideas, skills, and interests. They want to move beyond simply deriving status by being a member of a family, so they use the peer group to test their abilities, to experiment with various roles, and to "prove" their own worth.

The third process, *being exploratory*, deals with task-related issues. In this step, the person focuses on problem-solving itself rather than on the status to be gained from successful solution of a task. Because status is not the issue, even failure can be viewed as a positive learning experience. This level is not particularly common among adolescents and is far from universal, even in adulthood. This fact implies that no individual has to complete all three processes in sequence. Instead, people can get stuck at any point. So, for example, someone could be permanently resatellizing; such a person would be constantly trying to please others in order to win approval and gain assurance of his or her own self-worth.

Research Findings: The separation-individuation process does take place during the college years (Lapsley et al., 1989). Progress seems particularly likely if parents and child are able gradually to renegotiate the parent-child relationship. Letting go too abruptly leaves the child without a safety net of support, and holding on too tight impedes the process and perhaps forces the child to rebel (Offer & Offer, 1975).

Gilligan (1982a and b) has argued that separation means different things to men and to women. It is not surprising, then, that several studies have uncovered gender differences in how the parent-child relationship is renegotiated. For example, the relationship between father and son seems especially important in boys' separation. The son who is successful in individuation expresses disagreement with his father. He can also make direct suggestions to his father. His father seems at least tolerant of this assertiveness (Grotevant & Cooper, 1985). All of this may make it more difficult for the son to maintain parental ties during the transition period (Lapsley et al., 1989).

For girls, all family relationships (including those with siblings and the marital relationship between her parents) are important in the separation-individuation process (Grotevant & Cooper, 1985). They will usually show more dependence on parents than boys do. This is especially true of the relationship with their mothers (Lapsley et al., 1989). Unlike boys, however, girls' dependence on their mothers does not bode poorly for their adjustment.

In general, the relationship between college students and their parents appears to be quite comfortable. As was the case during adolescence, college students frequently consult their parents about major issues such as career options. However, communication on such issues seems to consist mainly of parents giving advice. Students do not seem to have a strong sense that their parents understand (or even seek to understand) their views (Hunter, 1985). They do believe, though, that their parents are concerned about their welfare.

Of course, communication is not easy in all families. It appears that boys who go away to college are more satisfied with interactions with their parents than are boys who live at home while attending college. Those living away from home also feel more affectionate toward their parents. Simultaneously, they feel more independent. Thus, it appears that going *away* to college (as opposed to simply being in college or being of college age) may facilitate the movement toward independent functioning without some of the conflicts (and therefore loss of positive parent-child interaction) that might occur if the parents were nearby (Sullivan & Sullivan, 1980).

Despite the generally positive tenor of parent-child communication, it is clear that peers gain in importance during the college years. College students believe their closest friends understand them better than their parents do (Hunter, 1985). This is hardly surprising, since college students seek to form friendships with empathetic peers, rather than for the status of being in a particular clique, as high school students do (P. Newman, 1982). Furthermore, parents' experiences and problems are less similar to the student's than peers' are, so there is more basis for empathy in the peer relationships.

Identity Formation

In his theory of personality development, Erik Erikson (1963; 1968) identified adolescence as the period marked by the crisis of identity versus role confusion (see Chapter 1). This concept of an "identity crisis" during adolescence has gained widespread popularity among both psychologists and lay people. While most of us think of the identity crisis as occurring during the high school years, research presents quite a different picture. Both cross-sectional and longitudinal data suggest that the critical years for identity formation occur during college. The issues most relevant to identity formation are typically first raised during college. Indeed, relatively little identity work goes on during junior high and high school. Furthermore, identity issues are most likely to be resolved during college, although many people continue the search for an identity throughout their twenties (Marcia, 1976 and 1980; Waterman, 1982; Tesch & Whitbourne, 1982).

In order to explore the nature of the identity crisis during college, we need to know what an identity is and what the possible outcomes of the identity crisis are.

Defining Identity: Erikson (1968) suggested that there are three components to an identity. First, there is a sense of continuity among past, present, and future identifications. Identity is not simply a one-time issue. You have always had some way of identifying yourself. Some of your identity has reflected roles you play, such as someone's child, a student, a Scout, a Catholic, or a member of a club. Your identity has also reflected your beliefs about yourself and your characteristics. You might have characterized yourself as ugly, honest, friendly, or intelligent. As a college student, some of these identifications will still fit; others won't. For example, many college students who breezed through high school are shocked at the difficulties they encounter in college work and rethink their "native intelligence" and academic talents. Past and present beliefs as well as future demands must be sorted through and reintegrated. Neither your background nor your future plans is deniable. Integrating all these roles and values is what Erikson means by establishing continuity.

In the process of reintegrating previous identifications, you typically achieve the second component of identity: You define yourself as unique. You are not your parents (though you probably share many of their values and beliefs). Nor are you your peers (though you probably also share some of their values and beliefs). Rather, you have forged a sense of yourself as being some combination of all the familial, peer, and cultural influences you have encountered. You see yourself as being different from everyone else you know. (The importance of uniqueness was emphasized in the earlier definitions of separation and individuation.)

Yet it is also important to see some similarities between yourself and others. You need to fit in somewhere. The final component of identity, then, is establishing a niche for yourself in the broader society. This niche may be defined in terms of occupation, political beliefs, sexual orientation, religion, or any number of other categories.

The process of establishing this identity is, according to Erikson, long and difficult. It is also not without risk. The dangers of the identity crisis are reflected in the four possible identity statuses used by researchers in this field (see, for example, Marcia, 1980, or Waterman, 1982). Two of these statuses are considered to be relatively positive: One is *identity achieved,* which is marked by a cohesive set of values concerning and a commitment to career, political, and religious beliefs, and sex role orientation. It is possible to be identity achieved in one area (such as career) but not in others (such as political and religious beliefs).

The second status, which is also considered positive, is *moratorium.* In this status, the person is actively seeking an identity, exploring various options and belief systems. The individual isn't ready to make a commitment yet, but is moving toward committing to certain goals and values. Theoretically, a person could stay in this status forever. If that happened, it would become maladaptive. In reality, though, the tensions associated with this status are probably too great to allow anyone to stay in it indefinitely. Indeed, the research indicates that it is the least stable of all identity statuses (Waterman, 1982).

The two "negative" statuses are *identity foreclosed* and *identity diffused.* Identity foreclosers look a lot like identity achievers. They are committed to a belief system, but they reach this commitment without going through a moratorium. Instead of establishing their own identity, they adopt one defined by someone else (typically, their parents). Identity diffusion looks a good deal like moratorium. The difference is that the identity diffused person is no longer searching for an identity. Rather, he or she has decided to live without committing to anything. Theoretically, this makes it impossible to establish a career or an intimate relationship.

Identity Status in College Students: A quick look at the data immediately supports the contention that the primary work of identity formation is done during college. It is exemplified in a longitudinal study of 53 men comparing their identity status at the end of freshman versus the end of senior year (Waterman, Geary, & Waterman, 1974). Both occupational and ideological status were evaluated. At the end of the freshman year, 2 percent of the men were considered identity achieved in both occupation and ideology; 38 percent were identity achieved in one of these areas; and 60 percent were identity achieved in neither area. As seniors, the numbers rose to 19 percent in both areas and 42 percent in either ideology or occupation. Only 38 percent had not achieved identity in either area.

Other researchers report similar findings (see Marcia, 1980; Waterman, 1982). This implies that a sizable number of students shift from one identity status to another during the college years. The largest shifts are from moratorium to one of the other statuses (Waterman, 1982). Which status one switches to appears to depend, at least in part, on which area of identity is being evaluated. College students do tend to shift from moratorium to identity achieved in terms of career issues. However, the findings concerning religious and political ideology are less clear. Preexisting religious beliefs are commonly called into question during college. A significant number of people shift out of the identity foreclosed status in religious ideology, but they do not necessarily achieve identity. Indeed, at least one study found they were likely to become identity diffused in terms of religion (Waterman & Waterman, 1971; Waterman et al., 1974). In terms of political ideology, many students do achieve identity or at least shift into a moratorium status (from foreclosure usually) (Adams & Fitch, 1982; Waterman et al., 1974). But many others seem uninterested in politics and become either identity diffused or foreclosed (Waterman & Goldman, 1976). So college attendance seems to be particularly valuable in resolving career identity issues. In terms of ideology, it at least exposes people to new options, though it may not always result in a positive resolution by the end of the college years.

Clearly, identity work is not always completed in college, even in terms of occupational interests. People who have been out of college for two to four years are more likely than college students to have achieved identity in all the areas (Tesch & Whitbourne, 1985). Furthermore, the data have two major limitations. First, several studies involved only male subjects. Because of Erikson's own theory, questions as to whether women's identity development is identical to men's have arisen. The second problem is that these studies tell us only about what happens to people who go to college. What about 18- to 22-year-olds who do not attend college? Are their patterns of identity formation similar to those of college students?

Identity in Women: Erikson (1963, 1968) believed that all people went through the same eight stages of development (see Chapter 1). This does not mean he believed there were absolutely no developmental differences between males and females. In terms of the identity crisis, Erikson thought the processes were similar for men and women. But, he argued, because of anatomical differences, the outcome is a bit different. Women, whose anatomy leads them to be interested in interpersonal relationships more than in competitive work, need to leave their identity a bit more open-ended than men do: ". . . the young woman's identity must keep itself open for the peculiarities of the man to be joined and of the children to be brought up" (Erikson, 1968, p. 283). This does not mean that young unmarried women are without identities; rather, women have a different focus in their identity development and a somewhat less clear-cut resolution to the crisis.

How do Erikson's ideas stand up after empirical investigation? In general, researchers have found few gender differences in the attainment of identity status (Schiedel & Marcia, 1985; Waterman, 1982; Tesch & Whitbourne, 1982). This is particularly true when the only rating of identity investigated is the "overall" category (as opposed to religious, sex-role, occupational, political). However, the data are limited and a few provocative gender differences have been uncovered that seem worthy of further investigation.

There appear to be more "paths" to identity for women than for men. James Hodgson and Judith Fischer (1979, 1981) have identified three different paths. There is the masculine path, in which identity is most likely to be achieved in the areas of occupation, politics, or religion. In the feminine path, identity is achieved in the sex roles or sex values areas. If identity is achieved in both masculine and feminine spheres, the person is following the androgynous path. In their study of identity development in 50 men and 50 women, they found females following all three paths, but not one man followed the feminine path.

The different paths available to men and women may even explain why the genders appear to be equal in overall identity status during college. There may be a group of women who follow either the male or androgynous path who complete their identities during college. Another group of women may follow the feminine path and not complete their identities until considerably later, after moving into the wife and mother roles (O'Connell, 1976; Schiedel & Marcia, 1985). This possibility is supported by evidence suggesting that college women who score high on masculinity (on sex role inventories) are more likely to have completed their identity formation (Orlofsky, 1977; Schiedel & Marcia, 1985). Thus, male and female college students who have not completed their identity formation may have different reasons for their status and may display different courses of development in the ensuing years. This question deserves further research attention (Schiedel & Marcia, 1985).

Which path a person follows to identity appears to have ramifications for other areas of functioning. Women who follow a feminine path may have higher self-esteem than those who follow the male route (Hodgson & Fischer, 1979, 1981). This finding is consistent with arguments that women do best when they do not deny their needs for interpersonal connection (Steiner-Adair, 1991). Men who choose the androgynous path have higher self-esteem than those who follow the masculine path (Hodgson & Fisher, 1979, 1981). So it remains possible that men and women do not form identities in the same manner. As we will see in Chapter 4, this has interesting ramifications for the way the genders approach marriage.

Identity in Noncollege Youth: The vast majority of research concerning identity formation has been done with college students. In fact, there has been only one study of identity in 18- to 21-year-olds who are not attending college.

Gordon Munro and Gerald Adams (1977) compared identity statuses in 30 college students and 27 working youths. Their results indicated that 44.5 percent of the working youths were identity achieved, whereas only 6.7 percent of the college students were. Conversely, 40 percent of the college students were identity diffused compared to 18.5 percent of the working youths. Surprisingly, these differences were primarily attributable to differ-ences in ideological rather than occupational identity status. Working youths were much more likely to have achieved identity in the religious sphere than were college students. Similar findings emerged for the area of ideological commitment.

Munro and Adams generated several explanations for these differ-ences. It could be that people who have not yet formulated an identity are particularly likely to go to college. Perhaps they think that college will help them find an identity. They may view college as a "holding pattern," a place where they can avoid making any commitments (at least temporarily). The latter explanation would help us understand why so many college students still have not completed identity formation at the time of graduation.

The causes of the differences between working and college youths can only be answered through further research. First, however, more research is needed to establish the precise nature of the differences, because there are methodological problems in the Munro and Adams study. For example, 50 percent of the college group was female, compared to 63 percent of the working group. Given Hodgson and Fischer's (1979, 1981) findings of gen-der differences in specific areas of identity achievement, this imbalance could be a problem. Furthermore, the Munro and Adams study was not longitudinal. We still do not know if there are differences between these groups in the process of identity formation. Similarly, we have no informa-tion on racial, social class, or ethnic differences in identity formation. So we do not know whether the transitional nature of the 18 to 22 period applies to everyone, or if it is specific to college students (especially white, middle-class college students).

Identity and Other Behaviors: You may be wondering why we have given so much attention to identity formation. One reason is that, within Erikson's framework, resolution of the identity crisis influences how later adult crises will be faced (see Chapter 1). For example, Erikson (1968) claimed that an identity diffused person is incapable of forming a truly intimate relationship.

Identity formation is also related to a number of concurrent behav-iors. College students in the moratorium status are more likely to use non-prescription drugs than those with foreclosed identities (Marcia, 1980). Col-lege students in the achieved or moratorium status show higher levels of achievement motivation and self-esteem than do foreclosures or diffusions (Orlofsky, 1978). Even choice of major seems to be related to identity. Iden-tity achieved women seem to choose more difficult majors (Marcia & Fried-man, 1970).

Finally, identity status appears to be related to level of moral reason-ing. Identity achieved college students' scores are more likely to be in Kohl-berg's postconventional reasoning level than those of other students (Rowe & Marcia, 1980) (see Table 3–1). Postconventional reasoning does not ap-pear to be necessary for identity achievement. Nor does identity achieve-ment necessarily cause postconventional reasoning (Waterman, 1982). In-

TABLE 3-1: Percentages of Different Aged Males at Each Stage of Moral Development

Stage	AGE					
	10	16–18	20–22	24–26	32–33	36
Preconventional	79.9	13.3	0	0	0	0
Transitional	14.3	17.8	9.4	8.0	0	0
Conventional	4.8	68.4	90.7	76.0	86.8	88.8
Postconventional	0	0	0	16.0	13.0	11.1

Source: Adapted from Colby, A., Kohlberg, L., Gibbs, J., & Lieberman, M. (1983). A longitudinal study of moral development. *Monographs of the Society for Research in Child Development, 48*, Ser. No. 200. © The Society for Research in Child Development, Inc.

stead, the two seem to coincide. This suggests, then, that the college years may also be marked by transitions in moral and ethical development.

MORAL AND ETHICAL DEVELOPMENT IN COLLEGE STUDENTS

Kohlberg's Model

The most influential model of moral development in recent years has been the one designed by Lawrence Kohlberg (1969). Kohlberg, building on Piaget's theory, outlined three levels of moral reasoning, with two stages within each level (see Table 3–2). Like Piaget's stages, these levels are assumed to constitute a hierarchy. Kohlberg also argues that each level is a discrete stage. Once a person reaches the third level, that person should make most (if not all) moral decisions in a manner consistent with that level and should not return to earlier levels of functioning.

The core concept reflected in each level is a changing sense of justice. At every level there is a sense of right versus wrong that becomes increasingly complex (Carroll & Rest, 1982). The first level is the *preconventional*. At this level, external factors guide moral decisions; the person follows commands from others. The decision whether or not to follow a request is based on the likelihood of reward or punishment. In the *conventional* level, the individual's moral decisions are guided by conformity to shared rules such as laws, regulations, or social norms. These rules are viewed as being for the good of society, as helping to maintain social order. While conventional reasoners expect to be rewarded for following the rules, their motivation is largely internal. They are truly interested in maintaining the status quo. *Postconventional* reasoners also tend to follow the rules of society. However, their compliance depends on congruity between the rules and their own individual set of principles, which are defined in terms of the good of humanity. These people will break a law if they see it as violating basic human rights. Martin Luther King, Jr.'s failure to abide by segregation laws can be interpreted as postconventional reasoning.

Kohlberg's model has been criticized as being both culture- and gender-biased (Gilligan, 1982a and b; Moran & Joniak, 1979; Simpson, 1974). Carol Gilligan (1982a) claimed that women will frequently score lower than men on Kohlberg's scale because they focus more on interpersonal relationships than on abstract, individualized principles. Women will try to resolve moral dilemmas through enhancing social communication rather than by direct challenges to authority (as a postconventional reasoner might do). Research indicates that when Kohlberg's methods are used, few gender differences have emerged in studies of moral development (Friedman, Robinson, & Friedman, 1987; Rest & Thoma, 1985; Snarey, Reimer, & Kohlberg, 1985; Walker, 1984 and 1986; see also Baumrind, 1986). However, when asked to recall and analyze a moral decision, women do seem to place more emphasis on caring and relationships than men do (Gilligan & Attanucci, 1988; Pratt, Golding, Hunter, & Sampson, 1988; Stiller & Forrest, 1990). Kohlberg's model, derived from work with an all-male sample, overlooks this component (Cortese, 1989).

The claims of culture bias are also relevant to our understanding of moral development during the college years. While there is still considerable debate as to whether there is culture bias, any bias that does occur is most likely to affect the assessment of the conventional and postconventional levels (Edwards, 1982; Snarey et al., 1985). These are precisely the levels of moral reasoning in question in discussions of moral reasoning in college students.

Another criticism of Kohlberg's theory is perhaps even more relevant to our consideration of the college years as a transitional period. Several researchers have failed to confirm Kohlberg's contention that the levels are discrete, hierarchical stages. Some research has suggested that males tend to skip from Stage 2 to Stage 4, while females tend to skip from Stage 3 to Stage 5 (Holstein, 1976). This finding suggests that there may be at least two paths, other than the one outlined by Kohlberg, for moral development. This finding, however, must be interpreted with caution, since most studies find neither stage-skipping nor gender difference in progression (Carroll & Rest, 1982; Snarey et al., 1985).

In addition, several researchers have reported that some college students show regressions in moral reasoning just before entering the postconventional level (Moshan & Neimark, 1982). Typically, this regression occurs in about 7 percent of the people tested (Carroll & Rest, 1982; Colby, Kohlberg, Gibbs, & Lieberman, 1983; Snarey et al., 1985). According to Kohlberg and his associates (Colby, Kohlberg, Gibbs, Candee, Speicher-Dubin, Hewer, & Power, 1983; Snarey et al., 1985), this is not a true regression; it simply reflects measurement error—that is, problems in rating responses.

College and Moral Reasoning

It is clear that moral development improves as people mature. These advances may continue at least into the mid-twenties (Carroll & Rest, 1982),

TABLE 3-2: Kohlberg's Stages of Moral Development

	CONTENT OF STAGE		
Level and Stage	What Is Right	Reasons for Doing Right	Sociomoral Perspective of Stage
Level 1: Preconventional: Stage 1. Heteronomous morality	To avoid breaking rules backed by punishment, obedience for its own sake, and avoiding physical damage to persons and property.	Avoidance of punishment and the superior power of authorities.	Egocentric point of view. Doesn't consider the interests of others or recognize that they differ from the actor's, doesn't relate two points of view. Actions are considered physically rather than in terms of psychological interests of others. Confusion of authority's perspective with one's own.
Stage 2. Individualism, instrumental purpose, and exchange	Following rules only when it is to someone's immediate interest; acting to meet one's own interests and needs and letting others do the same. Right is also what's fair, what's an equal exchange, a deal, an agreement.	To serve one's own needs or interests in a world where you have to recognize that other people have their interests, too.	Concrete individualistic perspective. Aware that everybody has his own interests to pursue and these conflict, so that right is relative (in the concrete individualistic sense).
Level 2: Conventional: Stage 3. Mutual interpersonal expectations, relationships, and interpersonal conformity	Living up to what is expected by people close to you or what people generally expect of people in your role as son, brother, friend, etc. "Being good" is important and means having good motives, showing concern about others. It also means keeping mutual relationships, such as trust, loyalty, respect, and gratitude.	The need to be a good person in your own eyes and those of others. Your caring for others. Belief in the Golden Rule. Desire to maintain rules and authority which support stereotypical good behavior.	Perspective of the individual in relationships with other individuals. Aware of shared feelings, agreements, and expectations which take primacy over individual interests. Relates points of view through the concrete Golden Rule, putting yourself in the other guy's shoes. Does not yet consider generalized system perspective.
Stage 4. Social system and conscience	Fulfilling the actual duties to which you have agreed. Laws are	To keep the institution going as a whole, to avoid the break-	Differentiates societal point of view from interpersonal agree-

Stage	Reasons for doing right	Social perspective of stage
Level 3: Postconventional or principled: Stage 5. Social contract or utility and individual rights to be upheld except in extreme cases where they conflict with other fixed social duties. Right is also contributing to society, the group, or institution. Being aware that people hold a variety of values and opinions, that most values and rules are relative to your group. These relative rules should usually be upheld, however, in the interest of impartiality and because they are the social contract. Some nonrelative values and rights like life and liberty, however, must be upheld in any society and regardless of majority opinion.	down in the system "if everyone did it," or the imperative of conscience to meet one's defined obligations. A sense of obligation to law because of one's social contract to make and abide by laws for the welfare of all and for the protection of all people's rights. A feeling of contractual commitment, freely entered upon, to family, friendship, trust and work obligations. Concern that laws and duties be based on rational calculation of overall utility, "the greatest good for the greatest number."	ment or motives. Takes the point of view of the system that defines roles and rules. Considers individual relations in terms of place in the system. Prior-to-society perspective. Perspective of a rational individual aware of values and rights prior to social attachments and contracts. Integrates perspectives by formal mechanisms of agreement, contract, objective impartiality, and due process. Considers moral and legal points of view; recognizes that they sometimes conflict and finds it difficult to integrate them.
Stage 6. Universal ethical principles Following self-chosen ethical principles. Particular laws or social agreements are usually valid because they rest on such principles. When laws violate these principles, one acts in accordance with the principle. Principles are universal principles of justice: the equality of human rights and respect for the dignity of human beings as individual persons.	The belief as a rational person in the validity of universal moral principles, and a sense of personal commitment to them.	Perspective of a moral point of view from which social arrangements derive. Perspective is that of any rational individual recognizing the nature of morality or the fact that persons are ends in themselves and must be treated as such.

Source: Kohlberg, L. (1976). Moral stages and moralization: The cognitive-developmental approach. In T. Lickona (ed.), *Moral development and behavior: Theory, research, and social issues*, pp. 31–53. New York: Holt, Rinehart and Winston.

though they do tend to plateau in early adulthood and after the completion of formal education (Rest, Davison, & Robbins, 1978). This is illustrated by the results of a 20-year longitudinal study by Kohlberg and his associates (Colby, Kohlberg, Gibbs, & Lieberman, 1983) (see Table 3–3). While this particular study included only males, such age-related changes have been found in both sexes and cross-culturally (Carroll & Rest, 1982; Edwards, 1981; Moshan & Neimark, 1982; Rest & Thoma, 1985; Snarey et al., 1985).

But is it just age that "causes" the improvement in moral reasoning? Of course not. Age in and of itself does not "cause" development. Rather, it is a marker of development, just as inches mark, but do not cause, height. What, then, might explain the changes?

There is evidence to suggest that people who continue their education after high school are particularly likely to advance in moral reasoning (Colby, Kohlberg, Gibbs, & Lieberman, 1983; Rest et al., 1978; Rest &

TABLE 3-3:   The Relationship Between Level of Moral Reasoning and Formal Education

Kohlberg's Stage	EDUCATION (PERCENT)			
	Finished High School Only	Some College	Four Years College and/or B.A.	Graduate School, M.A. and/or Ph.D.
			WORKING CLASS	
4/5	—	—	—	33 (N = 1)
4	—	17 (N = 1)	33 (N = 1)	33 (N = 1)
3/4	75 (N = 3)	83 (N = 5)	67 (N = 2)	33 (N = 1)
3	25 (N = 1)			
			MIDDLE CLASS	
4/5	—	—	14 (N = 1)	50 (N = 5)
4	—	33 (N = 1)	57 (N = 4)	50 (N = 5)
3/4	50 (N = 2)	67 (N = 2)	29 (N = 2)	—
3	50 (N = 2)	—	—	—

Data taken from age groups 28–36.

Source: Adapted from Colby, A., Kohlberg, L., Gibbs, J., & Lieberman, M. (1983). A longitudinal study of moral development. *Monographs of the Society for Research in Child Development, 48,* Ser. No. 200. © The Society for Research in Child Development, Inc.

Thoma, 1985). In fact, in adulthood, length of education is more strongly related to moral reasoning than age (Rest et al., 1978). More specifically, people with three or more years of college are more likely than those with less education to demonstrate postconventional reasoning (Rest & Thoma, 1985). Indeed, Colby, Kohlberg, Gibbs, and Lieberman (1983) reported that none of the men in their study achieved even the transitional level into postconventional reasoning without having completed college. Furthermore, none of their subjects achieved Stage 4 reasoning without having completed at least some college.

Why would college be positively related to moral development? One might think that because people who attend college have higher IQs and tend to come from more advantaged backgrounds, they would have developed more advanced moral reasoning even if they did not attend college. This is certainly possible, but does not seem to be the whole reason. College attendance seems to be more related to moral development level than either IQ or social class. Furthermore, college attendance appears to affect moral development positively, independently of IQ and social class (Colby, Kohlberg, Gibbs, & Lieberman, 1983).

James Rest and Stephen Thoma (1985) offer several possible explanations for why college might have such a positive impact on moral development. It may be, for example, that college students acquire verbal skills or specific information about moral philosophy that enables them to answer questions at the postconventional level. Or they may learn a more general "socio-moral perspective" that is rooted in postconventional reasoning. Or is may simply be that the general intellectual stimulation of college encourages cognitive development and thereby moral development. This view would be at least partially supported by findings that advanced cognitive development (namely, formal operational thought as defined by Piaget) is positively related to postconventional reasoning (Carroll & Rest, 1982). However, the evidence for this relationship is mixed, so all of Rest and Thoma's hypotheses remain plausible.

Other researchers have also suggested that college encourages the types of thought patterns needed to advance through the levels of moral reasoning. This is precisely the argument William Perry made in formulating his model of moral and ethical development.

Perry's Model

While Kohlberg's model has certainly dominated the research on moral development, it is not the only one available. William Perry (1970) has also presented an outline of moral and cognitive development, focused particularly on changes during the college years (see Table 3–4). Like Kohlberg's theory, Perry's is a stage model. He too presents three general levels of moral reasoning, with three substages at each level. He also includes temporary "escape" and "retreat" mechanisms that the developing individual may use if the process becomes too intense or threatening.

For our purposes, the most interesting aspect of Perry's theory is the role he assigns to college in facilitating moral development. Perry believes

TABLE 3-4: Perry's Levels of Moral and Ethical Development

Position	Description
1. Basic duality	The world is viewed in terms of absolute dualisms (right vs. wrong; we vs. others).
2. Multiplicity* prelegitimate	There is a perception of multiplicity but it is viewed as evidence of confusion or as alien. Someone with a different religious viewpoint might be acknowledged (as opposed to insisting that the person does not have an alternate view) but would be considered confused or unenlightened.
3. Multiplicity subordinate	Some of the implications of multiplicity are seen, but there is still some adherence to absolutes.
4. Multiplicity correlate or relativism† subordinate	Duality is restructured to include multiplicity, such as right-wrong vs. multiple views. Absolutes now doubted or viewed as unrealistic. May start to see the relativism of multiplicity, but no recognition that such relativism is rooted in knowledge rather than simply in authority.
5. Relativism correlate, competing, or diffuse	Relativism is seen as a viable strategy for dealing with moral/ethical issues, but it is applied in limited situations or without a sense of commitment.
6. Commitment‡ foreseen	Relativism is now applied to all secular issues; sees the need to commit to certain values, etc., within relativism.
7. Initial commitment	The first commitments are made. Person understands that commitments are rooted in own experiences. Only partial understanding of the implications of the commitment.
8. Orientation in implications of commitment	Some recognition of the implications of commitment leading to tensions in action vs. reflection, freedom vs. constraint, etc. Real sense of personal identity (in terms of values and style).
9. Developing commitment(s)	Growth orientation leads to restructuring or expanding commitment. Deeper sense of identity, including acceptance of own mood and perspective changes.

*Multiplicity refers to the plurality of viewpoints, perspectives, etc., within a particular issue or field. No one viewpoint is seen as superior to the others in that no inherent structure of the views is assumed.

†Relativism adds structure to the multiplicity so that the various viewpoints can be compared and evaluated.

‡Commitment refers to a conscious personal affirmation of specific values and perspectives.

Source: Adapted from Perry, W. (1970). *Forms of intellectual and ethical development in the college years.* New York: Holt, Rinehart, and Winston.

that a liberal arts education introduces a student to multiple views. Within various disciplines, such as history, English, or psychology, the students start to see that there are multiple viable explanations. For example, in explaining depression, one could look at learning models, psychoanalytic models, or cognitive models. None is completely right, but none is completely without merit. This exposure to a plurality of ideas triggers in most students a realization that the world is not black and white. It helps students see that there are always different perspectives and approaches.

Initially, this awareness of plurality will be applied only to academic disciplines, but slowly students will begin to realize that this concept applies to many real-life issues such as religion, values, and attitudes. It is this realization that starts students on the path to higher levels of moral and ethical reasoning.

Perry claims that most of this development will take place during the college years. He believes that most people are still functioning well within the first level when they arrive at college. By graduation, they may well be in the third level, though they would not typically have completed the entire sequence. He bases these claims on his own study of Harvard men, though he does not present hard data to back them up.

We should note that Perry does not claim that college is necessary for moral and ethical development to occur. Nor does he argue that attending college ensures that developmental progress will be made. Rather, he argues that, in general, the college atmosphere facilitates development. This is, of course, consistent with the data based on Kohlberg's model.

Moral Development and Behavior

Level of moral development, as assessed in terms of Kohlberg's theory, does appear to be related to actual moral behavior (Blasi, 1980; Carroll & Rest, 1982). It appears to be a factor in such diverse areas as conduct disorders, political issues, and support for capital punishment (Carroll & Rest, 1982). Of course, there is no one-to-one correspondence between moral development level and actual behavior. Many factors, such as religious beliefs, cultural norms, the availability of options, and even cohort may influence actual behaviors.

SOCIAL RELATIONSHIPS DURING COLLEGE

We have already seen that there are fairly dramatic changes in the relationships between college students and their parents. As separation-individuation and identity proceed, the emerging adult becomes more and more his or her own person. The break from parents is not a complete one, but it is crucial for optimal personal development. Furthermore, at least in our society, it is also a prerequisite for a socially acceptable marriage. We expect that even newlyweds will live "on their own," apart from parents. We also expect that the parents will leave the couple to make their own decisions and live their own lives. Indeed, in Chapter 6, we will see that such noninterference from parents is important if the couple is to make an adequate adjustment to marriage.

There is a second change in social relationships during this transition period, one that involves starting to get serious with one person. This means, among other things, that people begin looking for a relationship that could lead to marriage. While such a relationship is not necessarily sexual, in our society it often is. Thus, we must look at both separation from family of origin and dating relationships if we are to understand the transition to readiness to marry. Peers are also important for another reason. They provide the pool from which a partner for an intimate relationship will be chosen.

Intimate Relationships

Within Erikson's theory, a truly intimate relationship becomes possible only upon completion of identity formation. If a person is in the moratorium status, as many college students are, the best they can hope for is to form a pre-intimate relationship. Such a relationship would include considerable sharing of goals, ideas, and problems, but would lack the commitment involved in an intimate relationship (Orlofsky, Marcia, & Lesser, 1973). Individuals in a foreclosed or diffused identity status would form less adequate relationships. Their relationships may appear intimate, but they lack the real depth and sharing seen in intimacy. These are pseudo-intimate relationships. Or they may have few if any close relationships; that is, they may be considered isolated. (See Chapter 6 for a more detailed definition of these categories.)

Overall, research confirms this relationship between identity and intimacy, especially for men (Orlofsky et al., 1973; Hodgson & Fischer, 1979). College students are much more likely than adults in their mid-twenties to be in pre-intimate or isolated situations (Tesch & Whitbourne, 1982). However, college women are more likely than college men to be involved in intimate relationships (Hodgson & Fischer, 1981), and this is true whether the relationship is with a woman or a man. This finding is consistent with Gilligan's argument that women are oriented toward relatedness while men are oriented toward autonomy.

None of these relationships involves sexuality by definition, but most college students are involved in sexual relationships at some point. Therefore, it becomes important to understand the nature of college sexuality.

Rates of Sexual Behavior: Most college students engage in sexual intercourse. While estimates vary depending on the specific student population surveyed, about 70 to 75 percent of college men and 55 to 65 percent of college women report having sexual intercourse (Mittenthal, 1985; Phillis & Gromko, 1985; Sherwin & Corbett, 1985; Yalom, Estler, & Brewster, 1982). This reflects an increase in sexual behavior since the 1960s. For example, Sherwin and Corbett (1985) reported that in 1963, 75 percent of the college women surveyed were virgins. Only 38 percent of the women surveyed in 1978 were.

Relationships grow more intimate and committed during the transition to adulthood.

As you might expect, norms concerning when sexual intercourse is appropriate have also loosened up since the early 1960s. In 1978, for example, students were more likely to approve of intercourse between people who were dating steadily. Contrary to the popular stereotype, the norms have not become completely open-ended. Only 7 percent of the students surveyed in 1978 believed it was appropriate for people who were dating casually to engage in intercourse. Men tend to be somewhat more liberal than women in their sexual norms, but the difference is not great (Sherwin & Corbett, 1985). However, this difference may be one factor that contributes to the phenomenon of date rape, which is a considerable problem on today's college campuses.

In fact, the relatively liberal norms and behaviors of the 1978 students may be changing. The most recent data suggest that the percentage of women students who are virgins is increasing. Sherwin and Corbett (cited in Mittenthal, 1985) report that the percentage of college women who have not experienced intercourse rose from 38 percent in 1978 to 43 percent in 1984. Another study reported that 51 percent of the sophomore women studied in 1978 were engaging in sex at least once a month, but this figure had fallen to 37 percent by 1983 (Gerrard, 1987). This was very comparable to the 35 percent reporting sexual activity at least monthly in the early 1970s. Thus, we may be seeing a swing toward more conservative sexual behavior among college women, perhaps attributable to increased fear of disease (such as herpes or AIDS) or to the growing self-assurance of young women who feel less compelled to "please" boyfriends (Mittenthal, 1985). It may be that as social pressure to have sex has declined, women are more likely to follow their own belief systems and not engage in sex if they feel guilty about it (Gerrard, 1987). In other words, the high percentages reported in the late 1970s may be more indicative of social pressure than personal attitudes, whereas those from the early 1970s and 1980s reflect individual beliefs. This suggests that individual attitudes about sex may not have changed very dramatically over the last three decades.

In any case, there have been cohort shifts in sexual behavior, but these shifts are not really the core issue for this discussion. Rather, we are interested in how these relationships might prepare people for long-term sexual relationships. In line with this interest, let's examine the issues of responsibility and commitment.

The Use of Contraceptives: Sexual activity carries with it a number of risks, not the least of which is unwanted pregnancy. Without judging the morality of engaging in premarital intercourse, one can argue that individuals who recognize and deal with these risks are taking greater responsibility for their behavior than students who pretend that pregnancy cannot happen to them. Once again, we find evidence that the college years are a time of transition. College students appear to be somewhat more responsible in their sexual behavior, as reflected in their use of contraceptives, than high school students are. Research suggests that only about 40 percent of adolescent girls always use contraceptives during intercourse and about 20 percent never use birth control (Chilman, 1982). Estimates of contraceptive use among college students vary, but in general, more college students use some form of contraception (including rhythm) at least occasionally. For example, Patricia MacCorquodale (1984) reported that only 4 percent of the students and 7 percent of the noncollege youth she surveyed never used contraception.

It appears that women are somewhat more cautious than men about using birth control. In one study, twice as many men as women reported using no contraception (25 percent versus 12 percent) (Geis & Gerrard, 1984). It should be noted that the differences between high school and college students in contraceptive use do not simply reflect cohort differences. Rather, there seems to be significant improvement in the use of contraception with development. So, for example, although only 12 percent of college women were using no birth control, 42 percent of the women surveyed had not used contraception during their first sexual experience. Of course, there are many different forms of contraceptives available, and some are more effective than others in reducing the risk of pregnancy. Table 3–5 indicates the rates of use of various types of birth control among 336 students at a large university (Geis & Gerrard, 1984).

A number of factors influence choice of contraceptive, including personal as well as relationship characteristics. Men who are effective contraceptors, for example, tend to be well-informed about birth control, open-

TABLE 3–5:   Reported Methods of Contraception Used by College Students

Primary Method	Female Users	Male Users
Pill	57.6%	26.6%
IUD	0	0
Vasectomy	1.0	0
Condom	13.1	27.3
Condom and spermicide	1.0	3.0
Diaphragm	1.0	0.8
Rhythm	5.1	6.1
Withdrawal	3.0	8.3
Nothing	12.1	25.8

Source: Adapted from Geis, B., & Gerrard, M. (1984). Predicting male and female contraceptive behavior: A discriminative analysis of groups high, moderate, and low in contraceptive use. *Journal of Personality and Social Psychology, 46,* 669–680.

minded, older at the time of first intercourse, and currently involved in a stable relationship (Geis & Gerrard, 1984). For women, guilt and anxiety about sexual behavior seem to play a major role. Interestingly, sex guilt does not seem to influence rates of sexual behavior, but it does seem to influence contraceptive use (Geis & Gerrard, 1984). Women who use no birth control tend to report higher levels of sex guilt than those who use something (Mosher & Vonderheide, 1985). Similarly, women who are anxious about relationships with men (even of a nonsexual nature) are less likely to use birth control that requires preplanning in the form of a trip to a physician, such as the Pill, IUD, or diaphragm (Leary & Dobbins, 1983). Women who use diaphragms seem to have lower levels of guilt about masturbation than those using either other forms of contraception or no contraception (Mosher & Vonderheide, 1985). And women who rely on their partners for contraception (that is, men who use condoms) report more sex anxiety and sex guilt than those who assume the responsibility themselves (Geis & Gerrard, 1984).

One might think that gender role concepts are related to choice of contraceptive. It seems reasonable to suggest that students with more egalitarian attitudes about gender would be more likely to expect equal sharing of responsibility. Gender roles of both college and noncollege youth toward birth control are related to attitudes toward birth control, especially among men. So, for example, egalitarian men are more likely to believe that responsibility for birth control ought to be shared. This relationship is particularly strong among noncollege men. The relationship between gender role and actual behavior is much weaker. For example, gender role attitudes are not related to either use or method of contraception among college or noncollege women (MacCorquodale, 1984).

Commitment to Relationships: First of all, it appears that commitment to eventually marrying and having a family has not waned, at least among college women. Most college women evaluate marriage positively and plan to marry (Greenglass & Devins, 1982; Komarovsky, 1982; Long, 1983; Zuckerman, 1980). They are, however, planning to delay marriage until their mid-twenties. This is consistent with previously reported findings that most college students are not yet in an intimate relationship at least partially because they are still working on their identities. Women who perceive their parents' marriage as unhappy are less positive about marriage and less certain about their own marriage plans (Long, 1983).

The intention to marry does not appear to be affected by career plans, although the timing of marriage may be. For example, about one-third of the women surveyed by Esther Greenglass and Reva Devins (1982) said they would marry when they "meet the right man." Another one-third said they would wait until their education was completed, and another 19 percent planned to wait until they had established a career.

Career plans are, however, clearly secondary to having children. While the majority of college women plan to have both children and a career, they typically rate the children as taking precedence. For example, the most common answer to Greenglass and Devins' question as to when to have children was "when I feel like it." Most undergraduate women believe that couples should have children even when it will create a financial hardship or will interfere with the mother's career advancement (Straits, 1985). Thus, the data indicate that college women continue to view children as more important than career.

Most college women appear to be preparing for marriage in that most of them do date. For example, in Barbara Long's (1983) study, 95 percent of the women were dating and 65 percent were involved in "serious" relationships. How involved a couple is, in terms of emotional caring and the sharing of problems and experiences, predicts how stable the relationship will be. Furthermore, the chance that the relationship will end in marriage also predicts the stability of the relationship (Lloyd, Cate, & Henton, 1984). This again indicates the commitment college students have to marriage.

CAREER-RELATED DECISIONS

We have already seen that occupation-related values are part of the process of identity formation. It should not be surprising, then, that movement toward a realistic decision about a career is a major issue during the college years. Of course, this is not the first time a career is contemplated; the decision to go to college itself is indicative of a particular career orientation.

This continued interest in occupational future is underscored in Donald Super's model of vocational development (Super, 1953; Super, Starishevsky, Matlin, & Jordan, 1963). Super suggested that the entire period between ages 15 and 24 is focused on exploration of occupational options. This exploration becomes more realistic and evidence of a commitment begins to be shown during these years. From 15 to 17, the adolescent is in a *tentative* stage, during which temporary career choices are tried out in fantasy, work, and social interactions. During the *transition* stage, from 18 to 21, such choices are more constrained by reality, leading the individual to begin to prepare for "real" work through, for example, professional

Many occupations—and majors—still reflect gender divisions.

training. Between ages 22 and 24, Super claims the individual is in the *trial* phase. The person now actually tries out a job that he or she thinks might be of interest throughout adult life. By the end of this period, the individual is no longer interested in part-time jobs or in a job simply as a source of money. Rather, he or she is looking for a career. Should the trial job work out, the individual will move from the exploratory phase into the establishment phase of young and middle adulthood.

Among college students, there are two clear indicators of the movement toward commitment to a more realistic career goal: selection of a college major and tentative selection of an occupation. A variety of factors, including gender, race, socioeconomic status, political values, and personality characteristics, may influence these choices.

Gender and Sex Role

It should not come as a surprise that gender is a powerful influence on career choice. Traditionally, about 70 percent of all women have been clustered into "feminine" careers such as social work, teaching, nursing, and library science (Stockton, Berry, Shepson & Utz, 1980). As we will see in Chapter 7, feminine careers are lower in status and pay scale than the traditionally masculine careers. The feminine careers also tend to offer greater flexibility for part-time work (such as substitute teaching) or leaving and then reentering the field as family demands necessitate.

In recent years there has been some movement of women into masculine careers and of men into feminine careers. There have been some shifts in gender patterns of majors and career goals in college students. This cross-gender career orientation has been particularly evident in women; few men have opted for the lower-status, lower-paying feminine careers (Komarovsky, 1980; Stockton et al., 1980).

Of course, not all women opt for masculine (or nontraditional) majors and career goals. Indeed, most do not. What distinguishes college women whose majors and career goals are nontraditional from those choosing a more traditional path? Some research suggests that sex role orientation may play a role. Women with a more masculine orientation tend to select nontraditional careers. Women with androgynous sex roles are equally likely to choose a traditional or nontraditional career goal and major. Feminine women opt for the more traditional majors and careers. Among men, there is no relationship between career path and sex role; they all tend to select more masculine careers goals (Stockton et al., 1980).

Acceptance of the values of the women's movement also appears to affect college women's career orientation. Women with nontraditional goals are somewhat more likely to evaluate the women's movement positively and are much more likely to have taken women's studies courses (Komarovsky, 1980; Zuckerman, 1980).

While their mother's educational attainment appears to be positively related to higher career goals among college women (Zuckerman, 1980), the effects of other family characteristics, such as religious affiliation, are less clear. At least one study found that Catholic and Jewish women had

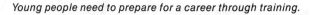

Young people need to prepare for a career through training.

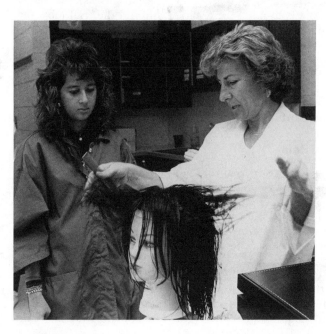

higher career aspirations (Zuckerman, 1980), while another found no relationship between religion and career orientation (Komarovsky, 1980).

It is also possible that the nature of education or training itself affects women's goals. For example, Daniel Levinson (1978) has outlined a theory of men's career development that emphasizes the importance of a mentor. A mentor helps students recognize their strengths and weaknesses, make contacts with people who may be instrumental in securing a job, get important career-related experience, and generally become more familiar with the way to get ahead in the field. A professor might bring a student onto a research project. This provides the student with research experience; it also opens up the possibility that the student will be a co-author on a paper based on the research. If the paper is presented at a professional conference, the professor may introduce the student to colleagues. All these opportunities improve the student's chances for admission to graduate programs or in finding a job.

The question is whether women get the same opportunities to be "mentees" that men do. At least among college students, it appears that men and women are about equally likely to have a mentor, but there seem to be important differences in the nature of the relationship to their mentors (Mokros, Erkut, & Spichiger, 1981). It appears that women, because they are more likely to have female mentors, typically have to initiate the mentor-mentee relationship themselves. Male college professors, on the other hand, seem to approach promising students. Perhaps this partly explains why male students are more likely to have the one highly influential mentor Levinson described.

Both male and female mentors spend a considerable amount of time on their students' professional development. However, women mentors are more likely also to give advice and be involved in their students' personal lives. Despite this extra involvement by female mentors, male mentors are more likely to keep in touch with their mentees after graduation. This may be related to women mentors' concern about being too influential or being seen as role models by students. Overall, then, it seems that female mentors may be a less powerful influence, in both the short and long term, than male mentors. This may put female mentees at a disadvantage in terms of professional development.

Thus, college women continue to differ from college men in terms of career orientation and goals, though the gap certainly is narrowing. Women are not, however, the only group that has traditionally displayed lower career achievement; racial minorities have also traditionally been overrepresented in less lucrative jobs.

Career Goals of Black Students

Much of the research on career orientation and goals among black students has yielded confusing results. No clear pattern has emerged other than that black men tend to prefer socially oriented careers (as opposed to technologically oriented) more than white men do (Slaney & Brown, 1983). Part of the reason for the confusion is that researchers have frequently failed to separate the influence of race from that of social class. Social class clearly has an effect on career choice, partially because it is related to one's ability to attend college (Slaney & Brown, 1983). When lower-class men have the opportunity to attend college, they tend to make career selections that are quite similar to those made by middle-class men (Slaney & Brown, 1983).

Robert Slaney avoided this error in two separate studies, one dealing with career issues of black women (Slaney, 1980), and the other with vocational issues of black men (Slaney & Brown, 1983). He found that when black women and white women shared similar family backgrounds, there were few differences in occupational choice. Both black and white women chose careers that seemed consistent with their personalities. Both groups were optimistic about the likelihood of success in attaining career goals, although the black women were somewhat more concerned about the possible negative effect of financial problems in reaching these goals. Overall, then, race does not seem to be a major factor in college women's career aspirations.

There do, however, seem to be differences between the career choices of black and white men (Slaney & Brown, 1983). Black men seemed to select artistically oriented careers more often than white men did. And white college men were more undecided than black men about career choices. This may simply be because white men see more options available to them. The differences are, however, outweighed by the similarities between the two groups.

We should note that career aspirations do not necessarily translate into career success. It is entirely possible that the black and white students will not, in the end, achieve comparable levels of salary and status. But the point here is that in college their aspirations are very similar.

Personal Characteristics and Career Choice

We have already seen that sex role values may play a role in career goals, at least for women. Researchers have investigated the impact of a variety of other personal characteristics on career aspirations and values. For example, students who rate themselves positively on problem-solving abilities are more optimistic about their potential for success and are more likely to have matched their talents to a particular occupation (Larson & Heppner, 1985). Students who are comfortable in the academic setting tend to have higher educational goals, including graduate school (Swanson & Hansen, 1985).

Political orientation also seems to be related to career goals, though this is less true now than it was in the late 1960s (McFalls, Jones, Gallagher, & Rivera, 1985). Liberals and left-wing radicals have increasingly adopted the vocational values of conservatives. However, the left-wing students still place less emphasis on "getting ahead." Their expectation of lower salaries is consistent with this value. And more radicals than any other group expected that involvement in national politics would be a major source of satisfaction in their lives. Despite these differences in values, radicals, liberals, moderates, and conservatives show very similar patterns of career selection.

Thus, we see that a variety of factors influence the career goals and values of college students. In many ways, these factors reflect the identity formation that is ongoing during the college years. Sex role and political values play a role, and the patterns of men and women show some differences. Yet it is clear that most students are moving toward adulthood by forming realistic career goals. Once again, however, these may be viewed as somewhat tentative choices. In Chapter 7, we will examine some of the factors related to the career a young adult actually enters.

DEPRESSION IN COLLEGE STUDENTS

We have seen that college is a time of major transition in individual development, social relationships, and career orientation. The individual is preparing to enter the world of adulthood. While it is a period of rapid and exciting change, it is also a time of considerable risk and stress. This was illustrated by the possible outcome of identity diffusion in Erikson's theory and by Perry's inclusion of deflection techniques in his model.

Rates of Depression

One indicator of this stress is the rise in depression during the college years. Among those actually seeking psychiatric help, the rate of clinical depression in 18- to 19-year-olds is more than double that of 15- to 17-year-olds (from 3.3 to 7.6 percent) (Weissman & Myers, 1978). More dramatically, Aaron Beck and Jeffrey Young (1978) have estimated that more than three-fourths of all college students will suffer "some symptoms" of depression during the academic year (see Table 3–6). For many of these people, the depression will be mild. But for about 46 percent, the depression will be sufficiently severe to lead them to seek help (Beck & Young, 1978). Some researchers have argued that measurement techniques have led us to overestimate the rate of depression among college students (Gotlib, 1984), but it is clear that depression is a major problem on campus.

Of course, the suffering associated with depression is enough justification to examine the phenomenon. However, depression in college students is associated with at least three other serious problems that intensify our interest. First, it is associated with suicide. The rate of suicide rises dramatically during the college years, from 7.6 per 100,000 in the 15–19 age range to 16.5 per 100,000 among 20- to 24-year-olds. And college students are 50 percent more likely than noncollege youths to commit suicide. Beck and Young (1978) argued that depression may be a factor in as many as 500 campus suicides every year.

Substance abuse is another problem often related to depression. While college students are quite comparable to their noncollege peers in drug use, they do seem to be more likely to abuse alcohol. Forty-five percent of the college students surveyed by the National Institute on Drug Abuse had drunk five or more consecutive drinks at least once during the preceding two weeks. Eighty percent had used alcohol in the previous 30 days;

TABLE 3-6:   Diagnostic Criteria for a Major Depressive Episode

A. At least five of the following symptoms have been present during the same two-week period and represent a change from previous functioning; at least one of the symptoms is either (1) depressed mood, or (2) loss of interest or pleasure. (Do not include symptoms that are clearly due to a physical condition, mood-incongruent delusions or hallucinations, incoherence, or marked loosening of associations.)

   (1) Depressed mood (or can be irritable mood in children and adolescents) most of the day, nearly every day, as indicated either by subjective account or observation by others

   (2) Markedly diminished interest or pleasure in all, or almost all, activities most of the day, nearly every day (as indicated either by subjective account or observation by others of apathy most of the time)

   (3) Significant weight loss or weight gain when not dieting (e.g., more than 5% of body weight in a month), or decrease or increase in appetite nearly every day (in children, consider failure to make expected weight gains)

   (4) Insomnia or hypersomnia nearly every day

   (5) Psychomotor agitation or retardation nearly every day (observable by others, not merely subjective feelings of restlessness or being slowed down)

   (6) Fatigue or loss of energy nearly every day

   (7) Feelings of worthlessness or excessive or inappropriate guilt (which may be delusional) nearly every day (not merely self-reproach or guilt about being sick)

   (8) Diminished ability to think or concentrate, or indecisiveness, nearly every day (either by subjective account or as observed by others)

   (9) Recurrent thoughts of death (not just fear of dying), recurrent suicidal ideation without a specific plan, or a suicide attempt or a specific plan for committing suicide

B. (1) It cannot be established that an organic factor initiated and maintained the disturbance

   (2) The disturbance is not a normal reaction to the death of a loved one (Uncomplicated Bereavement)

   Note: Morbid preoccupation with worthlessness, suicidal ideation, marked functional impairment or psychomotor retardation, or prolonged duration suggest bereavement complicated by Major Depression.

C. At no time during the disturbance have there been delusions or hallucinations for as long as two weeks in the absence of prominent mood symptoms (i.e., before the mood symptoms developed or after they have remitted).

D. Not superimposed on Schizophrenia, Schizophreniform Disorder, Delusional Disorder, or Psychotic Disorder NOS.

Major Depressive Episode codes: fifth-digit code numbers and criteria for severity of current state of Bipolar Disorder, Depressed, or Major Depression:

---

   1. *Mild:* Few, if any, symptoms in excess of those required to make the diagnosis, and symptoms result in only minor impairment in occupational functioning or in usual social activities or relationships with others.

   2. *Moderate:* Symptoms or functional impairment between "mild" and "severe."

   3. *Severe, without Psychotic Features:* Several symptoms in excess of those required to make the diagnosis, and symptoms markedly interfere with occupational functioning or with usual social activities or relationships with others.

TABLE 3-6: (continued)

4. *With Psychotic Features:* Delusions or hallucinations. If possible, *specify* whether the psychotic features are *mood-congruent* or *mood-incongruent.*

   Mood-congruent psychotic features: Delusions or hallucinations whose content is entirely consistent with the typical depressive themes of personal inadequacy, guilt, disease, death, nihilism, or deserved punishment.

   Mood-incongruent psychotic features: Delusions or hallucinations whose content does *not* involve typical depressive themes of personal inadequacy, guilt, disease, death, nihilism, or deserved punishment. Included here are such symptoms as persecutory delusions (not directly related to depressive themes), thought insertion, thought broadcasting, and delusions of control.

5. *In Partial Remission:* Intermediate between "In Full Remission" and "Mild," and no previous Dysthymia. (If Major Depressive Episode was superimposed on Dysthymia, the diagnosis of Dysthymia alone is given once the full criteria for a Major Depressive Episode are no longer met.)

6. *In Full Remission:* During the past six months no significant signs or symptoms of the disturbance.

0. *Unspecified.*

Note: A "Major Depressive Syndrome" is defined as criterion A.
Source: Reprinted with permission from the *Diagnostic and Statistical Manual of Mental Disorders, Third Edition, Revised.* Copyright 1987 American Psychiatric Association.

nearly a quarter had used marijuana; and almost 7 percent had used cocaine (USDHHS, 1986). Certainly not all of this is due to depression, but it is clear that depression plays a role.

Another problem that appears to be positively related to depression is eating disorders (see Table 3–7 for descriptions of bulimia and anorexia nervosa). Of course, depression is not the sole cause; many depressed women do not develop eating disorders and many bulimics and anorexics are not depressed. Furthermore, many symptoms of depression (irritability, weight loss, sleep disturbance) are also common outcomes of starvation. So it may be food deprivation rather than depression that accounts for the anorexic's symptoms (Swift, Andrews & Barklage, 1986). But there does appear to be an association. For example, Russell (1979) reported that 26 of his 30 bulimic patients appeared to be at least moderately depressed. It is probable that, in at least some of these cases, the eating disorder causes the depression, rather than vice versa (Swift et al., 1986). However, the finding that many women are depressed prior to the onset of the eating disorder and that depression "runs in their families" suggests that depression may put some women at risk for developing bulimia or anorexia (Pope & Hudson, 1984).

Causes of Depression

Ironically, it appears that the same aspects of college that facilitate development may contribute to depression. For example, separation from family and friends may trigger depression (Beck & Young, 1978). This is particularly likely if the student is accustomed to being cared for and has not

TABLE 3-7: Symptoms of Anorexia Nervosa and Bulimia Nervosa

Diagnostic Criteria for Anorexia Nervosa

A. Refusal to maintain body weight over a minimal normal weight for age and height, e.g., weight loss leading to maintenance of body weight 15% below that expected; or failure to make expected weight gain during period of growth, leading to body weight 15% below that expected.
B. Intense fear of gaining weight or becoming fat, even though underweight.
C. Disturbance in the way in which one's body weight, size, or shape is experienced, e.g., the person claims to "feel fat" even when emaciated, believes that one area of the body is "too fat" even when obviously underweight.
D. In females, absence of at least three consecutive menstrual cycles when otherwise expected to occur (primary or secondary amenorrhea). (A woman is considered to have amenorrhea if her periods occur only following hormone, e.g., estrogen, administration.)

Diagnostic Criteria for Bulimia Nervosa

A. Recurrent episodes of binge eating (rapid consumption of a large amount of food in a discrete period of time).
B. A feeling of lack of control over eating behavior during the eating binges.
C. The person regularly engages in either self-induced vomiting, use of laxatives or diuretics, strict dieting or fasting, or vigorous exercise in order to prevent weight gain.
D. A minimum average of two binge eating episodes a week for at least three months.
E. Persistent overconcern with body shape and weight.

Source: Reprinted with permission from the *Diagnostic and Statistical Manual of Mental Disorders, Third Edition, Revised.* Copyright 1987 American Psychiatric Association.

developed the skills (including social skills) to be self-sufficient. The breakup of an intimate relationship also increases the risk for depression.

Being separated from family and friends may contribute to a sense of loneliness, another factor involved in college student depression (Beck & Young, 1978). This can occur in a variety of forms. The student may feel excluded from the mainstream of social interaction. Such students may feel left out because they don't belong to a group or clique. They may feel that no one loves them. They may think they cannot express their feelings; they are keeping everything bottled up inside them. Finally, they may feel alienated, as though they do not have the same values, feelings, or interests as the other students.

Finally, academic stress may contribute to depression (Beck & Young, 1978). This is particularly likely in students who were "superstars" in high school but do only adequate work in college. Students who invest everything in their academic work may also be at risk. Such people have no support group, have nothing to live for except academic success. If academic success eludes them, they may well feel there is no reason to go on. Depression seems particularly likely if someone has to give up on an occupational dream (Gooden & Toye, 1984).

Of course, the factors that contribute to depression in anyone, such as the loss of a loved one through divorce or death, can also lead to depression in college students. Familial factors also seem to play a powerful role, especially in college women's depression. For example, witnessing domestic violence seems to predispose college women to depression (Forsstrom-Cohen & Rosenbaum, 1985). In fact, parental conflict in general seems to increase the likelihood of depression in college women, especially if it occurs in a father-dominated home and is accompanied by inconsistent love from the father (Schwarz & Zuroff, 1979). Nonetheless, college does seem to carry with it some additional risk factors. As we shall see with all developmental transitions, the college years can be stressful and can include mental disorders.

SUMMARY

The college years are truly a time of transition, with major changes in personality, moral judgment, familial ties, social and sexual relationships, and career orientation and goals. These changes prepare the college student to enter adulthood. Of course, these changes are not without their price; depression is a serious problem among college students. It is associated with other behavioral problems, including eating disorders and drug and alcohol abuse.

A variety of factors influence both the choices college students make and the ease of the transitions. The many influences underscore the point made in Chapter 1 that individual differences in adult development are both powerful and widespread. Gender has emerged as a particularly important factor in adult development, and we will see its impact throughout the book.

A word of caution: While it is clear that this is a transitional time for those who opt to attend college, it is not clear that this is as pivotal a time for those who choose to enter the working world after high school. There simply are not enough data available to make this judgment, so there is a serious gap in our knowledge about the transition from adolescence to adulthood.

By the end of the college years, most students are ready to enter the adult world. They are sufficiently committed to a career to begin supporting themselves. They are not quite ready for marriage, but are clearly moving toward it. And they are more ready than ever to take responsibility for their own values and decisions. These new skills and values will be critical in determining the path of development in young adulthood.

4 Physical and Cognitive Development

"Compared to young adults ..." may be the single phrase you will encounter most frequently as you read the remainder of this book. It reflects the widely held belief that young adults are at the peak of development physically, intellectually, socially, and emotionally. To use psychological jargon, young adults are our *baseline* group, the group to whom we compare all other adults.

In a sense, this tradition of using young adults as a baseline may simply reflect the emphasis on youth in our society. But our culture is not alone in believing that young adulthood is the epitome of development: The ancient Greeks also valued young adulthood (Lacey, 1968). They virtually idolized the young male body, and expressed consternation over Plato's argument that older women be allowed to participate in nude exercise. They apparently found the aging body (especially the aging female body) ugly.

The long-standing preference for youth might suggest that there must be some justification for the bias. If young adulthood were not the peak of human development, wouldn't we have stopped using it as a baseline by now? After all, many other ideas of the ancient Greeks (such as gender differences or Aristotle's explanation of reproduction) are no longer popular. The sheer staying power of this concept seems to support it. And there is indeed some basis for believing that the young adult years are our best ones. The brain, for example, has finally reached its full maturity and may be functioning at its optimal capability. We have survived the illnesses and physical vulnerabilities of childhood and have not yet begun to develop the maladies associated with poor life-style choices (the lung problems that result from smoking) or the aging process (arthritis). Behaviorally, we may have reached Piaget's final stage of cognitive development and Kohlberg's highest levels of moral development. Our social and emotional development is stimulated and challenged by our careers and our growing families.

All in all, it is an exciting period of personal growth and high-level functioning.

Young adulthood begins at about age 18 to 22 (the lower age is mainly for physiological functions) and ends at 35 to 40. But although there is some truth to the idea that this is the peak of human development, it is not the end of development. Young adults are not a homogeneous group; there are wide individual differences in virtually every area of development. Peak development will occur at different times for different people. Even within an individual, there will be differences in levels of functioning. And not all realms of functioning have been considered to peak in young adulthood. Personality theorists such as Erikson have often viewed later periods as peaks. This chapter, then, concentrates on the two areas where young adulthood has most commonly been viewed as the time of maximal functioning: physiological and cognitive development. Even here, however, much of the young adult "advantage" may be attributable to cohort effects. These and other factors will help us to understand that while the use of young adulthood as a baseline has some validity, we need to be cautious in idealizing this stage.

PHYSIOLOGICAL FUNCTIONING

Height and Weight

It may seem strange to include a section on height and weight in an adult development text. Yet many people are still growing when they reach adulthood, so it is absolutely appropriate. This is obvious in terms of weight. It is also true, albeit less dramatically, of height. In the United States, the average age for completion of skeletal growth in males in 21.2 years (Roche & Davila, 1972). Among females, who mature more rapidly than males, the average age is 17.4 years. These ages for completed growth are younger than they were at the turn of the century. Evidence suggests that men at that time continued to grow until they were about 26 (Roche, 1979).

This finding of more rapid maturation reflects a general secular trend in growth in the United States. *Secular trend* is a biological term that simply refers to changes in humans over an extended period of time (Roche, 1979). In this particular case, the trend is toward earlier maturation and larger size. While the size increases are particularly dramatic in childhood and adolescence, they are also evident in adulthood. Young American men are about 3.3 cm taller now than they were in the late 1800s. The increase is greater for black men, who are about 5.3 cm taller, than for white men, who are about 2.9 cm taller than nineteenth-century men. Similar trends emerge for women. Women born in 1941 were about 5.5 cm taller in their twenties than women born in 1895. This secular trend is not confined to Americans; it has also occurred in Holland, Japan, Sweden, and other industrialized countries. However, it is far from universal. Indeed, there has been evidence of secular decreases in some countries (such as Chile, India, and some African countries) (Roche, 1979). Currently, the average young American man

(25–34 years old) is about 5 feet 9 $\frac{1}{2}$ inches tall and weighs 173 pounds. The average woman is about 5 feet 4 inches tall and weights 142 pounds (HEW, 1985).

Physiological Systems

The Brain: In some ways, the brain is just finally finishing its growth. This is evident in neuron (nerve cell) development. Dendritic arborization, the branching of neuronal processes to interconnect neurons, may continue into the mid-twenties (see Figure 4–1). There is also evidence to suggest that myelination of neurons continues into the mid-twenties (Timeras, 1972). This involves the formation of a sheath of myelin around the cell body (soma) and the axons. The myelin sheath facilitates more rapid firing of the neuron and better conduction of messages through the neurons. This

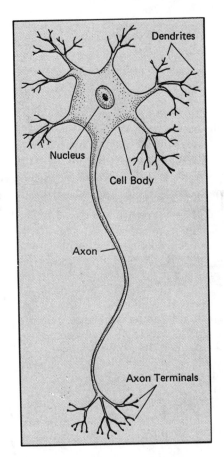

FIGURE 4-1:
The Neuron and Its Connective Processes.
An idealized diagram of a typical neuron. Actual neurons vary tremendously in shape and size.

Source: Darley, J. M., Glucksberg, S., & Kinchla, R. A. (1991). *Psychology,* 5th ed., p. 34. © 1991. Reprinted by permission of Prentice Hall, Englewood Cliffs, NJ.

may at least partially explain why the EEG waves of young adults are faster than those of either young children or the elderly (Woodruff, 1978).

At the same time, the neurons in the brain are beginning to show signs of aging. For example, lipofuscin, the age pigment, has begun to accumulate. Indeed, the accumulation of this yellow-brown pigment (whose function and effects remain unknown) is first evident in some brain structures as early as three months of age (Petit, 1982). Lipofuscin accumulation exemplifies the principle of *differential aging;* considerable accumulation is evident in some brain areas by age 10, whereas it is still negligible in other areas at age 60. Accumulation tends to be highest in the medulla and hippocampus and lowest in the cerebellum and neocortex (Petit, 1982). See Table 4–1 for summary of the functions of major brain areas.

Cardiovascular, Pulmonary, and Renal Systems: At least until age 30, the cardiovascular, pulmonary, and renal (kidney) systems are all typically considered to be operating at 100 percent efficiency. During the thirties, however, systems show some decline (Weg, 1975). For example, there is a reduction in maximum breathing capacity. But the declines are not large. In fact, all three systems are still operating at better than 90 percent efficiency at age 40.

Not all young adults have well-functioning hearts, lungs, and kidneys. About 3 percent of people aged 18 to 44 suffer from chronic heart conditions. Almost 6 percent suffer from high blood pressure. In fact, 11 of every 100,000 25- to 34-year-old men die from heart disease. This number jumps to 62 per 100,000 between 35 and 44 years of age (HEW, 1985).

Muscle Strength: Muscle tone and strength tend to peak somewhere between 25 and 30 years (DeVries, 1975). During the thirties, we begin to see minor declines. For example, hand grip strength may be about 95 per-

TABLE 4–1: Some Major Brain Structures and Their Associated Functions

Brain Structure	Function
Thalamus	Receives and relays sensory information to the cortex
Hypothalamus	Regulation of basic motivation (for example, hunger and thirst), basic emotions (for example, fight or flight), physical homeostasis
Hippocampus	Memory for new information
Cerebral cortex	Higher-order functioning including voluntary behavior, language, and interpretation of sensory information
Medulla	Controls involuntary functions (for example, breathing and heartrate)
Pons	A "bridge" carrying messages to other parts of the brain
Cerebellum	Controls balance, equilibrium, and muscle coordination

Muscle strength, cardiovascular functioning, and other capabilities all combine to make young adulthood the period of peak physical performance.

cent of what is was during the twenties. Most of the declines that occur during the thirties are of comparable magnitude (Welford, 1977), and if anything, are typically even less pronounced. Decline in muscle strength is very slow. In fact, even at age 60, it is frequently 80 to 90 percent of the 20-year-old level (DeVries, 1975).

Sensory Systems: Threshold is one common measure of sensory functioning. This is the minimum amount of stimulation an individual needs in order to experience a sensation. We might ask how loud a sound must be for an individual to hear it. The higher the level needed to experience the sensation, the higher the threshold. A low threshold is therefore indicative of good sensory functioning; higher thresholds indicate sensory losses.

In general, sensory systems appear to be functioning at their optimal level in young adulthood. Take the sense of taste, for example. Young adults' threshold for experiencing a sweet taste is lower than for either the elderly or young children (Engen, 1977). In other words, young adults need less sugar in a food in order to taste its sweetness. While not every sensory system declines with age (smell, for example, appears to be quite stable), none show consistent improvement across adulthood.

Hearing is also at maximal efficiency in young adulthood. This is at least partially attributable to the larger number of acoustic nerve fibers present in young adults. This difference makes young adults more sensitive to auditory stimuli in terms of both loudness and pitch perception (Corso, 1977). Indeed, the hearing of 20-year-olds is often used as a baseline for assessing hearing loss in older populations (Gulick, 1970).

The choice of 20 years old as a baseline is not accidental, for hearing does start to decline during the twenties (Corso, 1977). The losses are, however, quite minor. At lower frequencies (1000 hz or less), a 50-year-old's threshold for hearing is about 5 decibels higher than a 20-year-old's. For the higher frequency sounds, there is about a 10 decibel increase in threshold between 20 and 40 years (Corso, 1977). In either situation, however, the losses are minor. Indeed, the individual still may be within the "normal limits" of hearing, since the sound threshold may be as high as 25 decibels and still be considered normal. Typically, a loss of at least 15 decibels in threshold is needed to make a diagnosis of hearing loss. And even such a hearing loss will affect only the ability to hear faint noises, not normal conversation.

Certain aspects of visual functioning also begin to decline in early adulthood. People in their twenties are less efficient than teenagers in adapting to bright light (such as the headlights of an oncoming car) after being in darkness for extended periods of time (40 minutes or more) (Fozard, Wolf, Bell, McFarland & Podolsky, 1977). These changes too are typically not great enough to affect daily functioning. But other changes in vision may affect daily functioning. The eye's ability to focus begins to decline in childhood. The incidence of myopia (nearsightedness) increases between the ages of 1 and 20 (Fozard et al., 1977). This should come as no surprise to you. Certainly you know more people in college who wear glasses than you did in the first grade.

Sensory changes clearly exemplify the principle of differential aging. Some systems are at their maximal level of functioning in young adulthood; others begin to decline during young adulthood, having reached their peak during childhood or adolescence. So again, we need to be cautious in assuming that young adulthood is the best time of life.

Sexuality and Reproduction

Menstruation: Given that the average age of menarche (first menstrual period) is $12\frac{3}{4}$ years and that the average age for completing menopause is 47 years, it is safe to assume that the majority of young adult American women are menstruating. However, we should note that about 8 percent of all women complete menopause before they are 40, and an unknown number experience *amenorrhea* (absence of menstruation) because of malnutrition, stress, alcoholism, glandular dysfunction, or tumors (Christman & Thompson, 1980; Weideger, 1975).

A significant portion of young adult women suffer from at least some symptoms of a problem known as PMS (premenstrual syndrome). Surveys suggest that 30 to 40 percent of adult women think they suffer from PMS. Professional estimates of incidence vary, but it is commonly believed that up to 40 percent of menstruating women display some PMS symptoms and

2 to 10 percent suffer severely enough to warrant medical attention (PMS Action, 1983; Rose & Abplanalp, 1983). In the latter cases, a woman's family, work, and personal well-being may be seriously threatened. Indeed, the psychological effects of severe PMS can be so great that PMS has been successfully used as a defense in British courts (Dalton, 1980).

What is PMS? It is a vaguely defined syndrome. In fact, the list of potential symptoms is 150 items long (North Central Institute, n.d.). Virtually every symptom commonly seen in a general medical practice has at some point been associated with PMS (Rubinow, Roy-Byrne, Hoban, Growver & Post, 1985). Symptoms may be somatic, emotional, or behavioral (Abplanalp, 1983). Some of the more commonly cited symptoms include: tension, depression, anxiety or panic attacks, changes in sleeping habits, mental confusion, migraine headaches, cravings for certain foods (especially sweets, carbohydrates, and salt), bloating, alcohol craving, and clumsiness (North Central Institute, n.d.; PMS Connection, 1983). The key to diagnosis is not the presence of the symptoms per se, but rather their timing. They should appear at about the same time every month, typically between days 23 and 28 of the cycle, though they can occur anytime during the cycle and still be considered PMS (Hyde, 1985).

PMS is different from normal menstrual discomfort in that it significantly interferes with daily functioning. While both PMS and less severe menstruation-related problems exist, we need to be cautious in attributing too much to the cyclical hormonal fluctuations (Hyde, 1985). Most of the research in this area has been correlational and does not uncover cause and effect relationships. Do the hormonal shifts cause the tension, depression, and other psychological symptoms? Or do the psychological symptoms influence the hormonal shifts? The latter is a possibility. Every woman knows that tension can delay the onset of menstruation. This possibility is underscored by data indicating that women who have been led to believe they are premenstrual report more PMS-like symptoms than women who believe they are mid-cycle, even though the two groups are actually in comparable places in their cycles (Ruble, 1977).

To compound the problem, much of the research has been based on retrospective reports, which are very unreliable and may serve to overestimate both the incidence and the severity of PMS (Rubinow et al., 1985). Researchers have frequently failed to chart the actual ongoing relationship between menstrual cycle phase and mood changes.

We know very little about how women cope with PMS or less severe menstrual symptoms (Hyde, 1985) except that it is clear most women do cope. They continue to work, care for their families, interact socially, and so on. Thus, while we do not want to underestimate the real suffering experienced by some women, we do not want to give the impression that most women become dysfunctional at any point during their menstrual cycle.

Sexual Behavior: Married couples who are in their twenties have sexual intercourse two to three times a week; this rate gradually declines to about once a week by middle age (Hyde, 1986). These rates are averages, and there are wide individual differences. About 8 to 12 percent of couples in their twenties do not have intercourse at all (Wilson, 1975).

There is an interesting time-of-measurement effect in sexual behavior. It appears that the frequency of sexual intercourse among married couples has increased since the time of the original Kinsey report (Hyde, 1986). Furthermore, the nature of intercourse has also changed. Couples today seem to spend a longer time making love (because of increased time in foreplay), use a wider variety of positions, and engage in oral-genital sex more frequently than the couples surveyed by Kinsey in the 1930s and 1940s (Hyde, 1986). These changes seem to be particularly pronounced in younger, college-educated couples and so may reflect a cohort effect.

Sexual Dysfunction: It is always nice to begin a section with some statistics on the incidence of the problem under discussion. In the case of sexual dysfunction, we can only offer a guess. People suffering from sexual problems are often too embarrassed or ashamed to seek help. Yet only those people who seek treatment will be included in the statistics. This results in an underestimate of the incidence of sexual problems. To give you some idea of the scope of the problem, Masters and Johnson (1970) have estimated that as many as 50 percent of all marriages will be affected by sexual dysfunction.

Some of the more common types of sexual dysfunction are listed and defined in Table 4–2. Most are rooted in psychological problems; only about 10 to 20 percent of sexual dysfunctions have organic causes. For example, only 3.2 percent of the secondary erectile dysfunction cases reported by Masters and Johnson (1970) were organically caused. Of the 17 men treated for ejaculatory incompetence, none had physiological problems (Masters & Johnson, 1970). Painful intercourse in women (dyspareunia) is an exception to this general trend. It is frequently caused by organic factors including torn ligaments, vaginal or pelvic infections, or clitoral damage (Hyde, 1986).

Drugs may also contribute to sexual dysfunction. Alcohol, for example, is frequently associated with erectile dysfunction (Jones & Jones, 1977). The effects of marijuana on sexual functioning are unclear (Hyde, 1986).

There are five categories of immediate psychological causes of sexual dysfunction (Hyde, 1986):

1. Anxiety, particularly fear of failure or poor performance.
2. Building barriers that interfere with experiencing erotic feelings. An example is *spectatoring*, stepping outside of the sexual act to monitor one's own behavior.
3. Communication breakdowns between the partners.
4. Failure to engage in proper sexually stimulating behavior. This can often be solved by education in sexual techniques.
5. Negative thoughts, particularly about one's appearance or one's partner's characteristics.

Other psychological factors that may contribute to sexual dysfunction on a more long-term basis include previous learning, relationship conflict,

TABLE 4-2: Sexual Dysfunctions

Name	Description
Erectile dysfunction (Impotence)	Inability to have or maintain an erection. Primary erectile dysfunction refers to cases in which intercourse has never been possible. Secondary erectile dysfunction refers to cases in which the man has completed intercourse at least once.
Premature ejaculation	The man ejaculates too soon (either before penetration or within 30 seconds of penetration) and feels he cannot control his ejaculation.
Ejaculatory incompetence (Retarded ejaculation)	Inability to ejaculate following intense (and often lengthy) sexual stimulation.
Orgasmic dysfunction (Anorgasmia or pre-orgasmic or frigidity)	Inability of a woman to experience orgasm. In primary orgasmic dysfunction, the woman has never experienced an orgasm. In secondary orgasmic dysfunction, orgasms have been experienced at some time though not at present. In situational orgasmic dysfunction, women experience orgasm in some situations but not others.
Vaginismus	Spastic contractions in the outer third of the vagina often severe enough to prevent penetration.
Dyspareunia	Painful intercourse. May occur in men or women.

Source: Based on data from Hyde, J. (1986). *Understanding human sexuality,* 3rd ed. New York: McGraw-Hill.

fears of intimacy, or unconscious intrapsychic conflict (for example, wanting to have sex but feeling ashamed about engaging in sex) (Hyde, 1986).

Fertility: As we saw in Chapter 3, most college students plan to have children. In Chapter 6, this point will be underscored by a discussion of the less than 10 percent of all couples who currently remain childless by choice. But while over 90 percent of all couples want to have children, not all will be physically capable of reproducing. In fact, 10 to 15 percent of American married couples must face the problem of *infertility* (inability to reproduce) (Previte, 1983).

Women are almost twice as likely as men to be sterile from a variety of causes. The oviducts may be closed or blocked because of infections or inflammations. Oviduct blockage accounts for about 30 percent of the cases of female infertility. Cervical secretions may be too thick or too acidic to permit sperm to pass into the uterus. This is the cause of infertility in about 20 percent of the cases. About 15 percent of female infertility is attributable to hormonal problems that prevent ovulation (Previte, 1983).

In men, the major cause of infertility is a low sperm count or the production of too many abnormal sperm (Previte, 1983). This accounts for about 30 percent of the cases. A man is usually considered fertile if his sperm count is greater than 50 million sperm per milliliter of semen. Sixty percent of these sperm should be able to move quickly and easily. Less than

25% should be abnormal in appearance. The minimum sperm count possible for a man to be fertile is 20 million sperm per milliliter of semen. However, about half of the men with sperm counts between 20 and 40 million are sterile (Previte, 1983).

What causes a low sperm count? The testes may have been damaged by disease or radiation. Some men suffer from a congenital disorder in which the testes fail to descend into the scrotum. Hormonal disorders may also cause infertility (Previte, 1983). If the testes are too warm, the sperm count may become low temporarily. This can happen if men wear tight-fitting clothing that holds the testes too close to the body.

Pregnancy: We will consider the issue of adjustment to pregnancy in Chapter 6; here we are concerned only with the physiological aspects. Note, however, that the psychological and physical effects are not always clearly separable. A woman having a "difficult" pregnancy may have more trouble adjusting and vice versa.

A normal pregnancy lasts 38 to 40 weeks, or about 9 months. For the purposes of discussion, pregnancy is typically divided into three-month periods called *trimesters*. The most dramatic effects of pregnancy (aside from the weight gain) occur during the first trimester. There are large changes in hormonal levels, especially estrogen and progesterone. These changes cause the breasts to swell and the nipples to darken. Bowel and bladder functioning are also affected. The pregnant woman needs to urinate more frequently than usual and may experience constipation or bowel irregularity. Fatigue and sleepiness, probably due to the high levels of progesterone, are also common. Some women experience nausea or vomiting. While this frequently occurs in the morning (hence the term "morning sickness"), it can happen at any time of day (Hyde, 1986).

If a miscarriage (or spontaneous abortion) is going to occur, it will most likely happen during the first trimester (Hyde, 1986). Miscarriages usually occur because of natural causes, not because of anything the woman or her doctor did. No one knows how many pregnancies are miscarried because miscarriages may occur before a woman knows she is pregnant. Estimates of miscarriage rates range from 10 to 50 percent of all pregnancies, although a rate of around 20 percent seems to be most commonly cited.

Most first-trimester problems subside during the second trimester. There is, of course, rapid growth of the abdomen. Most women will need to start wearing maternity clothes by the time they are 5 months pregnant. By this time, they will also have felt some fetal movement. Constipation may continue to be a problem. This, in conjunction with the pressure of the pelvic organs on the rectal blood vessels, may cause the development of hemorrhoids. Some women may also experience *edema*, which is swelling due to water retention. The breasts complete their preparation for nursing and, around the nineteenth week, may begin to produce colostrum. This is a sticky, yellowish substance that is a precursor to milk (which will not be produced until after the baby is born) (Hyde, 1986).

During the third trimester, the uterus (and therefore the abdomen) becomes very large. The recommended weight gain during pregnancy is about 22 to 27 pounds. Weight gain and uterine enlargement have several effects. The uterus may press on the lungs and diaphragm, making breathing difficult. There is also pressure on the stomach, causing frequent indigestion. Many women are tired because of the strain on the heart and other physiological systems (not to mention just carrying that extra weight!). They feel clumsy, and indeed their balance is disturbed by the weight and its distribution (Hyde, 1986).

Late in the third trimester, women experience uterine contractions. Many women, especially those going through their first pregnancy, mistake these Braxton-Hicks contractions for the onset of labor. They can be quite strong and may last for an hour or more. However, unlike labor contractions, they gradually weaken and disappear.

Young adulthood is the time when most people establish intimate relationships. Sex becomes a regular part of their lives. It is also the time when many people will want to begin their families. Most people are physically capable of all of these things during young adulthood. However, a substantial portion will experience problems because of menstrual difficulties, sexual dysfunction, or infertility. Most of these problems have a psychologi-

The weight gain during the third trimester of pregnancy puts a strain on many physiological systems.

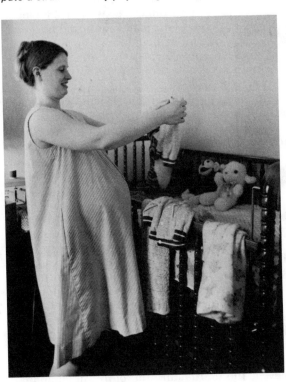

cal component. Indeed, as we shall see in Chapter 6, psychological adjustment to sex and pregnancy both influences and is influenced by physiological functioning.

A Look Ahead

With the exception of pregnancy, all the issues of physiological functioning just discussed will appear again in the chapters focused on physiological functioning in middle and old age. There are several points to keep in mind in reading those discussions. First, there are individual differences in physiological functioning in terms of height, weight, sexuality, fertility, and neurology. Second, not all systems are at the same level of development. Some (sexuality and hearing) peak during young adulthood; others (vision) have already started to decline. Even within a system (e.g., the brain) different structures may "age" at different rates. Finally, keep in mind that "decline" does not always mean "disability." A decline may be statistically significant and still have little impact on daily living.

COGNITIVE DEVELOPMENT

Not all new college students are equally well prepared for the collegiate academic experience. Some come to college with strong study, analytical, and writing skills. The basic tools needed to do well academically were formed during adolescence, and all that remains is to refine those skills and use them to accumulate more information. Other students appear to be at a disadvantage; they do not know how to study. They have never been asked to critique or integrate information. They find themselves falling behind because they not only have to acquire the new information, they also must develop new approaches to intellectual work. They often have particular difficulty dealing with abstract or hypothetical material.

These two groups of students seem to be presenting different pictures of intellectual functioning in young adulthood. One group seems to indicate that cognitive development, at least in terms of general cognitive structures, is virtually completed during adolescence. The other group seems to be undergoing considerable change in intellectual processes after adolescence. Which is representative of cognitive development during young adulthood?

There is little doubt that people continue to accumulate new information (such as vocabulary) throughout adulthood (Horn, 1970; Schaie, 1979). There are numerous debates concerning other elements of intellectual functioning in adulthood. For example, there is a question as to whether general intellectual functioning (as measured by a general or overall IQ score) remains constant. If it does not, does it decline or rise, and when does the shift occur?

Some researchers disagree with this entire approach. They do not view performance on intelligence tests as the central issue of cognitive development. They may believe that changes in intellectual functioning from childhood to adulthood are primarily *quantitative*—that is, best represented as improvements or increases in already existent processes—but they focus on general processes such as encoding and retrieving information rather than on IQ test performance. There are shifts, for example, in how information is encoded for entry into the analytical system. Some of these changes, which permit faster and more efficient analysis of more complex problems, occur during adulthood.

Still other theorists believe that the cognitive structures themselves change. *Cognitive structures* are general frameworks or approaches used in problem solving. They include processes such as what components of a problem are analyzed, how (and whether) the information from the components is integrated with other information (from other components and from previous experiences), and how such information is entered into memory. The question is whether there are *qualitative* shifts in the nature of these structures during adulthood. Some theorists, such as Piaget, argue there are not. The cognitive structures are typically formed before adulthood and are then simply refined and applied. Other theorists, including Klaus Riegel and Patricia Arlin, believe that the actual quality or nature of the approach to problem solving changes during adulthood. They therefore postulate adult stages of cognitive development.

These debates become particularly heated when discussing elderly adults, but they are also clearly in evidence in discussions of young adulthood. As with physiological development, young adult cognitive functioning is typically the baseline against which later abilities are measured. Since the definitions of cognitive development and the nature of its change during adulthood vary from theorist to theorist, the amount of change postulated will also vary.

Intelligence Tests

Structure of IQ Tests: When the word "intelligence" is used in discussing adult development, the writer is most often referring to performance on a full-scale or omnibus IQ test. The Wechsler Adult Intelligence Scale (WAIS) and the Primary Mental Abilities Test (PMA) are the IQ tests most commonly used in adult development research. These tests are divided into subscales designed to tap both specific information (for example, vocabulary) and the general skills used to solve problems (visual spatial skills or analogies). Table 4–3 summarizes the subscales of both the WAIS and the PMA.

The items on these and other IQ tests have been subjected to a statistical technique known as *factor analysis*. It allows the researcher to group various items into clusters which can then be labeled and interpreted. The factors are believed to represent different mental abilities (hence the name of the PMA). Researchers have identified at least 25 different primary mental abilities (Horn, 1982). Table 4–4 presents some of these factors.

Although various psychologists have long argued that IQ tests tapped a variety of mental abilities, they originally argued that only one form of intelligence, a general intelligence or g factor, was measured by these tests.

TABLE 4-3   Subscales of the Wechsler Adult Intelligence Test and the Primary Mental Abilities Test

Wechsler Adult Intelligence Scale (WAIS)

1. Information*	Taps culturally acquired knowledge (e.g., distance from New York to Paris)
2. Comprehension	Problematic situations for which a solution must be offered.
3. Arithmetic	Arithmetic problems.
4. Similarities	Examinee is asked how two things are similar.
5. Digit span	In the first part, the examinee must repeat 3–9 numbers that were presented orally. In the second part, the number sequence must be repeated in the reverse order in which it was given.
6. Vocabulary	Examinee is asked to define words.
7. Digit symbol	The examinee is given 9 symbols paired with 9 numbers. S/he must then match as many symbols and numbers as possible (using the "code") in 1 1/2 minutes.
8. Picture completion	The examinee tells what is missing from various pictures.
9. Block design	The examinee uses colored blocks to reproduce a presented pattern.
10. Picture arrangement	The examinee arranges pictures to represent a story.
11. Object assembly	The examinee arranges cards to make a picture of an object.

Primary Mental Abilities Test (PMA)†

1. Verbal meaning	A verbal recognition task in which the examinee is asked to match a target word (e.g., *big*) with the best synonym from a list of four words.
2. Space	The examinee must find the rotated form of a target design among several other designs.
3. Reasoning	The ability to recognize and generate logical rules is tested. For example, the examinee must identify which letter or number comes next in a sequence.
4. Number	The subject must indicate whether the given solution to an arithmetic problem is right or wrong.
5. Word fluency	The subject must write as many words s/he can think of that begin with the letter *S*.

*Subtests 1–6 can be used to calculate a "verbal IQ score"; subtests 7–11 can be used to calculate a "performance IQ score."

†All PMA subtests are timed. The scores of the subtests can be used to generate scores of overall intellectual ability and educational aptitude.

Sources: Schaie, K. W. (1979). The primary mental abilities in adulthood: An exploration in the development of psychometric intelligence. In P. Baltes & O. Brim (eds.). *Life-span development and behavior* (Vol. 2). New York: Academic Press. Wechsler, D. (1981). *Manual for adult intelligence scale.* New York: Psychological Corporation.

TABLE 4-4: Some of the Primary Mental Abilities

Factor	Tests defining factor
Verbal comprehension	Vocabulary, reading comprehension
Verbal closure	Scrambled words, hidden words
Associational fluency	Inventive opposites, figures of speech
Concept formation	Picture-group naming, word grouping
Induction	Classifications
Number facility	Addition, division
Spatial orientation	Card rotations
Perceptual speed	Findings a's
Visual memory	Monogram recall
Span memory	Digit span-visual, letter span-auditory
Meaningful memory	Recalling limericks, sentence completion

Source: Adapted from Horn, J. (1982). The aging of human abilities. In B. Wolman (ed.), *Handbook of developmental psychology,* p. 849. Reprinted by permission of Prentice Hall, Inc., Englewood Cliffs, NJ.

Over fifty years ago, Raymond Cattell (1941) first suggested that these tests actually measured two very distinct types of intelligence. He argued that some of the subtests actually measure *crystallized intelligence,* while others measure *fluid intelligence.* This theoretical distinction has been of critical importance in understanding adult intelligence.

Fluid intelligence is assumed to be biologically based (Cattell, 1963; Horn & Cattell, 1966). Cattell does not limit biological influences to genetic endowment; he also considers prenatal factors and the normal neurological declines associated with aging. The declines associated with aging may be developmental or they may be environmentally induced (Horn, 1970). So, for example, the decline in brain weight from an average of 1397–1480 grams during the twenties to just over 1200 grams in people over 70 would be expected to influence fluid intelligence (Horn, 1970).

What does fluid intelligence mean in behavioral terms? It refers to the ability to perceive relationships among words, pictures, concepts, and so forth (Cattell, 1963; Horn & Cattell, 1966). It also includes the ability to draw inferences from these relationships and to understand their implications (Horn, 1982). This requires both memory skills (in order to hold two or more items for consideration and analysis) and abstraction skills (in order to perceive the relationships) (Horn & Cattell, 1966; Horn, 1970). These skills are most accurately measured using *culture-fair tests*—that is, tests that do not rely heavily on specific learned information.

Crystallized intelligence, on the other hand, is defined as relying on acquired information and is tested by examining "knowledge" (vocabulary items, social conventions, or mechanical knowledge). It too involves perceiving relations, so it is not completely independent of fluid intelligence. But the relations here are not content-free, as they should be in fluid intelligence. If you wanted to measure fluid intelligence, you would try to find problems that are unfamiliar to the person. If you wanted to measure crystallized intelligence, you would work with information the person would know because of experience in the culture. As you might expect, education is a more important influence on crystallized than on fluid intelligence.

Before examining some of the data concerning fluid versus crystallized intelligence in young adulthood, two cautions must be offered. First, fluid and crystallized intelligence are not mutually exclusive; they are reciprocal influences. A person with stronger fluid intelligence can probably learn more and learn it faster than someone with weaker skills. On the other hand, education and experience, reflected in crystallized intelligence, can provide opportunities to develop tricks for the more efficient and complete use of fluid abilities. This overlap is illustrated in Table 4–4, where we see that several of the primary mental abilities seem to tap both fluid and crystallized intelligence.

Second, crystallized and fluid intelligence do not represent all the general factors measured on full-scale IQ tests. In fact, at least four other forms of intelligence have been identified. They include visual organization, auditory organization, short-term acquisition and retrieval, and long-term storage and retrieval factors (Horn, 1982). But since the impact of these factors has been much more limited than those of crystallized and fluid intelligence, our discussion of young adult intelligence will be restricted to crystallized and fluid factors.

Young Adult Performance: Cattell (1963) hypothesized that crystallized and fluid intelligence would show different age-related patterns. Specifically, he suggested that fluid intelligence would continue to increase until about 14 to 15 years. It would begin a steady decline around age 22. Crystallized intelligence would show gains until at least age 18 and possibly well beyond. Its decline would be later and less dramatic than that of fluid intelligence.

In general, the early cross-sectional studies tended to support Cattell's hypothesis. Fluid intelligence did indeed start to decline before age 20, while crystallized intelligence showed gains into the sixties (Horn, 1970). Longitudinal data, which were much less common, showed similar though less dramatic trends (Horn, 1970). However, more recent research has raised serious questions about these findings. Many researchers, including K. Warner Schaie (1979; Schaie & Hertzog, 1983) and Gisela Labouvie-Vief (1985), have argued that the actual age-related declines in any mental abilities come much later than early adulthood. Any seeming declines during young adulthood are, they argue, actually attributable to cohort differences.

Cohort differences, especially in education, may have a powerful influence on IQ performance. But cohort is not the only factor that may affect IQ performance. Older adults may be more cautious or less motivated in answering IQ items. This could yield an impression of intellectual decline when there is none. Similarly, fatigue and general test anxiety may negatively influence older adults (who are less accustomed to test-taking than students are) more than it does adolescents. Recent or frequent practice using the tested skills may be more common among younger adults (Den-

Education affects both cognitive functioning and test-taking skills.

ney, 1982). All these factors will be examined in more detail in discussions of intelligence in middle and old age. Suffice it to say that it is not at all clear when intellectual decline based on actual developmental physiological changes first appears.

This does not mean that no physiological changes influence IQ test performance. There probably are some. Instead, the effects of physiological decline occur after young adulthood. While there is still disagreement about the extent of cohort influence and timing of the decline in fluid intelligence, there does seem to be a growing consensus that young adulthood is, at worst, a time of stability in intellectual functioning. Furthermore, there is widespread agreement that crystallized intelligence actually increases during this period.

These studies and theories all focus on quantitatively measured IQ. Many psychologists have argued that such a conceptualization of intelligence is misleading and inadequate because it fails to capture the developmental changes in the nature of intellectual functioning. We turn now to these more qualitative approaches to adult intelligence.

Piaget's Theory

The Swiss psychologist Jean Piaget outlined a four-stage progression of cognitive development (see Table 4–5). These stages are normally com-

TABLE 4-5:   Piaget's Stages of Cognitive Development

Stage	Description
Sensorimotor (0–2 years)	Child moves from reflex-dominated behavior to a "practical" intelligence based on own actions with objects, people, and so on.
Preoperations (2–7 years)	Child can now use mental symbols, but the symbols are "static" and "inflexible." The child defines concepts in black and white terms. Ability to take other people's perspective is limited but improving.
Concrete operations (7–12 years)	Thought is now flexible. Child is able to use "reversibility" (for example, knows that addition can be reversed through subtraction). Is still tied to perceptible reality.
Formal operations (12+ years)	The logic that appeared in the previous stage is now extended to the abstract realm. The child is no longer tied to reality; can now form a variety of hypotheses about a situation and devise ways to test them. Becomes aware of the *possible,* not just the real.

Source: Based on data from Ginsburg, H., & Opper, S. (1979). *Piaget's theory of intellectual development,* 2nd ed. Englewood Cliffs, NJ: Prentice Hall.

pleted by about age 12 to 15 (Piaget, 1972). Piaget himself did not predict any major changes in cognitive structures after adolescence, which has led some psychologists (such as Reese & Rodeheaver, 1985) to question the applicability of his theory to adult intellectual functioning. While attempts to use a Piagetian framework to understand adult intelligence have been disappointing, most psychologists still see considerable value in Piaget's approach (Flavell, 1985; Neimark, 1981). Indeed, it has been the basis for considerable research and theorizing concerning adult cognition. Therefore, it is important to understand what Piaget suggested about adult intelligence.

According to Piaget (1972), the vast majority of adults function at the level of *formal operations.* There are three major features of formal operational thought. First, the formal operational thinker is able to transcend reality and think in abstract terms, no longer tied to the concrete, tangible aspects of a problem. Indeed, he or she can even envision "what if" situations. So, for example, when you try to imagine how an interpersonal encounter would have been different if you had said something other than what you did say, you are using formal operational thought.

Sometimes, before you go to meet someone, you try to imagine various scenarios. You think about various ways to handle the situation. In other words, you form hypotheses and deduce the potential outcomes of different approaches. This illustrates the second major feature of formal operational thought, hypothetico-deductive reasoning. Hypothetico-deductive reasoning is virtually identical to the scientific method used in biology, physics, chemistry, and psychology. You have a problem to solve. You generate hypotheses as to how that problem might be solved. Then you come up with ways to test those hypotheses. You know what kind of evidence will confirm a hypothesis and what will not. Again, all of this can be done mentally, that is, on an abstract rather than a concrete level.

In order to generate hypotheses effectively, you must be able to see the relationships among various components of the problem. This brings us to the third feature of formal operational thought, interpropositional thinking. John Flavell (1985) has provided an example of interpropositional thought. Let's say you have a phenomenon, W. You are asked to consider three factors (X, Y, and Z) that may cause W to occur. The concrete operational thinker could consider only one factor at a time. This person might, for example, check to see whether the presence of X causes W. If it doesn't, he would then check to see whether the presence of Y causes W, and so on. He can vary X, Y, and Z, but cannot covary them. In other words, he can imagine only within-proposition variation; his thinking is intrapropositional.

The formal operational thinker, on the other hand, can covary the propositions. She can imagine solutions such as Z may cause W, but only when X is not present. This is an example of a form of interpropositional reasoning known as conjunction. Real-life examples of conjunction often occur when we discuss the causes of disease. Exposure to a virus is necessary to contract many diseases, such as polio or measles, but the disease will

The ability to think abstractly and formulate hypothetical solutions, which develops during young adulthood, may trigger political involvement.

occur only if the person is susceptible to the virus—if the person's immune system cannot fight it. To contract polio, you must be exposed to the virus and have not been immunized against it. If you understand this, then you are using interpropositional thinking.

Formal operational thought, then, is marked by abstract, hypothetico-deductive, interpropositional reasoning. In addition to familiarity with these characteristics of formal operations, two facets of Piaget's theory need to be understood in order to appreciate the criticisms and revisions of his work. First, Piaget is a stage theorist. He believed there are qualitatively different, coherent cognitive structures at various points in development. The structures that underlie a child's thought are different from those that form the adult's approach to problem solving (see Table 4–5). They reflect a more flexible adaptation to environmental demands. Furthermore, these structures will be evidenced across a variety of situations (thought not every single one). In other words, it is accurate, within Piaget's view, to speak of a formal operational thinker. This individual will use formal operational approaches consistently in tackling problems.

Second, Piaget's theory focuses on competence. He was describing the optimal capability of thought at any given stage of development. Clearly, we do not always live up to our competence. In fact, the research suggests that adults are often ineffective, inefficient thinkers (Flavell, 1985). Any number of factors, including fatigue, illness, and distractions, may interfere with performance (Reese & Rodeheaver, 1985). Think, for example, of your own performance on exams. There must have been at least one occasion when you received a grade lower than what you expected. You thought you were prepared and knew the material, yet you got a low grade. Perhaps the questions were poorly worded. Or maybe someone talking in the hall broke your concentration. Or you might have been overly tired from pulling an all-nighter. Whatever the cause, your performance was different from your competence.

Formal Operations as a Universal Stage

Piaget argued that formal operations was a nearly universal, coherent stage of development. He believed that formal operational structures were qualitatively different from those used by young children. All these arguments have now been seriously questioned by the data.

First, formal operations, at least as it is traditionally measured, does not appear to be a universal phenomenon. Studies typically indicate that less than one-third of American adults tested have moved beyond the transition to formal operations (Kuhn, Langer, Kohlberg & Hann, 1977; Tomlinson-Keasey, 1972). Even college students do not all show formal operational thought (Gray, 1990; Neimark, 1981). For example, only 23 percent of the college women tested by Tomlinson-Keasey (1972) demonstrated the highest level of formal operational thought.

The cross-cultural data are even more discouraging. In many cultures, particularly in those that are not technologically oriented, researchers have found only limited evidence of concrete operations, let alone formal operations (Price-Williams, 1981). There are also some studies indicating that in any culture a number of groups are less likely to demonstrate formal operational thought. These groups include the poor, the less educated, and women (Neimark, 1981; Price-Williams, 1981).

Data concerning the coherence of formal operations as a stage are a bit more mixed. Studies that train people to use formal operations show that some people grasp the approach much too quickly to be acquiring it for the first time. This has been interpreted as indicating that the training may "release" already developing structures (Neimark, 1982). On the other hand, correlations among various tasks designed to measure formal operations tend to be moderate at best (Martorano, 1977). Use of formal operational thinking on one task does not ensure that other tasks will be approached similarly. Among Suzanne Martorano's (1977) 80 subjects, for example, only 2 used formal operational thought in solving all ten tasks administered. Furthermore, we are much more likely to use such thinking in our areas of expertise than in an unfamiliar situation (Flavell, 1985). The general conclusion of those reviewing the data concerning formal operations seems to be that there is, at best, questionable support for formal operations as a coherent stage (Flavell, 1985; Neimark, 1981, 1982).

Some psychologists seem ready to throw out the concept of formal operations altogether. But using statistical correlational techniques is only one way to examine whether or not formal operations forms a coherent system (Gray, 1990). We could look instead at the relationships among the various formal operations (of which there are 16). This is more consistent with Piaget's own approach. Furthermore, it is not clear that we should use formal operations all the time. Piaget suggested that intelligence was a process of adaptation, so the form of intelligence that best fits a situation is the most adaptive and therefore the most intelligent. For most daily situations, a formal operations approach is not necessary and may even be inefficient (Gray, 1990)

The question of the cohesiveness of formal operations as a stage brings us to a third empirically based criticism of Piaget's perspective. The question here is whether adult thought is qualitatively different from child thought. The evidence suggests that a substantial portion of the difference between children's and adults' cognition is due to the greater expertise and experience of adults (Flavell, 1985). When you question children about an area in which they have some expertise, they perform better than they normally would on problem-solving tasks. Conversely, when adults are faced with a problem in an area that is new to them, they perform more like children than like their own best thinking.

But there is reason to believe that, even under the most unfamiliar circumstances, the quality of adult thought is still generally superior to that of children (Flavell, 1985; Markham, 1979). This is clearly the case, for example, in the use of logic. Adults can overlook empirical evidence to evaluate just the logic of a statement; young children cannot (Moshman, 1990). Adults' maturation and experience have probably contributed to the development of more effective and efficient problem-solving strategies. Whether these strategies are sufficiently novel to constitute a new stage of development is questionable. Even more debatable is whether they are identical to those postulated by Piaget. Nonetheless, it is still possible that adult thought is qualitatively different from child thought.

There are, then, still some psychologists who think that Piaget's basic premise of qualitative shifts in cognitive development is tenable. These theorists, who are often called neo-Piagetians, fall into three camps. One group has tried to explain the data within the existing model. Some of these researchers, including Piaget himself, have appealed to methodological problems (the manner in which formal operations is assessed) in their explanations. Recognition of these problems has necessitated some rather minor modifications of the theory. Others have focused on the competence-performance distinction, developing models of "moderators of competence" to explain the findings (Neimark, 1979, 1981, 1985). These writers have expanded one component of the theory (the competence-performance distinction). The argument in both cases emphasizes how individual differences and testing circumstances might affect ability to demonstrate formal operational thought to an experimenter. Some of these writers emphasize external factors (such as testing situations), while others emphasize internal factors (which cognitive structures the individual finds most adaptive) in explaining the inconsistent use of formal operations (Gray, 1990).

A second group has tried to borrow broad themes from Piagetian theory. These psychologists, including Flavell, are doubtful of the validity of formal operations as a stage, but they do see qualitative differences between child and adult cognition. They generate lists of some of the differences without requiring that the differences constitute a cohesive stage of development. Finally, some psychologists have accepted the concept of formal operations (Arlin, 1975; Riegel, 1973). Their question is whether or not formal operations is the final stage of cognitive development. They have developed models of postformal stages.

Revisions of Piagetian Theory

Empirical Modifications: When data failing to support the universality of formal operations first appeared, Piaget (1972) continued to argue that virtually all normal adults do achieve formal operational thinking. The only exceptions would be people who lived in environments extraordinarily low in stimulation. But, he argued, our current means of assessing formal operations is incapable of tapping these thought patterns in many adults. This is because the use of the formal structures varies from one adult to another. The structures will be most evident within the adult's particular area of expertise, where the person will have sufficient information to envision relationships between concepts (interpropositional thinking).

Piaget himself recognized one shortcoming of this argument: It appears that formal operational thought does not generalize—that is, it is situation- (or topic area) specific. This, of course, is contrary to Piaget's view that the cognitive structures will be used in solving most problems. Piaget explains this inconsistency by suggesting that the structures will generalize as long as the tested content areas are of equal familiarity and interest to the subject. Thus, to assess formal operations reliably, we must frame the questions within the individual's areas of expertise.

Moderators of Competence: Edith Neimark (1981) argued that it is dangerous to constantly modify the theory to fit the evidence. What evidence is sufficiently strong to require modification? How much modification is permissible before the very nature of the theory changes? She therefore suggested an alternative approach, emphasizing moderators of competence, to explain the data within Piaget's general framework.

Neimark (1979) noted, as did Piaget, that there were sizable individual differences in the manifestation of formal operations. Do these individual differences seriously challenge Piaget's universality argument? Neimark says we cannot answer this question until we know the components of the individual differences. Neimark (1979; 1985) offers several possibilities. Intelligence may be a mediating factor, since mentally retarded people do not achieve formal operations (and may not even attain concrete operations). Cognitive style may be another. *Cognitive style* refers to the way a problem is approached rather than the ability to solve the problem (Brodzinsky, 1985). Does the individual rely heavily on contextual cues to define a problem (field dependence) or is the approach relatively independent of the environment (field independent)? Does the person attempt a solution quickly, without fully processing the information (impulsive), or is the approach slower and more deliberate (reflective)? While the roots of these differences are unclear, it does appear that there is some stability in cognitive style. A reflective person is likely to be that way starting in childhood, though there is generally some increase in both field independence and reflectivity during adolescence (Brodzinsky, 1985).

Cognitive style does appear to affect formal operational performance. The research suggests that reflective, field-independent people do better on formal operational tasks than impulsive, field-dependent people (Neimark, 1979). However, if David Brodzinsky's (1985) model of the relationship between cognitive style and cognitive structures is correct, this does not mean that impulsive, field-dependent individuals cannot achieve formal operational thought. Rather, they are likely to display it only on tasks that are low in ambiguity, complexity, and field effects. This indicates that cognitive style may affect performance rather than competence.

Gray (1990) has suggested that people may not use formal operations partially because they do not need to. Cognitive structures may be resistant to change, and people may "restructure" only when necessary. Concrete operations, the stage preceding formal operations, presents a powerful and sophisticated tool for dealing with the demands of the environment. The adaptations necessary to achieve formal operations may be more than most people are willing to make given the improvements in coping that will accompany the change (Gray, 1990).

Cognitive Trends: John Flavell (1985) is reluctant to accept the idea that formal operations constitutes a distinct *stage* of development. He does believe, however, that certain trends in cognitive development cause adolescent and adult thought to look different than child thought. Several of these are borrowed directly from Piaget. He agrees, for example, that adult thought is more abstract, interpropositional, and hypothetico-deductive than child thought.

Since Flavell seems to agree with Piaget's basic characterization of adult thought, why won't he use the stage label? Because he believes that children are capable of something close to these forms of thought. The reason adult thought looks so much more sophisticated than child thought is that adults have a greater capacity for processing information. They also have greater expertise in various content areas. Both factors make it possible for adults to process more complex information. Greater expertise allows them to use shortcuts in analyzing a problem, which frees some information-processing space. For example, if you are familiar with logic or physics, you can use standard formulas in approaching formal operational tasks. A child would first have to figure out the formulas. Furthermore, adults' greater awareness of cognitive processes (*metacognition*) allows them to self-monitor, and correct, their problem-solving approach. If you are trying unsuccessfully to pay your bills by paying the total amount due on each, you could shift to the strategy of paying only some bills. Or you could shift to the strategy of paying a portion of the total amount due on some or all of the bills.

Beyond Formal Operations: Several theorists have accepted Piaget's fundamental formulation of cognitive development but believe it is incomplete. They argue that there are levels of development beyond formal operations which constitute qualitatively different stages of cognition.

One of the earliest proponents of such a view was Klaus Riegel (1973), who argued that mature thought is marked by dialectical reasoning. In dialectic thinking, there is an awareness of the inherent contradictions of various situations, objects, people. One may realize, for example, that the Detroit Pistons are a better basketball team that the Indiana Pacers. But, in a particular game, the Pacers may beat the Pistons by a wide margin. This is a contradiction. You can bring temporary stability to the contradiction by saying that the Pacers played a better game that particular day, but that will not permanently solve the contradiction. The Pacers may, in two or three years, evolve to the point where they regularly beat the Pistons. This may cause you to reevaluate your ranking of the teams in order to achieve what is again a temporary stability.

The essence of dialectical thought, then, is conflict and change; stability is never more than a temporary status. This contrasts with Piaget's view that cognitive structures evolve to produce an increasingly stable balance (equilibrium) between the individual and the problems that person encounters. Piaget emphasized the development of stable structures that ultimately lead to clear-cut solutions to problems. Riegel emphasized the ambiguity of both problems and solutions.

Riegel argued that dialectical reasoning can, and does, appear during any of Piaget's four stages. So, for example, there is such a thing as "concrete dialectic operations." This enables an individual to achieve "formal dialectic operations" without actually passing through Piaget's stage of formal operations. Because formal dialectic operations does not rely on formal operations, it is not really a fifth stage of development. By definition, a fifth stage would have the fourth stage as a necessary, though not a sufficient, condition. That is, a person would have to pass through the fourth stage to get to the fifth, although reaching the fourth stage would not ensure attaining the fifth. Since this is not the case with Riegel's stage, it is somewhat inaccurate to claim that he postulated a stage beyond formal operations. It is more accurate to say that he suggested a form of thought that is different from, but develops parallel to, Piaget's stages (Commons, Richards, & Kuhn, 1982).

Patricia Arlin (1975) intended to identify a stage of cognitive development that truly was a fifth stage. She suggested that Piaget's formal operations was a problem-solving stage. Her fifth stage was a problem-finding stage. In this stage, creative thought would be applied to problems. This would lead, for example, to the formulation of generic problems and questions that move significantly beyond the presented problem. This process is what enables us to generate questions for scientific research (as opposed to how we approach those questions, which is what formal operations describes).

Arlin (1975) presented data indicating that there was indeed a problem-finding stage beyond formal operations. Formal operations did appear to be a necessary precondition for problem finding, in that none of the 12 subjects who scored high on problem finding were nonformal thinkers. Formal operations alone, however, did not ensure the development of problem finding (there were formal thinkers who did not become problem finders). Thus, Arlin's data met the criteria for establishing a fifth stage.

Other psychologists have questioned whether problem finding really is a fifth stage. There is some evidence that, like dialectic reasoning, problem finding can and does emerge in some forms during concrete and formal operations (Fakouri, 1976). In fact, Dennis Cropper and his associates failed to find any relationship between formal operations and problem finding (Cropper, Meck, & Ash, 1977).

Finally, Michael Commons and his colleagues (Commons et al., 1982) have described two levels of thought beyond formal operations. The first level, *systematic operations,* involves the ability to conceptualize all relations within a system (instead of two relations, as in formal operations). This allows the person to think about the system as a whole rather than simply the propositions within the system. The second level, *metasystematic operations,* involves being able to see the relationship of one system to another. In a sense, this is analogous to the intra- versus interpropositional advance from concrete to formal operations. Instead of being confined to intrasystem relations (as in formal operations), the metasystematic thinker can conceptualize intersystem relationships. This is illustrated in Einstein's theory of relativity, which integrated a system describing gravitational mass with one describing inertial mass. Both were complete systems, with multiple propositions and postulated relationships between those propositions, and Einstein's theory includes both.

Commons and his colleagues do present data supporting the existence of these levels. Their data also indicate that these levels appear only after formal operational thought has been achieved, though not all formal operational thinkers will advance to these levels. But we must be cautious in accepting these as new stages of adult thought. Commons and his colleagues used just one task. It is possible that, as in formal operational tasks, different tasks would yield different results. Perhaps a different task would find some systematic or metasystematic thinkers who were still at the concrete operations level.

Schaie's Model

K. Warner Schaie collected over twenty years of longitudinal data on adult intellectual development (see Chapter 13 for a discussion of his findings). On the basis of this research, Schaie (1977/78) has constructed a stage model of adult cognitive development that builds upon Piaget's theory and yet is quite different from it.

Schaie agreed with Piaget's argument that formal operations was the highest form of intellectual functioning, although not that cognitive development reached a plateau during adolescence. Instead, he suggested that Piaget's four stages described only the acquisition of knowledge. Knowledge *acquisition* might remain fairly constant throughout adulthood, but knowledge *use* would change. His stages of adult cognition describe changes in the use of knowledge.

Schaie outlined three or four stages of knowledge use (see Table 1–4). Young adults are in the *achieving* stage. They use intelligence primarily to solve real problems that have long-term implications, including career and family planning. Young adults must be aware of both the context and consequences of decisions. For example, in selecting a job, they must consider the relative importance of salary, job satisfaction, and promotion opportunities. There are no parents or teachers to "correct" the decisions. Rather, this is autonomous decision making.

By middle age, plans about career and family have been made and implemented. There is a shift in the type of problem being faced. During middle age, we enter the *responsibility* stage. Middle-aged people have responsibilities to spouses, children, co-workers, and to the community. These responsibilities must be considered when making major decisions. Most middle-aged people, for example, cannot just change jobs whenever they want to. They must consider how much moving at a certain time might affect spouses and children.

Some middle-aged people have more complex responsibilities than others. They might be executives or community leaders whose decisions affect hundreds of people. These people need to understand the structure and operation of an organization. When a company president decides to introduce a new product line, he or she must consider the risk (Could this cause the company to overextend itself?), whether the company can afford to produce the new product, how the change will affect the employees, and so on. Such a person is functioning at the *executive* stage. Of course, not everyone has the chance to use intelligence in this manner (which is why we say there are either three or four stages of adult cognitive development).

By old age, the uses of knowledge shift again. Elderly persons do not need to make long-range plans. Nor do they have as many family or job responsibilities. Because of this, Schaie suggested that elderly people become very selective in their use of intelligence. They learn about something or make a decision because it is of interest to them or because it helps them make sense of their lives. This, then, is the *reintegrative* stage during which people get back in touch with their own personal interests, values, and attitudes. They do not want to be bothered with meaningless tasks (which may affect performance on IQ tests and experimental tasks). They are less concerned with broad, abstract questions that have little meaning for daily functioning. This does not mean they cannot think abstractly. Indeed, they will if such thinking is relevant to their search for ego integrity.

What we see in Schaie's model is a pragmatic approach to cognition that emphasizes how intellectual capabilities are used rather than simply how they are structured. Thus, while there is a relationship between Piaget's and Schaie's models, Schaie has added a different dimension to our understand of adult cognition.

Information-Processing Models

All the approaches that have been discussed so far are, in one form or another, related to Piaget's model. Piaget's model, although certainly a major influence on our understanding of cognitive development, is not the only model available. Not all theorists believe there are qualitative shifts in intellectual functioning. Not all theorists postulate stages of development. Not all theorists make a distinction between competence and performance.

The information-processing approach draws an analogy between the human mind and a computer. Information is fed into the mind, where it is processed (or analyzed) to produce an output (behavior). This, of course, is the general outline of how a computer works. Note that the information can be *encoded* (can enter the mind) in a variety of ways. Similarly, a variety of rules (known as "procedural knowledge") can be used to process (organize, analyze, interpret) the information. For example, some information will be treated as a whole, while other problems will be broken down into component parts. The information can then be used to solve the problem or task at hand.

Information-processing theorists attempt to describe problem solving step by step. (In fact, they would like to be able to reproduce human thought patterns on a computer.) They believe that the fundamental steps involved in problem-solving remain the same throughout life. What changes are the limits of our processing capabilities and the power of the rules we use in solving problems.

MORAL DEVELOPMENT

One change from adolescence to adulthood is that we have to make moral decisions that have far-reaching effects for both our own lives and the lives of others. We may face exceedingly complex decisions about abortion, medical treatment, divorce, or career changes (see box on pp. 100–101). In Chapter 3 we described Lawrence Kohlberg's model of how such decisions are made. We saw that some theorists, notably Carol Gilligan, have argued that Kohlberg's model is incomplete. Kohlberg's model was based on research using an all-male sample and therefore reflects male moral development. Gilligan (1982a), working from research on abortion decisions, believes that women use a different framework in making moral decisions. Women, she argued, focus on interpersonal dependence and relatedness; men focus on independence and separateness.

Gilligan's stages of moral development in women, which are summarized in Table 4–6, parallel Kohlberg's. In the first stage, the focus is on self and survival. The woman feels alone in her situation and so does not consider the "rightness" of her decision or its effects on other people. She does what she wants to do. Such a woman would explain her decision to have an abortion quite simply: "I didn't want the baby."

The transition out of this level involves evaluating such decisions as selfish. Awareness of connection and responsibility to other people begins to emerge. The young woman starts to see that there is more at stake than her own interests. She sees the conflicts both within her own needs and between her needs and those of others. She might want to be independent and be loved by a baby. Furthermore, she might consider that having and keeping the baby, even though she wants it, might not be a good decision because she is incapable of being a good mother.

In the second level, these concepts of connectedness and responsibility become even more pronounced. The "maternal morality" of caring for others assumes center stage. Social norms and expectations, especially those concerning feminine behavior, are increasingly considered. The combination of care and social desirability leads the woman to want to do what is best for everyone. She wants the decision to be such that no one will be hurt. This, of course, often leaves her in an impossible dilemma. As Gilligan (1982a, p. 80) notes: "When no option exists that can be construed as being in the best interest of everybody, when responsibilities conflict and decision entails the sacrifice of somebody's needs, then the woman confronts the

TABLE 4-6:   Gilligan's Stages of Moral Development

Stage	Description
Level 1	Focus is on self and survival
Transition	Becomes aware of responsibility to others
Level 2	Tries to do what is best for all involved in the dilemma; often leads to self-sacrifice
Transition	Tries to redefine morality to more completely include own needs
Level 3	Recognizes the interdependence of self and others; considers own needs as well as needs of others

Source: Based on data from Gilligan, C. (1982). *In a different voice.* Cambridge, MA: Harvard University Press.

Abortion: Making a Moral Decision and Living with It

Every year, millions of American women face the question of whether to terminate a pregnancy. In 1985, 1,553,900 women had legal abortions in the United States (Britannica World Data, 1986). An unknown number decided against abortion. For some of these women, the choice was relatively easy. For others, it was tortuous with numerous changes of heart occurring during the process. This is indicated in a study of single black teenagers, 40 percent of whom changed their minds at least once while trying to decide (Bracken, Klerman, & Bracken, 1978). Carol Gilligan's (1982) interviews also reflect the difficulty of this decision for many women.

We can, then, conceptualize abortion as a decision-making process (Hyde, 1985). It is a process that clearly involves moral reasoning. Indeed, abortion seems to exemplify Carol Gilligan's definition of moral decision-making, " . . . the exercise of choice and the willingness to accept responsibility for that choice" (Gilligan, 1982, p. 67). There is a decision to be made, someone will be "hurt" by the decision no matter what it is, and ultimately the decision rests with one person—the pregnant woman.

If Gilligan's analysis of female moral development is correct, then abortion may be a particularly difficult moral dilemma. First, women are often not accustomed to making major decisions on their own. Indeed, some women will avoid responsibility for the decision by claiming that they only had the abortion to preserve the best interests of their lovers, parents, children, or husbands. Second, someone is going to be hurt by the decision. If the pregnancy continues, someone will have to support the child financially and emotionally. Some men and women are, at various points in their lives, incapable of providing such support. In these cases, both the parent(s) and child will suffer. On the other hand, abortion does terminate a potential life. For women, whose moral decisions may be based on the ethic of care instead of rights, this presents " . . . the seemingly impossible task of choosing the victim" (Gilligan, 1982, p. 80).

What factors do women consider in making the decision to abort? Research on the decision-making process itself is scarce (Hyde, 1985). But Gilligan's interviews provide some clues. Religion is an issue, particularly for Catholics. Life circumstances, including income, stage of career development, and the likelihood of the father's involvement, are considered. In fact, the man's wishes appear to be an important factor, with at least some women terminating pregnancies because the men want them to. Social norms may also play a role. Americans overwhelmingly support the right to abortion, but most qualify that support. For example, while about 80 percent support abortion when a woman's life is endangered, only about one-third (or less) approve of terminating a pregnancy for economic reasons (Lamanna, 1984). Some of these factors are illustrated in the statement of Sarah, one of Gilligan's subjects:

> Well, the pros for having the baby are all the admiration that you would get from being a single woman, alone, martyr, struggling, having the adoring love of this beautiful Gerber baby. . . . Cons against having the

baby: it was going to hasten . . . the end of the relationship with the man I am presently with. I was going to have to go on welfare. My parents were going to hate me . . . I was going to lose a really good job. . . . Con against having the abortion is having to face up to the guilt. (Gilligan, 1982, p. 92)

Sarah's last statement brings us to the issues of living with the decision. Research suggests that women experience few psychological problems after having an abortion, particularly when compared to women who were denied sought-after abortions (Osofsky & Osofsky, 1972). However, Janet Shibley Hyde (1985) has argued that such findings are questionable. She points out three major problems with the research. First, there is typically no assessment of pre-abortion adjustment. How do we know if women are coping well if we don't know what they were like before? Second, many of the studies have used mail questionnaires. It may be that women who felt comfortable about their abortions would be more likely to return such surveys. Those who had traumatic or difficult experiences might not want to discuss the abortion. Finally, women might want to avoid discussing negative aspects of the abortion because it would bolster the pro-life position or because they are grateful for the attention of a supportive, interested interviewer.

Hyde suggests that there is considerable stress involved in facing an unwanted pregnancy and an abortion. She outlines four possible sources of stress. First, the decision-making process itself may be stressful, at least for some women. Second, a strain may be placed on the relationship with the man and, to a lesser extent, with parents. Studies do indicate a higher rate of breakups of relationships following abortions (Cvejic et al., 1977). This was a fear expressed by several of Gilligan's subjects. Third, the actual abortion procedure is moderately painful and may cause stress (Bracken et al., 1978). Finally, women who have had abortions may need to mourn and may be prevented from doing so. Having made a "free" choice to have an abortion, a woman may find little sympathy for grief over losing the potential child.

seemingly impossible task of choosing the victim." Often, the "victim" will be the woman herself; her needs will be sacrificed to avoid hurting someone else.

It is difficult to go on sacrificing oneself forever. The imbalance between caring for others and the woman's own needs triggers the second transition. The woman reevaluates the meaning of relationships and tries to move away from the traditional definition of feminine "goodness" (self-sacrifice). She tries to redefine goodness so that it can include her own needs. One outcome of this shift is that she can no longer attribute her decision to what is right according to society. Instead, she must take full responsibility for her decision. The decision-making process then turns inward, and considers both self-needs and self-responsibility.

The assumption of responsibility leads the woman to the third level, in which she realizes that both her own needs and the needs of others must be considered. There is a recognition of the interdependence of self and other that results in a redefinition of caring. Care now involves avoiding exploitation and hurting all human beings, including the self. There is no longer a conflict between self and responsibility because the woman realizes that she is connected to the other people involved in the dilemma. In the midst of this caring for both self and other, however, is a clear awareness of the realistic dimensions of the situation that necessitates an active decision be made by the woman herself.

Gilligan argues that women's moral development focuses on caring and relationships, while men emphasize individual rights. Neither developmental path is right or wrong. Instead, we need to recognize the value of each approach and perhaps work toward a model that integrates both perspectives. Indeed, data indicate that, while both Kohlberg's and Gilligan's stages can be discerned in adult moral decisions, there are no dramatic gender differences in their applications when the experimenter defines the moral issue (Cortese, 1989; Friedman et al., 1987; Walker, 1984, 1986). Both men and women can employ the justice and the care orientation. However, when asked to generate a real-life moral problem, women are more likely to invoke a care orientation described by Gilligan, while men use the justice orientation described by Kohlberg (Gilligan & Attanucci, 1988; Pratt et al., 1988; Stiller & Forest, 1990).

SUMMARY

Throughout the text, you will see the phrase "compared to young adults." Now you have some idea of the level of physiological and cognitive functioning in young adulthood. Of course, the period of young adulthood spans 15 to 20 years, so some of the skills and systems change during the period itself. Furthermore, there are individual differences in psychological and physiological functioning. Some adults exhibit formal operational thought; others do not. The reasons for such individual differences are not always clear. However, they do remind us that the phrase "compared to young adults" is a bit simplistic. Young adults, like older adults, are not a unitary group in any sense other than that they are all the same age. Keep this in mind when comparing people of different ages.

Not so long ago people believed that development, at least in the sense of positive trends, ended in adolescence. It was frequently argued that development improved until young adulthood, when it either reached a plateau or began to decline. We have seen that this, too, is an oversimplification. There is growth-oriented development in terms of physiological systems and psychological abilities during young adulthood. Some areas improve, others plateau, and still others begin (or have already begun) to decline. Clearly, then, there is development, both positive and negative, after adolescence.

5 Personality

I think of myself as shy. In my opinion, I've always been shy. And I'll bet that if you asked my high school classmates, they'd agree that I was a shy teenager. But if you asked my current friends and colleagues, they'd say I was not shy. In fact, some of them actually laugh aloud when I claim to be shy. One of them even said I was one of the most outgoing people he'd ever met and that I was "naturally blabby." My own explanation for this discrepancy is that I've learned enough social behaviors to mask my shyness. My social psychologist colleagues argue that I don't know the meaning of the term "shy."

This personal note raises several issues about personality in adulthood. How continuous is it from adolescence? How much continuity is there between personality in young adulthood and middle and old age? Are our personalities composed of more or less permanent "traits"? Or do they change with our situation and stage of development? Is there a period of "optimal" personality development? If there is, does it occur during young adulthood?

The description also brings up questions about how to measure personality. If someone asked me, I'd say I was shy. If someone asked my friends, they'd say I wasn't. Who is correct? Given my own explanation of the diverging descriptions, would my behavior provide a realistic assessment of my comfort in social situations?

As in the preceding chapter, we need to establish a baseline. We need to see what personality looks like during young adulthood and how it is related to both earlier and later functioning.

THE ISSUE OF STABILITY

As we saw in Chapter 1, much of the research in adult personality functioning focuses on the issue of stability versus change. This issue provides a framework for analyzing much of what we know about personality in young adulthood. Many of the studies, for example, aim to demonstrate how personality changes from one phase of development to the next. This goal influences the choice of the personality characteristics to be examined. It has also fueled the search for information about how "life crises" contribute to personality change.

The Case for Change

Many life-span theorists have argued that there are major changes in adult personality. This approach probably began with Carl Jung (1931/1960) who suggested that, after middle age, people become less sex-role stereotyped in behavior and more focused on their own inner needs rather than familial and cultural needs. Erik Erikson (1963) later suggested that adults shift focus from intimacy to generativity to ego integrity as they age. Roger Gould (1972) and Daniel Levinson (1978) also offered stage theories of adult personality development.

Inherent Motives: Why would so many people argue that there is change in adult personality functioning? One explanation is that people are inherently motivated to continue to develop. Abraham Maslow (1971), for example, suggested that once certain basic needs are met, "growth motivation" drives human development. People strive to develop their intellect and emotional life simply for the challenge of doing so. Similarly, Karl and Charlotte Buhler (C. Buhler, 1935; C. Buhler & Massarik, 1968) argued that there is an innate tendency for "creative expansion" motivating human development throughout the life span.

Socialization: Other theorists have argued that the motivation for change is more socially based. As we pointed out in Chapter 1, socialization is a lifelong process that may affect adult personality in at least two ways. First, there are certain socially sanctioned role changes during adulthood. We expect young adults to establish a career, get married, and have children. These new roles may be stressful and may actually demand certain changes. David Gutmann (1975) argued that the birth of a child creates a "parental imperative." The demands of insuring the survival and optimal development of a child throw the parents into a state of emergency. To meet these demands, the parents divide the childrearing tasks such that one (typically the mother) is responsible for the child's emotional well-being, while the other (the father) procures the resources to provide food, shelter, medical care, and so on. This, according to Gutmann, causes young adults to be quite stereotyped in terms of sex-role behavior. After the children are raised the requirement for gender-based division of labor diminishes, resulting in the movement toward androgeny that Jung claimed marked later development. Gutmann's hypothesis, then, exemplifies how role changes (in terms of parenthood) might trigger personality changes (in terms of sex-role behavior).

This approach, emphasizing the impact of normal role changes on personality, is sometimes referred to as the *life crisis* model. It is an appeal-ing model because many of us intuitively believe that role changes cause personality changes. We've all seen single people feel disconnected from their newly married friends—"Joe just isn't as much fun since he married Kathy." Furthermore, it is a model that seems particularly applicable to young adulthood, since young adults experience more role changes than either middle-aged or elderly people do (Gurin & Brim, 1984).

Role changes are not the only aspect of socialization that may lead to changes in adult personality; there are also generalized expectations that adults will change. This is clear in terms of the expression of emotions (Av-erill, 1984; Malatesta & Haviland, 1985; Malatesta & Izard, 1984). There is an expectation in American society that we will generally display positive emotions (pleasure, joy, satisfaction) more openly than negative ones (anger, sadness, anxiety). After all, we don't want to upset other people, and it is certainly usually more disconcerting to watch someone cry or fight than to see someone smile or laugh. The expectation that the individual will follow this convention increases with age. We are not surprised when a 2-year-old throws a temper tantrum; we would be appalled to witness compa-rable behavior from one of our professors. It is easy to demonstrate that adults have internalized this convention. Think of how many times you've seen your parents laugh versus how many times you've seen them cry!

You probably have seen your parents smile even more than you've seen them laugh. This exemplifies a second convention about adult emo-tional expression—namely, that the expression should be more reserved, more blunted in adults than in children. This is especially true for adult men. As we gain more experience with social reactions to emotional expres-sion in various situations, we become more adept at meeting both social norms. Of course, changing the expression of emotions does not necessarily mean that the experience of emotions changes; you all know that you still feel joy, anger, and grief, often to extreme degrees. The situations that elicit such emotions are different now than they were in childhood, and your understanding of and reaction to the emotions have changed, but the emo-tions themselves are still there. Thus, within just one behavioral realm, we can make a case not only for change, but also for stability. Let's look more closely at this idea.

The Case for Stability

The belief in stability in adult personality can be traced to at least two different sources. First, early psychologists emphasized development as basically a childhood and adolescence process. Freud, for example, argued that personality development was virtually complete by about age 5, when the phallic period ended (see Table 5–1). Second, some theorists, including Gordon Allport and Hans Eysenck, have argued that each individual has a number of basic, innate personality traits that remain the same throughout life.

Traits and Types: Gordon Allport (1961) is probably the best known of the trait theorists. He argued that people consistently behave in certain ways: some are aggressive; others are shy. *Traits*, and the way in which they

TABLE 5-1:   Freud's Stages of Personality Development

Stage	Age	Description
Oral	Birth-1 yr	The oral area is the main source of pleasure. Difficulty in weaning can lead to permanent fixation at the oral stage, resulting in the development of an oral personality. These people are marked by immaturity, dependency in relationships, unusual friendliness and generosity, and the expectation that others will "mother" them. Oral fixation may also result in excessive eating and drinking.
Anal	1-3 yr	Pleasure is derived from retaining and expelling feces as libidinal energy is focused in the anal area. A child who experiences difficulty in toilet training may develop either an anal aggressive or an anal retentive character. Anal aggressives use hostile outbursts excessively as a means of coping. Anal retentives are stingy and stubborn as adults.
Phallic	3-5 yr	Libidinal energy is focused in the genital area. The Oedipal conflict occurs and should result in the formation of the superego. Inadequate resolution of this conflict may lead to an overactive or underactive superego, which would leave the person guilt-ridden and rigidly following rules. An underactive superego would result in inadequate concern with rules and societal values, possibly resulting in criminal behavior. These outcomes are more applicable to boys than to girls, since "normal" girls do not complete their superego development until later in life.
Latency	5-12	Sex drive (libido) is dormant and the child concentrates on acquiring the skills necessary to survive as an adult in his/her culture.
Genital	12-senility	Libidinal energy is again focused in the genitals, but now the energy is channeled into mature heterosexual relationships. Problems at this stage are attributable to early development.
	Senility-death	Regression to pregenital behavior.

are interrelated in a particular person, determine these characteristic ways of thinking and behaving. The key word here is "characteristic." People are stable and predictable in their reactions to situations, which allows us to describe an individual's reactions and typical behaviors. These are the characteristics that come to mind when you're asked to describe someone, and are called *central dispositions*. Each person has only a few such traits—probably ten or less is typical—and they appear in a wide variety of situations.

In addition to these central dispositions, we also have *secondary dispositions*, characteristics that are evident in a narrower range of situations. You would not be as surprised if someone violated these traits. A few people also have *cardinal dispositions*, traits that dominate the entire personality.

The pervasiveness of a cardinal disposition is best exemplified by the adoption of a person's name as the name of the trait; Christlike, sadistic, and Machiavellian are all examples.

The term trait is not assumed to be simply descriptive of some form of behavior; instead, Allport believed that traits actually exist within a person. Although we cannot look into someone's brain and see a trait, there is a neurophysiological and genetic basis for traits. According to Allport, a person is born not with a particular trait, but with a predisposition to develop certain traits. This is because physique, temperament, and intelligence are all relatively fixed at birth. These characteristics remain quite stable throughout life. They interact with the environment to produce the specific traits we see in an individual.

While Allport assigned a sizable role to the environment, Hans Eysenck (1975) has emphasized the role of genetics and constitutional factors in personality. He argued that there are *personality types*. These types are continuous dimensions, and given individuals fall somewhere along each dimension. The two major dimensions he identified are *introversion-extroversion* and *stability-instability*. Most people are neither extremely introverted nor extremely extroverted, but some do exhibit extreme extroversion. This type of person would exhibit high levels of sociability, activity, liveliness, and excitability. The stability-instability dimension refers to emotionality or excitability. Again, most people would not be at either extreme, but a stable person would tend to be easygoing, peaceful, and low in anxiety. A type thus represents a more general level of personality than a trait. You can characterize people by placing them in one of the four quadrants defined by the intersection of the two types. A person could, for example, be considered highly unstable and highly introverted or highly unstable and highly extroverted. Keep in mind, though, that most people do not fall into the extremes of either type.

There are data to support Eysenck's view. In several different reports, Paul Costa and Robert McCrae have presented evidence of certain stable traits in men's personalities (Costa, McCrae, & Arenberg, 1980; Costa, McCrae, & Norris, 1981; McCrae & Costa, 1986). They have identified five traits, three of which are particularly well documented: extroversion, neuroticism, and openness to experience. Each trait is actually quite similar to a "type" in that it consists of several specific characteristics. The characteristics of extroversion, neuroticism, and openness to experience are listed in Table 5-2.

The data that Costa and McCrae present are quite impressive. The correlations between the original personality assessments and measures taken 6 and 12 years later exceed .60 for each characteristic. In fact, these correlations are typically at least .70. The stability is as evident in men who were young adults at the time of the original testing as in men who were middle-aged and old (Costa, McCrae, & Arenberg, 1980).

Because Costa and McCrae's data are longitudinal, they are open to the criticism that the men tested are not truly a representative sample. Furthermore, only men were included in these analyses. However, other researchers have reported similar stability in both men and women (Costa &

TABLE 5-2:   Characteristics Associated with Costa and McCrae's Personality Factors

Extroversion*	Neuroticism	Openness to Experience
Warmth	Anxiety	Fantasy
Gregariousness	Hostility	Esthetics
Assertiveness	Depression	Feelings
Activity	Self-consciousness	Actions
Excitement seeking	Impulsiveness	Ideas
Positive emotions	Vulnerability	Values

*People showing each type will be rated high on the listed characteristics. So, for example, someone who is high on extroversion will be more warm, gregarious, etc., than someone low on extroversion.

Source: Based on Costa, P., & McCrae, R. (1984). Personality as a lifelong determinant of well-being. In C. Malatesta & C. Izard (eds.), *Affective processes in adult development and aging.* Beverly Hills: Sage.

McCrae, 1984), and cross-sectional studies fail to find age differences on many personality variables (Mellinger & Erdwins, 1985). Of course, not all researchers find such remarkable stability in adult personality (see Stevens & Truss, 1985).

In addition to extroversion and stability, Eysenck identified one other stable component of personality—*psychoticism,* a predisposition to be psychotic and/or psychopathic. It does not have bipolar opposites like introversion-extroversion or stability-instability. Rather, psychoticism simply exists to some extent in everyone. People who are high on psychoticism are more likely to develop untreatable mental illnesses. People with lower tendencies either don't develop mental illness or respond to treatment. Eysenck postulates a similar relationship between criminality and psychoticism. According to Eysenck, heredity determines the degree of psychoticism.

Genetics and Adult Personality: While Eysenck's view is more extreme, both Allport and Eysenck see genetics as influential in adult personality. Numerous studies of twins provide some basis for this assumption; they show that several dimensions of personality seem to be at least moderately affected by heredity (Goldsmith, 1983). Among young adults, these include aggression, impulsiveness, ego or self control, and sociability. The acquisition and maintenance of fears that are adaptive for survival (fear of death, water, loved one's misfortunes, dangerous places) also seem to be influenced by genetics (Rose & Ditto, 1983).

Some caution is needed in interpreting these results. First, it is important to remember that the reported genetic influence is moderate; all studies indicate a sizable environmental component in personality characteristics. Second, most of the research is cross-sectional. There is evidence to suggest that, at any given point in time, there is a genetic effect on personality functioning. However, if a person's score on personality measures changes, the change seems to be almost completely due to environmental events. Michael Pogue-Geile and Richard Rose (1985) reported such strong environmental influences for changes in scores measuring depression, introversion-extroversion, psychopathy, and religiosity in young adulthood. But they did find a strong genetic component for changes in the scale measuring schizophrenic tendencies. Overall, then, we may say   netics can influence (though not determine) certain personality cl rac istics, but the expression of those characteristics may change during \dult-hood. The change may be due primarily to environmental   nces rather than genetic tendencies.

In sum, while personality certainly can change, there is c   ble evidence that it typically does not, at least in terms of some cha ics (Costa & McRae, 1984; Gurin & Brim, 1984; Schaie & Parham, 19   ns & Truss, 1985; Woodruff & Birren, 1972). In addition to trait ex| s for this stability, developmentalists have focused on explanations   a-ble to those used to argue for change—namely, inherent motives a   l-ization.

Inherent Motives: Patricia Gurin and Orville Brim (1984) have that three basic needs lead to a tendency for stability: needs for c   t self-respect, and consistency of self. The need for control is easi plained. Imagine you have just heard that an acquaintance of your been raped. What questions would you ask the person telling you the s Chances are you'd want to know where she was, who she was with, how rapist got into the room, what she was wearing, and various other thi about her and her behavior. If you could, you would find some way of signing at least some of the blame for the rape to her, especially if you a a woman. Why? Because if you can convince yourself that she could ha controlled the rape, then you can continue to believe that you can contro the likelihood of becoming a victim yourself. "Blaming the victim," then, becomes comprehensible as an expression of our need for control. Such need for control has been empirically documented in a wide range of personality and social psychology research.

People also need to maintain self-respect and consistency in their impressions of themselves. They will alter their goals and distort experiences in order to maintain good images of themselves. It is not uncommon to take credit for success and blame others for failure. In fact, this tendency is one of the best established findings in psychology (Gurin & Brim, 1984). If you don't believe it, think of how you explain an A grade ("I worked hard" or "I have a knack for psychology") versus a D ("The test was too hard." "She asked nitpicking questions").

There can be a conflict between the needs for self-respect and consistency. If someone is low in self-respect, does he or she prefer praise or criticism? The praise would serve to bolster self-respect, but would be inconsistent with the person's self-image. The criticism would feed the need for consistency at the cost of self-respect. The evidence indicates that emotionally a person would prefer the praise, but cognitively could better attend to and comprehend the criticism (Gurin & Brim, 1984). This distinction shows us why a little bit of praise and support will not significantly raise people's self-respect. While they like it emotionally, they are unable to inter-pret it within their self-definition. This cognitive bias may even prevent them from remembering they were praised at all.

Socialization: If we do distort events to meet our needs for control, self-respect, and consistency, then it is easy to see how we would maintain stability in the face of the hundreds of daily encounters we all have. After all, each one is probably relatively small in the strain it puts on our person-ality. I can easily blame another driver for cutting in front of me and mak-ing me slam on the brakes. That doesn't make me think I'm a bad driver—much less a bad person. But what about the major role changes, the life crises, that we noted earlier? They mean great changes in our lives that continue to affect us day after day.

Stability proponents would answer "Not necessarily." To some extent, it depends on the properties of the life changes themselves. Many "life cri-ses" have age norms—that is, they typically happen at a certain time in life. We expect people in their twenties and early thirties to get married and have children. But those who have a first baby at age 42 may be faced with endless questions and have few friends in the same situation. Indeed, many of their friends may be enjoying a new-found freedom now that their chil-dren are growing up and leaving home.

According to Bernice Neugarten (1968), the timing of a life crisis is crucial. An "on-time" life crisis (like becoming a parent) need not provoke personality change. After all, people can prepare for it. This preparation, known as *anticipatory socialization,* helps to "steel" people for the changes and gives them a framework for interpreting and adjusting to them. We all know how much more difficult it is to deal with an unexpected change than with an expected one, even if it's a minor event. Think of the difference in your reaction to invited versus unexpected company, for example.

In addition, there is more social support for an "on time" event than for an "off time" one. If your friends' children are the same age as yours, you can talk about common problems in childrearing. You can exchange babysitting favors. You can take each other's children to school, to amuse-ment parks, to shows. Fifty-year-old parents of an 8-year-old can still do all of this, but they will be doing it with 35-year-olds instead of other 50-year-olds. Their own friends won't be involved. They may feel out of step both with the parents of their children's friends and with their own friends. In this case lack of support may be sufficient to mediate a personality change. For people following the usual path, the available social support will buffer the stresses of the role change and tend to minimize personality changes (Gurin & Brim, 1984).

Stability or Change?

The question of whether there is stability or change in adult person-ality is somewhat inappropriate and simplistic. It is clear that there is both stability and change. Some aspects of personality will change not only from one stage of adulthood to the next, but even within a particular stage. Still other characteristics will remain remarkably stable from the early twenties into the seventies and beyond. Given the complexity of human personality, this mix of stability and change should not be surprising.

Unfortunately, even this answer to the stability debate is too simplistic. We cannot formulate lists of characteristics that are stable and characteristics that change. First, there are individual differences in personality change. The timing of life events may affect whether or not those events "change" personality. There may also be gender differences in the stability of personality (Lowenthal, Thurnher, & Chiriboga, 1975). What we need to understand are what characteristics are likely to change, and under what circumstances.

Before we actually examine personality in young adulthood, a word of caution is needed. Much of the information about young adult personality comes from cross-sectional studies. This is risky because it is quite clear that there are cohort effects in personality functioning (Schaie & Parham, 1976). In other words, the differences between cohorts in terms of personality characteristics are sizable. For example, gender differences appear to be less pronounced in today's college students than they were in students of the 1970s, who showed fewer gender differences than students of the 1950s (Stevens & Truss, 1985). If you did a cross-sectional study, you might find that 55-year-olds were more stereotyped than 35-year-olds, who were more stereotyped than 25-year-olds. You might interpret this as a developmental trend when it may in fact be a cohort effect. Indeed, the 55-year-olds may actually be less stereotyped now than when they themselves were 25.

PERSONALITY CHARACTERISTICS

Many of the major personality development theorists, including Erikson, Levinson, and Gould, focus on issues of intimacy and career in discussing personality functioning in young adulthood. Since the next two chapters will deal exclusively with these topics, here we will look at some of the specific personality traits and psychological needs that have been examined in young adults.

Changes from Adolescence to Young Adulthood

In Chapter 3 we saw one of the major differences between adolescents and young adults. By sometime in their mid-twenties most adults have developed a fairly strong identity in terms of both career and personal values. Some evidence suggests that this may be more true for men than for women. This solidification of identity represents a major change in the underlying structure of personality. We might expect that it would be reflected in shifts in several specific personality traits.

High school boys' self-descriptions seem to reflect the confusion and discomfort of an unstable identity. When compared to young adult men's self-descriptions, teenage boys are more likely to see themselves as unhappy, dissatisfied, and generally insecure in terms of work and social relationships. Young adult men, on the other hand, see themselves as versatile and adventuresome. They seem to have endless energy and considerable faith in their ability to use that energy (Lowenthal, et al., 1975).

Similarly, high school girls view themselves as undecided, dependent, helpless, lazy, and unintelligent. Young adult women do not describe themselves in these terms. Yet they are not terribly positive in their self-descriptions; they see themselves as low in energy and high in jealousy (Lowenthal et al., 1975). The jealousy component seems to be tied to their interest in their families and reflects a desire to have more of their husbands' time. The emphasis on family is also evident in their portrayal of themselves as "warm" people. Carol Malatesta and L. Clayton Culver (1984) also reported that young adult women complained about lack of time with their husbands. This seems consistent with Erikson's (1980) argument that women's identities are forged within a marital relationship.

The relatively low energy level reported by young adult women in the Lowenthal study is interesting and may reflect mild to moderate depression. Many of the women in this study were mothers of young children. Several other researchers have reported that mothers of preschoolers are particularly susceptible to depression (Malatesta & Culver, 1984; Patterson, 1980), perhaps because of their relative isolation if they are at home full-time (Alpert & Richardson, 1980). These women have few social supports and feel that even their husbands are not particularly available to them. Their daily tasks, including housework, are often devalued by the general culture and involve constant repetition (Oakley, 1974). Think of how many times young homemakers wash the same dishes and clothes! Furthermore, young mothers are faced with many negative social interactions. Conflicts between mothers and their preschoolers may occur as often as once every three minutes, with major disagreements at a rate of as many as three per hour. Add to this approximately one major marital conflict per week (Patterson, 1980). Reliance on one role (in this case, motherhood) for all one's rewards and social supports is apparently a risky business (Rodin & Ickovics, 1990). So in many cases, despite the potential for work overload, women who work and have families frequently show better mental and physical health (Rodin & Ickovics, 1990; Tiedje, Wortman, Downey, Emmons, Biernat & Lang, 1990).

Longitudinal data on young women comparing personality functioning during college to that during young adulthood indicate some additional changes. Unfortunately, the findings do not give us a clear picture. For example, Malatesta and Culver (1984) reported that young adult women (around 30 years old) were less oriented toward success than were college women. On the other hand, Stevens and Truss (1985) found an increase in need for achievement in both men and women from the college years to age 30. During this same period, Malatesta and Culver's women subjects decreased their focus on aggression and anger. The women in the Stevens and Truss study showed no change in their need for aggression, though they did increase in their need to direct or dominate other people.

The data concerning changes in men's personality are somewhat more consistent. The longitudinal data indicate that men increase in their needs for aggression, achievement, and dominance and decrease in their need to apologize or "give in" (Stevens & Truss, 1985). These findings show some overlap with those of Lowenthal et al. (1975). Lowenthal's cross-sectional data indicated that young adult men were more hostile, more sarcastic, and less self-controlled than high school boys.

We should pause here to note that, while change obviously does occur, there is also considerable stability as people more from the adolescent/college years into young adulthood. For example, Stevens and Truss (1985) assessed 16 personality "needs" in their research. Eleven of these were either stable or showed such varied individual differences that no clear trend could be discerned. Similarly, there seems to be considerable stability throughout adulthood in individuals' judgments of their ability to affect the outcome of a situation (Gurin & Brim, 1984).

We have seen several changes from adolescence to young adulthood. There are also changes that take place during the young adult years. Malatesta and Culver (1984) reported a decrease in women's focus on success from age 18 to 31. By age 36, however, success is once again the dominant theme of women's self-descriptions. This resurgence of interest is underscored by the emergence of fear and anxiety concerning success (or, more accurately, lack of success) at age 34 and 36. Table 5–3 summarizes the major shifts in self-generated life themes at different points during young adulthood.

Masculinity-Femininity

The masculinity-femininity dimension of personality is a particularly interesting aspect of the stability versus change debate. There is, of course, the question of whether femininity, masculinity, or androgeny is an enduring characteristic of a given individual. Notice, by the way, that masculinity-femininity are not necessarily two opposite points on a scale. A person can

TABLE 5–3: Five Major Themes of Women's Self-Generated Descriptions of Their Lives

Age 17	Age 31	Age 33	Age 36
Success	Depression/ sadness	Affiliation (children)	Success
Anger/aggression	Lack of affiliation (husband)	Success	Illness
Domination/power	Success	Fear/anxiety	Affiliation (lover)
Affiliation (lover)	Affiliation (children)	Nurturance	Fear/anxiety
Lack of success	Success	Affiliation (lover)	Competence

Source: Adapted from Malatesta, C., & Culver, L. (1984). Thematic and affective context in the lives of adult women. In C. Malatesta & C. Izard (eds), *Emotion in adult development.* Beverly Hills: Sage.

exhibit both masculine and feminine traits, a state commonly referred to as *androgeny* (Bem, 1975). Indeed, several studies have found that androgynous people tend to score as better-adjusted. For example, O'Heron and Orlofsky (1990) reported that androgynous women scored lower on depression and anxiety than feminine women did.

The stability argument claims that there are socialized sex roles for men and women that each person adopts to a greater or lesser degree. The person would then be expected to exhibit that degree of masculinity, femininity, or androgeny throughout his or her life. Note, however, that within this perspective, individual stability is only as real as the stability of the social role. Gender roles, especially for women, have been changing rapidly during the past two decades and so may be quite unstable right now (Jacklin, 1989). One might therefore get a cohort effect in terms of the stability of a particular behavior or characteristic. Indeed, researchers have recently presented evidence for this (Hyde, Krajnik, & Skuldt-Niederberger, 1991). The change argument, on the other hand, suggests that level of masculinity or femininity differs as life circumstances change. Becoming a parent, for example, is frequently cited as a situation that elicits "feminine" (nurturant, warm, emotionally expressive) behavior.

The change theorists do not, however, agree on what causes shifts in sex role behavior. Gutmann (1975) argues that adults' sex roles become more differentiated with the birth of children. The demands of parenting require that women become more feminine and men more masculine. Abrahams, Feldman & Nash (1978) make a somewhat different argument. They too claim that parenting requires "feminine" behavior, but say that such behavior will appear in both men and women. Any adult actively involved in the care of young children should exhibit increased nurturing behavior. Similarly, they claim that any adult going into the working world will show increased aggressiveness and other masculine characteristics.

So we have three different hypotheses: (1) Sex roles may be stable; (2) sex roles may become more differentiated, at least temporarily, in young adulthood; (3) sex roles may change during young adulthood, with men and women responding similarly to new roles and situations.

At every stage of the adult life cycle, men typically rate themselves as more masculine and women as more feminine in terms of personality characteristics (Abrahams et al., 1978; Cunningham & Antill, 1984; Feldman & Aschenbrenner, 1983; Feldman, Biringen & Nash, 1981). However, cross-sectional data indicate that this difference is most pronounced in parents of young children (Abrahams et al., 1978; Feldman et al., 1981). This increased differentiation in self-rated sex role identity seems to be due primarily to changes in women. Men's masculinity ratings do not change dramatically during young adulthood. Women who are mothers of preschoolers do rate themselves as more feminine and less masculine compared to women who are not mothers or who are mothers of older (adult) children. Why would women change more than men? It can be argued that women may experience greater demands for change. Women may leave their jobs and lose adult social contacts when they become mothers. Men's lives may be less disrupted, particularly if they are minimally involved in childcare. Thus, men may feel less need to change their evaluations of themselves.

These data seem to lend at least some support to Gutmann's argument that parenthood increases sex role stereotyping. However, longitudinal data indicate a more complex picture that gives some support to the argument that parenthood brings out the "mother" in both men and women. Shirley Feldman and Barbara Aschenbrenner (1983) reported that both men and women increased in self-ratings of feminine identity and feminine role behavior as they moved from expecting a baby to actually caring for one. Men seemed to be as affected by parenthood as women were. In fact, men showed an increase in affectionate/tender feelings (a "feminine" personality trait) after becoming parents, while women showed no change.

Parenthood may also require certain "masculine" traits. Parents need to be able to take responsibility, make decisions, and act independently, particularly in emergency situations. Feldman and Aschenbrenner considered such abilities to be part of the personality trait called "instrumentality." Instrumentality increased for both men and women as they made the transition to parenthood. Another masculine trait, dominance, which seems irrelevant to parenting an infant, showed no change. The parents in the Feldman and Aschenbrenner study were more egalitarian than most in their division of housework and childcare, though the women were still primarily responsible for these tasks. The women in the study were fairly career-oriented. Yet like women in the cross-sectional studies, they became more stereotyped in their sex role identity. They increased in femininity and decreased in masculinity scores after becoming mothers. The men actually became less stereotyped as they showed increases in femininity while remaining stable in ratings of masculinity.

This all suggests that parenthood involves enough life changes to alter the behavior and personality of both men and women, but the personality shifts are not necessarily of the type Gutmann outlined. Men especially may become less stereotypic in their behavior (though they are, of course, still more masculine than feminine). And it may be that the increase in women's sex role stereotyping is due to the way we typically assign parenting roles. If women did not become "full-time" mothers while men were "part-time" fathers, such changes might not occur at all. Indeed, John Cunningham and John Antill (1984) found that involvement in the workforce seems dramatically to affect the degree of stereotyping in women and their spouses, independent of family status. Working women rate themselves as more masculine and less feminine than homemakers. While many of the working women in this study had children, Cunningham and Antill did not specifically examine the effects of parenthood on masculinity and femininity, so we cannot make a definitive statement about the impact of work versus parenthood on sex role identity.

EMOTIONAL DEVELOPMENT

Carroll Izard (1977) has argued that emotions are part of personality. In fact, some of the personality traits discussed earlier may simply be habitual combinations of a particular emotional state with a set of rules. A person may be "introverted" because he or she has repeatedly decided to deal with shame or distress by showing no emotion. Furthermore, emotions may influence other aspects of personality functioning. Think, for example, of the influence on sexual behavior of disgust versus interest versus fear versus enjoyment.

We have already seen hints of the widely held belief that motivation changes during the adult years. Recall, for example, the changing use of intellectual prowess outlined by Schaie in Chapter 4. Many theorists have argued that emotion is *the* major source of motivation in all people (Izard, 1977; Malatesta & Haviland, 1985). Indeed, in infants, motivation may be purely emotional. By adulthood, emotion combines with cognition to produce the motivation for behavior. Anger in an infant might lead to crying; adults can make decisions about how to release their anger. They can choose any form ranging from exercise to murder!

Freud argued that emotional development was completed during childhood and that adult behavior simply reflected the coping mechanisms, traumas, and experiences of childhood. But if we assume that emotions are largely socially defined, it becomes evident that Freud's view is overstated. Since socialization is a lifelong process, emotional development would be continuous. Childhood emotional development would not determine or even be more important than adult emotional development (Averill, 1984).

Physiology and Emotion

The view that emotional development is a life-span process has gained considerable popularity in recent years. But what is it that develops or changes? To answer this question, we must first examine the nature of emotions. Emotions have at least three components. First, there is a physiological component (Izard, 1977; Malatesta & Izard, 1984) that includes electrochemical activity in various brain systems, among them the cerebral cortex and the hypothalamus. It also involves the autonomic nervous system functioning that makes palms sweat, faces turn red, and hearts race. The number of basic emotions is limited (see Table 5-4), and each one is associated with a somewhat different physiological reaction (Izard, 1977; Malatesta & Haviland, 1985). There is little reason to believe that this physiological component changes very much with development. So we see immediately that, as with personality characteristics, some components of emotion will be stable throughout adulthood.

Feeling

The second component of emotion is the subjective experience of feeling. If you just looked at children and adults, you might be tempted to argue that adults feel emotions less intensely than do children. At the very least, you would claim that men are less emotional than children are. Yet Carol Malatesta and Carroll Izard (1984) have argued that, ideally, adults feel emotions more fully. They should learn to accept negative feelings and should also learn how to express them appropriately. In fact, several per-

TABLE 5-4:   Izard's Ten Basic Human Emotions

Emotional Dimension*

Interest–excitement
Enjoyment–joy
Surprise–startle
Distress–anguish
Anger–rage
Disgust–revulsion
Contempt–scorn
Fear–terror
Shame/shyness–humiliation
Guilt–remorse

*Each dimension represents a continuum from low to high.
Source: Izard, C. (1977). *Human emotions.* New York: Plenum.

sonality theorists, including Carl Rogers and Abraham Maslow, view this ability as a defining feature of optimal functioning.

An example might help to clarify this shift. When a little girl's feelings are hurt because another child doesn't want to play with her or because her father has expressed disapproval of her behavior, it is not unusual for her to say "I don't care." She may adopt a swaggering posture and claim that whatever the adult said is completely irrelevant. She may be fighting back tears while she's doing this. She feels the hurt, but tries desperately to repress it. On the other hand, when an adult's feelings are hurt, they typically acknowledge it. Certainly they cannot always express the pain immediately. They can't even always express it to the person who hurt their feelings. But they can somehow find a way to "admit" the emotion.

Emotional Expression

This brings us to the third component of emotion, its expression. This is probably the component that undergoes the most significant change. The change is not restricted to shifts that occur during childhood. Instead, we are constantly learning new rules about emotional expression. Some of these changes involve how we understand the emotion itself (Averill, 1984). What is causing us to feel angry? Is it something our spouse said? Is it something we ourselves did? Is it lack of sleep that makes us irritable? In addition to changes in how we make attributions about behavior, we change in how we appraise emotions. What do we hope to accomplish with this emotional display? Sometimes we just seem to want to make someone else feel good (or bad). At other times we want to change someone else's behavior. At still other times, we want some sympathy. And at yet other times we want to release tension. Such appraisals will influence how and when we display emotions.

What is changing, then, are the strategies we use in displaying an emotion. James Averill (1984) refers to these as the *heuristic rules* of emotions. Cognition obviously plays a major role here. We continually reorganize our definition of how to experience and express an emotion. We learn by observing how others react, by the consequences of our behaviors, and through our language (Malatesta & Haviland, 1985). So, for example, the availability of words to describe a particular emotion may influence our ability to appraise that emotion. Similarly, women, being permitted a wider range of emotional display (including verbalizing emotional states), may be better able to appraise and tolerate emotions, especially emotional ambiguities (Lowenthal et al., 1975).

That such rules about emotion are learned rather than innate is underscored by the consistent finding that women do not feel emotion any more intensely or any differently than men do (Malatesta & Haviland, 1985). This finding allows us to repeat the idea that we do not acquire new emotions, nor lose old ones. In fact, Izard (1977) suggests that there are only ten basic emotions, and that these are always with us. Through socialization, however, we continue to develop emotionally. We become better able to experience emotions fully and better able to express them appropriately.

LIFE CRISES AND COPING

Two things have become clear in our discussion of personality in young adulthood. First, young adults face a variety of life changes. In fact, there are normally more life changes in young adulthood than in middle or old age (Lowenthal et al., 1975). Second, there are at least some changes in personality functioning during young adulthood. This is true in terms of both personality traits and emotional reactions. Taken together, these two findings suggest that young adults may develop unique coping mechanisms.

Stressors and Coping Mechanisms

The Stressors: What are the stresses young adults face? We can suggest three major categories. First, there are the "normative" life crises: marriage, having children, and starting a career. Each of these includes considerable adjustment in daily living. Notice that these are not necessarily "negative" stressors; that is, they are not tragic or even bad events. This raises an important point about stressors. Stress is any event that requires adaptation, and it may be positive or negative. Some crises may involve threat or loss; others may simply present us with challenges (McCrae & Costa, 1986). Researchers are increasingly considering the differences in the demands of a positive versus a negative life crisis.

In addition to the normative crises, a young adult may be faced with a non-normative crisis. A woman may have a miscarriage or be raped. Parents may lose a child. Someone may become seriously ill or lose a job. A family may have to move. Someone might get a major promotion. Again, not all these events are negative, but they are non-normative. One implication is that there will not always be the widespread peer support that is available for on-time normative life crises.

Finally, there are *hassles* (Lazarus & Folkman, 1984). These can range from minor health problems, such as colds, to home or auto repair needs to unexpected company. None of these events is a crisis. No major shift in functioning is required. Yet all require time, energy, and decision making. Adults face hassles daily. Coping with them may be quite different from dealing with major life events.

Coping Mechanisms: Adults have a wide variety of ways of coping with both major and minor stressors. These range from praying to using alcohol or drugs to talking with friends. Robert McCrae and Paul Costa (1986) identified 27 different ways adults might cope with a life stress. Their list, presented in Table 5–5, is not exhaustive, but it does show the range of coping mechanisms frequently used by adults.

Table 5–5 also shows the effectiveness ranking of McCrae and Costa's

TABLE 5–5:   Rank Order of Mean Effectiveness Ratings for 27 Coping Mechanisms

Mechanism	EFFECTIVENESS		
	Problem Solving	Distress reduction	Average rank
Hostile reaction	1	3	2.0
Rational action	25	21	23.0
Seeking help	26	25	25.5
Perseverence	19	14	16.5
Isolation of affect	6	7	6.5
Fatalism	13	8	10.5
Expression of feelings	23	22	22.5
Positive thinking	16	18	17.0
Distraction	9	13	11.0
Escapist fantasy	4	12	8.0
Intellectual denial	17	15	16.0
Self-blame	5	1	3.0
Social comparison	10	16	13.0
Sedation	14	17	15.5
Substitution	15	24	19.5
Restraint	22	19	20.5
Drawing strength from adversity	20	26	23.0
Avoidance	18	10	14.0
Withdrawal	11	6	8.5
Self-adaptation	24	20	22.0
Wishful thinking	3	4	3.5
Active forgetting	7	11	9.0
Humor	21	23	22.0
Passivity	8	5	6.5
Indecisiveness	2	2	2.0
Assessing blame	12	9	10.5
Faith	27	27	27.0

Mechanisms ranked from least effective (1) to most effective (27).
Source: McRae, R., & Costa, P. (1986). Personality, coping, and coping effectiveness in an adult sample. *Journal of Personality, 54,* 396.

27 coping mechanisms. Interestingly, the same mechanisms that are effective in actually solving a problem (and, of course, not all problems can be solved) are also generally useful in reducing the distress that may accompany some stressors. Furthermore, certain coping mechanisms are apparently effective in a variety of situations. For example, patients experiencing stress syndromes, cancer patients, and families of cancer victims all found "seeking emotional support" the most effective way of dealing with their problem (Horowitz & Wilner, 1980). And people tend to agree on what types of reactions are most helpful, even if they themselves do not use them when faced with stress (McCrae & Costa, 1986).

Individual Differences in Coping

Rose Kennedy is something of a heroine to many Americans. She raised nine children (no small task in itself). One of the children was mentally retarded. She saw four of them die, two in public assassinations. Her husband suffered a stroke and eventually died. Her surviving son was the target of considerable public criticism following an automobile accident in which a female companion died. Her sons' and husband's private lives continued to be the focus of gossip and rumor, years after their deaths. Yet

People use a variety of means for coping with stress, including hostile reactions.

Rose Kennedy persevered. She also seemed to be a strong, committed, moral woman.

How is it that Rose Kennedy could endure all these tragedies while other people, facing much less obvious stress, develop psychological and physical illnesses, turn to drugs and alcohol, or even commit suicide? Since the evidence suggests that coping mechanisms are fairly stable throughout adulthood, this is a critical issue in understanding young adult personality.

There are at least two categories of variables to be considered in trying to understand reactions to a stressful event: episodic and dispositional variables (Lazarus & Folkman, 1984). Social factors, including roles and availability of support, may also be important.

Episodic Variables: Every stressful event has its own characteristics. We have already mentioned one dimension along which events vary—they may be positive or negative (or some mixture of the two). Some stressors, such as marriage or a job promotion, are desirable. Indeed, we actively seek them. In addition, some events can be prevented or at least effectively managed. You can often decide whether, when, and how to end a marriage. You usually cannot decide whether, when, and how a loved one will die. Furthermore, some events can be anticipated, and others cannot. A person may die after a long illness or suddenly in a car crash. Finally, some events may be one-time events, while others are chronic. My colleagues and I get paid once a month, and some months we run out of money before the month is over and have no disposable income for a few days. Sometimes we cannot pay a bill on time or buy all the groceries we want. This is difficult, but hardly comparable to chronic poverty.

Some researchers have suggested that the characteristics of the event itself influence how effectively and by what means a person copes. For example, Abigail Stewart and Patricia Salt (1981) argue that home versus work problems might have different outcomes for women. They viewed home-related problems as less controllable than work-related problems. Children's illnesses, spouse's job transfers and problems, and marital arguments are often only marginally within a woman's control. This lack of control could lead to a sense of helplessness, and helplessness, in turn, has been associated with the development of depression (Seligman, 1975). Job-related problems, on the other hand, are often controllable. After all, you can usually quit or find a new job more easily than you can get divorced or find a new spouse (Bergmann, 1981). Given that job stresses are more controllable and therefore less likely to result in helplessness, these stresses should show themselves in a form other than depression—perhaps physical illness (Stewart & Salt, 1981).

Stewart and Salt's results indicate that home- and job-related stresses are indeed differently related to depression. Home-related problems seem to result in depression more frequently than work problems. Conversely, work problems seem to lead to physical illness more often. Home problems are particularly likely to result in depression if a woman is a full-time homemaker. This makes sense, because full-time homemakers are less able to leave a difficult marriage than women who have their own income (Bergmann, 1981). Furthermore, working outside the home may give a woman another source of satisfaction and self-esteem when things are going badly at home that may reduce the negative impact of home-related problems (Fiske, 1982). Other researchers have also found that household problems are more likely to contribute to depression in full-time homemakers than in married women who work outside the home (Ilfeld, 1982).

Many of these studies focused on major events or problems. However, there are also all the hassles of daily living. A traffic jam or alarm clock failure may seem minor compared to marriage or an illness, but the data indicate that hassles are stressful. In fact, hassles are better than major life events in predicting both psychological and physical problems. Once again, however, this relationship is probably mediated by the individual's appraisal of the hassles and how generally pressured the person feels. Furthermore, as with major life events, poor coping tends to generate even more hassles (Lazarus & Folkman, 1984). So there are some similarities between reactions to hassles and to major life events.

Social Factors: The Stewart and Salt (1981) research indicates that social roles may have an impact on reaction to life stressors. Not only were homemakers more likely to experience depression than other women, but single career women were more likely than others to experience illness in the face of life stress. Married career women were less likely to develop either depression or illness despite experiencing higher levels of stress than the other women. Some researchers have found that the value of working outside the home is greater for young adult women than for middle-aged women. This may be a cohort effect. After all, today's young women are more likely to be truly committed to a career than women of earlier generations were. The commitment may increase the satisfaction associated with work. Furthermore, young women may face less job discrimination and social pressure to quit working than older women did (Fiske, 1982).

We have already explained why full-time homemakers might have more difficulty coping than other women do. But why would single women experience difficulty? Single people in general appear to be generally less happy than married people. One possible explanation is that they lack important social relationships to turn to for support. Social relationships appear to be crucial mediators of stress, especially for women (Belle, 1982; Chiriboga & Cutler, 1980: Rodin & Ickovics, 1990). Among coping mechanisms that adults find effective, seeking social support and talking to other people about the problem rank high (Horowitz & Wilner, 1980).

Both men and women rely heavily on social supports in times of stress. However, men tend to rely on their spouses, but women often turn to close friends (Rubin, 1985). In fact, wives are such an important buffer for men that marriage has often been called a "protective factor" for them (Belle, 1982). Married men are less likely than single men to develop psychological or physical problems, partially because wives serve as a sounding board for their husbands. Men find it easier to discuss problems with women than with other men. They feel they can "let their guard down" more. They do not have to maintain the self-sufficient masculine image they think other men expect (Rubin, 1985). So while men are less likely than women to be emotionally expressive under most circumstances (Malatesta & Haviland, 1985), they are best able to release their emotions and get support when they are married.

Women also seek emotional support from their husbands, but marriage is not the "protective factor" for women than it is for men. Indeed, married women are more likely to be depressed than single women are (Belle, 1982). However, women are more likely to have friends to turn to than men are. For example, three-fourths of the young adult single women in Lillian Rubin's (1985) study could name a best friend, but less than one-third of the single men could. Comparable statistics emerged for married men and women. Women are also more likely to seek and use social support from their work colleagues (Rodin & Ickovics, 1990). This difference between men and women may be especially crucial for certain types of stressors, such as divorce or death of a spouse. The wider range of support available to women may make them better prepared to deal with stress, but it is not without its risks. Too many social relationships may, in and of themselves, become a stressor (Belle, 1982).

Furthermore, certain types of support may be helpful in some situations but not in others. Carolyn Cutrona (1990) has suggested five different dimensions of social support: emotional support (caring), social integration (group membership), esteem support, tangible aid in the form of goods or services, and informational support. She has also identified four dimensions of stress. These include desirability of the stressor, controllability, duration of the consequence, and aspects of life affected by the stressor. She argues that controllability is the most important of these dimensions, but that all influence which types of support will be most helpful. Table 5–6 shows Cutrona's model of the optimal matching of social support and stress.

TABLE 5–6:   Optimal Matching Model of Stress and Social Support

Type of Stressful Event	Optimal Social Support
Controllable (Instrumental behavior can prevent event or lessen or eliminate its consequences)	a. Instrumental support b. Esteem support
Uncontrollable Life domain in which loss occurs: Assets Relationships a. Intimate b. Casual, group Achievement (work, school) Social role (loss, gain, or change)	a. Emotional support b. Tangible support c. Attachment d. Network support e. Esteem support f. Network support

Source: Cutrona, C. (1990). Stress and social support: In search of optimal matching. *Journal of Social and Clinical Psychology, 9,* 9.

Social roles and relationships do not develop independently of personality dispositions. Think, for example, of Erikson's theory. Intimate relationships, involving the kind of sharing and support needed to mediate stress, depend on personality development within his framework. Furthermore, our ability to use social support depends on our assessment of other people's behavior (Fincham & Bradbury, 1990). So, for example, if a husband is telling his wife about a disagreement he had with his parents and she praises his stand against them, he might interpret this as true support, fulfillment of an obligation, or a thinly veiled criticism of him as a wimp because he usually did not stand up to them or was not very effective (Fincham & Bradbury, 1990). This is similar to the argument made earlier concerning the impact of particular events on self-esteem.

Individual Dispositions: Our earlier discussion of Eysenck's theory clearly exemplifies the belief that personality functioning and coping are inextricably intertwined. And research supports Eysenck's view; people who score high on extroversion use more effective coping mechanisms, such as taking rational action and thinking positively. People high on neuroticism (comparable to Eysenck's instability) tend to use less effective mechanisms, such as hostile reactions, self-blame, wishful thinking, and withdrawal (McCrae & Costa, 1986). People who are high on neuroticism are more likely to be dissatisfied with life and to experience more negative than positive affect as well as more unfounded health complaints (Costa & McCrae, 1985, 1988).

Suzanne Kobasa (1979) has proposed a personality constellation that mediates the impact of stress. Some people, she claims, are more stress-resistant than others. These people display a personality structure that she calls *hardiness*. Hardy people tend to believe that they can control, or at least influence, the events in their lives; they tend to be very committed to the activities in their lives; and they view change as exciting and challenging rather than threatening. People who possess these characteristics are less likely to become physically ill when facing stress than people who do not. This is true even when people face the same types of stressors. Hardy people simply perceive events as more desirable and controllable than non-hardy people do (Rhodewalt & Agustsdottir, 1984).

The issue of controllability seems to be especially important to young adults who also possess Type A characteristics. Type A people, also known as cardiac-prone personalities, tend to be competitive, intensely desirous of recognition, deadline-oriented, and quick to act (Coleman, Butcher & Carson, 1984). Not surprisingly, people who are high on Type A and low on hardiness tend to be particularly negatively affected by uncontrollable stress (Rhodewalt & Agustsdottir, 1984).

The concept of hardiness and its relationship to stress outcomes underscores the importance of an individual's perception of a situation in determining reactions to an event. Marjorie Lowenthal and her colleagues (1975) also noted that different people had different approaches to stress. They identified four categories of coping, categories defined by the amount and severity of stress a person experiences and by the individual's preoccupation with that stress.

1. *Overwhelmed* people are high on stress and are preoccupied with it. They often focus on their stresses when describing themselves and their lives.

2. *Challenged* people, who may be comparable in some ways to Kobasa's hardy individuals, also face considerable stress, but they do not dwell on these events. Rather, they deal with the stressor and move on.

3. *Lucky* people experience less stress and are grateful for it. It may be that they arrange their lives to minimize stress, or they may simply fail to categorize events as being stressful when other people would.

4. *Self-defeating* people also experience relatively little stress, yet dwell on the stressors they do face and judge themselves harshly because of their inability to cope more effectively.

Table 5-7 shows the distribution of these coping categories among the young adults in Lowenthal's study. Men and women were quite equal in the amounts of stress they faced, but their coping styles were quite different. Young adult men facing considerable stress were more likely to be overwhelmed than challenged, a tendency that was much less pronounced among the women. On the other hand, when stress was low, men were likely to consider themselves lucky, while women more frequently fell into the self-defeating category. This latter finding may reflect the differences in young adult men's and women's roles and the perceived control over their stressors. In support of this argument, Anne Mulvey and Barabara Dohrenwend (1984) reported that young adult men experience more controllable life stresses than young adult women or people at any other stage of adult development.

Source of Individual Dispositions: Where do these coping strategies come from? First, note that there does seem to be some stability in the approach a person takes. Kobasa and her colleagues found that degree of hardiness was related to reactions to stressful events that occurred five years later (Kobasa, Maddi, & Kahn, 1982). Abigail Stewart's (1978) "self-defining" women are similar to Kobasa's hardy individuals in that they viewed problems as having identifiable causes that were within their control. Stewart

TABLE 5-7:   Coping Styles in Young Adults

Approach to Stress	Males (percent)	Females (percent)
Challenged	16	21
Overwhelmed	36	27
Lucky	32	21
Self-defeating	16	31

Source: Lowenthal, M., Thurner, M., & Chiriboga, D. (1975). *Four stages of life.* © 1975 by Jossey-Bass. Reprinted by permission.

found that women who were high on self-definition in college were more likely to cope effectively with problems that arose 14 years later. Finally, David Chiriboga and Loraine Cutler (1980), reporting follow-up data on Lowenthal et al.'s subjects, found little change in people's preoccupation with stress, despite changes in the types of stress they were experiencing.

Factors that contribute to an individual's typical reaction to stress include gender, marital status, and roles. The availability of social support seems especially important. The combination of job and family may also offer special protection, since a person can continue to derive satisfaction and a sense of competence from one realm when problems occur in the other (Fiske, 1982).

Exposure to stress also seems to play a role. As Lowenthal's typology suggests, stress exposure is not equal. By age 21, some inner city youths have had friends murdered, are parents, and have a long history of poverty. For other 21-year-olds, the only major stress experiences have involved going to college. People who are exposed to more stress may be more complex than other people: they appear to have greater inner resources; they demonstrate more competence, insight, and growth orientation; and they have stronger external resources and support systems. But they also tend to have more personal and social handicaps and deficiencies (Fiske, 1982). For example, people who lose their parents during childhood experience more stress as young adults. The loss of one's mother seems to be particularly linked to depression in young adulthood (Brown, Harris & Bifulco, 1986). Women whose mothers had died frequently marry early (before age 20) and experience premarital pregnancy. However, there are intervening factors in these relationships. For example, the higher rate of premarital pregnancy and early marriage is more true of working-class than middle-class women (Brown et al., 1986). Thus, early and frequent exposure to stress has both positive and negative effects that will be affected by other life circumstances.

Of course, personality characteristics also influence stress reactions. It is difficult to say how and why these characteristics develop; researchers cannot even agree on which characteristics are stable. And there are so many theories of personality that most colleges offer courses that look at nothing but these models. But we can say that there is some genetic component to personality. Some characteristics seem to emerge quite early in development. For example, Karen Matthews (Matthews & Siegel, 1982) has found evidence of Type A personality in young children, and the children seem to maintain these characteristics throughout childhood; we don't yet know what they are like as adults. Research has yet to establish the factors that contribute to the development of a hardy personality.

There are, then, a myriad of factors contributing to the means and effectiveness of an individual's coping responses. Most of us cope quite well with stress. Some people, however, are virtually incapable of coping with stress; in fact, the means they choose for coping actually add to their stress levels. Such is the case with alcoholics.

Alcoholism in Young Adults

Alcohol abuse is neither a new nor an exclusively American problem. It has been found at all times in history and in many cultures (Peyser, 1982). There is, however, no question that alcohol abuse is a major problem in the United States today. Fully 51 percent of young adult men (aged 18–27) drank five or more consecutive drinks within two weeks of a government study of alcohol use (USDHHS, 1986). Ten percent of the young adult men in this survey reported drinking daily. As many as 10 to 15 million Americans may experience frequent episodes of alcohol abuse (Coleman et al., 1984). The costs to the individual and society are tremendous. Physical disease, including brain disorders such as Korsakoff's syndrome, are more common among alcoholics. Alcoholics commit suicide 58 times more frequently than nonalcoholics. Half of all fatal car accidents involve a drunk driver. Alcoholism may cost industry over $10 billion annually because of lost workdays, industrial accidents, and general inefficiency. Even more dramatically, the overall cost of substance abuse in the United States may exceed $50 million per year (Peyser, 1982).

Alcohol abuse in young adulthood may carry some additional risks. Women who drink heavily while pregnant may produce infants with Fetal Alcohol Syndrome (FAS) or Fetal Alcohol Effects (FAE). Children with FAS or FAE often require extensive medical treatment and special schooling (Abel, 1984). Familial abuse is also often linked to alcohol. It is a common factor in wife battering, child beating, and child sexual abuse (Finkelhor,

Alcohol abuse is a common problem among young adults.

1984; Goodstein & Page, 1981; Kempe & Kempe, 1984). Thus, the developmental tasks of young adulthood (especially bearing and rearing children) may be significantly negatively influenced by alcohol abuse.

Of course, one could turn the last statement around and argue that the demands of young adulthood increase alcohol abuse. Alcohol is frequently used as a means of coping with stress (Peyser, 1982). Why? Any of you who have ever been drunk (and, if the statistics are accurate, most of you have) have some idea of the answer to this question. Psychologically, alcohol produces disinhibition. It makes a person feel less compelled to behave responsibly and increases both aggressive and sexual behavior (though it often actually interferes with sexual performance in men). There is a state of euphoria associated with alcohol intake, as well as relief from anxiety and depression. This is due to the sedative action of alcohol. In terms of its effects on the body, alcohol depresses central nervous system (CNS) functioning. In this respect, it is more like seconal, quaaludes, Valium, and Librium than LSD, PCP, marijuana, or cocaine. (see Table 5–8)

TABLE 5-8:   Symptoms of Dependence on Psychoactive Substances, Including Alcohol

Diagnostic Criteria for Psychoactive Substance Dependence

A. At least three of the following:

    (1) substance often taken in larger amounts or over a longer period than the person intended

    (2) persistent desire or one or more unsuccessful efforts to cut down or control substance use

    (3) a great deal of time spent in activities necessary to get the substance (e.g., theft), taking the substance (e.g., chain smoking), or recovering from its effects

    (4) frequent intoxication or withdrawal symptoms when expected to fulfill major role obligations at work, school, home (e.g., does not go to work because hung over, goes to school or work "high," intoxicated while taking care of his or her children), or when substance use is physically hazardous (e.g., drives when intoxicated)

    (5) important social, occupational, or recreational activities given up or reduced because of substance use

    (6) continued substance use despite knowledge of having a persistent or recurrent social, psychological, or physical problem that is caused or exacerbated by the use of the substance (e.g., keeps using heroin despite family arguments about it, cocaine-induced depression, or having an ulcer made worse by drinking)

    (7) marked tolerance: need for markedly increased amounts of the substance (i.e., at least a 50% increase) in order to achieve intoxication or desired effect, or markedly diminished effect with continued use of the same amount

    Note: The following items may not apply to cannabis, hallucinogens, or phencyclidine (PCP):

    (8) characteristic withdrawal symptoms (see specific withdrawal syndromes under Psychoactive Substance-induced Organic Mental Disorders)

    (9) substance often taken to relieve or avoid withdrawal symptoms

TABLE 5-8: (continued)

Diagnostic Criteria for Psychoactive Substance Dependence

B. Some symptoms of the disturbance have persisted for at least one month, or have occurred repeatedly over a longer period of time.

Criteria for Severity of Psychoactive Substance Dependence:

Mild: Few, if any, symptoms in excess of those required to make the diagnosis, and the symptoms result in no more than mild impairment in occupational functioning or in usual social activities or relationships with others.

Moderate: Symptoms or functional impairment between "mild" and "severe."

Severe: Many symptoms in excess of those required to make the diagnosis, and the symptoms markedly interfere with occupational functioning or with usual social activities or relationships with others.*

In Partial Remission: During the past six months, some use of the substance and some symptoms of dependence.

In Full Remission: During the past six months, either no use of the substance, or use of the substance and no symptoms of dependence.

*Because of the availability of cigarettes and other nicotine-containing substances and the absence of a clinically significant nicotine intoxication syndrome, impairment in occupational or social functioning is not necessary for a rating of severe Nicotine Dependence.

Source: Reprinted with permission from the *Diagnostic and Statistical Manual of Mental Disorders, Third Edition, Revised.* Copyright 1987 American Psychiatric Association.

Like tranquilizers, alcohol reduces awareness of both internal and external restraints and cues. This is why we say things when we're drunk that we would never say while sober. These effects may lead some people to view alcohol as a form of positive reinforcement: You are "rewarded" for drinking by being able to forget your problems and responsibilities (Coleman et al., 1984).

Beyond the possibility that alcohol abuse is a learned response to stress, there are several factors that may contribute to it. There may be a genetic component to alcoholism, as evidenced by the higher rate among children of alcoholics. However, as is the case with most genetic risk factors (for example, schizophrenia), most children of alcoholics do not develop the disorder themselves (Coleman et al., 1984). There is some evidence to suggest that personality may play a role. For example, men who later develop alcohol problems are more immature, impulsive, and antisocial in college than are other men (Loper, Kammeier & Hoffman, 1973). In general, however, the evidence for personality "determining" alcohol use patterns is weak. In most cases, the personality characteristics uncovered by researchers are so general that they also occur in many nonalcoholics. Furthermore, in many studies it is not clear whether the personality problems are a cause or an outcome of alcohol abuse (Peyser, 1982).

Alcohol abuse can be a self-perpetuating cycle. You use alcohol to alleviate stress. However, the use of alcohol may cause more stress in the form of family and job problems. This increases your need for alcohol. We should note that, although alcoholism is being discussed as part of young adulthood, the disorder can develop at any point in life. This is clear from the increased attention being given to alcohol abuse among children and adolescents (Sutker, 1982).

SUMMARY

The term *personality* is difficult to define concisely. It includes a variety of concepts that are united only by the goal of explaining what makes a person unique. To even try to begin to explain individuality, we need to consider roles, emotion, consistent characteristics, situational factors, stressors, and coping mechanisms.

In the field of adult development, we add yet another dimension to the study of personality—the developmental process. We are interested in how personality does or does not change throughout the adult years. This is primarily a descriptive process. We need to compare adults at various stages of development to outline which facets of personality change and which do not. In order to accomplish this, we need to establish some base-line of functioning. Our baseline is the young adult years because we assume that people will behave with at least some consistency once they have formed an identity.

We have seen that, in general, young adults are well-adjusted. They are energetic and problem-oriented. They face a variety of challenges, including marriage, childbearing and rearing, and launching a career. All of these are considered "normative" life crises, because our society expects that young adults will enter these roles. So the young adult faces these challenges with a broad-based support system that includes many peers who are dealing with similar issues. By performing these tasks "on time," the young adult probably unknowingly eases some of the stress inherent in the roles.

Yet some young adults adjust better to these roles than others. Some people facing many stressors are overwhelmed, while others feel challenged. Some facing fewer stressors feel lucky, while others are self-defeating. A variety of factors influence the young adult's ability to cope. Characteristics of the stressors themselves play a role. For example, controllability of stress may make it easier for young men to cope than for young women (especially young women who choose the homemaker role). Personality characteristics, including hardiness, Type A behavior, extroversion, and neuroticism, also have an impact.

Some of these personality characteristics are fairly stable, at least throughout the young adult years. This does not mean that there is no personality development during these years; there is evidence of change in emotional expression, gender roles, rates of depression (especially for women), and various other aspects of personality. Many of these changes are attributable to socialization processes, including the assumption of adult roles. In later chapters, we will see how continued socialization results in further changes.

Even in this brief summary of the chapter, we have moved from pure description to an explanation of the stability and change in personality functioning. Proponents of both stability and change models use similar explanations. For example, both view socialization as important. However, the stability proponents view socialization pressures as forcing predictable behavior, while the change proponents focus on life crises and role acquisitions. Both also look to internal motivation for explanations. In addition, stability proponents point to genetic factors. And indeed there do seem to be some personality characteristics that are influenced by genetic predispositions.

Given the importance of roles in a variety of explanations of adult personality functioning, it is appropriate to turn to an in-depth exploration of two of the major role changes—those involving family and those involving career. This is the focus of the next two chapters.

6 Family and Social Relationships

Every now and then, a letter appears in a Dear Abby or Ann Landers column that runs something like this: "Dear Abby (or Ann): I am a (fill in Jewish, Catholic, Italian, or any other group label) woman. I've just started dating a man who is (a member of another group). My parents want me to quit seeing him because they're afraid I'll marry him and they don't want me to marry a non-(whatever). I don't want to marry a non-(whatever) either. But I do want to keep seeing Joe (not his real name). We have a lot of fun together. It's not serious and I'm sure I won't marry him. This is causing a real problem between my parents and me. What should I do? Signed, Confused." Abby's and Ann's answers generally point out that you shouldn't date someone you'd be opposed to marrying because you can't control "falling in love."

Are Abby and Ann right? Is "falling in love" an irrational decision over which we have little or no conscious control? And what about poor "Confused"? If she does fall in love with this inappropriate man, will she marry him? If she does, will the marriage be doomed by the differences in their backgrounds, beliefs, or values? Will her parents try to break up the marriage in the hope that she will find a more appropriate man? Will they disown her? And what impact does their reaction have on the marriage's chances for success?

This fictional letter raises a variety of issues about how and why we decide to marry and the factors that influence the course of the marriage. Many theorists have posited that marriage, or at least the establishment of an intimate relationship, is the central task of young adulthood. Thus, the answers to these questions are crucial in understanding social development during young adulthood.

MARRIAGE

You may have noticed that some theorists, such as Erik Erikson, discuss the establishment of intimacy as the core crisis of young adulthood, but others, such as Robert Havighurst, focus specifically on marriage. Are marriage and intimacy synonymous? A definition of intimacy is necessary before that question can be answered. Erikson himself defined the ideal intimate relationship as one in which there is:

1. mutuality of orgasm
2. with a loved partner
3. of the other sex
4. with whom one is able and willing to share a mutual trust
5. and with whom one is able and willing to regulate the cycles of
   a. work
   b. procreation
   c. recreation
6. so as to secure to the offspring, too, all the stages of a satisfactory development. (Erikson, 1963, p. 266)

Erikson's definition sounds a lot like an ideal marriage, with its focus on heterosexual sexuality, mutual trust, and childrearing. The definition is, however, limited by its emphasis on the ideal and the vagueness of some of its terminology. Orlofsky and his colleagues (Orlofsky, Marcia & Lesser, 1973) have been somewhat more specific in their definition. Someone who has achieved intimacy is able to have close mutual relationships, and usually has several close friends. This person listens to their problems, concerns, achievements, and they listen to his or hers. At least one of these friendships is likely to be a heterosexual love relationship. While the couple may not have yet made a final commitment (marriage), there is real depth to their relationship. People who have achieved intimacy demonstrate self-awareness, are genuinely interested in others, and show little defensiveness. They are distinguished from people who are pre-intimate (conflicted about commitment or ambivalent about sexual relationships), stereotyped (in superficial stereotypic relationships), or isolates (who have no real friends) (Orlofsky et al., 1973).

Looking at these definitions should make it clear that marriage and intimacy are not interchangeable terms. Many unmarried couples are "intimate" in that they share feelings, values, friends, activities, and perhaps even a home with children. On the other hand, many marriages are "devitalized." Couples stay together out of a sense of obligation or convenience rather than a real desire to be together.

Given this, why do some theorists seem to equate intimacy and marriage? The answer is simple statistics. In the United States, marriage is the most common form of intimate relationships among adults. Despite declines in the marriage rate over the last decade, the vast majority of Americans will be married at least once (Glick, 1984). Probably about 90 percent of the men and 88 percent of the women who were between 25 and 29 in

Marriage is still the most common expression of adult intimacy and commitment.

1980 will marry (Glick, 1984). This is down from the 96–97 percent rate in the cohort that was 25 to 29 in the 1950s, but still constitutes a clear majority. Marriage, then, is a normative behavior. Yet, as we shall see, it is one that requires considerable adjustment. And it carries with it substantial risks, including infidelity, divorce, widowhood, and domestic violence. Why, then, do so many people choose to get married?

Why Marry?

We start this discussion with the assumption that most people freely choose to get married. This is a valid assumption in the United States, and, indeed, in most of the world. Even if it was not, we would still need to explain why parents arranged marriages for their children. The explanations might be somewhat different. For example, arranged marriages probably involve financial considerations more often than freely chosen marriages (especially since increasing numbers of women do not need a husband in order to survive financially). And freely chosen marriages involve "love" more often than arranged marriages. Yet other explanations, particularly those involving procreation, would probably apply equally well to both types of marriage.

If you ask why people marry, you typically get two general responses.

The first is that the couple is "in love." Why do people who are in love get married? Their answer always is that it is expected, love and marriage simply go together. This, then, is the second explanation: There is social pressure to get married. It is expected, especially if you are in your twenties and are in love. While these points are valid, they do not tell the whole story. Most notably, they leave us wondering why society would so heartily endorse marriage as an institution.

Sociobiological Explanation: Sociobiology starts with the premise that our main goal is the protection of our genetic endowment (Barash, 1979; Dawkins, 1976; Wilson, 1975). In its most basic form, this involves protecting ourselves and maximizing our own well-being. But none of us lives forever. Therefore, ultimately our genes can survive only if we pass them on, if we procreate.

Now, we could follow the lead of many animals and procreate with a variety of partners as often as possible and leave behind us a long line of descendants. According to sociobiologists, this is precisely what men would like to do (Meredith, 1984). But such an approach would be maladaptive for women. Why? Theoretically, men can produce an infinite number of offspring. They are fertile from their mid-teens until they die. Their fertility is not limited by time, pregnancy, or lactation. Women, on the other hand, could produce a maximum of 35 to 40 offspring. (This is a theoretical estimate. Most women's bodies could probably not tolerate this number of pregnancies.) Their role in reproduction is much more extensive than men's. Each offspring renders them infertile for at least the nine months of pregnancy and frequently for the first few months of lactation (though lactation is not a reliable method of contraception). Furthermore, they lose their fertility in middle age when they complete menopause. Finally, the infant relies on the mother's milk for survival. While technology has negated this reliance in industrialized countries, it is still true in much of the world and is considered part of the evolutionary endowment of human beings.

These differences mean that women invest a lot more in each offspring than do men. Therefore, women are extremely interested in ensuring the success of each child. Theoretically, men could risk the "failure" of many offspring (even if many of them died, the man could easily father more children). So it is up to women to enforce a system that will maximize the survival chances of their children.

This is where marriage comes in. The one thing that women have that men need in order to reproduce is sex. In marriage, they trade their sexual exclusivity for protection and support from a man. They may also require his sexual exclusivity, though as polygamous societies amply demonstrate, this is often less important than the protection and support. In order to maximize the survival of their own genes, women force men into marriage or a marriagelike relationship. In societies where men cannot be so constrained, women will develop other child supportive systems, such as some form of matriliny (Maccoby, 1991).

Sociobiologists point to a variety of human and animal data in support of this argument. For example, they claim that, by nature, women are more monogamous than men. Lesbian and heterosexual women have comparable numbers of lovers. But gay men, unbridled by women's restraining influence, have many more lovers and extrarelationship affairs than heterosexual men do (Blumstein & Schwartz, 1983; Meredith, 1984). Furthermore, gay men are much more likely to be in open relationships than lesbian women are (Bell & Weinberg, 1978).

The sociobiology perspective has met with considerable criticism. Often this criticism is aesthetic, religious, or political in nature. Sociobiologists (Barish, 1979) reject the criticism on the basis that science is not bound by value systems. However, there have also been more scientific criticisms (Straumanis, 1986). There is little reason to believe that substantial amounts of human behavior are so controlled by instinct and evolution (though the behavior of many animals may be). Human brains are very flexible, allowing us to adapt to a variety of situations. We can process large amounts of diverse information and make rational decisions based on that information. Indeed, Jay Belsky and his colleagues (Belsky, Steinberg, & Draper, 1991) have recently argued that marriage will only be selected as a means of optimizing genetic survival under certain circumstances. This does not mean that the protection of children plays no role in the decision to get married. Rather, it means that protection of the genetic endowment may not be the driving force behind marriage.

Personal Growth: It is also possible that society recognizes the importance of close interpersonal relationships for personal growth and therefore encourages marriage relationships. This is certainly part of your parents' interest when they "pressure" you to get married. It is also implied in the judicial system's willingness to not force spouses to testify against one another in criminal cases.

How might marriage encourage personal growth? We have already seen one theoretical model of the importance of intimacy for adult development in Erikson's theory. Other psychoanalysts have followed Freud's lead in describing intimate relationships as important. For example, Blanck and Blanck (1968) outlined several facets of personal development that might be facilitated by marriage. First, they suggest, marriage may allow a final resolution to the sexual prohibitions and inhibitions of childhood, especially from the Oedipal conflict. After all, people are not only permitted but encouraged to engage in sexual activity in marriage. Refusal to engage in sexual intercourse is one of the few permissible grounds for divorce in the Catholic Church. If you don't believe that marriage is still seen as a form of "permission" for sex, think about the terms we normally use to describe sexual relationships. We have premarital sex, extramarital sex, and in this day of high divorce rates, even postmarital sex. Yet we rarely talk about marital sex (other than in research studies) because the term seems almost redundant to us.

Blanck and Blanck also argue that marriage facilitates the development of a new level of "object relations." Early in development, objects (people) are loved only because they fulfill our needs. Indeed, in infancy we don't even recognize people as distinct from their fulfillment of our needs (Mahler, Pine & Bergman, 1978). So, for example, psychoanalytic theorists argue that the mother only exists for the infant while she is feeding, changing, or comforting the baby. In a marital relationship, however, we are potentially able to overcome defining love for others on the basis of their fulfillment of our needs. Instead, we are able to consider the other person as an individual and can value our spouse's characteristics and abilities even when we are not in a state of need. This does not mean that the spouse's ability to fill needs is irrelevant to the success of the marriage; rather, need fulfillment is no longer the sole criterion for staying in a relationship.

A third reason marriage is important is because it completes another level of separation from parents. At least in most American families, newlyweds move into their own home and become self-supporting. Indeed, marital status is the characteristic that best distinguishes adult children who live with their parents from those who do not (Aquilino, 1990; Glick & Lin, 1986). Keep in mind that this is a *potential* outcome of marriage. Many young couples rely heavily on their parents for financial assistance and may even live in the parents' home. There is limited evidence of some cultural influences also in that Chicano families may have more of a preference for parent–adult child co-residence (Aquilino, 1990). Many newly divorced adults face a similar situation. Indeed, if a parent is living with adult children it is more likely that they are living together in the parent's than in the children's home and that they share residence because of needs of the children (Aquilino, 1990).

Fourth, marriage allows us to exercise personal autonomy in a way that dating relationships do not. In a marriage, there is a public commitment and public pressure to stay together. This sense of security may "free" a person to say, do, and try things he or she might be reluctant to do otherwise. This kind of freedom is more common in marriage than in a cohabitation relationship and may be one reason why success rates of cohabiting couples are more similar to those of dating couples than to marital partners (Macklin, 1978; Sternberg, 1986). The financial status of married couples may also provide some personal opportunities that would otherwise be unavailable. For example, a spouse's job may enable the other to attend law school. Finally, marriage may provide an opportunity for identifying with the positive characteristics of a spouse. You might, for example, develop more patience dealing with other people after watching a spouse interact with friends and family. Or you might become more aware of prejudice against women from talking to your spouse and seeing her involvement with the rape crisis hotline or the domestic violence center.

Of course, none of these positive outcomes is automatic. A person's ability to benefit from marriage depends greatly on previous development. However, it is evident that society could view these outcomes as beneficial not only to the individual but also to children, parents, and the community. This perspective is even clearer in another model emphasizing personal growth in marriage, Orville Brim's role theory.

Brim (1968) suggested that changes in adult social roles contributed to changes in adult personality. The socialization process itself causes an adult to change. Since the goal of socialization is to mold the individual to fit the society's needs and values, the stake of society in adult socialization is clear. But how is marriage related to adult socialization? Brim argued that the primary agents of adult socialization are one's partners in adult interaction. These include one's spouse, employer, and children. Each partner tries to alter the other's behavior in a way that increases the other person's desirability as a partner. In other words, each partner tries to get the other to fill their social roles in the best possible manner. While any adult has numerous partners in social interaction, the marital relationship is viewed as the most influential (Brim, 1968). As we have noted before, and will see again in greater detail, marriage requires considerable adjustment on the part of both individuals. Parenthood, which often is also a part of marriage, requires additional adjustment. Thus, the role changes associated with marriage lead to adjustments which in turn alter an adult's personality.

Although both the psychoanalytic and role theory models have some appeal, there is little actual research from either perspective. So, while there are some theoretical arguments about the benefits of marriage for personal development, we have little direct evidence that these benefits commonly occur.

Love: Most Americans would claim that you get married because you are "in love." Clearly, love is not the only element in the decision to marry. Many people who are in love never marry. And people who are not in love often marry or at least stay married after the love has waned. Even so, there is no doubt that love plays an important role in American marriage and that one cannot be understood without understanding the other.

There are probably as many different definitions of love as there are people; we will probably never all agree what constitutes love. Research does provide some picture of how people in love differ from those who are simply involved in friendships. People who are in love seem to need the presence of the loved one in order to be completely happy. People in love are willing to tolerate the other's faults. And they trust each another to be caring, tolerant, and supportive. Perhaps most important, they care for and about each other. They truly want their loved one to be happy and work to ensure that happiness. Trust and care are also elements of friendship. The need and tolerance aspects of friendship are less obvious than those of love. And care is less clearly the core of friendship than of love (Kelley, 1983). These facets of love are reflected in its manifestations. Trust is evidenced in self-disclosure of intimate thoughts, facts, and feelings. Care is indicated in willingness to give nonmaterial (emotional support), material, and physical expressions of love (Kelley, 1983).

The issues of need, care, tolerance, and trust also can be used to categorize models of different types of love. Harold Kelley (1983) has suggested three general models of love: passionate love, pragmatic love, and altruistic love. Each general model describes a different type of love. As Table 6–1 indicates, each type emphasizes a different component of love. Passionate

TABLE 6-1: Three Types of Love

Type of Love	Emphasis	Course
Passionate	Need-related issues such as sex, loneliness, self-esteem	Tends to have a sudden onset and a brief duration.
Pragmatic	Trust and tolerance	Develops slowly out of trusting, satisfying interactions, as when friendship blossoms into love.
Altruistic	Internally motivated caring, as opposed to caring in order to get a response (such as love from the other person)	Unclear but probably long-lasting, as in "mother love."

Source: Based on Kelley, H. (1983). Love and commitment. In H. Kelley, E. Bercheid, A. Christensen, J. Harvey, T. Huston, A. Levinger, E. McClintuck, L. Peplau, & D. Peterson, *Close relationships*. New York: Freeman.

love, for example, is centered on the need aspects, while pragmatic love focuses on trust and tolerance.

Robert Sternberg's (1986) triangular theory of love demonstrates the interrelationships among various types of love. Sternberg suggests that love has three components. First there is intimacy. Intimacy, for Sternberg, is the feeling of closeness that occurs in love relationships. It is the sense of being connected or bonded to the loved one. Intimacy is evidenced in several different ways. We want to do things to make life better for people we love. We genuinely like them and are happiest when they are around us. We count on them to be there when we need them and we try to provide the same support to them. We share our activities, possessions, thoughts, and feelings with them. In fact, sharing activities may be one of the most crucial factors in turning a dating relationship into a loving marital relationship (Duck, 1983).

Passion is the second component of love (Sternberg, 1986). This refers to the forms of arousal that lead to physical attraction and sexual behavior in a relationship. Sexual needs are important here, but they are not the only forms of motivational needs involved. For example, needs for self-esteem, affiliation, and succorance may also play a role. Sometimes intimacy leads to passion; at other times, passion precedes intimacy. In still other cases, there is passion without intimacy (as in an encounter with a prostitute) or intimacy without passion (as in a sibling relationship).

The final component of Sternberg's triangle is decision/commitment. This component consists of a short-term and a long-term aspect. The short-term aspect is reflected in the decision that you love someone. The commitment to maintain that love is the long-term facet. While decision and commitment are not necessarily related, in most marriages the decision that one is in love predates the commitment to the relationship. In fact, marriage, in a sense, combines the decision and the commitment in that it "... represents a legalization of the commitment of a decision to love another

TABLE 6-2: **Taxonomy of Kinds of Love Based on Sternberg's Triangular Theory**

	COMPONENT		
Kinds of Love	Intimacy	Passion	Decision/commitment
Nonlove	−	−	−
Liking	+	−	−
Infatuated love	−	+	−
Empty love	−	−	+
Romantic love	+	+	−
Companionate love	+	−	+
Fatuous love	−	+	+
Consummate love	+	+	+

+ = component present; − = component absent.
These kinds of love represent limiting cases based on the triangular theory. Most loving relationships will fit between categories, because the various components of love are expressed along continua, not discretely.

Source: Sternberg, R. (1986). A triangular theory of love. *Psychological Review, 93,* 119–135. Copyright © 1986 by the American Psychological Association. Reprinted by permission.

throughout one's life" (Sternberg, 1986, p. 123). Again, the relationship of decision/commitment to the other two components of love varies. In some relationships (like arranged marriages), commitment may lead to intimacy and passion. More commonly, however, intimacy and passion lead to the kind of commitment seen in American marriages.

We have already seen that not all relationships involve all three components of love. Sternberg (1986) has developed a taxonomy of the types of love (see Table 6–2). Clearly, we all hope that our marriages will be formed from consummate love. We would further hope that consummate love continued to be evidenced in our marriages. Of course, this ideal is not always achieved. In many marriages, the passion dies and the marriage is marked by companionate love. And more than one couple has mistaken infatuated love for consummate love.

Even if we assume that the issues we have discussed, including love, account for why people marry, we are left with many questions. Foremost among these is why we marry who we marry. Indeed, understanding marital choice may help us to understand why we marry. After all, many unmarried people will tell you that they are still single because they haven't met Mr. (or Ms.) Right. How do you know when the right person has come along? And how does a relationship develop from the first introduction to a wedding?

Marital Choice

Once again, we could answer the question of "who do you marry" with the answer "whoever I fall in love with." But that would be too simple. Why do we fall in love with someone? Here is a perfect example of a behavior for which common sense provides no answer. Although folk wisdom tells us that "birds of a feather flock together," it also says "opposites attract." Can psychological research resolve this conflict?

The Role of Similarity: There is little doubt that people tend to marry people who are similar to them in a variety of ways (Murstein, 1982). The similarities tend to be most visible in terms of demographic variables such as religion, race, educational level, age, and socioeconomic status. Such similarity is not only evident in the choice of a marital partner, but also shows some relationship to marital success.

While similarity plays a role in marital choice, the nature of that role is unclear. First, similarity may not really tell us much about why we marry a specific person. Think, for example, of a college student. Even if he is in a relatively small college, he is likely to meet a hundred or more women during his four years. They will, by and large, be his age, race, educational level, and probably socioeconomic level. Yet at most, only one of them will be chosen as a spouse and he would view only a few as even potential wives.

Furthermore, it is not clear that people find similarity attractive. Other factors, such as physical attractiveness and whether the other person likes us, play an important role in attraction. In addition, many people marry others who do not even share demographic similarity. Many Catholics marry non-Catholics, for example, and these heterogamous couples do not seem to be less happy than homogamous couples (Shehan, Bock & Lee, 1990). This all tends to indicate that similarity is not a critical factor in choosing a spouse. Rather, it may simply serve to limit the pool of available spouses. In other words, you are more likely to meet people who are like you. They are the people who attend your school, your church, and your clubs and live in your neighborhood.

Complementary Needs: Winich's (1958) theory of complementary needs was an early attempt to resolve the seeming conflict between similarity and differences in marital partners. He suggested that we are most likely to marry someone who best satisfies our psychological needs. He identified needs within the framework of Henry Murray's (1938) personology. In some cases, this means we will be attracted to someone whose personality is quite the opposite of our own. A man who has a high need for dominance would not want to be married to a woman with high dominance needs, since the two would be in virtually constant conflict. Instead, a high dominance person is likely to marry a low dominance person. This condition of "opposites attracting" is called Type I complementarity.

In cases of Type II complementarity, two people have needs that coincide. It is not that they are at opposite ends of the spectrum in a particular need; rather, they each have a need that is served by a different need of their partner. For example, a man with a high nurturance need might be attracted to a woman with a high need for succorance (Murstein, 1982). Winich does not require that either member of the couple be conscious of these needs in order for complementarity to operate. Winich's (1958) own research offered some support for his theory. However, there were methodological problems in this work, and later attempts to replicate the findings have generally been unsuccessful (see Murstein, 1976 & 1982 for some of the criticisms). This does not mean that there is no evidence for complementarity of needs. There is. Rather, this particular theory is not strong enough to explain marital choice.

Stimulus-Value-Role Theory: Bernard Murstein (1976; 1982) has formulated the Stimulus-Value-Role (SVR) theory to explain the development of all dyadic relationships, including courtship, friendship, and marriage. SVR is an *exchange theory.* This means that, given free choice, people will make relationship decisions on the basis of the balance of assets and liabilities of each member of the couple. Assets are characteristics that are rewarding to the partner. Liabilities are personal characteristics which cost the partner in some way.

In other words, people do not like to feel that they are giving more than they are getting out of a relationship. And they do not like to feel that their partner is somehow "holding them back" in terms of job progress, social opportunities, and so on. Of course, the appraisal of the fairness and advantageousness of a particular "exchange" is always made by the individual, and is made in relative rather than absolute terms (Duck, 1983; Murstein, 1976). That is, people try to get the best relationship they think they can. This is an important point to remember. Some people have low self-esteem and will settle for a bad or even abusive relationship because they think it is what they deserve and the "best they can do." Furthermore, equity in an exchange does not always mean equality on a particular characteristic (Murstein, 1982). A very attractive woman may marry a less attractive man who has a good sense of humor and is supportive of her career. Even though he incurs a "debt" in terms of attractiveness, he "pays her back" with his supportiveness and humor.

Murstein conceptualizes a relationship as developing through three stages. The *stimulus stage* accounts for the initial meeting and decision to see the person again. Physical attractiveness plays a major role here, particularly in dating relationships. We tend to associate positive personality characteristics with physical attractiveness. When we say that someone looks like a nerd, for example, we are commenting on more than physical appearance. We tend to prefer people who are physically attractive. This will not always be true, of course. We may already know something about a person before meeting him or her that will compensate for physical appearance. Or our own self concept may be such that we feel uncomfortable or inadequate in approaching a very attractive person (Duck, 1983; Murstein, 1982).

In order for the stimulus stage to be completed successfully, the two people must perceive an equity in these relatively superficial characteristics (including social status, physical appearance, and poise). If this happens, the dyad can move on to the *value-comparison stage.* In this stage, the couple discovers and compares personal values, attitudes, and opinions in a variety of areas. At first, the issues that are discussed may be relatively unimportant (such as political affiliation or college major), but eventually, they will get to very intimate concerns (such as wanting children or understanding each other's needs).

This exchange of information involves considerable self-disclosure. The members of the pair do not necessarily self-disclose at the same rate; one member may be much more forthcoming than the other. As long as both partners continue to find the relationship rewarding, this imbalance is acceptable. In fact, pushing a person to self-disclose before he or she is ready may destroy the relationship. And disclosing too much too fast can be as damaging as withholding information. The timing and control of self-disclosure is crucial if the relationship is to progress (Duck, 1983). Eventually, both must disclose their intimate feelings, fears, and beliefs if the relationship is to succeed. Furthermore, the success of the relationship relies heavily on the couple reaching some kind of consensus on fundamental values (Murstein, 1982).

As the value-comparison stage progresses, the importance of stimulus values begins to wane. The individuals are already beginning to test their role compatibility. This involves assessing what types of roles each person will play in relation to the other and to the broader community. Again, there must be some equity here, although the roles are not necessarily identical or complementary. Eventually, role comparison becomes more important than value comparison and the couple enters the *role stage*. It is not necessary that the couple enter this final stage before marrying. Indeed, many people will decide to marry on the basis of the value comparisons (Murstein, 1982). Furthermore, this stage would virtually never be completed before marriage. Indeed, it is probably a lifelong stage because people are always changing roles or adding new ones (such as becoming a parent or going from student to worker).

People have a variety of methods of making both value and role comparisons. Verbal communication is, of course, critical here and is the primary mode of information exchange (Duck, 1983; Murstein, 1982). But sharing activities is also very important (Duck, 1983). The nature and frequency of these activities change as the relationship develops. For one thing, the activities become increasingly public as the couple lets friends, family, and the general community know that they are "getting serious." On the other hand, more private activities are also shared. For example, they may watch more TV together and share more household tasks. In fact, the couple may decide to live together prior to (or instead of) marrying. Indeed, about one-quarter of all college students will *cohabit* at some time (Macklin, 1978).

Murstein's model provides a plausible outline of how a relationship develops into marriage. There is some empirical support for the model (see, for example, Murstein, 1976, 1982). However, like any model of marital choice, it cannot completely predict when people will marry and who they will choose, partially because factors outside the people involved influence these decisions. For example, you may find someone you might want to marry and then have to move to another city. Or your family may force you to break off a promising relationship. Indeed, it is important to realize that families probably play a major role in mate selection (Milardo & Lewis, 1985). From a very early age, children are taught what type of spouse is

Taking time to discuss values is an important component of the development of an intimate relationship.

acceptable. Some of this learning comes from simply observing the parents. Some of it comes from direct parental training. In some sense, parents even provide the opportunities one has for meeting a potential spouse by determining neighborhoods, school, and club participation.

Even during adolescence and adulthood, parents and family continue to exert an influence. For example, they may actively support the couple by inviting them to family gatherings, creating opportunities for them to be alone together, and so on. Or they may actively undermine the couple, even going so far as threatening to disown their child if the couple continues to see each other. Thus, while characteristics of the individual members are important in determining who will marry who, familial influences can also play a large role.

Adjusting to Marriage

The decision to marry in some ways marks the beginning of a new relationship. Marriage differs from dating or even cohabiting relationships in many ways (see, for example, Macklin, 1978; Rubin, 1977). There will be new social pressure for the couple to stay together. Expectations concerning sexual behavior, both within the couple and from the society, may change (girlfriends are supposed to say "no"; wives aren't). There may be pressure to have children. The members of the couple are supposed to make accommodations and compromises for each other and for the good of the relationship.

Marriage is going to require considerable adjustment even for couples who have been together a long time. In fact, couples who have been slow to decide to marry may have more trouble adjusting (Duck, 1983), because such couples have often had difficulty working out values and roles. Since working out roles is a continuous process, the difficulty would bode poorly for the marriage.

Most of the adjustments to marriage will be made during the first two or three years. The difficulty of this period is underscored by the fact that this is the most common time for couples to divorce (Norton, 1983). Theories of primary relationship development also emphasize the strain of the first few years. In McWhirter and Mattison's (1984) model, for example, the first year constitutes the blending stage. This stage is characterized by high sexual activity, romantic love, and merging. The next two years make up the nesting stage. During this stage, there is a decline in romantic love, the search for compatibility, setting up of a home, and feelings of ambivalence. The third stage is the maintaining stage and is marked by an increase in individuality, risk taking, establishment of traditions, and coping with conflict. This occurs during the fourth and fifth years of a relationship.

The first year is often a euphoric one. Sexual activity among married couples tends to be higher now than later in the marriage (Blumstein & Schwartz, 1983). In Philip Blumstein and Pepper Schwartz's study of 3,603 married couples, 45 percent of those married less than two years had intercourse at least three times per week. Only 27 percent of those married 2 to 10 years and 18 percent of those married over 10 years had intercourse this frequently. Furthermore, the first year of a marriage is marked by higher levels of relationship quality (as perceived by the spouses) and more uniformity between the spouses in their evaluations of the quality of the relationship than couples in the nesting stage (Kurdek & Schmitt, 1986; MacDermid, Huston & McHale, 1990). The couples also share more activities and have more positive interactions during the first year (MacDermid et al., 1990). This suggests that both members of the couple are most likely to be happy during the first year. Unfortunately, people's expectations for the rest of married life may be formed during this time. Especially for women, expectations of romance and comfort that are very high during the first year are related to greater marital distress during the third year of marriage (Kurdek, 1991).

The nesting stage seems to be particularly difficult. Indeed, relationship quality rises again during the maintaining stage, though there is still less uniformity in the individual spouses' ratings of quality than during blending (Kurdek & Schmitt, 1986). This does not necessarily mean that there are no stresses during the first year. Rather, the glow of romance may temper the impact of those stressors. Once that glow has diminished, the problems become more obvious.

The major source of stress is adjustment to new roles. The couple must define the boundaries of their relationship (Boss, 1983). When spouses either fail to define boundaries or disagree as to what the boundaries should be, there is confusion about how to behave. This, of course, creates stress.

What types of boundaries need to be defined? First, the boundaries between the spouses themselves must be clear (Boss, 1983). The husband, for example, may expect that his wife will always be around. He may expect her to have all of her meals with him, spend all evenings and weekends with just him, and generally be constantly available to him. She, on the other hand, may need some "private time" to go for a walk by herself or work on her hobbies. Or she may want to have lunch with friends or spend an occasional evening at an organization meeting. His expectation, then, is that the couple will function almost as one person. Hers is that they will retain some individual friends and interests. Their clashing expectations create ambiguity and stress. So, for example, she may be uncertain whether to risk his anger and have lunch with a friend or give up the lunch and resent his intrusion on her individuality.

Sexuality also becomes an issue in drawing boundaries. There is typically a loss of privacy (Zuengler & Neubeck, 1983). The bathroom and the bedroom now belong to both of you. Your spouse will not only see you nude but will also see you using the bathroom, performing your grooming routines, and so on. Some people find this frustrating and embarrassing.

There may also be questions about who initiates sex and when you can refuse sex. While the man still is the more common initiator in the vast majority of married couples, there is usually some initiation by the wife (Blumstein & Schwartz, 1983). Some men actively dislike women initiating sex and some women are very uncomfortable doing so (Blumstein & Schwartz, 1983; Rubin, 1976). There may also be conflicts concerning the frequency of intercourse and what types of sexual activity (for example, oral sex) are appropriate. Such conflicts may lead to performance anxiety or general dissatisfaction with one's sex life.

Sexual attraction to other people may also be an issue (Zuengler & Neubeck, 1983). There will inevitably be people to whom you are attracted. Some individuals will feel guilty about such attraction. Others will tell their spouses, who may react negatively. Still others will act upon the attraction. Indeed, about 15 percent of people married less than two years report at least one episode of extramarital sex (Blumstein & Schwartz, 1983).

Boundaries must also be drawn between the families of origin and the couple (Boss, 1983). "Miss Manners" recently answered a letter from a woman who was complaining that her husband's weekly hour-long long-distance phone calls to his parents were making it difficult for them to pay for their new car and house, much less to buy other items. Apparently he is more involved with and closer to his parents than she would like him to be. They have not yet reached an agreement about his obligations to his parents versus his obligations to the couple. Notice that there is no right or wrong solution. Some wives would not object to this level of contact between their husbands and in-laws. Rather, the individuals in the couple must draw the boundaries concerning such obligations and commitments. While such boundary-making difficulties are often considered "in-law problems," the problem really lies within the couple's failure to communicate clearly with each other.

Not all in-law problems are exclusively couple communication issues, however. The couple may have clearly decided between themselves what type of contact they want with their in-laws. The in-laws may fail to respect this line and intrude with advice, visits, and so on. In such cases, it is up to the couple to communicate their wishes as a couple to the offending in-laws.

Boundaries also need to be drawn between home and work (Boss, 1983). In some cases, the failure to define such boundaries is related to the question of expectations. Think back to the man in the previous example who wanted his wife constantly available. Now imagine that she was a high-powered workaholic executive. She may rarely be home in the early evenings. To make matters worse (from his perspective), she may frequently bring work home with her. Again, there is no single appropriate solution to this problem, but there is a need for clear communication between the spouses to resolve it.

Work boundary problems may take on special meaning in dual-career couples (Boss, 1983; Skinner, 1983). The couple may compete to see who can get raises faster, be appointed to more important committees, and so on. Such competition may foster jealousy. There may also be conflict over whose job is more important. This issue is particularly likely to come up when one spouse's time is needed for non-job-related work (such as grocery shopping, entertaining, housework) or if one spouse needs to move in order to advance in his or her job.

Finally, there are economic boundaries to be drawn. Most married couples, including newlyweds, favor pooling their financial resources (Blumstein & Schwartz, 1983). Indeed, even when they don't, the government often automatically pools the resources through community property laws. In many states, all resources are considered the equal property of the spouses, and each spouse may be held accountable for bills incurred by the other.

Not all spouses, however, agree about pooling their money. Men are more willing to pool than women (Blumstein & Schwartz, 1983). This may be because women are more reluctant to give up the freedom that having their own money gives them. People who are concerned that the marriage may not last are also less willing to pool resources. This may partially explain why couples who fail to pool their money during the first years report greater marital distress during the third year of marriage (Kurdek, 1991). Furthermore, even if the couple agrees to pool their money, there may be conflicts about how the money should be spent. This is underscored by the fact that married couples fight more about money than any other issue (Blumstein & Schwartz, 1983). Such fighting may be more frequent when there is no egalitarian control over the resources or if one or both members of the couple is dissatisfied with the family income.

The question of dissatisfaction with income may be particularly stressful for newlyweds. It is expensive to set up housekeeping. If the wife leaves her job (perhaps because of pregnancy), the loss of her income may make the situation even more difficult.

Clearly, then, newlyweds have a number of adjustments to make. They must get accustomed to having another person around virtually all of the time. They must work out their expectations of each other and their relationships to their families of origin. They must adjust to new economic realities. Some couples will face more of these difficulties than others, and these problems are hardly restricted to the newlywed period. They do tend to be particularly intense during the first two or three years of marriage. Similarly, it is during the first two or three years that couples most frequently decide how labor and decision making will be divided. This brings us to the issue of marital roles.

Alternate Life Styles

Of course, not all young adults marry. Some choose to live together without being legally married. Others establish a gay or lesbian relationship. Still others choose to remain single, living alone, with friends, or with their parents. The use of the term "alternate life styles" to describe such living circumstances underscores how normative marriage is. But the term may also be misleading, because nonmarital households are not only fairly common, they are growing in popularity.

Heterosexual Cohabitation: The number of unmarried persons of the opposite sex living together has grown rapidly since 1970. In 1970, there were about 523,000 cohabiting couples. By 1981, there were 1,808,000 cohabiting couples (Spanier, 1983). And the trend shows no sign of abating (Glick, 1984; Spanier, 1983). Indeed, cohabitation is becoming such a common phenomenon that researchers argue we should no longer consider it an alternate life style. Instead, they way, we should consider it an increasingly common step in the progression from dating to marriage (see, for example, Gwartney-Gibbs, 1986; Spanier, 1983).

Who are the cohabitors? Are they really on the road to marriage? Various data seem to indicate that they are. First, most cohabitors are fairly young (under 35 years old). About half of the couples involve two people who have never been married and almost three-fourths of them have no children (Spanier, 1983). Thus, cohabitors seem to be people who are marriage material.

Cohabitation does indeed seem to be a prelude to marriage for many couples. In examining marriage licenses in one county, Patricia Gwartney-Gibbs (1986) found that 53 percent of the couples applying for licenses were currently cohabiting. It appears that couples who wish to delay marriage for some reason (such as finishing one's education or just "making sure") are particularly likely to cohabit. In Gwartney-Gibbs' sample, for example, the cohabitors were consistently older at the time of marriage license application than the noncohabitors.

It is difficult to say exactly how many cohabiting couples eventually marry. It is widely believed that most of them either marry or break up (Macklin, 1978). In other words, few of these couples cohabit permanently. Indeed, in Blumstein and Schwartz' (1983) study of American couples, they were not able to find enough cohabiting couples who had been together for over 10 years to use this group in their data analysis (though they were able to find enough gay and lesbian couples who had been together this long). The breakup rate among cohabiting couples appears to be higher than among married couples. For example, Blumstein and Schwartz (1983) recontacted married and cohabiting couples 18 months after their original survey. Of those couples who had been together 0 to 2 years at the time of the original survey, 4 percent of the married and 17 percent of the cohabiting couples had broken up. About 29 percent of the cohabiting couples had gotten married during this time.

Are cohabiting couples different from married couples? Yes, they are, although the differences seem to have declined during the past decade (Spanier, 1983). In a cohabiting versus a married couple, both members are more likely to be employed or seeking employment. It is relatively rare for a member of a cohabiting couple to be completely out of the labor force. Almost all the women work or are actively seeking work. And it is more common for a cohabiting woman than for a wife to be supporting an unemployed partner (Spanier, 1983). These economic differences between cohabiting and married couples may help to explain the greater unwillingness of cohabitors (especially the women) to pool their incomes (Blumstein & Schwartz, 1983).

Female cohabitors seem to be more independent than wives in other ways, too. For example, they are more likely to attend club meetings without their partners. And they are more likely than wives to have at least one affair, regardless of how long the couple has been together. Male cohabitors are also more likely than husbands to be unfaithful to their partners (Blumstein & Schwartz, 1983).

There are, however, many similarities between married and cohabiting couples. Although cohabitors view themselves as more egalitarian and androgynous than married couples, the gender roles within the relationships are actually quite similar (Duck, 1983; Macklin, 1978). Furthermore, the two types of couples seem to move through the same relationship stages. As in married couples, cohabiting couples in the nesting stage were less happy than those in the blending stage (Kurdek & Schmitt, 1986). Cohabiting couples tend to be as satisfied with their relationships as married couples are (Macklin, 1978), although questions about commitment may lead to somewhat more tension among the cohabiting couples (Kurdek & Schmitt, 1986). Such tension would seem particularly likely in cohabiting couples where one partner, typically the woman, has a stronger commitment than the other (Macklin, 1978).

While cohabitation appears to be quite similar to marriage, it does not seem to be replacing marriage (Macklin, 1978). Instead, most couples seem to be cohabiting as a form of trial marriage. As has already been noted, many of these couples never make it to marriage. Furthermore, as a trial marriage, cohabitation seems to be of limited usefulness. There is little evidence to suggest that marriages between cohabitors are more stable than other marriages (Macklin, 1978). On the other hand, there is little evidence indicating that such marriages are less stable. The factors contributing to marital stability seem to be too diverse to be dramatically affected by a cohabiting experience.

Gay and Lesbian Couples: It is always difficult to estimate how many Americans are homosexual, because the number one comes up with depends on the definition you use. The percentage of people who are *exclusively* homosexual (that is, have no heterosexual experience) is probably quite small. Probably about 4 percent of all men and 2 percent of all women are exclusively homosexual. But 4 percent of all men translates to about 2 million people, so we are not talking about just a few Americans. Furthermore, many more Americans have had at least some homosexual experiences. About 37 percent of all men and 13 percent of all women have had at least one same-sex experience that resulted in orgasm (Hyde, 1986).

Many homosexuals are in relationships. In one study, almost 40 percent of the gay men and over 60 percent of the lesbian women were in a same-sex relationship (Bell & Weinberg, 1978). More than half of these gay men were members of an open couple in which monogamy was not required. Most of the lesbians were in a closed couple in which monogamy was expected (Bell & Weinberg, 1978). This underscores one difference between homosexual and married couples. Gay men are much more likely than husbands to have at least one extra-couple affair. During the first two years of the relationship, 66 percent of gay men but only 15 percent of husbands had such an encounter (Blumstein & Schwartz, 1983). On the other hand, lesbian women are about as monogamous as wives are. About 15 percent of the lesbians and 13 percent of the wives had sexual relations with someone other than their partner during the first two years of the relationship (Blumstein & Schwartz, 1983).

While lesbian couples are more like married couples in terms of monogamy, gay couples are more like married couples in terms of money issues. In both gay and married couples, the person with the higher income tends to hold the power. And in both gay and married couples, dissatisfaction with income tends to translate to overall relationship dissatisfaction. In lesbian couples income does not seem to be related to power or relationship satisfaction (Blumstein & Schwartz, 1983). However, gay and lesbian couples both differ from married couples in their willingness to pool their incomes. Married couples are about twice as willing to pool incomes as are gay and lesbian couples, though this difference declines somewhat the longer the same-sex couples are together (Blumstein & Schwartz, 1983).

Gay and lesbian couples seem to go through the same relationship stages as cohabiting and married couples (Kurdek & Schmitt, 1986). Once again, then, the first year seems to be happier than the second and third, which is followed by an upswing in happiness during the fourth and fifth years. Furthermore, although gay and lesbian couples are more likely than married couples to break up, many of them do stay together for extended periods of time. If a homosexual couple does stay together for more than 10 years, the likelihood of their breaking up is not dramatically different from that of married couples (Blumstein & Schwartz, 1983).

Not all gays are in same-sex relationships. Estimates suggest that about 20 percent of all gay men enter into heterosexual marriages (Bell & Weinberg, 1978; Ross, 1983). Even higher percentages of lesbians (probably over

Many gay men and lesbian women are involved in long-term, monogamous relationships.

one-third) get married. The marriages of the gay men tend to last somewhat longer than those of the lesbians, but in both cases the marriages tend to be less happy and of shorter duration than those between two heterosexuals. It is of some interest to note that most of these gay-straight marriages produce at least one child (Bell & Weinberg, 1978). Since homosexuality has been used as grounds to deny a parent custody (Hyde, 1986), this situation probably contributes to an underestimation of the number of homosexuals who are involved in heterosexual marriages. After all, admitting homosexuality could lead to the loss of contact with one's children.

Gay men seem to marry for largely the same reasons that heterosexual men do. The largest group (26.2 percent in Ross' 1983 study) marry because they think they are in love. Others marry in the hope that it will "cure" their homosexuality, because their girlfriends are pregnant or pressuring them to marry, or because they want children (Ross, 1983).

While our understanding of gay and lesbian couples is quite limited, several things seem clear. Many homosexuals are as interested in long-term relationships as heterosexuals are. And many of them are interested in having children. The interest in loving, secure relationships is not a function of sexuality; rather, it seems to reflect some more basic human need.

Single Adults: Not all young adults are in marriage or marriage-like relationships, however. In 1980, about 30 percent of the men and 20 percent of the women under 30 had not yet married (Glick, 1984). Most of these people will eventually marry, but about 10 percent of all men and 12 percent of all women currently in their twenties will never get married. This means that about three times more people will remain single throughout their lives than in their parents' generation (Glick, 1984).

In addition to the never-marrieds, a substantial number of young adults are single because of divorce. As of 1980, 20 percent of the men and 24 percent of the women aged 25 to 34 had already divorced or separated from their spouse (Glick, 1984). Most of these people will eventually remarry, but about 15 to 20 percent will remain single. More divorced men than women will eventually remarry (Glick, 1984).

One interesting outcome of the increase in the number of single people is that more adults are living with their parents. As of 1984, there were 50 million Americans between the ages of 18 and 29; 18 million of them lived with their parents (Glick & Lin, 1986). Thus 37 percent of these young adults live with their parents, up from 34 percent in 1970. About 30 percent of all parents have a co-resident adult child (Aquilino, 1990).

About one third of the young adults living at home are 18 or 19; about one half are 20 to 24; and one sixth are 25 to 29. They live with their parents for a variety of reasons. Most have never been married and are employed. These people may be living at home until they save enough money to strike out on their own or until they decide to marry. Almost one third of the young adults living with their parents are either unemployed or out of the labor force. A little less than one fourth of these people are students. Apparently their parents are supporting them (Glick & Lin, 1986). Parental health seems to play little role in whether adult children live with their parents. The arrangement is usually designed to meet the needs of the adult child rather than the parents (Aquilino, 1990).

Of the young adults who had ever been married, about half of those living in their parents' homes were still married. These young married couples are particularly likely to reside in the wife's parents' home. The other half are separated or divorced. Somewhat surprisingly, more divorced men than women return to their parents' home to live. People who are separated, as opposed to legally divorced, are more likely to move back home, perhaps as a temporary measure while they are waiting to see if the marriage can be reconciled. For the sake of clarity, however, it is important to emphasize that the vast majority of ever-married adults, regardless of current marital status, maintain their own homes (Glick & Lin, 1986).

In fact, a substantial group of singles is among the most successful career women. Women who have graduate level education are less likely to marry than the other women (Houseknecht et al., 1987). So, for example, in 1979 15 percent of the women aged 35 to 54 who had post-bachelor's education were not married. Generally, unmarried women represent 5 percent of the female population. Among men, education seems less likely to deter marriage; highly educated men's rate of singlehood is identical to that for the general male population (8 percent) (Houseknecht et al., 1987). At the very least, these women seem to be delaying marriage. They may, of course, remain single throughout their lives. While them motivation for these decisions is poorly understood, it is clear that women who are not married have higher levels of career achievement than women who are. This is true across a variety of measures of achievement and success both in terms of education and career. It is also true whether the woman is never-married or divorced (Houseknecht et al., 1987).

HAVING CHILDREN

American values concerning having children are changing. People are having fewer children than in the past. In 1960, the fertility rate was 3.7 births per woman. Since 1976, it has fluctuated between 1.7 and 1.9 births per woman (Stengel, 1985). This decline implies at least two things. First, more people are opting to have only one child. The popular press' increasing attention to "only children" reflects this trend. Second, more women are not having children at all (thus lowering the average number of births per woman). Indeed, some estimates suggest that as many as 25 percent of today's childbearing age women will never have children (Stengel, 1985). Sometimes this is an involuntary decision; the couple is, for any number of reasons, unable to conceive. In other cases, there is a conscious, voluntary decision, made early in adulthood, not to have children. Still other people meant to have children but somehow never got around to it.

The increases in only children and in "accidental" voluntary childlessness are at least partially caused by another change in childbearing trends. Women are waiting longer to have their children. For example, between 1972 and 1982, the rate of first births to women aged 30–34 more than doubled. The more educated a woman, the more likely she is to delay childbearing. So, for example, 25 percent of all college-educated women have their first baby when they are in their thirties. Even at 30 to 34 years of age, nearly a third of women with graduate education still have not had their first child (Roosa, Fitzgerald & Crawford, 1985). These women are opting to establish their careers before they begin having children. Furthermore, increasing numbers of women want to continue working after they have children. Over half of the women who work during pregnancy are back at work within one year of giving birth (Kamerman, Kahn, & Kingston, 1983). Most women with preschool children work outside the home. Combining childrearing with career demands places limits on how many children you will have. And it is clear that career interests are a major contributor to the decision to remain voluntarily childless (Houseknecht 1977, 1982).

There is one other noteworthy trend in American attitudes toward childbearing. Traditionally, we have thought of having children as an event that follows marriage. We think of *couples* as making the decisions about when and how many children to have. But by 1982, fully 20 percent of all births were to single women. While these women certainly face more difficulties than couples raising children together, it is evident that single mothers are now a well-entrenched phenomenon. Indeed, some people believe that this trend will only increase as more women who did not marry during their twenties decide in their thirties that they will have children even if they do not have a husband.

Deciding to Have Children

With the development of reliable, readily available contraceptives and the legalization of abortion, childbearing became an increasingly planned event. In fact, somewhere between 85 and 95 percent of all pregnancies that occur within marriages are at least somewhat planned (Entwisle, 1985). Even a substantial number of pregnancies occurring among single women are planned or actively wanted, although it is more difficult to estimate a percentage in these cases. Furthermore, studies of young college women indicate that the vast majority plan to have children someday. So, while it is certainly the case that some pregnancies are "accidents" (due to failure to use birth control or to contraceptive failure), it is clear that many people actively choose to have babies.

It is not always obvious precisely why people decide to have children at all much less how they decide on the timing. Certainly, there is a social norm that suggests we will have children beginning sometime in our twenties. As was the case with marriage, some people are probably heavily influenced by this norm and simply have children because it "seems like the thing to do." Some people can give only vague explanations as to why they are having a child. They may say that children give meaning to one's life. Or they may be seeking the lifelong affectional bond we associate with having a child. This may be particularly important to unwed teenagers, who often feel that no one else loves them. It may also be important to those who perceive marriage as so unstable and unpredictable that only having a child can ensure that they will always have someone to love who loves them back (Entwisle, 1985).

It is also possible that people somehow believe that children are important for their own development. Erik Erikson (1963) has suggested that having children is the easiest and most common route to generativity in mid-life. This does not mean that having children guarantees generativity or that not having them prevents it. Nonetheless, generativity is more commonly achieved among parents (including adoptive parents) than among nonparents, suggesting that children can indeed facilitate adult development (Snarey, Son, Kuehne, Hauser & Valliant, 1987).

Studies of people who delay having children or who choose voluntary childlessness can provide some additional clues about how the childbearing decisions are made (Daniels & Weingarten, 1982; Houseknecht, 1977 & 1982; Roosa et al., 1985). These people often are more aware of how they made their decisions. While there is a myriad of specific reasons involved in the decision-making process, three broad categories seem to summarize the major factors.

First, there is the issue of psychological readiness. Until identity formation is complete, people may not be certain whether having children is part of their value system. They may not know whether they are sufficiently mature, responsible, and interested in making the financial and time sacrifices involved in having children. Their priorities regarding children versus career may seem unclear. As was pointed out in Chapter 3, the definition of identity may take longer for those who attend college than for those who do not. Thus, it is not surprising that college-educated women are more likely to delay childbearing.

Second, many people are worried about the impact of children on the marriage. This concern is well-founded; the divorce rate is higher in marriages formed because of pregnancy. Even in established marriages, there is a decline in marital satisfaction following the arrival of the first child. Some research suggests that this decline may be an artifact of the normal timing of childbearing. Most couples have their first child within a couple years of marriage when a decline in the "romantic" nature of the relationship is already occurring (Kurdek & Schmitt, 1986). However, there are reasons why children may contribute to decreased marital satisfaction. A couple with children has less privacy for conversation, sex, and recreational activities. Taking vacations or going out for an evening requires planning. Hiring a babysitter adds to the costs of such recreation and may force many couples to reduce the frequency of these activities. Indeed, financial resources in general will be affected by children. Children are expensive. They must be clothed, fed, and given medical care. A larger house or apartment may be needed. There are books, toys, music lessons and, for many people, college expenses to be covered. It has been estimated it costs three to four times a family's annual income to raise a child to age 18 (Miller & Myers-Wall, 1983). Some of this money will be made and spent at the expense of the parents' time together. Thus, people may decide to have children only when they feel ready to make these sacrifices.

Finally, career achievement plays a role in deciding when and if to have children. Most women today work outside the home. In some cases, this is because of a desire to experience the satisfactions associated with work. But it is important to note that about 39 percent of the total family income in the United States is provided by women (Kamerman et al., 1983). Furthermore, 23 percent of all American children (and over 50 percent of all African-American children) live in single-parent homes (Stengel, 1985). Women's income, then, is often essential to the survival of the family.

Given the increasing desire and necessity of women to work, it is not surprising that more women are waiting until they have established their careers before they have children. Many women wait until they can take at least a short maternity leave without jeopardizing their jobs (Roosa et al., 1985). Most women, however, are not eligible for a maternity leave (Kamerman et al., 1983). In other words, leaving their job to have a baby may well mean losing their job. And some women want to stay home the first year or so anyway. In these situations, a couple may wait until they have been able to save enough money to be temporarily without the woman's income. Furthermore, the decision to take time off to care for an infant may permanently impair a woman's earning capacity. This is true even for professional women who take relatively short (less than 6 months) maternity leaves (Hewlett, 1984).

Thus, several factors play a role in making the decision to become parents. Although the decision is typically made by both husband and wife, we know much more about the woman's concerns than the man's. Perhaps this is because in making the joint decision, men usually follow their wives' lead. Indeed, half of all voluntarily childless men say they would change their minds if their wives wanted children (Roosa et al., 1985). Or maybe the research emphasis on women's decision-making processes simply reflects our bias that women are more interested in children than men are.

Adjusting to Pregnancy

Pregnancy involves substantial physical and life-style changes for a woman. There will be weight gain, fatigue, and gastrointestinal problems. In some cases, the woman's health, and even her life, may be threatened. If she is conscientious, she will be careful about smoking, drinking, nutrition, and using medications during pregnancy (for example, Smolak, 1986). It is not surprising, then, that women need to make some adjustments during pregnancy.

However, it is important to remember that the prospective father's life is also changing. He is affected by his wife's physical and psychological changes during pregnancy (for example, Feldman et al., 1983; Shapiro, 1987). And he is concerned about what things will be like after the baby is born (for example, Fein, 1976; Shapiro, 1987). Thus, pregnancy is also a time of transition for the man.

The Mother's Adjustment: Adjustment to pregnancy may be conceptualized as a gradual process. Although the medical confirmation of pregnancy is a discrete tangible event, the physical and psychological demands of pregnancy necessitate continued reassessment of self, the developing child, relationships, and future responsibilities.

The first few weeks are often a time of mixed emotions. The woman may be thrilled to be pregnant, but she is also likely to have doubts, especially if it is her first pregnancy. Concerns about the fetus run high during this time because she has no clear indicators that the baby is developing normally. Women may not really feel pregnant yet. They may find it impossible to start to plan for the baby. Others are so concerned that they develop superstitions. They may refuse to talk about the pregnancy or tell anyone about it for fear that they will "jinx" the pregnancy. The woman may also have doubts about her ability to be a good mother. Indeed, she may not yet be able to envision herself as a mother or her husband as a father. One of the tasks of this period is for the woman to accept the pregnancy and change her perceptions of herself and her husband to be more in line with parenthood (Atkinson & Rickel, 1984; Turrini, 1980; Alpert & Richardson, 1980).

As the woman moves into the second trimester, and particularly after she feels the fetus move and hears the fetal heartbeat, some of these concerns abate. She becomes less anxious about her ability to mother. She can see herself in the role more easily. She starts to think of herself, the father, and the baby as a family. She even feels better physically. Some of this phys-ical improvement is real and some is psychological. Women often report they have the most energy during the second trimester and the beginning of the third trimester (Atkinson & Rickel, 1984).

Many women find that pregnancy affects their relationship with their own mother. The years immediately preceding pregnancy are often marked by a gap between mother and daughter as the younger woman tries to estab-lish herself as a separate, responsible individual. The birth of a child is perhaps the clearest and most widely accepted indicator of adult status in the United States (Entwisle, 1985). Thus, the daughter often no longer has anything to prove to her mother. Furthermore, the pregnant woman (and new mother) may develop a new level of respect for her own mother. Both women may feel they have more in common now. All this may serve to bring mother and daughter closer together (Alpert & Richardson, 1980).

The last few weeks of pregnancy may be particularly difficult for the woman. She is beginning to tire of being pregnant. She may find it difficult to get around and may have begun her maternity leave. This may leave her feeling isolated and bored. She may feel more tired and her back may ache much of the time. Furthermore, she will have completed any childbirth edu-cation classes. She will have made arrangements for the birth and probably for bringing the baby home. In other words, she is psychologically and phys-ically ready to deliver the baby (Turrini, 1980). Yet all there is to do is wait.

Not all women adjust equally well to pregnancy. Some, for example, never fully accept the fact that they are pregnant and so never seek prenatal care or make arrangements for the birth. Other women are worried about their own health or the fetus's well-being throughout their pregnancy. Still others simply wish they were not pregnant and that the baby would never arrive. These examples of poor adjustment provide some clues as to the factors that influence how well a woman copes with pregnancy.

The woman's psychological preparedness to be a parent, the planned-ness of the pregnancy, her health and the fetus's development, the family's financial resources, the parents' age, and the availability of social support all contribute to adjustment. For example, women who receive little sup-port from husbands, family, and friends seem to show poorer adjustment to both pregnancy and motherhood (Atkinson & Rickel, 1985; Feldman et al., 1983). Pregnancy or delivery complications may negatively influence adjustment (Entwisle, 1985). The smoothness of the pregnancy may, in turn, be related to whether or not it was planned. Planned pregnancies seem to proceed with fewer perceived difficulties, especially during the first trimes-ter (Entwisle, 1985).

Throughout pregnancy, then, the woman becomes more aware of the developing child. She also redefines her own and her husband's roles. She may find a new closeness with her own mother. Women do not, however seem to focus on what life will be like after the baby is born. In fact, fathers-to-be seem to be more aware of how many changes there will be after the baby arrives (Alpert & Richardson, 1980). This reflects one difference be-tween male and female adjustment to pregnancy.

The Father's Adjustment: Pregnancy represents a major life transition for men, too. Indeed, fathers are often more stressed during pregnancy than mothers (Fein, 1976; Miller & Myers-Wall, 1983). One reason is that he may feel "left out." The pregnant woman receives a considerable amount of attention, even from strangers, and he is under some pressure to provide some of this support. He also has less constant reassurance than the woman does that the baby is developing normally. He cannot feel the baby move as early in the pregnancy as the woman can. Furthermore, she feels every movement; he feels them only occasionally (Shapiro, 1987). Thus, he may perceive a mother-child relationship developing but not yet a father-child relationship.

In addition to his concerns about the fetus's health, the father may also be worried about his wife. If something should go wrong, he could lose both of them. Since most men do not regularly accompany their wives for their prenatal checkups, they do not get direct reassurance and information from medical personnel. Even when they do go with their wives, they may feel like outsiders because they know so little about obstetrics and gynecology (Shapiro, 1987). Related to this is the common fear of being unable to perform well during the labor and delivery (which most men plan to attend). Many men worry that they will faint or forget what to do (Shapiro, 1987).

It is not only health issues that concern the prospective father. Men often worry about what life will be like after the baby is born, financially, socially, and sexually. Men who will be the sole support of the family tend to be particularly worried about financial issues. They become concerned about things like life insurance and taking physical risks (Shapiro, 1987). Women tend to be so focused on the pregnancy itself that they don't think as much about what it will be like to actually have the baby around. Indeed, this may be one reason why women are so much more susceptible to postpartum depression than men are (Alpert & Richardson, 1980; Fein, 1976).

All these feelings may be intensified by cultural norms that prevent men from expressing their fears and worries, especially to their friends. Since they often don't want to worry their wives and feel they can't talk to their friends, men may feel isolated and confused. Some men make an effort to get closer to their own fathers (Alpert & Richardson, 1980) in order to fill this void.

Of course, not every feeling that the man has is going to be negative. Men are like women in that there is typically a variety of emotions associated with pregnancy. They too feel elation and anticipation about the awaited birth. They too may develop a closer relationship with their father. But in general, pregnancy is a time of unrecognized stress for men.

Adjustment to the Baby

The first few hours following a baby's birth are a time of elation, mixed, perhaps, with exhaustion. Parents report feeling little stress during the actual hospital stay (Parke & Sawin, 1980). Indeed, assuming the birth has gone as expected, fathers may feel better after the baby is born (Fein,

1976). After all, their fears about the mother and baby's health as well as their own performance during labor and delivery are now alleviated. Furthermore, new parents are engrossed with their newborns (Greenberg & Morris, 1974). They are fascinated by the baby's appearance and spend large amounts of time talking about the baby and planning the future. Of course, these reactions can be tempered or even reversed by birth complications or problems with the baby's health. But, typically, this is a very happy and satisfying time for the parents.

Very soon, and somewhat abruptly, however, reality will set in as the parents begin to care for their newborn. Most new parents find babies very demanding in terms of time and physical exertion. It is a task for which most middle-class parents, at least, have little formal training. The realization that parenthood is an irrevocable decision sets in. Women in particular seem to be surprised by how difficult it is to have a small baby around. Thus, there are adjustments to be made (Entwisle, 1985; Miller & Myers-Wall, 1983).

The need for adjustment becomes even clearer if you think of the family as a small social system. Family members have established roles. Establishing such roles is one of the tasks of adjusting to marriage. Similarly, in the course of adjusting to marriage, the couple has established values and priorities. The introduction of a new family member will require some reevaluating and shifting of roles. It is not unusual, for example, for a new mother to assume a more traditional feminine role and for the new father to assume a more masculine role (Gutmann, 1975; Miller & Myers-Wall, 1983). Even in countries where men are eligible for paternity leave, like Sweden, women assume most of the infant care responsibilities (Kalleberg & Rosenfeld, 1990). The loss of time and privacy associated with a new baby may contribute to a decline in marital satisfaction. Women especially seem to perceive an increase in marital stress, particularly in terms of how much attention they receive from their husbands (Miller & Myers-Wall, 1983).

All this may leave the impression that adjustment to a new baby is an extraordinarily difficult task. Indeed, early researchers labeled this period a "crisis" (for example, Dyer, 1963; LeMasters, 1957). A majority of the couples in these studies reported "severe" adjustment difficulties. However, such extreme problems appear to have been a cohort effect. Parenthood was somewhat glamorized during the 1950s. As attitudes and education about children have changed, so has the difficulty of adjusting to a new child.

Most researchers now conceptualize this as a "transitional" period (for example, Entwisle, 1985; Hobbs, 1965; Hobbs & Cole, 1976; Miller & Myers-Wall, 1983; Russell, 1974). The decline in marital satisfaction appears to be less dramatic now than it was in earlier cohorts (Entwisle, 1985). And the majority of couples now report only "slight" difficulty in adjusting to a new baby (Hobbs, 1965; Hobbs & Cole, 1975). Furthermore, there are individual differences in adjustment such that some couples' marital relationships *improve* after the birth of a baby (Belsky & Rovine, 1990; see Table 6–3). When adjustment problems do occur, they are more likely to be evident in the mother than in the father.

TABLE 6-3: Various Patterns of Change after the Birth of a Baby on Relationship Scales

	Accelerating Negative Change	Gradual (linear) Negative Change	No Change	Modest Positive Change
Wife				
Love	15.6%	26.6%	46.1%	11.7%
Conflict	6.3	42.1	21.9	30.2
Ambivalence	9.3	22.5	47.3	20.9
Maintenance	12.7	47.5	25.4	14.4
Husband				
Love	11.1%	35.0%	43.6%	10.3%
Conflict	5.2	25.2	33.9	35.7
Ambivalence	6.7	27.7	32.8	32.8
Maintenance	14.7	45.9	24.8	14.7

The scales all measure dimensions of an intimate relationship. Love taps feelings of affection and belongingness; conflict assesses arguments, fights, etc.; maintenance measures behaviors (such as communication) intended to enrich and hence maintain the relationship; and ambivalence refers to feelings about your partner.

Source: Belsky, J., & Rovine, M. (1990). Patterns of marital change across the transition to parenthood: Pregnancy to three years postpartum. *Journal of Marriage and the Family, 52,* 12. Copyright 1990 by the National Council on Family Relations. Reprinted by permission.

Mothers' Adjustment: Contrary to popular belief, not all mothers experience postpartum depression. It is unusual for any depression that does occur to be severe enough to require treatment. About 10 to 20 percent of all new mothers experience no depressive reaction; a comparable percentage experience moderate to severe depression. The majority of mothers (perhaps up to 85 percent but more likely 55 to 60 percent) experience only a temporary case of "the blues." New mothers with the blues are usually teary, despondent, and anxious. They have trouble concentrating. The problem usually begins 2 to 4 days after the birth and in most cases, lasts only 2 or 3 days. There are no known long-term consequences (O'Hara, Zekoski, Philipps & Wright, 1990; Pitt, 1982).

Recent research indicates that new mothers are no more likely to experience a "true, clinical" depression than a matched sample of women who have not had babies (O'Hara et al., 1990). However, the new mothers do show poorer social adjustment and more depressive symptomology (such as mild dysphoria and fatigue). Thus, while a full-blown depression may be unusual, negative feelings are not. Women usually find the birth process and childcare more physically stressful than they had anticipated and report feeling exhausted during the first few weeks of motherhood (Entwisle, 1985; Miller & Myers-Wall, 1983; O'Hara et al., 1990). They may feel isolated, since it is often difficult to go out with a new baby (Atkinson & Rickel, 1984). They may be disappointed in their own mothering ability or their baby's behavior. This seems to be particularly likely among middle-class mothers, who often have no experience with small babies and therefore have unrealistic expectations about what this time will be like (Entwisle, 1985).

Women who have returned to work may feel guilty about leaving the baby with someone else (DeMeis, Hock, & McBride, 1986; Miller & Myers-Wall, 1983). Working mothers may also face conflicts as they try to resolve career-motherhood conflicts by compartmentalizing their roles and establishing priorities (Miller & Myers-Wall, 1983). But these women, many of whom gave considerable thought to having their children, may be quite well equipped to handle these multiple roles.

A variety of factors influence how well and how quickly a new mother adjusts to her role. Social support, especially from the husband, appears to be crucial (Crockenberg, 1981; Cutrona & Troutman, 1986; Miller & Myers-Wall, 1983). Women who are happy in their marriages have easier postpartum adjustments (Atkinson & Rickel, 1984). The needed spouse support seems to be more in terms of attention and affection than actual assistance in childcare tasks (Entwisle, 1985; Miller & Myers-Wall, 1983). Such social support seems to protect a woman from depression by increasing her sense of competence as a parent (Cutrona & Troutman, 1986).

Infant temperament also plays a role, with mothers of difficult infants being more prone to depressive reactions (Cutrona & Troutman, 1986). This, however, seems to be a cyclical relationship, since dissatisfied mothers seem to have infants who become more difficult as time progresses.

Issues concerning the pregnancy, delivery, and baby's health may also play a role. Unplanned pregnancy may increase the risk of postpartum depression (Atkinson & Rickel, 1984). Similarly, birth complications, such as a Cesarian section, may increase the risk (Entwisle, 1985). And health problems in the babies, including prematurity, may lead to poorer adjustment (Smolak, 1986).

Finally, some researchers believe that biological factors, including the hormonal fluctuations associated with pregnancy, childbirth, and lactation, as well as genetic influences, may play a role in postpartum depression (Atkinson & Rickel, 1984; Kaplan, 1986; Pitt, 1982). While the precise nature of a physiological component remains the subject of debate, the general literature on depression suggests that it does play a role, especially in more extreme reactions. On the other hand, it is clearly not the sole determinant of postpartum adjustment in women.

Father's Adjustment: Fathers also get the "baby blues," though this issue has received less research attention than maternal postpartum depression. Martha Zaslow (Zaslow et al., 1981) reported that about two-thirds of the fathers she studied suffered mild to moderate postpartum blues. None suffered true depression. So, both the rate (about 67 percent for men vs. 80–90 percent for women) and the severity of postpartum blues is less for men than for women.

Some men, though, have more negative reactions to the birth than other men. About one-third of the men in the Zaslow study had the blues for more than 8 days. The men experiencing the more extended blues reported problems with their wives and in their new roles as fathers. They seemed to be uncertain of what to do or how to help their wives. This is consistent with Fein's (1976) report that fathers with a well-defined role in relation to newborn care were more likely to adjust well during the postpartum period. Note that the nature of the father's role is less important than the existence of a role for him. Fein found that it didn't matter whether the father assumed a traditional breadwinner role or became an active participant in parenting; he simply needed a defined role. It may be important, however, that the father's attitude and role are consistent. Parents who hold traditional division of labor attitudes but actually have less traditional role assignment report more conflict and less love within their marriages after the baby is born (MacDermid, et al., 1990).

The other major finding of Zaslow's research—that is, that the husband-wife relationship is important in the father's adjustment—also meshes well with other empirical findings. Susan Feldman and her colleagues (Feldman et al., 1983) found that maternal characteristics were slightly more powerful predictors of the father's behavior than were his own characteristics. Men's playfulness with their babies, their involvement with caretaking, and their satisfaction with fatherhood were all related to their wives' characteristics. The mother's assessment of the marriage and her adjustment to pregnancy were both positively related to her husband's satisfaction with fatherhood. Wallace and Gotlib (1990) have reported that wives' prenatal marital adjustment is an important determinant of husbands' postpartum marital satisfaction.

In a similar vein, Rob Palkovitz (1985) has suggested that the effects of the father's attendance at the birth may affect his early interactions with the baby *indirectly* at least as much as directly. This means that the early experiences with the birth process may affect the father-mother relationship, which may in turn affect the father-infant interaction. Palkovitz hypothesizes that this may be why fathers who were unexpectedly absent from the birth seem to be more actively involved in the baby's care. They may be trying to make it up to their wives for not being with them during the delivery. Researchers have also suggested that fathers may not be more involved in infant care because the mothers interfere with or event prevent (perhaps unconsciously) such help (Barnett & Baruch, 1987a). This may be particularly true of older mothers (Feldman et al., 1938). Thus, mothers may contribute to the fathers' feeling of being left out and having no clear role in the new family.

While new fathers do have adjustments to make, mothers apparently have a more difficult transition. This is probably partially attributable to the hormonal changes and physical exhaustion women experience (Pitt, 1982). Furthermore, men may be more psychologically prepared for their new role than women are. After all, during pregnancy they were more focused on it (Chester, 1979). Indeed, the birth of the baby may actually reduce stress for men (Fein, 1976). In addition, the woman typically assumes much greater responsibility for the physical care of the newborn. Not only is this a strain on her physically, but it also puts her in a position of relative social isolation. She may find it difficult to go out of the house regularly, much less resume her normal social or work life. In other words, the mother may experience more extensive role changes than the father and be psychologically less prepared for them.

Marital Happiness: If you look just at group averages, you will find that marital satisfaction decreases after the birth of a baby (Belsky & Rovine, 1990). Some of this decrease seems to be attributable to the normative decline in couples' happiness after the first year or so together (MacDermid et al., 1990). As Table 6–3 shows, however, there are substantial individual differences in both the direction and degree of changes in marital satisfaction in the immediate months after the baby is born.

Not surprisingly, marital adjustment during pregnancy is one of the best predictors of postpartum marital happiness for both husbands and wives (Wallace & Gotlib, 1990). As we have noted, the wife's adjustment seems to affect the husband's. The self-esteem of the parents as well as their interpersonal sensitivity also plays a role. For example, decline in marital quality postpartum has been associated with lower paternal interpersonal sensitivity and lower self-esteem in both parents (Belsky & Rovine, 1990). Finally, the baby's characteristics play a role (Belsky & Rovine, 1990; Wallace & Gotlib, 1990). Babies who are more demanding and more difficult to care for have parents with lower marital satisfaction.

Parenting Preschool and School-Age Children

With the decline of the physical demands of caring for an infant, parenting may become somewhat easier. Even financial demands may abate as the child requires fewer visits to the doctor, no longer requires special food, and outgrows toys and clothing less rapidly. In some ways, the period of parenting preschool and school-age children may be viewed as a plateau in terms of stress. However, it is not without its risks and strains (Alpert & Richardson, 1980).

Women who are at home full-time with young children may be particularly "at risk" (Alpert & Richardson, 1980; Ilfeld, 1982). Such work is not held in high esteem by society and tends to be very repetitive. The same clothing gets washed over and over; favorite stories may be read aloud repeatedly; almost every lunch may be peanut butter and jelly. Furthermore, there is considerable task fragmentation. Young children frequently interrupt whatever their mothers are doing. At the very least, they need to be checked regularly. Indeed, the monotony, fragmentation, and time pressures have been compared to factory work (Oakley, 1974). Furthermore, the mother may feel that she rarely gets to talk to adults (even her phone conversations will be interrupted) and may also feel that she has little interesting to discuss when the opportunity does arise. Thus, she may be suffering from psychosocial deprivation.

Since women who work outside the home are still typically their children's primary caregivers, they too face these problems, and some of them feel overwhelmed by the combined responsibilities of home and work (Belle, 1982). On the other hand, work may serve as a buffer against the strains of raising young children. When things are going poorly at home, for example, the woman may still find a source of reward and self-esteem in her work. And, of course, work provides the woman with income which in turn gives her greater social status.

Having young children also raises the possibility of another challenge. If you have another baby, the children as well as the parents need to adjust. So, while certain concerns (about one's ability to parent, for example) may be lessened, new ones arise. There is the issue of how to give each child the attention she or he wants. The older sibling may heartily resent the new baby. Illnesses may be passed around the family. Thus, it is not surprising that although the risk of postpartum depression seems to be somewhat less after the birth of the second child compared to the first, it actually seems to rise again when a woman has three or four children (Atkinson & Rickel, 1984).

CHILDLESSNESS

Not every adult has children; even many married couples are childless. In some cases, this is involuntary because there is a fertility problem (see Chapter 4) that prevents the couple from having children. Some couples, however, simply opt not to have children.

Involuntary Childlessness

Americans routinely expect people to want to have children. When they want to but cannot, our sympathy is aroused. In fact, we may view involuntarily childless couples more positively than any other type of family (Polit, 1978).

There is some justification for our sympathetic view. Infertile couples may go through a grieving process similar to that seen following a death (Roosa et al., 1985). There may initially be denial of the problem as the couple goes from doctor to doctor trying to find a cure. This may be followed by anger, guilt, and bitterness. The partners may blame themselves and each other for their inability to have children. This can be stressful to the individuals and to the marriage. Sexual relations may be impaired, for example, as the couple tries to "regulate" sex (in accordance with the woman's ovulation cycle) in an attempt to conceive.

This part of the process may take some time and may interfere with the couple's seeking appropriate advice and options. It is not until the grief is resolved and the couple can accept the problem that adoption, for example, can be considered. Even other options for having a child (such as surrogate mothering or artificial insemination) cannot be considered until infertility is accepted.

Accepting infertility does not necessarily end the couple's problems. Artificial insemination seems to create guilt in some women who feel strange about conceiving a baby with "another man." And the husband may feel some ambivalence about the impregnation. But, in general, making the decision and going through the process of artificial insemination seems to draw the couple closer together (Roosa et al., 1985).

Voluntary Childlessness

As much as Americans tend to sympathize with involuntarily childless couples, we are suspicious of those who can have children but do not. No family type is viewed more negatively than the voluntarily childless couple (Polit, 1978). In general they are viewed as selfish, immature, independent, self-centered, rebellious, and unconventional (Roosa et al., 1985; Polit, 1978). They are also seen as less friendly, wholesome, and good-natured than those who want children. Voluntary childlessness is thought of as not only nontraditional, but also as deviant.

In some ways, this stereotype of voluntarily childless couples is correct. The women are more career-oriented. These couples often do not want the responsibility of children and may be unwilling to have their independence restricted by a baby. They may not want the financial burden of children despite the fact that, typically, these are well-educated people with good incomes. In fact, as income of the wife rises, her fertility rate drops. They are also concerned that a child will have a negative impact on their marital relationship (Houseknecht, 1977, 1982; Roosa et al., 1985). Certainly many people would view these reasons as indicative of immaturity, selfishness, and irresponsibility. And women who do not want children are untraditional. They know they will be under pressure to have children but feel comfortable ignoring the social norms (Houseknecht, 1977).

But these are not the only reasons people opt not to have children. Some couples are concerned about population control or world conditions and believe it is morally inappropriate to have children. Others may be concerned about the woman's health, even though she is capable of pregnancy and childbirth (Roosa et al., 1985). Furthermore, these are not people who are incapable of loving and giving. Indeed, they tend to have happier marriages and higher levels of communication within their marital relationships than people with children (Roosa et al., 1985). Voluntarily childless couples do have friends. In fact, a strong social support group is typically needed in order for a couple to buck tradition and decide against having children (Houseknecht, 1977).

Some people decide very early not to have children. At least the women in this group tend to show the characteristics just described; they are career-oriented and have a social group that supports their decision. They tend to be less traditionally feminine than other women and have more of a feminist orientation. They are more distant from their parents psychologically and have fewer memories of a warm, loving early childhood (Gerson, 1980; Roosa et al., 1985).

But some voluntarily childless couples did not originally intend not to have children. They simply planned to delay childbearing, perhaps until they were financially established or until their marital relationship was established. Originally, they probably had a timetable. Perhaps, for example, they planned to have a child when they had been married for 5 years. Then, for a variety of reasons, the time was delayed and the timetable became less clear. They still plan to have children but they're not sure when. Age is starting to catch up with them. They may be concerned about the wife's health or their ability to adjust. The pressure from their families to have children starts to abate after 5 or 6 years of childlessness. These factors may lead the couple to consider and ultimately decide on childlessness (Roosa et al., 1985).

Those couples who move from "delayers" to voluntary childlessness are different from people who make the decision early. They are closer to their families, are less achievement-oriented, and are less likely to make the decision "permanent" by undergoing a sterilization procedure (Roosa et al., 1985). In other words, these couples fall somewhere in between early decision makers and those who do have children in terms of their attitudes about family, work, and women's roles.

DIVORCE

Around 1960, the number and rate of divorces among American couples began to rise. The number of divorces tripled from 1962 to 1981 (Caldwell, Bloom & Hodges, 1984), and the divorce rate increased by 113 percent between 1966 and 1976 (Kelly, 1982). The increases occurred in all races, socioeconomic classes, and family types (with or without children) (Kelly, 1982). While the rate has apparently been more or less stable since the early 1980s, there are still over 1 million divorces every year in the United States (Caldwell et al., 1984).

It is difficult to know whether the increased frequency of divorce caused a relaxing of social and legal attitudes, or vice versa. Nonetheless, it is evident that people facing divorce in the 1980s were in a very different situation from those who divorced prior to the 1960s. Divorcing couples in the 1950s apparently had much more dramatic and compelling reasons for ending their marriages than those in the 1980s (Kitson & Sussman, 1982). Reasons for divorce in the 1950s were more likely to include drinking, nonsupport, and desertion; in the 1980s there was an increased frequency of complaints concerning personality differences, home life, and values conflicts.

Divorce is more socially acceptable now. Legally, it is much easier (and much less expensive) to obtain a divorce than it used to be. School systems, social service agencies, and even family counselors are much better equipped to deal with divorce. And since many of us know divorced people, the individual going through a divorce is more likely to have role models and support systems for postdivorce life.

All this means that the early research concerning divorce may not be very helpful in understanding what today's separating couples face (Kelly, 1982). This is a good example of a time-of-measurement effect. We may also be seeing a cohort effect as successive generations of Americans have more experience with and acceptance of marital disruptions. It is still the case, of course, that most marriages do not end in divorce. Certain factors, including age at marriage, wife's income, and premarital pregnancy, are associated with divorce risk. Table 6–4 summarizes these relationships.

The Divorce Process

The increased acceptability and frequency of divorce has not erased its impact on the people involved. Divorce still requires considerable readjustment in terms of roles, relationships, and emotions. While there are some positive aspects of divorce, the experience is, in general, a difficult one. The amount and types of adjustment required vary depending on the stage of the divorce process. For the purposes of analysis, three stages can be delineated: the preseparation phase, the decision to divorce, and postdivorce adjustment (Caldwell et al., 1984).

Preseparation: Certainly there are cases in which there is virtually no preseparation phase; the decision to divorce is made impulsively and suddenly. It is much more common, however, to find a long period of marital dissatisfaction preceding the separation. In the California Divorce Study, for example, 20 percent of the divorcing couples reported they had been unhappy for 5 to 8 years, 33 percent for 8 to 12 years, and almost 15 percent for more than 12 years (Kelly, 1982). Most of these marriages were miserable for an extended period of time marked by " ... strident incompatibilities, long unmet and competing needs, lack of respect and intimacy, dishonesty, hostility, abuse, and total failure in communication ... " (Kelly, 1982, p. 739). Women in particular seem to be unhappy during this period. They report higher rates of psychological disturbances (Caldwell et al., 1984).

TABLE 6-4: Factors Contributing to Marital Instability

Factor	Relationship to Marital Instability
Age	Men who marry before age 20 and women who marry before 18 are about twice as likely to divorce
Education	Men and women who fail to complete high school are more likely to divorce.
Premarital pregnancy	Increases risk of divorce.
Work	Instability of husband's employment or marked decline in his income is related to increased likelihood of divorce. Wives with higher incomes are more likely to divorce (although in some cases, this may represent a preparation for divorce rather than a contributing factor).
Intergenerational transmission	Children of divorce may be more likely to divorce but only under certain circumstances related to their postdivorce adjustment (how happy they thought their parents' remarriages were).

Source: Based on data from Kelly, J. B. (1982). Divorce: The adult perspective. In B. Wolman (ed.), *Handbook of developmental psychology,* pp. 734–750. Englewood Cliffs, NJ: Prentice Hall.

They also seem to be more unhappy for longer periods of time than the men are (Kelly, 1982).

If the marriages are so unsatisfactory, why does it take so long to decide to get a divorce? For one thing, the individual(s) involved must realize that the marriage is the root of the problem (Ahrons, 1983). Initially, there may be strong denial that the marriage is in trouble. A couple may think that a new house or job will solve the problems. They may think that once the children get older things will settle down. The American tendency toward privacy may also contribute. Since most of us do not know the intimate details of other peoples' marriages, we may think that the problems we are facing (such as a decline in intimacy or communication) are normal (Kelly, 1982).

Tension during this period runs high (Ahrons, 1983). The couple may start to blame each other for various family problems but are not yet ready to give up their marital roles. This situation can go on for years; indeed it can go on indefinitely, creating a very difficult scenario for all family members. Eventually, however, many couples realize that the marriage is ending and start to distance themselves emotionally from their partners and begin some of the role changes that will be necessary after the separation (Ahrons, 1983). Even at this point, tension runs high because neither the marital nor the postdivorce roles and emotions are entirely appropriate.

Decision to Divorce: Every marriage faces difficult periods when divorce could be seen as a viable alternative. During any crisis period, the individuals have at least four options (Rusbult, Johnson & Morrow, 1986). They can "exit" the relationship by separating, divorcing, or threatening to leave. They can respond with "voice," trying to actively change the situation through discussions or counseling. A "loyalty" response such as waiting for things to change or defending the spouse's behavior to others is a possibility. Or, they can simply engage in "neglect" by refusing to discuss the problem or ignoring the partner.

A variety of factors influences the likelihood of each of these responses (Rusbult et al., 1986). For example, the greater the satisfaction with the relationship prior to the problem, the more likely a "voice" response will occur. On the other hand, exit responses are more likely if the offended partner saw other life-style options (including single living) as preferable to the current relationship. Older people, those who have been in relationships longer, and those with lower education levels are less likely to engage in exit or voice behaviors.

The severity of the crisis also plays a role (Rusbult et al., 1986). In many separations there is a "last-straw" phenomenon (Kelly, 1982). Common examples of these are an extramarital affair or some external event (such as a job change). But in many other couples there is no identifiable precipitating event; instead, there is just a growing recognition of divorce as a viable option (Kelly, 1982). Table 6–5 summarizes some of the reasons men and women give for seeking a divorce.

Given that women tend to report greater marital dissatisfaction prior to the divorce, it should not be surprising that they are much more likely

TABLE 6-5:   Common Marital Complaints from Divorcing Couples

Women	Men
Feeling unloved	Wife was inattentive to husband's needs
Husband belittled wife's competence and intelligence, wife eventually felt she could do nothing right	Incompatibility of interests, values, and goals from the beginning of the marriage
Husbands hypercritical of everything (clothing, appearance, ideas)	Sexual deprivation due to wife's disinterest or frigidity
Sexual deprivation due to husband's disinterest or infidelity	Chronic nagging or anger from wife
Chronic anger or nagging by husband	
Husband not home enough	

Source: Based on data from Kelly, J. B. (1982). Divorce: The adult perspective. In B. Wolman (ed.), *Handbook of Developmental Psychology*, pp. 734–750. Englewood Cliffs, NJ: Prentice Hall.

to initiate the separation (Caldwell et al., 1984; Kelly, 1982). Furthermore, men are more likely to oppose the divorce than women are (Kelly, 1982). Few divorces are truly mutual decisions. Indeed, often one spouse is caught off guard by the request for separation.

Who initiates the divorce has both short- and long-term consequences. Initiators may feel guilty or sad but also have a sense of control over the situation. They do not feel the rejection or humiliation the noninitiator experiences. They have had a chance to mentally rehearse and prepare for the role changes. Thus, it is common to find that the initiators adjust to both the separation and the divorce more easily. They show fewer psychological problems. Indeed, having made the decision may be such a relief to them that psychological and psychosomatic symptoms actually abate at the time of separation. In other words, the preseparation period may be most stressful for the initiator, while the postseparation period may be the most difficult for the noninitiating partner (Kelly, 1982).

Postdivorce Adjustment: During the early months of the separation the divorcing partners are likely to experience considerable anger (Kelly, 1982; Caldwell et al., 1984). Some of this is attributable to the legal system. Divorce is set up as an adversarial process in which one person "fights" the other for custody, visitation rights, and property. The plaintiff's lawyer will encourage him or her to protect their self-interest for now and the future. The defendant's lawyer will be giving similar advice.

Anger is also fueled by some of the difficulties encountered in the first few months. Women, for example, are likely to experience economic problems (Caldwell et al., 1984). Indeed, some women, especially those who had been homemakers married to professional men, find that their standard of living has dropped dramatically (Kelly, 1982; Weitzman, 1984). Divorcing women often have problems finding appropriate employment and planning their careers (see Chapter 11). They are more likely than men to switch jobs in an attempt to increase their incomes. As the more frequent custodial parent, women are also more likely to find homemaking responsibilities burdensome (Caldwell et al., 1984). Such problems can contribute to bitterness toward the soon-to-be ex-spouse, who is often blamed for the difficulties.

Depression is also a common reaction during the early phases of separation (Kelly, 1982). For women, the depression seems to be rooted in a feeling of being overwhelmed by new responsibilities (vis-à-vis the children and economic level) and roles. For men, the loss of contact with their children seems to be a primary contributor. Other commonly cited problems include loneliness, breaking attachment bonds to the former spouse, establishing new social networks, and resolving conflicts with the ex-spouse. Women tend to have stronger social support systems than men do, but both genders report losing some old friends following the divorce (Caldwell et al., 1984). Furthermore, many divorcing people do not have close relationships or social networks on which to rely. For example, approximately two months after the separation, only about one-third of the participants in the Caldwell et al. study were dating. In fact, many men view their ex-wife as the person who could be most helpful to them in making their adjustment. They have no one else they feel understands them as well. This lack of relationships or social outlets may contribute to the sense of loneliness and, in some cases, isolation, felt by newly separated individuals (Kelly, 1982).

Not all effects of divorce are negative. Many women report a sense of relief and a feeling of having a "new chance" when they divorce. And many men find that their relationships with their children actually improve after a divorce (Kelly, 1982; Caldwell et al., 1984). Psychological health often improves for both men and women, though it is important to note that happily married people typically enjoy better psychological and physical health than do divorced people (Kelly, 1982; Bloom et al., 1979; Caldwell et al., 1984). And the majority of both men and women view the divorce positively 5 years later (Kelly, 1982). Women particularly were likely to be more contented and have higher self-esteem than they had prior to the divorce. Not all problems were gone. There is a sizable minority who, 10 years after the divorce, are bitter and isolated. Some men have virtually lost contact with their children and, despite adequate resources, refuse to help with their children's education expenses. However, the decision to divorce seems to have been a good one for at least one member of the majority of couples (Wallerstein & Blakeslee, 1989).

Life Styles after Divorce: Eventually the difficulties associated with divorce begin to abate. Roughly 2 years afterward, men typically feel their lives are more or less back in order. It takes longer, approximately 3 years, for the average divorced woman to regain this sense of stability. The healthier a person was psychologically prior to the divorce, the more likely it is that a sense of stability will eventually be attained (Kelly, 1982).

Finances may continue to be a problem, especially for women with small children. While court-ordered child support payments are made more regularly now than in the past, they are still often sporadic. For example, in 1978 48.9 percent of the women who were supposed to get child support received their full payment, 22.7 percent received some of the money, and 28.4 percent got none of it. By 1983, these figures had risen to 50.5 percent (total payment), 25.5 percent (partial payment), and 24 percent (none). This means that about 958,000 women did not receive child support in 1983, so that America's children were owed a total of $3 billion by their noncustodial parents. Whites were both more likely to be awarded support payments and to receive at least some portion of them than were African-Americans or Hispanics (*Columbus Dispatch*, July 12, 1985).

Loneliness can continue to be a problem for a long time after a divorce. While it is tempered by time and the establishment of new social relationships, it still causes measurable discomfort, especially for women. Women who are mothers of young children or who lost considerable social status through their divorce are particularly likely to suffer (Kelly, 1982).

Of course, many divorced people eventually remarry. Indeed, approximately 79 percent of them will (Stengel, 1985). But, as we will see in more detail in Chapter 10, these remarriages are often difficult. Divorce is considerably more frequent in remarriages than in first marriages, especially if stepchildren are involved.

SUMMARY

Every major theorist of personality or social development during the young adult years makes the formation of a long-term intimate relationship a cornerstone of healthy development. In the United States, a voluntary marriage, based on romantic love, is the most common form of this relationship. Yet the process by which the decision who and when to marry is made is only moderately well understood. Social expectations, including age roles, certainly play a major role. However, there also may be biological factors involved as people seek to find the optimal situation in which to reproduce their genes.

Marriage is a widespread phenomenon in the United States, but it is not the option chosen by everyone. First, there are other forms of intimate relationships that may serve the purposes of marriage. These include heterosexual cohabitation and lesbian and gay relationships. While these relationships are similar to marriage, they differ in important ways in terms of economic sharing, sexual fidelity, and duration of the relationship. They are different from marriage simply in terms of social acceptance and legality. Indeed, these social issues may in part determine some of the differences between marriage and other forms of intimate relationships. Cohabiting couples may be less likely to pool incomes, for example, because they are not automatically guaranteed receiving a percentage of the money upon dissolution of the relationship the way married couples are.

Some people opt to remain single. In fact, this seems to be a growing trend, although the percentage of people choosing this life style remains small. There is, at present, little information on why people make this choice and how it affects their long-term development.

People who do form intimate relationships, married or not, must make adjustments in terms of privacy, social relationships, and a number of other areas. These adjustments are influenced by the individuals' age, social skills, and support systems. The first year or two is particularly difficult, although it is not usually a time of real crisis. Rather, it is a transition period.

Becoming a parent is also a transition period. It not only introduces a new social relationship (parent-child), but it alters existing ones. The time, energy, and financial resources required by a new baby can take a toll, especially on marital satisfaction and the adjustment of the mother. Again, a variety of factors, including infant temperament and social support, will mediate these effects. As with marital adjustment, this is not typically a crisis period.

Once again, however, we see individual differences in life style decisions. More and more women are choosing to have their children later in adult life, and many of these women are having only one or two children. A minority of married couples opt not to have children at all. Some of these couples make the decision early in marriage; others seem to make it by default. Those making such a choice typically are quite career-oriented and need a strong social support system in order to go against the normative trends.

Whether they have children or not, many married couples will eventually divorce. This difficult decision generally triggers a period of crisis in the individual's lives. It requires social, emotional, and economic adjustments that may take years to make. The adjustment frequently seems to be more difficult for women, perhaps because they typically have custody of the children, despite the fact that they more frequently initiate the divorce. However, substantial numbers of divorced women also report considerable benefits from the divorce, particularly in the realm of enhanced self-esteem. Factors influencing adjustment to divorce including financial status, predivorce adjustment, and social support systems.

This chapter has focused on the formation of the family during the young adult years. Note, however, that every transition during this period is facilitated by a strong social support system. Friends and relatives continue to play an important role in a person's well-being even after marriage. As we saw in Chapter 5, women are more likely to have these close friendships. And they seem to be more likely to rely on them as they move through these transitions. Men, on the other hand, often seem to view their wives as their best friends, an approach that can be particularly devastating in cases of divorce.

7 Work

Jennifer decided late in high school that she wanted to be a psychologist. She went to college immediately after graduating from high school and declared a psychology major within her first year. After college, she went straight into a Ph.D. program. She now teaches psychology on the college level.

John's high school career choice was architecture. He went to college for one year but could not apply himself to the task and left. At 19, he joined the Army. Although it was not his original intention, he eventually became a career soldier. He could have left the Army at 39, but opted to stay in a few more years. Now, in his early forties, he must decide how to spend the remainder of his work life.

In her early twenties, Marcia entered a Ph.D. program in history. While in the program, she got married and had her first child. Her husband's job required that they move some distance from her university. The combination of the move, the baby, and her dissatisfaction with the Ph.D. program led her to withdraw after completing the work for her masters' degree. She and her husband decided that she would stay at home and raise their children. When the youngest child enters school, Marcia plans to return to college for an as yet undetermined degree. At the time she returns to college, she will have been out of the job market for about 13 years.

Mark began working in his family's restaurant while he was in his early teens. This experience led him to work in restaurants throughout his late teens and early twenties. He held a variety of jobs ranging from busboy to cook to assistant manager. But he always viewed such work as temporary, simply a way to make a living, and did not hold any of them for more than a few months. Several other jobs, including a stint in the Army and working for a delivery service, were viewed similarly. In his mid-twenties, he went to work as a handyman's apprentice. He learned carpentry, plumbing, and a variety of other skills. He was particularly interested in the cabinetmaking he had learned and tried to establish a business using this skill. When that was unsuccessful, he tried general contracting. As his own business waxed and waned, he would occasionally work for other companies. As he got older, he wanted more job stability and settled into working for one company. However, with age also came the realization that his body would not tolerate the physical strain of carpentry work indefinitely. Now, in his late thirties, he is trying to move into a more managerially oriented position in carpentry.

These experiences clearly demonstrate the variety of paths in selecting and developing a career. Some people make a decision fairly early in adult life and stay with it; others find the career they have chosen is not the best one for them; still others have a difficult time finding a niche. And then there are those who find a career but who want to change it later in life.

The choices we make in terms of career have far-reaching implications. The amount of time people spend working makes it a major influence on life satisfaction. Even though people today work shorter hours and fewer days than in the past, the average American man spends over half of his life at work (Havighurst, 1982). It should not be surprising that such a time-consuming activity is often a source of status, self-esteem, and friendships. Indeed, for some people, work is the thing that gives meaning to their lives (Havighurst, 1982). And, of course, work determines a person's standard of living and thereby influences housing, health care, leisure activities, and even life expectancy.

PEOPLE AT WORK

Who Is Working?

Most people in the United States who want to work do hold jobs. Even at the height of the Great Depression in the 1930s, nearly three-quarters of those interested in working were employed. This statement is not intended to trivialize the problem of unemployment. As Table 7-1 indicates, al-

TABLE 7-1: Seasonally Adjusted Unemployment Among People Aged 16 and Over

		UNEMPLOYMENT RATE				NUMBER OF UNEMPLOYED (in thousands)	
Year	Total	Black Men	White Men	Black Women	White Women	Men	Women
1950	5.3	NA	4.7	NA	5.3	2239	1049
1960	5.5	NA	4.8	NA	5.3	2486	1366
1970	4.9	NA	4.0	NA	5.4	2238	1855
1980	7.1	14.3	6.1	14.0	6.5	4267	3370
1986	7.0	14.5	6.0	14.2	7.1	4530	3707

Source: Council of Economic Advisors (1987). *The economic report of the President,* pp. 282, 288. Washington, D.C.: Government Printing Office.

TABLE 7-2:   Americans Who Worked, 1954-1986

Year	Total	RATE OF LABOR FORCE PARTICIPATION White Men	Black Men	White Women	Black Women	NUMBER WORKING (in thousands) Total	Men	Women
1954	58.8	85.6	NA	33.3	NA	60,109	41,619	18,490
1960	59.4	83.4	NA	36.5	NA	65,778	43,904	21,874
1970	60.4	80.0	NA	42.6	NA	78,678	48,990	29,688
1980	63.8	78.2	70.3	51.2	53.1	99,303	57,186	42,117
1986	65.3	76.9	71.2	55.0	56.9	109,597	60,892	57,569

Source: Council of Economic Advisors (1987). *The economic report of the President,* pp. 282, 286. Washington, D.C.: Government Printing Office.

though rates of unemployment are relatively low, the actual number of people involved is substantial. Furthermore, the problem is more pronounced for some groups than for others. So, for example, young black men have a very high rate of unemployment.

Unemployment rates cannot give us the full picture of who is working in the United States. If we look solely at the rates, we might get the impression that the U.S. economy has not made any strides in providing more job opportunities, but in fact more jobs are available now than at any other time in history. And more people are working than ever before (see Table 7-2). The rate of unemployment stays high because of the influx of workers who would not have sought jobs in the past. Most notably, women have entered the job market in record numbers during the past two decades, especially married women and women with small children. The labor force participation of wives, for example, more than doubled between 1960 and 1982 (Kamerman et al., 1983).

Why Do People Work?

Just as most people get married, most of us work. And you might suspect, it is often difficult for people to pinpoint why they work. There is, of course, the obvious answer that we work to make the money we need to live. But it is clear that work is a much more integral part of the human experience than this rationale implies. Erik Erikson (1968) and the researchers using his theory (such as Marcia, 1980) include work as part of their definition of identity. Indeed, one entire childhood stage of development in Erikson's model, industry versus inferiority, is devoted to acquiring the skills one needs to function as an adult.

Similarly, Freud (1961/1930) viewed work as crucial to healthy adult functioning. Indeed, Freud's definition of a healthy adult was someone who could work and love. Psychologists have long believed that income is only one reason why people work. However, since it is the most obvious reason, it makes an appropriate starting point for a discussion of why people work.

Survival: Sociobiologists (Barash, 1979) argue that the desire to pro-tect one's genetic endowment is the major determinant of human behavior. Research confirms that substantial numbers of people work primarily to get the money they need to live (Friedman & Havighurst, 1954; Havighurst, McDonald, Perun, & Snow, 1976). Certainly, work can be viewed as increas-ing the likelihood of survival for both oneself and one's offspring. The in-come derived from employment is necessary to purchase food, clothing, shelter, and medical care. Of course, not all work in all cultures in done for pay. In some societies (and even among some individuals in the United States), some work is done to produce the goods used to survive. People may farm, weave, sew, or construct their own homes. They may also barter the goods they produce for other necessities.

The patterns of career development may also be seen as supporting a sociobiological perspective. It may not be coincidental that people tend to settle into a stable career pattern around the time they begin to have chil-dren. In fact, may prospective fathers are acutely aware of the importance of a well-paying job and being able to provide financial security for their families. Such issues were a concern to over 40 percent of the expectant fathers interviewed by Jerrold Shapiro (1987).

Personal Satisfaction: Income, though important, is far from the sole reason people want to be employed. This is evident from the number of people who work in lower-paying jobs by choice. For example, college pro-fessors could work in industry or government at considerably higher sal-aries than schools can pay. In 1978, the average starting salary for a new Ph.D. psychologist in academia was about $3,000 per year less than in the business world (Stapp et al., 1981). The amount of volunteer work people do underscores the fact that the rewards of work go far beyond a pay check.

One of the primary reasons people work is for personal satisfaction. This includes being able to be creative, being involved in decision making, feeling that your work makes a difference, and being intellectually chal-lenged on the job (Havighurst, 1982; Yankelovich & Clark, 1974). Since the 1960s, interest in a fulfilling job has increased among both white and blue-collar workers (Yankelovich & Clark, 1974). Indeed, among young blue-collar workers, having an interesting job is just as important as being paid well. And having a self-fulfilling job is equally important to college and noncollege youth, although the latter may find it more difficult to secure such employment.

People often see their jobs as a source of respect and status (Havig-hurst, 1982). Certainly, we all have heard derogatory comments about people who do not work, particularly those on welfare. Economic self-suffi-ciency is an indicator of full adult status in our society. The respect associ-ated with working and earning a salary is emphasized by men's reactions to their wives' working. It appears that men's mental health suffers when their wives work primarily because they feel inadequate as breadwinners (Staines, Pottick, & Fudge, 1986). Put another way, it appears that they lose some of the self-respect and status they would otherwise gain from their jobs.

A person's reasons for working include survival, personal satisfaction, and friendship.

Friendship: Finally, many people enjoy working because it gives them the opportunity to interact with other adults. This may be important to women who would otherwise be at home all day with young children (Rodin & Ickovics, 1990). Indeed, this may be one reason why mothers who work outside the home are frequently happier, and suffer fewer mental and physical health problems, than those who do not.

Friendships established at work may also be especially important to people who are in "low ceiling" jobs (Kanter, 1977). While their pay may be adequate, these people cannot expect to climb the ladder of success. Socializing with other employees may therefore become more important. This may be why there are more picnics, sports leagues, and organized recreation for factory employees than for professionals, although professionals too derive considerable pleasure from associating with colleagues (Havighurst, 1982).

CAREER DEVELOPMENT

Stages of Career Development

Super's Model: Donald Super (1957) has outlined five major stages of career development, which are summarized in Table 7–3. The late teens and early twenties are devoted to *career exploration;* by the end of this period, the individual has made a tentative commitment and has probably completed at least some training toward that goal. The training may take the

TABLE 7-3: Super's Stages of Career Development

1. *Growth Stage* (birth to 14 years):	A period of general physical and mental growth.
a. Prevocational substage (to 3):	No interest or concern with vocations.
b. Fantasy substage (4–10):	Fantasy is basis for vocational thinking.
c. Interest substage (11–12):	Vocational thought is based on individual's likes and dislikes.
d. Capacity substage (13–14):	Ability becomes the basis for vocational thought.
2. *Exploration Stage* (15 to 24 years):	General exploration of work.
a. Tentative substage (15–17):	Needs, interests, capacities, values, and opportunities become bases for tentative occupational decisions.
b. Transition substage (18–21):	Reality increasingly becomes a basis for vocational thought and action.
c. Trial substage (22–24):	First trial job is entered after the individual has made an initial vocational commitment.
3. *Establishment Stage* (25 to 44 years):	The individual seeks to enter a permanent occupation.
a. Trial (25–30):	A period of some occupational change due to unsatisfactory choices.
b. Stabilization (31–44):	A period of stable work in a given occupational field.
4. *Maintenance Stage* (45 to 65 years):	Continuation in one's chosen occupation.
5. *Decline Stage* (65 years to death):	
a. Deceleration (65–70):	Period of declining vocational activity.
b. Retirement (71 on)	A cessation of vocational activity.

Source: Huyck, M., & Hoyer, W. (1982). *Adult development and aging,* p. 344, Belmont, CA: Wadsworth.

form of college attendance, vocational school, an apprenticeship, or actual work experience.

The *establishment phase* of vocational development begins in the mid-twenties and is divided into two substages. Through the mid-/and late twenties, people continue in the trial period. They may change jobs in order to find the specific constellation of responsibilities, salary, and work hours that best fit their needs. In some cases, this may mean redirecting their careers; in others, job changes are simply the best way to move up the ladder.

Because getting started in a field often requires considerable investment of time and energy, this may be a very difficult period for the young adult. At the same time, the person may be trying to start a marriage and a family (Havighurst, 1982). Women may feel guilty about leaving a young baby at home while they go to work (DeMeis et al., 1986). Furthermore, women often end up working a "double shift" because they do a disproportionate amount of the housework and childcare in addition to working full-time (Hochschild, 1989; Kalleberg & Rosenfeld, 1990). This is especially true for women with small children. Middle-class men and women may also face intense conflicts during this period because their ability to retain their socioeconomic status depends almost exclusively on their ability to build a successful career (Havighurst, 1982).

Sometime in the early to mid-thirties, the person enters the *stabilization phase.* A career choice has been made, and work patterns become less changeable. Not only is there less likelihood of a career change (only about 10 percent of men over 40 change careers), but there is also less movement to new jobs within a career path.

Among the examples given at the beginning of this chapter, Mark's career development most closely approximates Super's model. But a quick inspection of the examples and of your own personal experience makes it clear that not everyone follows the same steps in establishing a career.

Levinson's Model: Daniel Levinson (1978, 1986, 1990) has postulated very different phases of career development. Keep in mind, however, that Levinson's model does not deal exclusively with career development. Rather, his "seasons" and transitions cover all major aspects of adult development. While Levinson (1986) admits that a wide variety of issues may consume an adult's energy and time, he claims that two—career and family—seem to be the overriding concerns of most Americans. Thus, much of his model does focus on career issues.

Levinson's theory describes development in early and middle adulthood. As Table 1–4 indicated, his developmental phases are tied to specific ages. This is somewhat unusual; most developmentalists resist tying stages or accomplishments to specific ages because they fear people will interpret age as a causal factor. Yet Levinson claims that across a wide variety of American adults he and others have studied, these age ranges emerge consistently. He views the timetable as being tied to evolutionary forces. They should occur universally, although it remains to be seen whether cross-cultural data will validate his model.

These phases represent different periods in the development of the individual's *life structure,* the underlying organization of an individual's life at any given point in time (Levinson, 1986). The pattern is determined mainly by the person's relationships in the outside world, and these relationships change over time. This is true whether the relationship is with an institution (such as school or church), an individual (such as a spouse, boss, friend, or child), a historical or mythological figure, or a force (such as nature or God). These relationships and the changes in them shape every aspect of our lives, from the content of our daily activities to levels of self-esteem.

In early adulthood, then, the overall goal is to build a life structure that is appropriate for adult living during these years. Note two things here. First, the life structure is constructed to be appropriate; it must meet both social demands and the needs of the individual. Second, it is a life structure appropriate for young adulthood. The relationships and interests that serve us well during this period will be inadequate for middle age and later life.

The first three phases of early adulthood, starting with the early adult transition at age 17–22 and ending with the age 30 transition at age 28–33, constitute the *novice phase*. In order to form a successful life structure, the individual must negotiate four tasks (Levinson, 1978). First, a *Dream* must be formed, a vague but not completely intangible vision of what the person would like his or her life to be like. It is not a fully articulated plan, but it is more than a feeling or intuition. The Dream will usually include both family and career goals or hopes, although these two elements are not necessarily in balance.

How powerful and important is a Dream? Sylvester Monroe (1987), a journalist, wrote of his Dream and the role it played in guiding him from a poor childhood in urban housing project to a successful career in journalism:

> When I left Chicago for St. George's School in the fall of 1966, through an outreach program ... I wanted to be a writer. I read ... Fitzgerald and dreamed of authoring my own novel.... The dream gave me hope. And my mother convinced me that without an education the dream was impossible.

> What strikes me most about retracing the lives of the boys from 39th Street is how easily our lives could be interchanged ... Steve also had a chance ... (he) was also in the ... program ... but he got into drugs, then living off women, and hasn't had a job since 1979 ... what is clear to me now, is that where dreams come together with opportunity, a chance for success follows. Where they do not, the inevitable occurs. I wondered what Steve's life ... might have been had ... [his] abilities to dream not been circumscribed by race. (Monroe, 1987, pp. 20–21).

The second task is forming mentor relationships. A mentor will help to guide and advise the person in the pursuit of the Dream. He or she will provide both practical advice and social-emotional support. It is the combination of a Dream and a mentor that allows a person to accomplish the third task, forming an occupation. This involves more than simply making a career choice; it includes finding a way to translate values, interest, and abilities into an occupation. Forming an occupational identity ("I am a carpenter" or "I am a psychologist) is also part of the process. This may happen quite quickly, but more commonly it is a complex task that requires several years to complete. There may be several false starts along the way. Or it may take some time to move up the ladder to a job that really approximates the Dream.

The final task of the novice phase is forming love relationships by marrying and having a family. The complexity of this task was examined in Chapter 6. This too involves assessing one's skills, attitudes, and beliefs to form relationships that meet both societal standards and individual needs.

By age 34, these tasks have been completed. Sometimes the established life structure is satisfactory to both society and the person. In other cases, it is adequate from society's perspective but not from the individual's (or vice versa). So, for example, a person may be in a respectable, well-paying job but be disappointed with the level of intellectual challenge the job pro-

A mentor can be important in career adjustment and advancement.

vides. Or someone may be in a career, such as art or music, that does not pay enough to support a family. Of course, it is also possible that neither society nor the individual will be satisfied with the life structure—for example, unemployment or a career cycle that involves less and less important jobs.

In any case, the adult will have established a life structure which he or she then lives with for several years (the culminating life structure for early adulthood phase). During this time, the person enjoys the fruits of his or her efforts (at least in a relatively positive outcome). At the same time, preparation is beginning for the next transition, which will lead into middle life.

Career Choice

From research, we know that factors other than salary play a role in determining career choice. People sometimes choose careers they find challenging or fulfilling. Family needs may play a role, especially for women. Just as a variety of factors influence the selection of a college major, many influences determine career selection. They include personality, parental influences, job characteristics, and gender.

Personality: Holland (1973) suggests that personality is a major determinant of career choice. He outlined six different types of personality: realistic, investigative, artistic, social, enterprising, and conventional (see Table 7–4). He also described work environments that would fit each of these personality types. The goal is to match the work environment to the personality type. If the match is a good one, the person will be satisfied in the job; mismatches increase the likelihood that the person will change jobs.

One of the best-known tests of vocational interests, the Strong-Campbell Interest Inventory, is based on Holland's model. The Strong-Campbell consists of over 300 items that evaluate attitudes about leisure, occupations, and academic subjects. On the basis of the answers to these questions, an individual can be categorized as realistic, investigative, and so on. As is the case with Holland's model, Strong-Campbell can be quite helpful in career planning. This is why it is frequently given in high schools. However, it has two drawbacks as a device for actually selecting a person to work in a given job. First, interests do not always coincide with abilities and skills. Second, a person can lie about his or her interests in order to appear better suited for a particular job (Schultz & Schultz, 986).

Thus, the Strong-Campbell is not usually a very effective way to test the compatibility of Holland's model and actual job selection. Furthermore, it is very difficult to test Holland's model among people who have been on the job for any length of time, because work tends to influence values and beliefs. The longer people have been at a particular job, the more they tend to like it (Havighurst, 1982). Certainly some of this difference is attributable to the increased likelihood of staying with a job you like. But part of it is probably due to changing attitudes to justify job tenure. Indeed, this is what social psychological theories, such as cognitive dissonance theory, would predict.

Furthermore, general societal norms may influence the evaluation of a job. During the mid-1970s, there was a noticeable decline in worker satisfaction. Some of this decline may be explained by the serious economic recession that occurred at this time (Havighurst, 1982), but some of it may have been due to the changing criteria for evaluating job worth (the challenge and fulfillment offered by the job rather than income level). Thus, there may be cohort differences in how people evaluate the satisfaction they derive from their work that are independent of the personality-environment match.

Parental Influences: Parents may affect career choices in a number of ways. Most parents frequently and willingly give advice on career issues. In the most dramatic cases, the young adult child adopts parental values and beliefs unquestioningly and forms a foreclosed identity. Such individuals are expected to follow (or at least attempt to follow) whatever career their parents deem most appropriate for them.

Of course, this is not the case with most people, but most parents do have an impact on their children's career choice. For example, they can influence *achievement motivation.* This concept refers to simultaneously excelling at one's work and doing something that is important or valuable (Hyde,

TABLE 7-4:   Holland's Personology of Job Choice

Personality-Environment Types	CHARACTERISTICS	
	Environment	Personality
Realistic	Stimulates people to perform tasks Fosters technical competencies and achievement Encourages a world view in simple, tangible, and traditional ways Rewards people for showing conventional values	Conforming, frank, persistent, practical, stable, uninsightful
Investigative	Stimulates people's curiosity Encourages scientific competencies and achievements Encourages a world view in complex, abstract, independent, and original ways Rewards people for displaying scientific values	Analytic, critical, curious, independent, intellectual, introspective, introverted, methodical, passive, pessimistic, precise, rational, reserved
Artistic	Stimulates artistic activities Fosters artistic competencies and achievements Encourages a world view in complex, independent, unconventional, and flexible ways Rewards people for displaying artistic values	Unassuming, unpopular, complicated, disorderly, emotional, imaginative, impractical, impulsive, independent, introspective, intuitive, nonconforming, original
Social	Stimulates social activities Fosters social competencies Encourages a world view in flexibly cooperative social ways Rewards people for showing social values	Cooperative, friendly, generous, helpful, idealistic, insightful, kind, persuasive, responsible, sociable, tactful, understanding
Enterprising	Stimulates enterprising activities Fosters enterprising competencies and achievement Encourages a world view in terms of power, status, and stereotypical ways	Acquisitive, ambitious, argumentative, dependent, energetic, flirtatious, impulsive, pleasure-seeking, self-confident, social

TABLE 7-4: (continued)

Personality-Environment Types	CHARACTERISTICS	
	Environment	Personality
Conventional	Rewards people for showing power, status, and money	
	Stimulates conventional activities	Conforming, conscientious, defensive, efficient, inhibited, obedient, orderly, persistent, practical, self-controlled, unimaginative
	Fosters conventional competencies and achievements	
	Encourages world view in simple, constricted ways	
	Rewards people for showing conventional values of money, dependability, and conformity	

Source: Hultsch, D., & Deutsch, F. *Adult development and aging*, p. 277. New York: McGraw-Hill. Copyright © 1981 McGraw-Hill, Reprinted by permission.

1985). People with high achievement motivation are more likely to seek high-status jobs that require considerable work and commitment (such as a profession career). Indeed, differences in achievement motivation have frequently been used to explain the variation in career success of men versus women and first-born versus later-born children (Hyde, 1985; Sutton-Smith & Rosenberg, 1970).

Many authors have argued that attitudes about achievement are formed early in life (Dweck & Elliott, 1983). It is not surprising, then, that parental behavior and style affect achievement motivation. Children whose parents provide warm, supportive, nurturant, and intellectually stimulating homes seem more interested in doing well in school (Belsky, Lerner, & Spanier, 1984). This seems to carry over into adulthood; high achieving women, for example, are more likely to come out of stable homes with fathers who took an active interest in their education and development.

Maternal employment also influences achievement motivation, especially in girls. Research has long shown that daughters of women who work outside the home are more likely to aspire to careers themselves and show higher levels of achievement motivation (see, for example, Hoffman, 1979). On the other hand, boys whose fathers are successful and achievement-oriented tend to show higher levels of achievement (for example, Radin, 1981). Perhaps no one exhibits this trait more clearly than the Kennedy sons. Their father was a self-made millionaire who eventually entered political life (as an Undersecretary of the Navy and Ambassador to the Court of St. James in England). His rise from poverty to status and wealth served as an example to his four sons, all of whom were remarkably successful. This implies that Joseph Kennedy, Sr., was a role model for his sons. In other words, children tend to identify with their parents' work-related characteristics and eventually are likely to exhibit them in their own careers.

Holland (1973) reported that parenting styles had some limited impact on the personality type the individual developed. Mothers who were very authoritarian—that is, who made rules and enforced them with little explanation to or input from the child—tended to raise children who were conventional types (see Table 7-4). Parents who were more democratic, who considered the child's perspective in making decisions, were more likely to have investigative sons though there was no systematic effect on the daughters. This finding is consistent with Diana Baumrind's (1971) findings indicating that parenting style is more likely to affect male achievement orientation than female.

Job Characteristics: Many people choose jobs or careers that are related to their reasons for working in the first place. Intuitively, it would seem that the status and income level associated with a job would be major determinants of job selection. Of course, for some people they are. Status would be likely to be important, for example, to people whose parents held highly respected jobs. But many people work at low-status jobs. And this is not because they are confused about the status of various jobs; by high school, most people tend to rate the status of jobs similarly. Thus, for most people, status will not be the major rationale for selecting a job.

Income seems to be a major issue only until some acceptable minimum level is achieved. So when money is tight or jobs are scarce, as in a depression or in the case of lower-class workers, the highest paying job will frequently be the most desirable one (Schultz & Schultz, 1986). In such situations, people are more concerned about survival than personal satisfaction.

Similar statements could be made about the importance of job security. The more options people have, the less likely they are to be concerned about job security. Having a "future" in a career field is not unimportant, but young adults who do not have families yet (or whose spouses work) are in a particularly good situation to base job and career decisions more on personal interests and needs than on income and security. Well-educated young adults are especially likely to do this, not only because they are less apt to be married with children, but also because more opportunities are available to them. Compared to previous cohorts and less educated workers, today's college-educated young adults are more likely to look for work that is challenging and interesting. They want to be involved in making decisions. They also want a job that allows them time to participate in leisure pursuits (Donovan, 1984; Jackson & Mindell, 1980). So, for example, they may not want to work nights or weekends on a regular basis. Less educated workers may well prefer such jobs because they tend to pay better than the regular day shift does.

Although most young adults seek challenging, interesting jobs or careers, they often do not find them immediately. Entry-level positions rarely involve the sort of challenge and responsibility they seek. Indeed, some authors have suggested that many young adults suffer a "reality shock" when they take their first job. They are surprised at how much time is spent on menial work (such as filling out forms or answering mundane questions for customers). This is probably one reason why job satisfaction tends to be lower among young workers than among middle-aged and older employees (Schultz & Schultz, 1986).

Gender: Back in the 1950s, when children played, little girls got to be the "nurses" while little boys were the "doctors"; boys were the "bosses," girls were their "secretaries." The working women we knew (and there weren't all that many) were elementary school teachers, babysitters, nurses, and secretaries. Most of us knew few men who held these jobs. The men were doctors, dentists, police officers, car mechanics. Our career aspirations reflected these experiences. Have times changed?

In some ways they have. Women are entering traditionally male fields in record numbers. For example, in 1970, 8 percent of all doctors were women; by 1986, this figure had nearly doubled. Even more dramatically, only 5 percent of all lawyers and judges in 1970 were women; by 1988, 19.5 percent were women, and fully 29 percent of the lawyers and judges under 35 were female (Council of Economic Advisors, 1987, U.S. Dept. of Commerce, 1990). Table 7–5 documents comparable changes in the gender distribution of a variety of occupations.

Table 7–5 also shows that women continue to dominant certain professions. From 1970 to 1986, the percentage of women nurses declined only

TABLE 7-5:   Percentage of Female Employees in Selected Occupations

			1986	
Occupation	1970	1980	All	Under 35 Years
All occupations	38	43	44	45
Managerial and professional	34	41	43	49
Mathematical and computer scientists	17	26	36	41
Natural scientists	14	20	23	28
Physicians	8	12	15	24
Registered nurses	97	96	94	NA
Lawyers and judges	5	14	18	29
Technical, sales and administrative support	59	64	65	66
Engineers and related technicians	9	17	18	22
Sales occupations	41	49	48	54
Secretaries and typists	97	98	98	98
Service occupations	60	59	61	58
Law enforcement	6	13	14	NA
Bartenders	21	44	49	NA
Waiters	91	88	85	NA
Farming, forestry, fishing	9	15	16	14

NA indicates "not available."

Source: Adapted from Council of Economic Advisors (1987). *The economic report of the President,* p. 219. Washington, D.C.: Government Printing Office.

3 points (from 97 percent to 94 percent). And the proportion of women secretaries remained steady (97 percent in 1970; 98 percent in 1986) (Council of Economic Advisors, 1987).

Thus, while women seem to be moving into "male" occupations, men are not moving into "female" occupations. The reasons for this are fairly straightforward. Female occupations tend to be lower both in pay and status than the traditional male careers. They also tend to involve less intellectually stimulating work and less decision-making responsibility. A doctor, for example, decides what the patient's treatment will be; a nurse administers the care according to the doctor's orders. A secretary types the reports the boss has written. In fact, the fastest typists do not even read the words in the report; instead they type letter by letter.

Women are not abandoning the traditional career choices. Over half of all women still work in those fields: teaching young children, clerical work, social work, and nursing (Rodin & Ickovics, 1990). And even when they do enter male fields, women frequently choose a more "feminine" subspecialization. So, for example, female psychologists are much more common in developmental than in physiological psychology (Stapp et al., 1981).

In today's job market, women are no longer relegated to certain types of jobs.

And women doctors are most likely to be pediatricians or obstetricians. In the natural sciences, there are more women biologists than physicists. The reasons for such gender differences in career choice are covered later in this chapter.

GETTING AHEAD

There are many ways to define success on the job. As you might expect, the values an individual holds about what makes a "good" job are similar to those used to evaluate the job. For unskilled or semiskilled workers, success might be represented primarily by rising salary and job security. Indeed, these are often the primary issues in union negotiations by factory workers, miners, and others. For more educated executive types, however, pay increases may not be enough, and job stability is often not an issue at all. Instead, they want promotions that will give them increased responsibility and challenges.

Of course, responsibility and salary often go hand in hand. For many workers, the only way to get a really good pay raise is to move into a different job. So people are generally interested in receiving promotions. Some jobs are "dead-end" or "low ceiling" by nature. People enter them knowing there is limited room for advancement. A secretary in a corporation, for example, may be eligible to move up a few notches in the secretarial ranks, but is not likely to move into an administrative or management position where there is greater responsibility and remuneration (Kanter, 1977).

Selecting the Right Job

Only certain jobs, then, afford the opportunity for considerable advancement. The person who wants to get ahead needs to select a job carefully. This includes not only the starting position, but also promotions within an organization. Rosabeth Moss Kanter (1977, p.131) provided an example of this from her corporate research: "The manager of a staff function, an organizationally savvy man, turned down a corporate directorship in personnel, despite high pay and elevated title, because it was a dead end." Jobs that do not have much room for promotion are called "low ceiling" positions. Selecting a low ceiling position was the single greatest reason people did not get ahead in Kanter's (1977) study. Keep in mind that the definition of a low ceiling job may vary from corporation to corporation. That is why the phrase" ... an organizationally savvy man ... " in the preceding example is such an important one.

The "ceiling" of a job is not the only factor involved in the likelihood of promotion. While a job may offer a path to success, there may also be considerably more competition in one placement than in another. Some individuals will be in high ceiling jobs but will fail to move up. While this is sometimes attributable to poor performance, it is more frequently caused by the availability of more qualified people than there are high-level slots (Kanter, 1977).

Academia provides an interesting example of this phenomenon. Virtually all people who plan to make college teaching a career want to hold tenure-track positions. Some colleges offering such positions will grant tenure to anyone who proves to be qualified. These colleges do not mind giving tenure to everyone in a department; there is little concern about what percent of the faculty is tenured. Other colleges have tenure quotas. Their administrations have decided that a certain number of faculty positions must be left open. They may hire five people in a particular year, all in tenure-track positions, and intend to grant tenure to only four of them. All five may be qualified, but there are only four openings. Thus, the five must compete for the positions in a way that faculty members at schools without tenure quotas do not. A new Ph.D. who is knowledgeable, then, will always ask whether there are tenure quotas and weigh this as part of the job decision.

Finally, there are high ceiling jobs from which people do not move because they followed the wrong path to get to the job (Kanter, 1977). The next step up the ladder requires education or experience they do not have. This often happens to people who work their way out of low ceiling jobs. In the corporation Kanter studied, secretaries and plant workers occasionally made their way into the sales division. For new college graduates, the sales division offered an excellent opportunity for moving into administration. But the former secretaries and plant workers did not have college degrees, and they were often too old to be considered for the climb up the corporate ladder. Movement out of the sales division was virtually impossible for them.

There are, then, three mistakes people can make in terms of job selection: (1) they can chose a low ceiling job; (2) they can opt for a job where the competition for promotion is too great; (3) they can select a job where they are not qualified for the next level up. All these mistakes are related to characteristics of the job itself. And at least some of them could be avoided if, like the man in the earlier example, one is " . . . organizationally savvy. . . . "

Mentors

But how do people obtain information about an organization? The most common way is through a mentor. A mentor teaches the young adult the job and social skills he or she will need to succeed. The mentor also provides the young worker with contacts and opportunities that would otherwise be unavailable. There is no one good synonym for the term mentor. Daniel Levinson (1978) offers possible alternatives ranging from guru to teacher and them dismisses them all as capturing only a portion of the role. Perhaps "guardian angel" is the best substitute.

How important is a mentor? To quote a manager who did not get ahead: "In any corporation, nine times out of ten, you need an angel to watch over you if you're going to get ahead" (Brown, 1979, p. 132). In fact, this man attributed his own failure largely to the loss of his mentor: "I had an angel, but when a new regime came in . . . my angel got his wings clipped

... " (Brown, 1979, p. 132). In his view his mentor's decline led to his own gradual discrediting and demotion.

It might seem to you that this man was rationalizing and placing blame for his own failure on someone else, but research suggests that his appraisal may well be correct. Daniel Levinson (1978) argues that establishing a mentor relationship during young adulthood is crucial to career success. When Rosabeth Kanter (1977) tried to distinguish sales people who were promoted from those who simply got raises, she found that "fitting in socially" was a critical variable. The salespeople who got promoted were perceived as team players who fit in with their peers and the organization. These are skills and perceptions that would be facilitated by a mentor. The more crucial factor in salary increases, exceptional job performance, is not necessarily influenced by a mentor. As long as knowing how to play organizational politics is critical to success, having a mentor will be a major determinant in an individual's career path.

And this is where the problem arises, for not everyone has equal access to mentoring relationships. Some people seem to be selected for the fast track as soon as they enter a job (Kanter, 1977). The reasons for this are unclear, although at least in some situations they seem to include preconceived ideas about who will succeed. So, for example, an Ivy Leaguer may be tapped while a state college grad is not. Or someone who comes from the right kind of background may fit the mold best. In any case, these people receive special attention and opportunities, including the increased possibility of establishing mentor relationships.

Gender and race may also play a role. For one thing, women, minority members, and ethnic or immigrant Americans may not fit people's ideas about fast trackers. In addition, mentors tend to be the same gender as their mentees (Levinson, 1978). Since people generally find similarity attractive, it would not be surprising if a similar tendency occurred among blacks, Hispanics, and other groups. Most corporate administrators are white males. This, then, decreases the number of potential mentors for women and minority members. Finally, there may be subtle or overt discrimination. While discrimination on the basis of sex or race is illegal, the number of complaints lodged by women and blacks indicates that real discrimination continues to exist. This can be a factor at any stage of career development, including hiring, establishing mentor relationships, and promotion.

Women may have special problems in establishing mentor relationships with men. Male supervisors often worry about how their relationship with female subordinates will be perceived (Kanter, 1977). They do not want to be seen as "dating" a woman employee or as trying to seduce her (or being seduced by her). Such fears are particularly likely to arise in situations where a man has not worked with women before. When one women proves to a man or a corporation that she can do the job and get the promotions without reference to gender, it becomes easier for women to move up in that corporation. Among the reasons for this is that the men become more comfortable serving as women's mentors.

Personal Characteristics

It would be a mistake to leave the impression that the reasons that people get ahead in a job are unrelated to their own characteristics. Career success is not completely determined by opportunities for promotion and mentoring. Indeed, even these opportunities do not operate independently of the individual's own attitudes and behaviors.

One factor that seems to be important is commitment to a job and achievement in it. Douglas Bray and Ann Howard (1980) reported that high work standards, enjoying leadership roles, and wanting to move ahead within the company (all as assessed at the time of hiring) predicted managerial level twenty years later. And entry-level managers will often report that they do extra work because they see it as a way of getting ahead. They also note, however, that they often enjoy the work, demanding though it may be (Kanter, 1977). So degree of interest and commitment is probably fueled by an occupational "dream." Without such a dream, career success seems unlikely (Levinson, 1978).

However, if commitment to a particular job makes the person too narrow, it may actually hamper the likelihood of moving up the ladder (Bray & Howard, 1980; Kanter, 1977). Good executives need to know more than technical skills; they also need to be interested in financial issues, interpersonal relations among employees, employee motivation, and so on. And a significant promotion may require a willingness to learn new technical skills. Thus, it is not surprising that having a wide range of interests is also a good predictor of career success. Furthermore, the abilities that make such flexibility possible, such as cognitive functioning and creativity, are good predictors of career achievement (Bray & Howard, 1980).

GENDER DIFFERENCES IN WORK

It should be clear by now that the experience of career development and work is not the same for women as for men. Three sets of statistics capture these differences demographically. First, women are less likely than men to work outside the home and are less likely to work full-time. Second, women make less money than men do, even within the same occupations. Third, some careers are viewed as appropriate for women and others are seen as more fit for men. Included here are the careers of homemaker and full-time parent.

The Demographics

Women in the Labor Force: We can begin by looking at the employment statistics for adults over age 20 who are not in the military. In 1988, there were 54.7 million women over age 16 working in the United States, and approximately 66.9 million men (U.S. Dept. of Commerce, 1987). This represents about 76 percent of the adult males but only 57 percent of the adult females in the United States.

Women's labor force participation has increased dramatically during this century. As Table 7-6 indicates, only 17.4 percent of women aged 20–64 were employed in 1890; by 1986, this figure had risen to 66.4 percent. Employment rates are even higher among young women; about 72 percent of women in their twenties are working. These shifts have many implications and raise new issues for developmentalists to consider: dual-career families, delay in marriage and parenthood, and households headed by single women. They also imply that there may be significant cohort effects in women's career development. Many of the existing theories and data concerning women's work lives may simply not apply to today's young women.

When they do work, women are more likely than men to work part-time. About two-thirds of the part-time employees in the United States are women (U.S. Dept. of Commerce, 1990). Women at all levels of employment are susceptible to this difference. For example, only 4.6 percent of the males but 12.3 percent of the females receiving Ph.Ds in psychology in 1978 worked part-time during their first postgraduate year (Stapp et al., 1981). This has important implications for women's financial well-being. Part-timers obviously make less money overall. They are also likely to be paid less per unit of work. A part-time professor earns less per course taught than a full-timer does. Furthermore, part-time workers are less likely to be eligible for such benefits as health insurance and retirement funds.

Women's preference for part-time work may be indicative of their attempts to balance career and family. Indeed, in countries where part-time work is more of an option (Sweden and Norway), women (but not men) with young children are likely to reduce their work hours (Kalleberg & Rosenfeld, 1990). Similarly, research with first-time mothers suggests that many of them would prefer to work part-time if the option were available (Behrman, 1982).

Wages: As a group, women make less money than men do. The median annual income of full-time white male workers in 1988 was $28,262. The comparable figure for white women was $18,823 (Council of Economic Advisors, 1990). Put another way, women received approximately $0.69 for

TABLE 7-6:   Percentage of Women Who Were Employed, 1890–1986

	WOMEN AGED 20–64			ALL WOMEN	
Year	All	White	Black and Other	20–24	25–34
1890	17.4	14.9	38.4	30.2	16.8
1920	22.9	20.7	43.1	37.5	23.7
1940	29.4	27.9	42.9	45.6	33.3
1960	42.3	40.9	54.0	46.1	36.0
1980	60.8	60.5	62.8	68.9	65.5
1986	66.4	66.3	66.4	72.4	71.6

Source: Adapted from Council of Economic Advisors, (1987). *Economic report of the President,* p. 211. Washington, D.C.: Government Printing Office.

every $1.00 men got (Council of Economic Advisors, 1987). Even within specific professions, including traditionally "female" careers, men typically receive higher salaries (see Table 7-7).

People will sometimes argue that women earn less than men because they work fewer hours. As has already been noted, women are part-time employees more frequently than men are. But even restricting statistics to full-time employees leaves a substantial male-female wage gap. Indeed, the differences just cited are based on full-time employees. Full-time male workers do work about 6 percent more hours than full-time female workers (Council of Economic Advisors, 1987), but females earned 30 percent less. The hours differential does not explain the entire wage gap.

Another oft-cited factor, that women and men tend to be in different careers, also can only partially explain the wage differential. First, the delineation of male versus female careers is becoming hazier. Second, even within careers, women make less than men do. This, of course, implies that differences in educational levels cannot fully explain the wage gap. Years of experience is also of limited value as an explanatory variable. Stapp (Stapp et al., 1981) found, for example, that new Ph.D. psychologists taking their first academic position averaged a salary of $18,500 if they were male but only $17,533 if they were female. Women taking jobs in school settings earned $17,000; men accepting such appointments earned $19,975.

This is not meant to suggest that factors such as education, experience, and number of hours worked play no role in explaining the wage gap. Men as a group have more education, more work experience, and work more hours than women do. The point is that while these differences cannot be ignored, they also do not account for the whole wage gap. The largest single factor in explaining the wage gap is work interruptions (Hewlett, 1984). Women are more likely to interrupt their careers, at least temporar-

TABLE 7-7: Median Salaries of Men and Women in Various Professions (1984, Full-Time, Year-Round Employees Only)

Occupation	Male	Female
Accountants and auditors	30,327	19,273
Engineers	35,310	27,857
Health technologists and technicians other than LPNs	22,194	17,744
Computer equipment operators	25,012	15,742
Secretaries, typists, and stenographers	19,384	14,711
Cleaning and building services, except household	14,233	10,215
Motor vehicle operators	20,111	11,911
Executive, administrative, and managerial occupations:		
Manufacturing	40,829	20,943
State and local government	24,934	17,191
Retail trade	23,625	14,621

Source: U.S. Dept. of Commerce, Bureau of the Census, (1986). *Money income of households, families and persons in the United States: 1984.* Washington, D.C.: Government Printing Office.

ily, to bear and raise children. With only a minority of companies offering maternity leave, this often means that women come back to lower-paying jobs or miss out on promotions. This is true even though the interruptions often amount to no more than a year or two out of a 40-year career (Hewlett, 1984).

Career Choice: Salary is one way of measuring job status. We frequently think of higher-paying jobs as having more status than lower-paying ones. So, for example, a physician is held in higher esteem than a sanitation worker. This is not only because the doctor makes more money; a college professor has higher career status than a factory worker, but at least in certain industries, the factory worker may well make more money. Education is certainly a factor here. So is responsibility. One reason we value doctors so highly is because they can save lives. And college professors train the doctors and lawyers whose service we value.

Again, however, such obvious factors do not tell the whole story. Nurses, for example, are also involved in saving lives, but nursing is a relatively low-status career. And full-time mothers are responsible not only for their children's health and safety, but also for their early education and socialization. Yet few careers hold lower status than being "just a housewife." Kindergarten and elementary school teachers are paid less and held in less esteem than college professors. Secretaries, who must have a variety of specialized skills, are viewed as lower in status than carpenters or plumbers. Indeed, the latter are called "skilled labor," while the former are "clerical workers."

It thus becomes possible to argue that women's careers are lower in status and pay because so many women are in them. The reasoning in this statement may sound circular—yet the highest-status "female jobs" (such as nursing and social work) are considerably lower than status in the highest-status "male jobs" (such as physician or business executive). Even within a profession, the areas where women are heavily represented (such as pediatrics) are seen as lower in status than those where men more clearly dominate (such as surgery). Education and responsibility, once again, fail to explain the difference.

Clearly, then, women and men show different rates of labor force participation, earning power, and involvement in particular careers. Because the work that women tend to do is lower in both pay and status, women are frequently viewed as having lower career achievement. Let us now turn to some explanations for this idea.

Achievement Levels

Explanations of the differences in males versus female career attainment tend to fall into two categories. The more common type of explanation focuses on why women choose lower-status careers. Here we can include issues such as commitment to family, personality characteristics, and vocational issues. Some researchers view these explanations as a form of "blaming the victim"; they suggest that women have lower career achievement because of societal forces such as societal definitions of achievement and status as well as job discrimination.

The Importance of Family: It is often argued that women enter the job market with different expectations from those of men. Women's career goals are seen as different. Women, it is argued, often look for ways to combine career and family. In particular, women with young children or those planning to have children seem to value both flexibility in work hours and shorter work hours. They choose careers such as teaching which allow them to be home with their children during the summer and after school. If they plan to take time off to raise their children, which many women still do, they may look for careers that can be interrupted without high cost. So, for example, a year or two out of the secretarial field has fewer repercussions than a year or two out of engineering or medicine. Finally, some women want to be able to accommodate any moves their husband's career progress might demand. This leads them to choose careers that have easily transferable skills. Nurses and secretaries are in demand in virtually any part of the country; transferring a legal or medical practice is not so easy.

Research suggests that women do indeed want to stay home with their children. For example, Debra Behrman (1982) interviewed 70 couples about their plans for work after their first baby was born. While 95 percent of the husbands planned to keep working full-time, only 23 of the 70 wives did. Twenty-one of the women planned to work part-time and 26 planned not to work outside the home at all for at least 18 months. Furthermore, only 8 of the 23 wives planning full-time employment actually wanted to follow this path. Of the remaining 15 women, half would have preferred part-time work and half would have preferred to be at home full-time. In the majority of these cases, the women were going back to full-time employment primarily out of financial necessity.

Behrman's study examined *plans* for continuing to work. As you might expect, plans and behavior do not always coincide. Ellen Hock and her colleagues found that nearly a quarter of the women who planned to stay home with their babies returned to work within a year. On the other hand, about 13 percent of the women in this study who had planned to work ended up at home full-time within a year (Hock, Morgan, & Hock, 1985). Apparently, some women find full-time parenting less rewarding than they expected and return to work. Others feel more and more uncomfortable about leaving their babies in someone else's care and withdraw from the labor force (Hock et al., 1985). It is important to note here that most of the women in Hock's study followed through with their plans.

Somewhat surprisingly, it is not clear that women who wish to stay home with their babies choose different types of careers than those who plan to continue working. In Behrman's study, for example, about 46 percent of the women who planned to keep working full-time were in "traditional" female careers. The comparable figure for those who were planning to stay home was 42 percent. Furthermore, there were no differences in job flexibility for the full-time worker versus the full-time mother. Only those who opted for part-time work had greater flexibility (which is probably why they could fulfill their desire to work part-time). Women who planned to continue full-time employment were, however, in more prestigious careers than the other women.

Women who are more committed to their careers may be more inclined to work continuously, whereas those who believe their infants need the care only they can provide may be more likely to interrupt their careers and stay home (Behrman, 1982; Hock et al., 1985). Attitudes about family, especially childrearing, may well influence whether or not a woman interrupts her career. In this sense, family commitments may influence career achievement, since women who interrupt their careers will accrue less experience and may therefore ultimately earn lower salaries and fewer promotions.

Freudian Theory: Sigmund Freud (1961/1930) viewed work as a service to society and to civilization. Commitment to work was guided by the "moral arm" of the personality, the superego. People with strong, healthy superegos would work because it was the socially appropriate thing to do. Healthy superego development depends on the resolution of the Oedipal conflict, and Freud viewed women as incapable of a clear-cut resolution of this conflict. Boys, he suggested, have a real motivation, castration anxiety, for ending their sexual attachment to their mothers. This enables them to identify with their fathers and form a superego. Girls, on the other hand, have no comparable impetus for terminating their sexual attraction to their fathers. They never completely identify with their mothers; instead, they continue to resent the mother's interference with their relationship with the father. They also continue to long for the penis that they believe their mother denied them. The only way for them to get a penis is by having a boy baby (subconsciously, they would prefer that their father sire the baby).

All this leads a girl to develop a less adequate superego and, therefore, a lower interest in serving society through work. In fact, Freud thought that narcissism was a common quality in women, who were more interested in serving their own needs than those of society. Not only are women less likely to be committed to careers, but they also actively interfere with men's work life:

> Furthermore, women soon come into opposition to civilization and display their retarding and restraining influence—those very women who, in the beginning, laid the foundations of civilization by the claims of their love. Women represent the interest of the family and of sexual life. The work of civilization has become increasingly the business of men, it confronts them with ever more difficult tasks ... of which women are little capable.... (Freud, 1961/1930, p. 50)

Thus, Freud saw women's lower career attainment as an outcome of their developmental process. Indeed, lower career attainment was virtually inevitable if a woman accepted her femininity. Freud's ideas may well seem outmoded to us now, but he is not alone in arguing that lower career attainment is a natural outcome of the female role.

Sociobiology: Sociobiologists tend to see the woman-as-parent, man-as-provider division of labor as a natural outcome of the *parental imperative* (Gutmann, 1975). This theory was described earlier (Chapter 6). The division of labor requires that woman use (and, perhaps, refine) skills that are incompatible with career success. More specifically, women become nurturant and emotionally supportive rather than aggressive and competitive. Men show the reverse pattern, allowing them to become increasingly career-orientted and more successful. As we noted in Chapter 6, there is some empirical support for these patterns of "feminine" versus "masculine" behavior following the birth of a baby, although the findings are not unanimous.

In addition to fostering characteristics that may be incompatible with career achievement, the parental imperative may also compel women to withdraw from the labor force, at least temporarily. Even relatively short work interruptions of a few months may inhibit career achievement. For example, the woman may have to look for a new job and may well have to accept a position lower than the one she left. Furthermore, lengthy absences might require considerable reeducation, at least in certain fields. Imagine, for example, the changes in medicine or law during a five-year period. Indeed, some people have suggested that this is one reason women frequently chose fields that do not change rapidly or dramatically, such as clerical work or elementary school teaching (Council of Economic Advisors, 1987). While intuitively this seems like a sensible explanation for women's lower career achievement, some researchers have reported that the "gender gap" in salary is just as large for women who never interrupted their careers as for women who did (Hewlett, 1984).

Socialization: Socialization theories also suggest that women do not develop the characteristics or skills needed for high levels of career success. However, this is not seen as the result of a biological function such as the parental imperative. Rather, the socialization process shapes women's work attitudes and behaviors.

We have already seen several ways in which this might work. First, achievement motivation in girls may be hampered by subtle cues from teachers (Dweck & Elliott, 1983). They may develop less confidence in their abilities. This can carry over into career decisions. For example, Ware and Steckler (1983) studied freshmen in a major university who planned to major in science. Both men and women had comparable credentials, including similar backgrounds in high school science. At the end of freshman year, however, 69 percent of the men but only 50 percent of the women actually declared a science major. This difference seemed to be attributable to the women's greater sensitivity to mediocre (by their definition) performance in introductory science courses. While women were discouraged by a C grade, men were not. The men were convinced they could work harder and would be successful; the women's confidence was undermined. This is consistent with teacher reactions to girls' versus boys' work (Dweck & Elliott, 1983). Elementary school teachers tend to praise boys' ideas and criticize their effort level; they criticize girls' ideas and praise their neatness, punctuality, and so on. In addition, there is some evidence to suggest that even at the college level instructors are more likely to discourage women from pursuing "prestigious" degrees such as premed or engineering.

The availability of role models is a second aspect of socialization. Role models not only provide inspiration, but also exemplify the skills and behaviors that can be used to succeed. It is not surprising, then, that girls whose mothers work outside the home show higher levels of achievement motivation than those whose mothers are full-time homemakers (Hoffman, 1979). While parents are always powerful role models, the influence of the mother in this case may be increased by the relative lack of societal role models for women's career success. Girl children may never (or rarely) meet female executives, doctors, dentists, and so on. Television's portrayal of women still frequently relegates them to less successful career roles. Even when a female television character is career-oriented, she is often in a minority at work, in need of "rescuing" by a male colleague, or simply never shown actually engaging in her work. Such a dearth of role models might prevent a girl from constructing a sex role concept that includes female career success (see, for example, Kohlberg's 1966 theory of how sex roles are constructed in childhood).

Discrimination: All the preceding explanations focused on factors in female development, roles, and behavior that might lead women to have lower career achievement than men do. But look back to the statistics on salary. In occupation after occupation, men make more money than women do. This is true in jobs that have predominantly female employees (nursing or secretarial work), predominately male employees (engineering), require little formal education (meter readers or cleaning) or considerable education (dentists and physicians). It is true when we control for the age of the employee, and it is true when we control for education level. And, of course, all the statistics reported here apply only to full-time, year-round workers.

It is difficult to believe that independently of age, education, and occupational choice, women work so much less effectively than men that they *deserve* to be paid less. There should be some job, it seems, that women do better. For example, it is generally assumed that jobs requiring physical strength are better done by men while those that require finger dexterity are better done by women (Bielby & Baron, 1986). Indeed, employers seem to hire men and women on this basis despite court decisions in the early 1970s that outlawed such practices as discriminatory. It is not surprising that there are more women than men in occupations such as typist or telephone operator and more men than women who are carpenters, laborers, and freight handlers. Yet in all these occupations, men are paid more.

This seems to suggest at least two things. First, men and women are still seen as appropriate for different jobs. This is true within occupations and organization, in that men and women are rarely equally likely to be assigned that same job title within a corporation (Bielby & Baron, 1986). The job titles more commonly assigned to men carry higher salaries. Yet, in research by William Bielby and James Baron (1986), differences in job title assignment did not appear to be attributable to skills, training, or turn-over costs to the business. Their explanation for the differences was dis-crimination. Employers, they argue, have expectations and stereotypes that set up self-fulfilling prophecies. They think, for example, that women are less achievement-oriented, less loyal to their work, and less willing to put in long hours. So they assign women to dead-end, low-challenge jobs. Not surprisingly, such jobs do not hold the women's interest for long (if at all).

Another study, by economists Marianne Ferber and Carole Green and sociologist Joe Spaeth (1986) also indicated that subtle discriminatory fac-tors seemed to contribute to the wage gap. Using data collected in 1982 from over 400 men and women, they found that the salary reward structure for men and women was different. Men, for example, were much more likely than women to receive higher salaries if they were more educated. Women were more likely to receive higher salaries for supervising other workers (which is more common among men than women). Women were also likely to receive more rewards for having a male supervisor. (This may represent a ceiling effect, since 94 percent of the men had male supervi-sors.)

Using these data, Ferber and her colleagues were able to construct a formula that predicted men's salary levels. They found that they needed a different formula to predict women's salary levels. They then used the wom-en's formula to try to predict what men would make if they were rewarded as women are. Although men in the study actually had an average income of $24,158, Ferber and her colleagues found that the average male salary would have been $18,634 had it been generated by the same system that determines female salaries. On the other hand, the average female salary would rise from $12,799 to $18,247 if it were based on the reward system used to generate male salaries. In other words, the gender gap in wages would virtually disappear (men's salary would average only about $400 more per year instead of about $11,000 more) if the reward systems were reversed. Notice, though, that the women's salary does not equal the men's even when the same reward structure is applied, indicating that discrimina-tion alone cannot explain the wage gap.

These data, then, suggest that employers may discriminate against women in initial hiring, job assignment, and salary increases. While formal discrimination is now illegal, more subtle discrimination clearly continues. Indeed, finger dexterity versus physical strength, for example, is now a slightly greater discriminating factor in male and female job assignment than it was prior to court decisions outlawing it (Bielby & Baron, 1986). So it does appear that women's lower career attainment is far from exclusively due to "problems" in women's attitudes or abilities.

RACIAL DIFFERENCES

There are also substantial differences in the incomes of African-Americans and whites (Council of Economic Advisors, 1990). Median annual incomes for white workers were given earlier. For African-American men, the median annual income for full-time, year-round employees in 1988 was $20,716. This is roughly 73 percent of the comparable white male figure. African-American women's median annual income was $16,867, or roughly 60 percent of the white male figure and 90 percent of the white female figure. Furthermore, the poverty rate is considerably higher among African-American than white *workers*. The rate of poverty among white workers is just under 5 percent; among African-American workers, it is just over 13 percent (Klein & Rones, 1989). Even these figures may be too rosy. A higher percentage of African-Americans than European-Americans are either unemployed or have dropped out of the labor market completely. Hence, the African-American economic picture may be even worse than it seems (Jaynes, 1990). This is exemplified by the fact that today the majority of African-American children will spend at least half of their childhood in poverty (Ellwood & Crane, 1990).

As with the male-female wage gap, numerous explanations have been offered for the racial wage gap. One is educational differences. The actual difference between median number of years of education for African-Americans and whites is quite small now. As of 1980, young black adults attained a median of 12.6 years, while white young adults attainment was 13.0 years. This is a dramatic improvement over the racial educational gap of two or three years that existed in 1940 (Jaynes, 1990). Even a difference this small, however, can be significant. For example, African-Americans are more likely to drop out of high school and less likely to complete college than are European-Americans (Blau & Ferber, 1986). In 1988, among men aged 25–34, 91 percent of the whites and 83 percent of the African-Americans had completed high school. In addition, 28 percent of the whites but only 15 percent of the African-Americans had finished college (O'Neill, 1990).

Nonetheless, even when educational level is equated, African-Americans often earn less than European-Americans. Table 7–8 shows family poverty rates by race and sex at various educational levels (Klein & Rones, 1989). As you can see, even among college graduates, African-American families are at least twice as likely as white families to be living in poverty. This is especially true among women because African-American

TABLE 7-8: Familial Poverty Rates for Varying Levels of Education by Race and Sex

	MEN		WOMEN	
	White	Black	White	Black
Total	4.7	10.5	4.8	16.0
< 4 yr high school	11.7	17.4	11.8	28.7
4 yr high school	4.4	9.6	5.0	17.8
1–3 yr college	3.0	7.4	3.4	8.6
≥ 4 yr college	1.6	3.5	1.3	3.2

Source: Klein, B., & Rones, P. (1989). A profile of the working poor. *Monthly Labor Review,* 3–13.

women are much more likely than white women to be the sole support of their families. In 1988, 47.8 percent of the African-American women between ages 15 and 44 had ever been married compared to 67 percent of the white women. Over 60 percent of African-American births in 1988 were to unmarried women; the comparable figure for whites was just under 16 percent. Thus, many of the African-American women do not have a man's salary to lift them out of poverty. This is where the race and gender wage gap intersect to create a particularly insidious problem. Why African-Americans opt not to marry is unclear, although the relatively weak financial status of black men may be at least a small part of the reason (Ellwood & Crane, 1990).

In the early part of the twentieth century, both amount and quality of education probably contributed to the substantial black-white wage gap. These have not been such important factors since about the 1960s (O'Neill, 1990). Indeed, up until the 1980s, African-Americans were making considerable progress in closing the wage gap. African-American women continued to make progress relative to white women (Jaynes, 1990). Among African-American men, however, the gap reopened during the 1980s. This was especially true among young male high school and college graduates. African-American men in this group were more likely than white men to be in blue-collar manufacturing jobs and so were apparently hit harder (and have not recovered from) the recession of the early 1980s. Furthermore, additional education and skills apparently do not open doors as quickly for African-American men as for whites. This is evident in a lower rate of return per year of education and experience for African-American men (O'Neill, 1990).

Racial discrimination in wages has declined since early this century. Indeed, in 1940, 55 percent of all white Americans surveyed said that white people should be given jobs before blacks, just on the basis of race. By the 1970s, virtually no one would agree with this position (Jaynes, 1990). Nevertheless, it is clear that substantial racial wage differences still remain and that discrimination plays a role in creating the gap.

DUAL-EARNER FAMILIES

At least two things should be clear by now. First, men and women have traditionally assumed different roles in the society in general and in the family in particular. Women have been responsible for childcare, housework, and decisions related to the household and children. Men have been the "good providers" (Bernard, 1981). They provided financial support for the family and made decisions regarding major expenditures (including housing) and life style. For the most part, they were only tangentially involved in childrearing and housework. Simply put, men were career-oriented and women were family-oriented. In fact, several major theories of adult development treated such differences as a given. It was these differences that the theories sought to explain in much the same way that child developmentalists seek to explain language development or temperament.

Second, women have entered the labor force in record numbers. This increase is especially dramatic among married women. In 1960, for example, only 27 percent all wives worked. By 1982, this figure had risen to 56 percent. Even married women with young children were entering the labor force. In 1975, 30.4 percent of married women with children under 2 were working. In 1981, 41.8 percent of married mothers of children under 2 were employed outside the home (Kamerman et al., 1983). By the mid-1980s, half of all married mothers of infants under one year old were working (Council of Economic Advisors).

These two trends seem to be opposed. It would appear to be unlikely that women could simultaneously work outside the home and continue their level of exclusivity in childcare and housework and still be attentive, available wives. Dual-earner families should, then, face different problems and adjustments from traditional, single-earner families. As the number of dual-earner families has increased, researchers have become interested in describing the interaction patterns and stresses in these families.

Before we examine their findings, however, it is important to note that this empirical interest is fairly new. We have little longitudinal data available on how these families ultimately fare. Furthermore, there may well be cohort differences in the stresses reported. Certainly, social acceptance, and therefore social support for dual-earner families has increased in recent years. And it appears that such support will become even more tangible in the future as the government moves to improve maternity leave and childcare (Trost, 1986).

Furthermore, much of the research is on the dual-career family, a particular subgroup of the dual-earner family. In the dual-career family, both spouses are pursuing outside work that requires considerable training and commitment. They are working at careers rather than jobs. In the past, most dual-earner families had at least one spouse (almost invariably the wife) whose work was limited to a 40-hour (or less) work week, leaving evenings and weekends free for childcare and housework. In such families, the spouse with the secondary career assumed most of the responsibility for such tasks. Since this was usually the wife, traditional sex roles were, for the most part, maintained. In dual-career families, however, both members have jobs that require longer hours, travel, and so on. The wife cannot easily continue to do all the housework and childcare. Probably only about 5 percent of all American families are dual-career (Berardo, Sheehan, & Leslie, 1987). They face special challenges. For example, if husband and wife are to both have truly equal careers, neither one will be able to assume the "traditional wife's" role of carrying the primary responsibility for housework and childcare (Berardo et al., 1987). These unique problems, along with the assumption that dual-career families are a growing breed, have stimulated considerable research and social policy interest.

The Couple

In the 1950s and 1960s, there was typically a sharp distinction between the roles of husband and wife. The wife was responsible for housework and childcare; the husband supported the family financially. Her work in providing a supportive home atmosphere enabled him to work long hours in order to make the most money. Similarly, her lack of involvement in the labor force enabled him to take new positions that required relocation or more time away from the family. In some ways, all members of the family were served by this arrangement (as long as the relationship worked well). Anything that advanced the husband's career also improved the family's standard of living. And the work provided by the wife in the home in many ways made that career advancement possible. Indeed, many corporations set up career ladders in a way that assumed that there was a "wife" who would perform social, domestic, and familial functions (Hunt & Hunt, 1982).

It is obvious to everyone that the women in these families were not combining career and family. What is sometimes forgotten is that the men did not "have it all" either. They did not get to spend "quality time" with their children. In fact, they were often relatively absent from their children's daily lives. Even in the dual-earner families of the period, the husbands were more oriented and committed to time at work than time in the family. And the wife supported this orientation (Hunt & Hunt, 1982).

In most dual-earner families today, this continues to be the case. The wife is responsible for most childcare and household tasks, even if she holds a "professional" job. Of course, she is often spending fewer hours performing these tasks than does the full-time housewife. The full-time homemaker married to a blue-collar worker spends about 44 hours a week on housework, while the full-time employed wife with a nonmanagerial husband spends about 33 hours. In all cases, however, the wife is clearly responsible for most of the housework. This is true even in dual-career families (Berardo et al., 1987). Indeed, some studies indicate no significant difference between the percentage of housework done by employed versus nonemployed wives (Bergmann, 1986; Walker & Wallston, 1985).

Even when studies do report greater husband involvement in families where the wife is employed, the differences do not tend to be dramatic. In a survey study of over 1500 couples, dual-career and dual-earner wives were responsible for about 70 percent of the housework, compared to the 80 percent done by full-time homemakers (Berardo et al., 1987). Rosalind Barnett and Grace Baruch (1987a) found that husbands with nonemployed wives were alone with their children 20 percent of the time; the comparable figure for husbands of employed women was 30 percent. Furthermore, only 12 of the 160 fathers in their study were "responsible" for (were expected to plan for or schedule) two or more of the eleven childcare tasks investigated. In terms of traditionally feminine household chores (laundry, meal preparation, housecleaning, meal cleanup, and grocery shopping), the men whose wives worked did approximately 19 percent of this work, while those whose wives were at home full-time did about 16 percent of it. And 150 of the 160 men in the survey were not responsible for any of these tasks.

It should be noted that husbands' failure to participate more is not necessarily due to their unwillingness to help or to some form of sexism on their part. Women's attitudes about men's roles are better predictors of husbands' involvement than men's own attitudes are. In other words, many women seem uncomfortable with a high level of husband involvement in childcare and housework. This seems to block greater participation by the husband (Barnett & Baruch, 1987a).

The husband's work continues to have a higher priority than the wife's in most dual-earner families. This is indicated by the wife's greater willingness to give up her job if her husband needs to relocate (D. Skinner, 1983; Walker & Wallston, 1985). This does not mean that the couple does not consider the wife's career in making such a move. Indeed, couples in which the wife has a strong career are less willing to relocate (Walker & Wallston, 1985). However, if a move is made, it is more likely to be for the husband's career than for the wife's (D. Skinner, 1983).

While the maintenance of more or less traditional marital roles is true in all types of dual-earner families, it may be less pronounced in the dual-career families. In these families, there tends to be a greater commitment to equality of the spouses (Hertz, 1986; D. Skinner, 1983). Since both spouses have demanding, potentially high-paying jobs, there is no longer a clear distinction between breadwinner and dependent. The rationale for one person doing all (or most) of the homemaking so that the other's career can advance is gone. However, the burden of housework and childcare still falls to the wife (Berardo et al., 1987).

It is still clearly the case that single women have higher levels of career achievement than married women (Houseknecht et al., 1987). This may indicate that the responsibilities of being a wife, especially when combined with motherhood create a "drag" on a woman's career. Indeed, one recent study concluded by suggesting that couples either hire household help or avoid having children in order to enable the wife in dual-career families to truly have equal emphasis on her work (Berardo et al., 1987). Given the limited value and acceptance of these options, dual-career couples will need to find new ways of dividing household tasks, worktime, and childcare if they are to have both careers and families (Berardo et al., 1987; Hertz, 1986; Hunt & Hunt, 1982; D. Skinner, 1983).

This is where the problems can begin. Obviously, couples who are truly trying to combine careers and family have few role models. Even friends who are experiencing the same difficulties can be of only limited help, partially because such couples have little time to spend socializing with others (D. Skinner, 1983). Social supports for such couples are limited. Although some companies are offering childcare, flexible schedules, and parental leave, most are not (Hertz, 1986; Hunt & Hunt, 1982; Kamerman et al., 1983). Indeed, some researchers argue that there is still active social resistance to the idea of mothers of very young children working (Hertz, 1986).

Where does this leave the dual-career couple? Most have to work out their own solutions (D. Skinner, 1983; Hochschild, 1989). Some opt not to have children; most opt to have only one or two children (Berardo et al., 1987; Hunt & Hunt, 1982). It is clear that having children creates a major problem for dual-career couples in that marital satisfaction is lower in these spouses than in childless dual-earner families (Walker & Wallston, 1985).

When they do have children, the burden tends to fall on the mothers, who feel guilty about leaving their children while they work and feel responsible for being active parents. Fathers do not usually share either this guilt or this sense of responsibility (Hertz, 1986). In fact, Janet and Larry Hunt (1982) argued that fathers never will feel this strongly about parenting because the societal rewards are so low and the price to their career is so high. They predict, therefore, that couples will do one of two things. If the woman is strongly committed to her career, they will simply forego having children. Otherwise, they will continue in the more or less traditional patterns. The Hunts do not foresee a substantial rise in truly egalitarian marriages. For the moment, their predictions appear to be substantiated.

In addition to working out daily routines, the dual-career couple faces several other problems. By the time they have finished their work and household chores, there is little time left for socializing, even with other family members (D. Skinner, 1983; Walker & Wallston, 1985). There may also be the sense that nothing is getting done well. They feel that they are not "good" parents because they are not always available to their children. And they cannot achieve optimal career development because of family obligations. They may also feel conflicted about trying to break the traditional marital role mold (D. Skinner, 1983; Walker & Wallston, 1985). Furthermore, and perhaps most important, there is often little time for them as a couple. They may find it difficult to find time to talk about anything other than scheduling. There may be little time for romance or even sex (D. Skinner, 1983; Walker & Wallston, 1985).

Given all these difficulties, it is somewhat surprising that these marriages are not clearly more unhappy than other marriages. Indeed, several studies have found higher levels of marital satisfaction among employed than nonemployed wives in working-class and professional families (Burke & Weir, 1976; Walker & Wallston, 1985). Other studies have found no differences in marital adjustment or marital discord when the wife is employed. In fact, there have been reports of better communication and higher commitment among dual-earner than single-earner families (Walker & Wallston, 1985). For example, both the husbands and wives in Ronald Burke and Tamara Weir's (1976) research reported higher levels of communication concerning their own personalities and their sex lives in families where the wife was employed. The dual-earner couples in this study also reported better agreement on values and behaviors as well as disagreement resolution based on mutual give and take rather than one person always "winning."

We wouldn't want to paint too rosy a picture, however. Several studies have found that marital satisfaction of husbands is lower when the wife is employed (Burke & Weir, 1976; Osheron & Dill, 1983; Staines, Pottick, & Fudge, 1986; Walker & Wallston, 1985). While the wife's working per se may not affect marital satisfaction, the family's ability to accommodate her career may (Walker & Wallston, 1985). And certainly not all families are equally able, or willing, to make the adjustment. Indeed, the Hunts (1982) foresee increased marital instability as more and more couples come into direct conflict over the wife's career and family obligations. Remember, right now the wives appear to be doing a good deal of the compromising, though men are making some contributions. Should wives become more stringent in their demands for career time, families may be decreasingly able to accommodate them (Hunt & Hunt, 1982). Such compromises could become even more difficult if women are unable to become more accepting of male involvement in the household tasks. In other words, women will need to give up their guilt about "neglecting" childcare and housework (Hertz, 1986) before true equality in marital roles can be achieved.

The Wife

It has already been noted that women who work outside the home are still primarily responsible for childcare and housework. This situation could, it would seem, easily lead to "role overload" (D. Skinner, 1983). This means that the number of roles the woman is filling simply demand more time than she has available (Walker & Wallston, 1985), leaving her feeling overworked and inadequate. The employed wife might also feel *interrole conflict* (Walker & Wallston, 1985). Such a situation occurs when the demands of two roles are incompatible. So, for example, she may have a meeting at work during her child's soccer game. She obviously cannot be in both places at once.

Yet it is clear that not all employed wives feel either overloaded or conflicted by work-home demands. Feeling overloaded appears to be a subjective matter unrelated to the actual number of hours worked (Tiedje et al., 1990; Walker & Wallston, 1985). It could be that women are simply socialized to accept high levels of working hours (at home or on the job) as "normal." Or it may be that certain forms of work, such as childcare, are so enjoyable to women that they don't feel the strain. Perhaps women simply refuse to acknowledge an overload (Walker & Wallston, 1985). In any case, many employed wives do not feel overloaded most of the time.

The lack of role conflicts in some women is somewhat easier to explain. Women who have high self-esteem, strong social and spousal support, and some control over their work schedules tend to experience less interrole conflict (Walker & Wallston, 1985). Thus, personality characteristics in conjunction with family and work dimensions determine how often family and work demands clash.

What all of this adds up to is that women who work outside the home do not always suffer psychologically because of it. In fact, several studies have indicated that women in dual-earner families are actually healthier, psychologically and physically, than full-time homemakers (McBride, 1990; Repetti, Matthews, & Waldron, 1989; Rodin & Ickovics, 1990; Walker & Wallston, 1985). Ronald Kessler and James McRae (1982), for example, found that employed wives were less likely to show psychological distress in terms of depression, anxiety, low self-esteem, and physical symptoms (such as ulcers). This was especially true if the employed wives did not have children. However, if children were present and the husband shared in the childcare, the employed wives continued to have an advantage (in terms of psychological well-being) over the full-time homemakers. This is probably at least partially due to a reduction in role conflicts because of the husband's assistance.

While Kessler and McRae (1982) found that spousal assistance with childcare was an important factor in determining the effects of employment on the wife's mental health, help with housework was not. This tends to suggest that whatever guilt women feel about leaving their traditional roles focuses more on their role as mother than as housewife. This has some interesting implications for social policy. Both the government and industry might well be able to alleviate some of the concerns of working mothers if quality childcare was more readily available. This, in turn, might improve the mental health of these women.

The Husband

Employed wives, then, tend to have higher levels of marital satisfaction and better mental and physical health than full-time homemakers. Work outside the home seems to improve their sense of autonomy, self-esteem, and well-being. Women appear actually to *benefit* from employment. We might expect that their husband too would do better. After all, we have seen several instances in which the wife's attitude heavily influences the husband's behavior and adjustment. Furthermore, the increase in family income when the wife works raises the husband's standard of living too, enabling him to take better vacations, own newer cars, and so on.

Yet men do not seem to clearly benefit from their wives working. In fact, Kessler and McRae (1982) reported that the husbands of employed wives showed higher levels of depressive symptoms and lower self-esteem than do husbands of full-time homemakers. Similarly, Burke and Weir (1976) found that the husbands of employed wives seemed to worry more, have lower spirits and more physical illnesses. Men who help their employed wives with childcare seem less distressed, but it is unclear why (Kessler & McRae, 1982). Kessler and McRae thought this might indicate a greater acceptance of the wife's employment. It is also possible, however, that the wife's better adjustment in such cases simply influences the husband's attitudes. Indeed, Kessler and McRae's interpretation is questioned by other findings indicating that the husband's self-reported acceptance of his wife's employment does not improve his job or marital satisfaction (Staines et al., 1986).

Several studies have found higher marital and work dissatisfaction among men with employed wives (Burke & Weir, 1976; Osheron & Dill, 1983; Staines et al., 1986; Walker & Wallston, 1985). Some of the findings related to these general ones are somewhat confusing. For example, men in dual-career families who have children feel more self-actualized and successful at work than those who are childless (Osheron & Dill, 1983). This seems counterintuitive, given the extra demands placed on his time (and income) by the presence of children. Indeed, not all studies have found that the presence of children reduces the negative effects of the wife's employment (Staines et al., 1986). Also, the same men who report lower marital satisfaction indicate that they have better communication with their wives and are more likely to resolve conflicts by mutual agreement rather than by one partner's dominance (Burke & Weir, 1976). In other words, in terms of behavior, the marriages seem to be happier. Yet the men said that they were less happy in their marriages. In fact, they said they were having more trouble communicating with and showing affection toward their wives, even though they actually communicated more than did the husbands of housewives.

How can we reconcile these conflicting findings? Quite simply, we can't. The dynamics underlying the effects of wives' employment on their husbands are poorly understood. The only clue we have is that men whose wives work seem to feel less adequate as "breadwinners" (Staines et al., 1986). Perhaps this is why the dual-career men with children do better. At least if there are children, he has *someone* he is supporting. We might also suggest that involvement with childcare is helpful to dual-career men because it gives them a clearer role in the family. After all, if a man's "good provider" role is reduced by his wife's employment and he is unable (or unwilling) to participate in childcare, then how is he important to the family? We have seen the importance of clear role definition in men's adjustment to parenthood (see Chapter 6). There is little reason to doubt that it is equally important here.

Thus, while dual-earner families face a myriad of difficulties, most couples seem to fare reasonably well. The wives especially are likely to benefit. Husbands, on the other hand, may actually suffer psychologically and physically. Considerably more research will be needed before we understand how these families cope and how the status of these husbands can be improved.

THE OTHER CAREER: HOUSEWIVES

Throughout this chapter, attention has been given to the growing number of women who are employed outside the home. The movement of women into the labor force has been particularly dramatic among wives and mothers of young children. Yet in describing these trends it is easy to lose sight of the fact that approximately half of all women opt to be full-time homemakers for at least a portion of their adult lives. In some cases, they will be at home only for a year or so. Others will stay home until their youngest child enters school. In any case these women have chosen to do a full-time job that carries no salary and precious little social status.

The Job

We have an image of a housewife as someone who watches soap operas all day while eating chocolates or talking on the phone. On the other hand, there is the old adage that " ... a woman's work is never done." The latter actually seems to be a more accurate description of the housewife/mother. It has been estimated that the full-time homemaker works somewhere between 40 and 55 hours per week (Bergman, 1986; Piotrowski 1982). If there are young children in the house, of course, the hours can be even longer. Indeed, the mother may be "on call" virtually 24 hours a day.

Since an increasing number of women are full-time housewives only when their children are very young, a point made by Piotrowski (1982) is of particular interest. The jobs of homemaker and mother are often oppositional. Full-time homemakers are expected to keep clean houses. But children make messes. And they often interrupt their mother's work, making it difficult for her to complete any task, particularly on any sort of schedule (as is expected with meals, for example). Futhermore, the more control the mother has in setting the daily routine (in order to complete the daily housework), the less control the child has. This may bring mother and child into conflict.

Children also may restrict a woman's movement outside the home. She may be restricted by their naptimes, mealtimes, and so on. Indeed, housewives often report feeling isolated (Oakley, 1974). They complain that tasks are monotonous or repetitious. The same clothes, dishes, and floors get washed day after day after day. Such tasks require little intellectual attention or creativity. And those tasks that might permit some personal involvement, such as cooking, are often interrupted by the child or are performed under a time constraint that prohibits creativity (Oakley, 1974).

Many people believe that the amount of time homemakers spend on family tasks has decreased over the years. Time-saving devices, such as microwaves, washers, and refrigerators, have ostensibly cut housework. And women have fewer children than in the past. The family is also no longer a producer of goods; rather, it is a consumption unit. Indeed, some research indicates that the number of housework hours has decreased (Bergman, 1986). Other researchers, however, have argued that there has been no significant decrease in the time spent on housework. Instead, they suggest, the nature of household work has changed (Cowan, 1983). less suppor

First, our standards of cleanliness and health have changed. People didn't used to bathe or wear clean clothes every day. They didn't polish floors and furniture. They didn't scour bathtubs and toilets. These are things we take for granted (Cowan, 1983). And full-time housewives may feel particularly pressured to do an outstanding job of cleaning. Consider the comments of one of Oakley's subjects:

> . . . I can't say I *like* washing floors: kneeling on the floors, washing them . . . I do it to keep it clean. Stephen's all over the floor, and if they're not done, he's going to get filthy. These floors . . . show every mark . . . I feel it ought to be done. I've never been able to go out and leave anything. I could never leave washing up in the sink or anything like that. . . . (Oakley, 1974, pp. 109–110)

This woman washes her floors every day so her baby won't pick up any dirt from the floor. Houses used to have dirt floors.

Second, things that used to be delivered to the house, ranging from milk to medical care, now have to be "picked up." Similarly, items that used to be produced in the home (such as food or clothing) now must be purchased at stores. Transportation of goods and family members has become a major element of housework (Cowan, 1983).

Job Satisfaction

There are two things most housewives don't like about their jobs: housework and the low status ascribed to the job (Oakley, 1974). Actually, the two are related. One of the reasons homemakers don't like housework is that it carries no external rewards: You don't get paid for doing it well. You rarely even get praised. Housework is most commonly noticed when it is not done (Piotrowski 1982; Oakley, 1974). Thus, most of the rewards have to be internal and self-generated. This is, of course, difficult to maintain. Furthermore, as we already noted, housework is monotonous, fragmented, and performed under time pressure. Indeed, Ann Oakley (1974) found that it was very comparable to factory assembly work. Just as these job characteristics can cause dissatisfaction in industrial workers, they contribute to the homemaker's dislike of housework.

On the other hand, many homemakers do enjoy taking care of their children (Oakley, 1974). Indeed, many of them are home in order to care for their children. They see mothers as special, as able to provide intangibles that enrich a child's development (Hock et al., 1985). And they want to teach the child their own values. At least temporarily, they are willing to sacrifice income and the other benefits of working outside the home in order to have this impact on their children.

The other thing homemakers like about their jobs is that, to a large extent, they can set their own schedule (Oakley, 1974). Certainly, there are constraints of their children's and husband's needs. But they do not have to sit behind a desk from 9 to 5 with a half-hour break for lunch and two coffee breaks. They can do their housecleaning early in the day and shopping in the afternoon. Or they can reverse the schedule. Or they may choose not to leave the house at all on a particular day. While their freedom is far from complete, it is much greater than that experienced by many employees.

Given the pros and cons of being a homemaker, it is not surprising that depression is common among young housewives. On the other hand, it is not surprising that many women still opt to "hold the position." The difficulties of the job are great, but so are the rewards.

SUMMARY

Most Americans work for pay throughout much of their adult lives. This is now true of both men and women. We work for a variety of reasons. Some of these, of course, are related to survival. We work to make the money we need to support ourselves and our families. Some of the needs filled by work, however, are psychosocial. Work gives us status and may contribute to self-esteem. It also provides a place for us to meet and interact with people.

People do not all show the same pattern of career development. Some select an occupation, and perhaps even a specific job, very early in adulthood and stay with it until retirement. Others need considerably more experimenting before making a final decision. In fact, some people may never really settle on one occupation. This is true of both men and women, but because of societal roles and expectations, women are less likely to show permanent commitment to a job or occupation and are more likely than men to interrupt their work lives in order to be at home with the children. There are large individual differences, however, in the choices and the timing of these choices.

Of course, individuals not only choose different patterns of career development, they also select different occupations. Gender, personality, achievement motivation, parental values, and a myriad of other factors seem to contribute to this choice. Once a choice is made, certain variables affect the likelihood of career success. Some of these are job-related characteristics, such as how much competition there is for advancement. Other factors are more related to personal characteristics and choices.

Despite societal advances in women's rights, women still make considerably less money than men do. Again, some of this difference is probably due to personal choice. So women are more likely than men to want to take time off from work or work part-time when their children are young. We should note that these choices are constrained by social roles and expectations.

Job discrimination probably also contributes to the gender gap. Employers, like the rest of us, hold beliefs about what men and women are best able to do. Certain job titles continue to be more apt to be assigned to men than to women (and vice versa). Furthermore, employers may use different criteria in evaluating men and women for promotion.

The rapid influx of married women into the labor force has created a dramatic increase in the number of dual-earner families. Some of these are actually dual-career families, in which both partners are strongly committed to their careers. This equal commitment can create problems in terms of time and energy allocation for housework, childcare, and family life. It appears that, in most of these families, such household tasks are not equally allocated but instead fall mainly to the wife. This may be one reason why married women tend to have less career success than do single women.

Finally, when we talk about work, we usually mean work for pay. Yet substantial numbers of women work in the home, cleaning, cooking, running errands, providing childcare, and so on. The hours are long, the work often boring and fragmented, the financial rewards undependable, and the social status of the job almost nonexistent. Yet women continue to be housewives, thereby choosing a different life course than most men and than many other women.

8 Physical and Cognitive Development

You're not as young as you used to be, and there are all sorts of reminders of it: middle-age spread, empty nest syndrome, midlife crisis, the "change," screenings for breast and colon and prostate cancers. Is there nothing positive about being middle-age?

Of course there is. While some physiological systems do begin to decline, by and large these are healthy years. Children leaving the home can provide adults with a new sense of freedom as well as a sense of accomplishment at having successfully completed childrearing. Menopause means no more risk of pregnancy, a thought that makes sex more enjoyable for many women. And it's not at all clear that there is any such thing as a midlife crisis, at least not in the sense of a traumatic upheaval.

This may indicate that many of our negative impressions about middle age are little more than stereotypes. Premenopausal women, for example, are considerably more negative about "the change" than postmenopausal women (Neugarten, Wood, Kraines, & Loomis, 1963/1968). Our youth-oriented society may be oblivious to the more positive aspects of aging. On the other hand, it is also possible that people adjust their expectations of physical functioning, family relationships, and so on downward as they age. Perhaps middle age is as bad as the stereotypes have suggested, and human beings simply rationalize it away.

While many people are very happy in middle age, others are very dissatisfied. In fact, suicide rates among white women peak during middle age (Manton, Blazer & Woodbury, 1987). This underscores the wide range of individual differences in both the form of and adjustment to changes. Early life style choices, including marital status and partner, diet and exercise, alcohol and tobacco use, and career path, all begin to yield costs or benefits now. And because most of us have families, these effects, and our methods of coping with them, have an impact on others that in turn affects us. By middle age we are participants in a complex set of interrelated social systems (B. Newman, 1982) which serve as a support or a drain on our resources (Belle, 1982).

But what is middle age? It is difficult to identify a particular physical, psychological, or cultural event that marks the beginning or end of middle age. The boundaries are somewhat arbitrary (though some theorists, such as Daniel Levinson, believe they may be evolutionarily set; see Chapter 9). For our purposes, we will define middle age as extending from approximately 40 to 65 years of age. Note that this definition may be culturally specific to some extent; it is not clear whether middle age would occur at the same time in societies where life expectancies are either much shorter or much longer than ours. We do not know whether people in cultures with shorter life spans deal with the middle life issues at all (B. Newman, 1982). The point is particularly important in this chapter, since many of the changes discussed here are related to life styles that might not even exist in other societies.

PHYSICAL CHANGES

There are a myriad of physical changes during the middle years. Some of these changes have, at most, only minor implications for daily living; others mark the beginning of bodily decline that will ultimately require medical intervention or may even be fatal. Some of the changes are "normal" in that they seem to be an outcome primarily of the aging process. Still others appear only in cases of illness; that is, they represent "pathological" aging. Normal changes at midlife are typically not very dramatic. Furthermore, they can often be corrected or ameliorated through medical intervention or minor adjustments in daily living.

There are substantial individual differences in aging. Just as some women have their first menstrual period at 11 and others at 15, some women finish menopause at 46 and others do not even begin menopause until 52. Some men never lose their hair to any substantial extent; others are virtually bald at 40. And it doesn't take an expert to tell you that Joan Collins, Elizabeth Taylor, and Paul Newman look better than many other people their age. Such differences are not confined to external changes. There is considerable variation in male testoterone levels during adulthood, for example (Comfort, 1980). And while kidney functioning declines in most people, some research subjects actually show improved renal functioning with age (Shock et al., 1984).

There is also intra-individual variability in aging. Not all bodily systems age at the same rate. This is dramatically illustrated by the changes in the female reproductive system versus those in virtually any other bodily system. Even within a physiological system, decline is not uniform. So, for example, the middle-aged heart does not recover from exercise as quickly as the young heart does, but the differences between the resting heart function of young and middle-aged adults may be negligible (Shock et al., 1984).

Exterior Changes

We all have an image of middle-aged men and women. The men are balding, with pot bellies. The women have gray hair and wrinkled faces. Words such as "middle-age spread," "crow's feet," and "laugh lines" become increasingly evident in our vocabularies as we enter middle age.

Hair and Skin: As people get older, their hair is more likely to turn gray. This is attributable to a decline in tyrosinase activity (Previte, 1983). Tyrosinase is an enzyme intrumental in the formation of melanin, the black to brown pigment that gives color to human skin, hair, and eyes. It can be converted into other pigments to produce hair colors other than black or brown. In any case, since melanin is involved in skin, hair, and eye color, it is not surprising to find that there are "color" changes in all three. Eye color seems to fade, so that the eyes look gray (Weg, 1975). As if to compensate for the loss of pigment production, some pigmentation cells in the skin enlarge. This produces the "age spots" or "liver spots" often seen in elderly people (Kart, Metress, & Metress, 1978).

Not everyone's hair grays at the same rate. Since hair color is controlled by genetic functioning, it is not surprising that there are wide individual differences. Some people will begin to gray in their teens or twenties; others will not gray until their seventies or older. Graying is therefore not perfectly correlated with age. However, there is a strong relationship.

The hair not only grays, it loses some of its luster. This is partially due to the loss of pigment and partially due to the decline in the functioning

Although external changes such as hair loss and wrinkles may create consternation in the middle-ager, they do not signify a serious health problem.

of the sebaceous glands that produce oil for hair and skin (Kart et al., 1978; Previte, 1983). There may also be some hair loss. Some of this is due to reduced blood flow to the scalp (Kart et al., 1978). However, most hair loss in middle age is genetically mediated (Previte, 1983). This explains why there are such large individual differences in amount and timing of hair loss. Male pattern baldness is a sex-linked genetic trait; the genes controlling it are activated by testosterone. Typically, this condition first becomes evident as a man enters middle age.

The changes in the skin are also quite dramatic. As early as the twenties, evidence that the face is used to produce various expressions is clear from the "worry lines" around the eyebrows or the "laugh lines" around the mouth. By 40 or so, these expressive lines become quite obvious. These and other wrinkles are caused by a variety of factors (Kart et al., 1978). The skin loses some of its elasticity, so it doesn't snap back from changes in facial expressions. More important, there is a gradual loss of subcutaneous fat. Eventually, this loss of subcutaneous fat is evident all over the body as wrinkles appear everywhere, not just on the face. Furthermore, the subcutaneous fat loss is what makes elderly people's hands, feet, and faces (and, eventually, chests, arms, legs) appear so thin and bony. This "thinness" is not obvious in middle age, of course. Thus, the changes in skin that we see in middle age are simply part of a longer process that began in the twenties and will continue well into old age. As the loss becomes more severe, additional associated symptoms, such as temperature regulation problems, will appear (Kart et al., 1978).

Weight: There seems to be some disagreement as to whether people typically gain weight as they age. Some researchers have reported weight loss after middle age (Shock, 1972); others have reported weight gain (Brozek, 1952, cited in Weg, 1975). Such conflicting findings may reflect cohort or other sample differences. Recent national statistics (see Table 8-1) indicate that weight typically increases until about the mid-thirties, when it reaches a plateau. There may then be a decrease in weight after about age 65 (Statistical Abstracts, 1986). Of course, these are cross-sectional data, so the age differences may be due to cohort rather than development.

It is clear, however, that obesity becomes an increasingly common problem. Indeed, the peak rates of obesity are found in men 45–54 years old and women 55–64 (Bernstein, 1983). Much of the decline in obesity rate after these ages is due to the death of overweight people rather than to individual weight loss with age.

It is easy to understand why age-related weight gain might occur. Basal metabolism rate (the "resting" energy use of the body) decreases with age. There is about a 2 percent decline per decade in basal metabolism after age 50 (Previte, 1983). This, in conjunction with lowered levels of activity, results in a decreased need for calories. There is approximately a 5 percent reduction in calories needed to maintain a healthy weight and bodily functioning for every decade past age 55. After age 75, the caloric needs are probably reduced about 7 percent per decade (Kart et al., 1978). Not everyone makes the appropriate caloric reductions, and thus they gain weight.

TABLE 8-1: Average Weights for Men and Women of Different Ages

	AGE					
Height	18–24	25–34	35–44	45–54	55–64	65–74
Men						
5'2"	130	139	146	148	147	143
5'3"	135	145	149	154	151	148
5'4"	139	151	155	158	156	152
5'5"	143	155	159	163	160	156
5'6"	148	159	164	167	165	161
5'7"	152	164	169	171	170	165
5'8"	157	168	174	176	174	169
5'9"	162	173	178	180	178	174
5'10"	166	177	183	185	183	178
5'11"	171	182	188	190	187	182
6'0"	175	186	192	194	192	187
6'1"	180	191	197	198	197	192
6'2"	185	196	202	204	201	195
Women						
4'9"	111	120	131	129	132	132
4'10"	114	123	133	132	135	135
4'11"	118	126	136	136	138	138
5'0"	121	130	139	139	142	142
5'1"	124	133	141	143	145	145
5'2"	128	136	144	146	148	148
5'3"	131	139	146	150	151	151
5'4"	134	142	149	153	154	154
5'5"	137	146	151	157	157	157
5'6"	141	149	154	160	161	160
5'7"	144	152	156	164	164	163
5'8"	147	155	159	168	167	166

Source: *Statistical Abstract of the United States, 1986,* p. 120. Washington, D.C.: Government Printing Office.

Note that you do not need to eat more as you age in order to gain weight. Eating the same amount of food you ate as a young adult will result in weight gain.

Regardless of whether or not someone actually gains weight, middle-aged and older people do not usually look as "lean" as young adults. This is because lean body mass declines with age so that proportion of body fat at a given weight increases (Bernstein, 1983). This process probably begins in the thirties (DeVries, 1975). This means that a 20-year-old who weighs 120 pounds has less body fat than a 60-year-old who weighs 120 pounds. The change is more dramatic for women than for men. Both the increase in fat and the decrease in basal metabolism is greater for women than for men (Rodin, Silberstein, & Striegel-Moore, 1985). Obesity (as assessed by percentage of body weight that is fat) may actually be more of a problem in the middle-aged and elderly than we currently believe, since we now base our estimates solely on weight (Bernstein, 1983).

The decline in lean body mass represents a loss of total muscle mass. This loss is more evident in the skeletal muscles than in the smooth muscle of the digestive tract or blood vessels (Kart et al., 1978). Muscle strength therefore declines (DeVries, 1975). This, of course, leads to sagging (including in the abdomen and the face). The decline probably begins in the thirties, but the rate is quite slow until age 60 or so. This means that the middle-aged person will not be able to exert as much muscular force for as long a time as the young adult will. However, under normal circumstances, the impact of this decline is quite limited until old age, and exercise can help alleviate these changes (DeVries, 1975; Kart et al., 1978).

Sensory Functioning

While changes in hair color, skin, and physical appearance may be important psychologically to some people, they have little influence on how we live our lives. After all, many of these changes can be alleviated or camouflaged by hair dye, skin cream, exercise, or fashion tricks. With the exception of obesity, none of these changes has implications for our ability to function normally in our daily routines. Sensory changes, while not life-threatening or debilitating, have the potential to have a greater effect.

Vision: A common joke among the middle aged is that their arms are getting too short. They keep holding books farther and farther away in order to be able to read them. Eventually, they run out of arm; they can't hold the book far enough away to be able to read it. So they go to an optometrist who will prescribe glasses, typically bifocals.

This farsightedness that commonly appears in middle age (usually in the forties) is called *presbyopia* (Previte, 1983). It is attributable to a declining ability of the lens to change shape so as to focus light properly on the retina. This decline actually begins around age 8; so once again, we see that the changes evident in middle age are simply part of a long developmental process. The lens doesn't just lose some of its flexibility; it actually hardens. There is also some yellowing of the lens, making it more difficult to distinguish "cool" colors such as green or blue (Kart et al., 1978). The lens loses some of its transparency (Kline & Scheiber, 1985), so that less light gets into the eye. Short wavelength light (as in blue and green) is particularly likely to be filtered out, contributing to the problems in distinguishing color. This reduced transparency is evident in about two thirds of 51- to 60-year-olds and 96 percent of those over 60. It is not surprising, then, that visual acuity is fairly steady from young adulthood until about age 50. Then it begins to decline quite rapidly (Kline & Scheiber, 1985).

What causes all these changes in the lens? The lens has no blood vessels in it. Therefore, it relies on the fluids around it for nutrition. The fluids nourish best the cells on the surface of the lens. Those beneath the surface gradually die, but there is no mechanism for removing the dead cells. They simply build up. In fact, the lens continues to grow throughout life, roughly tripling in size by age 70. These aging and dead cells eventually are the center of the lens (having been buried by newer cells), which is now opaque and hard (Previte, 1983).

If the opacity becomes too great and virtually blinds the individual, we say that person has developed cataracts. This usually occurs in first one eye and then the other, although the amount of time between the appearance of cataracts in each eye tends to decline with age. So, for example, there is about four years between the cataract development in 45-year-olds but only about two years in 65-year-olds and one year in 75-year-olds (Kline & Scheiber, 1985). Cataracts develop when pigmented compounds accumulate, a process apparently exacerbated by repeated exposure to bright sunlight (Kline & Scheiber, 1985; Previte, 1983). Diabetes also increases the likelihood of developing cataracts (Kline & Scheiber, 1985). There have been claims that all of us would develop cataracts if we simply lived to be old enough (Kart et al., 1978). Others, however, argue that there are important physiological differences between cataracts and normal aging (Kline & Scheiber, 1985). In about 95 percent of all cases, cataracts can be corrected by replacing the damaged lens with an artificial one.

In addition to declines in visual acuity, middle-aged and elderly people typically experience some difficulty in adapting to darkness and glare (Kline & Scheiber, 1985). The problems in adapting to darkness, which begin in the thirties but become particularly marked after age 60, are probably attributable to the changes in the lens. Sensitivity to glare, which also appears to be due to the the increased opacity of the lens, increases sharply after age 45. These two changes may make night driving increasingly difficult because the eye reacts more strongly to the glare of headlights and then takes longer to adapt to the darkness after the car has passed. Such problems may be intensified by declines, after about age 50, in the size of the visual field and in depth perception.

Aside from cataracts, all the changes discussed thus far are more or less part of "normal" aging. One other eye disease commonly begins during middle age and deserves to be mentioned here. Glaucoma is a disease that involves a buildup of the aqueous humor (the fluid in the eyeball). This creates pressure on the optic nerve, causing irreparable damage to the optic nerve and retina. Glaucoma, which can actually take several different forms, is a leading cause of blindness in the middle-aged and elderly (Kart et al., 1978; Kline & Scheiber, 1985).

There are no signs of glaucoma until the blindness starts to become noticeable. First peripheral vision becomes deficient. A person might, for example, bump into the edges of doorways because he or she can't see them clearly. The condition gradually worsens until tunnel vision develops. Eventually the sufferer will become totally blind. Prior to the loss of peripheral vision there is no pain, discomfort, discharge, visual dysfunction or any other symptom. However, evidence of pressure buildup is present in a thorough eye exam. If you are over 40, and particularly after 50, eye exams that include glaucoma testing should be done regularly. This is especially true if you have suffered a serious eye injury or disease or if you have close relatives with glaucoma. While the disease is not curable, it is treatable.

Early diagnosis can greatly increase the number of years of serviceable vision (Kart et al., 1978; Kline & Scheiber, 1985).

Audition: Hearing losses are not as widespread as visual declines. Nearly 90 percent of all Americans over the age of 45 wear glasses (U.S. Statistical Abstracts, 1986), but only about 13 percent of people over 65 have significant hearing loss (Kart et al., 1978). Even anecdotally, you are never surprised to find out that an adult wears glasses. They are a common phenomenon in a high school or college classroom. Hearing aids, however, are still unusual enough to attract attention.

Furthermore, many of the changes in the auditory system that may interfere with hearing do not occur until old age. So, for example, both the atrophy of the ear canal and certain types of receptor cell damage do not commonly occur until after age 60 (Olsho, Harkins, & Lenhardt, 1985). Thus, hearing problems are not widespread among the middle-aged.

That does not mean that the middle-aged suffer no hearing problems. The most common hearing impairment is *presbycusis* (Kart et al., 1978; Olsho et al., 1985), a disorder that interferes with the ability to hear high frequency sounds. Men are more likely than women to experience this problem. In some sufferers, the losses will be confined to high frequency sounds. In others, the losses will ultimately extend into the lower frequencies. This is because there can be different causes of the initial loss. In either case, overall hearing will gradually deteriorate, although people suffering losses at all frequencies will probably encounter greater difficulty (Kart et al., 1978; Olsho et al., 1985).

Initially, these losses have little impact on daily life because they do not impede speech perception (Kart et al., 1978). As deterioration continues, speech perception may also worsen, particularly in terms of distinguishing among consonants. This typically does not happen until old age and may be alleviated by a hearing aid. The effects of presbycusis may also be mediated by the speaker's volume. It is not wise for speakers to raise their voices, because that does nothing to lower the frequency of speech into a more discernible range. Lowering the volume of the voice does lower the frequency, making the speech more comprehensible to the listener (Kart et al., 1978; Olsho et al., 1985).

Physiological Systems

Cardiovascular System: Most people are aware that there is an age-related increase in heart problems (including fatal heart attacks) that becomes noticeable during the middle years. As we shall see, much of the increase during middle age is apparently due to life-style and personality characteristics. Some portion is attributable to the gradual aging of the heart.

As we age, our heart rate slows and there is a decrease in the amount of blood pumped by the heart. The cardiac muscles themselves also diminish in size and strength (Kart et al., 1978; Previte, 1983). Some researchers (Shock et al., 1984) however, have argued that these declines are more apparent than real. They claim that the observed declines are due to inclusion in the samples of people with heart disease who lower the mean scores. If observation is confined to those with no heart disease, there is little or no cardiac decline into old age (Shock et al., 1984). It is important to note that, even if there actually is an age-related decline in cardiac functioning, the heart normally continues to pump enough blood to maintain a healthy body. The heart is not the only physiological system that is "slowing down"; basal metabolism rate, for example, has also decreased.

While the heart continues to operate well while at rest, there are more noticeable changes in cardiac functioning following exercise or exertion. The maximum heart rate achieved during exercise (and therefore the amount of blood reaching parts of the body) declines with age, beginning probably in the twenties (Previte, 1983; Shock, et al., 1984). The aging heart thus reacts less well to stress.

Lungs: As we age, the air sacs in our lungs become less elastic and therefore probably cannot expand to their maximum level as easily as when we are younger (Kart et al., 1978). Indeed, research indicates that our maximal breathing ability, in terms of both rate and oxygen intake, decreases with age. This decline becomes more marked after about age 50 (Shock et al., 1984). As was the case with the heart, functioning remains adequate to maintain normal daily activities. However, the lungs may not react as well when they are stressed—for example, during exercise.

These findings apply, of course, to healthy individuals. More specifically, they describe the pulmonary functioning of healthy nonsmokers. People who smoke have lower lung capacity even when the lungs are at rest. This is true at all ages and even when the smoker has not developed any lung disease. The evidence indicates, however, that quitting smoking improves the lung capacity (Shock et al., 1984). That is why quitting smoking not only reduces risk for diseases, but also improves ability to climb stairs, exercise, and so on.

Reproductive System: Perhaps the most dramatic physical change during middle age occurs in the female reproductive system. "The change,"— menopause—has been given such a central role in psychological theory, medicine, and societal belief systems that it is treated separately later in this chapter.

Men do not go through any comparable change in their reproductive system. They may never lose their fertility or their ability to perform sexually. However, there typically are some changes in the male reproductive system and its functioning that can influence a man's sexual enjoyment and self-confidence.

Sometime around 40 years old, a very gradual decline in testosterone production begins. This process is sometimes called the *male climacteric.* Although the rate of decrease will become more dramatic after age 50, it will not result in the complete termination of testosterone production. Even at age 80, there is enough testosterone to allow a man to father a child (Asso, 1983; Previte, 1983). There will be fewer viable sperm, however, making it less likely that an older man will father a child. The higher rate of birth defects among the offspring of older fathers may also be attributable to poorer quality sperm.

In addition, there are changes in the testes themselves (Kart et al., 1978). They become smaller and less firm. They produce fewer sperm. The prostate gland, which provides a component of the seminal fluid, may become enlarged, which can interfere with normal urination (Previte, 1983). If the enlargement becomes too great, surgery may be required. The surgery is extremely common, especially after age 65, when it becomes one of the five most common reasons men are hospitalized (Statistical Abstracts, 1986). The surgery does not usually prevent later sexual activity (Previte, 1983).

Although impotence does increase in frequency with aging, most men can attain an erection even when they are in their seventies (Newman, 1982). It does, however, take men longer to attain an erection, and they may need direct penile stimulation in order to become erect (Comfort, 1980). However, older men can maintain an erection longer than younger men (B. Newman, 1982; Weg, 1975). They reach orgasm much as young men do, although the ejaculation itself may be less forceful (Comfort, 1980; B. Newman, 1982). Older men do need a longer refractory or recovery period following orgasm before they can again achieve an erection (B. Newman, 1982). In fact, in some older men, the refractory period may eventually become as long as 24 hours.

Several points need to be emphasized here. First, there are substantial individual differences in both the timing and the degree of these changes (Comfort, 1980). Second, there is probably nothing inherent in the normal aging process that physically precludes sexual pleasure. While impotence does become more common as men age, it is not necessarily directly attributable to aging per se. More likely it is due to disease (especially diabetes), psychological problems (such as depression), or drug effects (Comfort, 1980; Rossman, 1980). Men experiencing impotence, then, should seek medical attention, because the condition may be reversible.

Although there is a decline in male sexual activity after about age 30, many healthy men continue to have sex regularly into their seventies and beyond (Rossman, 1980; Shock et al., 1984). Contrary to popular mythology, these are not "dirty old men." Instead, they tend to be physically healthy married men who enjoyed sex when they were younger (Pfeiffer & Davis, 1972; Shock et al., 1984). In fact, the strongest predictor of middle-aged and older men's frequency and enjoyment of sexual activity is their frequency and enjoyment during young adulthood. Physical health, life satisfaction, and availability of a partner are also important factors in predicting male sexuality in middle and old age.

Menopause

Few life events are so common and yet so poorly understood as menopause. All women go through menopause if they live long enough. In fact, a substantial portion of women's lives now occurs in the postmenopausal years. Right now, over half of all women live to be at least 75 years old. This means that the postmenopausal years constitute fully one-third of their lives (Asso, 1983). The frequency of such a lengthy postmenopausal life has increased substantially during the twentieth century. Indeed, at the turn of the century female life expectancy was about 48 years. Given that the average age for menopause is around 50, and has probably been in the late forties to early fifties for generations, this means that many women died before reaching menopause or shortly thereafter (Asso, 1983; Goodman, 1980).

Since most women now live through and for a long time after menopause, it is important to understand both the short- and long-term effects of the event. For many years, Americans have typically thought of menopause as an almost tragic occurrence that causes a variety of physical and psychological symptoms. Furthermore, we have often viewed it as the first marker of old age, since we have traditionally associated youth with fertility. Thus menopause has carried negative implications because of what it caused (in terms of physical changes) and because of its link to aging.

Definitions and Research Caveats: At first glance, menopause seems easy to define. It is the cessation of menstruation. Most researchers will require that menstruation has not occurred for 12 consecutive months in order to consider a woman postmenopausal. This must be caused by an end to ovarian function (as opposed to pregnancy or a disease) in order to be considered menopause. Menopause marks the end of a woman's reproductive capability. She can no longer become pregnant.

Certainly the end of menstruation is a tangible, discrete event that should be easy to assess. However, several problems arise in trying to do research on menopause (Asso, 1983; Bardwick, 1971). First, while the definition relies on the cessation of menses, the actual process of hormonal and ovarian function changes begins long before (perhaps 10 to 15 years) menstruation actually stops. And menstruation usually stops gradually rather than abruptly. A woman's periods may be less frequent, shorter, and lighter for several years before they end. Furthermore, certain changes continue after menopause. For example the level of the pituitary-produced hormones FSH (follicle stimulating hormone) and LH (lutenizing hormone) rises during menopause and continues to be elevated for several years afterward (Asso, 1983).

Researchers have not typically wanted to consider the entire period of physical change as menopause for several reasons. Not all the physical changes occurring during this period are associated with the changes in reproductive capability. Indeed, as we shall see, many of the changes, such as decreasing bone mass and increasing risk of heart disease, also occur in men. In addition, the changes prior to the cessation of menses are so subtle that most women do not notice them. They do, of course, notice missed periods. Thus, the psychological effects will vary during this period of time. This has led researchers to distinguish between the climacteric (or climacterium) and menopause. The *climacteric* refers to the longer period of more diverse physical changes associated with, though not necessarily causally related to, menopause. The term *menopause* is reserved for the shorter period of time when the menses are actually ending. A researcher might, for example, consider a woman who has not had a period for 3 to 12 months to be in the midst of menopause, a woman who has had two consecutive periods premenopausal, and one who has not had a period for at least 12 months postmenopausal (Goodman, 1980).

Investigators do not always use the same definitions of menopausal phases. Even if they did, there would be problems. Much of the research involves at least some retrospective report. Either all of the women are being asked to remember when symptoms started or at least the postmenopausal group is. Retrospective reporting is generally undesireable but there is, in addition, evidence suggesting bias in women's memory of other aspects of their reproductive history, such as menarche (Goodman, 1980) as well as menopause itself (Asso, 1983), making such methodology particularly suspect in research on menopause.

As was noted earlier, some physical and psychological changes during these years are not attributable to menopause. Yet researchers have rarely attempted to separate the effects of aging from the effects of menopause (Asso, 1983 Goodman, 1980). Some methods for separating age and menopause effects cannot be used. For example, age-matched groups are not a viable method. Young (35–40 years old) premenopausal women cannot be compared to young menopausal women because the two groups would be expected to differ in ways other than menopausal status. After all, the former group would be within the "normal" range for menopause, while the later group would not (Goodman, 1980). Indeed, a substantial number of the postmenopausal young women may have experienced "artificial" (surgically induced) menopause, a very different event than "natural" menopause.

Researchers could, of course, compare male to female development to get some idea of age and menopause effects. They could also look at symptomology reported by pre- and peri- and post-menopausal women. Neither approach is perfect. The latter approach, for example, might involve cohort confounds that may be particularly powerful in terms of women's attitudes toward their bodies in general (Goodman, 1980; Grossman & Bart, 1979; Parlee, 1978). Nonetheless, including such "control" groups would be of some help in defining the effects, yet they have only occasionally been used (Asso, 1983; Goodman, 1980).

Finally, even within the menopausal group itself, sampling procedures have often been poor. It is very common to find that the menopausal women are all drawn from a gynecological sample. This is particularly true of research done prior to the late 1970s. This is a problem for several reasons. First, not all women go to doctors for menopause-related problems. While the data are not always in agreement, probably at least one-third and perhaps as many as 80 percent of all women do not go to a doctor even for relief from hot flashes, the most common symptom (Grossman & Bart, 1979; Nathanson & Lorenz, 1982). Probably only about 15 percent require any medical treatment for their symptoms (Shepard & Shepard, 1982). We can expect, then, that such clinically based studies will indicate more severe physical problems during menopause than most women actually experience. Furthermore, women with psychological problems (such as depression or anxiety) are more likely than psychologically healthy women to go to gynecologists independently of physical symptoms (Asso, 1983). This means that research relying on clinical samples will overreport psychological disturbance during menopause. All of this has contributed to an emphasis on the negative aspects of menopause and to a conceptualization of menopause as a disease, though it is actually a natural process.

Timing and Causes: A female newborn's ovaries have all the eggs (ova) she will ever have. They are in an immature form (known as follicles) and, after puberty, mature under the influence of FSH. As they mature, the ova produce substantial amounts of estrogen. Indeed, they are normally the major source of estrogen. The estrogen, in combination with LH, leads to ovulation (the release of a single egg from the ovary). Immediately following ovulation, there is an increase in the production of progesterone by the ovaries. If the egg is not fertilized, there will be a rapid drop in estrogen and progesterone which, in turn, will cause the lining of the uterus (the endometrium) to be shed. In other words, the woman will menstruate.

Since menopause in the cessation of menstruation, something must happen that interferes with these hormonal mechanisms. The disruption is caused by the gradual loss of ovarian functioning (Asso, 1983). As a woman ages, more and more of her ova are lost. By age 45, she has only 5,000–20,000 follicles (compared to about 400,000 at birth) (Asso, 1983; Hyde, 1986). Many of the remaining follicles are not sensitive to FSH and will not mature and produce estrogen. Without the estrogen, there will be no menstrual period. Note that it is the lack of estrogen (and therefore progesterone) production by the ovary that breaks the cycle. The FSH and LH produced by the pituitary gland continue to be present. Indeed, their level rises during menopause because estrogen is not present to turn off their production. The point here is that menopause does *not* represent a generalized malfunctioning or dysfunctioning or even decline of the endocrine system; only the ovaries no longer function as they did in early adulthood (Asso, 1983).

The median age for menopause in American women is approximately 50–51 years. This figure seems also to apply to at least industrialized countries (Asso, 1983; Nathanson & Lorenz, 1982). As with any physical phenomenon, there are wide individual differences in the timing. Menopause may occur any time between about 45 and 55 and still be considered "normal" (Shepard & Shepard, 1982). The age at menopause has apparently not changed very much across generations, although there is some debate about this issue (Asso, 1983; Giele, 1982a). Thus, it seems less susceptible to the nutritional and health factors that have gradually decreased the age at menarche (first menstrual period) (Asso, 1983).

Several factors do appear to be related to age at menopause (Asso, 1983). Women who smoke tend to have earlier menopause. This may be at least partially due to their lower weight compared to nonsmokers. Heavier women tend to go through menopause later. So do taller women. Women who are married and those who have had children also tend to experience later menopause. Neither socioeconomic status nor the use of birth control pills seems to be associated with age at menopause.

By and large, it appears that menopause is set through genetic or evolutionary forces (Asso, 1983). And menopause occurs well before the end of the maximum human life span (the maximum number of years a human being could possibly live). Indeed, as we already noted, nowadays it occurs well before most women die. From an evolutionary or sociobiological perspective, this differential between the end of reproductive capability and the end of life may seem strange. What evolutionary purpose would be served by women living so long beyond their reproductive role? The answer to this question is unclear (Asso, 1983). It might be noted, however, that motherhood and mothering-type roles are not necessarily over with menopause. In certain societies, it is not unusual for grandmothers to raise their grandchildren while the mothers work (for example, Suggs, 1987). Indeed, this is not uncommon among African-Americans. About three times as many African-American as European-American children are raised by a grandparent (U.S. Bureau of Census, 1989). On the other hand, Carl Jung (1931/1960) argued that these postparental years were crucial in the completion of an individual's personal growth and development (see Chapter 9).

Physical Symptoms: Whatever the explanation for women's longevity beyond reproductive capability, it would certainly not make much sense for them to be physically incapacitated for much of that time. In other words, given that a third of adult life remains, we would not expect that menopause would routinely cause serious permanent physical damage or deficits. Furthermore, since all women experience menopause, it would be inefficient (to say the least) for the process itself to be physically debilitating. What state would society be in if every women had to take a year or more off in order to go through menopause?

It is surprising, then, that American physicians have commonly thought of menopause as a disease rather than a natural phenomenon (see, for example, Grossman & Bart, 1979; Parlee, 1978). In fact, through the 1970s, doctors routinely prescribed estrogen to alleviate menopausal symptoms, even if the woman involved had not reported any (Grossman & Bart, 1979). Such attitudes have probably contributed to the fears of menopause expressed by women who have not yet lived through it (Neugarten, 1968; Neugarten et al, 1968).

While they are not as severe as popular mythology would suggest, there are some physical symptoms associated with menopause. The most common one, occurring in probably about 75 percent of all women, is hot flushes (Asso, 1983; Grossman & Bart, 1980). Not only is it the only symptom that occurs in a substantial majority of women, hot flushes (and the related night sweats) seem to be the only symptoms that "peak" during menopause (Nathanson & Lorenz, 1982). As the name implies, a woman experiencing a hot flush feels very warm in her face and upper body, but her face does not typically turn red from the warmth. In fact, research indicates that there is no change in skin temperature during a flush. However, the woman will often break out in a sweat and perhaps even shiver. She may also experience heart palpitations. The hot flush starts suddenly, although women often know when one is about to occur. Flushes usually last less than 4 minutes and can vary in intensity. The immediate cause is not known, although the phenomenon appears to be related to the rate of loss of estrogen (Asso, 1983).

Beyond this, menopause is a bit like PMS (see Chapter 4) in that virtually every physical symptom seen among middle-aged women has been attributed to it. There have been reports suggesting that menopause causes an increase in headaches (especially migraines), urinary frequency, insomnia, weight gain, dizziness, and heart palpitations (Asso, 1983; Grossman & Bart, 1980; Shepard & Shepard, 1982). The research suggests that none of these is directly caused by menopause, although insomnia may be a problem in women who suffer extensively from night sweats (which are related to menopause). In other words, none of these symptoms appears to be attributable to the menopausal estrogen decline. This is not to say that menopausal women do not experience such problems. But those who do tend to have a history of the problem or be having a particularly difficult menopause (perhaps because of difficulty adjusting to the idea of being sterile or aging). The latter possibility is bolstered by empirical findings indicating that women who tend to have one symptom (other than hot flushes) tend to have several.

Long-term Physical Effects: Thus far the focus has been on physical symptoms occurring during menopause itself. Are there any long-term effects other than sterility? The research suggests two well-established long-term effects of estrogen loss and possible a third. The two established effects are changes in bone mass and the genitals. The more controversial outcome is coronary disease.

The mineral mass of bones peaks somewhere between about 25 and 40 years of age and then is steady for several years. Both men and women experience a loss in bone mass as they age, but the loss is about twice as great and occurs more rapidly in women (Asso, 1983). Furthermore, bone fractures associated with the bone loss are 6 to 10 times more common in women than in men after age 50 (Nathanson & Lorenz, 1982). Women's loss of bone mass accelerates greatly after menopause, and this appears to be due to estrogen deprivation rather than aging. There are several reasons for this conclusion. First, estrogen therapy slows the rate of bone loss. Second, when women of the same age who are pre- versus post-menopausal are compared, the former have much smaller bone loss than the latter. Finally, men, in whom estrogen depletion occurs much later, suffer less and later bone loss.

The question of bone loss is important because it leads to increased rates of fractures and is associated with osteoporosis (Asso, 1983). In *osteoporosis*, the spine gradually degenerates, leading to back pain, curvature of the spine, spinal and hip fractures, and reduced height (Shepard & Shepard, 1982). The fractures can be fatal or can be a contributing factor to death (Nathanson & Lorenz, 1982). The disease is particularly frequent in women over 60 years old and may develop to some extent in as many as half of all postmenopausal women (Asso, 1983; Shepard & Shepard, 1982). Estrogen replacement therapy does appear to be of some value in slowing or even stopping the progress of the disease, but it does not reverse the damage already done (Shepard & Shepard, 1982).

The second well-established physical change involves the genitalia. With the decrease in estrogen, vaginal atrophy occurs. The tissue of the vagina, as well as the labia and other tissue surrounding the vagina, shrinks, thins and dries. There will be less lubrication available during intercourse. The vagina may also become shorter and narrower. These and other changes may result in pain or bleeding during intercourse (Asso, 1983; Shepard & Shepard, 1982).

Such changes need not signal an end to sexual activity, however. First, the changes are gradual, so that the menopausal or immediately postmenopausal women can easily continue intercourse. Second, if the atrophy is mild, a lubricating cream or jelly can be used to facilitate intercourse (and, of course, intercourse is not the only form of sexual expression). Third, estrogen replacement therapy will alleviate and even reverse many of these symptoms (Asso, 1983; Shepard & Shepard, 1982). Thus, postmenopausal women can continue to enjoy sex.

The more controversial long-term effect concerns the relationship between cardiovascular disease and menopause. Before age 50 (premenopause), coronary disease is relatively rare in women compared to men (Asso, 1983; Nathanson & Lorenz, 1982). Men are roughly three times more likely to die from heart attacks than women are. And women who don't smoke almost never have heart attacks before age 50. After menopause, however, the rate of cardiovascular disease in women rises. The gap between male and female deaths from myocardial infarction drops to 2:1. Some of this shift may be attributable to the rise in cholesterol in the postmenopausal years, since high levels of cholesterol have been associated with increased risk for heart problems.

However, it is not clear whether any of these changes is attributable to menopause itself. Estrogen replacement therapy does not clearly reduce the risk of cardiovascular problems in either men or women (Asso, 1983; Nathanson & Lorenz, 1982). Indeed, some research has indicated that estrogen treatment may actually increase the risk of heart attacks (Asso, 1983). Also, arguing that estrogen depletion contributes to increased cardiovascular problems implies that estrogen serves some kind of protective function. This would further imply a gap between the rates of cardiovascular problems in men and women during young adulthood. As we have seen, such a gender gap exists in the United States, but it does not exist in countries such as Japan (Nathanson & Lorenz, 1982). Thus, although there is a rise in the rate of cardiac problems among women following menopause, it is not at all clear that the two events are related.

Psychological Symptoms: There is a widespread belief that menopause causes women to behave in unpredictable, abnormal ways. This is true among both men and women, who often feel that they have insufficient information about what really happens during menopause (see, for example, Neugarten 1968 and Neugarten et al., 1968 for women's specific concerns). Even medical professionals have traditionally endorsed this belief. The following quote from a conference on menopause captures this attitude:

> ... Dr. (Howard W.) Jones (Professor of Obstetrics and Gynecology, The Johns Hopkins School of Medicine) characterized menopausal women as being a caricature of their younger selves at their emotional worst.... (Parlee, 1978, p. 223, quoting from Ryan & Gibson, 1971, p. 3)

The most commonly cited psychological problem is menopausal depression (also known as involutional melancholia). However, professionals have also mentioned increased anxiety, tension, unpredictability, and irritability as "normal" symptoms of menopause (Asso, 1983; Parlee, 1978). Such conclusions were based on clinical samples and, as we noted earlier, these samples are probably biased toward finding problems. Indeed, research using more diverse, nonclinical samples has failed to support this picture of psychiatric disturbance. Women do not feel more stressed, depressed, or irritable. Women who do encounter difficulty tend to be preoccupied with aging or the loss of social roles (such as motherhood), rather than suffering from an extreme or unusual loss of estrogen (Asso, 1983). Indeed, some researchers have actually reported a decrease in psychological problems during and after menopause compared to the years immediately preceding it (Asso, 1983).

Since Bernice Neugarten's groundbreaking work in the 1960s (Neugarten, 1968; Neugarten et al., 1968), it has been clear that most women do not respond negatively to menopause. Many actually are glad to not have to worry about menstrual periods or pregnancy anymore. They are also happy that their active mothering role is ending because their time will now be more their own. Even women who are not particularly pleased are not very worried or distressed. In fact, they are more likely to be worried about widowhood than menopause (Neugarten, 1968; Neugarten et al., 1968).

It has been suggested that Neugarten's findings might be too optimistic, that perhaps women of that cohort did not feel comfortable complaining about menopause or women's roles. However, more recent research has yielded similar conclusions. For example, half of the menopausal and postmenopausal women in one survey reported that the change was "easy" or "moderately easy" (Grossman & Bart, 1980). And the decreasing prescription of estrogen for menopausal problems underscores the shifting beliefs held by doctors about the incidence of psychiatric problems among menopausal women (Giele, 1982a; Shepard & Shepard, 1982).

The long-term effects of menopause are similar. Many women feel freer and more in control of their own lives (Goodman, 1980; Neugarten et al., 1968). Rates of first admission to hospitals for virtually any type of psychiatric disorder (except organic brain syndromes) drop during the menopausal and postmenopausal years (LaRue, Dessonville, & Jarvik, 1985).

There is some evidence that memory impairment in postmenopausal women responds to estrogen treatment (Asso, 1983). Such data are severely limited, however. And since we know there are age-related trends in memory functioning, considerably more research will be needed to ascertain whether or not there is a link between memory and menopause.

PHYSICAL ILLNESS

We have already seen some evidence that illness rates begin to increase in middle age. Cataracts, impotence, prostate problems, and changes associated with menopause provide examples. This does not mean that the body is falling apart. Nor does it mean that everyone develops some form of serious illness during middle age. Indeed, increasingly, most people are quite healthy.

In fact, it is not even the case that all diseases become more common in middle age. For example, may acute conditions actually occur less frequently as we age. In 1982, upper respiratory infections occurred in over 90 percent of children under 6 but only about one-third of people between 17 and 44 had them. The rate of upper respiratory infections continued to drop with age so that about one-fourth of 45- 64-year-olds and less than one-fifth of the people over 65 had them (Statistical Abstracts 1986). Furthermore, many middle-aged people report that they have more energy and feel better now than they did when they were younger (Neugarten, 1968). Keep in mind that there are no longer any sick children around to keep parents up all night or to give them the flu.

Nonetheless, it is important to understand the developmental nature of illness. Too often people have confused the effects of illness with aging. The classic example is severe memory loss in old age. People used to believe that this was a normal outcome of the aging process. Now we believe that memory loss due to aging is relatively small and that the severe memory losses seen in senility are actually attributable to organic brain syndromes. We need, then, to distinguish primary aging, which reflects normal development effects, from secondary aging, which reflects the effects of illnesses that become more common with age (Busse, 1978).

Of course, we cannot overlook the effects of a serious or chronic illness on the sick person. Nor should we underestimate the impact of someone's illness or death on their family. Clearly, then, it is important to understand both the causes and effects of illness.

Statistics

Chronic conditions and illnesses requiring hospitalization both begin to increase during middle age. Table 8–2 indicates that there are dramatic increases in heart conditions, hypertension, diabetes, arthritis, and hearing problems. Many of these continue to show substantial increases in frequency in old age. And, as Table 8–3 indicates, middle-aged and elderly people with these disorders are much more likely than young adults to be

TABLE 8-2:   Rate per 1000 People of Chronic Conditions in Different Age Groups in 1982

Chronic Condition	AGE			
	Under 18	18–44	45–65	>65 Years
Heart conditions	17.2	34.7	136.8	256.8
High blood pressure	2.9	58.9	245.7	390.4
Chronic bronchitis	33.7	24.5	44.2	52.0
Asthma	40.1	29.0	36.3	40.8
Hay fever, allergic rhinitis without asthma	55.1	109.3	87.5	64.5
Dermatitis	40.0	40.3	38.2	24.9
Arthritis	2.7	55.3	276.2	495.8
Diabetes	1.4	9.2	57.6	88.9
Migraine	7.8	47.0	49.9	19.2
Visual impairments	13.1	31.2	53.4	101.1
Hearing impairments	19.7	48.8	142.7	299.7

Source: Statistical Abstract of the United States, 1986, p. 116. Washington, D.C.: Government Printing Office.

debilitated by them. Note, though, that other chronic conditions, such as migraines, asthma, or visual impairment, show much smaller increases. Still others, such as hay fever and certain skin diseases, actually show decreases. This again serves to emphasize that aging does not always bring illness and that different systems of the body age at different rates.

Given the increases in chronic disorders, it is not surprising that middle-aged and elderly people are more likely than children and young adults

TABLE 8-3:   Causes and Levels of Activity Limitations by Age Group, 1982

Condition	AGE		
	<45	45–64	>65 Years
Percent limited by:			
Heart condition	4.7	20.1	26.0
Arthritis	4.8	22.0	30.5
Hypertension	3.2	16.4	16.8
Back/spine impairment	13.9	9.9	4.6
Percent of all persons with:			
No activity limitation	93.0	75.0	59.3
Activity limitation	7.0	25.0	40.7
in major activity	4.7	18.9	27.0

Source: Statistical Abstract of the United States, 1986, p. 117. Washington, D.C.: Government Printing Office.

to be hospitalized. The duration of the average hospital stay also increases with age. Table 8–4 shows the rate of hospitalization and duration of stay for various age groups; the table also indicates why the people were hospitalized. Note that the reason for hospitalization tends to become more life-threatening with age. So, for example, the most common reason for hospitalizing young adult women is childbirth. In fact, none of the five most common reasons for hospitalization in this group (delivery, benign neoplasms, psychoses, menstrual problems, miscarriage) is usually life-threatening. This is not meant to imply that such illnesses cannot be serious or that surgery ought to be treated lightly under these circumstances. But compare these reasons for hospitalization to those for middle-aged women. Now, in addition to gall bladder problems, psychoses, and benign tumors, we also find heart disease and cancer, the two leading causes of death in the United States. Heart disease alone accounts for about one-third of all American deaths (Booth-Kewley & Friedman, 1987).

Gender differences also are evident. Heart disease becomes a major cause of hospitalization sooner for men than for women. And, as Table 8–4 indicates, young adult and middle-aged men stay in the hospital longer than women do. However, women are more likely to report being ill and to seek medical help. This does not necessarily mean that women are less healthy than men; it may simply reflect women's greater willingness to admit illness (Nathanson & Lorenz, 1982).

Gender and age differences are also apparent in the mortality statistics. As we noted in Chapter 1, women have a longer life expectancy than men. Table 8–5 shows the rate and cause of death for men and women of various ages. With the exception of female suicide (which peaks in middle age), the death rate increases with age independently of the cause of death. Middle-aged men are about twice as likely as middle-aged women to die. And men and women die of different causes. For example, men between the ages of 25 and 54 are about three times more likely than women to die from heart disease. The difference narrows somewhat between age 55 and 64 (when about 2.7 men die for every 1 woman), but even after 65 the rate is slightly higher for men than women (Statistical Abstracts, 1986). On the other hand, women between 35 and 44 are slightly more likely than men to die of cancer. Table 8–6 further indicates that men and women are susceptible to different forms of fatal cancers.

Life-Style Factors in Illness

We have already seen that, in general, physical deterioration associated with normal aging is *not* sufficient to explain the increases in illness and death during the middle years. As is the case with health and longevity throughout the life span, genetics plays a role. Diabetes is a genetically transmitted disease. And various forms of cancer (including uterine and breast cancer) and heart disease may involve genetic predispositions, although they are apparently not genetically transmitted (Previte, 1983; Shepard & Shepard, 1982). Many of the health problems commonly emerging during the middle years, however, are substantially affected by life-style fac-

TABLE 8-4: Hospital Discharges and Days of Care, by Sex, Age, and Diagnosis, 1987

Age and First-Listed Diagnosis	DISCHARGES Number (1,000)	DISCHARGES Per 1,000 Persons	Days of Care per 1,000 Persons	Average Stay (days)
Male				
All ages*	13,568	116.0	805.7	6.9
Diseases of heart	2,016	17.2	115.0	6.7
Malignant neoplasms	868	7.4	66.9	9.0
Fracture, all sites	519	4.4	36.7	8.3
Pneumonia, all forms	468	4.0	31.7	7.9
Cerebrovascular disease	392	3.4	32.3	9.6
Under 15 years*	1,537	57.3	269.9	4.7
Pneumonia, all forms	114	4.2	13.6	3.2
Acute respiratory infection	113	4.2	18.6	4.4
Bronchitis, emphysema†	105	3.9	12.7	3.3
Congenital anomalies	79	2.9	15.9	5.4
Chronic disease of tonsils and adenoids	77	2.9	3.5	1.2
15–44 years*	3,874	68.7	441.1	6.4
Fracture, all sites	274	4.9	36.8	7.6
Psychoses	231	4.1	51.4	12.5
Alcohol dependence syndrome	160	2.8	30.9	10.9
Diseases of heart	157	2.8	15.8	5.7
Intervertebral disc disorders	157	2.8	14.8	5.3
45–64 years*	3,528	163.1	1,099.1	6.7
Diseases of heart	795	36.7	218.8	6.0
Malignant neoplasms	275	12.7	114.2	9.0
Intervertebral disc disorders	103	4.8	29.5	6.2
Cerebrovascular disease	102	4.7	47.3	10.0
Inguinal hernia	88	4.0	8.8	2.2
65 years old and older*	4,629	381.9	3,163.3	8.3
Diseases of heart	1,054	87.0	639.0	7.3
Malignant neoplasms	485	40.0	374.0	9.3
Cerebrovascular disease	273	22.5	206.3	9.2
Pneumonia, all forms	222	18.4	180.9	9.9
Hyperplasia of prostate	206	17.0	96.4	5.7
Female				
All ages*	19,818	158.9	968.0	6.1
Delivery	3,911	31.4	96.1	3.1
Diseases of heart	1,720	13.8	99.9	7.2
Malignant neoplasms	1,011	8.1	67.7	8.3
Fracture, all sites	543	4.4	41.0	9.4
Pneumonia, all forms	456	3.7	29.6	8.1
Under 15 years*	1,150	45.0	209.9	4.7
Pneumonia, all forms	90	3.5	15.5	4.4
Acute respiratory infection	76	3.0	8.9	3.0
Chronic disease of tonsils and adenoids	69	2.7	3.1	1.2
Bronchitis, emphysema†	67	2.6	9.3	3.6
Congenital anomalies	57	2.2	15.8	7.0
15–44 years*	9,268	160.3	669.7	4.2
Delivery	3,897	67.4	206.6	3.1
Pregnancy w/abortive outcome	297	5.1	11.3	2.2
Psychoses	216	3.7	52.0	13.9
Inflammatory disease of female pelvic organs	184	3.2	13.9	4.4
Benign neoplasms	180	3.1	14.1	4.5
45–64 years*	3,571	151.2	1,040.5	6.9
Diseases of heart	441	18.7	121.8	6.5
Malignant neoplasms	383	16.2	125.0	7.7
Benign neoplasms	113	4.8	25.3	5.3
Cholelithiasis	109	4.6	28.2	6.1
Psychoses	108	4.6	64.9	14.3
65 years old and older*	5,830	329.1	2,938.6	8.9
Diseases of heart	1,186	66.9	511.0	7.6
Malignant neoplasms	468	26.4	250.6	9.5
Cerebrovascular disease	392	22.1	236.8	10.7
Fracture, all sites	307	17.3	203.0	11.7
Pneumonia, all forms	223	12.6	126.9	10.1

*Includes other first-listed diagnoses, not shown separately. †Includes asthma.

Represents estimates of inpatients discharged from noninstitutional, short-stay hospitals, exclusive of federal hospitals. Excludes newborn. Based on sample data collected from the National Hospital Discharge Survey, a sample survey of hospital records of patients discharged in year shown; subject to sampling variability.

Source: Statistical Abstract of the United States, 1990, p. 109. Washington, D.C.: Government Printing Office.

TABLE 8–5: Deaths in 1986 from Various Causes by Age and Sex

	Heart Disease	Cancer	Accidents	Cerebrovascular Diseases	Liver Disease
Males					
25–34 yrs	2.5	2.9	13.5	.5	.8
35–44 yrs	9.4	6.6	7.9	1.3	2.3
45–54 yrs	24.5	18.9	5.2	2.4	3.2
55–64 yrs	65.6	54.8	5.3	6.3	4.7
65–74 yrs	110.6	83.1	5.1	14.1	4.0
75–84 yrs	114.3	62.5	4.9	21.3	1.5
85+ yrs	62.2	19.3	2.8	13.0	.3
Females					
25–34 yrs	1.2	2.7	3.4	.5	.4
35–44 yrs	3.0	8.3	2.4	1.1	.9
45–54 yrs	8.5	18.9	1.8	2.2	1.4
55–64 yrs	28.7	44.0	2.4	5.5	2.4
65–74 yrs	70.1	63.7	3.4	14.3	2.5
75–84 yrs	124.7	54.1	4.7	30.7	1.4
85+ yrs	137.1	25.4	4.2	35.9	.3

The numbers represent deaths in thousands. Remember that there are more women than men, especially in old age.

Source: *Statistical Abstract of the United States,* 1990, p. 80. Washington, D.C.: Government Printing Office.

TABLE 8–6: Death Rates for Various Forms of Cancer by Sex and Age

	Respiratory	Digestive Tract	Breast	Lymphatic	Urinary Tract
Males					
35–44 yrs	9.8	9.0	.1	4.7	1.3
45–54 yrs	69.4	40.1	.2	10.3	7.3
55–64 yrs	229.2	126.6	.5	23.9	21.8
65–74 yrs	423.2	268.6	1.1	55.4	49.7
75–84 yrs	567.9	465.3	1.8	93.9	105.8
85+ yrs	472.9	665.0	3.1	110.8	174.8
Females					
35–44 yrs	6.0	5.6	18.3	2.2	.7
45–54 yrs	35.1	25.4	45.4	6.4	3.1
55–64 yrs	94.4	72.7	80.9	16.5	9.2
65–74 yrs	152.0	162.5	109.9	38.3	19.0
75–84 yrs	146.3	303.1	136.2	67.2	39.1
85+ yrs	113.0	482.1	180.0	77.1	62.0

The numbers represent deaths per 100,000 population in the specified group in 1986.

Source: *Statistical Abstract of the United States,* 1990, p. 84. Washington, D.C.: Government Printing Office.

tors, including diet, exercise, and smoking. In fact, the Surgeon General has suggested that the causes of more than half of all diseases and disabilities could be controlled by the affected person, thereby preventing the illness (Siegler & Costa, 1985). There is also evidence that personality may play a role in illness.

Diet: Compared to many other cultures, Americans consume a relatively high-fat, low-fiber, high-calorie diet. Many Americans also use excessive amounts of salt and sugar. Of course, they are not always aware of this, since Americans also frequently eat packaged or fast foods which may be high in sodium or fat. Poor eating habits may leave a person malnourished *and* overweight. Obesity is particularly a risk if the individual does not exercise regularly.

What difference does all of this make? Before outlining some of the links between diet, weight, and disease, it is important to emphasize that the discussion here concerns *risk factors* rather than causes. For example, high sodium intake is associated with heart attack (myocardial infarct) (Feldman, 1983; Previte, 1983). But sodium does not cause heart disease. In fact, sodium is necessary for normal bodily functioning. Sodium deficiencies can, for example, cause muscle cramping (this is especially likely in hot weather) or kidney failure. The heart attack itself is due to the death of heart muscle cells, not to high levels of salt.

Although there is still considerable debate concerning the role of diet in heart disease, there is a growing consensus that high levels of fat intake increase the risk (Feldman, 1983). More specifically, the cholesterol contained in animal fats seems to be dangerous. High levels of cholesterol in young adults and middle-aged persons (under about 55 years) seem to bode especially poorly (Feldman, 1983). Cholesterol contributes to a buildup of fat in the coronary arteries. This may damage the artery walls (atherosclerosis) so that the risk of heart attack is increased. There are genetic differences in the processing of fat, so that simply assessing a person's diet is not sufficient as a means of monitoring cholesterol. Middle-aged people, especially those with a family history of heart disease, should have their cholesterol levels checked by a physician.

High cholesterol levels do not doom a person to a heart attack. As was noted earlier, this is a risk factor, not a direct causal agent. Furthermore, cholesterol levels can be reduced. Even the buildup of fatty deposits in coronary arteries is reversible (Blankenhorn et al., 1987) through a low-fat diet and cholesterol-reducing drugs.

Obesity also increases the risk of heart attack (Feldman, 1983). Some of this risk is attributable to the higher levels of cholesterol and other fats in the blood of overweight people. In addition, the heart of an obese person has to work harder in order to supply oxygen to all the body tissues. Again, obesity is not a death sentence; its effects can be reversed through permanent weight loss (accomplished by a combination of exercise and diet).

Excessive sodium use may be associated with high blood pressure, another condition that can damage the arterial walls and lead to heart attacks (Feldman, 1983). High salt intake alone cannot cause high blood pressure. It creates a risk when combined with a genetic predisposition for hypertension. The risk is heightened if the high salt use is a lifetime habit and if it is accompanied by a low level of potassium in the diet (Feldman, 1983). In fact, the ratio of sodium to potassium may be more crucial than the absolute level of salt intake.

Heart attacks are not the only potentially fatal disease affected by diet. There is some evidence, albeit mixed, that high fat consumption contributes to the development of colon cancer (Smith & Brubaker, 1983) and breast cancer (Nash & Wilwerth, 1991). It has also been suggested that low fiber consumption may increase the risk of colon cancer. However, the support for this theory is very sparse. On the other hand, there is evidence that eating cruciferous vegetables (such as cabbage, broccoli, brussels sprouts, and turnips) reduces the risk of colon cancer (Smith & Brubaker, 1983).

Correlation population studies suggest that foods containing nitrites (such as dried, smoked, and salted meats or fish) are associated with the development of stomach cancer. Diets low in fresh fruits and vegetables also are correlated with higher rates of stomach cancer (Smith & Brubaker, 1983).

It is important to reiterate that these dietary factors *increase the risk* of cancer and heart attacks; they are not direct causes in the way that the measles virus causes measles. Rather, they interact with other factors, including genetic predispositions, to create the conditions that allow the disease to develop.

There are a few other effects of diet, including obesity, that deserve at least brief mention (Bernstein, 1983). People with high cholesterol diets, especially overweight women, are at increased risk to develop gall bladder disease. Overweight persons are more likely to develop diabetes, assuming that they have the genetic predisposition. They are also more likely to develop osteoarthritis (especially in the joints that bear the person's weight) and various respiratory problems.

Cigarette Smoking: Cigarette smoking, like diet, does not seem to significantly endanger health during the adolescent and young adult years. In other words, these young smokers do not suffer from serious lung disease, yet their lungs are being damaged, and by middle age the damage starts to become evident.

Cigarette smoking has long been implicated in the development of lung cancer. Indeed, it is often cited as a primary factor in the higher rate of lung cancer in men over women and as the reason that lung cancer is now increasing among women (Nathanson & Lorenz, 1982). Lung cancer is one of the most serious forms of cancer and is the leading cancer killer among middle-aged and elderly men. Among women, it is second only to breast cancer in 45-to 54-year-olds and is the leading cancer killer in 55-to 64-year-olds (*Statistical Abstracts*, 1986). Stopping smoking at any point prior to the onset of the disease seems to significantly reduce the risk of lung cancer (Kart et al., 1978).

Cigarette smoking also increases the risk of chronic obstructive lung disease, or chronic bronchitis and emphysema (Kart et al., 1978). Both are marked by a shortness of breath and a chronic cough. Contrary to popular opinion, shortness of breath is not a normal occurrence among the middle-aged and elderly. If it appears chronically, it should be medically evaluated. These conditions are treatable through exercise, drugs, and respiratory therapy. However, they cause permanent irreversible damage to the lungs. Eventually, people with emphysema often die of heart failure (Kart et al., 1978).

Sun Exposure: Part of the American ideal of beauty is a good tan. The comic strip *Doonesbury* had a series about the "ultimate tan." There are tanning booths and salons for those of us who can't get to the beach, and for people who don't even have time to get to the tanning salons, creams and lotions provide the appearance of a tan.

Although a tan may give a young person a "glow of health," it is actually quite dangerous. By middle age, the effects of years of exposure to the sun's ultraviolet rays begin to take their toll in the form of increased risk of skin cancer (Kart et al., 1978). There are actually three types of skin cancer; basal cell carcinoma, squamous cell carcinoma, and malignant melanoma. The last of these is the most serious and is also the one least likely to be heavily influenced by sun exposure (though it does seem to play some role). Basal and squamous cell carcinoma are not usually fatal unless left untreated for extended periods of time, although the latter is more likely to metastasize (spread to other organs). However, they can be painful and disfiguring. People who have had extensive exposure to the sun's ultraviolet

Life-style habits, including drinking and smoking, begin to take their toll in middle age.

rays, particularly those who have suffered sunburns that blistered, are at increased risk for these forms of skin cancer.

Type A and Heart Disease

Personality has been implicated as a causal factor in a variety of diseases ranging from asthma to ulcers to cancer. But no personality-disease relationship has attracted the attention of the potential link between Type A and heart disease. In preparing a statistical review of the relationship, Stephanie Booth-Kewley and Howard Friedman (1987) identified 150 studies of personality and heart disease done between 1945 and 1984. Furthermore, even laypeople have a concept of such a relationship. We routinely associate heart attacks with middle-aged men (much more so than women) who are ambitious, somewhat mean, driven workaholics. Even the term Type A has become a part of mainstream American language.

What is Type A? First, it does not seem to be a true personality type. There does not appear to be a large genetic component. Nor is there a constant, inherent difference between the physiology of Type As versus Type Bs. In fact, the behavior of Type As and Type Bs differs only under very specific circumstances, typically situations designed to challenge the person (especially intellectually) or elicit competitiveness (Carver & Humphries, 1982; Rosenman & Chesney, 1982). Second, it is not the equivalent of stress. Stress implies some form of emergency or unusual strain (internal or external) that requires physical or psychological adaptation. Type A, on the other hand, is more a style of approaching situations or problems that

Type A men may be at increased risk for cardiovascular disease.

may be challenging but not necessarily stressful (Rosenman & Chesney, 1982).

Type A, also known as the Type A behavior pattern or the TABP, is a constellation of characteristics, attitudes, and behaviors. Most commonly it is defined to include ambition, competitiveness (in a "hard-driving," aggressive manner), and impatience. Such people tend to talk and do things very quickly and be easily irritated. Though they may often appear to be tense, they are not anxious or frightened by challenges (Rosenman & Chesney, 1982). People who do not show these characteristics are labeled Type B.

Why TABP should increase the risk of coronary heart disease (CHD) is not completely clear. However, it does appear that certain physiological reactions in Type As are similar to those that contribute to artherosclerotic disease (thickening of the arterial walls, which eventually leads to blockage or damage). For example, Type As tend to show elevated or unstable levels of blood pressure, catecholamines, and cholesterol. All of these are also associated with artery damage (Carver & Humphries, 1982; Rosenman & Chesney, 1982). Recent evidence suggests that cholesterol may somehow interact with Type A personality to produce elevated levels of cortisol and catecholamines under stress. This is not true for Type Bs (Suarez et al., 1991). Other evidence suggests that Type A men may have chronically elevated sympathetic nervous system and neurohormonal activity (Williams et al., 1991).

Early research (prior to the mid-1970s) consistently showed a moderate correlation between TABP and CHD. Indeed, in 1978 a government panel concluded that the link was empirically established (Cooper et al., 1981). More recent research has frequently failed to find a link between TABP and CHD, creating a controversy as to whether the relationship exists at all (see Booth-Kewley & Friedman, 1987; Fischman, 1987). There are several possible explanations for the differences in results.

First, researchers do not always agree on a definition of Type A. They do not even agree on the underlying components of Type A. Physiological reactivity, need for control, and need for productivity has each been suggested as the core concept in TABP. There have also been different measures used to assess TABP with the easier-to-use but less reliable Jenkins Activity Scale gaining in popularity (Booth-Kewley & Friedman, 1987). And CHD actually involves several different problems, including artherosclerosis, myocardial infarction (heart attack), angina, and cardiac death, raising yet another possible definitional confound.

An analysis by Booth-Kewley and Friedman (1987) helped sort out the effects of these and other methodological problems. They concluded that there was a real and reliable relationship between TABP and CHD. This effect is smaller than the original studies estimated, but sufficiently large to warrant attention from public health officials. The relationship is more or less independent of gender, smoking, age, education, and blood pressure. This suggests that TABP's association with CHD is not due to any relationship to one of these other risk factors.

Not all aspects of TABP are equally associated with CHD (Booth-Kewley & Friedman, 1987). Aggressiveness and competitiveness (in a driven

small groups focus class
decide on + teach to
Physical and Cognitive Development **239**

style) seem to be particularly strongly associated with CHD. On the other hand, job commitment is not. The stereotype that "all work and no play" leads Jack to have a heart attack is apparently wrong (see also Chapter 11). Other researchers have similarly reported that competitiveness, especially when coupled with hostility, is a particularly strong predictor of CHD (Rosenman & Chesney, 1982).

The TABP-CHD relationship is weaker in prospective than in cross-sectional studies (Booth-Kewley & Friedman, 1987). This may indicate that TABP does not actually in any way "cause" CHD. Instead, the behaviors associated with TABP somehow co-occur with CHD. However, the small number of prospective studies make it impossible to draw a definitive conclusion.

Booth-Kewley and Friedman also looked at the relationship between CHD and several other personality factors. Interestingly, they found that depression was about as strongly related to CHD as TABP. In fact, in prospective studies depression was actually a stronger predictor of CHD. This is consistent with other findings that depression often immediately precedes sudden death (Carver & Humphries, 1982). Other, less dramatic associations were found between CHD and hostility, anger, and anxiety (Booth-Kewley & Friedman, 1987). Recent evidence indicates that lack of spousal support and high levels of masculinity may result in poor recovery from heart attack (Helgeson, 1991).

All this would seem to suggest a relationship between personality and CHD. The personality component may not be TABP as traditionally defined, but at least certain components of TABP seem to be concomitants of CHD. TABP, as well as depression, are certainly amenable to intervention (Roseman & Chesney, 1982), making this one of those "controllable" factors that contribute to the death of middle-aged Americans.

COGNITIVE DEVELOPMENT

By and large, cognitive skills are at a plateau during middle age. At least in terms of psychometrically measured intelligence, people have reached their peak levels of performance and have not yet begun to show the declines sometimes associated with old age. Research by stage-oriented theorists such as Arlin or Commons (see Chapter 4) has not typically extended into middle age. Rather, they have simply tried to establish whether a postformal operational stage exists. There are two exceptions to this trend. First, there is some research on whether there is a regression back through the Piagetian stages. In other words, researchers have examined whether or not people revert to concrete and even preoperational thought as they age. Again, the bulk of this research is with elderly adults.

Decision Making

The other exception is K. Warner Schaie's (1977/1978) theory. As we outlined in Chapter 4, Schaie argued that while the structure of adult thought did not change dramatically, the function or use of thought did. In middle age, we are in the *responsible stage.*. We make long-range plans, as we did in young adulthood. But now those plans are tempered by consideration of our family's needs and desires. So, we might turn down a transfer, even if it involves greater potential for advancement, if our spouse has a job that would be difficult to replace or if the schools are not as good as the ones in which our children are currently enrolled.

Some people are responsible for more than just their family's well-being. Their positions mean that their decisions affect other employees of the company or, in the case of government leaders, perhaps an entire community or nation. Such people must evaluate the effect of their decisions within this more complex context. These people are in a substage of the responsible stage known as the *executive stage.* (Schaie, 1977/1978).

It is easy to imagine how someone in the executive stage may have to decide to "sacrifice" one component of a constituency for another larger component or for the "common good." In some sense, this is what leaders are doing when they make the difficult decision to send young men and women off to war to protect or defend their nation. It may be less obvious that all middle-aged adults are faced with similar conflicts, albeit on a smaller scale. Middle-aged adults are involved in a variety of interpersonal systems (Levinson, 1986; Newman, 1982). These include family relationships, intimate relationships, and business relationships. There may be conflicts within or across the systems. A business trip with a colleague of the opposite sex may cause some jealousy within an existing intimate relationship. Or the demands of an ill parent may be more than children or spouse

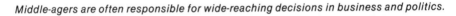

Middle-agers are often responsible for wide-reaching decisions in business and politics.

or job can accommodate. Decisions must be made as to who "wins" and who "loses" in such situations.

The decisions to be made during middle age are both practical and complex. They have ramifications for both the individual and colleagues and family. While middle-aged people certainly have the intellectual capability to deal with such problems, it may be surprising that more of them do not feel overwhelmed by the nature of the problems they face. Barbara Newman (1982) has suggested at least two reasons why they don't.

Problems as Stimulation: The problems that face middle-aged individuals involve families, friends, and jobs. Often the solutions have long-term implications for a variety of people. Middle-aged people know all of this. They know that choosing the right pension plan, or failing to establish one at all, will affect not only their old age, but the quality of life of their loved ones. Of course, this is true of many of the decisions they must make. In other words, there is a continuity between, or at least a similarity among, the problems they face. They need to establish a set of principles, a life plan or philosophy, that will give continuity to their decisions (B. Newman, 1982). Such a plan might include an ordering of priorities, goals for oneself and individual family members, the values one most wants children to learn, or the standard of living one wants for oneself and one's family.

Since problems are seen as interrelated, they become something of an energizing source for cognitive growth (B. Newman, 1982). We might, for example, recognize a discrepancy between reality and ideals, leading us to try to generate new solutions to old problems. In seeking such solutions, we may discover heretofore unnoticed relationships or answers to other problems. Newman provides an example of a woman trying to figure out why she cannot stick to a diet who in the process of examining her eating habits begins to realize the strong influence of her husband on most of her daily life and choices.

Trying to implement newly made decisions may also prove stimulating as we compare, evaluate, and revise. This problem solving, then, is challenging and stimulating. We have a strong motivation—our concern for ourselves and our loved ones—to resolve problems effectively and efficiently. The problems are not just inconveniences or mental exercises; they are an interrelated chain of meaningful decisions.

Metacognition: Not all of a middle-aged individual's time and mental energy is used in solving immediate, pressing problems. Indeed, such a situation would be exhausting and would impede the process of formulating a life philosophy. Defining (and refining) a life plan requires reflection. It requires time to daydream, reminisce, evaluate past decisions, and try to predict the future (B. Newman, 1982).

In other words, we must be able to monitor our thought processes. We need to analyze our decisions and how we made them. What went wrong? What went right? People who have suffered through a divorce often think about the decision (and how they made it) repeatedly. Indeed, the decision-making process itself is often drawn out over several years as the person thinks and rethinks about the marriage and spouse (Kelly, 1982). We look for flaws in our reasoning. Are we being too harsh in judging our spouse? We look for alternative solutions. Would counseling be helpful?

In analyzing our decisions, we are engaging in metacognition. *Metacognition*—thinking about thinking and thought processes—also involves introspection. Newman (1982) argues that these metacognitive processes become more dominant during middle age as people try to define a philosophy of life. She is not alone in suggesting this. As we shall see in Chapter 9, many theorists, beginning with Jung, have argued that greater introspection is an outcome of the midlife crisis.

Experience and Skills

There is considerable debate among researchers in cognitive development concerning the role of experience and practice in achieving and maintaining intellectual skills (Denney, 1982). Most of the research, and even theorizing, on this issue has focused on the elderly and so is discussed in Chapter 12. Although the research on this issue is extremely limited (Salthouse, Babcock, Skovronek, Mitchell, & Palmon, 1990), its implications for cognitive functioning in middle age are worth mentioning.

As we saw in Chapter 4, several theorists (notably Horn and Cattell) have identified various components of intelligence. Some of these, such as crystallized intelligence, seem to improve with age; others, such as fluid intelligence, seem to decline. The assumption has been that basic reasoning processes somehow are not maintained during aging and that perhaps this is due to lack of use (Denney, 1982; Salthouse & Mitchell, 1990; Salthouse et al., 1990).

It does seem to be the case that certain forms of reasoning depend on experience. Take, for example, statistical and methodological reasoning (Lehman & Nisbett, 1990). Statistical reasoning involves principles that indicate an understanding of the law of large numbers and its derivatives (regression to the mean and that large samples yield more stable and reliable results). Methodological reasoning concerns understanding the role of confounding variables in evaluating a problem. Such reasoning is valuable in daily life when we need, for example, to evaluate the claims of advertisers. Research has indicated that specific types of academic training, especially in the social sciences, are helpful in developing these skills. Similarly, development of conditional reasoning skills, a form of deductive reasoning, is particularly facilitated by study in the natural sciences and the humanities (Lehman & Nisbett, 1990).

Such findings suggest that experience is helpful in the acquisition of various types of reasoning. But is it helpful in the maintenance of such skills? The issue of statistical reasoning and propositional logic has not been directly addressed. However, Salthouse and his colleagues (1990) demonstrated that men with substantial visual-spatial experience (architects) had better visual-spatial skills than those with less experience. Nonetheless, in both groups of men, older men showed poorer performance than young men. By age 60, the men scored 1 to 2 standard deviations lower than young men on various visual-spatial tasks. This does not suggest that older men were no longer competent architects. It does, however, indicate that certain cognitive skills apparently suffer age-related decrements even in the face of considerable use and experience (Salthouse et al., 1990). In another study using self-reports of visual-spatial skills use, Salthouse and Mitchell (1990) also found that age-related declines in spatial-visualization measures were similar across various levels of experience. Other skills, including prose recall (Rice & Meyer, 1986) and visual-manual transcription (Salthouse, 1984), also seem to show age effects that are independent of experience. Thus, while an experienced person may have better skills than an inexperienced agemate, the experience does not guarantee maintenance of the skills. Of course, this does not mean that all skills decline independently of how frequently they are used.

SUMMARY

The physical changes that occur during middle age are easy to see. Hair turns gray. Many men lose some hair. Wrinkles become more obvious. Fat-muscle ratio shifts so that the middle-aged often look flabby compared to young adults. More people wear glasses more of the time. And a noticeable number develop a disease or disorder.

Yet most of these changes do not have a substantial effect on daily functioning. In some sense, then, they are more apparent than real. Certainly, the decline in physical strength and sensory acuity may limit performance on some jobs. But only some jobs are so affected, and even in these cases experience can often compensate for the losses. Ability for self-care is certainly not lost. Indeed, middle-aged people often shoulder more responsibility for others than any other cohort. This is evident in Schaie's description of this as the "responsibility" stage of adult cognitive development.

One ability that is lost is female reproduction. Menopause marks the end of a women's fertility. Myths about menopause abound among both women and men of all ages. Our image of "the change" as a time marked by depression and anxiety seems, in general, to be inaccurate. Most women move through menopause with few physical symptoms. The most common of these, hot flushes, has little effect on daily activities. Other symptoms may be less attributable to menopause as a physical event and more due to the woman's self-image and understanding of her role. Most women do not react very negatively to the loss of reproductive capability. Indeed, they seem glad to no longer have to be concerned about unwanted pregnancy.

While most middle-aged people are quite healthy, a fair number do develop serious, even fatal, conditions. Many of these illnesses are at least partially caused by life style. Most of the relevant life-style variables, such as a poor diet, too much sun, or cigarette smoking, have a cumulative effect, so their negative impact is evidenced in the middle years. Among the diseases that rise rapidly in rate during this time are heart disease and cancer. Men seem more susceptible than women, particularly to coronary disease.

This initial chapter has already established one of the dominant themes of the section on middle age: Americans are very youth-oriented, devaluing the positive aspects of aging while emphasizing the negative ones. It is not surprising, then, that our concept of middle age is biased in reflecting it as a time of decline and disintegration. The evidence actually indicates that, for most of us, it is a period of strength and good functioning. As we will see, this is a true in the realms of personality, family, and work as in physical development.

9 Personality

A middle-aged man decides to leave his job and family. He starts to do something he always wanted to do—maybe travel or paint—instead of being involved in the rat-race. He falls in love, and perhaps even moves in with, a younger woman. Everyone says it is sad, but his wife commonly hears that this is a phase he's in, that it will pass. He is, she is told, having a "midlife crisis."

This popular image of midlife crisis is best exemplified by the life of the painter Paul Gauguin (1848–1903) (Colarusso & Nemiroff, 1981). Gauguin was a French banker with a wife and four children who, at age 43, abruptly left them and moved to Tahiti to paint native women. He achieved great fame, "proving" that one should follow one's dream rather than society's image of what is appropriate. Gauguin's midlife crisis, accompanied by a career shift and leaving his family, was "successful."

Or was it? As Calvin Colarusso and Robert Nemiroff (1981) point out, this version of Gauguin's life is more myth than reality. He did leave his family and job and move to Tahiti to paint. But it was not a sudden decision; he left his job some eight years before he left for Tahiti. And he did not actually leave his job; rather, he lost it during the Paris stock market crash and, instead of getting another brokerage position, he decided to devote his time to painting. He did not leave his wife at this point. The family, with no available means of support since Gauguin was not yet successful in selling his work, lived with his wife's parents. Six years before he left for Tahiti, his marriage fell apart. It is worth noting that Gauguin tried to talk his wife into going with him. She, however, was more interested in a traditional, middle-class life style and refused to go.

Even these additional facts do not sufficiently capture the lack of suddenness in Gauguin's decision. Gauguin had been painting and taking art lessons for several years prior to losing his job. And he had been a serious collector of impressionistic works. Thus, he had a longstanding interest in art. But why go to Tahiti? Gauguin had lived with his mother in Peru as a young child, in a wealthy and comfortable setting. Though they left when Gauguin was still a young child, it has been argued that he romanticized this period of his life and was left with the image of his beautiful mother in a tropical paradise. Furthermore, his grandmother, Flora Tristan, had been something of a revolutionary who railed against middle-class society and felt herself an outsider to it. Gauguin apparently identified with her. Thus, we can find a longstanding resentment toward middle-class, material-istic French society, accompanied by a longing for a tropical Paradise Lost. This information makes Gauguin's decision seem much less abrupt and mysterious (Colarusso & Nemiroff, 1981). His identification with his grand-mother may also help us to understand why he died an unhappy man who thought of himself as an outcast who was not sufficiently appreciated by middle-class society.

Gauguin's life serves to make several points. First, he apparently did go through a change at mid-life. As we shall see, many theorists (such as Jung, Erikson, and Levinson) see such change as normative. Indeed, Daniel Levinson (1978) provides numerous examples of midlife transitions in such writers as Eugene O'Neill, Lillian Hellman, and William Shakespeare. He also provides examples from lives of academicians and factory workers so that we are not left with the impression that only temperamental artists experience the transition. But there is still considerable debate as to how common and how severe (or crisis-like) this change is.

Paul Gauguin's "Women of Tahiti," painted in 1891 after he moved to Tahiti.

Second, the change is not sudden or surprising. Typically, there will be patterns of dissatisfactions, interests, or characteristics that will contribute to the nature and extent of the change. One of Levinson's (1978) interviewees, for example, left his secure factory job and became a mental health worker at age 45. The man's father was a minister and he had wanted to continue his father's legacy of serving people. Thus, his new occupation was more in line with values that had developed in childhood.

Third, various aspects of one's life may be touched by mid-life changes. In Gauguin's case, both family and career were altered. In some cases, only one or the other is affected, and many people make no major changes in their lives at all. Trying to understand what types of changes are made—or are not made—is a major task of theorists investigating midlife.

Of course, all this assumes that there is some form of midlife crisis or transition. And not all theorists agree that there is. Many researchers argue that middle age, and indeed all of adulthood, is marked by substantial stability in personality functioning (Atchley, 1989). Who is correct? Or is there a way to reconcile the stability versus change debate?

MIDLIFE CRISIS: THEORETICAL MODELS

The term midlife crisis appears both in the media and in daily conversation. The notion of a midlife crisis, or, more aptly, midlife transition, was first introduced to psychology by Carl Jung in the 1930s. Jung was a former student of Freud and his ideas reflect psychoanalytic theory. Other theorists who have described midlife transitions, including Erik Erikson, Daniel Levinson, and George Valliant, also were influenced by psychoanalytic theory. The impact of psychoanalytic thought on our understanding of midlife change should not be surprising, since psychoanalysts have long believed that there are stages of development (which would, of course, be marked by transitions) and that early influences will resurface to shape adult life.

Jung's Model

It would be grossly misleading to characterize Jung's theory as merely an extension of Freud's. Jung introduced a variety of new concepts that were significantly different from those presented by Freud. Among them are the belief that development continues significantly beyond childhood and that behavior is guided by intrapsychic symbols known as *archetypes*. Both concepts are important in Jung's model of midlife.

Stages: Jung (1931/1960) divided the life span into four broad stages: childhood (birth to puberty), youth (puberty to the late thirties), maturity (middle age), and extreme old age. He argued that one needed to subdivide adulthood into stages because life must have a purpose for the individual and for the species. Yet the purpose of life changes throughout adulthood. In the early adult years, the purpose or goal is to establish a career and a family. Doing so not only facilitates individual growth and well-being, but also serves the society. These cannot be the goals of middle and old age. The children have been born and raised. A secure career has been established and, by old age, has been finished.

Jung sees old age primarily as a time of dependence and disability. Middle age, then, is the stage during which the highest functioning is attainable. As societal (including familial) demands for childrearing and work decline, middle-aged individuals gain the time and freedom to look at their own needs. The sense of freedom to think of themselves first is given a significant boost by the death of their parents (Jung, 1931/1960). Their death frees people from the "dutiful child" role, allowing them to serve their own wishes rather than those instilled in them by their parents.

Introspection and Integration: In middle age, then, we are truly allowed the luxury of introspection. Introspection enables us to develop *wisdom*, which Jung defined as being in touch with the primordial images that make up the *collective unconscious* (the universal groundwork for personality). Gaining harmony with these symbols further permits us to integrate components of our personality. For example, all of us have symbols of masculinity (animus) and femininity (anima) that are an unconscious part of our personalities. In youth, we deny the opposite gender component; men are often afraid to show feminine values or behavior and women avoid masculine characteristics. Some of this is because of parental and societal demands to fill gender-based roles. But in midlife these demands wane and we are able to allow the "opposite" gender side of us to emerge.

Jung's ideas permeate virtually all the modern theories of midlife transition. Jung suggested that there would be a major shift in personality around age 40. This shift would involve a movement toward greater concern with the self than with the family or work. This is not a totally selfish interest; family and work are not necessarily renounced or neglected. Rather, there is an increased introspectiveness and desire to understand one's own needs and serve them. Previously denied components of personality will emerge. There may be gender role shifts, for example. Part of understanding one's own needs, however, is understanding one's connectedness with others (through the primordial symbols, for example). So there is a sense of humanity that leads to greater tolerance and even wisdom. People who fail to achieve such wisdom usually have failed to accept the aging process itself and are, for some reason, trying to cling to or regain their youth. They are often constricted, intolerant, and unhappy people. To borrow the terms that Erikson will employ to describe them, they are stagnant and despairing.

Erikson's Model

Erikson's seventh stage of psychosocial development, focusing on generativity versus stagnation, is often characterized as occurring during middle age. This is not quite accurate. Erikson himself distinguished between young adulthood and adulthood without drawing any specific age boundaries (Erikson, 1982). Instead, generativity concerns arise once intimacy (the focus of the sixth stage) has been established. This small distinction is worth raising for two reasons. First, Erikson does not believe that the "crises" are age-determined, though they are age-linked. He envisions a wide age range for the achievement of any of the adult stages (Erikson, 1982). While most theorists would agree that age itself is not a causal agent, there is considerable debate as to how strongly it is related to adult transitions (Levinson, 1986).

The other reason for making the distinction is to note that Erikson, like Jung, seems to see the middle adult years as the time when real "maturity" can first be attained. *Now* the individual is an adult, with no qualifier. Those personality theorists who believe in a midlife transition universally see it as a time of growth. Contrary to many popular myths, youth may not be the best time of life. Real maturity in personality functioning may occur only later.

Generativity: While Erikson himself did not develop a full-scale model of a midlife transition, his idea of generativity versus stagnation has been seminal in other models. *Generativity* refers to " . . . establishing and guiding the next generation" (Erikson, 1980, p. 103). This is commonly achieved through having and rearing one's own children (including adopted children) (Snarey et al., 1987). But generativity may also be exercised by guiding or contributing to other peoples' children through community service, career choices (such as teaching), or mentoring. New ideas and new products that serve the broader community may also be elements of generativity. Note that simply having children does not guarantee that one is being generative (Erikson, 1980; Snarey et al., 1987). Rather, there has to be an unselfish interest in caring for the next generation. In fact, care is the "virtue" that emerges from this crisis (Erikson, 1982).

The negative side of this crisis is stagnation (Erikson, 1982), marked by failing to care for others, by rejecting them as unworthy of attention. There will always be some failure to care for others. After all, you typically could not care for your own children adequately if you were trying to support every child in the world. This, then, exemplifies the principle that there needs to be a balance between the two antitheses (in this case, generativity and stagnation). But stagnation represents rejection carried to an extreme, as in the psychological or physical abuse of one's own children or racial or ethnic prejudice.

Valliant's Model

Unlike Jung and Erikson, whose work is based primarily on clinical impressions, George Valliant's (1977) ideas about midlife change are rooted primarily in an empirical study of 95 healthy, white, college-educated men. It could be argued that these men had "easier" lives than many other people. At least they had more opportunities than most of their contemporaries (women, blacks, non-college-educated) did. Indeed, graduating from college between 1939 and 1944, as these men did, automatically placed them in a select minority.

On the other hand, the men did not all live model lives. There were disturbed parents (alcoholism or chronic depression) and even parental death, for example. And Valliant suggests, and many others would agree, that long-term ineffective parenting can be a major life stressor associated with negative outcomes. Thus, there is some variability among the life experiences of the men studied. The areas of variation may be sufficiently important to reduce concerns about generalizability of the findings. In other words, the variations may be in areas that have particularly crucial implications for adult development.

Valliant (1977) interprets his findings as supportive of Erikson's theory. He therefore views midlife as a stage marked by generativity concerns. Recall, however, that Erikson himself had been somewhat unclear about the precise timing of the generativity conflict. Although generativity is typically seen as a midlife issue, it does directly follow the intimacy crisis, which will usually be resolved in the twenties. Therefore, either the intimacy conflict is extended, generativity issues are raised before middle age, or there is a gap between the two.

There may also be a stage between intimacy and generativity. This is Valliant's argument. He suggests a stage of *career consolidation*. This stage is an adult analogy to Freud's latency stage or Erikson's industry versus inferiority crisis. It is a period of relative quiet in terms of inner development. Instead of dealing with internal psychic conflicts, the individual works on learning a job, establishing a place in a chosen field, and providing for a family. In many ways, Jack (or Jill) *is* all work and no play:

> In working hard ... the ... men tended to sacrifice play. Rather than question whether they had married the right woman, rather than dream of other careers, they changed their babies' diapers and looked over their shoulders at their competition. (Valliant, 1977, p. 216)

In the forties, however, careers are fairly established and families are substantially raised. This permits a return to identity issues. Just as there is a reassessment of childhood values and goals during the adolescent identity crisis, the midlife crisis involves the reassessment of adolescent and early adult beliefs and accomplishments. As Erikson and other ego psychologists have argued, then, Valliant views development as a lifelong process of identity formation and re-formation.

Such questioning will, in healthy people, lead to generativity. But both the questioning and the generativity are made possible by the maturation of the ego defenses. Valliant's (1977) data indicated that adolescents were twice as likely to use immature ego defense mechanisms (projection or acting out) as mature defenses (dissociation, sublimation, or altruism). By young adulthood, this ratio had reversed. And by middle age, the men were four times more likely to use mature rather than immature defense mechanisms. Of course, the men did not uniformly show this pattern. Indeed, some of the men, dubbed the "Perpetual Boys" by Valliant, failed to show any developmental shift in defense mechanisms from adolescence through midlife. They never became generative. Valliant views child-parent relationships, the nature of the adolescent identity crisis, and current environmental supports as playing a role in these individual differences.

What triggers the reevaluation and the increased generativity? Valliant does not single out one event or factor. He does give special attention, as Jung did, to parental death. Parental death can free a middle-aged person from various constraints and allow a new look at values and goals. So, for example, one of the men in Valliant's study could not admit that he was at all like his father or that his father had any impact on his life. This was apparently because the man was trying to establish himself as a person who was distinct from his father. Paternal death facilitated this process.

Parental death will not be a factor for everyone. Many people sufficiently resolve the issue of separation from parents during adolescence and young adulthood. Indeed, this may be why Valliant suggested that people who refuse to face the adolescent identity issues will have particularly difficult midlife transitions. This is not to say that a full-blown adolescent identity crisis is preferable. In fact, such crises are associated with vulnerability to mental instability rather than with good adjustment. Similarly, Valliant does not view a traumatic upheaval as necessary, or even desirable, during the midlife transition. He even suggests that such "crises" are rare in nonclinical samples. Rather, he argues, this is a transition period, just like so many stages of life. Adaptation and adjustment are needed. Whether or not the person successfully adapts will depend on environmental support and previous development.

Valliant also introduced a stage occurring later in the middle years, between Erikson's stages of generativity and ego integrity. This stage is marked by the conflict of *keeping the meaning versus rigidity*. There is a waning of the internal questioning and a recognition of sociocultural values, their role, and how they can (and should) be perpetuated. The person is moving toward the tolerant attitude that marks ego integrity, but has not quite achieved it. Thus, there is often some complaining still about the younger generation's lack of appreciation for the "older" or more "traditional" values. There is also some concern with one's own deteriorating physical status. Although this has not yet typically led to concerns about death, the physical declines do lead a person to question what is important and valued and to reorder use of time.

Valliant, then, outlines ten stages of ego development rather than the eight suggested by Erikson (see Table 9–1). He sees the transitions as attributable to biological evolution, environmental factors, and personality development. The midlife transition, like the other transitions, represents maturation in ego functioning and adaptation to changes in life circumstances.

Levinson's Model

Daniel Levinson's theory, too, is based on empirical work. Levinson's stage theory marks middle adulthood as beginning at 40 and ending at 65 (Levinson, 1986). Unlike many other theorists, Levinson views the stages as heavily constrained by age. He is unwilling to assign a wide age range to the stages and is very specific about the duration and timing of the periods.

TABLE 9-1:   Valliant's Modification of Erikson's Stages

Conflict/Stage	Age
Trust versus mistrust	Infancy
Autonomy versus shame and self-doubt	Toddler
Initiative versus guilt	Preschool
Industry versus inferiority	School-age
Identity versus role confusion	Adolescence
Intimacy versus isolation	Twenties
Career consolidation	Thirties
Generativity versus stagnation	Forties
Keeping the meaning versus rigidity	Fifties
Ego integrity versus despair	Old age

Valliant introduced two new adult stages (career consolidation and keeping the meaning) and modified the ages associated with the adult stages.

Source: Based on Valliant, G. (1977). *Adaptation to life.* Boston: Little, Brown.

Life Structure: The focus of Levinson's theory is changes in life structure. This is neither a personality structure nor a social structure (Levinson, 1986); instead, it is the pattern that underlies a person's life, serving as a boundary and mediator between personality and society. The life structure goes through a series of developmental periods that occur in a fixed sequence (see Chapter 1). Some of these periods represent transitions, during which an existing life structure is ended and the groundwork is laid for a new one. Other periods are for structure building. A transition period normally lasts about 5 years. Building periods are a bit longer, lasting 5 to 7 years. Thus, although building periods last somewhat longer than transitions, it is still the case that almost half of adulthood is spent in transition periods. This is important because it makes the midlife transition less unusual. After all, it is not the only one that occurs during adulthood.

A *life structure* is composed mainly of the person's relationships with the outside world (Levinson, 1986). Relationships may be stable or temporary, with a single person or a large group, reciprocal or unilateral. There are infinite variations in relationships, which explains why the specific content of the life structure varies from individual to individual. Someone may have a large number of relationships in many different settings, but typically only one or two can really command full attention. For most people, the relationships involved in marriage-family and occupation are the core components of the life structure. However, there is both inter- and intra-individual variability in content and balance of the life structure. For example, occupation may be a more central component in young adulthood than in old age. Indeed, occupation may be a negligible component of the life cycle of many retirees.

Midlife Transition: The midlife transition begins at about age 40 and ends at about age 45. In dismantling the young adult life structure and laying the groundwork for the middle-age structure, a person faces three tasks: reappraising young adulthood, testing options for middle age, and integrating personality polarities. Ideally, all of these tasks move the individual further along the path toward maturity and individuation (Levinson, 1978, 1986).

Reappraisal of young adulthood enables a person to become more realistic (Levinson, 1978). Young adulthood is a time of illusions. We think that achieving a dream, be it career success or a large home or marriage, will ensure happiness. We think that hard work and persistence will ensure success. And we think that success is an all or none event. Such illusions help to fuel our goals in young adulthood, but if we were to cling to them indefinitely, we would grow bitter, tired, and disappointed, for they are simply not true. We would be crushed under the weight of these illusions. So the *de*-illusion (as opposed to disillusion) that comes in midlife may be something of a disappointment, but it can also be a relief (Levinson, 1978). The mixed reaction we have to it leaves us with reason to continue living and allows us to change our life structure to one that is more productive for us.

As we move toward completing the reappraisal of young adulthood, the emphasis shifts from the past to the future. Will the life structure that is currently in place serve our newly defined goals and priorities? Is the marriage we are in worth being in? Does our job meet our needs for self-expression? Some of the external aspects of the life structure will be changing on their own: children will leave home, parents will become ill or die, friends will move. There are also internal shifts in values and goals because the individual has reappraised the past and is developing toward greater individuation.

In Levinson's scheme, *individuation* is a lifelong process of defining one's self in relation to the environment. The task is never complete. At midlife, individuation proceeds through the integration of four polarities. The four polarities are young/old, masculine/feminine, destruction/creation, and attachment/separation. Each pair represents somewhat oppositional tendencies, one of which tends to assume dominance at various points in the life span until middle age, when they start to be integrated. Levinson's concept is quite similar to Jung's, then, in that he argues that the introspection of middle age allows the individual to more fully develop, or at least acknowledge, all aspects of his or her personality.

The Polarities: The integration of the polarities is in many ways the central task of middle age. Levinson (1978) particularly emphasizes the young/old polarity.

In Chapter 8 we saw that there are many visible signs of aging that occur in middle age. There is no denying thinning or graying hair, presbyopia, menopause, and the increased rates of illness and death among peers. Children are also a constant reminder of aging. They are now adults, leaving home and starting their own careers and families. Our parents, too, remind us not only that time marches on, but also what it has in store for us. They are becoming more frail, perhaps even developing chronic disorders. They may need our care. At work, we are no longer the junior faculty or the junior executives. We have seniority as well as a good sense of what our final level of career achievement will be. This all reminds us that we are getting older. Of course, this is not the first time that realization has hit us. Many people feel old as they graduate from high school or college and realize that the carefree days of being financially supported by their parents are over. Even children lament not being able to do things they did when they were younger. The young/old polarity, then, is a recurring issue in development. Indeed, Levinson, agreeing with Jung, represents the issues as archetypes, with *puer* being the young and *senex* the old archetype. But now the recognition of aging carries with it a sense of mortality. There is not only the awareness of age but also of death and the end of the life span. Although there are still many good years left, more living is behind than ahead of most people.

It is important that people accept the aging process and become middle-aged rather than staying young adults. However, they should not define themselves as too old. Instead there should be " ... an increase in the Old qualities of maturity, judgment, self-awareness, magnanimity, integrated structure, breadth of perspective ... vitalized by the Young's energy, imagination, wonderment, capacity for foolishness and fancy ... " (Levinson, 1978, p. 212). Indeed, middle age is the "center" of life in that there should be an optimal balance of Young and Old.

Balance is the key to the integration of the other polarities, too. In the attachment/separation polarity, for example, the balance is between the needs of self (separation from the world) and the needs of others (attachment to the world) (Levinson, 1978). Carol Gilligan (1982a) has argued that integration of this particular polarity will be quite different for men and women. Men's development, she suggests, emphasizes separation, independence, and assertiveness. Women's development focuses on relationships and serving the needs of others, especially family. Levinson seemed to imply this difference by pointing out the role of a "special woman" who supports and serves the young man's quest for his "dream." At midlife, then, women may develop more interest in separateness and men may become more "attached."

Indeed, Levinson (1978), like Jung (1931/1960), argued for an even more substantial shift in gender roles. Jung seemed to suggest a veritable crossing-over

> ... what has broken down is the masculine style of life which held the field up to now, and that what is left over is an effeminate man. Contrariwise, one can observe women ... who have developed in the second half of life an uncommonly masculine tough-mindedness which thrusts the feelings and the heart aside. (Jung, 1931/1960, p. 398)

Levinson's formulation (1978) is less dramatic. He does not claim that men become feminine or that women become masculine. In fact, he believes it is erroneous to consider the shift as quantitative. Rather, there is a qualitatively different integration of the masculine and feminine components of personality such that both are now expressed. Note the similarity of this argument to that made by sociobiologists in their "parental imperative" (Gutmann, 1975; see Chapter 6).

One outcome of the new masculinity/femininity balance is that a man may be better able to mentor a woman (Levinson, 1978). After all, he no longer has to prove his masculine prowess. The integration of the destruction/creation polarity also improves the ability to mentor others because it leads to a better balance between power (representing destruction) and love (representing creation). Add to this the recognition of one's own seniority (in the young/old integration) and the balancing of attachment/separation, and it becomes clear that concern for the next generation is growing and is more easily expressed. Thus, Levinson seems to be agreeing with Erikson in emphasizing generativity and guidance for the next generation.

Cytrynbaum's Model

Solomon Cytrynbaum and his colleagues, like many other theorists, view the midlife transition as one of several developmental transitions faced during the life span (Cytrynbaum, Blum, Patrick, Stein, Wadner, & Wilk, 1980). They believe that comparable transitions occur in both men and women, though the timing and specific content may vary from individual to individual. Indeed, some people will actually experience a crisis. This will occur when the person's inner psychological resources and external means of support are inadequate to deal with the developmental tasks he or she faces.

Predispositions: The midlife transition does not occur in a vacuum. Both previous personality and social systems influence the timing, strength, duration, and outcome of the transition (Cytrynbaum et al., 1980). People who have coped effectively in the past will probably do well now. Some people, for example, like to be challenged by stress and change; others feel easily overwhelmed by it; still others seek to avoid change and stress altogether. People who are preoccupied with stress will probably deal less effectively than those who are less concerned about it (Fiske, 1982). Similarly, Paul Costa and Robert MacCrae (1985) have presented evidence indicating that a sense of happiness and well-being is fairly stable across adulthood. This stability appears to be largely attributable to consistency in personality traits. Indeed, Atchley (1989) has argued that there are both internal and external pressures to maintain such continuity. He, then, expects consistency to be the norm.

In the same vein, social supports can serve to mediate midlife transition. As was the case in young adulthood, multiple roles seem to increase the likelihood of coping well (see Chapter 7). One role can provide a sense of well-being and competence if things are not going well in the other. Thus, women who are married and work seem more satisfied at midlife than those who fill only one role (see, for example, Baruch & Barnett, 1986a). On the other hand, too many demands from other people can be draining (Belle, 1982). This may be a particular risk at middle age, when aging parents and adolescent/young adult children may drain one's physical, financial, and psychological resources.

In addition, some social systems are more flexible and tolerant of aging than others are (Cytrynbaum et al., 1980). A professional athlete, for example, may find aging a much more serious threat than would an executive. In some professions, there is still considerable room for advancement after middle age; in others, there is none. Similarly, some cultures assign a place of honor to older members of the society or family; other cultures treat them as useless or burdensome. Such differences in social systems can affect our perception of our own aging.

Triggers: A number of changes that occur at midlife may trigger the transition (Cytrynbaum et al., 1980). Some of these are biological, ranging from hair loss to menopause to the onset of a chronic disease. Some are career-related, as when an academician's tenure decision is made. Others are familial, as both children and parents age. Some people will experience primarily normative events; others will be faced with unusual traumas, such as widowhood or a heart attack. Although the specific events will differ, both in form and number, all of us will be reminded that half of our life is over. There will be a shift, then, in time perspective and a greater awareness of death. Time no longer seems unlimited.

All these factors serve to trigger the reappraisal of the midlife transition (Cytrynbaum et al., 1980). There is rarely one single event that does it. Certainly there is no single trigger that is universal. Given the individual differences we have already seen in family, career, and biological development, this should not be surprising.

Tasks: These changes have led Cytrynbaum and his colleagues to postulate five major developmental tasks to be mastered during midlife. Indeed, the willingness and dedication to deal with these tasks indicates the onset of the midlife transition. The tasks are:

1. Acceptance of death and mortality
2. Recognition of biological limitations and health risks
3. Restructuring of sexual identity and self-concept
4. Reorientation to work, career, creativity, and achievement
5. Reassessment of primary relationships (Cytrynbaum et al., 1980, p. 467)

Working through these issues can lead to a new integration of personality components, sometimes to the point of considerable personality change. This outcome is similar to those suggested by Jung and Levinson as the optimal results of the midlife transition. Not everyone is successful in negotiating these tasks. People who do not adapt at midlife may show a variety of long-term symptoms of distress and dissatisfaction with life. These include depression, alcoholism, and psychosomatic symptoms (Cytrynbaum et al., 1980). Again, Levinson (1978) had suggested similar symptoms, indicative perhaps of a loss of interest in continuing, as negative outcomes of a midlife transition.

Sequence: Cytrynbaum and his co-workers suggest that the process of the midlife transition consists of four steps. These are summarized in Table 9-2. Some of these processes occur on a conscious level, while others are less clearly within our awareness. Many of the triggers of the transition are conscious; on the other hand much of the reassessment occurs at a subconscious level.

Table 9-2 also lists some of the behavioral changes that can occur as a result of the midlife transition. Again, they are similar to those suggested by Jung, Erikson, Valliant, and Levinson, with a substantial emphasis on generativity.

Methodological Note: All these models have generated considerable interest in the midlife transition. The empirically based models are often particularly popular, given our society's faith in science. Of course, the method of choice in studying midlife transition is typically a longitudinal design. As we noted in Chapter 2, selectivity of the subjects creates a problem in such studies. Often it is difficult to generalize the findings to a broader population.

This external validity problem is exacerbated when the subject pool is intentionally restricted. Unfortunately, this is true of the databases of both Levinson and Valliant's models. Levinson's is based primarily on a study of 40 men through young adulthood and into middle age. Valliant's subjects were all white, male college graduates who were selected precisely because of their promise. Keep in mind that the men in Valliant's study completed college between 1939 and 1944, when college attendance was considerably less common than it is today.

The failure to include women in the samples has generated considerable criticism (Gilligan, 1982a, b). Women's biological, work, family, and personality development all seem to show some differences from men's. This, then, may well lead them to face midlife differently. Gilligan, for example, argues that women must learn to give more time, energy, and credence to their own needs, rather than just serving the needs of others as they age. While for men maturity has meant autonomy, for women it has meant interdependence. In middle age, some of that interdependence declines, and women can become more autonomous. Men, on the other hand, seek greater interdependence and less power. While the outcome may be similar for both men and women, in that both ideally achieve a balance of interdependence and autonomy, the paths for getting there may be quite different. We need a clearer model of how women's developmental processes may differ from men's (Gilligan, 1982b).

The issue of gender role development provides an interesting example of such a possibility. Assume, for the moment, that what happens (or is supposed to happen) at midlife is a movement toward androgeny. In other words, the individual starts to value "masculine" and "feminine" characteristics more equally. But what if women are more commonly androgynous

TABLE 9-2: A Schematic Overview of Major Personality and Social Systems Parameters and Processes During the Midlife Transition

Predispositions	Developmental Processes			Outcomes
Personality Differences in personality (ego strength, narcissism, coping strategies, defenses, etc.) which predispose individuals to respond differentially to the midlife transition Interacts with ←→ **Systems** Extent to which primary systems (couples, family, work organization) can adapt and support individual member's engagement with midlife tasks as assessed by system's flexibility, communication, boundary management, leadership, role differentiation, culture and myths; vary by social class, racial, ethnic background, etc.	**Precipitators or Triggers** **Individual:** Encounter death anxiety; shift in time orientation. **Stressful or Unanticipated Life Events:** Biological changes; illness or death of parents, spouse, friends; life-threatening illness. **Social System:** Reduction in parental imperative; work organization or professional culture signals limitations on mobility and rewards or pressures to retire.	**Developmental Tasks** Accept death and mortality. Accept biological limitations and risks. Restructure self-concept and sexual identity Reorientation to work, creativity, and achievement. Reassess primary relationships.	**Developmental Processes** Destructuring → Reassessment Reintegration and restructuring → Behavioral and role change ↑	**Adaptive** Acceptance of mortality; achieve a sense of individuation and coherent identity; integration of creative and destructive forces; attain a sense of community; integrate masculine, feminine, and related emergent components of personality; reinvest narcissism in self. Able to cope with developmental tasks of the second half of life. **Maladaptive** Failure to establish sexual bimodality which integrates male and female components of personality; failure to transfer narcissism; inability to accept mortality and associated losses. Casualties of one's own developmental potential expressed in midlife-related symptoms (depression, anxiety, decreased appetite for food and sex, poor concentration, fear of homosexuality, alcoholism, psychosomatic disorders) or in vulnerabilities and predispositions to distress and maladaptive symptoms as older adults

Source: Cytrynbaum, S., et al. (1980). Midlife development: A personality and social systems perspective. In L. Poon (ed.), *Aging in the 1980s*, p. 465. Copyright © 1980 by the American Psychological Association. Reprinted by permission of the APA.

than men as they approach middle age? Or what if androgeny during young adulthood has different meaning for men than for women? Would such differences affect the path of the midlife transition? These are interesting questions because several theorists (for example, Pleck, 1977) have argued that women have more gender role flexibility throughout the life span.

It is not unusual for researchers to find that more young women have masculine attitudes than young men have feminine ones (O'Heron & Orlofsky, 1990). Indeed, there is some evidence that young men may actually be afraid to show femininity (O'Neil, Helms, Gable, David, & Wrightsman, 1986). Furthermore, androgeny in young women (or, more specifically, adherence to some masculine traits no matter what the level of femininity) is associated with positive adjustment for women (Bem, 1985; O'Heron & Orlofsky, 1990). However, young men who are low on masculine characteristics tend to be poorly adjusted (O'Heron & Orlofsky, 1990). Thus, the meaning and rigidity of gender roles may be different for men and women as they approach midlife. To use the terminology of Cytrynbaum et al., they may have different predispositions.

At various points, Levinson (1986), Valliant (1977), and Cytrynbaum and his colleagues (1980) have all claimed that there are considerable similarities between male and female development and that their theories have general applicability. Levinson's recent (1990) report of his own data concerning women's midlife development raises some questions about these claims. While he notes that the general sequence of life structure periods holds for both sexes, he also claims there are powerful gender differences in resources, constructs, and composition of the life structure. Indeed, these differences are so marked that Levinson uses the term "gender splitting" to describe the rigid division between men and women. The splitting is evident in the domestic and work spheres. It is also evident in masculine versus feminine conceptions of self.

From 1980–1982, Levinson interviewed three groups of 15 women. All 45 women were 35 to 40 years old at the time of the interviews. The first group were traditional homemakers. As they approached midlife, they felt restrained by their domestic role; only 20 percent were still satisfied homemakers in intact marriages. The remainder were either divorced or trying to somehow revise their marriages to accommodate careers. The second group were faculty women who found themselves lost behind their academic husbands' identity at midlife. They had originally thought they could function as faculty wives, but the role was neither stimulating enough nor satisfying. These women were trying to make their own careers more central as they came into midlife.

The first two groups, then, were women who had tried to place family before career. At middle age, they were trying to combine the two. The third group were businesswomen who had intended to establish their careers and then have children. Not surprisingly, many of them (60 percent) never did have children. Those who did found combining career and family more difficult than they had expected. Although some felt their solutions to the problems were adequate, none reported being truly satisfied with the career-children balance (Levinson, 1990).

One thing that is noteworthy about Levinson's data is the more complex Dream that women develop. Women also seem to have more trouble achieving their Dream. This is probably because of the greater family demands faced by women (even career women). More research is needed to uncover the full effects of these differences on strategies and outcomes of development.

As is true of research on women, we need more research concerning working-class adult development. This may seem unnecessary. After all, if people with opportunities and privilege face a "crisis" or "transition," wouldn't those with more difficult and more stressful lives encounter even greater difficulty at midlife? Perhaps they would, although we'd expect considerable individual variability. Furthermore, some sociologists have suggested that the midlife crisis is less a natural developmental phenomenon than a result of too much leisure time combined with a great deal of emphasis on the self. It is possible that people whose time continues to be consumed by survival and "making ends meet" (as the middle-class man's is during the Career Consolidation stage) never have a midlife transition." Similarly, adults in cultures that emphasize the group over the individual may face less of a personal crisis in middle age. Such issues require further investigation before we can truly understand the nature of the transition.

The work of Jung, Erikson, Valliant, Levinson, and Cytrynbaum emphasizes change in the middle adult years. One might think, therefore, that these theorists see little continuity in adult functioning. Looking back over the models, we can see this is not true. All of the theorists ascribe a major role to previous personality. Indeed, it is a reformation of the existing personality, rather than the introduction of bizarre or incongruent values and goals, that occurs during midlife. Think back to the example of Gauguin's life. Even such a dramatic shift in behavior and roles actually reflects substantial continuity.

The models also share other features. They suggest multiple triggers of a transition, rather than one particular event. This underscores the great individuality in development that is evident by middle age. All of the triggers might, however, be considered to reflect what Bernice Neugarten (1968) has referred to as a shift in time perspective. With roughly half of life behind them, adults reorder priorities and reevaluate goals and values such that they fit the needs of the remainder of life.

And that is the other similarity across the models: All clearly reflect a belief that development does continue in adulthood. The development here is not simply change. It is positive change, a movement toward greater maturity, at least in psychologically healthy individuals. Here we have a realm in which older adults may actually function better than younger ones.

PERSONALITY FUNCTIONING

Perhaps the major question concerning personality functioning in middle age is whether stability or change is dominant. As we noted in Chapters 1 and 5, and as will be evident again in Chapter 13, this is a core issue of personality research across adulthood. Given the dominance of both the popular and theoretical image of middle age as a time of crisis and change, however, this question takes on special urgency in understanding personality. A major problem has been deciding how to define and determine stability. There are various statistical methods that can be used to address the issue (Bengston et al., 1985). You could compare group averages at two (or more) points in time, and if there is no change in the averages, you can argue that the characteristic is stable. Or you can look at the correlation between scores at different times. If the correlation is high, you might also argue that the characteristic is stable.

If you performed both types of analyses and found stability in both cases, you could probably feel quite confident about your conclusions. But it is not unusual to find that the two analyses yield different outcomes. There can be a change in the overall group averages while the relative rankings of the individuals (which is what the correlation looks at) remain stable. In this situation you would find a change in the group averages, perhaps indicating lack of stability, but stability in ranks.

Which finding is correct? Researchers and theorists cannot always agree (Bengston et al., 1985). Even when they agree on the question there may be problems. For example, two researchers may agree that the important issue is whether rankings are stable. But they may disagree on how large the correlations need to be to indicate stability. Some researchers may accept any statistically significant finding as indicative of stability. Others may require that the correlation be large (usually greater than .70) to indicate meaningful stability. As we noted in Chapter 2, a correlation does not necessarily have to be large to be significant.

The lack of agreement on how to assess stability, as well as what level of group differences or correlation indicates stability or change, has contributed to the conflicts in the adult personality literature. Keeping this in mind, let's turn to an examination of several specific aspects of personality.

Self System

Beginning with Jung, theorists suggesting a midlife transition have argued that it will result in changes in the self-structure. They have often argued, for example, that the personality becomes more integrated so that the person is less concerned about being masculine *or* feminine. Following the transition, people also supposedly become more introspective and in touch with their own values, feelings, and so on.

All these hypotheses suggest changes in the self-system. By self-system, self-structure, and self-concept we mean the beliefs or ideas that someone holds about himself or herself. It is what Bengston refers to as the "cognitive component" of self. Although it consists mainly of our own thoughts about who and what we are, it also includes some information about other people's reactions to us (Bengston et al., 1985). So, both the statements "I am shy" and "Other people think of me as shy" may be seen as tapping into the self-system. The self-system may be assessed by direct questions about self beliefs, as in Bernice Neugarten's (1968) interviews with 100 men and women about how it felt to be middle-aged. Projective techniques such as the Rorschach or the Thematic Apperception Test (TAT) may be used to get at unconscious beliefs about self (Neugarten & Gutmann, 1958/1968). Even self-report personality inventories, used to assess general traits, may be viewed as measures of self-concept since they assess the person's ideas about his or her own functioning (Bengston et al., 1985; McCrae & Costa, 1982). Not surprisingly, different techniques yield different results.

Bernice Neugarten's research indicated that middle-aged people do view themselves as different from young adults (Neugarten, 1968). They apparently realize that they have more and different experiences than do young adults. These differences can serve to create a boundary, and sometimes, perhaps, a gap, between the middle-aged and the young. As one of Neugarten's interviewees noted:

> I graduated from college in the middle of the Great Depression. . . . Everybody was having trouble eking out an existence. . . . Today's young people are different. They've grown up in an age of affluence. When I was my son's age, I was much more worldly, what with the problems I had to face. . . . But my son can never understand all this . . . he's of a different generation altogether. (Neugarten, 1968, p. 94)

Similarly, middle-aged people may begin to feel closer to their parents' generation than to their children's. This is partially because the middle-aged no longer identify themselves as "young" and partially because they now realize that older people understand and have lived through what the middle-aged person is now facing (Neugarten, 1968).

The popular press image of middle-aged parents and their children might have us believe that such distancing between the two generations is bad, that it fosters a "generation gap." But the generation gap is much more myth than reality. Furthermore, the distancing may serve a valuable purpose. Generativity may be impossible without the sense that the young are different. This belief gives the middle-aged the basis for providing the young with access to their experience. While such a role may initially be frightening, most middle-aged people see it as their responsibility to provide guidance to the young for the good of both the young adults and society in general.

Neugarten's interviews also point out a change in time perspective during middle age. You begin to realize that time is finite, that you are not immortal. In the words of one of Neugarten's participants:

> Time now is a two-edged sword. To some of my friends, it acts as a prod; to others, a brake. It adds a certain anxiety, but I must also say it adds a certain zest in seeing how much pleasure can still be obtained, how many good years one can still arrange, how many new activities can be undertaken. . . . (Neugarten, 1968, p. 97)

One interesting effect of this shift in time perspective may be that middle-aged and older adults are less happy, but more satisfied, with their lives than are young adults (Andrews & Withey, 1976; Campbell, Converse, & Rodgers, 1976). This may be because of different expectations about how much can be accomplished. So, for example, young adults believe their lives have improved more during the past few years and will continue to improve more dramatically than do older people (Andrews & Withey, 1976). As you realize time is limited, you may develop more appropriate expectations about what it will allow you to do.

So it is evident that there are some changes in self-image as one moves through middle age. However, the bulk of the research evidence indicates that there is considerable stability in self-concept throughout the middle years. Longitudinal research suggests that self-image is steady throughout the adult years (Bengston, et al., 1985; Busse & Maddox, 1985). In fact, not only the specific characteristics but also the structuring or grouping of those characteristics appears to be fairly stable with age (Bengston et al., 1985; Pierce & Chiriboga, 1979). So, for example, Robert Pierce and David Chiriboga reported that all six factors that emerged in a study of self-concept were evident in a follow-up of the subjects five years later. The factors, which are shown in Table 9–3, were not identical, but there was considerable overlap. Once again, then, we see stability but with room to accommodate the adaptations adult life requires.

TABLE 9–3:   An Example of Stability of Factor Structure in Adult Personality

Characteristics* in Original Factors	Five-Year Follow-Up Factors
Factor 1: Personal Insecurity	
Easily hurt	Easily hurt
Touchy	Easily embarrassed
Easily embarrassed	Touchy
Jealous	Timid
Worried	Confident[†]
Timid	Defensive
Factor 2: Amiability	
Considerate	Fairminded
Cooperative	Reasonable
Hostile[†]	Self-controlled
Sincere	Cooperative
Fairminded	Unworthy[†]
Reasonable	Rebellious[†]
Factor 3: Assertion	
Assertive	Bossy
Bossy	Assertive
Shrewd	Impulsive
Competitive	Stubborn
Ambitious	Rebellious
Guileful	Dramatic

TABLE 9-3:   (continued)

Characteristics* in Original Factors	Five-Year Follow-Up Factors
Factor 4: Self-control	
Reasonable	See the second dimension in this
Self-controlled	column
Calm	
Impulsive	
Self-pitying	
Wise	
Factor 5: Hostility	
Resentful	See the third dimension in this column
Rebellious	
Defensive	
Sarcastic	
Self-pitying	
Impulsive	
Factor 6: Social Poise	
Charming	Warm
Poised	Friendly
Dull[†]	Likable
Sophisticated	Considerate
Reserved	Tactless[†]
Warm	Charming

Three additional factors emerged at the five-year follow-up that had not been represented in the original analysis. The order of emergence of the factors at the follow-up was not identical to the order of the original analysis.
*Characteristics are listed in the order of their importance in defining the factor/dimension.
†This characteristic is inversely related to the factor/dimension.

Source: Pierce, R., & Chiriboga, D. (1979). Dimensions of adult self-concept. *Journal of Gerontology, 34,* 80–85.

Personality Characteristics

Most of the studies of adult personalities functioning have at least included self-report personality inventories as a measure. It has been argued that these inventories reflect, and may even be determined by, self-concept (Bengston et al., 1985; McCrae & Costa, 1982). However, there is considerable similarity between the scores of self-reported personality inventories and ratings by others, including trained observers and spouses (McCrae & Costa, 1982). This suggests that personality, even as it is measured in self-reports, may be more than simply self-concept. Therefore, the research on personality characteristics is considered separately here.

The bulk of this research suggests considerable stability throughout adulthood (see Chapter 5). This is especially true of studies that have used correlational analyses and are longitudinal in design (see, for example, Bengston et al., 1985; Busse & Maddox, 1985; Costa, McCrae, & Arenberg, 1983; Siegler, George, & Okun, 1979). Indeed, it appears that cohort differ-

ences in personality characteristics may be larger than age differences (Bengston et al., 1985; Schaie & Parham, 1976; Woodruff & Birren, 1972).

As we saw in Chapter 5, the work of Paul Costa, Robert McCrae, and Douglas Arenberg, using the data from the Baltimore Longitudinal Study, suggests that there is stability in personality inventory scores over long periods of time. Costa and McCrae have focused on three components of personality: extraversion, neuroticism, and openness to experience (Costa & McCrae, 1984; Costa, McCrae, & Arenberg, 1980, 1983; McCrae & Costa, 1982). The research has been quite convincing in demonstrating stability, especially in neuroticism and extraversion. The stability has been evident in cross-sectional, longitudinal, and sequential analyses. Cohort, time of measurement, and assessment error do not appear to account for the stability. The stability has been demonstrated in terms of the structure of the three traits, as well as individual rankings on the traits.

Other researchers have also found neuroticism and anxiety level to be stable facets of personality. Indeed, these may be the most consistent findings of the personality research (Bengston et al., 1985). This is of considerable interest because of the negative relationships between neuroticism and health (Costa & McCrae, 1980) and between neuroticism and a sense of well-being (Costa & McCrae, 1984). Extraversion has also been found to be related to happiness across the life span (Costa & McCrae, 1984), and although the findings are somewhat less consistent, it too has shown remarkable stability across studies. Other characteristics or aspects of self that appear to be fairly stable across age include: sense of security or adjustment; sociability; competence and achievement orientation; and openness to experience (see Bengston et al., 1985).

Even when the analyses have included a wider range of characteristics, as in the 10 traits measured by the Guilford-Zimmerman Temperament Survey, stability has been the rule for the men of the Baltimore Longitudinal Study. For example, in an analysis of seven-year longitudinal data by Karen Douglas and David Arenberg (1978), only 2 of the 10 traits, masculinity and general activity level, showed age-related declines that did not appear to be attributable to cohort or time of measurement. And in both cases the absolute decline was relatively small and probably had virtually no effect on the men's daily lives (Costa et al., 1983).

The consistency of the stability findings has lead Costa, McCrae, and Arenberg (1983) to conclude that change is the exception, not the rule, in adult personality development. This does not mean people cannot change. Certainly with therapeutic intervention or under extreme circumstances, people can change their personalities. And some people may indeed go through a midlife crisis that can affect personality, though this, according to Costa and colleagues, is more attributable to neuroticism than to development. Indeed, Costa and his co-authors call for rethinking the meaning of personality so that we conceptualize it more as a cause or independent variable than as an effect or dependent variable. Rather than explaining only what affects personality changes in adulthood, which are few and far between, we might expend more energy on explaining how personality influences health, well-being, adjustment to life crises, and so on.

What might cause personality to be so stable? There are several possibilities. As Atchley (1989) has noted, there are both internal and external pressures toward stability. Stability allows us to develop expectations and habits of behavior. We know who we can count on. We don't have to spend a lot of time figuring out daily interactions and can put our cognitive capacities to other uses.

Scarr and McCartney (1983) have suggested a genetic-environmental basis for stability. They argue that the nature of genetic-environmental interactions changes with development. In infancy, the relationship is passive. The goodness of the match between the baby's genetics and the environment is out of the baby's control. Early in development, there also comes to be a reactive relationship, in which the environment reacts differently to children of different genetic predispositions (and vice versa). For our purposes, the most important relationship comes as children begin to achieve the right to make real choices—about work, friendships, and so on. Scarr and McCartney (1983) claim that such choices will reflect genetic predispositions. The maturing individual will engage in "niche-picking." A very sociable person will select a job that involves considerable contact with other people; a shy or unsociable person will look for a career that involves working alone. Insomuch as genetic dispositions are stable, the individual will select the same environmental characteristics over and over. With both the genetic disposition and the environment evincing stability, it is no wonder that personality characteristics will be stable.

It would be erroneous to leave the impression that stability prevails throughout adulthood. First, as was noted earlier, there is considerable debate as to what constitutes stability (in a statistical sense). Second, the data are at least somewhat conflicting for most of these variables. Indeed, the measures vary so dramatically from study to study that it is often difficult to make comparisons and draw a conclusion. For example, Bengston and his colleagues (1985) reviewed 21 studies of self-structure in adulthood that used self-concept scales (this does not include studies that used personality inventories). A total of 16 different measures of self-concept were used in the 21 studies. Only 4 of the scales were used in more than one study. Third, certain aspects of personality, including the ego functions often emphasized by psychoanalytically oriented theorists, have received little attention (Costa et al., 1983). In fact, there is regrettably little overlap between the constructs from the theories of midlife transition and the empirical work on adult personality.

Finally, there are findings that indicate change during adulthood, especially from young adulthood to middle age. For example, the 20-year follow-up of the AT&T managers has indicated considerable change in personality (Bray & Howard, 1983). The men seemed to become less dependent on the approval of others and showed an increased need for autonomy. They were also less interested in making friends or understanding the feelings or motivations of other people. They expressed less guilt when they made mistakes and were more likely to want to take charge of a situation. Overall, then, the men seemed to become more independent, more their "own man," even if it was at someone else's expense. It is possible that some of the increased "toughness" demonstrated by these men was the result of their managerial experiences. After all, "nice guys finish last." Indeed, the men themselves cited things like supervisory experience and successful self-assertion as the reasons for the changes.

A Methodological Note: As was the case with the studies that formed the basis for the theoretical work in midlife, many of the empirical findings that have just been discussed can be generalized only to white, middle-class men. Both the Baltimore Longitudinal and AT&T studies included only white men in their original samples. Although new, more diverse waves of participants have now been added, they have not been in the studies long enough to yield longitudinal data. There is some evidence to suggest that, at least in old age, males and females show different patterns of self-concept development (Schmitz-Scherzer & Thomae, 1983). There is also evidence that life satisfaction, which appears to be affected by personality (Bray & Howard, 1983; Costa & McCrae, 1984) shows different age-related patterns for white men than among African-Americans or women (Campbell et al., 1976). All this underscores the importance of reevaluating the "established" developmental patterns with samples that include African-Americans and women.

Sex Roles

Sex roles could easily have been included in the discussion of self-concepts, since they are clearly a part of our identity and self-image. Indeed, our sense of ourselves as masculine or feminine can be a major identifying characteristic (Bem, 1985). Think of the multitude of words in our language that define sex-role-related personality features: wimp, macho, swish, vamp, bimbo, belle, dyke, wuss, sissy, tomboy, and numerous unprintable terms. Sex roles also deserve special treatment because of the theoretical and empirical emphasis they have received.

As we have seen, explanations of why sex roles ought to change at midlife fall into two groups. The first emphasizes the "parental imperative," arguing that parenting requires a male/female division of labor (Gutmann, 1975). Once the children are grown and leave home, there is no longer so strong a need for a "protector/provider" and a "nurturer." Both parents are free to drop some of the restrictions of their parenthood roles and develop more cross-gender characteristics. The second explanation focuses on middle-age as a time of introspection that leads ultimately to a reintegration of both the masculine and feminine sides of the personality (Jung, 1931/1960; Gould 1972; Levinson, 1978).

The data on whether there actually is a change in sex-role behavior during or after midlife is mixed, although reviewers seem to continue to conclude that the bulk of the research indicates change (Bengston et al., 1985). It is interesting to note, however, that a recent study indicates that women who believe they had become more "masculine" during middle age viewed the end of parenting as the cause of the change (Cooper & Gutmann, 1987). As one of the participants noted:

> I became more independent when my youngest left home. There was a need in me all along to be more myself ... it took my kids growing up before I could have the conflict in my marriage so that I could act as a self-determining kind of person. There was some secret part of me that was locked away and then, at that time, was freed. (Cooper & Gutmann, 1987, p. 351)

It would be risky to conclude that men and women do move toward androgeny after middle age. After all, this is an area of personality functioning that is quite likely to be affected by cultural changes, yielding the possibility of cohort or time-of-measurement effects. And life experience factors, such as social class or work environment, which vary from study to study, may affect how much a particular sample has been affected by the social changes in men's and women's roles during the last twenty years. The roles people choose to play ("niche-picking") may have an influence. In one recent study, traditional homemakers did not show the same increase in independence and assertiveness from age 27 to 43 that women who worked outside the home did (Helson & Picano, 1990). All these possibilities may help us understand why even the longitudinal data seem to conflict on this issue. The scientists and professional men who formed the sample for the Baltimore longitudinal study seemed to show age-related decreases in masculinity (Douglas & Arenberg, 1978). The somewhat broader, but still middle-class, sample of the Duke Longitudinal Study, which included both men and women, showed no age-related shifts in sex role (Siegler, George, & Okun, 1979). If we consider increased autonomy and "toughness" indicative of increased masculinity, then the male managers of the AT&T study actually showed increases in masculinity during middle age (Bray & Howard, 1983).

Even if we did argue that there is a shift toward androgeny, we would be left with the question of the meaning of that shift. Do men become "feminine" or women "masculine"? Do they even achieve androgeny? The Baltimore Longitudinal Study men showed a statistically significant decline in masculinity scores, a decrease that was not attributable to cohort or time of measurement. Indeed, this is one of the most consistent findings of developmental change in this sample. Yet in real life terms, the change is small. There was a change of about one-eighth of a standard deviation over a seven-year period. At that rate, it would take the average man in the sample over a hundred years to drop down to the masculinity score of the average college woman (Costa et al., 1983).

LIFE SATISFACTION

Middle-aged people are facing life changes that make them realize they are no longer young. And especially in our society with its emphasis on youth, that can be a sobering thought. The question, then, is how happy are the middle-aged? Are they able to accept, and even enjoy, the changes that are occurring in their physical, family, and work lives? One of Bernice Neugarten's interviewees offered this commentary:

There is a difference between wanting to *feel* young and wanting to *be* young. Of course it would be pleasant to maintain the vigor and appearance of youth; but I would not trade those things for the authority or the autonomy I feel— no, nor the ease of interpersonal relationships nor the self-confidence that comes from experience (Neugarten, 1968, p. 97)

Such statements led Neugarten to conclude that people viewed middle age as a time when one's ability to handle complicated problems was at its peak. After all, a person now has experience and expertise well beyond those of the young adult but still maintains more of a physical and psychological "edge" than the elderly typically have. This perspective is also captured in Schaie's (1977/1978) middle-aged stage of cognition, the organization function (see Chapters 4, 8).

In general, middle-aged people are at least as satisfied with their lives as young adults are (Andrews & Withey, 1976; Campbell et al., 1976; Faver, 1984). This is true in a variety of realms, including satisfaction with housing, family, marriage, the amount and usefulness of education, community and neighborhood, and life in the United States. There is some evidence to suggest that life is particularly satisfying after age 50 when, for example, marital satisfaction has begun to rebound from the plateau achieved after adjusting to having children (Campbell et al., 1976).

Health is the exception to this overall sense of well-being (Andrews & Withey, 1976; Campbell et al., 1976). This is not surprising, since there are real declines that create concern. The illnesses, and even deaths, of peers exacerbate such worries. Of course, not everyone experiences the same de-

Many middle-aged people are very satisfied with their lives and find they have the time and expertise to pursue special interests and make meaningful contributions.

gree of concern. First, different people age physically at different rates, so that the decline is greater in some middle-aged people than in others. Second, personality will influence a person's perception of health. Research from the Baltimore Longitudinal Study indicates that men who are high on masculinity and emotional stability are not likely to complain of angina pains (a heart condition), even when electrocardiograms indicate that they should. On the other hand, men low on these characteristics may complain of pains even when their ECGs are normal (Costa et al., 1983). There can be such a difference between "objective" and "perceived" health that many studies consider them as separate variables.

Stressful Events

The stereotype of middle-aged people is that they are unhappy because of certain events. We have already seen in the previous chapter that menopause does not typically carry the negative ramifications popular mythology expects. Similarly, nest-emptying does not appear to "break parents' hearts." Indeed, many people find the launching of the last child a real relief. In fact, marital satisfaction actually starts to rise at this point. Both men and women often react with increased happiness and life satisfaction (Busse & Maddox, 1985), although it is also quite common for this event to have no real impact on life satisfaction (Andrews & Withey, 1976; Faver, 1984).

A non-normative stressor in middle age may produce lower life satisfaction. For example, middle-aged widows show more signs of stress than older widows do (Busse & Maddox, 1985). They are less satisfied and are more likely to become ill, including fatally ill, than the older women are. This appears to be attributable to the non-normative nature of the event (see Chapter 5) and because many of these deaths are relatively sudden. For the older widow, a spouse's death may actually be a relief, bringing an end to a long period of disability and pain. Even in these very stressful circumstances, however, many women adapt more than adequately in the long run (Busse & Maddox, 1985).

The reactions to non-normative stressors imply the importance of appraisal in coping with and adapting to stress. When people are able to anticipate, and thereby prepare for, a stressor, they are less likely to experience it as extremely stressful (Lazarus & DeLongis, 1983; Whitbourne, 1985). When an event is "on time" developmentally, such cognitive preparation can take place. Indeed, active preparations can be made. Parents can make decisions on how to spend their time once the children have left home. They can even begin to institute some of these plans before the children are gone. A woman who was a full-time mother might begin to attend college while her children are in middle or high school and then become a full-time student or employee once they have left. This will fill the "empty" time left by no longer having to care for the children and will make the transition easier. However, when an event is "off-time," as when a young or middle-aged woman is widowed, such preparation is impossible. So age plays a role in how we interpret events and whether we judge them to be stressful or routine.

Middle-aged people appear to face fewer life events than do young adults (Lazarus & DeLongis, 1983; Lowenthal et al., 1975). In some ways this is not surprising. After all, young adults are more likely to be forming (or dissolving) marital relationships, starting or changing jobs, having children, and so on. Middle-aged people seem to be more "settled" in their lives. But, this does not necessarily mean that the middle-aged face less stress. First, there may be methodological biases such that the stressors more commonly faced by younger adults are emphasized. What about caring for aging or ailing parents? Is having a child in college stressful? Is preparing for your children's marriage stressful? Such items do not appear on life events scales. Second, as we discussed in Chapter 5, daily hassles may actually have more impact on psychological and physical well-being than major life events (Lazarus & DeLongis, 1983). And there is no reason to believe that daily hassles decline during the middle years. Indeed, as we have seen, the middle-aged seem to have very complex responsibilities to work, family, and community.

In addition, there is some evidence to suggest that having a sense of personal control is important in coping effectively with stress (Lazarus & DeLongis, 1983). And there may be some loss in the sense of control late in middle age (after about age 50). This could lead to more frequent appraisals of events as stressful, although, as we have seen, the research on life satisfaction certainly does not indicate that older people are more unhappy. Perhaps this too reflects a way in which age-related expectations influence the appraisal of stress.

Overall, there seems to be little change in the way people cope with or adapt to stress as they age (Lazarus & DeLongis, 1983). However, the use of ego defense mechanisms does undergo some change such that the less "mature" defenses like fantasy become less common in middle age (McCrae, 1982; Valliant, 1977). General styles of coping, such as being "challenged" or "overwhelmed" by stress, appear to be maintained throughout adulthood (Fiske, 1982).

SUMMARY

Two major issues need to be considered in discussing personality functioning and development during middle adulthood. The first is whether there is a midlife crisis and, if there is, what its beginning, middle, and outcome look like. The second issue, not totally independent of the first, is how much change there is in personality during the middle years.

It is ironic that folk wisdom seems to send us a conflicting message about personality during this time. One tells us "You can't teach an old dog new tricks" and assumes that adults' interests, values, coping skills, and personality traits do not routinely change. Yet, on the other hand, we also assume that people face a "midlife crisis" during which they might leave their spouse, change jobs, take up new hobbies, and join new organizations. Which image is accurate?

The simplest, almost-correct answer would be that the former is more realistic for most people than the latter is. Researchers have consistently reported considerable stability on major personality traits, such as extraversion and neuroticism, throughout adulthood. Few people, especially men, voluntarily change careers, and divorce is less common now than it was during early adulthood. Furthermore, people do not routinely report extremely high levels of stress at this time. In fact, they seem quite happy or at least satisfied with their lives. They have more free time now that their children are grown, and yet they are still relatively healthy. They may even face fewer stressors than do young adults, although methodological problems make it impossible to make a definitive statement on this.

Yet theorists including Jung, Erikson, Valliant, Levinson, and Cytrynbaum continue to argue that there is a significant transition during the middle years. These theorists do not all require that the transition be marked by turmoil and upheaval. Yet they all claim there will be significant questioning and at least some restructuring as people pass the midway point in life. Part of this restructuring will be greater consideration of their own needs and values (as opposed to those of spouse, children, parents, or co-workers). Indeed, there is some evidence that the middle-aged are more introspective and perhaps in touch with their own needs than younger adults are. Again, a decline in parental responsibility would certainly facilitate such a shift.

It has also been suggested, by Jung and Levinson for example, that there is a new integration of personality components. Theorists and researchers have argued that there is a move away from very rigid sex roles. Note that women do not become masculine, nor do men become feminine; rather, each moves closer to androgeny. The research concerning this shift is not unanimous.

Two major methodological shortcomings make it extremely difficult to draw a conclusion about the nature of midlife personality. First, a disproportionate amount of the research, especially the longitudinal studies, has been conducted only with men (especially white, middle-class men). It is difficult to know whether their developmental pattern is indeed the prototype for all human development. Second, it is difficult to determine what constitutes stability. Of course, it is easy to determine what level of cross-age correlation is statistically significant. However, researchers cannot agree on what level of correlation indicates meaningful (in terms of daily life) stability or change. Thus, even researchers such as Paul Costa, who argue a strong case for stability, must admit that a significant amount of personality test scores do not appear to be stable.

PART III: MIDDLE AGE

10 Family and Social Relationships

Being a parent to an adolescent is supposed to be very trying. There are constant fights about dating, clothes, schoolwork, friends, cars, household chores, and almost anything else that can possibly be debated. Parents worry about drugs, alcohol, pregnancy, and automobile accidents. According to the popular mythology at least, these have to be some of the most difficult years in the parent-child relationship. The only thing that could possibly be worse is not having the child around at all. And that is the other element of middle-aged parenting: letting go of the children. Optimists call it "launching"; pessimists discuss the "empty nest" and its accompanying syndrome. Is there nothing positive about parenting during middle age?

To make the picture bleaker still, many psychologists consider middle-aged people to be part of the "sandwich generation." They continue to face the pressures of active parenting, especially in financial terms. They are also being pressured by demands, especially for financial assistance, from aging parents. Just as their children begin to gain independence, their parents are becoming more dependent. Indeed, parents may become completely disabled by a stroke, Alzheimer's disease, or some other serious illness that will require the middle-aged person to care physically for a parent.

All of this can, of course, put pressure on a marriage. The children are gone. What do the spouses have in common now? There are no grades or children's baseball games to discuss. The spouses may well find that while the children were growing up, they were growing apart. And now one of their mothers-in-law needs attention or assistance. The possibility of considerable unhappiness seems significant. But listen to the middle-aged themselves:

> Just about now we have a comfortable home, two children, a grandchild, and I feel relaxed. That is a rather comfortable feeling—to be our age—to live for each other. (Deutscher, 1968/1964, p. 266)

273

Things are coming up now . . . These will be great years . . . We are both interested in our home and we look forward to taking a trip by boat. (Lowenthal & Chiriboga, 1982/1972, p. 335)

As always, the popular images are not always correct. Middle age is not a time of disintegration of familial relationships. However, the images are not groundless either ; there are stresses and strains in family life. And some families are at risk for dissolution.

MARITAL RELATIONSHIPS

By middle age, most people are married. Indeed, most people have been married for a long time (10 years or more). We certainly would expect their marriages to differ from the relationships of newlyweds or couples who have just had their first child. After all, adjustments to living together, including decisions about power, money, and sex, have been made. The children are older, and perhaps gone from the home, leaving more time to the parents as a couple. Furthermore, many of the most incompatible, unhappy couples will already be divorced. From a less positive perspective, the couple is aging, and physical infirmities or psychological disappointments in career or family may have set in. Resentments over long-unresolved differences may be taking their toll. Or the couple may have settled into a comfortable rut so that they take each other for granted. Thus, there are rationales for expecting middle-aged marriages to be happier than others. There are also reasons for expecting them to be less happy.

The "Average" Marriage

Parenting adolescents and the actual launching of children from the home can be quite stressful for a marriage. Thus, particularly in the early years of middle age, marital satisfaction is often quite low, especially for women (Harris et al., 1986; Lowenthal et al., 1975). Indeed, marital satisfaction is usually at its nadir during the school and adolescent years of the children. Typically, however, satisfaction rises after the children have left home (Campbell et al., 1976; Glick, 1984; Harris et al., 1986). While this is true of both men and women, middle-aged men appear to be more satisfied with their marriages than middle-aged women (Campbell et al., 1976). This sex difference may be a cohort effect, however, in that the middle-aged women in these samples had built their primary adult roles around being a wife, homemaker, and mother. It may be that, in such cases, the increasing demands on the husband's time from his career and the departure of the children could contribute to general dissatisfaction with family life. Ravenna Helson and James Picano reported that middle-aged women who had opted for traditional roles showed greater declines in psychological well-being than other women did. The traditional women also had developed more chronic health problems by the time they were 43 (Helson & Picano, 1990). With increasing numbers of women working outside the home throughout adulthood, we may eventually see the middle-age marital satisfaction of men and women moving toward equality. Indeed, recent research indicates that work satisfaction mediates the effects of adolescent development on middle-aged parents' well-being (Silverberg & Steinberg, 1990).

On the other hand, it has long been argued that marriage is more beneficial to men than to women (Bernard, 1981). For example, men's family roles appear to be less demanding than women's. Women may actually attempt to protect their spouses from family problems (Baruch, Biener, & Barnett, 1987). As men's health problems increase, the familial demands on women's time and energy become even greater. Indeed, one of the most distressing facets of the wife role for middle-aged women is the husband's health (Baruch & Barnett, 1986a). It is possible, then, that women have fewer reasons than men to be satisfied with their marriages.

Sexuality

Physical changes that might influence sexual behavior were described in Chapter 9. The conclusion was that normal physical aging does not interfere significantly with sexual intercourse and certainly should not result in the termination of sexual activity. Nonetheless, surveys consistently indicate that frequency of marital coitus does decline with age (Blumstein & Schwartz, 1983; Hunt, 1974). While the extent of the reported decline seems to vary depending on cohort, gender (women always report lower frequency), and other sample characteristics, the general trend is invariant.

There are huge individual differences in coital frequency. Some couples report no sexual activity during the year, others several hundred lovemaking sessions. Health, attitudes toward sex, and general marital satisfaction will all influence frequency. Compare the attitudes of two middle-aged people concerning sex. The first is from a woman who has been married for 30 years; the second is from a man who has been married 20 years.

> I don't like all this discussion about sex—even in the better magazines. I hope your study will help to put it in its proper perspective. I expected to perform sex in marriage, but both before and since, I'm willing to admit that it's a much overrated activity. Now and then, perhaps it's better. I am fortunate, I guess, because my husband has never been demanding about it, before marriage or since. It's just not that important to either of us. . . . (Cuber & Harroff, 1986/1965, p. 267)

> I love my sex and I've got a wife that loves it just as much as me. . . . Nowadays, even after twenty years of marriage, it's still about three times a week—and with the kids finally all in school, we've even started up again on the lunchtime. . . . My wife puts some of that . . . perfume on and I know right away that she wants it tonight and that really gets me going. . . . (Hunt, 1974, pp. 225–226)

Of course, marital sex is not the only possibility. By middle age, a significant portion of men and women have engaged in extramarital sex. Indeed, many people think of an "affair" as indicative of a midlife crisis.

The majority of Americans do not approve of extramarital sex. And, not surprisingly, they particularly disapprove of their spouses engaging in sex with someone else. Indeed, probably over 80 percent of Americans are opposed to their spouses engaging in extramarital sex (Hyde, 1985). But attitudes toward extramarital sex are not very good predictors of whether or not someone has an affair. Men appear to be more likely than women to engage in extramarital sex, with about 50 percent of the men and 25 percent of the women reporting having at least one encounter (Hyde, 1985). Of course, this may be a reporting bias, and the difference between men and women may not be so great. Furthermore, there may be a cohort effect, since younger women's reports of extramarital sex are more comparable to men's, while the gap continues between middle-aged and older men and women (Blumstein & Schwartz, 1983). We should note, however, that all major surveys considered here predated awareness of AIDS. It is entirely possible that there will be a decline in extramarital sex comparable to the shifts seen recently in premarital sex.

Why Do Marriages Last?

The problem with describing "average" marriages is that we are left with the impression that marriages are comparable. This is simply not the case. We tend to think of marriages that have lasted as "successful." In some sense, of course, they are—after all, one of the goals of newlyweds is to stay married. But staying married does not mean that the partners are blissfully happy; it does not even mean they are truly satisfied.

Types of Marriages

John Cuber and Peggy Harroff (1986/1965) identified five types of marriages among couples who had been married more than 10 years and had never contemplated divorce. Their study predated the huge rise in divorce in the United States, but the shift in divorce patterns should affect only the frequency, not the types of marriages themselves.

The *conflict-habituated marriage* is marked by considerable fighting and bickering. The fighting may be done mainly in private, or it may erupt when others (including the children) are present. There is typically considerable tension in the marriage, and the couple sees themselves as not agreeing very often. In other words, the spouses know they fight more than others do. Yet they do not leave or wish to leave. Some researchers and clinicians have suggested that such couples have a "neurotic" need to stay together (Cuber & Harroff, 1986/1965; Klagsbrun, 1985).

A much more common type of marriage is the *devitalized*. Indeed, many middle-aged people think a devitalized marriage is normal. In this type of marriage, the magic is gone and reality has set in. The couple's time together revolves around family and social obligations. Their conversations may, for example, center on the children and bills. They do not fight a great deal, and both share genuine concern about the children and careers. A housewife in her late forties described her devitalized marriage for Cuber and Harroff:

Judging by the way it was when we were first married—say the first five years or so—things are pretty matter-of-fact now—even dull. They're dull between us, I mean. The children are a lot of fun ... and even the company parties aren't always so bad. But I mean where Bob and I are concerned—if you followed us around, you'd wonder why we ever got married. We take each other for granted. We laugh at the same things sometimes, but we don't really laugh together—the way we used to....

Now I don't say all of this to complain.... There's a cycle to life. There are things you do in high school. And different things you do in college. Then you're a young adult. And then you're middle-aged ... you get the children and other responsibilities.... You have to adjust to these things and we both try to gracefully.... Anniversaries though do remind you kind of hard.... (1986, pp. 265–266)

The perceived change in the marriage, from being exciting to now being matter-of-fact, marks this as a devitalized marriage. A *passive-congenial* marriage, on the other hand, was never particularly exciting or romantic. These couples, like the devitalized, do not fight very often. They are comfortable in their marriages and will occasionally point out that they have certain "common interests." But there is not now, and apparently never was, passion in their marriage. While this is sometimes intentional, as in a marriage of convenience, it probably usually just happens because the couple is more interested in other aspects of life, such as career or having children or doing community work. Indeed, the passive-congenial marriage can fit societal needs quite well. Think, for example, of the "traditional" couple, with a busy professional man and the dutiful wife raising the children and providing a comfortable home for him. This type of marriage is not for everyone, but it certainly does work well for some people's needs.

The fourth type of marriage is the *vital*. These couples share virtually everything and truly enjoy each other's company. In fact, being together is what makes an activity or event fun for them. They are willing to give up other things, such as job advancement or social invitations, in order to do things together. Of course, they are still separate people whose needs and achievements will sometimes clash. But when they fight, they work to resolve the issue. This is different from the conflict-habituated couple, who never seem to finish fighting over any given issue. This type of marriage may be best summarized as one that emphasizes the importance of the couple over any other single aspect of life.

In the *total marriage*, there is virtually nothing in life other than the couple. They share everything. They work together, play together, raise the children together, and so on. They do not really have "separate" identities and interests, as is evident in this husband's description:

She keeps my files and scrapbooks up to date ... I invariably take her with me to conferences around the world. Her femininity, easy charm and wit are invaluable assets to me ... she's indispensable to me ... she'd go along with me even if there was nothing for her to do because we just enjoy each other's company—deeply. You know, the best part of a vacation is not what we do, but that we do it together. We plan it and reminisce about it and weave it into our work and other play all the time. (Cuber & Harroff, 1986/1965, p. 271)

As his description implies, one spouse must virtually build his or her life around the other's, and the recipient of such attention must find it enjoyable and helpful rather than smothering. As you might expect, then, such marriages are quite rare.

Formula for a Happy Marriage?

It should be clear that there is no one single type of long-lasting marriage. There is not even one single type of happy marriage. Many of the passive-congenial couples interviewed by Cuber and Harroff were perfectly satisfied with their marriages. One could easily envision others who would immediately leave a marriage if it were not marked by excitement and sharing. Indeed, Cuber and Harroff (1986/1965) found such couples and noted, therefore, that the seemingly "happier" types of marriage (the vital and the total) were not more stable than the others.

It is not surprising, then, that there is no single formula for building a successful marriage. But couples who have been married for a long time and are relatively satisfied and happy in their marriages do share certain common characteristics. After interviewing 87 couples who had been married at least 15 years, Francine Klagsbrun suggested that the more happily married couples shared eight characteristics.

First, Klagsbrun argues, these couples are able to accept change. They recognize that roles, needs, values, and so on change as children are born, promotions are won, parents age. They are able to adapt to these changes and accept them as an inevitable part of development. This does not mean that these people are passive victims of fate. Instead, they view themselves as having and making choices and being willing to accept the consequences of those decisions. They believe they chose to be married, and they continually reaffirm that choice.

At the same time, these couples are able to live with things they can't change (Klagsbrun, 1985). Successful couples are able to ignore certain faults in each other or the marriage. This too is evidence of the adaptability of these individuals. If you read Dear Abby or Ann Landers, you will often see them advise people not to marry someone who has a particular habit they dislike. Peoples' values and behaviors do not change because they get married, as domestic violence illustrates. It is highly unusual for a man to beat his girlfriend and then never hit her once they are married (Goodstein & Page, 1981). Similarly, premarital sexual behavior is one of the best predictors of the likelihood of engaging in extramarital sex (Hyde, 1985). On a less crucial level, people are not likely to stop biting their nails, snoring, and so on when they get married. You have to accept people as they are or not marry them.

One of the reasons successful couples are able to accept the imperfections in their spouses and marriages is because they work from the assumption that the marriage is permanent. This is more than a hope; for these couples, divorce is not an option. Some of this may be a cohort effect. Many of the couples in Klagsbrun's sample were married when divorce was much less acceptable. Usually one partner is particularly vehement in the belief that the marriage *must* survive and will make more compromises, changes, and so on than the other. Nonetheless, the commitment is not one-sided. Indeed, which person has the greater commitment may actually vary from time to time.

A fourth characteristic of happily married couples is that they trust each other (Klagsbrun, 1985). This does not apply just to sexual relations; they trust that their spouse will not ridicule their appearance, concerns, accomplishments, accidents, and good fortune. It is this trust that allows the intimacy noted by theorists such as Erikson (1980) and Sternberg (1986).

Similarly, a balance of dependencies facilitates intimacy. The members of the couple need each other. This characteristic is similar to Winich's concept of complementary needs (see Chapter 6). But this balance is not necessarily based on specific characteristics. Rather, the spouses meet each other's needs in a variety of areas. And the marriage itself also meets needs (socially, for example).

Sixth, the couples enjoy each other's company. They like to do things together, although they don't necessarily do everything together. These couples spend a good deal of their time together just talking, although they are also comfortable enough with each other to sit in silence and enjoy it. They will make compromises, such as alternating vacation sites or types of movies they see, in order to be together.

Eventually, couples build a history. Among happy couples, this history helps bind them together. They focus on the good times, particularly when the marriage is under some stress. Of course, young couples do not have this history to rely on and so it may be more difficult for them to envision how good marriage can be. One might say that the shared history gives a couple some perspective on problems. It also enables the individuals to recognize that they may be doing most of the giving right now, but that there were times when the spouse gave disproportionately.

Finally, there is an element of luck in successful marriages. Job loss, handicapped children, serious mental or physical illness, or financial catastrophe can strain a marriage to the breaking point. Many couples never have to face such stressors until the marriage is well-established. Recall, for example, Lowenthal's findings (Fiske, 1982; Lowenthal et al., 1975) concerning the different levels of stress individuals face during their lives. There is also, of course, an element of luck in choosing the right spouse. There are no guidelines for making a choice (which is probably one reason psychologists have been relatively unsuccessful in generating models of marital choice).

These characteristics apply to happy, long-lasting marriages whether they are first or second marriages (Klagsbrun, 1985). However, the rate of divorce is higher in second marriages than in first ones, particularly if one or both members of the couple have children (Glick, 1984).

Couples in successful marriages enjoy spending time together just talking.

Remarriage

Almost a third of marriages are remarriages. The vast majority of these are post-divorce rather than post-widowhood second marriages. Indeed, the vast majority of divorced people, perhaps 70 percent or more, will eventually remarry. The people least likely to remarry following a divorce are well-educated women (Glick, 1984). This is important to remember because some portion of divorced women probably remarry, perhaps too quickly, because they cannot adequately support themselves and their children. This will certainly affect adjustment to remarriage. Men with custody of their children are likely to remarry more quickly than noncustodial men (Glick, 1984). This trend too may have implications for the likelihood of a successful second marriage. We might expect, for example, that people who remarry quickly have not adjusted to divorce as well as those who delay remarriage.

One might expect that adjustment to remarriage is actually easier than it is for first-time marrieds. After all, the couple has experience in living with someone of the opposite sex. The partners are older and (one hopes) more mature (Goetting, 1982). But the previous experience is often one of the problems. When people are married for the first time, their values, ways of doing things, beliefs about division of labor, and so on are rooted in their parents' examples. Remarried people not only have these biases, but also the actual patterns they had established with the first spouse. And especially when children from a first marriage are present, those earlier patterns tend to be repeated (Goetting, 1982). This can create difficulties because it interferes with the couple's discovery of the patterns and roles that best fit the two of them.

Ann Goetting has suggested six components to adjusting to remarriage. The first, *emotional remarriage*, involves establishing a new emotional bond in a heterosexual relationship. This means overcoming fears that this relationship too will fail. In some ways, a remarriage is emotionally less risky than a first marriage. The individuals find divorce to be an acceptable solution to marital problems, and they know they can survive a divorce. On the other hand, one marital failure can be attributed to the other person, to unusual circumstances, to interfering in-laws, or to any number of factors other than one's own inadequacies. Two or more marital failures, however, start to raise questions about ability to get along with people. In this sense, remarriage presents a greater emotional risk.

The second task of remarriage is *psychic remarriage*. This means moving from identity as an individual to identity as a couple. For many people—especially, perhaps, women who married at a young age—this means giving up the first real freedom and autonomy they have ever had. A middle-aged woman who has been divorced for 4 years after a 13-year marriage describes the feeling:

> I don't rely on anyone but myself. I have my own needs and my own goals ... I won't make compromises in my life anymore. I have had three men ask me to live with them in the last four years, and I have said no. I want to live with myself. I will share some of my time and space with people I care about, but I won't have anyone else calling my shots ... I don't want to remarry. (Klagsbrun, 1985, p. 297)

For some people, on the other hand, the shift back to couple status is welcome. They were lonely while divorced. Indeed, loneliness is probably the most common complaint of divorced people (Kelly, 1982). Many people feel more a part of the "normal" adult community when they are married, since so many activities assume that couples will participate.

This assumption is related to the third component, *community remarriage*. Society at least indirectly encourages remarriage by making marital roles clearer than roles for divorced persons. However, remarriage also has its social costs. Often the friends who saw you through the divorce are lost because they are single. There is usually some loss of contact with friends, even after a first marriage, but losing touch with people who were important to you during a major life crisis can be particularly difficult (Goetting, 1982).

The fourth component, *economic remarriage*, is probably second only to parental remarriage in terms of difficulty. Having enough money is not usually a big problem, since the incomes of two households are now combined (Goetting, 1982). However, conflicts over how to spend the money may be particularly vituperative, especially if there are children from a previous marriage. Who should pay those children's expenses? Men whose stepchildren live with them while their biological children do not may feel particularly conflicted. Their stepchildren may enjoy a better standard of living than their biological children do, for example. On the other hand, if he pays enough child support to provide his children with opportunities, does he also have to ensure those opportunities to his stepchildren, even if their father is inconsistent (or worse) in his support payments? The mothers themselves often feel guilty and embarrassed about the cost of their children to their new husband. Whether this type of problem is alleviated by the increase in dual-earner (and, especially, dual-career) couples remains to be seen.

The couple must also accomplish *legal remarriage*. This refers not only to the legally sanctioned union, but to decisions about inheritance and legal responsibilities. Again, this is particularly difficult if children are involved. Even if they are not, questions may arise about whether or not the first spouse deserves any portion of the resources. For example, what if the newly remarried man is a doctor whose degree was made possible by his first wife's financial support? Does he owe her part of his income for the remainder of his professional life? What about life insurance policies or retirement funds that were started jointly by the original couple? All these questions need to be resolved, and there are few, if any, legal guidelines about how to do this.

Finally, if there are children, *parental remarriage* must occur. This is probably the most difficult task of remarriage and is probably the one most likely to endanger the new union.

The Stresses of Stepparenting

The presence of stepchildren makes the adjustment to remarriage more difficult. And the adjustment to stepparenting is the most difficult component of adjusting to remarriage. There are a number of reasons for this difficulty (Goetting, 1982; Visher & Visher, 1983).

Stepchildren symbolize the tie involved in a spouse's previous marriage. In fact, they typically require that the tie be maintained. Thus, because of the children, the new husband or wife will continue to have contact with the previous spouse. This may provoke feelings of jealousy or conflicted loyalty for one or both members of the new couple.

The presence of stepchildren also means that the new couple has no time to adjust to each other as a couple. Instead, they are a family right from the beginning. They do not have the privacy, free time, or financial freedom that first-time newlyweds enjoy. They are, in some ways, comparable to couples in which the woman is pregnant at the time of marriage. And the evidence clearly indicates that such couples are at greater risk for divorce (Kelly, 1982). The time alone that most first-time couples have allows them to work out roles, discuss options, and just get to know each other. Couples with stepchildren may not have such time because the children are always around.

Of course, the stepchildren may intentionally or indirectly undermine the new marriage. If the remarriage occurs quickly after the divorce, the child may not yet have given up hope of reuniting the parents (Wallerstein, 1983). Such a child might attempt to bring his mother and father back together. He might also try to present his new stepparent in a negative light, complaining about the stepparent's disciplinary tactics, interests, interference with family routines, and favoritism toward stepsiblings. On the other hand, a mother and her daughter (more so than her son) may develop a very close relationship in the divorce-remarriage interval (Hetherington, 1989). The daughter may become something of a confidant and companion. She may be given unusual (for a child) responsibilities. The arrival of a stepfather may interfere with this relationship, and this may be why daughters typically have more difficulty adjusting to stepparents than sons do (Hetherington, 1989). Thus, questions of discipline and change in family routines are real issues for remarried couples. Furthermore, the existing parent-child relationship can interfere with the new couple presenting a united front to the children concerning these questions. In such cases, the parent-child coalition may supersede or override the parent-parent coalition, a situation that bodes badly for the marriage.

Most stepparents and stepchildren eventually make positive adjustments (Clingeempl & Segal, 1986; Visher & Visher, 1983). The image of children or stepparents being hated or maltreated by one another is simply not true for most families. Love is not instant, of course, and loving a person does not mean you will automatically love their children. But apparently that love is sufficient to help most people make the adjustments and sacrifices required by stepparenting. Furthermore, stepparenting is rarely a "surprise"; the new spouse knew about the children and probably knew the children themselves prior to the marriage. Therefore, there was time to prepare at least cognitively for stepparenting and for the couple to discuss how they might handle certain situations.

PARENTING

The period of middle age covers roughly 25 years (from about 40 to 65 years of age). Parent-child relationships change quite dramatically during that time. At the beginning of middle age, most people will still have children living at home. In fact, the children may be quite young, particularly given recent trends toward delaying childbearing. Typically, though, the children are at least preadolescents (10–13 years old) as the parents embark on middle age. And virtually every middle-aged parent will, sooner or later, be dealing with an adolescent child.

Parenting Adolescents

Thanks in large part to theorists such as G. Stanley Hall and Erik Erikson, adolescence is commonly conceptualized as a period of great psychological stress. Adolescents are searching for an identity and so behave in an erratic and unpredictable way. They are questioning their parents' values so that they can decide what their own values will be. They are somewhat rebellious, but such rebellion is, in Erikson's view, not only necessary but healthy (Erikson, 1968).

If this portrayal of adolescence is correct, then we can expect considerable strife between parents and teenagers. There will be a serious generation gap. The disagreements will be intensified by the adolescents' cognitive development (Kidwell, Fischer, Dunham, & Baranowski, 1983; Smetana, 1988). They can now envision rules and values that are different from those of their parents and will want to know why their parents have adopted the attitudes and beliefs they have.

This type of challenge may be particularly difficult if the parent is already questioning his or her value system (Kidwell et al., 1983). In other words, if the parent is in a midlife transition or crisis, dealing with an adolescent may be almost intolerable. This is partially because teenagers have their entire lives ahead of them, while the middle-aged parents may be feeling the pressure of time. Certainly more than one teenage daughter has listened to lectures about how many more opportunities are open to her than her mother had. This could lead a parent to envy the adolescent. Similarly, the physical and sexual vigor of the teenager could cause jealousy on the parent's part (Kidwell et al., 1983). This may be one reason some parents disapprove of virtually anyone their son or daughter dates.

The combination of the child's and parents' developmental needs helps explain why some studies report that this is the least happy period in an adult's life and in a marriage (Lowenthal & Chiriboga, 1982/1972; Nock, 1982). The parents are in conflict with and about the teenager, as evidenced by one mother's statement:

> ... the main thing we really have our big arguments about is over our daughter ... because he feels that I'm taking her side too much.... And I feel that I ... want to protect her from him, because I think he gets too belligerent to her, instead of trying to talk sensibly. (Lowenthal & Chiriboga, 1982/1972, p. 338)

Parents report fights with teenagers on a wide range of issues. But the data indicate that most of the fights are over trivial issues such as hairstyles or clothing (Smetana, 1988). Although teenagers and parents feel less positive toward each other than they did in the past, their orientation is still predominantly positive (Jurkovic & Ulrici, 1985; P. Newman, 1982). Teens actually value their parents' opinions, especially on life issues such as careers (P. Newman, 1982; see also Chapter 3). Furthermore, midlife is not usually a time of significant crisis. The data indicate that adolescence is not particularly crisis-ridden either (Offer et al., 1984; Peterson, 1987). Thus, the developmental conflicts predicted by theory do not seem as likely once the data are examined.

Indeed, most parents do not report the adolescent years as the time of the most fights with their offspring. Rather, the bickering seems to peak in the pre-adolescent years, just as puberty begins (Jurkovic & Ulrici, 1985:

Steinberg, 1987). By mid-adolescence (about 15 or 16) most of the rules about dating and so on have been worked out, so the fighting actually declines. The research, then, suggests that parent-teenager conflict has been exaggerated. It does occur, but is probably confined primarily to trivial issues and better described as bickering. This certainly can be annoying—one mother depicted it as " . . . like being bitten to death by ducks" (Steinberg, 1987, p. 36)—but it does not threaten the integrity of the familial system.

Some families, of course, face more serious problems (Kidwell et al., 1983; Offer & Offer, 1975). These tend to be families in which the parents have trouble letting go of the children (Kidwell et al., 1983). In fact, such families are more likely than others to produce children who do experience a problem-filled adolescence (Offer & Offer, 1975; Friedlander & Siegel, 1989). Of course, the adolescent's problems will cause greater family conflict. But the conflict will continue even after the child has left the home.

Launching the Children

It is no surprise to parents that children grow up and leave home. Since birth, the parents have been gradually preparing the child to play a role in adult society. In the process, they have also prepared themselves (Rubin, 1980). The decisions made in infancy about weaning and toilet training as well as those in adolescence about dating and curfews were all steps toward letting the child go.

In fact, the launching of the children may actually be a relief for many parents. As one father pointed out: "It took a load off me when the boys left. I didn't have to support 'em anymore" (Deutscher, 1968/1964, p. 265). Finances are only one burden that may be reduced. More dramatic, perhaps, are the reductions in household labor. There are no children to be cooked for, cleaned up after, chauffeured around, or supervised. One mother in Deutscher's (1968/1964) study expressed it well:

> There's not as much physical labor. There's not as much cooking and there's not as much mending and, well, I remarked not long ago that for the first time since I can remember my evenings are free. And we had to be very economical to get the three children through college. We're over the hurdle now; we've completed it. Last fall was the first time in 27 years that I haven't gotten a child ready to go to school. That was very relaxing. (p. 265)

Parents repeatedly express that, while they are glad they had children, the increases in freedom, privacy, and available resources once they are gone make this a pleasant time in their lives (Alpert & Richardson, 1980; Cooper & Gutmann, 1987; Deutscher, 1968/1964; Lowenthal & Chiriboga, 1982/1972; Nock, 1982; Rubin, 1980).

Of course, such freedom is available *after* the children have left the home. Are parents equally positive about the launching period itself? Keep in mind that there may be several years between the time that the first child leaves home and the departure of the youngest one. This entire time constitutes the *launching period*.

Just as the birth of a baby causes shifts in family roles (see Chapter 6), the departure of the children will necessitate changes. Time use and household chores will need to be reallocated. There will be less to do, but not all parents will perceive this positively. Women who have built their lives— and their identities—around the homemaker/mother role may particularly suffer (Rubin, 1980). This may be why middle-aged women who occupy multiple roles as wife, mother, and worker seem to be happier than those who fill only one or two of the roles. Furthermore, among midlife women at least, motherhood itself does not appear to be a real source of satisfaction (Baruch & Barnett, 1986a). This may be at least partially attributable to the transitions occurring in the mother role.

That this is a time of transition seems quite clear. Rochelle Harris, Abbie Ellicott, and David Holmes (1986) defined a *transition* as " . . . a confluence of several psychosocial changes, often interrelated, that clustered together within the span of a few years" (p. 410). Both external behavioral changes and internal alterations in values or attitudes were considered. Using this definition, about 80 percent of the women interviewed experienced a major transition sometime during the family life cycle. Nearly half of these transitions occurred during the launching period, considerably higher than the rate reported at any other phase. The next highest percentage occurred during the postparental period (33 percent) followed by the preschool (28 percent), adolescent (17 percent), school-age (10 percent), and no children (8 percent) phases.

But Harris and her colleagues make the point that transitions are not necessarily negative—nor do they have to be difficult. Such a view is consistent with that of a number of theorists. However, their data indicate that most of the transitions that occurred during the launching phase did have a negative tone. Other data also indicate that, at least for women, this is often an unhappy time of life (Lowenthal et al., 1975). The unhappiness does not appear to be due primarily to the children's departure (Harris et al., 1986); instead, the difficulties were usually attributable to a marital problem or changes in work status (including reentering the work force). Many women felt that a period of both internal and external stability was ending. The nature of the transitions showed so much inter-individual variability, however, that no sweeping generalizations about causes can be made (Harris et al., 1986).

There is some suggestion that men may actually experience more of a sense of loss at the departure of the children (Rubin, 1980). In a traditional family, men have considerably less daily involvement and contact with the children than women do. Therefore, they are less aware of the children's gradual movement toward independence. The young father may be too busy establishing a career to spend much time with the child. By the time the father actually has spare time to spend with his children, they may be off with peers and not be readily available to him. This gives some fathers the sense that they have "missed" their children's growing up.

Some mothers are, of course, quite distressed by the departure of their children (Harris et al., 1986; Rubin, 1980). This is particularly likely if the mother is "overinvested" in the mother role—that is, if most or all of her identity is rooted in motherhood (Alpert & Richardson, 1980; Rubin, 1980). Such women have trouble letting go and fear that they are useless without children to mother. Fathers may have similar reactions if they were unusually attached to a particular child. Parents may also react negatively if they feel like failures as parents (Rubin, 1980). If the children seem ill-prepared to care for themselves or to contribute to society, the parents might wish for a second chance or might feel guilty and try to figure out "where we went wrong." Such families are, luckily, the exception rather than the rule.

As we have already indicated, the years following the departure of the children tend to be good ones. People feel more positive about themselves and their lives (Harris et al., 1986; Lowenthal, 1975). Women feel more assertive and, unless a relative's illness impedes it, freer to explore their own interests (Harris et al., 1986; Lowenthal, 1975). Thus, "emptying the nest" can trigger transitions. Roles and relationships are altered. There seems to be some temporary upheaval, particularly for women, but this appears less attributable to missing the children and more to the new roles the woman faces. The end of this transition brings most people a renewed sense of well-being and freedom.

GRANDPARENTING

Most people think of grandparents as elderly people. In one sense, the stereotype of the white-haired grandmother is correct. Over 75 percent of people over 65 are grandparents (Hagestad, 1985). However, grandparents may easily range in age from about 30 to 110. Most people become grandparents for the first time sometime during their forties or fifties (Burton & Bengston, 1985; Troll, 1985). So grandparenting is an issue for the middle-aged. And the nature of grandparenting is undoubtedly quite different for middle-aged and elderly (over 65 years) grandparents (Johnson, 1985; Troll, 1985).

The impact of age on grandparenting style is well-established. Indeed, some of the earliest work on grandparenting indicated that age was an important influence, with younger grandparents being more involved and playful than older ones (Neugarten & Weinstein, 1964/1968). Age is only one factor affecting the attitudes, involvement, and behaviors of grandparents. Indeed, there is probably no other role that is so nearly universal yet so heterogeneously defined as grandparenthood.

Grandparenting Styles

Most people feel fairly comfortable in the role of grandparent, and most grandparents are in regular contact with their grandchildren (Neugarten & Weinstein, 1964/1968; Troll, 1985). A common reason for discomfort with the role is inability to envision oneself as a grandparent. Whether we realize it or not, we all have expectations for our lives (Troll, 1985). Among those expectations is the age at which we expect to become grandparents. Yet the actual decision that makes us grandparents is out of our control. It is entirely possible to become a grandparent well before you feel "ready." Participants in a study of young adult and middle-aged black grandmothers by Linda Burton and Vern Bengston (1985) exemplify the conflict that the "off-time" grandparenting role can create:

> I could break my daughter's neck for having this baby. I just got a new boy-friend. Now he will think I'm too old. It was bad enough being a mother so young—now a grandmother too! (28-year-old grandmother; p. 61).

> This is the best time for me to become a grandma. I'm not too young to regret it and I'm not so old that I can't enjoy it ... I have the time, the money, and the knowledge to deal with my grandchild. ... (46-year-old grandmother; p. 73)

These quotes exemplify one of the few "normative" aspects of grand-parenthood—namely, that it occurs at a certain age. As with other life events, we can consider our entrance to grandparenting "on time" or "off time." Beyond that, the role is poorly defined (Johnson, 1985; Troll, 1980, 1985). It is one that is determined by the values, needs, and commitments of both the grandparent and the parent of the grandchild. So, for example, a working grandmother might play a different role than a non-working grandmother (Troll, 1985). Or a divorced mother might need more help from the grandmother than one whose husband is available (Bengston, 1985; Johnson, 1985). The role is in many ways personalized and idiosyn-cratic.

It should not be surprising, then, that research has indicated a variety of "styles" of grandparenting. The earliest taxonomy came from Neugarten and Weinstein's (1964/1968) study (see Table 10–1). They identified five types of grandparenting:

1. *Formal*: These grandparents clearly distinguish themselves from the grand-child's parent. They typically assume neither the responsibilities nor rights of par-enthood. So, for example, they rarely babysit or offer advice to the parents. They are, however, interested in their grandchildren.

2. *Fun seeker*: These grandparents view their grandchildren as playmates, taking

TABLE 10-1:   Frequency of Various Styles of Grandparenting

Style of Grandparenting	Grandmothers (N = 70)	Grandfathers (N = 70)
Formal	22	23
Fun-seeking	20	17
Parent surrogate	10	0
Reservoir of family wisdom	1	4
Distant figure	13	20
Insufficient data	4	6

Source: Neugarten, B., & Weinstein, K. (1964/1968). The changing American grandparent. In B. Neugarten (ed.), *Middle age and aging*, p. 282. Chicago: University of Chicago Press.

them fishing, on vacation, out to eat, and so on. Note that these are activities that will be enjoyed as much by the grandparent as by the grandchild. Authority over the child is rarely a central issue. Fun is the major concern.

3. *Surrogate parent*: As the name implies, these grandparents (or, more accurately, grandmothers) assume major parental responsibility for their grandchildren. They actually provide the discipline, caregiving, guidance, and so on that usually comes from the parent. The grandchild may live with them. In some cases, the grandchild's parents may not even live with the grandchild and grandparent on a regular basis.

4. *Reservoir of family wisdom*: This is an authoritarian type of role that is almost invariably played by grandfathers rather than grandmothers, although it is not common even among men. In many ways, however, it is the stereotypical grandfather role: a source of good advice and information as well as skills. Even the parents will defer to the grandfather in such cases.

5. *Distant figure*: In some ways this grandparent resembles the "formal" type. Both types are not intimately involved in daily decisions about the grandchild and assume a somewhat removed status in relation to the grandchild. However, contact between the grandchild and the formal grandparent is much more frequent than between the distant figure and the grandchild. In fact, the distant figure grandparent may see the child only on holidays and special family occasions.

At the time of Neugarten and Weinstein's research, the parent surrogate role was fairly rare (see Table 10-1). Several authors have recently made the point that this may be changing (Bengston, 1985; Johnson, 1985). As divorce and single parenthood become more common, grandparents (again, particularly grandmothers) may be called upon to help in the care of their grandchildren. African-American grandmothers may be especially likely to help raise their grandchildren (Harrison et al., 1990). Middle-aged rather than elderly grandmothers are likely to be asked to provide assistance, mainly because the grandchildren of the middle-aged grandparent are more likely to require care (Johnson, 1985).

Note, however, that such help will typically be provided only upon request, for at least two reasons. First, the middle-aged grandparent is likely to be quite busy with job, spouse, household, and perhaps children still at home. Second, there is a widely held belief, at least among grandmothers, that one ought not to interfere in one's child's and grandchild's lives (Johnson, 1985). Middle-aged grandmothers, particularly, make an effort to be nonjudgmental and accepting of their children's decisions, though this is not always easy for them (Johnson, 1985; Troll, 1985). This may be a cohort effect based on parenting through the 1950s, 1960s, and 1970s. But it does mean that these women do not emphasize the importance of "passing on" family values. They view such socialization as the parents' responsibility (Johnson, 1985). The idea of parents as exclusive socializers may, however, be more common among middle-class Euro-American families than in extended African-American families (Harrison et al., 1990).

These styles summarize some of the actual patterns of interaction between grandparents and grandchildren. Behaviors are not always directly correlated with attitudes. A low correlation is particularly likely in the case of grandparenting because the playing of the role depends heavily on the "permission" of others (namely, the parents of the grandchild). It is there-

fore important to consider what grandparents believe they ought to be doing with their grandchildren because it gives us some idea of why they are
or are not satisfied in the role. It also helps to clarify how much of the role
is socially defined.

The Meaning of Grandparenting

Like many other roles, our expectations and beliefs about grandparenting have been influenced by the way our parents played the role. Nonetheless, social changes, especially in women's roles, and in divorce, have
altered the needs of both grandparent and grandchild. Furthermore, the
role has always been marked by the ambiguity of wanting to help but not
wanting to interfere (Bengston, 1985). Such ambiguity may be heightened
in divorce, for example, where the grandparents' rights and responsibilities
(even for visitation) have yet to be defined (Hagestad, 1985).

Grandparents see their sheer presence as a major component of their
role (Bengston, 1985). The presence of a grandparent gives the family a
sense of continuity, of rootedness, and, perhaps, of an ability to survive
adversity. After all, the grandparent is evidence of the resilience and persistence of people. In addition, the presence of a grandparent typically offers
assurance that there is *someone* who cares what happens and will be willing
to help.

Of course, some grandparents are more active and more clearly available than others. They make it clear that they are ready to give financial,
social, or personal help. In many families, of course, this readiness is purely
symbolic. The children and grandchildren rarely call on the grandparents
for help. But if help is requested, it is more likely to be asked of the middle-
aged rather than the elderly grandparent.

Grandparents also apparently see it as their role to maintain a certain
level of intergenerational contact (Hagestad, 1985). This does not mean that
they are constantly, or even frequently, calling their grandchildren in order
to see them. But as the efforts of grandparents whose children divorce indicates, they will try to have regular contact with the children. Indeed, grandparents may become closer to their ex-daughter-in-law in order to maintain
contact with their grandchildren. This, of course, could create conflict between the son and the grandparents.

More commonly, the grandparents' desire to maintain intergenerational communication is evident in the type of interactions they have with
their grandchildren. As the grandchildren get older, there are "demilitarized zones" of conversation (Hagestad, 1985). These are issues that are
avoided because they might precipitate conflict. With a younger child, such
issues might include difficulty at school or a parent-child conflict about
having a party; with adolescents, demilitarized zones might focus on sex,
drugs, or dating.

Grandparents, then, view themselves as a stabilizing force in the family. They provide backup to the parents, a sense of continuity for the family,
and protection from external forces (Bengston, 1985; Hagestad, 1985). This
is what grandparents think they mean to their families. But what role does
grandparenting play in their lives?

Table 10-2 indicates some of the meanings attached to the grandparent role (Neugarten & Weinstein, 1964/1968). The categories are not mutually exclusive; some grandparents fit more than one category. There is also overlap between these and the styles of grandparenting outlined earlier.

Grandparenthood may be significant because it is a *source of biological renewal and/or continuity*. It may be through grandchildren that the grandparent feels young again or feels connected to the future. This meaning of grandparenthood would probably be more salient to older grandparents. Indeed, among younger grandparents, the role may actually make them feel old (Burton & Bengston, 1985).

Some grandparents may also feel *emotional fulfillment* in the role. It is a new opportunity for a successful interpersonal relationship. Many grandfathers, for example, find that they can be close to their grandchildren in a way they couldn't be with their own children. Both career demands and the necessity of being a disciplinarian might have precluded real closeness with their own children (Neugarten & Weinstein, 1964/1968). In a related vein, grandparenthood might provide *vicarious achievement*. This is especially likely when the grandchild is seen as having an opportunity to accomplish something that neither the grandparent nor parent could.

Some grandparents relish their role as *resource person*. They enjoy giving advice or providing financial aid. This gives them a sense of importance and usefulness. According to Neugarten and Weinstein (1964/1968), few people seemed to attach much significance to this aspect of grandparenting.

The final group is grandparents who are *remote*, who attach little or no personal significance to the role. This might happen because of problems between the grandparent and his or her own child. Or, especially among grandmothers, the lack of preparedness to assume the grandparent role might be important. As one of the participants in Neugarten and Weinstein's study said: "It's great to be a grandmother, of course—but I don't have much time. . . . " (1964/1968, p. 283). Note her near-apology for her attitude. This too is a common component of the remote grandparent's attitude.

While most grandparents are not remote, research does indicate that

TABLE 10-2:   The Significance of Grandparenting Role to Grandparents

Significance of Grandparent Role	Grandmothers (N = 70)	Grandfathers (N = 70)
Biological renewal/continuity	29	16
Emotional self-fulfillment	13	19
Resource person to child	3	8
Vicarious achievement through child	3	3
Remote; little effect on self	19	20
Insufficient data	3	4

Source: Neugarten, B., & Weinstein, K. (1964/1968). The changing American grandparent. In B. Neugarten (ed.), *Middle age and aging*, p. 282. Chicago: University of Chicago Press.

few of them view the relationship with their grandchildren as central (Troll, 1980). Grandparents are glad to see their grandchildren; they are also glad to see them go home. Young grandchildren, particularly, require consider-able expenditure of energy and close supervision. Visits may actually be draining or exhausting to the grandparents. Raising one set of children (their own) was enough for most grandparents; they do not wish to raise their grandchildren. And many grandparents, especially the middle-aged ones, have conflicting obligations to jobs, friends, each other, and in many cases, their own parents. It would almost be impossible for them to build their lives around their grandchildren, even if they wanted to.

Factors Influencing Diversity

Grandparenthood may be viewed as a tenuous role (Burton & Bengs-ton, 1985). It is a role that is recognized and has a status within a family, yet it carries few rules or norms. Therefore, most grandparents are left to define the role themselves.

Grandparents are a very diverse group of people demographically, so-cially, and behaviorally. Some are young (under 30), others are very old (over 100). Some are employed, others retired, and still others (especially grandmothers) were never employed. Some have good relationships with their adult children; others do not. Some have a spouse and children at home to care for and interact with; others live alone.

As might be expected, this diversity is reflected in the attitudes and grandparental style of the grandparent. We have already seen the influence of several factors. People who become grandparents "on time" appear more accepting of the role than those who view themselves as too young or too old (Neugarten & Weinstein, 1964/1968; Burton & Bengston, 1985). The di-vorce of the grandchild's parents may affect both the extent and nature of the grandparent role (Johnson, 1985). Women are more likely to assume a surrogate parent role than men are, and men are more likely to be distant, though neither style is particularly common.

Several researchers (see Bengston, 1985; Hagestad, 1985; Troll, 1985) have suggested more pervasive gender differences in grandparenting. In general, grandmothers report closer relationships with their grandchildren, especially their granddaughters. The grandmothers assume more of an af-fective role in the family, keeping family members in contact (and on good terms) with one another. In other words, grandmothers are more likely than grandfathers to be the negotiators in the family. Grandfathers, on the other hand, are more likely to view themselves as advice givers or as simply need-ing to stay out of the way. These gender differences seem to reflect tradi-tional sex roles in American society. Therefore, we might expect that they are influenced by cohort and perhaps time of measurement. In other words, future generations of grandparents may not show such marked sex differ-ences.

Social class differences are also evident (Troll, 1985). Grandparent-hood is likely to occur at an earlier age among the lower class. As is often the case when the parents of the grandchild are younger than average, lower-class grandparents (especially the grandmother) are more likely to assume a surrogate parent role. Lower-class grandparents are more likely than middle-class grandparents to be squeezed financially and in terms of time. Their own parents are less likely to have adequate retirement income, health benefits, and so on. And their children are less likely to be employed and have adequate health insurance. Their grandchildren are more likely to need health care. The burden on the lower-class grandparent may be great.

The employment status of the grandparent may also play a role (Johnson, 1985; Cherlin & Furstenberg, 1985; Troll, 1985). This is more true for grandmothers than grandfathers. One might expect that working grandparents would have less time to spend with their grandchildren. Research does not indicate that non-working grandmothers actually have more contact with their grandchildren. Of course, the working grandmothers are likely to be younger and in better health than the non-working ones, and both age and health are positively related to grandmother-grandchild contact (Aldous, 1985). Contact is not the only variable that might be affected; working grandparents may have more money and more family status. Either of these might affect their relationships to their grandchildren (Troll, 1985). Perhaps even more significant, working grandmothers do not view their grandchildren as being as central part of their lives as non-working grandmothers do (Kivnick, 1985). This too might be expected to affect grandparent style.

Thus, a variety of factors may contribute to the style of grandparenting. Many other factors, such as personality, probably also play a role; few of the influences are well understood.

RELATIONSHIPS WITH FAMILY OF ORIGIN

Thus far our definition of familial relationships has been focused on, if not restricted to, spouses and children. In other words, the emphasis has been on the family of procreation. Certainly, this emphasis reflects both the theoretical models and the daily experiences of adulthood. However, such an approach is incomplete. Relationships with the family of origin do not dissolve as soon as a marriage occurs; both parents and siblings continue to play a role in our lives.

Sibling Relationships

The sibling relationship is unique (Cicirelli, 1980, 1985). First, for most people, it is the longest-lasting relationship they have. With increased longevity, it is not unusual for a sibling relationship to last 80 or 90 years. Second, siblings share many intimate experiences, especially in childhood. Siblings themselves cite these shared experiences as the basis of their closeness (Dunn, 1984). Their traditions, values, and attitudes are forged in very similar environments. They live in closer quarters than they will with anyone else, except perhaps a spouse. They know each other's strengths and

Middle-aged people often have extensive, complicated family relationships that include parents, siblings, spouses, children, and grandchildren.

weaknesses in a way that others cannot. Finally, the sibling relationship is, at least eventually, more egalitarian than most others. After all, neither sibling is "in charge" of the household; neither controls the finances or makes most of the major decisions; neither one can "hire" nor "fire" the other.

There is little doubt that siblings serve as important role models in childhood (Dunn, 1983) and that they help socialize and support each other. But how important are these relationships in adulthood? Do siblings continue to be particularly important people in the lives of most adults?

Siblings are not as important as spouses or even parents (Cicirelli, 1985). For example, they are only rarely consulted on decisions not directly related to the family of origin. The closer a person is to a spouse, the less likely he or she is to be very close to siblings. The majority of siblings report a decrease in closeness once one of them marries (Dunn, 1984). In fact, too much sibling involvement could interfere with spousal relationships or social relationships in general. Thus, it is expected that the sibling relationship will not be the central one for most adults.

On the other hand, sibling relationships do not disappear during adulthood. The majority of adults have at least one sibling. This is true even of elderly (over 80) people. Furthermore, at least during young and middle adulthood, most of us have at least one sibling living within 100 miles of us (Cicirelli, 1980). The closer our siblings live, the more likely we are to have contact with them. Higher levels of emotional closeness and feelings of responsibility to siblings also contribute to greater sibling contact and interaction (Lee, Mancini, & Maxwell, 1990).

Siblings typically do feel some sense of obligation to one another

(Goetting, 1986; Lee et al., 1990). They will help each other in times of need, though it is more common for people to turn to spouses or parents or even their own children. Siblings also provide emotional support, as they did when they were children, although the amount of such interaction certainly decreases as family of procreation obligations increase (Goetting, 1986).

Older adults report feeling closer to their siblings than do middle-aged people, who are closer to their siblings than are young adults (Cicirelli, 1980, 1985). It is not yet known whether these differences reflect a developmental or a cohort effect, since virtually all the research on adult sibling relationships is cross-sectional. It does seem, however, that while closeness may be maintained or increased throughout adulthood, it rarely *originates* then (Dunn, 1984). A similar trend exists for sense of compatibility, which increases across age groups. Compatability is not always (or even usually) identical for all sibling pairs in a family. Most people report feeling closer to one sibling than to others. Most commonly, this is a sister and a middle child (Cicirelli, 1980).

The amount of conflict and rivalry decreases across age groups (Goetting, 1986), although this is less true for brothers than for sisters. It is probably attributable at least partially to the decreased contact among siblings in old age. Some researchers have suggested that the decrease in rivalry may be more apparent than real. Perhaps adults believe it is socially unacceptable to compete with their siblings and so report that they do not. Of course, conflict and rivalry can, and often do, arise in certain situations, particularly those involving the care of aging parents or the settling of parental estates.

Siblings are clearly emotionally attached to each other (Cicirelli, 1985; Goetting, 1986; Lee et al., 1990). Indeed, it is very unusual for people to lose or break off contact with siblings. Yet, they only occasionally provide real aid or assistance. Again, there is some increase in the amount of mutual aid provided across age groups. Some sisters will, for example, virtually replace a widowed brother's wife temporarily. Siblings will also often support each other in times of crisis, such as illness or death. But such help is often limited by the proximity of the siblings and the lack of close contact between them. In a sense, siblings seem ready to help, but rarely are actually asked to do much.

What purpose do sibling relationships serve in adulthood? The relationship implied thus far is significant. Knowing there is someone available to help can be a great comfort. And the sibling may actually be called upon. In addition, siblings are used to reminisce, a function particularly important to the elderly or the dying who are in the process of life review (Goetting, 1986; see also Chapter 17). In addition, siblings may still be contributing to one another's socialization. They may provide role models for each other in terms of how to handle certain problems with children, jobs, or spouses. They may also continue to serve as "pioneers" in relationships with parents. The behavior of one sibling may pave the way for another. The first one to go to college may help convince the parents that moving away from home is a good experience for the adolescent. The first child to get divorced may face pressure that later ones do not because the parents have become more accepting of the idea. Certainly, siblings are not the major socializing agents during adulthood, but they may continue to contribute to development. Siblings may also work together to provide care for aging parents (Goetting, 1986).

Relationships with Parents

One outcome of increased longevity is that large numbers of middle-aged people have living parents. These aging parents often develop health problems. Many (indeed, most) of their mothers will be widowed and need help with a variety of daily activities. At the very least, aging parents will find it increasingly difficult to get out to visit children and grandchildren. Therefore, responsibility for personal contact will fall to the adult child.

In the United States, the government does provide some aid to the elderly. Most of this assistance is financial, in the form of Social Security and Medicare. These and other government programs relieve some of the financial burden. However, in many cases the Social Security money is not sufficient. Furthermore, someone has to help elderly people apply for and secure the government money. Middle-aged children often serve as mediators between government agencies and their parents (Aizenberg & Treas, 1985). If problems develop and a visit to the Social Security office is needed, for example, the middle-aged child is often called upon to provide the transportation.

The fact of the matter is that currently most services to the elderly are provided by family members (Aizenberg & Treas, 1985; Brody, Kleban, Johnsen, Hoffman, & Schoonover, 1987; Giordano & Beckman, 1985). These services may range from driving the older adult to the grocery store and doctors' appointments to providing full-time care to a bedridden parent (Brody et al., 1987). The time, energy, and financial demands of caring for an aging parent may pressure a middle-aged adult who is already being pushed (or pulled) by providing aid to his or her own children. This is what Elaine Brody (1981) meant when she coined the phrase "middle generation squeeze."

Filial Maturity: These arguments make it sound as if most people will someday have to provide some care or assistance to their aging parents (or parents-in-law or grandparents). In fact, this assumption is so widely accepted that Blenkner (1965) has suggested that a normal task of adulthood is the achievement of *filial maturity*: the adult child's recognition that he or she is an adult and therefore has certain responsibilities. Furthermore, aging parents are seen as "colleagues," not authority figures. There is now a reciprocal relationship; the child can either give or receive aid. Of course, the parents too must recognize the child as an adult and must see the reciprocal nature of the relationship for this process to be successful (Aizenberg & Treas, 1985; Giordano & Beckman, 1985).

Filial maturity implies that the adult children view themselves as autonomous yet connected to their parents (Aizenberg & Treas, 1985; Feldman & Feldman, 1984). Not all adult children achieve this perspective. They may instead be *role-determined* in their relationship to their parents (Feldman & Feldman, 1984). In other words, they continue to act like obedient, dependent children. They may provide assistance, but it is often out of a sense of guilt or fear or wanting to please (Aizenberg & Treas, 1985). Other children may reject their filial responsibility altogether. These are often people who felt rejected and unsupported as children or who are currently seeking their own identity (Feldman & Feldman, 1984).

Filial maturity is *not* the same as a role reversal. Caregiving children do not normally become parental figures to their parents (Giordano & Beckman, 1985). The parents still typically do many things for themselves and usually retain control of their finances. The vast majority of the elderly live in their own homes, thereby continuing a level of privacy and decision making that is not routinely available to young children. The child does not become a parent to the parent. Rather, he or she becomes an adult who is offering aid to another adult. And, at least in middle-class families, the adult child is often still the recipient of some aid from the parent. Once again, this underscores the reciprocal nature of the relationship.

The Caregivers: Daughters are the family members most likely to provide care or assistance to the elderly (Brody et al., 1987) This continues to be true despite the rise in number of working women, In fact, there is little difference between the aid provided by working and non-working women (Brody & Schoonover, 1986). Working daughters provide comparable amounts of help with tasks such as shopping, transportation, and emotional support. Non-employed daughters are, however, more likely to help with cooking and personal care.

It would be difficult to argue that it is only the employment status of the daughter that influences how much care her parent (usually her mother) receives from her. First, we know that factors such as the daughter's marital status and the living arrangements of the elderly parent play a role. Married daughters whose parents do not live with them provide less care than daughters who are single or residing with their parents (Horowitz, 1985; Lang & Brody, 1983). Furthermore, the parent's needs will influence how much care is given.

The level of the parent's needs may conflict with the daughter's own life, especially her work. The Long-Term Care Survey (Stone et al., 1986, cited in Brody et al., 1987) indicated that over one-third of caregiver daughters had rearranged their work schedules in order to provide care. A quarter of them had taken unpaid time off from work to help their parents. A British survey indicated that about one-fifth of part-time women workers did not work full-time because of their parents' needs (Rossiter & Wicks, 1982 cited in Brody et al., 1987). Even more dramatically, about 12 percent of daughters taking care of their parent quit their jobs in order to do so (Brody et al., 1987). In fact, caring for ill relatives is the second most common reason middle-aged women give for leaving the workforce (the first is their own illness).

Such women are particularly likely to show the strain of caring for an ailing parent. They report more of their own health problems than do caregiver daughters who have either never worked or continue to work. And yet some of the women who continue to work may be considering giving up their jobs. These tend to be women whose mothers' cognitive functioning is impaired (Brody et al., 1987). A substantial number of these women try hiring someone to care for their mother, but this kind of help does not seem to relieve the stress they experience. Some of this stress is due to the interference with their work created by the mother's illness.

It is possible, of course, that the role assumed by daughters will change as more and more women work at careers rather than jobs. Indeed, Elaine Brody and her colleagues found that the caregiving daughters who did not leave work saw their jobs as having a very central role in their lives. Perhaps in the future there will be greater egalitarianism between men and women in the care of their aging parents.

Middle-aged Recipients: It would be a mistake to leave the impression that middle-aged children simply provide care to their parents. Many older parents are continuing to provide financial assistance to their middle-aged children and to their grandchildren (Hill, Foote, Aldous, Carlson, & Macdonald, 1970; Giordano & Beckman, 1985). This may be particularly true in upper-middle-class families in which the oldest generation controls substantial family resources (Troll, 1982). As we noted earlier, this may also be particularly true in divorced families. Recent research (Wallerstein & Blakeslee, 1989) indicates that middle-class divorced fathers may often refuse to pay for their children's college educations. It is possible that, in the future, grandparents will step in to pay some of the tuition bills.

Keep in mind also that the earlier discussion of grandparenting indicated that some grandparents may provide help with childcare. Again, this may be particularly true in divorced or dual-earner families. It is also possible that such aid is provided sporadically to a wide range of couples. So, for example, many couples who wish to vacation without their children may ask their parents to take the kids. Similarly, help may be given in terms of caring for the middle-aged child's home or in cases of illness. However, it is much more common for middle-aged children to provide these forms of aid than to receive them.

SUMMARY

Family life during middle age does not appear to be nearly as bleak as the opening paragraphs of this chapter suggest. Relationships with spouses remain strong. Some marriages lose some of their passion but, as was the case from the beginning, there are wide individual differences among couples as to the roles they assume in their marriage. Such diversity exemplifies the principle that there is no one, single correct path to normal development or life satisfaction. It is not surprising, then, that no formula for a successful marriage was identified. There are, however, certain characteristics that marked long-married couples. These include flexibility, a commitment to the marriage, and a willingness to accept flaws.

Not all marriages are successful; many result in divorce. Remarriage presents challenges that are quite different from those faced in a first marriage. Two of the most difficult are economic and parental remarriage. These are interrelated challenges, inasmuch as many of the economic conflicts are likely to revolve around the support of children from previous marriages. Most of these issues are eventually resolved, and the relationship between stepparent and stepchildren usually ends up being at least adequate.

Middle-aged parents, biological or not, find themselves faced with adolescent children. Again, the strains of parenting adolescents have probably been exaggerated. There are conflicts to be settled, and the economic burdens can be very great. This is probably one of the reasons that marital satisfaction is often quite low at this period. Keep in mind, however, that parenting itself, not just parenting adolescents, is associated with low marital satisfaction.

Furthermore, for most couples marital satisfaction will rise dramatically (almost to newlywed levels) once the children are launched. The departure of the children provides new freedom, privacy, and financial flexibility. Of course, it also brings a need for a redefinition of roles and responsibilities. And for parents who have built their identities around parenthood (more typically women) or feel they have missed out on their children (more commonly men), this may be a difficult adjustment. This again underscores the fact that individual differences among adults are rooted in earlier development and decisions.

Parent and spouse are not the only family roles played by the middle-aged. Many of them are grandparents. Once more we see marked individual differences in styles of grandparenting as well as in its importance in a particular person's life. In general, the middle-aged are glad to be grandparents, but they don't usually build their lives around this role. They are often still working themselves, and they are frequently both physically and financially able to enjoy life now.

Finally, there are relationships with the family of origin. Siblings may be viewed as an available resource, but they are rarely called upon for help. Aging parents may provide assistance to their middle-aged children. More commonly, though, the middle-aged child is asked to help the parent(s). Government resources for helping the sick or disabled elderly are woefully limited; most of the responsibility falls to the family, particularly daughters or daughters-in-law. This can create time, energy, and financial drains on the middle-aged child, especially if the aged parent has suffered intellectual declines.

11 Work

There is little doubt that work is at the core of adult experiences. It determines or influences our standard of living, our self-esteem, our social status and acceptability, our place of residence, and our social connections. It fills a tremendous portion of our waking time. It provides the context for much of our adult development. Furthermore, our society offers virtually no alternative to work (Garfinkel, 1982). You either work or are out of work. Certainly, unemployment is viewed negatively. Even retirement often seems suspect, particularly given its connotations of uselessness and declining competence. Full-time homemaking/parenthood, which might be viewed as an alternate, is frequently demeaned because it is not "work."

If young adulthood represents a period of deciding what type of career or work is desirable, middle adulthood represents living with that choice. As we noted in Chapter 7, few middle-aged men change their jobs, much less their careers. Probably only about 10 percent of men between the ages of 40 and 60 hold a variety of different jobs (Havighurst, 1982). This is not a negligible number, of course, but clearly the vast majority of men stay in their jobs. They are in a period of career stabilization (Super, 1957, 1985).

Stability does not mean there are no interesting questions to be asked. Do they stay, for example, because they are happy in their jobs? Or because age discrimination narrows their options? Or are there personality changes or family demands that cause middle-aged men to value stability above many other job characteristics?

You might notice that we have been discussing men but not women. This is because women often follow different career paths. As we saw in Chapter 7, women are more likely to take time off to care for children. Some may rejoin the work force only during the middle years (Havighurst, 1982). While today's trend is not for women to stay home, the available research is typically based on women who were middle-aged in the 1960s,

1970s, and even 1980s. We have considerable data on women who did stay home, since among those cohorts, women who worked their entire adult lives were something of a rarity.

Women are also more likely to feel conflicted in the face of career and family demands. In conjunction with work history and career choice differences, this conflict may make work in the middle years a different experience for women than for men. It is therefore important to remember that information gathered from male workers may not reflect the attitudes or behaviors of female workers.

WORK MOTIVATION

Arthur Miller's (1957) characterization of Willy Loman captured many of the stereotypes about the middle-aged worker nearing retirement. Loman has worked for the same company for many years. He is loyal to it, a "company man." He likes his job and believes he understands it and does it well. Yet he is actually incompetent, no longer able to keep up with changes in the market or with the sales levels of the younger personnel. How accurate is this portrayal of the older American worker?

A Theoretical Framework

In order to understand how workers of different ages approach and evaluate their jobs, it is important to have a general understanding of what leads people not just to work, but to do the best they can. There are many applicable theories. Some are general motivational theories, such as Maslow's hierarchy of needs. In Maslow's theory, certain survival needs must be met first (food, shelter, physical safety). Then the person will automatically be motivated by more psychological needs, specifically belongingness and love needs and esteem needs. All four of these needs may contribute to interest in or willingness to work. After all, work provides the funds to purchase housing, food, and clothing. It is also a source of friendships and companionship. And, of course, a job done well and rewarded may bolster self-esteem.

Maslow's hierarchy of needs provides us with some understanding of why people work, but it does not tell us why someone might be satisfied, highly motivated, and work hard at a particular job. That is really the question of interest here.

J. Richard Hackman and G. R. Oldham (1976) have developed the *job-characteristics theory of work motivation*. This theory, which is summarized in Figure 11–1, specifies several variables related to attitudes about work and job performance. As the name of the theory implies, many of the variables are job characteristics. Three of these—skill variety, task identity, and task significance—combine to provide information about the meaningfulness of the job. These include the number and variety of skills needed to perform the job. The more complex the job, the more challenging and rewarding it is. Task identity refers to whether the worker completes a job (or

FIGURE 11-1:   Job Characteristics Theory of Work Motivation.

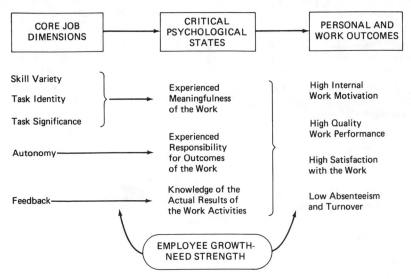

Source: Hackman, J., & Oldham, G. (1976). Motivation through the design of work: Test of a theory. *Organizational Behavior and Human Performance, 16,* p. 256.

product) or just does part of it. Most people find it more meaningful to be involved in the whole job. Imagine how frustrating it can be to see the same component of a car engine over and over without ever seeing the completed engine, much less the car. Such job fragmentation is one of the things that makes assembly line work monotonous and unrewarding.

The third is the importance of the task. This is one reason that doctors' work is perceived as meaningful. What task could be more important than saving human lives? Compare this to the ticket-taker at the movie theater. In general, a worker who views a job as important will be more likely to be motivated to do it well.

Jobs also differ in how much responsibility is assigned to a worker and how much feedback is available to that worker. These characteristics are also related positively to work motivation. The relationship between job characteristics and worker behavior is not independent of the worker; the employee's own need for growth is a mediating factor. Furthermore, the combination of high responsibility and poor feedback from management may be detrimental. Indeed, this combination has been associated with a variety of health problems, including coronary disease and gastrointestinal problems (Repetti et al., 1989).

The job characteristics model, like most models of work motivation, emphasizes the importance of an interesting, challenging job for worker satisfaction. Presumably, people with greater responsibility and authority should be more satisfied. So should people whose jobs are complex and important.

Job Characteristics and the Older Worker

A quick look at the job characteristics model might lead us to hypothesize that the middle-aged worker will be more satisfied than the younger worker. The middle-aged worker is likely to be in a job that utilizes his or her skills. If the skills are not well matched to the job, the person probably would have changed jobs long ago. Furthermore, the middle-aged person is apt to have moved up the job ladder at least a little. Therefore, the job is often more complex and skilled than that of the younger worker. Recall from Chapter 7 that one of the most common complaints of the younger worker is that the work is mindless and tedious. Being a trainee is not the same thing as being a manager!

Along with the greater complexity comes greater autonomy. Because middle-aged workers have experience and have proved themselves, they are less likely to be actively and directly supervised. Indeed, there is some chance that they are now supervisors themselves. There is at least one possible exception to this. If the employer begins to suspect that the biological aging process is affecting the worker's capabilities, supervision might actually be increased.

It is important to note here that the comparisons being made between younger and older workers are *within* job types. There are many differences across jobs that operate more or less independently of age. In fact, job characteristics of the type outlined in Hackman and Oldham's model are probably more important determinants of work attitudes and behavior than age (see Rhodes, 1983; Schultz & Schultz, 1986). Nonetheless, age has been consistently shown to be correlated with at least some job-related attitudes, behaviors, and values.

Job Attitudes

How do most people feel about their work? This is not a trivial question. What we do is an important component of who we are. It should not be surprising, then, that researchers frequently find that job satisfaction is related positively to life satisfaction (Bray & Howard, 1980). Of course, job satisfaction is not the sole determinant of life satisfaction. Family, leisure activities, commitments to church or community work, and a myriad of other activities can significantly add to or detract from life satisfaction (Stagner, 1985). But work is an important contributor. Employers are also interested in increasing job satisfaction (Schultz & Schultz, 1986; Stagner, 1985). As the work motivation model presented earlier suggests, job satisfaction is related to productivity and commitment to work.

Most Americans are satisfied with their jobs. Post-World War II Gallup polls consistently indicate that between 87 and 90 percent of workers hold positive attitudes about their jobs. This does not necessarily mean they think their jobs are ideal; significant numbers of blue-collar workers, for example, would like to change jobs. They believe better jobs might have more to offer. But they do not see their jobs as inherently poor; workers are satisfied when they see few negative aspects of their jobs (Schultz & Schultz, 1986).

Most middle-aged workers are satisfied with their jobs.

Job satisfaction is influenced by a variety of factors, including the job characteristics outlined earlier. In addition, personal characteristics and goals may influence satisfaction (see Figure 11–2). We have already seen that job characteristics may vary with age. It is also possible that personal values may change with development. But age-related changes in job satisfaction must be described before we can examine their causes.

Job Satisfaction: The research is quite consistent in finding that older workers are more satisfied than younger workers with their jobs (Campbell et al., 1976; Havighurst, 1982; Rhodes, 1983; Schultz & Schultz, 1986; Stagner, 1985). The positive relationship between age and job satisfaction ap-

FIGURE 11–2:   Factors Influencing Job Satisfaction.

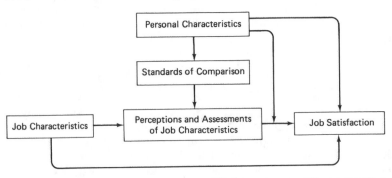

Source: Campbell, A., Converse, P., & Rodgers, W. (1976). *The quality of American life.* © The Russell Sage Foundation. Reprinted by permission of the Russell Sage Foundation.

pears to hold true up until at least age 60. At that point there may be some decline, although the data are mixed (Rhodes, 1983). The relationship is particularly evident among black workers, with the gap between older and younger workers' satisfaction being considerably larger than among whites (Stagner, 1985). Furthermore, although the pattern is uniform for male workers of various professions, the data concerning the relationship between age and job satisfaction are much more mixed for women (Rhodes, 1983).

The age-job satisfaction correlation exists even when other variables are controlled. Multivariate studies indicate, for example, that the age-job satisfaction link holds for both white-collar and blue-collar employees. Older people report greater job satisfaction independently of occupation, status, educational level, or number of years of experience (Rhodes, 1983). This means, for example, that if a 25-year-old and a 50-year-old have both been working for the same firm at the same job for five years, the 50-year-old is likely to report greater job satisfaction than the 25-year-old.

These data are all based on direct measures of job satisfaction, but there are other indicators that older workers are more satisfied (Rhodes, 1983). For example, age is consistently related to job involvement. Older workers tend to be more committed to the firm or organization for which they work and have less intention of leaving it. They also report higher levels of internal motivation to do their jobs well. Such attitudes frequently fit together, as indicated in Hackman and Oldham's model (Figure 11–1).

The consistency of the research makes it tempting to draw the conclusion that age somehow "causes" greater job satisfaction. One almost immediately begins to generate hypotheses as to why that might be the case. Perhaps older workers are better matched to their jobs. Maybe they have more realistic expectations. But caution is needed here. The overwhelming majority of the research on age and job satisfaction is cross-sectional. In Susan Rhodes's (1983) review of the literature, she examined over 60 studies looking at age and job satisfaction, and *all* were cross-sectional. This means that the supposed age effects may actually be, at least in part, cohort effects. This seems quite likely, given that the young adults in these studies typically grew up in "times of plenty" (the fifties and sixties), whereas the older adults lived through the Depression and World War II. One might expect that the older workers had different values and attitudes, even when they themselves were young adults. In fact, limited research does suggest that some portion of the age-job satisfaction relationship is actually attributable to cohort (see Rhodes, 1983).

Job Characteristics and Job Satisfaction: The age-job satisfaction relationship can be analyzed in terms of job characteristics. This may help us to better understand why older workers are more satisfied with their jobs; the information is also of potential use to employers who wish to improve job satisfaction as a means of increasing worker productivity.

Older people tend to like the work itself more than younger workers do (Rhodes, 1983). Perhaps people who don't like a job leave it, so that the older workers (in a cross-sectional study) are simply those who always liked the job and chose to stay in it. Or it is possible that people "rationalize" their choices so that, having been on a job for a while, they start to like it more (Havighurst, 1982). It is also possible that older workers are looking for something different in a job. Perhaps challenge or opportunity for advancement is more important to younger workers. Longitudinal research with middle-aged AT&T managers indicates that their interest in advancement and other external rewards for work had decreased over the twenty years of the study (Bray & Howard, 1983). Challenging work, however, remained an important source of motivation for them.

Other job characteristics do not appear to be age-related (Rhodes, 1983). For example, older employees are not clearly more satisfied with their salaries or promotions. Nor do they like or get along with co-workers or supervisors better. These job characteristics, then, do not appear to mediate the age-job satisfaction relationship. It is interesting to note, however, that older managers seem to care less about these facets of work. Their interest in making friends, understanding other peoples' motives, and gaining approval from supervisors and peers all decreased from young adult levels (Bray & Howard, 1983).

Work Values and Job Satisfaction: Of course, personal characteristics may also influence the age–job satisfaction relationship. These characteristics include values and needs related to work itself. Some people have a greater need for achievement than others (Schultz & Schultz, 1986). This affects not only what type of job they choose, but what they need to accomplish through the job in order to feel satisfied.

Work values as a research topic have not attracted as much attention as job satisfaction itself (Rhodes, 1983). The limited available research does indicate, however, that older workers have a greater need for security. This makes sense. The middle-aged worker is more likely to have family obligations and is supposed to be making an active contribution to family and community. Furthermore, the older worker may be more concerned about the problem of finding a new job. This is not an unfounded worry; there is no doubt that the older worker (40 or older) has a harder time finding a job (Kelvin & Jarrett, 1985). Workers in their forties seem to be aware of this, and they are concerned about what could happen if they do lose their jobs (Stagner, 1985). While this has always been true, technological advances may now make workers obsolescent at a younger age than ever before.

Technological advances may also make it more uncomfortable for the older worker to change jobs (Bray & Howard, 1983; Stagner, 1985). It would mean acquiring new skills, which may be disconcerting to many older workers. After all, their "performance edge," compared to younger workers, comes from familiarity with job, clients, territory, and so on (Salthouse et al., 1990). The rewards of the job change may not seem worth the costs. Their current level of income may well be acceptable to them, and the hassle of moving, the aggravation of learning new skills and taking on new responsibilities, and the limited likelihood of substantial rewards may all make them reluctant to want to change jobs (Bray & Howard, 1983).

*Middle-aged and older workers
like jobs that give them considerable autonomy.*

This all assumes, of course, that a new, technologically oriented position would be available to them. The research suggests that this is unlikely,
either in their current firm or with a new employer (Stagner, 1985). Employers are reluctant to invest training money in middle-aged or older employees. The stereotype of the "elderly" as slower to learn and as poorer per-
formers is seen as applicable to 50-year-olds. And employers don't believe
that the middle-aged worker will be with the firm long enough to pay back
the training investment.

Younger employees, on the other hand, may have stronger needs for
self-growth and self-actualization (Rhodes, 1983). Again, this makes sense.
As was suggested in Chapter 3, many young adults are still forming their
identities. Chapter 7 pointed out that newly employed young adults often
have very unrealistic expectations about how challenging work will be. In
other words, they expect that work will provide them with all sorts of opportunities for building self-esteem and identity. This does not mean that older
workers do not care whether their work is challenging or meaningful; they
certainly do (Bray & Howard, 1983; Rhodes, 1983). However, they apparently do not have the same expectations about dramatic self-growth
through work. They are more realistic and less naive than they were as
young adults (Bray & Howard, 1983). But they still care who is in charge or
whether there is self-enhancement from the work. Indeed, the greatest sin-

gle attitude change among the AT&T managers in Bray and Howard's study was an increased need for autonomy at work. This was true at all levels of management and was independent of education. Younger workers may be more dissatisfied than older workers are with the amount of control they have at work (Stagner, 1985). This may be because the younger worker typically has less control, because the older worker has experienced a relative increase in independence during a career, or because of cohort differences in expectations about autonomy. In any case, the older worker clearly does not like external control. In fact, many older workers will choose early retirement rather than be "bossed around" by someone else (Stagner, 1985).

WORK BEHAVIORS

Many employers still have a mandatory retirement policy. While there are many reasons for such policies, a major one certainly is the expectation that older workers are less able to do the job than younger ones are. Think, again, of Willy Loman. We have just seen fairly convincing evidence that older workers' job-related attitudes ought to make them *better* workers. We certainly expect, consistent with Hackman and Oldham's model, that people who are satisfied with their jobs will work harder and more efficiently at them. But any good social psychologist will tell you that the relationship between attitudes and behavior is often very slight. Furthermore, the realities of physical aging may make it impossible for the older worker to continue to perform a job competently.

Direct Measures of Job Performance

All of us who work have been subjected to performance evaluations. Indeed, many of you have probably helped to evaluate someone—namely, one of your professors. You may well have completed a course evaluation form or written a letter that was somehow used to decide whether your professor was hired, retained, or promoted. But think about some of the questions you addressed. Some might have been very general ("Was this a good course?"), others very specific ("Were the lectures well-organized?"). But virtually all of them were subjective. All sorts of factors could influence your answers, and no inter-rater reliability is ever established to see if students interpret or rate the evaluation questionnaires consistently.

Job performance evaluations almost always carry a heavy element of subjectivity, and this may be particularly critical in understanding performance ratings of older adults. After all, we are a society marked by negative attitudes about age. The existing research has been very poor in terms of controlling for such influences; indeed, researchers rarely even use the same measures of performance evaluation. Furthermore, much of the research is cross-sectional (Rhodes, 1983).

Given the methodological problems, it is little wonder that the results of the research are mixed. Some studies have found improvements in performance with age, others decreases, and still others no differences. Job experience appears to be a mediator in the positive findings. In other words, when older workers perform better, it may simply be because they have more experience (Rhodes, 1983). While this is a valuable piece of information, it does not negate the advantage of the "average" older worker. Typically, the older worker will have more experience, since only a minority of workers change jobs after age 40.

One would expect that certain kinds of jobs would be more affected by the aging process than others (Rhodes, 1983). Given the physical changes in middle age, we might expect that jobs requiring great physical strength or agility might be better done by younger workers. Some of the relevant declines are outlined in Table 11–1. Jobs that require monitoring high-pitched noises (as an indicator of a machine malfunction, for example) or separating a particular signal (a supervisor's orders) from a good deal of background noise (machinery) might also be more difficult for the older worker to perform well (Stagner, 1985). Of course, there will be individual differences even in these jobs, since there are large individual differences in both the rate and extent of physical decline. Furthermore, practice and experience might compensate for any physical losses that do occur.

Indirect Measures of Job Performance

Indirect measures of job performance include rates of turnover, absenteeism, and accidents. We may assume that there is some correlation between these behaviors and the attention being given to work. Certainly, these measures are less direct indicators of job performance and are, in that respect, less adequate than evaluations. On the other hand, these indirect measures are less subjective. Multiple raters can easily agree on whether someone resigned or was absent from work. It should be noted, however, that researchers do not always agree on the specific behaviors that should

TABLE 11–1: Potential Effects of Physical Decline on Work Level

Age-Related Decline	Work Effect
Loss of high-frequency hearing	Difficulty understanding verbal instructions, especially in noisy settings; difficulty hearing alarm systems or certain types of machine malfunctions.
Visual decline	Not typically crucial because correction is usually available. Unlike auditory declines, visual declines are not clearly age-related.
Memory declines (typically in short-term or working memory)	In nonpathological aging, these are relatively minor and easily compensated for.
Motor decline	May affect learning a new motor skill but apparently less important in well-established skills. Again, experience may compensate for decline.

Source: Based on Stagner, R. (1985). Aging in industry. In J. Birren & K. Schaie (eds.), *The handbook of the psychology of aging,* 2nd ed., pp. 789–817. New York: Van Nostrand Reinhold.

be included in calculating these rates (Rhodes, 1983). Some researchers include all voluntary resignations in turnover rates, and others exclude resignations due to maternity or retirement.

Recall that older workers are less likely to want to leave their jobs. This attitude is reflected in actual behavior; older workers are less likely to actually leave their jobs (Rhodes, 1983). It does not appear to be the case that older workers are completely committed to work and generally reluctant to leave it. Although normally full retirement benefits are not available until age 62 and the mandatory retirement age is 70, the median age for retiring from industry is around 58 (Stagner, 1985).

Older male workers are less likely than younger men to take time off from work when it is not necessary. In other words, there is a negative correlation between age and avoidable absences (Rhodes, 1983). Again, this may reflect a greater level of commitment on the part of the older men mediated by loyalty to the organization, higher levels of responsibility, or stronger family responsibility. The research is not yet available to explain this relationship. Yet it would seem to be a particularly interesting one to investigate, because it does not hold for women. The data concerning the relationship between age and avoidable absenteeism among women employees are much more mixed (Rhodes, 1983). Unavoidable absence is also related to age. Here, however, the older men are more likely than the younger to miss work. This may be because they have more chronic diseases. Furthermore, although older workers appear to be somewhat less likely to have industrial accidents, they need longer to recover from them. They are also more likely to suffer a permanent disability from an accident (Rhodes, 1983).

Once again, the pattern for women is different. It is not clear that there is any relationship among women workers between unavoidable absence and age (Rhodes, 1983). It is possible that there is no linear relationship between age and unavoidable absence, but there may be a curvilinear or even a bimodal relationship. Some evidence does suggest at least one peak in absenteeism, when women are aged 26–35. This is the time when children are often preschoolers or school aged and need to be watched if they become ill (as they frequently do). Childcare responsibility typically falls to the mother. The unavoidable absenteeism rate may then drop off until biological aging begins to take its toll. Since this may be later for women than for men, the peak may be less pronounced. These possibilities require further research.

A Warning about the Data: Data concerning job attitudes and behaviors are crucial in the debate over mandatory retirement. They are also critical in the larger conflicts about age discrimination. If the data indicate that older workers are more responsible and committed, for example, then it becomes harder to suggest that they ought to be relieved of their duties. On the other hand, the data concerning accidents may lead employers whose jobs involve heavy machinery or physical labor to be cautious about allowing older workers to continue.

Any such policy decisions based exclusively on the available data would be premature. The data, as we have noted, are overwhelmingly cross-sectional (Rhodes, 1983), which presents problems in terms of generalizing the findings to older workers of different cohorts. Second, many of the studies have used questionable measures. This is particularly true of the job performance studies. Third, researchers often assume that the age-work relationship will be linear and direct. These assumptions are not always valid and may lead to inappropriate analyses. Finally, many of the investigators did not consider men and women separately. While men and women are often similar in attitudes and behaviors, there are enough differences to mandate separate consideration of the genders in this case.

WORK AND HEALTH

In Chapter 8, we noted that life-style habits begin to take their toll in middle age. Health can be affected by diet, smoking, drinking, and exercise patterns. Exposure to toxins or damaging environmental factors (such as asbestos or coal dust) at work often must continue for years before the effects are noticeable, and these effects will frequently show up in middle age.

Garfinkel (1982) has argued that work is a major environmental context for adult development. Fully a third of life is spent at work (Schultz & Schultz, 1986). If this is true, then work may be seen as a potential source of stress, self-esteem, life satisfaction, and conflict. Any long-term effects of such psychological dimensions of work may also show up in middle age. Or they may interact with the developmental tasks of the period to produce unique short-term effects.

Job-Related Illness

A nuclear plant accident, such as the ones at Three Mile Island and Chernobyl, will generate a huge amount of press coverage. One of the things everyone will want to know is how many people were killed or injured. Experts will try to estimate how many employees will eventually develop cancers or blood disorders as a result of radiation exposure. Such illnesses are, however, difficult to link directly to the nuclear accident, since they may take twenty years or more to appear.

While these are certainly dramatic examples of work-related illnesses, they are by no means the only ones. The EPA has identified over 16,000 workplace substances that are known to be toxic (Lambrinos & Johnson, 1984). Every year, nearly 400,000 people develop work-related sicknesses, and over 100,000 die (Schultz & Schultz, 1986). The financial cost of illness is also very high. Shipyard workers who develop asbestos-related illnesses, for example, may lose as much as $156,000 each in lifetime wages (Lambrinos & Johnson, 1984).

As Table 11-2 indicates, many of these work-related illnesses are forms of cancer. As is always the case with cancer, it takes many years for the symptoms to appear, so these work-related illnesses typically first show up in middle age. Indeed, the length of time it takes the symptoms to occur leads to many questions about potential causal agents and has therefore

TABLE 11–2:   Hazardous Substances and On-the-Job Diseases

Potential Dangers	Diseases That May Result	Workers Exposed
Arsenic	Lung cancer, lymphoma	Smelter, chemical, oil-refinery workers; insecticide makers and sprayers—estimated 660,000 exposed
Asbestos	White lung disease (asbestosis); cancer of lungs and lining of lungs; cancer of other organs	Miners; millers; textile, insulation and shipyard workers—estimated 1.6 million exposed
Benzene	Leukemia; aplastic anemia	Petrochemical and oil-refinery workers; dye users; distillers; painters; shoemakers—estimated 600,000 exposed
Bischloromethylether (BCME)	Lung cancer	Industrial chemical workers
Coal dust	Black lung disease	Coal miners—estimated 208,000 exposed
Coke-oven emissions	Cancer of lungs, kidneys	Coke-oven workers—estimated 30,000 exposed
Cotton dust	Brown lung disease (byssinosis); chronic bronchitis; emphysema	Textile workers—estimated 600,000 exposed
Lead	Kidney disease; anemia; central nervous system damage; sterility; birth defects	Metal grinders; lead-smelter workers; lead storage-battery workers—estimated 835,000 exposed
Radiation	Cancer of thyroid, lungs and bone; leukemia; reproductive effects (spontaneous abortion, genetic damage)	Medical technicians; uranium miners; nuclear power and atomic workers
Vinyl chloride	Cancer of liver, brain	Plastic industry workers—estimated 10,000 directly exposed

Source: Pelletier, K. (1984). *Healthy people in unhealthy places: Stress and fitness at work,* p. 90. New York: Delacorte.

often made it difficult for workers to collect compensation or other job-related benefits (Lambrinos & Johnson, 1984).

One of the best known of these work-related diseases is black lung disease (pneumoconiosis), a debilitating disease caused by exposure to coal dust. Over 200,000 miners have been exposed to this risk. And should they manage not to develop this particular disease, miners are still at risk for other lung problems. Death from respiratory illness is five times more common among coal miners than among other workers (Schultz & Schultz, 1986). Similar lung problems (from inhaling fiber and chemicals) have been noted in female cotton mill workers (Repetti et al., 1989).

Work-Related Stress

Many people assume that some jobs are more stressful than others. Typically they believe that fast-paced, responsible, or very competitive jobs are particularly stressful. We would routinely think of medicine, business, or the law as stressful. On the other hand, clerical or assembly line work would be thought of as less stressful because the employee is under less "real" pressure on a daily basis. We might expect, then, that business executives would be more likely than their secretaries to show both the physical and psychological effects of long-term stress.

This conceptualization is too simplistic for several reasons. First, most theorists now agree that stress is subjective rather than objective (see Lazarus & Folkman, 1984). In other words, the stress is in the "eye of the beholder," and a task or characteristic of a job that is stressful to one employee may not be for another (see Chapter 9 for a discussion of different styles of assessing and coping with stress). Job characteristics will interact with experience, personality, and even family situation to produce the perception of stress. The question is not whether the job itself is stressful, but whether the person's needs, abilities, social support systems, and so on fit with the demands of the work (Holt, 1982). The family-work conflicts that many women experience exemplify this situation.

Furthermore, it is easy to underestimate the stress of a boring, low-status job. High amounts of autonomy in a job are actually associated with lower stress. The higher a management position is in an organization, the less likely that the job is perceived as stressful (Schultz & Schultz, 1986). Similarly, high levels of job satisfaction are correlated with low levels of stress. And we have already seen that jobs with high levels of challenge and autonomy are more likely to be perceived as satisfying (Bray & Howard, 1983; Schultz & Schultz, 1986; Stagner, 1985). These relationships help explain the somewhat surprising ranking of jobs as stressful. According to the National Institute of Occupational Safety and Health, the three most stressful jobs are laborer, secretary, and inspector. All these factors may also help to explain why men who are physicians or professionals are healthier than the general population (Repetti et al., 1989).

Is the older worker any more susceptible to stress than the younger worker? Do years of work at a stressful job culminate in physical or psychological problems? The answers to these questions are not clear. *Burnout*, for example, is considered to be the result of consistent stress from overwork (Schultz & Schultz, 1986). But the duration of the exposure needed to produce burnout varies considerably from person to person. Many burnout victims are middle-aged, but many others are still in their twenties.

The results of research on mental health and aging among workers are ambiguous (Stagner, 1985). Some studies find that older workers suffer fewer psychiatric symptoms and show better mental health than younger employees; other studies show the reverse. It is understandable how both could be true. There is, for example, a positive correlation between job satisfaction and age. There is also a positive correlation between job satisfaction and mental health. So we would expect that mental health and age would be positively correlated. On the other hand, job satisfaction alone cannot guarantee a happy life. Health and family problems may be the cause of the mental health problems. Indeed, at least some research indicates a negative correlation between life satisfaction and job satisfaction (see Stagner, 1985, but also see Bray & Howard, 1980). Perhaps people who are very satisfied with their work find it the sole source of fulfillment in their lives.

It may also be that, although they are more satisfied with their jobs, older workers may experience special stressors. They may find it difficult to adapt to working with (or for) women, for example (Schultz & Schultz, 1986). They may be concerned about the increasing role of technology, feeling that their skills are falling further and further behind those necessary to do a job well. This means that rumors of layoffs, reorganizations, or plant closings may be more stressful to the older worker, who will have more difficulty finding a new job.

Of course, the younger worker also has some special stresses. He or she may be learning the job or learning how to fit in at work. The older worker does not have these concerns. Juggling children and work demands may also typically be greater problems for young adults, who are more likely to have infants or preschoolers at home (Repetti et al., 1989).

NEW CAREERS AT MIDLIFE

Thus far, the focus has been on the "average" middle-aged worker, the one who has been in the same job for many years. Some middle-aged people, however, are starting a new job or career. There are at least three common reasons for this. One is the loss of a job; second is a midcareer shift in which a worker voluntarily decides to change careers. The third pattern, which is restricted almost exclusively to women, is entering the job market for the first time. All these patterns can be expected to require considerable adaptation by both the individual and the family and should therefore create substantial stress for the new employee. Furthermore, we might think of these new employees as being "off-time" in that career decisions and initiation are commonly thought of as the developmental tasks of young adults.

Unemployment

We have already noted several times that work is an integral part of our lives, self-definition, and social status. Self-esteem is strained because we (and society) define the unemployed as inadequate, inflexible, or lazy (Sinfeld, 1985). The stress may be particularly marked for the middle-aged worker who is justifiably concerned about finding a new position with pay, status, and responsibility similar to those of the job that was lost. It should not be surprising, then, that the loss of a job can be an extremely stressful event. Consider this statement from a recently-returned-to-work man in his fifties:

> It affected me a lot when I was unemployed. I didn't think I was going to get another job. . . . It was degrading—in the dole office or when people asked me what I was doing. People would say "are you still unemployed?". . . . I was looking. It was very degrading. I have worked all my life and got angry. People who have never been unemployed don't know what it is like. . . . When you are unemployed you are bored, frustrated, and worried, worried sick: at least I was. . . . (Sinfeld, 1985, p. 194)

Unemployment does not affect everyone in the same way. Factors such as previous experience with unemployment, current household income, health status, and availability of social support all affect adjustment. As might be expected, duration of unemployment may be a factor (Kelvin & Jarrett, 1985). Many researchers believe that people are initially very stressed by job loss but adapt fairly quickly (Kasl & Cobb, 1982; Kelvin & Jarrett, 1985). This enables the worker to look for a new job and plan for the future. However, if a new job is not found, hopelessness, resignation to the unemployed status, and apathy about looking for work may set in (Kelvin & Jarrett, 1985). Although the worker may not initially blame himself or herself for the loss of the job, self-blame may develop if unemployment lasts more than six months (Kasl & Cobb, 1982). Finally, as unemployment drags on, benefits and savings run out, creating additional stressors (Bolte & Fowler, 1991). These are very real risks for a middle-aged worker who is likely to have considerable difficulty in finding a new job.

Many factors determine how likely a worker is to find a new job. Contacts play a very important role (Kelvin & Jarrett, 1985; Sinfeld, 1985). Often the contacts are relatives, including the middle-aged person's own children. Health and social support also play a role. In general, family support is helpful in adapting to unemployment and in finding a new job. However, for older men in poor health, family support may actually deter job-seeking (Kasl & Cobb, 1982). The family may express greater concern about the worker's health and well-being than about finding a new source of income. Occupation plays a role too. In recent years, workers in heavy manufacturing, such as the auto industry, have lost jobs permanently as well as temporarily (Bolte & Fowler, 1991).

Regardless of how the new job is found, chances are that the older worker will have to settle for lower status and pay (Kelvin & Jarrett, 1985; Sinfeld, 1985). This seems to be true in a wide variety of occupations and professions. People who, despite lack of educational qualifications, have worked their way up in a company may be particularly vulnerable to this loss of status, since their skills are often company-specific (DuBrin, 1978). Even if a comparable replacement position is found, the worker has missed out on promotions, training programs, and other advancement possibilities while looking for work. This puts him or her at a disadvantage in competing with younger, better trained workers (Sinfeld, 1985). In fact, some workers will take early retirement rather than settle for a lower-status position or continue to try to compete:

> At the peak of my career I was the company controller, the highest ranking financial manager in my company. . . . When the company . . . went public . . . it became . . . apparent . . . they really didn't want me working as a controller. I made fewer and fewer decisions until I was functioning as an accountant. Soon I was given the option of working as a plant accountant or taking early retirement. Rather than take any more punishment to my ego, I chose retirement. (DuBrin, 1978, p. 182)

Although this woman was not "officially" fired from her company or even her position, being eased out of a job and demoted is a form of job loss.

Midcareer Shift

A small minority of people decide voluntarily to change careers in midlife. Some return to school or undergo specialized training in order to get a better job. They change jobs only when their education is complete, so there is little risk to them. This is so understandable that researchers have spent little time or effort trying to explain such behavior (see, for example, Stagner, 1985). Others, however, are like Paul Gauguin, whose biography was briefly recounted at the beginning of Chapter 9. They leave careers that, by societal standards, are very successful. Their new careers are often lower in status, security, and pay. Even when they are not lower in status, as when an executive opts to become a lawyer (Levinson, 1983), there is still an extended period of lowered pay and considerable risk to life style. Gauguin, for example, was a banker and became a painter. A 48-year-old supervisor at Polaroid left to become a golf course owner; a 52-year-old pilot left TWA to run a boatyard (Schultz & Schultz, 1986). Note that these changes are not just moving from one position to another comparable one. Rather, they involve dramatic changes in life course.

Why would anyone walk away from a good, secure career? There are a number of possible explanations (Levinson, 1983). The work may no longer be challenging or interesting; tasks that used to be exciting may now be routine. Perhaps career advancement has leveled off. It may be clear to the person that he or she has reached the highest rung of the ladder within this career. The person may feel his or her talents are being underutilized or even wasted. All these feelings may lead a person to consider switching careers.

In some cases, the sense of dissatisfaction is less defined. A 40-year-old corporation president expressed it like this: "I keep feeling more and more depressed, and I can't figure out why. I've gone as high as I can go, there's nothing wrong with my life, but I just can't seem to shake the feeling of, 'So here I am, so what?'" (Schultz & Schultz, 1986, p. 321). One might suggest, as Harry Levinson (1983) does, that such people are suffering from a "midlife crisis" in which they are evaluating their commitments to family, career, and themselves. While most people do not undergo a real crisis at this point in their lives, some people certainly do.

Some career changes are attributable to burnout. This phenomenon is not restricted to middle age (Stagner, 1985); burnout is the result of too much emotional involvement or too many responsibilities and problems at work. In other words, the burnout victim feels overwhelmed (Schultz & Schultz, 1986; Stagner, 1985). The overinvolvement in work may indicate a self-esteem or self-confidence problem. Work performance is affected, as the worker becomes less and less productive despite longer hours. The dissatisfaction associated with burnout leads many people to change jobs or careers (Stagner, 1985). However, people who blame their jobs for dissatisfaction that is actually more attributable to their own personality flaws are likely to be disappointed. They are apt to find their new career just as overwhelming and draining as the one they left (H. Levinson, 1983).

Workforce Reentry

Women who married and had children during the 1950s, 1960s, and even into the 1970s typically dropped out of the workforce. Their husbands provided the income for the family while they cared for the children and made home a "safe haven" for all. Some of these women never intended to work again. Others thought they might eventually return to work. Today's cohort of young wives and mothers is less likely to leave the workforce. However, it is still not uncommon for women to take substantial amounts of time off to raise children. The only difference is that most of these women plan to return to work eventually.

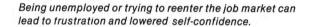

Being unemployed or trying to reenter the job market can lead to frustration and lowered self-confidence.

Many women who stopped working unexpectedly find themselves returning to the labor force. They may have discovered that the intersection of increased longevity and decreased fertility simply left them with too much life to live and too little to do after the children went to school or left home. For many women, the situation was made desperate by divorce or widowhood (Blau, Rogers, & Stephens, 1978; Nestel, Mercier, & Shaw, 1983; Sommers & Shields, 1978). Consider these two examples:

> In 1974 my husband died suddenly and in a matter of a few horrible hours I became a 55-year-old widow. I spent $33\frac{1}{2}$ years . . . making a home for my husband and three children. I have developed no working skills and have been unsuccessful in finding any sort of a job. . . . Consequently my funds grow smaller along with my shrinking ego. The $2\frac{1}{2}$ years until I reach 60 stretch interminably. My husband's social security will be no big deal. . . .

> I am a 65-year-old Christian lady whose husband, after 32 years of marriage, divorced me 2 years ago to marry his secretary. . . . The divorce cut me off from our Blue Cross-Blue Shield. . . . (R)aising five children I never worked out to establish Social Security, so I am not eligible for Medicare. . . . I now own half of my three bedroom home. My ex and his wife live across the street from me. I go out to work as a baby sitter in their home. That's the only job I could get. . . . (Sommers & Shields, 1978, pp. 88–89)

Women who are suddenly divorced or widowed are often not prepared to find a job. These "displaced homemakers" face a myriad of problems, including employer attitudes. They often have neither the work experience nor the education to compete effectively in the job market (Nestel et al., 1983; Sommers & Shields, 1978). Whatever skills they once possessed may well have eroded, since many of these women have not worked outside the home for ten years or more. Volunteer experience may be discounted. A middle-aged woman described her experience:

> I've answered dozens of ads and tried the unemployment office where they send me to the job board . . . after I fill out an application I never hear from them again. They say I have no experience. Well, I thought raising six fine children and working on school bond campaigns and electing the right candidates to Congress was experience, but I guess not. They look at you like a piece of discarded junk. (Sommers & Shields, 1978, p. 91)

Even when these women find work, it is likely to be very low-paying. For some of them, the pay will be so low as to make working futile (DuBrin, 1978; Nestel et al., 1983). For example, one study found that labor force participation actually dropped for black women who were widowed or separated (Nestel et al., 1983) because the combination of low wages and child-care demands was too overwhelming. These women opted instead to rely on AFDC (Aid For Dependent Children). But this is only a stopgap measure. When the children reach their majority, the AFDC will end and these women will have to return to work after an even more extended absence.

The rise in divorce rates in recent years makes this a fairly common experience. In the early 1960s, only about 4 percent of all divorces involved marriages that had lasted for fifteen or more years. Now about a fifth of divorces are between long-married couples (Weitzman, 1984). Child support awards are most common and highest for custodial mothers with very small children, a situation that does not typically describe a woman who has been married for fifteen years or longer. Laws do recognize that these women may have been out of work for a long time (in order to care for children and the home) and require that this be considered in awarding alimony. Older full-time housewives are more likely to be awarded alimony than other women are. But as many as a third of these women receive no alimony, and those who do may receive it for a very limited time or in very small amounts (Weitzman, 1984). For such women, their economic situation may border on the desperate.

But what of women whose labor force reentry is more planned and voluntary? Do they face comparable problems? In some ways, they do. Their salaries, for example, are often quite low. Indeed, this is the most common reason for leaving the workforce after reentry (Shaw, 1983). They too will face ageism and sexism in looking for work. And the fears and anxieties about finding work are similar for all reentering women (DuBrin, 1978). They are concerned, for example, about competing with younger, better-trained women. They worry about their skills and their appearance. They worry about their children and homes and the conflict between career and family.

Why do these women go back to work? Many have always planned to return to jobs for which they have trained and in which they are interested. Chapter 6 clearly demonstrated the advantages of working for a women's self-esteem, coping, and health (Baruch et al., 1987; Repetti et al., 1989; Rodin & Ickovics, 1990). However, it would be a mistake to assume that women return to work just for "fulfillment" (although one would think that would be a sufficient reason). Most families need the money that can be generated by the wife working. The women wait to return to work until their children are in school. Among other things, this reduces childcare expenses. They usually return as soon as the children are settled in school rather than waiting for the nest to empty (Shaw, 1983).

How much do women lose by interrupting their work lives? The answer to this question is not completely clear, but it appears to be "not much." Women who reenter in their fifties, for example, find their wages comparable to those of women who reenter in their thirties (Shaw, 1983). In other words, the extra years out of the workforce did not cost them anything at entry level. Some researchers argue that the gender gap in earnings (see Chapter 7) appears to be about the same whether women have worked continuously or interrupted their careers (Giele, 1982b). There are limited data to indicate, however, that work interruptions (including relatively short ones) are the single greatest contributing variable in explaining the gender gap (Hewlett, 1984).

Life satisfaction too seems to be comparable, probably because women make career and family decisions that reflect their own attitudes and values. For example, a couple may regret having to give up certain material goods so that the wife can stay home with the children, but will think the positive effects on the children are worth the sacrifice. Conversely, women who do not stay home may believe that their children have "missed out" on something but that the opportunities bought by money and the parent's own sense of fulfillment balance this out. In other words, adults recognize and accept tradeoffs in their lives (Giele, 1982b).

None of this implies that having a family has no effect on women's careers. It certainly does. In fact, having children does tend to lower career achievement. Researchers consistently find a negative correlation between the presence of children and women's earnings (Blau et al., 1978). However, this is true even when a woman does not interrupt her career to bear and raise the children (Giele, 1982b). The specific path chosen to combine career and family, then, seems less important than the decision to combine them. As long as there is a fit between preferences and options, the paths all seem to work fairly well. This may be because society does not prescribe one reasonable or acceptable path any more. Women are not violating social norms by working continuously or by interrupting work; both are acceptable and will receive some support.

LEISURE

Life is not all work, at least not for most of us. What do Americans do in their leisure time? The answer to that question reflects the variations in our definitions of leisure:

> Father, age 53: I like to watch almost any type of sporting event, live or on television. I like to swim, and I read all types of books and magazines, when I have the time. I love to drive a car and travel to different towns and cities in the state. (Troll, 1982, p. 214)

> Mr. X is a fifty-year-old executive, with a pattern of leisure activities which is the prototype of the community-centered style of leisure. He is president of one country club, a member of another, a Shriner, and a member of the executive council of a national Boy's Club movement and of a number of charity organizations. Mr. X's favorite leisure activity is to go on trips during his vacation, to New York City to see the Broadway theater, and to see exhibitions of modern art. He is active in encouraging the local art museum to acquire . . . modern art. He enjoys playing golf . . . playing cards, painting his garage, and entertaining business people both at home and at the club. . . . He goes with his wife to the movies and to . . . musical comedies. . . . With his wife he goes out to eat once a week and entertains other couples. (Havighurst & Feigenbaum, 1968/1959, pp. 350–351)

> Mother, age 50: Sleep. The way things are now I don't have the time to do a lot of things. I'm tired when I get home from work. I don't have a car so that's limiting. I watch TV, listen to my daughter sing, and go to church, of course. (Troll, 1982, p. 222)

We colloquially define leisure as nonwork (Blanchard & Cheska, 1985; Burrus-Bammel & Bammel, 1985). Notice, however, that one of Mr. X's leisure activities is "entertaining business people." This activity is not clearly distinct from work. In fact, many people might consider it work. Even if we restrict ourselves to examples of nonwork, the meaning of leisure is apparently quite broad. It includes travel, reading, serving on committees, attending plays, watching sporting events, sleeping, and entertaining. There are some activities many of us would routinely consider appropriate for leisure, such as participating in sports, going for walks, playing music, or spending time with family, that are not represented here. While we may be willing to include all of these as leisure activities, we also intuitively recognize that there are some important differences among them.

Figure 11–3 helps to illustrate some of these differences. Work can be differentiated from leisure on the basis of goal. Work has a external goal, such as status or money; leisure is oriented toward self-growth and regeneration. The pleasureableness of the activity also needs to be considered in order to understand leisure versus work, and to distinguish play from nonplay. Work can be playful, as is often the case with professional athletes, who derive obvious pleasure from their jobs. Or leisure can be non-playful, as when someone is bored by a television show or by dinner company.

We need, then, to distinguish leisure from recreation. *Leisure* is a broad term including the attitudes and time spent on personal growth activities. *Recreation,* on the other hand, refers to specific activities, some of

FIGURE 11–3:   Relationships among Leisure, Work, and Play.

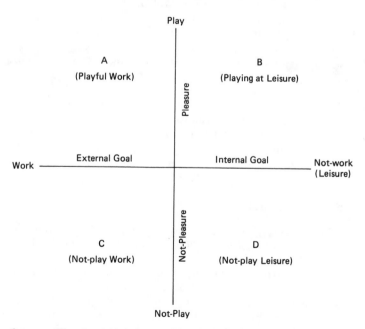

Source: Blanchard, K. & Cheska, A. (1985). *The anthropology of sport.* Reprinted by permission of Greenwood Publishing Group, Inc., Westport, CT. Copyright © and published in 1985 by Bergin & Garvey.

which promote personal growth (talking with friends) and some of which do not (watching old cartoons on TV). All leisure is "re-creational," but not all recreation is leisure (Burrus-Bammel & Bammel, 1985).

The Relationship between Work and Leisure

In ancient times, leisure was more important than work. It was during leisure that people had time to think and develop new concepts of themselves and their world. The Greeks, for example, viewed leisure as something to be pursued and work as something to be avoided (Blanchard & Cheska, 1985).

As societies became increasingly industrialized, the value of work and leisure changed. We are a work-oriented society. Surveys suggest that the vast majority of us would continue to work even if we did not have to for survival (Burrus-Bammel & Bammel, 1985). Americans routinely rate leisure activities as less important than work and family. For example, Table 11–3 shows that 90 percent of the 50-year-old men rated work as important or very important to their quality of life. Half or fewer gave a similar rating to creative expression, socializing, or passive recreation such as watching TV. In fact, the five components most highly rated are health, work, close spousal relationships, children, and self-understanding. Only the last of these is clearly related to leisure, although family relationships may be. The lowest ratings were assigned to socializing, creative self-expression, active and passive recreation, and participation in government. These are all leisure activities. Other research indicates that health, a good marriage, a strong family life, and work are more important to most people than leisure activities (Campbell et al., 1976).

Americans not only place more value on work, they claim to derive more satisfaction from it. In a sample of 47- to 71-year-olds, for example, only 13 percent of the men and 16 percent of the women said they got more satisfaction from leisure than from work (Pfeiffer & Davis, 1971). And the Quality of American Life Survey (Campbell et al., 1976) found that higher satisfaction ratings were given to marriage, family life, housework, and jobs than to non-work activities. Table 11–4 also indicates that people are generally less satisfied with their opportunities for learning and self-expression than with work (Flanagan, 1980, p. 165).

Leisure and Life Satisfaction

Despite the low rankings given to the importance and pleasure of leisure, leisure activity appears to be significantly related to life satisfaction. So, for example, John Flanagan (1980) found active recreation, socializing, creative expression, and learning to be important predictors of quality of life among 50-year-olds. They were less important predictors than work or spousal relations but more important than raising children. These findings were surprising, given that socializing, active recreation, and creative self-expression were among the five lowest-rated components in terms of perceived importance. Thus, at least in Flanagan's sample, the elements of liv-

TABLE 11-3:   The Importance of Quality of Life Dimensions

Component	MALE			FEMALE		
	30 yrs	50 yrs	70 yrs	30 yrs	50 yrs	70 yrs
Physical and Material Well-Being						
A. Material comforts	80	86	88	75	84	86
B. Health and personal safety	98	96	95	98	97	96
Relations with Other People						
C. Relationships with relatives	68	64	62	83	76	79
D. Having and raising children	84	85	82	93	92	86
E. Close relationship with a spouse	90	90	85	94	82	43
F. Close friends	71	76	74	79	80	88
Social, Community, and Civic Activities						
G. Helping and encouraging others	60	73	65	71	75	80
H. Participating in local and national government	47	64	65	42	60	57
Personal Development and Fulfillment						
I. Learning	87	69	52	81	68	59
J. Understanding yourself	84	85	81	92	91	87
K. Work	91	90	58	89	85	60
L. Expressing yourself creatively	48	40	37	53	54	60
Recreation						
M. Socializing	48	46	51	53	49	62
N. Passive recreation	56	45	53	53	56	64
O. Active recreation	59	52	47	50	52	51

*For all age groups the question read, "At this time in your life, how important to you is _____?"

Percentages of 1,000 30-year-olds, 800 50-year-olds, and 800 70-year-olds reporting the importance of 15 quality of life dimensions to them at the present as "very important" or "important."

Source: Flanagan, J. (1980). Quality of life. In L. Bond & J. Rosen (eds.), *Competence and coping during adulthood.* Hanover, NH: University Press of New England.

ing that people perceive as important are not exactly the same ones that actually appear to influence their life satisfaction.

The Quality of American Life Survey (Campbell et al., 1976) also supports this conclusion. In fact, reported satisfaction with non-work activities was more highly correlated with a person's global sense of well-being than was any other variable, including work and marriage (see Table 11-5). A somewhat different slant on this issue is provided by research indicating a lack of correlation between career success and life satisfaction (Bray & Howard, 1980). Despite Americans' interest in a successful career, they are apparently very capable of being happy without it. This is partially attributable to their investment in avocational activities. Indeed, the rate of avocational activities showed an increase for the less successful managers over the twenty years of the AT&T study, while such interests were steady for the more successful men (Bray & Howard, 1980).

TABLE 11-4: How Well Are Needs Met?

Component	MALE			FEMALE		
	30 yrs	50 yrs	70 yrs	30 yrs	50 yrs	70 yrs
Physical and Material Well-Being						
A. Material comforts	26	27	24	24	32	26
B. Health and personal safety	14	17	15	14	18	20
Relations with Other People						
C. Relationships with relatives	19	29	27	19	30	31
D. Having and raising children	20	14	18	17	14	16
E. Close relationship with a spouse	16	19	13	19	28	31
F. Close friends	19	19	20	18	21	22
Social, Community, and Civic Activities						
G. Helping and encouraging others	39	28	28	38	26	26
H. Participating in local and national government	46	38	36	46	38	39
Personal Development and Fulfillment						
I. Learning	42	36	27	50	44	35
J. Understanding yourself	26	26	24	29	25	20
K. Work	21	26	24	21	32	24
L. Expressing yourself creatively	40	32	26	43	32	28
Recreation						
M. Socializing	27	28	27	26	31	27
N. Passive recreation	29	27	18	30	26	21
O. Active recreation	36	41	36	37	40	35

Percentages of a sample of 1,000 30-year-olds, 800 50-year-olds, and 800 70-year-olds reporting their needs as moderately, only slightly, or not at all well met for each of the 15 quality of life components. For the 50- and 70-year-olds, the question read "How well are your needs and wants being met in this regard?" For the 30-year-olds, the question read "How satisfied are you with your status in this respect?"

Source: Flanagan, J. (1980). Quality of life. In L. Bond & J. Rosen (eds.), *Competence and coping during adulthood.* Hanover, NH: University Press of New England.

Individual Preferences

There are age, gender, and social class differences in what people prefer to do during their leisure time. For example, middle-aged and older people are more likely than young adults to prefer solitary activities (Gordon, Gaitz, & Scott, 1976). Although they may actually devote more time to leisure, they tend to have less varied leisure pursuits (Gordon et al., 1976; Lowenthal et al., 1975). Middle-aged people are particularly likely to spend time at home, working around the house or watching TV (Gordon et al., 1976). It is tempting to assume that this means they are spending "quality time" with their families or are at the very least sharing activities with spouses and children. However, we need to be cautious in making that assumption. For example, many families (over 50 percent) now own VCRs. If asked, about 75 percent will agree that watching the VCR is a good way for the family to spend time together. Yet one study found that about 60 per-

TABLE 11-5: The Proportion of Variance in an Index of Well-Being, Explained by Individual Domain Satisfaction Scores

		Proportion of Explained Variance (r^2)
G3.	Non-working activities	29
J1.	Family life	28
G15.	Standard of living	23
	Work	18
	Marriage	16
G16.	Savings and investments	15
H3.	Friendships	13
A21.	City or county	11
B11.	Housing	11
E4.	Amount of education	9
A22.	Neighborhood	8
C6.	Life in United States	8
E5/6.	Usefulness of education	8
G11.	Health	8
	Religion	5
	National government	5
	Organizations	4

Note: The number of cases upon which each estimate of explained variance is based ranges from 2,106 to 2,160, with three exceptions: Family life (2,077 cases); Amount of education (1,975 cases); and Organizations (1,783 cases).

Source: Campbell, A., Converse, P., & Rogers, W. (1976). *The quality of American life.* © The Russell Sage Foundation. Reprinted by permission of The Russell Sage Foundation.

cent of the actual viewing was done by a solitary person (Gunter & Levy, 1987). Television watching was more family-oriented, though almost 25 percent was done by a lone viewer and only 17 percent included both parents and children as viewers (Gunter & Levy, 1987). Thus, the preferences of older adults may not simply reflect their interest in spending time with their families.

Although data often indicate age-related shifts in leisure activities, we need to be cautious about interpreting aging as a causal factor. First, many of these studies are cross-sectional (Gordon et al., 1976). Therefore, the differences may well be cohort differences (Burrus-Bammel & Bammel, 1985). The likelihood of cohort differences is increased by the fact that there are educational differences between the age groups, and education has been shown to be a major determinant of leisure interests. Furthermore, not all studies even find age effects (Burrus-Bammel & Bammel, 1985; Havighurst, 1961). Those that do often uncover very small effects that account for less than 5 percent of the variance. This means that less than 5 percent of the differences among people on measures of leisure activities is explained by their age.

Gender also affects choice of leisure activity. Women are more likely to be dissatisfied with the amount of leisure time they have (Hochschild, 1989; Pfeiffer & Davis, 1971). In Table 11-4, for example, women indicate more dissatisfaction than men do with learning and socializing opportunities. Consistent with sex-role stereotypes, women are more likely to work around the house and men more likely to watch sports or use guns as forms of leisure (Gordon et al., 1976), although it is possible that some of these differences will disappear with increasing equality of roles.

Although there are some gender differences in activity choice, men and women appear to be more similar than different. This is demonstrated in Table 11-6. Part of the reason is that at least in middle-class families, husbands and wives tend to share their leisure time. Social class may also affect leisure activity choices. Robert Havighurst and Kenneth Feigenbaum (1959/1968) found that upper-middle-class people tended to be community-centered. These people's leisure was dominated by family activities but also included a substantial amount of community service or participation in clubs and civic associations. Interaction with friends was also quite high. Lower-middle and working-class people, on the other hand, were more likely to be home-centered, so most of the activities involved members of the family. The specific activities, of course, vary considerably from one family to another and include fishing, going to a church event, or watching TV. Even the vacations of the community-versus home-centered people are quite different. The former tend to go to resorts or sightseeing; the latter usually visit relatives.

The lowest social classes may not fit either of these patterns (Havighurst & Feigenbaum, 1959/1968). As we noted in Chapter 6, gender-role differentiation is often quite strong in these families (Troll, 1982). This role division extends into leisure activities. The men are more likely to go out to the bar or go bowling "with the boys," while the women may embroider or get together with "the girls." American society is marked by some social mobility, so these social class divisions are not absolute. Havighurst and Feigenbaum (1959/1968) estimated that 10 percent of the population had

TABLE 11-6:   Mean Hours Spent per Week on Various Activities

Activity	Men	Women
Working	36.8	34.5
Eating	9.8	9.8
Caring for oneself	7.7	8.4
Watching television	11.6	13.2
Reading	8.3	9.0
Engaging in sport hobby	3.9	3.4
Engaging in sport in person	0.6	0.3
Attending church and meetings	2.3	2.9
Volunteer work	0.7	1.1
Socializing	4.8	7.2
Doing activity around house	5.7	3.6
Doing other activity (specified)	0.7	0.6
Just sitting around	3.3	2.6

Source: Pfeiffer, E., & Davis, G. (1971). Use of leisure time in middle life. *Gerontologist, 11*, 187–195. Copyright © The Gerontological Society of America.

leisure patterns typical of a higher social class than their own, while 5 percent had patterns more common to a lower social class.

Social class is not the sole determinant of differences in leisure patterns. Havighurst and Feigenbaum found, for example, that personality influenced leisure use independently of social class and place of residence (suburban versus urban). People with more active leisure roles tended to be better-adjusted. But there were exceptions to this trend. Men who were unhappy at work or in their marriages tended to have low adjustment but high leisure scores. Apparently they were trying to find satisfaction through their leisure activities. This finding fits with other data, such as Bray and Howard's report that less successful AT&T managers increased their leisure activity while more successful men did not change their level.

Some people have virtually no leisure; they devote all their time to work (including homemaking). These people are, of course, what most of us call *workaholics*. Contrary to popular opinion, these people may be quite happy and well-adjusted (Burrus-Bammel & Bammel, 1985; Havighurst & Feigenbaum, 1959/1968; Schultz & Schultz, 1986). It is not necessarily the case that their marriages are unhappy. Nor are they failing to find sources of self-renewal or growth. Rather, they so enjoy their work and find it so challenging that it provides a path for development, even in noncareer realms.

SUMMARY

Choices made early in adulthood can influence paths, rates, and outcomes of development in a variety of realms. Looking at work during the middle years clearly illustrates the effects of such individual differences. Yet, as always, it also underscores certain similarities in development.

At least among men, the middle years are a time of career stability. Middle-aged men generally like their jobs, a phenomenon that is probably a function of both self-selection and rationalization. It is not surprising, then, that they are less likely than younger men to be voluntarily absent from work or to quit their jobs. Their reluctance to change jobs, however, is influenced by factors other than affection for their work. They also believe that it would be difficult to find new, better jobs. And they are right. The middle-aged are the first victims of ageism. Employers do not want to invest in training an older worker. And they may believe that the older worker is less willing or able to learn a new job.

The physical effects of aging may influence a middle-aged person's ability to do a job. He or she may not hear a machine well enough to detect a malfunction, or strength for lifting heavy objects may be diminishing. But such effects are typically small and easily compensated for by the worker's years of experience.

It is fairly safe to assume that middle-aged men have a number of years of experience at their jobs. This assumption is less widely applicable to women. Even today, many women come out of the labor force for extended periods of time to raise children. In fact, women who married in the 1940s,

1950s, and 1960s commonly believed they would never work for pay again after their children were born. If these women become displaced home-makers through divorce or widowhood, they can face an uphill struggle in finding work. Even if they always planned to return to work, the competi-tion against younger, yet more experienced and better trained, women can put them at a serious disadvantage and may completely discourage them.

Similar problems are faced by workers who become unemployed. Our work-oriented culture makes long-term unemployment difficult to accept. And, of course, there are the attendant financial problems. Many middle-aged people find themselves accepting less responsible, lower-paying jobs simply to return to the workforce.

Individual differences are also evident in leisure activities. Both gen-der and class seem to influence choice of leisure activities. Even career suc-cess appears to have some impact. While most of us may need leisure time in order to regenerate, some workaholics do not.

12 Physical Development

The title of this chapter may seem bit odd. Physical *development?* Isn't the issue really physical *deterioration?* Think of the images of the aged. Whistler's Mother spending her days in her rocking chair. Or elderly people so crippled by disease that the only solution their spouses can find is to kill them. And the "nameless" elderly, sitting in institutions, just waiting to die.

But what about Ronald Reagan, Paul Newman, Katherine Hepburn, the British Queen Mother, and the countless other elderly who seem to have full lives? They may have infirmities, certainly. Hepburn has medication-controlled Parkinson's disease and Reagan has had several cancer surgeries. But they still function more than adequately in daily life.

Talking to the elderly themselves does not provide a clearcut answer:

> I am seventy-four years old and have been married for fifty-two years. We are fortunate to have good mental as well as physical health. This is not entirely a matter of luck. We have worked at it. . . .

> At sixty I am more vigorous and healthy than I was twenty years ago. My eighty-five-year-old mother shows me that by the eighties certain things in your body do start to give way, but . . . she's certainly . . . healthy.

> I went to visit a ninety-four-year-old friend who lives in a nursing home. She was recently diagnosed as having various ailments which require anywhere from three to ten pills a day. . . .

> . . . my vision was so impaired. Driving home in the dusk was scary. I felt as though I had my nose right up against the windshield.

> For three years, I was confined, caring for a sick husband twenty-four hours a day. Then my doctor said I had to send him to a nursing home because my blood pressure was rising. (Boston Women's Health Collective, 1984, pp. 452–463)

Who then is truly representative? What are the physical changes that accompany aging? Which are part of the aging process, and which are pathological? These questions are not always easy to answer. Some people are very healthy in old age. Many have some physical problems, but the problems are correctable. Still others require constant care. Do not expect, then, to find a narrowly defined age curve for physical development among those over 60. The norm is more likely to be individual differences.

Methodological Caveats: Much of our stereotype of the elderly as infirm, incompetent, and helpless is attributable to our failure to separate aging from illness. This is particularly obvious in the area of mental functioning. We often speak of "senility," particularly in the form of memory loss, as if it were a normal part of aging. In fact, only a fraction of the elderly suffer from serious memory impairment, and this is due to organic brain syndromes rather than normal aging.

The confounding of illness and aging is also evident in gerontological research. It is indeed difficult to separate the two. First, health problems do become more common as people age, and some are widespread. Well over half of the elderly population suffers from heart disease (Lakatta, 1985), for example. This means that a sample must be carefully screened in order to evaluate non-disease-related coronary changes. Such a sample will in many ways reflect the most elite of the elderly, a form of selectivity that may introduce its own problems.

Screening for health problems is not always easy. In the case of coronary artery disease (CAD), for example, both resting and stress measures are available. The resting measures are much easier to obtain and so have formed the basis for screening in many studies. Yet this measure may underestimate CAD compared to the stress method (Lakatta, 1985). Even when measures themselves are reliable, other issues may make results questionable. Take, for example, hearing tests. The cautiousness of the elderly and their unfamiliarity with task demands might lead them to respond less to sounds that are barely perceptible—but they may in fact hear these sounds. This, in turn, might lead to an overestimate of the decline in their hearing (Olsho et al., 1985).

Our measures of physiological functioning have become increasingly sophisticated. We no longer have to rely exclusively on EEG readings; evoked potentials, PET scans, and CAT scans can provide much more specific information about brain functioning. But most of the available research is not based on this technology. Longitudinal studies, so important for their ability to track individual differences and avoid cohort effects, are often technologically outdated before they are completed (Busse & Maddox, 1985). We certainly cannot throw out the information these studies provide; we simply need to exercise caution, to integrate the less sophisticated but longitudinal findings with the more advanced but cross-sectional results as they emerge.

Finally, we need to recognize that we are attempting to associate physical and behavioral changes using a predominantly correlational method. Sometimes the two sets of data are not even collected together. Rather, a

Although they may experience declines in hearing, vision, and manual dexterity, most older people retain enough functioning to participate in a wide range of activities.

normative trend in physiology is used to explain a normative behavioral shift. Given the individual differences in the aging process, this is very risky. Even when the two measure are taken together, the risks of associating physiology with behavior are great. Many of the measures in both realms are quite nonspecific (EEG or reaction time), or their meanings are unclear. Autopsy results must be treated with special caution, given the redundancy and interconnectedness of function as well as the plasticity of central nervous system functioning (Busse & Maddox, 1985). Both causes and effects of brain "damage" can be difficult to pinpoint.

Indeed, it is often difficult to ascertain whether a particular physical change even has an effect, because there appear to be changes that have little or no meaning for daily functioning. For instance, the eardrum becomes less elastic with age, but this has no known functional significance (Olsho et al., 1985). Information about physical changes is nonetheless important because it helps us understand how the system might react to insult or illness. However, we do need to avoid becoming so overwhelmed by a list of physical declines that we lose sight of the fact that most elderly function adequately on their own.

PHYSIOLOGICAL SYSTEMS

The Brain

Anatomical Changes: Some of the best-documented changes in the central nervous system are those that affect neurons (nerve cells). First, some neurons are lost, though the losses are relatively small, probably in the range of about a 1 percent loss of cortical neurons every year after age 70. The losses are not uniform throughout the brain; certain areas of the brainstem seem to suffer little or no loss with normal aging. In general, losses are greater in the frontal cortex than in the diencephalon, cerebellum, and brain stem (Bondareff, 1985).

Degenerative phenomena may also be observed in the CNS neurons (Bondareff, 1985; LaRue & Jarvik, 1982), including the accumulation of lipofuscin pigment in the cytoplasm of the neurons. The function of this "age pigment" is unknown (Petit, 1982). The number of amyloid or granulovacular bodies increases. These protein accumulations may block blood vessels and even lead to strokes. Although present in "normal" elderly brains, they are particularly common among Alzheimer's patients (Wurtman, 1985). The neurofibillary tangles and senile plaques found in Alzheimer's victims' brains are evident in the normal aged brain (LaRue & Jarvik, 1982). *Neurofibillary tangles* are masses of twisted neuronal filaments. Often these damaged neurons are surrounded by *senile plaques* which are areas of amyloid and other debris that become particularly numerous after the sixth or seventh decade (Feinberg et al., 1980; Wurtman, 1985).

This makes it seem as if the difference between Alzheimer and normal brains is simply quantitative; Alzheimer victims show greater deterioration than the normal elderly do. But this is an oversimplification. First, there may be a threshold of loss. If this threshold is not reached, there will be no interference with normal functioning. In other words, the relationship between degenerative phenomena and functional decline is not completely linear (LaRue & Jarvik, 1982). Second, as will be evident in the more extended discussion of Alzheimer's disease later in this chapter, there are significant differences between the victims' brains and those of normal elderly. For example, the sites of damage are often different, as are the number of neurological abnormalities. It would be uncommon, for example, to find senile plaques, neurofibillary tangles, *and* amyloid bodies in a "normal brain," whereas it is typical to find all of them in an Alzheimer's brain (Wurtman, 1985).

In the normal elderly, neuronal degeneration may be due to changes within the neuron itself or to external forces (Bondareff, 1985). External factors contributing to degeneration might include change in blood vessels or the cerebrospinal ventricles (Bondareff, 1985). It is not unusual for the volume of cerebrospinal fluid to increase with age, causing a dilation of the brain ventricles or sulci (Jernigan, Zatz, Feinberg, & Fein, 1980; LaRue & Jarvik, 1982). The pressure from the expansion may damage neurons. However, the extent of the dilation is not a very good predictor of cognitive losses in either normal or Alzheimer's patients (LaRue & Jarvik, 1982).

Neuronal interconnections may also be lost because of the loss of *Purkinje cells,* which are neurons located in the cerebellum. Each one typically receives impulses from over 80,000 other neurons. These cells are rather like telephone relay stations, integrating, connecting, and coordinating large amounts of information (Previte, 1983). The number of Purkinje cells declines gradually until about 60, and then begins to fall more rapidly (Bondareff, 1985).

Neuronal communication may also be affected by changes in the *neurotransmitters,* chemicals that carry messages from one neuron to the next. There are several different neurotransmitter systems in the human brain, including acetylcholine, dopamine, norepinephrine, and serotonin. Each of these systems shows different age-related changes (Rogers & Bloom, 1985). Norepinephrine levels, for example, tend to drop most dramatically in the brainstem, while lowered dopamine levels are more evident in the striatum. It is not only the amount of transmitter available that may be affected by age. Both dopamine and acetylcholine have fewer receptor binding sites in the elderly brain. This means that there are fewer sites to receive the messages being carried by these neurotransmitters (Rogers & Bloom, 1985).

Neurons are not the only components of the aging brain that change. Blood flow to the brain may decrease by as much as 23 percent between ages 33 and 61 (Wurtman, 1985). The older brain, however, appears to be more efficient at extracting oxygen from the blood, so that the decreased blood flow does not normally cause a serious problem.

It is worth pausing a moment here to make two points about the patterns evident in age-related neuronal changes. First, there are wide individual differences. Some individual "normal" elderly will suffer more severe losses of certain types than some individual Alzheimer's victims (LaRue & Jarvik, 1982). Second, losses are not uniform within an individual. Talking about overall neuronal loss has limited meaning, since the losses are quite different in the cortex and in the brainstem.

EEG Changes: The slowing of EEG activity is a long-known, frequently replicated finding (see Busse & Maddox, 1985; Woodruff, 1985). Table 12–1 shows the young adult speed (in cycles per second, or cps) of the four levels of EEG activity (Woodruff, 1985). Alpha rhythms, associated with alert wakefulness, slow about 0.5 to 0.75 cps for each decade after 60.

TABLE 12-1: Types of EEG Waves

Wave Name	Cycles Per Second (cps)	Level of Arousal
Delta	1–3	Deep sleep
Theta	4–7	Light sleep
Alpha	8–13	Alert wakefulness
Beta	14–30+	Thinking and problem solving

Source: Woodruff, D. (1985). Arousal, sleep, and aging. In J. Birren & K. Schaie (eds.), *The handbook of the psychology of aging.* New York: Van Nostrand.

By 70, the average alpha is around 9–9.5 cps. After 80, alpha is commonly in the 8.5–9 cps range. Women show a faster average alpha rhythm than men. There are no well-established cognitive declines associated with the alpha slowing (Busse & Maddox, 1985).

Alpha declines are more marked among the institutionalized elderly, where the average alpha rhythm may be less than 8 cps. This is particularly true of patients with cerebral, vascular, or neurological disorders. Dementia (Alzheimer's, Pick's, Crutzfeld-Jakob's) patients may show even more dramatic slowing, with an average of less than 7 cps (Busse & Maddox, 1985). Depending on how rigidly one adheres to the categories outlined in Table 12–1, this may no longer be considered true alpha (Woodruff, 1985). In any case, among the dementia population, amount of alpha decline is correlated with amount of impairment (Busse & Maddox, 1985).

In addition to the overall slowing of alpha, there is the appearance of scattered slow waves (6–8 cps) during the alpha interval. If the alpha slowing is slight and the slow waves are very scattered, there appears to be no negative meaning. However, if slowing is moderate (6–8 cps) or severe (more than 10 percent of alpha is at 4 cps or less), brain dysfunction is likely. There is a greater decline in alpha among terminally ill patients (Busse & Maddox, 1985). Thus, fast activity seems to bode well for both cognitive ability and longevity.

The speed of the alpha rhythm appears to be positively correlated with both oxygen consumption and blood flow in the brain. This may explain why *slightly* elevated blood pressure is associated with both faster alpha and better cognitive functioning among the elderly. The slightly increased pressure may compensate for the narrowing of the vessels, resulting in adequate (closer to young adult) blood flow (Busse & Maddox, 1985). *Severe* hypertension or decompensative heart disease, however, is associated with poorer cognitive functioning (LaRue & Jarvik, 1982; Schaie, 1979).

The Heart and Circulatory System

It is clear that there are more abnormalities in the electrocardiograms (ECG) of the elderly than of middle-aged or young adults (Shock et al, 1984). What is not clear is which of these changes, if any, is an outcome of "normal" aging and which are due to disease. Over half of all elderly suffer from some form of heart disease, but some of this disease is not clinically evident and could lead them to be included in a "normal" group. Thus, we must be extremely cautious in interpreting the available data on the heart (Lakatta, 1985).

This is exemplified by the findings on cardiac output. Early studies reported a decrease in cardiac output, in the range of about 1 percent per year (see DeVries, 1975). More recent data, however, suggest no specific age-related decline in cardiac output. Rather, the decline reported in earlier studies seems to be attributable to hidden heart disease (Lakatta, 1985).

This does not mean that there are no age-related changes in heart structure or function; the heart apparently shows some enlargement after age 50, though the enlargement is more pronounced in those with heart disease (Shock et al., 1984). The cardiac arteries, including the aorta, are less elastic, and systolic blood pressure is higher. These changes lead to a thickening of the left ventricle wall. This, in turn, causes more stroke work and greater oxygen consumption by the heart muscle (Lakatta, 1985). In other words, the elderly heart is less efficient. As might be expected, the efficiency is even more affected in those with heart disease.

It is interesting that both the causes and the effects of cardiovascular disease seem to change with age (Busse & Maddox, 1985). Three of the factors associated with myocardial infarction in middle age—obesity, cigarette smoking, and high cholestrol—do not seem to predict infarctions in the elderly. High blood pressure and personality factors, on the other hand, appear to be risk factors at all ages (Bierman, 1985; Busse & Maddox, 1985; Kannel, 1985). In terms of cardiovascular diseases' effects, the middle-aged heart patients' cognitive functioning tends to be more impaired than the elderly patient's.

Atherosclerosis: Arteriosclerosis is a broad term referring to the thickening and hardening of the walls of the arteries. Atherosclerosis is a form of arteriosclerosis that affects the large arteries, including those of the heart. Atherosclerosis can cause, among other things, myocardial infarction, angina pectoris, and cerebrovascular accidents, and hence is classified as the leading cause of death among Americans over age 65 (Bierman, 1985).

Atherosclerosis is age-related in the sense that it becomes more marked over time. Similarly, the processes that contribute to atherosclerosis are cumulative. So, for example, one widely accepted theory of atherosclerotic development is the reaction to injury hypothesis. This theory suggests that various factors, including high blood pressure and cigarette smoking, can cause damage to the innermost layer of the blood vessels. When this damage is chronic (recurring over time), the middle layer grows out and over the inner layer. This abnormal growth, with an accompanying layer of fat, accumulates until blood flow is altered (Bierman, 1985).

There is some evidence that the blood vessels change with age. For example, the walls may become more rigid with age. And the wear and tear cited in the reaction to injury hypothesis is real; it leads to a dilation and elongation of the arteries and may contribute to the development of aneurysms. *Aneurysms* are weak spots in the arterial wall, often resembling bubbles or balloonings, which can break. Places where the blood vessels curve or branch seem particularly vulnerable. Aneurysms can be fatal if they burst (Bierman, 1985).

These changes, however, are not sufficient to account for atherosclerosis. Atherosclerosis, though widespread among Americans, should not be considered a normal (that is, inevitable or positive) outcome of the aging process. Instead, it is a pathological state whose origins are traceable to lifestyle habits, such as too much cholesterol and too little exercise. While the earliest signs of atherosclerosis are evident in American children, even the elderly of more "primitive" societies may not show any symptoms of the disease (Bierman, 1985).

Hypertension: Hypertension is like atherosclerosis in several ways. First, it is a major contributor to cardiovascular disease across the life span. It may cause the damage that leads to atherosclerosis. Certainly, people with hypertension are at greater risk than "normotensives" for dying of heart attacks or strokes (see Table 12-2). Second, most people experience an increase in blood pressure with age. However, this is more true of "affluent" than "primitive" societies and does not appear to be an inevitable consequence of aging. Indeed, even within Western cultures, the rise in blood pressure is more predictable from early blood pressure and from weight gain than from age alone (Kannel, 1985).

Hypertension generally refers to a level of blood pressure higher than is considered "safe." Blood pressure is measured in two components, systolic and diastolic. When blood pressure is taken, the first or top number represents the systolic pressure and the second or bottom number is the diastolic pressure. Hypertension can affect only one component, or, more commonly, both. There is no single definitive set of numbers that defines hypertension, but the Framingham Study (the best-known longitudinal study of cardiovascular risk) defined systolic pressure of greater than 160 or diastolic pressure exceeding 95 as hypertensive. At the outermost limits, systolic pressure of over 200 and diastolic pressures over 120 would constitute hypertension (Kannel, 1985).

Systolic and diastolic pressure do not show identical developmental curves. Systolic pressure rises steadily (at least among Americans), whereas diastolic pressure typically begins to decline after about age 65. Furthermore, hypertension involving only systolic pressure may appear after age 55 and still be considered a primary form of hypertension. On the other hand, essential hypertension, involving both components, almost always appears prior to age 55. If it begins after 55, it is usually secondary to some other disease or disorder, such as kidney problems (Kannel, 1985).

One other age-related blood pressure change deserves mention here. With age, there is increased *lability* of blood pressure (Kannel, 1985). This means that the readings fluctuate more dramatically in older than in younger adults. So it is important to obtain multiple readings in making a

TABLE 12-2: Risk of Specified Cardiovascular Events According to Hypertensive Status (Person Aged 65-74)

Blood Pressure Status	STROKE		CORONARY DISEASE		PERIPHERAL ARTERIAL DISEASE		CARDIAC FAILURE	
	Men	Women	Men	Women	Men	Women	Men	Women
Normotensive	12.4	5.4	2.7	0.6	6.2	2.6	3.9	3.2
Borderline	24.0	13.7	8.1	6.4	5.9	2.6	6.8	6.3
Hypertensive	28.4	22.1	18.9	16.4	7.0	5.9	18.1	9.7

Source: Kannel, W. (1985). Hypertension and aging. In C. Finch & E. Schneider (eds.), *Handbook of the biology of aging,* 2nd ed., pp. 859-877. Copyright © 1985 by Van Nostrand Reinhold. Reprinted by permission.

diagnosis of hypertension. As long as the average blood pressure level is not hypertension level, the lability itself does not appear to be a problem.

Skeleton and Bones

One of the best-known physiological risks among the elderly is broken bones. We have all heard of cases in which an elderly person took a spill and broke a bone, often a large one such as the hip. Fractures of the femur, the largest single bone in the human body, double for every five years past 50 (Exton-Smith, 1985). Less severe trauma or impact is needed to break a bone in the elderly, and they are more likely to suffer a break near a joint than a young person is. Elderly women are considerably more susceptible to fractures of all sorts than are elderly men (Exton-Smith, 1985). This sex difference is probably at least partially attributable to the higher rate of osteoporosis among elderly women. This difference, which first appears after menopause, was discussed in Chapter 8.

Osteoporosis is a frequently misused term. Many people think it refers to a particular disease, but it actually indicates a condition, skeletal loss, rather than a particular pathological state (Exton-Smith, 1985). It has multiple causes and in over half of all cases, no specific explanation can be found. Osteoporosis is considered a pathological state and can be distinguished from other bone diseases (osteomalacia), as well as from normal age-related declines (osteopenia).

The decline in amount of bone usually begins during the forties, with a very steady loss after about 45. Different people lose bone at different rates. Indeed, some individuals have more bone in old age than others have at the age of skeletal maturity (around 30). Nonetheless, it appears that there is always some bone loss. With age, the long bones (such as the femur) become more porous and thinner. Flat bones also become more porous and therefore less strong. Bone loss is due both to a slowing in bone formation and an increased rate of bone resorption (Exton-Smith, 1985).

What factors influence the rate of bone loss and the final amount of bone? One seems to be bone mass at skeletal maturity. As has already been implied, some people's bones are denser at maturity than other people's, and this difference apparently continues throughout adulthood. This is probably one reason why men are less susceptible than women to fractures and osteoporosis. Beginning in childhood, males have a greater amount of bone than females (Exton-Smith, 1985). Hormonal differences also contribute to the gender difference in bone loss.

Nutrition may also play a role. The ability to absorb calcium, a mineral that is instrumental in bone formation, decreases with age. In fact, calcium absorption in children may be two or three times greater than in adults. And postmenopausal women may need about 50 percent more calcium daily than premenopausal women. The elderly, then, are particularly susceptible to calcium deficiency. Since vitamin D is important in maintaining calcium's balance in the body, a deficiency will exacerbate a calcium deficiency. Housebound elderly, who do not get vitamin D from the sun, seem to be particularly at risk. Furthermore, the elderly who are house-

Regular exercise may be beneficial in a number of ways, including slowing bone disease and maintaining pulmonary functioning.

bound are often immobile, and immobility can itself produce localized osteoporosis (Exton-Smith, 1985).

Individual differences are clearly evident in skeletal status among the elderly. Once again we see that both internal and external factors influence these differences. In fact, these differences are so great that researchers often report a group increase in bone amounts after age 80 because of the strength and good health of the "survivors" who make up such groups (Exton-Smith, 1985).

Vision

It is no surprise that researchers report that visual acuity declines with age (Busse & Maddox, 1985; Kline & Schieber, 1985). For most people, glasses will solve the problem, but a significant number will become legally blind. Estimates suggest that as many as 376,000 elderly people will be legally blind by the year 2000, while another 1,760,000 will have severe visual problems. It is little wonder that vision losses are second only to cancer as a feared outcome of aging (Kline & Schieber, 1985).

Anatomical Changes: Declines in visual acuity can be explained by changes in the eye's structures and alterations in the neural components of aging. Figure 12–1 shows the structure of the eye and the neural pathways that carry visual information to the brain. Table 12–3 outlines the major structures of the eye, their functions, and age-related changes (Kline & Schieber, 1985). There are significant changes in all the eye structures. The

FIGURE 12-1:   A Cross Section of the Eye.

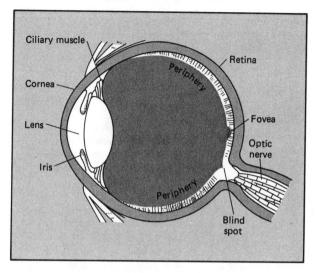

Ciliary muscle

Cornea

Lens

Iris

Retina

Periphery

Fovea

Optic nerve

Periphery

Blind spot

Source: Darley, J., Glucksberg, S., & Kinchla, R. (1991). *Psychology*, 5th ed. © 1991. Reprinted by permission of Prentice Hall, Englewood Cliffs, New Jersey.

outermost portion of the eye, the cornea, flattens and yellows as part of normal aging; the lens also yellows and loses some of its transparency. These changes affect not only acuity, but also color vision.

Some of the changes evident in the visual system appear to be related to life-style patterns; they may not truly be outcomes of aging. For example, the decline in light receptors in the retina is probably largely attributable to ultraviolet exposure. Wearing appropriate sunglasses might help to reduce this loss. The detachment of the vitreous body from the retina is usually due to a jolt or a blow. Therefore, workers who are subject to sudden jolts (such as truck drivers) may be at particular risk for developing the problem (Kline & Schieber, 1985).

Functional Changes: Many of the changes in visual processing first become evident in the middle years (see Chapter 8). These changes then become more pronounced with advancing age. Light sensitivity declines, which in turn reduces color sensitivity. Changes in the lens are primarily responsible for the decreased sensitivity to light. More specifically, an increased level (or threshold) of light is needed before the elderly person can see. Their dark adaptation is therefore poorer than that of a young adult. At the same time, the elderly person's ability to adapt to glare is decreasing, again due mainly to increasing lens opacity. It also takes older people longer to recover from glare, with those in their seventies needing about two-thirds more time than young adults in their twenties. The glare of car headlights has been specifically investigated, and it has been found to be common for older drivers to experience special difficulties at night. They

TABLE 12-3:   The Major Structures of the Eye and Their Age-Related Changes

Part of the Eye	Function	Age-Related Change
Cornea	Bends light onto the retina	Flattens → decreased refraction of light and luster of eye. Increased waviness, irregularity, and corneal deposits. Yellowing in the very old. Increased corneal astigmatisms.
Iris and pupil	Regulates amount of light	Decreased pupil diameter (senile miosis) → decreased light to retina. Because pigment decreases, light entering the eye is more diffuse.
Lens	Focusing for various distances	Old cells are not lost, so new ones push old to center → decreased lens transparency. Yellowing. Decreased accommodative power.
Vitreous body	Maintains shape of eye	Posterior vitreous detachment, usually due to a jolt, blow, etc., can be caused by age-related changes in vitreous fluid. This can → light flashes (w/o stimuli), blurred vision, floaters, and sometimes hemorrhaging or retinal detachment.
Retina	Begins visual processing in photoreceptor cells (rods and cones)	Decreased photoreceptors, especially cones. This is probably due to UV light exposure. Other changes have no apparent functional effect.
Visual brain	Portion of cortex that is primarily responsible for visual processing	25% reduction in neurons in macular projection of visual cortex by 70, with continued decline until at least 87. Also fewer dendritic spines and neurotransmitters. Visual perceptual process slows. These effects are lessened by redundancy of brain functions.

Source: Based on Kline, D., & Schieber, F. (1985). Vision and aging. In J. Birren & K. Schaie (eds.), *The handbook of the psychology of aging,* 2nd ed., pp. 296–331. New York: Van Nostrand.

see less well in the dark and are more disturbed by oncoming headlights than are younger adults (Kline & Schieber, 1985).

The field of vision also constricts (Kline & Schieber, 1985). There is a decline in peripheral vision that could affect performance on a variety of tasks, including driving. The field of vision is constant until about age 35, shows slight decline until about 50, and then a more rapid loss. Visual field loss is particularly pronounced after age 75 and continues into the nineties.

As we noted in Chapter 8, significant declines in visual acuity begin in middle age, commonly in the form of presbyopia. The ability to see both stable and moving objects is affected (static versus dynamic acuity). Static acuity probably begins to decline after about age 45 and is reversible with glasses and proper illumination if there is no visual pathology. Dynamic acuity shows more dramatic declines that seem to affect driving ability. Older people will, for example, have more difficulty reading highway signs. Contrary to what intuition might tell you, static and dynamic acuity declines are not highly related. We cannot always predict dynamic declines from static losses, and dynamic, not static, acuity changes predict driving ability (Kline & Schieber, 1985). These losses may combine to affect elderly people's ability to attend selectively to objects and events within their visual field. These declines in visual attention, combined with cognitive declines, help explain the higher rate of auto accidents among older adults (Owsley et al., 1991).

Older people are aware of these visual declines (Kosnik, Winslow, Kline, Rasinski, & Sekuler, 1988). They report more problems than younger adults with following moving targets, extracting information from moving sources, seeing in poor light, adjusting to glare, completing visually oriented tasks quickly, and finding a particular object in a group of objects. Depending on the specific visual task in question, self-reports of visual difficulties are two to six times greater as people age. Seeing in dim light, using dynamic vision, and speed of processing visual information show fairly steep declines. Losses in near vision and visual search speed, however, seem more gradual to people. In other words, people experiencing normal aging do not suddenly lose their vision. In their opinions, the losses vary in both rate and extent, according to the skills involved (Kosnik et al., 1988).

It is clear that such losses can interfere with daily life, especially driving. They may also make it more difficult for some people to work if their jobs require rapid processing of visual information. Older people do report such problems more frequently.

Pathologies: Diseases or disorders of the eye are not an outcome of aging itself, but they do become more common with age. The most common visual pathology, cataracts, is eight times more frequent among the elderly than in the general population. Similarly, glaucoma is eight times more common, and retinal disorders (other than diabetic retinopathy) are six times more frequent among the elderly population (Kline & Schieber, 1985). Both cataracts and glaucoma (see Chapter 8) are even more common among the elderly than among the middle-aged. There is, for example, a linear increase in the rate of glaucoma between ages 60 and 85. Screening for glaucoma is particularly crucial among older people.

A third disorder is so much more frequent among the elderly that its name implies that age is a factor: senile macular degeneration (SMD). The *macula* is an area of the retina. *Cones* (the receptors used in color vision) are concentrated here, especially in the center of the macula (an area known as the *fovea*). Indeed, visual acuity is highest when the "stimulus" is focused onto the macula. It is here, for example, that detail such as fine print will be discriminated (Kart et al., 1978; Kline & Schieber, 1985).

In SMD, there is a systematic deterioration of the macula and loss of visual acuity, usually down to the 20/50 to 20/100 range on the Snellen chart. The disease usually affects both eyes and is not treatable; retinal areas are actually destroyed. Its cause is unknown, although conditions such as diabetes or hypertension may contribute in some cases (Kart et al., 1978; Kline & Schieber, 1985). Victims of SMD are not completely blind; only the macula is affected. The areas of the retina that enable peripheral vision are generally left intact, which allows the SMD victim to get around. However, tasks that require finer discrimination, such as reading or opening medicine bottles or telling time, will be difficult or impossible. Magnifying glasses may give some people sufficient acuity to perform some of these tasks (Kart et al., 1978; Kline & Schieber, 1985).

Audition

Presbycusis, loss of the ability to hear high-frequency sounds, is one of the major sensory declines associated with human aging (see Chapter 8). About 80 percent of people over 45 have some presbycusis, with more than half of these being over 65. It has been estimated that about 20 percent of people aged 45–54 and 75 percent of 75- to 79-year-olds have some high-frequency hearing loss. In more severe cases, this can lead to difficulties in localizing sound, discriminating speech, and remembering long sentences (Olsho et al., 1985). It is not clear how much of these hearing losses is due to aging and how much to life style (such as exposure to loud noises).

Structural Changes: Figure 12–2 shows the structure of the ear and the neural pathway that carries auditory information to the brain. Table 12–4 outlines the major structures of the ear, their functions, and their age-related changes (Olsho et al., 1985). Note that there are changes in virtually every structure, but these changes do not all have functional implications. There is some lessening of flexibility in the eardrum, but this has no known effect on hearing. Changes in the hair cells, which are the actual receptor sites for hearing, and their related structures (such as the basilar and tectorial membranes) seem particularly likely to reduce hearing acuity.

Some caution is needed in interpreting these changes (Olsho et al., 1985). Research on audition is surprisingly limited. We do not yet know much about the function of some of the structures. There seem to be specific cells that respond to specific stimuli, but these are poorly mapped at the present time. Furthermore, there have been sampling problems. As with

FIGURE 12-2:   A Diagram of the Ear.

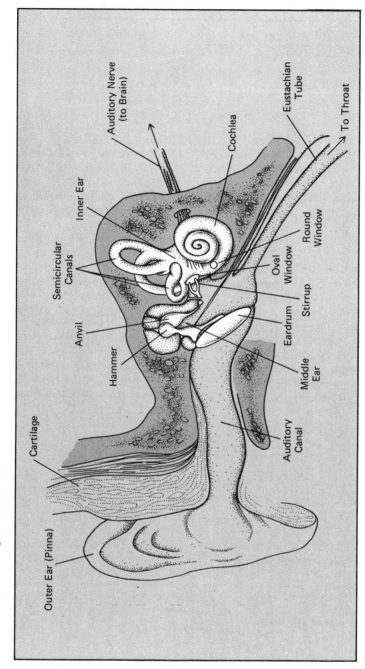

Source: Darley, J., Glucksberg, S., & Kinchla, R. (1991). *Psychology,* 5th ed. © 1991.
Reprinted by permission of Prentice Hall, Englewood Cliffs, New Jersey.

343

TABLE 12-4: Structures of the Auditory System and Their Age-Related Changes

Part of the Ear	Function	Age-Related Change
Outer Ear		
Pinna	Sound localization	Some changes in size, shape, and flexibility, but with no known functional implications.
Auditory canal	Sound localization Attenuation of loudness of sounds > 1000 Hz (i.e., high frequency sounds)	Atrophy of walls → (a) Wax buildup → conductive hearing loss; (b) Collapsed walls → loss of high frequency hearing.
Middle Ear		
Eardrum (tympanic membrane)	Sound amplification	*Possible* decreased elasticity with no known functional significance.
Ossicular chain	Sound amplification	Some thinning and calcification with no known functional significance.
Eustachian tubes	Pressure equalization; fluid drainage	Mixed reports, but no changes established. Increased rate of colds in the old may → clinical impression of more blockage in the old.
Inner Ear		
Basilar membrane	Differentially stimulates outer hair cells	Decreased flexibility. When extreme, there can be a hearing loss (low frequencies first), known as inner-ear conductive presbycusis.
Tectorial membrane	Base for outer hair cells	Increased thickness. When extreme, can result in inner ear conductive presbycusis.
Hair cells	Sensory receptors	Decline, may begin by 20. Can → hearing loss, especially at high frequencies.
Stria vascularis	Capillary system within the cochlea; necessary for neuronal transmission	May atrophy → increased pigment and calcium deposits, decreased cell organelles and (when severe) cells and capillaries → strial presbycusis.

Source: Based on Olsho, L., Harkins, S., & Lenhardt, M. (1985). Aging and the auditory system. In J. Birren & K. Schaie (eds.), *The handbook of the psychology of aging,* 2nd ed. New York: Van Nostrand.

brain-behavior studies, many researchers have looked at either structural or functional change, rather than at both simultaneously. In addition, there is much more information available about changes in deaf elderly than in the mild to moderately impaired individual. It is possible that there are just quantitative differences between these groups; however, it is also possible that there are qualitative differences. Finally, the cautiousness, attention problems, and lack of familiarity with tasks that often mark the performance of the elderly may result in overestimates of any functional decline that does occur.

Functional Changes: The best-documented functional change is a decline in pure tone sensitivity (presbycusis). This is especially evident at higher (1000 hz or greater) frequencies. The losses are more common and more severe in men than in women, but there is no single pattern of presbycusis (Kline & Schieber, 1985). This raises suspicions about the "normality" of the decline. In fact, there are four forms of presbycusis: sensory, neural, metabolic, and inner ear conductive. (Table 12–4 shows the different structures involved in these forms.) Noise exposure is known to play a role, although it is not a necessary precursor of the loss. Furthermore, it is not clear that noise exposure is implicated in all four forms of presbycusis. The roles of genetics, diet, and disease are unknown. Even the "cause" of the sex difference is not known, since noise exposure alone cannot explain it. So although presbycusis is routinely considered as a "normal" outcome of aging, it is not clear that it is actually inevitable.

These hearing losses do not usually have much effect on daily living. Most "important" sounds are less than 4000 hz in frequency. In fact, research indicates that speech is still intelligible if all sounds exceeding 1800 hz are removed. Typically, hearing loss is mild at frequencies of 250–2000 hz and only moderate up to about 4000 hz. Therefore, it is not the pure tone losses that are the culprit in most hearing difficulties (Olsho et al., 1985). Furthermore, hearing aids may be helpful in the more severe cases (Kart et al., 1978).

There is a decline in the ability to discriminate among frequencies (Olsho et al., 1985). This may affect speech perception, because many speech sounds are distinguished primarily on the basis of frequency (vowels) or intensity (stop consonants). So it may become more difficult to distinguish a *b* from a *p* sound or a short *i* from a short *e* (as in *pin* and *pen*).

Overall, speech perception is only slightly impaired. Under ideal conditions, the loss of speech intelligibility is in the range of 5–10 dbs. This means the sounds must be 5–10 dbs louder for older than for younger adults to discriminate speech sounds. Sentences are usually more difficult for presbycusis sufferers to repeat than individual words. The losses are more pronounced under adverse conditions, such as when the speech is rapid, interrupted, or reverberated (Olsho et al., 1985).

The causes of the speech perception losses are not known. It could be that changes in the ear itself contribute to decreased sensitivity. Perhaps there is a slowing in neural transmission and processing of speech. This in conjunction with memory problems could make it difficult to process sentences or paragraphs. It is possible that both sensory and neural mechanisms are involved (Olsho et al., 1985).

In any case, hearing losses should be carefully evaluated, because many of them are treatable. Those under 80 may be helped by hearing aids, though for older elderly the aids may exacerbate the problem (Olsho et al., 1985). In some cases, a buildup of ear wax is contributing to the problem, and its removal can improve hearing. Some forms of hearing problems, such as a hardening of the stapes, can be surgically corrected (Kart et al., 1978).

Other Sensory Systems

Vestibular: The vestibular sense is involved in maintaining balance. While not one of the five senses, it is an important sensory process. Falling is a major problem among the elderly (Ochs, Newberry, Lenhardt, & Harkins, 1985). Given the common phenomenon of weakening of the bones, it is not surprising that falls among the elderly may have serious results. Falls can be fatal, especially for those over 75. Approximately 70 percent of all deaths from falls occur among people over 65, and in people over 75, falls are the most frequent cause of accidental death, surpassing automobile fatalities. They can also lead to decreased mobility, increased dependence on the family, and in some cases, institutionalization.

But do elderly people actually fall more than young adults do? Or are they simply more susceptible to injury when they do fall? The data indicate a positive correlation between age and falling (Ochs et al., 1985). This is true even in nonfatal falls. Although falling is more common and more serious among institutionalized than among community-dwelling elderly, both groups fall more often than younger people. Even among the community dwellers, who are assumed to be fairly healthy, about a third of those over 65 fall at least once a year. Women are more likely to fall than men and are more likely to sustain serious injury (probably at least partly because of their osteoporosis problems). Men, however, have a higher death rate from falls.

What causes falling? Some of the factors are extrinsic, such as broken sidewalks, unfamiliarity with the environment, and so on. Others are disease-related. Cardiac arrhythmia, postural hypotension, and drug side effects can all cause falling. Often disease and environmental factors will interact. And many times the cause is simply unknown (Ochs et al., 1985).

In addition, the aging of the vestibular system itself may contribute to falling (Ochs et al., 1985). As people age, they may suffer from a loss of equilibrium, a condition known as *presbystasis*. Vestibular sensory receptors seem to be involved in presbystasis. The otoliths, which detect gravity changes, show a more than 20 percent decline in receptors and neurofibers. The semicircular canal receptors, which respond to head position changes, decline by about 40 percent after age 50, but the relationship of these declines to prebystasis has not been clearly established.

Other balance problems include *vestibular ataxia* (a feeling of constant disequilibrium when walking), inability to recover from the beginning of a fall, and increased body sway when standing (Ochs et al., 1985). It is not yet clear which of these constitute normal aging phenomena and which are disease or disorder related. Vestibular ataxia, which is particularly common among the very old, seems to have a genetic component. People who suffered from motion sickness in their younger days are more likely to exhibit this ataxia. Balance requires the integration of vestibular, motor, and visual information. Some of the declines in the visual system may contribute to balance problems. Integrating information may also be a problem (Ochs et al., 1985).

Taste and Smell: Nutritional problems are fairly common among the elderly. One potential culprit in these difficulties is a declining sense of taste. It may be that things just don't taste as good as they used to. Some of this change may be due to disease and some to medication, but it is also possible that there is an actual decline in gustatory ability.

Taste thresholds appear to be fairly stable throughout life, especially the ability to discern a sweet taste (Bartoshuk & Weiffenbach, 1990). It does appear that there is a decline in the ability to discern a bitter taste (Spitzer, 1988). Sour and salt discrimination may also be more difficult for the elderly, although the data for this are equivocal. The ability to detect various flavors within blended food also declines. However, this may be more attributable to losses in the sense of smell than to taste declines (Bartoshuk & Weiffenbach, 1990). Smell seems to decline more consistently and dramatically with age than taste does.

It is interesting to note that people with hypertension seem to have even more trouble tasting salt than other elderly do (Spitzer, 1988), perhaps because of their medication. But Mary Spitzer (1988) has also hypothesized that these people may have always had high salt discrimination thresholds and may therefore have needed more salt in their diets in order to taste it at all. This in turn might contribute to the onset of the hypertension. It is known that there are genetically mediated differences in taste thresholds.

What causes the age-related acuity losses? Cross-sectional research suggests that it is not due to a loss in taste bud density. There may, however, be some loss in the sensitivity of the taste buds (Miller, 1988). Given the individual differences in taste sensitivity, longitudinal research is needed to determine whether or not a decline exists.

CAUSES OF AGING

It is clear that there is a certain amount of physical degeneration with advancing age. What causes these declines is less obvious. Several explanations have been offered, but none has received unequivocal empirical support.

Biochemical Explanations

At least three major biochemical models of aging have influenced research during the past two decades (Rothstein, 1982): the free radical theory, the error catastrophe hypothesis, and the cell senescence model.

The basic premise of the *free radical theory* (Harman, 1956) is that oxygenation produces derivatives that damage physiological structures. More specifically, the perioxidation of unsaturated fatty acids leads to the formation of free radicals, which then accumulate and cause damage. The existence of free radicals has been documented. Furthermore, lipid perioxidation results in the production of lipofuscin, the "age pigment." As we saw in Chapter 4 and earlier in this chapter, there is more lipofuscin in the brains of elderly adults. However, it is not clear that it actually affects brain functioning, nor is it clear how any free radical might cause any system to age.

The *error catastrophe hypothesis* suggests mistakes in protein synthesis (Orgel, 1970), which is controlled by the genes. The proteins then control every cell in the body (Previte, 1983). Some even provide "feedback" to keep the genetically controlled process of protein synthesis moving. Mistakes in some proteins would not cause serious damage, but over time the mistakes could accumulate. If the proteins feeding back into the process were erroneously coded, the damage could be particularly devastating. This type of "catastrophic error" would cause a physiological breakdown. Research tends to indicate that protein errors do not seem to accumulate to dangerous levels with age, and no form of catastrophic error has been identified (Rothstein, 1982).

The third model concerns *cell senescence* (Hayflick & Moorhead, 1961). It used to be believed that cells in culture (in laboratories) were immortal. In other words, aging was not a built-in process, but would have to be induced. However, beginning in the 1960s, it became clear that this was not true. Cell division gradually slows down until it stops. This is true when the cell is in a laboratory culture, presumably free from whatever might damage cells in the human body. The life span of cells themselves is limited. However, it is not clear how the behavior of individual cultured cells is like overall aging in the organism. Furthermore, the mechanism guiding the "aging" of the cells is not clear. Genetics may provide an answer to that question.

The Role of Genetics

Geneticists have addressed several questions relevant to aging. The first is whether specific genes trigger and control the process. There might actually be a gene (or, more likely, a set of genes) that directly turn on the aging process (McClearn & Foch, 1985). Such genes might be like those involved in Alzheimer's disease or in syndromes such as Werner's disease that mimic some of the physical symptoms of aging (Kirkwood, 1985; Martin & Turker, 1988). To date there has been considerable success in locating genes involved in age-related pathologies such as Alzheimer's disease. But there has not been any substantial advance in the identification of "aging" genes.

Why would we expect to find such genes? Assuming that genetic influence is guided by natural selection processes, we would have to argue that aging is somehow an adaptive process (Kirkwood, 1985). Aging is a way to ensure reduction of the population so that there is not too much competition for limited resources. Proponents of this view also point out that limiting the life span through aging allows for a faster generational turnover, so that genetic adaptations to the environment can be made more quickly. Neither argument is very convincing. First, most animals do not live to be "old" if they are in their natural environments, so there would be little need to build in a natural system of elimination. Furthermore, it is difficult to understand why a longer life would not be advantageous. In other words, why would long life be associated with deterioration? Indeed, some researchers have argued that long life is a genetically selected-for trait—that longevity is positively influenced by genetics (see T. Johnson, 1988).

Such concerns have led other researchers to suggest that aging itself is not an adaptive process (Kirkwood, 1985). In fact, they argue that there is no direct selection for aging. Instead, aging is a by-product of other genetic effects. One possibility is that characteristics selected for because they were positive in early life are negative in later life (T. Johnson, 1988). So, hypothetically, a gene that led to strong bone calcification in childhood might contribute to arterial clogging in old age (Kirkwood, 1985). This genetic action is called *antagonistic pleitropy* (T. Johnson, 1988). While not documented, it seems plausible because of the known multiple actions (pleitropy) of many genes (McClearn & Foch, 1985).

The second possibility, called *mutation accumulation,* is that some genes have no effect in young organisms but do have a negative effect in older ones (T. Johnson, 1988). Because these problems do not interfere with reproductive fitness, they are not selected out. In other words, natural selection simply fails to operate (Kirkwood, 1985). This is plausible because it is known that certain genes are not operative at birth and "turn on" later in development (McClearn & Foch, 1985; Plomin, 1983). Furthermore, a number of disorders, most notably Huntington's Chorea, seem to underscore the possibility of such a mechanism. Huntington's Chorea is a fatal neurological disease that is transmitted by a dominant gene, the symptoms of which do not appear until middle age.

While research is far from conclusive, it does tend to support the more nonselectionist views (Johnson, 1988). There is little evidence for genes that actually cause aging; instead, it appears to be a by-product of other genetic actions. For example, in the Drosophilia (fruitfly), delaying reproduction results in increased longevity. Apparently early reproduction, which is the norm, depletes metabolic reserves (Johnson, 1988). This example, however, illustrates at least two problems. First, the available research is severely limited and is often in species whose relationship to human functioning is unclear. Second, we may have to wait for a process-by-process examination in order to understand aging. The genetic influences on one system may be different from those on another (Martin & Turker, 1988). Given the wide range of aging effects across systems, this possibility is not surprising.

There is yet another whole set of possibilities for the role of genes in aging. It may be that genetic effects do not "cause" aging. It has been argued that the genetic material itself—the DNA, RNA, or chromosomal arrangements—somehow deteriorates with age, thereby causing faulty protein synthesis and cell functioning. This, in turn, results in aging (e.g., Kirkwood, 1985; McClearn & Foch, 1985; Tice & Setlow, 1985).

The most common of these explanations is that the repair ability of DNA breaks down with age. DNA breaks and errors are common at any age. The damage may be due to external factors, such as exposure to ultraviolet rays or to hydrocarbons. Or internal factors may cause the damage. For example, free radicals might damage the genetic apparatus (Rothstein, 1982). In any case, without repair, mutation and eventually death of the cell result. The errors are so common that, left unrepaired, DNA function would be impaired, and perhaps destroyed, within one year (Tice & Setlow, 1985).

Failure to repair the breaks would be associated with deterioration of the sort seen in aging (Tice & Setlow, 1985). It could be that there is a gradual accumulation of unrepaired breaks that are simply missed by the system. After enough time, the number of oversights would reach a critical level, and functional losses would occur. Or the repair mechanism itself might be lost, so that repairs would be less frequent and less adequate. In the former case, decline would be gradual; in the latter, it would be abrupt. This is similar to the argument of the error catastrophe hypothesis.

The evidence is that the rate of repair is fairly constant across the life span (Tice & Setlow, 1985)—but this is not the whole story. Some cells show less repair capability throughout the life span, and among these the neuronal and muscular cells seem to be most negatively affected by age. So, if DNA damage is a factor at all in aging, it is probably on the level of specific cells or tissue, rather than an overall or gross loss of DNA. Once again we see that physiological aging is not really an all-or-nothing phenomenon, even within a particular individual.

The results for RNA are similar (Reff, 1985). There is no good evidence for gross RNA deteriorations. On the other hand, chromosomal arrangements do appear to be affected (Martin & Turker, 1988; Schneider, 1985). For example, the normal human cell has 46 chromosomes (23 pairs). Among older adults, there is an increased number of cells with too many (hyperdiploid) or too few (hypodiploid) chromosomes. Hypodiploidy is more common; it increases from about 3 percent to about 9 percent of all cells when children are compared to those over age 65. But the effect of this and other problems in chromosomal arrangements is not clear (Schneider, 1985).

Genetic research is an exciting potential source of explanations for the aging process. But not everyone is ready to jump on the bandwagon. There are still those who believe that genetics play no role in normal aging. They view aging as an outcome of wear and tear, including exposure to ultraviolet rays, predators, disease, and toxins (McClearn & Foch, 1985). This argument would imply that aging would not occur in a perfect environment. Once again, then, we see the difficulty in separating normal aging from pathological processes. Clearly the biochemical and genetic models are interrelated. After all, genes control the biochemical processes. Part of the question is where in the biochemical process the "breakdowns" associated with aging occur. Is it right at the beginning, in the genetic code? Or is it further down the line—for example, in the by-products of biochemical processes? Another issue is whether the "damage" results primarily from internal or external factors.

HEALTH AND AGING

As we saw in Chapter 8, serious diseases begin to become noticeably more common during late middle age. Death rates also rise, only partly because of the higher rate of serious diseases such as cancer or heart disease. In addition, the immune system is less able to fight infections that may complicate a disease or make an infectious disease more serious than it would be in young adults. These immune system declines may also contribute to blood vessel injuries (Hausman & Weksler, 1985). Finally, life-style choices begin to have an impact. However, these choices, such as smoking or obesity, often take their greatest toll in middle age or very early old age. They may not always be the risk factors for the elderly that they are for younger adults (Busse & Maddox, 1985), perhaps because the people with such habits who have survived into old age are, for some reason, less susceptible to their effects than most people are.

Many statistics documenting the decline in health that accompanies aging were provided in Chapter 8. In those over 65, the rates rise steeply. The rate of people suffering from chronic heart problems rises from 137/100,000 people in the 45–64 age group to 257/100,000 in the over 65 group (*Statistical Abstract of the United States,* 1986). The death rate from heart disease among women aged 55–64 is 244/100,000 and 724/100,000 in the 65–74 category (*Statistical Abstract of the United States,* 1990). While the increase does not occur in every single category, it is an irrefutable trend.

These statistics are of concern for at least four reasons. One, of course, is that there is an interest in extending the life span as long as possible. People simply do not like to die or to lose their loved ones to death. Second are the economic concerns. There is considerable fear, both on the part of individuals and the government, that the elderly are not receiving sufficient health care and that there is no one to pay the cost. Research confirms that financial status can be a factor in elderly women's delaying seeking medical attention (Eve, 1988). This concern is intensifying as the population ages and is certainly one impetus for the catastrophic illness health insurance bill signed by the president in 1988. Third, the impact on the entire family can be great. As we will see in Chapter 15, most of the daily care for the ill elderly is provided by family members. This can cause stress, job interruption, and less than optimal care. The fourth issue is the effect of deteriorating health on the quality of life for the elderly.

Quality of Life

The elderly are, in general, as satisfied with their lives as young and middle-aged adults are. Health is the exception to this trend (Campbell et al., 1976). The elderly are less satisfied, more concerned about, and spend

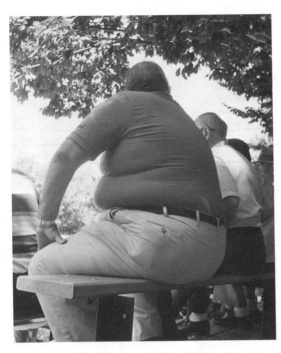

Obesity can negatively affect health, increasing the risk of hypertension, heart attacks, and other diseases.

more time discussing their health than other groups do. Complaints about sensory, cardiovascular, and genitourinary systems particularly seem to increase with age (Costa & McCrae, 1985).

The elderly often have more than one health problem. In many cases, at least one of these problems will be chronic and require both life-style changes and medication. A diabetic may have to monitor both diet and exercise and need insulin daily, either orally or by injection. Degree of debilitation will also vary. Someone with arthritis may have only occasional pain or may virtually lose the use of a hand. Furthermore, the elderly will often suffer multiple symptoms, both mental and physical, making disorders harder to diagnose and treat. Some of the diversity of symptoms is probably due to drugs or drug interaction effects, since most elderly, even those living in the community, take two or more different drugs daily (Vestal & Dawson, 1985). Women are more likely than men to be taking several drugs (Rodin & Ickovits, 1990).

People with chronic health problems might be expected to have particularly low quality of life. Many are disabled to some extent. Furthermore, many victims of chronic illness are in pain much of the time. Finally, there is considerable expense, for prescriptions and medical care, involved in many cases of chronic illness.

However, recent research suggests that many people with chronic illnesses do not view their health as particularly worse than that of other people their own age (Pearlman & Uhlmann, 1988). They actually report their health to be between "good" and "fair" and see themselves as only slightly disabled. This perception of disability may be the key. This particular study included only ambulatory patients.

The effects of chronic illness on quality of life may be mediated by a variety of factors (Pearlman & Uhlmann, 1988): financial status, interpersonal relationships, and levels of psychological distress (depression and anxiety). Indeed, these factors may be more important than physical health in determining quality of life for many elderly people.

Self-Ratings of Health

Quality of life is, of course, a subjective rating; people are asked whether they think their life is better or worse than most other people's. Therefore, it is not surprising to find that self-ratings of health are related to quality of life ratings (Kaplan, Barell, & Lusky, 1988; Pearlman & Uhlmann, 1988). Subjective self-ratings of health show moderate correlations with more objective ratings of health (based on physicians' reports and lists of symptoms or conditions). However, the two are not identical. It is difficult to know whether one is more "accurate" than the other.

Perhaps even more important, self-perceptions of health seem to be related to survival rates among the elderly (Kaplan et al., 1988; Mossey & Shapiro, 1982). For example, in a survey of elderly Israeli community dwellers, Kaplan and colleagues found that those who rated themselves as "very sick" were five times more likely to die during the five-year follow-up than those who considered themselves healthy. Again, it needs to be emphasized that those who rated themselves as "very sick" were more likely to have multiple illnesses, to take more drugs, and so on. In other words, they actually *were* sicker than other respondents. Nonetheless, even when objective health status and age were controlled, subjective self-ratings of health seemed to predict survival. When people of equal age and objective health are compared, we expect that those who rate themselves as healthier would have higher survival rates (Kaplan et al., 1988).

Personality dispositions appear to influence how people rate themselves. In a series of studies, Paul Costa and Robert McCrae have consistently found that neuroticism predicts self-reports of health (Costa, Fleg, McCrae, & Lakatta, 1982; Costa & McCrae, 1980; Costa & McCrae, 1985; Costa, McCrae, Andres, & Tobin, 1980). Notice that only self-reports of health are predicted. *Objective* measures, such as electrocardiogram readings (ECG) or blood pressure, are not predicted by neuroticism.

For example, in one of their studies (Costa et al. 1982), 123 men were classified into four groups. One group reported no angina pain and had negative ECG readings (no indication of heart dysfunction); the second had both angina pain and positive ECG readings; the third reported pain but had negative ECGs; and the fourth reported no pain but had positive ECGs (Costa et al., 1982). Groups 1 and 2 did not differ from each other in terms of neuroticism. In other words, people who are verifiably suffering from heart problems are not more neurotic than those who have healthy hearts. Group 3, however, did score higher on neurotic scales. Neuroticism and symptom reporting, then, seem to go together.

Several caveats are in order here. First, there are methodological problems. Costa and McCrae's data are analyzed from a variety of perspectives (longitudinal, cross-sectional, time-sequential, and cross-sequential). Their findings are quite consistent across analyses. However, all but one of their analyses were conducted on participants in the Baltimore Longitudinal Study of Aging (BLSA). This was a select, very healthy, very well-adjusted group of volunteers. In fact, in some studies, Costa and McCrae made the sample even "healthier." In their study of hypertension, for example, they omitted all men who were receiving hypertensive medication at any time during the study (Costa et al., 1980). This may have biased against finding the most dramatic associations between personality and health. Furthermore, it may be argued that their measures were not appropriate for testing the aspects of personality most likely to be associated with heart disease or hypertension. Using self-report, as they did, makes characteristics such as "repressed anger" difficult to assess.

Even if we accept their findings, caution in interpretation is needed. Pain, including angina, is often a major and crucial symptom of a problem. Sometimes it is the only indicator. Indeed, it is not clear that people high in neuroticism are not suffering from any illness. If this were true, various studies would not have reported high correlations between psychological functioning and hypertension (Costa et al., 1980). Instead, it seems that high neuroticism is more likely to lead to reporting and diagnosis of a disease (Costa et al., 1980; Costa & McCrae, 1985). Patient reports of pain should never be ignored.

Hypochondria

People sometimes think that the link between neuroticism and self-reports of poor health gets stronger as people age. They may be inclined to dismiss or downplay the older person's complaints about pain, discomfort, or dysfunction. They may even consider older people to be *hypochondriacs,* people for whom there is virtually no relationship between subjective and objective health (Costa & McCrae, 1985).

The issue of whether older people are more hypochondriacal than younger ones is important for several reasons. If we first assume that they are, then older people are using valuable medical time. The cost of unnecessary medical care is one concern; in addition, the hypochondriac may submit to (or even demand) unnecessary medical tests or procedures. There seems to be a link, for example, between neuroticism and undergoing arteriography (McCrae et al., 1982). These tests are expensive and may be dangerous. Some of the drugs that the elderly take willingly may be unnecessary and may actually undermine their health (Rodin & Ickovics, 1990). Finally, there is the loss of time to the elderly and to those who might be assisting them by taking them to doctors, hospitals, and so on.

Now let's assume that hypochondriasis is not more common in the elderly than in younger adults, but that people *think* it is. Under these circumstances, the elderly might not get the help they need, even if they do see a doctor. If the complaining is assumed to be indicative of anxiety or depression, psychoactive drugs might be prescribed, drugs that can have dramatic side effects. Finally, the person's self-esteem might be affected as others belittle the complaints. The high rate of prescription of psychoactive drugs to elderly women may indicate how much even physicians ascribe their reported symptoms to psychological problems (Rodin & Ickovics, 1990).

Some researchers have argued that hypochondriasis is indeed common among the elderly (Busse & Blazer, 1980). It may be particularly pronounced in depressed oldsters. The combination of hypochondriasis and depression may increase the risk of suicide (LaRue et al., 1985). Those who believe that hypochondriasis increases with age view it as a response to increased stress (Busse & Blazer, 1980). It may be a reaction to a situation involving prolonged criticism or to a decline in marital satisfaction due to a spouse's illness. The latter circumstance may explain why hypochondriasis appears to be more common among elderly women than men. Other researchers, however, argue that hypochondriasis does not increase as people age (Costa & McCrae, 1980; Costa & McCrae, 1985). Instead, they suggest, hypochondriasis seems to be a fairly consistent aspect of personality across adulthood. In other words, the older person who is a hypochondriac or even a neurotic complainer probably was one as a young adult. The documented age-related increases in physical symptoms probably primarily reflect real health problems (Costa & McCrae, 1980).

The Influence of Drugs

In the United States, the elderly buy a disproportionate number of both prescription and nonprescription drugs. About 11 percent of the American population is over 65; yet they buy 20 to 25 percent of the drugs sold in this country. By the year 2030, they are expected to be buying 40 percent (Vestal & Dawson, 1985). The most common nonprescription purchases are for analgesics. The most common prescription drugs used by the elderly are cardiovascular agents and psychoactive drugs. Most take two or more drugs on a daily basis—which is not surprising, since many diseases are treated with multidrug therapies. Hypertension, for example, is often treated using a combination of a diuretic, a sympatholytic drug, and a vasodilator (Rudd & Blaschke, 1985). Women are more likely than men to be taking a variety of drugs related to anxiety reduction (tranquilizers and sedatives). They are also more likely to become addicted to such drugs. This is particularly disconcerting, since over 80 percent of acute drug reactions among the elderly are a result of tranquilizer and sedative misuse (Rodin & Ickovics, 1990).

Nursing home clients are especially likely to take multiple drugs. In fact, it is not unusual for them to be taking multiple psychoactive drugs, such as an antipsychotic (thioridazine) and a hypnotic (fluorazepam) (see Table 12–5). Charges have been made that such prescriptions are designed more to control behavior than to alleviate patient suffering. In fact, it has been argued that these multiple psychoactive prescriptions are more likely to be given to clients with high intelligence and low physical disability (Vestal & Dawson, 1985).

Gray - Beta-blockers can cause Insomnia!

TABLE 12-5: Some Side Effects of Commonly Used Drugs*

Drug (Brand Name)	Therapeutic Use	Physical Side Effects	Behavioral Side Effects	Drug Interaction Effects
Diazepam (Valium) Chlordiazepoxide (Librium)	Tranquilizer; sedation	Drowsiness, weight gain	Confusion, hostility, irritability, increased anxiety (esp. in patients concerned about sedative effects)	Additive effects with other CNS depressants
Tricyclics (Amitril, Elavil, Janimine, Totranil)	Antidepressant	Dry mouth, sour or metallic taste, blurred vision, tachycardia, palpitations, dizziness, constipation, excessive sweating, weakness, fatigue, postural hypotension	Manic excitement, confusion (in over 30% of patients 50+ yrs) tremor	Potentiates the effects of alcohol and other sedatives; blocks the effect of clonidine (used to treat hypertension)
Digitalis (Digoxin, Digitoxin)	Cardiac (treatment of congestive heart failure)	Nausea, vomiting, diarrhea, abdominal pain, pain in lower face, headache, fatigue	Loss of appetite, disorientation, confusion, aphasia, hallucinations, (esp. in patients with atherosclerotic disease)	Increased risk of toxic reaction when prescribed with quinidine, verapamil
B-blockers (Propanolol, Nadolol, Timolol)	Antihypertensive	Cardiac depression, dizziness, headache	Insomnia, confusion, disorientation	

Aspirin Acetaminophen (Tylenol) Ibuprofen (Medipren)	Analgesic, anti-inflammatory, fever reduction	*Toxic reaction:* Dizziness, ringing in ears, high tone deafness, nausea, vomiting *Chronic use:* Gastric ulceration, potassium depletion, increased blood clotting time	*Toxic reaction:* confusion, stupor, psychosis
Antacids (a) Aluminum-based Magnesium-based (Milk of Magnesia) (Most common antacids combine aluminum and magnesium (Mylanta, Maalox, Gelusil, Di-Gel)	Digestive problems	Constipation, bowel perforation, bowel obstruction	Generally affects availability of other drugs, esp. iron, tetracycline, digoxin, fat-soluble vitamins, phenothiazines, prednisone
Antacids (b) Calcium-based (Tums)		Constipation, belching, flatulence, nausea	Decreases availability of fluoride, iron, phosphate, tetracycline, phenothiazine

*This table is not exhaustive either in the drugs chosen or the side effects listed. The frequency of side effects varies from drug to drug.
Source: Based on data from Gilman, A., Goodman, L., Rau, T., & Murad, F. (eds.), (1985). *The pharmacological basis of therapeutics,* 7th ed. New York: Macmillan.

The statistics and allegations are worrisome for several reasons. First, adverse drug reactions are two to three times more common among people over 60 than among those under 30 (Vestal & Dawson, 1985). Sometimes they are severe enough to warrant hospitalization (including psychiatric admission). Some of these reactions may actually be attributable to errors in following a doctor's orders. People taking multiple medications may generally be more susceptible to making such mistakes. The very elderly (over 75) who suffer some memory impairment may also be likely candidates for making errors. Furthermore, the actual physical reactions to at least some drugs appear to change with age (Rowe, Andres, Tobin, Norris, & Shock, 1976; Salzman, 1982; Vestal & Dawson, 1985) (see Table 12–6). The changes include decreases in drug absorption, slower and less complete drug distribution, and slower clearance of the drugs from the system. There may also be increases in receptor site sensitivity. These changes may render the elderly more susceptible to both the therapeutic and the toxic effects of some drugs. Therefore, it is often advisable to start elderly patients with lower dosages than would typically be prescribed for a younger adult. Furthermore, the changes in rate of absorption and clearance may influence the timing and likelihood of drug interaction effects. Age does not affect the metabolism of all drugs. In other words, we cannot simply say that all older people will always absorb less of every drug. This is why research using elderly populations is crucial in understanding pharmacological effects. It is also why all drug use in the elderly ought to be supervised, or at least checked, by a professional.

Reactions to drugs or their interactions can be very dramatic (see Table 12–5). They may cause dementia-like symptoms of memory loss, confusion, and disorientation. Some of the anticholinergics used to treat ulcers and glaucoma and the antiadrenergic drugs used in treating hypertension have been associated with erectile dysfunction (Hyde, 1986). Tricyclic antidepressants may produce dry mouth problems in the elderly. This discomfort may decrease the likelihood that they will continue the drug. Dry mouth may also contribute to poor-fitting dentures or the loss of porcelain fillings (Salzman, 1982). Tricyclics are associated with cardiac impairment, which may have more severe results among the elderly. MAO inhibitors, also used to treat depression, may interact with other drugs to produce severe hypertension. Anti-anxiety agents have been associated with drowsi-

TABLE 12–6:   Drugs Whose Dosage Requirements or Side Effects Vary with Patient Age

Psychoactive Drugs	Cardiovascular Drugs	Analgesics	Others
Tricyclics (esp. imipramine)	Digitalis	Morphine	L-Dopa
Fluorazepam	Diuretics	Pentazocine	Antihistamines
Diazepam	Methyldopa		Antibiotics
Alcohol	Propanol		
Nitrazepam	Hydralazine		
Lithium			

ness and loss of motor coordination (Salzman, 1982). These examples underscore the variety of possible reactions.

Not all drug reactions (or interactions) are immediately apparent. In some cases, drugs need to build up to a toxic level before any side effects are evident. This may take days, weeks, or in rarer cases, months or years (see Gilman, Goodman, Rall, & Murad, 1985, for examples). This is why any psychological disturbance evidenced by a person using any drug, prescription or nonprescription, on a frequent basis ought to be investigated as a drug reaction by a physician.

ORGANIC BRAIN SYNDROMES

Senility is an integral part of the image of the elderly. Many people believe that memory loss is a normal part of aging. They will talk in a surprised tone about their 80-year-old grandmother who is "still sharp as a tack, though." It is often surprising to learn that only about 5 percent of the elderly population suffers from moderate to severe "senility." Even if we include mild cases, the percentage rises to only 15 percent.

Of course, senility is not the technical name for the severe memory loss, confusion, and so on that laypeople use the word to mean. Indeed, even the more technical sounding "senile dementia" is not as broadly used as it used to be. Increasingly, professionals and the general public recognize that these elderly are suffering from one of several types of organic brain syndromes (OBS). OBS does *not* constitute normal aging; it is a pathological state.

Deliriums

There are two general categories of OBS. *Reversible OBS,* also known as *delirium,* is caused by a temporary malfunctioning of some significant portion of the cortex. Probably about 10 to 20 percent of all OBS cases fall into this category (LaRue et al., 1985). Table 12–7 lists some of the common causes of delirium. One is metabolic dysfunction. For example, the kidneys or liver may be failing, and either case will lead to a buildup of toxins in the system. Behavior will be affected. Other frequently implicated metabolic problems include diabetes, hypoglycemia, hypothyroidism, and vitamin deficiencies (especially B12 and folic acid). The effects can be very dramatic. The severe memory losses and confusion associated with chronic alcoholism (Korsakoff's syndrome) appear to be the result of vitamin deficiencies.

Reversible OBS is also frequently induced by drugs. The problem may be drug intoxication or a drug interaction effect, because problems in drug absorption, breakdown, and excretion can make the elderly particularly susceptible to drug effects. Some of the drugs associated with delirium are diuretics, cardiac drugs, steroids, hypertensive medication, and psychotropic drugs (such as tranquilizers or antidepressants).

The important point about delirium is that it is reversible. The victim may show the same behaviors that we associate with the irreversible brain

TABLE 12-7: **Some Common Causes of Reversible Delirium**

Cause	Type
Drugs	Diuretics, sedative-hypnotics, analgesics, antihistaminics, antiparkinsonian agents, antidepressants, neuroleptics, cimetidine, digitalis glycosides
Alcohol intoxication or withdrawal	
Cardiovascular disorders	Congestive heart failure, myocardial infarction, cardiac arrhythmias, aortic stenosis, hypertensive encephalopathy, orthostatic hypotension, subacute bacterial endocarditis
Infections	Pneumonia, urinary tract infection, bacteremia, septicemia, cholecystitis, meningitis
Metabolic encephalopathies	Electrolyte and fluid imbalance; hepatic, renal, and pulmonary failure; diabetes and other endocrine diseases; nutritional deficiency (especially of vitamin B complex); hypothermia and heat stroke
Cerebrovascular disorders	Transient ischemic attacks, stroke, chronic subdural hematoma, vasculitis
Cerebral or extracranial neoplasm	
Trauma	Head injury, surgery, burns, hip fracture

Source: Lipkowski, Z. (1983). Transient cognitive disorders (delirium, acute delusional states) in the elderly. *American Journal of Psychiatry, 140,* 1426–1436. Copyright 1983 The American Psychiatric Association. Reprinted by permission.

syndromes—disorientation, memory loss, denial, depression, and habit disturbance. Behavior alone is *not* a reliable indicator of whether or not a brain dysfunction is reversible; medical tests of metabolic functioning and drug levels are necessary.

Dementias

The types of brain dysfunction that are irreversible are rooted in cell loss, blood vessel damage, or injury to the brain structures. What causes such loss is not always clear. The course of an irreversible OBS may be mediated by environmental response, but deterioration will continue, at least given our current medical knowledge.

There are several types of irreversible OBS. *Multi-infarct dementia* is the result of a series of small strokes. The blood vessels in the brain are breaking and causing injury to the surrounding tissue. This probably accounts for about 15 to 25 percent of all irreversible OBS cases. It can often be definitively diagnosed through CAT scans and EEG readings (LaRue et al., 1985). Creutzfeldt-Jakob disease, which afflicts mainly people in their sixties and seventies, is a rare disorder occurring at a rate of about 1 new case per 1 million people (making it 5000 times less common than Alzheimer's).

Creutzfeldt-Jakob appears to be caused by a slow-moving viruslike infectious agent known as a *prion* (Prusiner & Benheim, 1984). Pick's disease is another rare neurological disorder that shows similar behavioral symptoms but somewhat different brain pathology than Alzheimer's disease. Finally, although much of the dysfunction associated with Korsakoff's syndrome can be alleviated by proper diet, there is some permanent damage.

Table 12–8 lists various medical tests that can be used to identify which type of dementia is present and to differentiate reversible from irreversible cases. Note that many of these tests evaluate metabolic functioning. There are also some behavioral differences between delirious and demented clients (see Table 12–9). For example, a delirious patient will be unable to focus attention (Seltzer, 1988) and will probably be virtually untestable. The demented client, particularly one in the early stages of disease, may be cognitively impaired but will be able to attend to questions. It is crucial that cases of delirium be appropriately diagnosed; failure to do so may result in permanent brain damage (Seltzer, 1988).

These tests and behavioral symptoms are not infallible, however. Indeed, Alzheimer's disease is typically the diagnosis when the tests fail to support anything else conclusively. In other words, Alzheimer's is a "default" diagnosis. Performance on various mental status questionnaires and screening instruments that evaluate memory, attention, and reality orientation is also considered in making a diagnosis (LaRue et al., 1985).

Alzheimer's Disease: Alzheimer's is by far the best known and most widely publicized of the irreversible OBS. It accounts for at least 60 percent of irreversible OBS cases and afflicts over 3.5 million Americans. The number affected will rise as the elderly population increases, since it is primarily, though not exclusively, a disorder associated with old age. About 4 to 8 percent of all Americans over 50 suffer from Alzheimer's, with the percentage increasing to 25 percent or more in those over 80.

Many people do not realize that Alzheimer's is a fatal disease. It is the fourth leading cause of death in the United States and claims over 100,000

TABLE 12–8:   Screening Tests for Evaluating Dementia

1. Complete blood count with sedimentation rate
2. Analysis of urine
3. Stool examination for occult blood
4. Serum urea, nitrogen, and glucose; serum electrolytes, (sodium, potassium, carbon dioxide content, chloride, calcium, phosphorus); bilirubin; serum vitamin B12, folic acid.
5. Tests for thyroid function
6. Serological test for syphilis
7. Roentgenogram of the chest
8. Electrocardiogram
9. Computerized tomography (CT scan) of the brain

Source: Small, G., Liston, E., & Jarvik, L. (1981). Diagnosis and treatment of dementia in the aged. *The Western Journal of Medicine, 135,* 477.

TABLE 12-9: Differences between Symptoms of Delirium and Dementia

Feature	Delirium	Dementia
Onset	Rapid, often at night	Usually insidious
Duration	Hours to weeks	Months to years
Course	Fluctuates over 24 hours; worse at night; lucid intervals	Relatively stable
Awareness	Always impaired	Usually normal
Alertness	Reduced or increased; tends to fluctuate	Usually normal
Orientation	Always impaired, at least for time; tendency to mistake unfamiliar for familiar place or person	May be intact; little tendency to confabulate
Memory	Recent and immediate impaired; fund of knowledge intact if dementia is absent	Recent and remote impaired; some loss of common knowledge
Thinking	Slow or accelerated; may be dream-like	Poor in abstraction, impoverished
Perception	Often misperceptions, especially visual	Misperceptions often absent
Sleep-wake cycle	Always disrupted; often drowsiness during the day, insomnia at night	Fragmented sleep
Physical illness or drug toxicity	Usually present	Often absent, especially in primary degenerative dementia

Source: Lipkowski, Z. (1983). Transient cognitive disorders (delirium, acute delusional states) in the elderly. *American Journal of Psychiatry, 140,* 1426–1436. Copyright 1983 The American Psychiatric Association. Reprinted by permission.

lives every year. It has been estimated that by the year 2000, Alzheimer's will cost the United States $50–75 million annually.

Alzheimer's disease progresses through three stages (Reisberg, 1983; Schneck, Reisberg, & Ferris, 1982). The first is forgetfulness. Memory is affected in ways that may be irritating and worrisome, but the losses may not be sufficiently severe to signal the seriousness of the problem. People may forget to turn off the stove. They may forget where they put their keys or an appointment book. Of course, everyone does this sometimes. But Alzheimer's victims will often forget in more unusual ways. One man, for example, could not remember how to turn the windshield wipers on in his car. A woman forgot how to turn on the stove at her own home. These people just don't seem alert. They often become nervous and defensive about their problems and so may seem combative or depressed. Denial, by both the victims and their families, is still possible at this stage.

In the second phase, confusion, the denial starts to break down (Reisberg, 1983; Schneck et al., 1982). Memory, especially short-term memory, becomes markedly impaired. The person tends to "lose his train of thought" in conversation and repeats things. Communication becomes disturbed. The victim is aware that something is wrong. This awareness, probably in conjunction with the brain damage, results in personality disturbances. The person may become paranoid or depressed, irritable and restless, and yet will still try to deny the problem and blame others. This can also interfere with getting whatever help is available. The victim may view such evaluation and assistance as a threat. The family is faced with difficult and frightening situations and decisions.

It takes anywhere from about three to ten years to reach the third stage, which is marked by full-blown dementia (Reisberg, 1983; Schneck et al., 1982). Convulsions may occur; so might incontinence, an effect that can be particularly difficult to deal with. Long-term memory loss is evident. Eventually, even the names of family members will escape the victim, as may his or her own name. Language will grow increasingly impaired and may ultimately be lost. Confusion becomes so complete that sufferers can no longer be trusted to perform basic tasks or routines. Eventually they cannot brush their teeth, bathe themselves, or be left alone. Finally, there is death, typically five to fifteen years after the onset of the disease.

People sometimes think that Alzheimer's might not be such a difficult disease for the sufferer. They believe the person does not know or recognize what is going on and so feels no sense of loss. This is clearly not true during the first two stages. The sufferer is anxious, distressed, embarrassed, and depressed. One described it as looking into your mind and finding a black hole. They are suffering. The woman who made the following statement has a father who suffers from Alzheimer's. It is clear that "suffers" really is an appropriate term:

> Last August ... my father didn't know where he was.... He'd sleep for an hour ... and then be up for 12. He'd tear the sheets off his bed.... He used to cry a lot and say I want to go.... (*Wall Street Journal*, February 14, 1989, p. A16)

Although it is more difficult to document the pain during the third stage, the patients appear to be lonely, and frequently weep, moan, or cry out. As difficult as it is for the victims, however, it is probably even worse for the families (see Chapter 15).

What causes Alzheimer's disease? The immediate cause is brain pathology. The damage is concentrated in the cerebral cortex and in the limbic system (especially the hippocampus). The three most common forms of damage are neurofibrillary tangles, senile plaques, and amyloid bodies. These are also all found in normal aged brains; it is the sheer number of tangles, plaques, and amyloid bodies, as well as their co-occurrence, that distinguishes an Alzheimer's brain from the normal one. In addition, blood flow through the brain is about 30 percent less in an Alzheimer's patient than in a normal person. Unlike the normal elderly brain, the Alzheimer's victim does not show increased efficiency in oxygen consumption to compensate for the decreased blood flow. There is a significant loss of neurons in the more primitive areas at the base of the brain. There seems to be a shortage of the neurotransmitter acetylcholine. However, other neurotransmitters may also be at low levels, particularly in some of the subcortical areas. Finally, there is some evidence of increased levels of aluminum. However, the aluminum is concentrated around the neurofibrillary tangles and may indicate little more than an affinity between the two (LaRue et al., 1985; Wurtman, 1985).

The problem is that no one knows what causes these neurological symptoms. There are several hypotheses (Wurtman, 1985). Genetics seems to play a role, at least in some cases. The risk of developing Alzheimer's if a family member (older than 50 years) developed it is about three times greater than if there is no family history of the disease. Furthermore, victims of Down's syndrome, which is caused by a chromosomal aberration, virtually always develop Alzheimer's disease if they live past about age 40. Nonetheless, people with no family history of Alzheimer's do develop the disorder. This has led some researchers to postulate that there are actually two forms of the disease: one that is genetically mediated and a milder form that occurs primarily in very old people (over about 80).

Other explanatory models have focused on levels of the neurotransmitter acetylcholine, blood flow, and abnormal brain proteins. All of these models have received some empirical support. Two other proposed models, those emphasizing an infectious agent and toxins, seem particularly shaky. The commonalities between Creutzfeldt-Jakob disease and Alzheimer's led to the suggestion that the latter might also be caused by prions. However, attempts to "infect" laboratory animals with Alzheimer's have been unsuccessful. Of course, it is possible that the disorder is transmissible under certain as-yet-unknown circumstances. The toxin that received some attention was aluminum. Could Alzheimer's be caused by the ingestion of high levels of aluminum? The research indicates it is not; media scares about using aluminum products are unwarranted.

The causes of Alzheimer's disease remain unknown, and it may be some time before an answer is found. The disease is often diagnosed only after it has progressed to at least the second stage, and by then it is difficult to separate out which physiological changes are causes and which are effects or even concomitants of the disease. Noninvasive techniques for exploring the brain and its functioning, such as the PET scan, are becoming more widely available. And unfortunately, the disease is becoming more common as more people live to be old. These two factors should improve the likelihood that an explanation will be uncovered.

CREATING A LIVING ENVIRONMENT

The evidence clearly indicates that many people experience losses in physical functioning as they age. It is not clear, of course, whether such losses are inevitable. There are ways for people to maintain and improve their health even in old age. However, whatever their cause, declines are common and often necessitate alterations in the living environment. After all, life satisfaction is affected by the "fit" between a person's capabilities (real and perceived) and the environment (Lawton, 1987; Parr, 1980; Windley & Scheidt, 1980).

Elderly people suffering from severe disabilities, such as those associated with strokes or Alzheimer's disease, may need constant supervision or attention. They may need assistance with even the most basic tasks of daily living. Those who are still able to live on their own in their own homes may also benefit from environmental modifications. Since there are wide individual differences in both type and degree of decline, it is impossible to offer a single prescription as to the optimum environment for an older person; individual needs must be considered. What follows are a few suggestions for modifications that might compensate for some common physical declines.

Social Contacts

As will become clear in Chapters 14 and 15, most of the elderly want to maintain social contacts with friends and family. Such contact may become a necessity if illness develops. Telephones should be within easy reach. If the house is large, there should be several phones. After all, falls that might break a bone are most likely to occur in the home, and the injured person will not be able to climb or descend a flight of stairs to get to a phone. A phone with computerized calling to emergency numbers might be helpful. The sound of the bell, visibility of the numbers, and ease of dialing should also be considered in making a purchase.

Driving a car is another way of making or maintaining social contacts. Surveys indicate that the majority of elderly people do maintain valid drivers' licenses (Sterns, Barrett, & Alexander, 1985). While overall auto accident rates for the elderly are low, accidents per mile driven are relatively high. This suggests that some elderly have difficulty driving. As the earlier discussion of vision indicated, night driving may be particularly difficult. Access to safe public transportation (including taxis) or private assistance from families and friends is important. In some cases, the person may be a capable driver, but be so concerned about driving skills (especially vision) that he or she stops driving (Sterns et al., 1985). Regular eye exams may help to alleviate such concern and return a certain level of independence (and perhaps self-esteem) to the individual.

Accidents

Falls and burns are among the most common injuries in the home (Sterns et al., 1985). Some accidents may be unavoidable, as when an illness causes an older person to faint. However, many are preventable.

Stairs are especially likely culprits in falls. Older people typically need higher levels of illumination in order to see well. Therefore, stairways should be well lit. Handrails can provide support. Risers should not be too high, treads should not be too narrow, and the angle of the staircase should not be too steep (Parr, 1980; Sterns et al., 1985). Falls may also occur in the bathroom. Tub devices, including rails and seats, are available to make getting in and out easier. There are also "extenders" for toilet seats that re-quire less bending of the knees (Windley & Scheidt, 1980).

Burns typically occur in the kitchen (Sterns et al., 1985). The older person may accidentally turn on a burner or fail to turn one off. Easily visible, well-marked controls can diminish the likelihood of such accidents. Manipulability of the controls may also be a consideration if the person has arthritis. Scalds from hot tap water can be prevented by simply turning down the thermostat on the water heater.

Drugs are implicated in many of these accidents. We have already seen that accidental overdose is more likely when people are taking multiple medications, as is often the case with the elderly (Sterns et al., 1985; Vestal & Dawson, 1985). Furthermore, many frequently prescribed drugs have side effects such as postural hypotension (a drop in blood pressure when the person stands after sitting or lying down), dizziness, or fainting that could cause falls (see Table 12–5). The confusion that results from some drugs may contribute to virtually any type of accident. Therefore, people taking multiple drugs should be assisted or monitored. A chart of which drugs are taken when might be helpful. Any evidence of side effects should be checked with a physician. And if a person is taking a drug known to pro-duce dangerous side effects, family members or friends should check in regularly in an unobtrusive way (Paar, 1980).

SUMMARY

There is little doubt that most major physiological systems show some age-related decline. However, in many cases the declines are minor in terms of their impact on daily living or can be ameliorated. Glasses, hearing aids, medications, and so on can all facilitate the continuation of an active life style well into old age.

It is not clear, however, what components of these declines are actually due to aging alone. Both habits and disease take their toll on our bodies over time. For example, many middle-aged and elderly Americans have heart problems. Most of these seem to be due to diet, smoking, and exercise patterns or genetic predispositions rather than to any built-in aging blue-print. The same can be said of many sensory losses; sunlight can damage the eyes and loud noises can contribute to hearing losses.

Given that damage and disease cause a substantial proportion of the decline, it is not surprising that there are large individual differences in the timing, type, and degree of loss. After all, different people have different habits, disease exposures, and genetic predispositions. The importance of recognizing these individual differences cannot be overestimated. Some el-derly will be able to drive, work, care for themselves and others, and gener-ally participate in various activities at a level very comparable to that of younger adults. Old age does not automatically mean physical or mental debility.

On the other hand, serious problems do become more common with age. The rate of organic brain syndromes rises. Of these, the irreversible

Alzheimer's disease is perhaps the most common and therefore the most frightening. The presence of such diseases reminds us once again that severe memory loss, confusion, and other signs of mental deterioration are not part of "normal" aging. We should also be reminded that sometimes such syndromes are reversible. They may be secondary to other diseases or be caused by drugs. Other physical problems also become more common. In general, level of health and functioning is related to life satisfaction, and self-perceptions of health seem especially important.

Findings about biological changes in old age have practical implications. They indicate, for example, how people might alter their life styles early to prevent some of the damage. Of course, such changes will not prevent aging or death, but they may help us to maintain productive happy lives well into old age. These findings also suggest ways that we might alter homes, workplaces, and public facilities to make them more accessible and safe for the elderly.

13 Cognitive Development

Imagine you are participating in an experiment on problem solving. You are given the following problem:

> Downstairs, there are three rooms: the kitchen, the dining room, and the sitting room. The sitting room is in the front of the house, and the kitchen and dining room face the vegetable garden at the back of the house. The noise of the traffic is very disturbing in the front rooms. Mother is in the kitchen cooking and Grandfather is reading the paper in the sitting room. The children are at school and won't be home til teatime. Who is being disturbed by the traffic noise? (Cohen, 1979)

How would you answer? One possible answer is "the grandfather." Supposedly, this answer reflects an analysis of the logical relations of the problem: it is the middle of the day so traffic noise is likely to be high, the noise is greatest at the front of the house, so that people in the front of the house are most likely to be disturbed by the noise. In this case, that person is the grandfather. This is precisely how most young adults solve the problem.

Another possibility is to answer that no one is being disturbed. The grandfather may be at greatest *risk* for being disturbed, but apparently is not. After all, why would he continue to sit there and try to read? Why not just move to another room? Perhaps he is deaf, or maybe the traffic noise isn't particularly bad right now. Or he could be the kind of person who is not easily distracted, who can "tune out" extraneous noise. This is the type of response older people tend to give.

Which answer is right—or better? Traditionally, researchers and theorists argued that the older people's responses were indicative of a loss of ability to reason logically (Cohen, 1979). The view that old age is marked by meaningful decline in intellectual abilities is still widely held. It is embodied in Horn's (1982) model of the aging of intellectual abilities. Since the mid-1970s, however, another interpretation has gained a foothold. These gerontologists argue that the differences in answers are indicative of cognitive restructuring, similar to that described for childhood by Piaget's stages. For example, the older people's responses can be viewed as more realistic and therefore more adaptive to real situations (Labouvie-Vief, 1985). Such arguments are consistent with Schaie's (1977/1978) model of intellectual development during adulthood.

This example captures one of the major issues in the area of cognitive functioning during adulthood. Should adulthood be conceptualized as primarily a period of intellectual decline, or as sequential restructurings that result in both gains and losses (Baltes, 1987)? Answering this question involves making several other decisions. Are laboratory findings, using nonsense syllables or word lists, as important as those of studies using "real-life" stimuli? Are longitudinal studies more valid than cross-sectional studies? How much should individual differences be considered? Which individual differences are relevant? Should we, for example, be particularly swayed by findings which suggest that declines are much later or less severe for some groups than for others? What about research which demonstrates that some "declines" can be reversed with training? What does this tell us about intellectual development and functioning in old age (Lerner, 1990; Willis, 1990)?

These questions are of great importance to society and to individual people. They affect work-related policies, including retirement and eligibility for training programs. They might affect how educational policies for the elderly are designed. The more optimistic view, if supported by research, could play a major role in combatting prejudice. It could also affect the self-esteem of individuals since it is clear that right now the elderly are harsh in their own judgment of their cognitive functioning (Zarit, Cole, & Guider, 1981).

Methodological Caveats: The debate between the "decline" and "restructuring" positions is neither small nor particularly friendly. Consider, for example, some of the articles that have defined the parameters:

> The myth of the twilight years. (Baltes & Schaie, 1974)
> On the myth of intellectual decline in adulthood. (Horn & Donaldson, 1976).
> On the plasticity of intelligence in adulthood and old age: Where Horn & Donaldson fail. (Baltes & Schaie, 1976)
> Faith is not enough: A response to the Baltes-Schaie claim that intelligence will not wane. (Horn & Donaldson, 1977)

While the reasons for the differences are complex, much can be explained by understanding methodological emphasis.

You may recall that Schaie is one of the major proponents of sequential designs (see Chapter 2). He has argued that cross-sectional data can only demonstrate group differences; they cannot provide information about developmental change. Longitudinal studies, on the other hand, do trace individual development. Therefore, longitudinal data can provide developmental information. Schaie recognizes, of course, that the longitudinal sample is biased in favor of healthy, well-motivated, better-functioning participants. Sequential designs are better, but impractical.

Longitudinal data are likely to show smaller, later declines than cross-sectional results. But if you are truly interested in general or common patterns of aging, mightn't the cross-sectional results be more accurate? After all, the samples are more representative. This is what Horn (1982) argues. In his opinion, the exclusivity of the longitudinal sample misleads us about what aging usually looks like. Furthermore, he argues, the decline is evident in longitudinal data, albeit less dramatically. In Horn's opinion, cross-sectional and longitudinal data show the same general trends. Thus, the two camps also differ in how much weight they place on the timing and degree of the declines that do occur.

Timing and degree of decline are important, inasmuch as they provide clues about the mediators of the changes in intellectual functions. If the declines are mediated by external factors (including task demands), then they are not really declines, are they? Indeed, many researchers have proposed that factors such as motivation, familiarity with task materials, relevance of task materials and incentives, time allotted to perform the task, and other task characteristics are major determinants of the differences between younger and older subjects (Denney, 1982; Horn, 1982; Labouvie-Vief, 1985; Poon, 1985). In fact, as will become evident shortly, many of these variables do affect the size of the "decline." Those who argue against the notion of decline tend to interpret such evidence as indicative of the flexibility of adult intellectual functioning. Those who see decline suggest that the losses are specific to certain skills.

This raises the issue of *ecological validity*. The question here is how the documented declines affect daily living. Much of our information is based on laboratory studies. Participants in this research might be asked to recite a span of numbers backwards (a memory task) or to determine what letter comes next in a sequence like SUXBGM (a test of fluid intelligence). The elderly perform more poorly on such tasks than younger adults do (Horn, 1982). It can be argued that this indicates a decline in intellectual functioning. Proponents of restructuring, however, are quick to point out that such differences disappear when the elderly are asked to remember the gist of a meaningful passage. This, they argue, demonstrates that the elderly are simply more oriented to the realistic and the practical (Labouvie-Vief & Schell, 1982). The question is, does that mean the laboratory findings are meaningless or unimportant? In the same vein, how much of a loss is necessary before it begins to affect daily living or cannot easily be compensated for (as in making lists to help memory)?

Finally, the discussion thus far has lumped together all cognitive abilities. This is appropriate, because the issues under consideration are important in research and theorizing about all types of cognition. It is misleading inasmuch as there is no universal aging pattern that applies to all forms of cognition. Paul Baltes (1987) has warned that development is a multidimensional and multidirectional process, and has used cognitive functioning to exemplify this. Indeed, even within cognitive realms such as memory, different aspects do not show a common pattern. This is reminiscent, and perhaps reflective, of the patterns seen in biological aging. Given these differences, in the remainder of this chapter we will treat memory, problem solving, psychometric intelligence (IQ), concept formation, language, and learning separately. Note, however, that this division is artificial; the various cognitive skills are interrelated. For example, certain memory declines seem to be important in explaining losses in fluid intelligence (Horn, 1982). Furthermore, some theorists have argued that many of the losses reflect deterioration of a more general skill, such as slower speed of processing (Salthouse, 1985) or reductions in developmental reserve capacity.

MEMORY

No skill has generated more interest among researchers than memory (Poon, 1985). This is hardly surprising. After all, the belief that memory abilities decline significantly with age is widely held, even among the elderly. Compared to young adults, older people report more memory failures and are more distressed by them (Cavanaugh, Grady, & Perlmutter, 1983; Zarit et al., 1981). And these failures are not trivial: They include forgetting names, locations, appointments, addresses, and other components of daily life. Such failures may have negative results, such as medication overdoses. On the other hand, many of the failures can be remediated by the use of memory aids (such as lists), which the elderly do report using more frequently than young adults do (Poon, 1985).

It has been assumed, then, that memory losses are widespread and can affect daily living. This alone would be reason for pinpointing the nature and causes of the losses. However, memory is also viewed as essential for other cognitive functions such as problem solving and language. Indeed, Horn (1982) classifies both short- and long-term memory among the second-order intellectual skills (along with fluid and crystallized intelligence). The role of memory in such skills is brutally apparent in the Alzheimer's victim.

The Information-Processing Model

Research in aging and memory has been facilitated by the presence of a strong, dominant model: information processing. This model has been heavily used by those seeking to define the precise location of age-related declines in memory.

The information-processing model makes three assumptions (Poon, 1985). The first is that the individual is an active processor who can influence both learning (encoding) and retrieval processes. This underscores the belief that there are indeed different strategies (procedures) for organizing information to get it in and out of memory. Some strategies may be more efficient than others. It becomes possible, then, that a memory deficit could be due to encoding or retrieval problems, rather than to deficiencies in storage capacity. This further implies that not everything gets into memory.

In other words, some things may never be encoded. It is possible that young adults encode different aspects of a situation than older adults do, and this could result in differential performance on memory tasks.

These implications are also relevant to the second assumption: that memory functioning can be analyzed both quantitatively and qualitatively. The efficiency of qualitatively different strategies can be compared. Comparison will often be done through quantitative measures, such as how many pieces of information are recalled. Types of information recalled can also be analyzed, again exemplifying a more qualitative approach. So, for example, some researchers have argued that younger adults may be more attentive to specific contextual cues than older people are (Craik & Simon, 1980; Puglisi, Park, Smith, & Dudley, 1988).

The final assumption is that there are different stages of information processing, often referred to as memory stores. Four are commonly differentiated: sensory memory, primary memory, secondary memory (sometimes subdivided into secondary and working memory), and tertiary or remote memory. Table 13–1 provides a brief description of the function, capacity, and duration of three of the stores. Note that the flow of information is usually conceptualized as unidirectional, moving from sensory through primary, then secondary, and finally into tertiary. Proponents of the restructuring perspective view this emphasis as inappropriate, as we shall see.

TABLE 13-1: Differences among Three Stages of Memory in an Information Processing Model

Feature	Sensory Register	Short-Term Storage (Primary Memory)	Long-Term Storage (Tertiary Memory)
Entry of information	Pre-attentive	Attention required	Rehearsal
Maintenance of information	Impossible	Attention Rehearsal	Repetition Organization
Format of information	Literal copy of input	Phonemic Probably visual Possibly semantic	Largely semantic Some auditory and visual
Capacity/trace duration	Large/.25–2 seconds	Small/up to 30 seconds	Unlimited?/ minutes to years
Information loss	Decay	Displacement Decay?	Loss of trace or loss of accessibility?
Retrieval	Readout	Probably automatic Items in consciousness Temporal/ phonemic cues	Retrieval cues Possibly search mechanisms

Source: Adapted from Craik, F., & Lockhart, R. (1972). Levels of processing: A framework for memory research. *Journal of Verbal Learning and Verbal Behavior, 29,* 671–684.

Sensory Memory: Sensory memory simply receives and temporarily records an ongoing event; it is a faithful reproduction of information about a stimulus. But, as Table 13–1 indicates, it is very short-lived, typically lasting less than 2 seconds. It is considered a "pre-attentive" store in that we do not have to be paying attention to a stimulus for it to enter our sensory memory. Some stimuli do catch our attention and therefore undergo further processing; others receive no attention and fade from sensory memory. That is why we don't remember everything that happens around us. It is also one reason why police investigating a crime often get responses such as "I just didn't see anything," although the person was in the same room as the perpetrator.

Each sense has its own sensory memory. In the general memory literature, two sensory registers have received research attention. The register for auditory stimuli is known as *echoic memory*. The one for visual information is called *iconic memory*. Iconic memory has received much more attention in the aging literature than echoic memory has. Indeed, we can say almost nothing about age-related changes in any sensory register but iconic memory.

We saw in Chapters 8 and 12 that there are commonly substantial changes in the visual system as people age. It would not be surprising, then, to find that iconic memory changes dramatically too. After all, vision would affect the information that gets in to the sensory register. Yet there seem to be only modest declines in sensory memory (Fozard, 1980; Labouvie-Vief & Schell, 1982; Poon, 1985). It may take the elderly longer to identify stimuli, particularly if the material is very complex. So it takes longer to identify a string of numbers than to identify a single letter. This decreased processing speed would be detrimental when fast recognition is important, as in reading highway signs. In most situations, however, the impact of limited decreases could be alleviated if the sensory image or icon was held in the register longer. Indeed, some research suggests that the icon persists longer in older than in younger adults (Poon, 1985). It may last long enough to allow identification under most circumstances. Furthermore, in many everyday situations, the stimulus remains available so that the individual does not have to rely exclusively upon iconic memory in order to identify the object or event.

Primary Memory: Primary memory is a very limited store, in terms of both capacity and duration. Imagine you are at a party and a friend says to you, "Alfred, I'd like you to meet Martha." Your sensory memory allows you to recognize this series of sounds as words in an introduction. It is your primary memory that allows you to respond using Martha's name. Without rehearsal, which may simply involve calling Martha by name several times, the information will be lost. If you run into Martha later in the evening, you will have already forgotten her name. Primary memory, then, is more a processing than a storage component. Information is held only briefly as organizing and processing begins in order to transfer it to secondary memory.

Generally, research indicates that the old are as proficient as the young in retrieving information from primary memory (Fozard, 1980; Poon, 1985); there is apparently little or no age-related decline in capacity (Labouvie-Vief & Schell, 1982; Poon, 1985). But while storing information in primary memory seems unaffected by age, processing abilities may not fare so well. Several studies have found processing problems in older adults. The elderly tend to be slower in recall (Poon, 1985). More important, they may have more trouble organizing information. So, for example, the elderly will typically perform similarly to young adults on forward digit-span tasks. In other words, when asked simply to repeat a short string of numbers, they do fine. However, there are age differences on backward digit-span tasks, where the respondent is asked to repeat the string of numbers in the reverse order in which they were given (Fozard, 1980; Labouvie-Vief & Schell, 1982). The elderly seem to have a more difficult time manipulating information.

Familiarity with the stimuli or the patterns organizing the stimuli seems to mediate this effect. The less familiar the to-be-remembered information is, the greater the difference in the performance of old versus young adults (Labouvie-Vief & Schell, 1982). Most Americans are more likely to remember correctly a name like James than a name like Bhutto. Again, this has important implications for daily living, since most of what we need to remember is more or less familiar to us. Even new things, such as phone numbers or names of new people, are typically organized in familiar patterns.

Secondary Memory: At this level, we can truly say that the information is entering the main memory system. This is a storage place for newly acquired information. It can hold more information, and hold it longer, than primary memory can. It would be secondary memory that allows you to call Martha by name after meeting ten other people at the party. This is also where most of the work of organizing and processing the information for transfer into long-term (tertiary) memory occurs. It is sometimes described as having a storage component (secondary memory) and a processing component (working memory). It is also the area of memory where the greatest age-related deficits have consistently been reported (Fozard, 1980; Labouvie-Vief & Schell, 1982; Poon, 1985).

The age difference is particularly evident when retrieval cues are limited. In other words, the difference is greater in recall than recognition situations. The difference is also more pronounced on rote tasks. In such tasks, the respondent is asked to remember a passage word for word. The performance of the elderly is more similar to that of young adults if only the gist of a passage needs to be remembered.

This and other evidence has led researchers to suggest that the age-related problems are in processing rather than storage (Craik, 1977; Fozard, 1980; Labouvie-Vief & Schell, 1982; Poon, 1985). But is it in encoding or retrieval? In fact, the two processes are only theoretically distinguishable. There is little doubt that efficacy of retrieval is dramatically affected by encoding. That is one reason why you remember things for an exam better if you have a way of organizing and relating the material. Supposedly, the "deeper" your organization and analysis during encoding, the better your ability to recall (Craik & Lockhart, 1972). This "depth of processing" argument has often been used as an explanation for the relative deficits seen in the elderly; it has been argued that young adults use "deeper" processing methods.

This argument has several corollaries. First, we might expect that the elderly would do poorly when the to-be-remembered material requires considerable processing. They might do worse at garnering an implied rather than an explicit message from a passage and then remembering it. Research suggests that the elderly recognize an implicit message, such as some of those contained in advertisements, about as well as young adults do (Rebok, Montaglione, & Bendlin, 1988). Furthermore, under relatively straightforward conditions, memory for implied statements is similar. However, if there are long or unexpected delays before recall is attempted or if the task requires memory of very specific details, the elderly perform less well (Reder, Wible, & Martin, 1986).

Another implication is that the elderly do not organize information as effectively as young adults do. It may be that young adults are better able to exploit the "logic" of an event. So, for example, they may make better use of superordinate-subordinate category relationships or temporal ordering. Research has indicated such processing advantages for young adults (Ratner, Padgett, & Bushey, 1988). However, these age differences appear consistently only when *spontaneous* use of organizing principles is being examined. In other words, older people are less likely to use temporal ordering or categorical relationships to organize material if the experimenter does not tell them to do so. With more explicit instructions, the age difference often diminishes or even disappears (Poon, 1985; Ratner et al., 1988).

Lynn Hasher and her colleagues (Hasher & Zacks, 1988; Hasher, Stoltzfus, Zacks, & Rypma, 1991) have suggested another way in which organization might be a problem. Their argument is that the elderly are less effective at selectively encoding information. Therefore, too much irrelevant and misleading information gets processed in working memory, which makes encoding more demanding and retrieval more difficult.

On the other hand, it is possible that part of the problem in retrieving information from secondary memory is due to the fact that it never got in there. For example, age differences are more pronounced under conditions of divided attention (Puglisi et al., 1988; Ponds, Brouwer, & van Wolffelaar, 1988). Older people's ability to process events, including daily situations such as those encountered in driving, may be taxed beyond its limits in such conditions. Part of the information may never get into the system. Similarly, the elderly may make use of nonessential environmental cues only when they are very salient (Sharps & Gollin, 1988). For example, a colorful map may be more easily remembered than a black-and-white one.

Age differences are also less dramatic if the elderly participants have high verbal skills. Familiarity with both materials and procedures helps too; practice will reduce the age difference (Poon, 1985). Memory may also vary with the type of material. Both actions and pictures seem to be more easily recalled than words (Puglisi et al., 1988; Ratner et al., 1988). Such factors do not necessarily erase the differences, though. In fact, some researchers have argued that the "best" performance by the "average" older person will still be poorer than the "best" performance by the "average" younger adult (Denney, 1982). This is exemplified in a training study by Campbell and Charness (1990). Both the young and old subject groups improved on a working memory task. The elderly improved so much that they were performing at the young adults' pre-training (baseline) level. But the improvement in the young adults' performance meant that the elderly never caught up. Even more dramatically, some studies (Kliegl, Smith, & Baltes, 1990) show an actual increase in the age gap with training because the young improve more than the elderly do.

There are no doubt losses in secondary memory functioning, but the cause of this deterioration remains unclear (Labouvie-Vief & Schell, 1982). It may be rooted in brain losses (Horn, 1982). Or the slowdown observed in most areas of cognitive processing may be to blame (Botwinick, 1978; Salthouse, 1985). Similarly, the implications of these memory losses are poorly defined. Losses are minimal when the person is dealing with familiar information in a routine context. Even in situations where information may be forgotten, simple memory aids, such as lists or putting something where you will be sure to see it, often minimize the risk of forgetting. Indeed, people of all ages use such memory aids, although elderly people use more of them (Poon, 1985). So memory losses may not cause significant inconvenience for many older adults in many situations. They will need more reminders. And they may experience more embarrassing lapses, although part of the embarrassment is attributable to their greater sensitivity about memory functioning. But overall they will find their memory functioning to be more than adequate for daily living.

Tertiary Memory: The other name for this store, long-term memory, better captures its function and structure. This is the repository for all processed information. It contains everything from vocabulary to information about public and private events to how to read facial expressions. Without tertiary memory, linguistic, cognitive, and social functioning would virtually cease. You would not remember how to carry on a conversation, drive a car, or use a bathroom.

As Table 13–1 indicates, information can be stored in tertiary memory for years. In fact, some theorists have argued that once something gets into long-term storage, it is there for good. Of course, some information is more easily retrieved. Some of it is virtually inaccessible. But much of it can be retrieved under certain circumstances. For example, you may be hard pressed to remember the names of all of your sixth-grade classmates. Your memory might be improved by looking at a picture of them. You may do even better if you have a former classmate to discuss the names with.

There is no doubt that information accumulates over the life span so that a 10-year-old has less in long-term memory than does a 20-year-old, who has less than a 30-year-old, who has less than a 40-year-old, and so on. What this means is that the older you are, the more information you have to sort through in order to get to the specific word, event, or person that you are trying to remember. It would not be surprising, then, to find that older people are less likely to retrieve things from tertiary memory or that at least it takes them considerably longer to do so. It is the case that old people tend to take longer to retrieve memories from long-term storage than younger ones do (Hyland & Ackerman, 1988). This may simply reflect the slower rate of processing found in most cognitive realms (Botwinick, 1978; Salthouse, 1985). Or it may be indicative of the greater number of associations each cue generates in an older person. Given a cue such as Thanksgiving, a young adult may have only one or two memories that come to mind. An older person may have a dozen or more and so may need more time to decide which one to report.

There do not seem to be large age differences in the amount that can be retrieved from tertiary memory. In fact, for certain types of events, older people may outperform younger ones. For example, when the older participants actually lived through a public event (such as the bombing of Pearl Harbor or the Kennedy assassination) whereas the younger ones only learned about it second-hand, the older person's memories may be more accurate (Poon, 1985). For more recent events, the data are more mixed. Some studies find slight advantages for young adults, and others do not. Of course, this may reflect salience of the events for the different age groups as much as it reflects memory functioning (Poon, 1985). When asked to generate their own memories in response to a cue, young adults are more likely to generate more recent memories. However, older adults are capable of generating recent memories, too (Hyland & Ackerman, 1988).

The information-processing model has been the most frequently employed paradigm for investigating memory functioning across the life span. Its use has focused us on the *site* of memory loss. Once the losses are localized, attempts are made to explain them in terms of storage, encoding, and retrieval. The research from this perspective has indicated that the greatest losses occur in secondary memory, a short-term store where considerable processing takes place. The elderly, it seems, do not use the same organizational tools that young adults do. They are able to recall less and have fewer details in their reports than do younger adults.

Yet even these findings, reliable though they are, are conditional. There seems to be considerable variation in the size of the age differences, depending on whether the task requires rote memorization or simply recalling the gist of the story. The familiarity of the material and the verbal skills of the respondent also seem to matter. To some researchers, such factors indicate that there is no absolute decline in memory (Labouvie-Vief & Schell, 1982; Poon, 1985). Rather, there are changes in the approaches people take to remembering or in the relationships between person-task-environment that require a different approach to understanding memory functioning across the life span.

Contextual Hypotheses

Some theorists have suggested that the findings from information-processing research may not really indicate losses. Consider what is "lost" for a moment: verbatim memory skills, nonessential details, ease of remembering completely novel information. Couldn't we look at this list and suggest that memory simply becomes more tuned to normative, daily tasks? Wouldn't such a shift be adaptive (Lerner, 1990)? After all, why waste time developing or maintaining (at peak level, at least) skills you rarely use? Given that there are limits on everyone's cognitive processing capabilities, wouldn't it be most efficient to "streamline"? Surely, something is lost in the process, but isn't something also gained? These are some of the questions that led Gisela Labouvie-Vief and David Schell to suggest an alternative to the information-processing model.

Taking a cue from Piaget's and Schaie's models of cognitive development, Labouvie-Vief and Schell (1982) argue that cognitive restructuring continues across adulthood. Just as in childhood, this may mean that certain "skills" are lost. For example, younger children are more likely to "pick up" nonessential information, such as color or position of an object when these are unimportant, than are older children. Yet this is not seen as a "loss," because ignoring such information allows the older child to focus on the solution to the problem. The older child, in other words, is more efficient in completing the task:

> As new modes of information analysis supersede old ones, a trade-off is being made by which old modes lose in efficiency. It is important, however, to examine such restructuring with a view toward potential gains as well. Thus we would predict that adults, even ones quite advanced in age, will display modes of information processing which are not only coherent but also highly efficient in selected circumstances. (Labouvie-Vief & Schell, 1982, p. 838)

More specifically, Labouvie-Vief and Schell argue that older people are more focused on the ecologically salient and relevant. This, of course, is similar to Schaie's (1977/1978) model of intellectual development during adulthood, which emphasizes the *functions* of intelligence. The adult's memory functioning may be geared toward the pragmatic. This is why age differences are less dramatic when material is familiar and meaningful. The consistent finding that type of material reduces age difference indicates that there is no generalized loss of functioning.

This approach also explains why the elderly do all right if only the gist of a discourse passage needs to be recalled but perform significantly less well if details need to be recalled. This is an example of the tradeoffs that are often seen as new structures develop (see the earlier example; see also Baltes, 1987). This can be interpreted as exemplifying Werner's orthogenetic principle of development, that development moves toward increasing differentiation (specificity) and hierarchical integration. So, the elderly will demonstrate greater specialization in memory function. They will also have more complex associations within memory systems (Labouvie-Vief & Schell, 1982).

How can we be certain that these are reorganizations and not permanent losses? Perhaps the elderly have lost all ability to process details and remember them. If this is so, then it would affect what jobs they can hold, what family tasks they can be expected to complete, and so on. The research consistently shows that elderly people can improve their performance on many types of tasks with changes in directions or training. For example, Ratner and her colleagues (1988) reported that older people reported fewer details of a structured event than did young adults. The experiment was repeated with a different group of participants. This time, however, the instructions included a model showing how much detail to provide as well as repeated, explicit instructions to provide as much detail as possible. With these instructions, no age differences emerged. Apparently the elderly people did not really believe the experimenter wanted to hear all those "boring details." Again, this may be interpreted as an approach that will be more efficient and pragmatic in situations other than psychology experiments.

Thus, the elderly typically adopt a particular approach to memory tasks, an approach marked by general (as opposed to detailed) encoding of the event. They are more likely to do well with familiar information and will frequently adopt a pragmatic attitude to both encoding and retrieving the information. There is some plasticity in their memory functioning, of course, indicated by the ability to modify their approach when it is clear that modification is necessary or beneficial. All of this leads Labouvie-Vief and Schell to conclude that the elderly have evolved an efficient, practical format for dealing with memory requirements that should be viewed as an advance for daily functioning rather than as the deficit seen in psychology experiments.

The Interactive View

It might appear that the information-processing proponents have been too pessimistic in their evaluation of aging and memory. On the other hand, the contextual approach may be too optimistic. After all, the elderly may not always be dealing with familiar material. And there may not always be instructions or training to make it clear how much detail needs to be remembered. Furthermore, their plasticity in responding to training is not unlimited and may not be as great as that of young adults (Campbell & Charness, 1990; Kliegl et al., 1990). While the losses in memory functioning may not affect every aspect of life, they are real and can be important.

Poon (1985) has suggested that the most fruitful, and realistic, approach might be an interactive view. From this perspective, the task demands, the environment, and the individual all interact to produce performance. There may be deficits, but their effects will be greater for some people than for others. Those with high verbal skills, for example, seem less affected. And some people will find very effective ways of compensating for the losses by leaving themselves notes, setting timers to remind them of appointments, enlisting help from friends and family in remembering to take medicine, and so on. Still others will find that their environments make few unusual memory demands. They may have a fairly comfortable routine and may have extensive support systems to help them cope when that routine is disrupted.

The relative importance of task demands versus environment versus individual characteristics is not known. It is not clear how adequate most people find their memory functioning to be. Furthermore, it is not clear how much memory functioning can be improved (or impaired) by changes in circumstances. These are all questions for future research.

INTELLIGENCE

Several thorny issues are involved in any attempt to discuss intelligence. The first is simply trying to define the term. We could take the easy route and suggest that intelligence is what intelligence tests (IQ tests) measure. What we really mean here is that intelligence is so difficult to define that we will restrict our definition to our measures. There is some wisdom to this approach, in that it overtly acknowledges our inability, as a discipline, to agree on a broader, more abstract definition of this crucial term.

On the other hand, we need to have some sense of what the IQ tests are intended to measure. So we return to the question of what constitutes intelligence. First, we assume that intelligence involves adaptation. Faced with a problem, human beings must develop a solution. They must, in other words, adapt or change either themselves or the problem. In Piagetian terms, adaptation involves accommodation (changing one's intellectual structures to meet the environmental demands) and assimilation (changing the environment to meet the constraints of one's intellectual structures). As a simple example, let's say you are about to visit a friend in a nearby town. You turn on the radio and hear that the route you most commonly use has been closed by a snowstorm. You have several options. You could "force" the environment to change by borrowing tire chains or a four-wheel drive vehicle. You could modify your own behavior by staying home or taking a different route. In any case, you adapt to the situation.

A second assumption is that intelligence is multifaceted, with several important components that are frequently referred to as the primary mental abilities. Table 4–4 listed some 25 primary mental abilities that have been empirically defined. As you might expect, this long list of abilities has often proved difficult to work with, especially in gerontology, since over a half-century of research has indicated different age functions for the various abilities (see Schaie, 1979, for a summary of the early research). Intelligence is multidimensional and multidirectional in its development (Baltes, 1987). Therefore, more abstract abilities, again based on empirical work, have been generated. These are summarized in Table 13–2. Pay particular attention to *crystallized intelligence* (Gc) and *fluid intelligence* (Gf). They are at the core of much of the research on intellectual functioning in adulthood.

Tables 4–4 and 13–2 capture what might be termed the *structure* of intelligence (Horn, 1982); they describe the basic abilities we use in coping intellectually with our environment. Analyzing this structure and its developmental changes has been the thrust of gerontological research using intelligence tests. However, changes in the structure of intelligence are not

TABLE 13-2: Major Second-Order (More Abstract) Mental Abilities Functions

Factor	Factor Name	Description
Gc	Crystallized intelligence	Involves performances indicating breadth of knowledge and experience, sophistication, comprehension of communications, judgment, understanding conventions, and reasonable thinking. Primary mental abilities involved include verbal comprehension, concept formation, logical reasoning, and general reasoning.
Gf	Fluid intelligence	Abilities include seeing relationships among stimulus patterns, drawing inferences from relationships, and comprehending implications. Primary abilities involved include induction, figural flexibility, integration, logical reasoning, and general reasoning.
Gv	Visual organization	Reflects fluency in perception of visual patterns as opposed to inferring the patterns. Primary abilities involved include visualization, spatial orientation, speed of closure, and flexibility of closure.
Ga	Auditory organization	Represents fluent perception of auditory patterns. Tests include speech perception under distracting conditions, tonal series, repeated tones.
SAR	Short-term acquisition and retrieval	Processes involved in attending to and retaining information long enough to do something with it. Primary abilities include span-memory, associative-memory, and meaningful memory.
TSR	Long-term storage and retrieval	Processes involved in forming associations for encoding for long-term storage and using associations or forming new ones for retrieval. Primary abilities involved include association fluency and object flexibility.

Source: Adapted from Horn, J. (1982). The aging of human abilities. In B. Wolman (ed.), *Handbook of developmental psychology.* Englewood Cliffs, NJ: Prentice Hall.

the whole story; there may also be age-related differences in how we use our abilities. Perhaps approaches to solving problems change. This is, of course, in line with Labouvie-Vief's arguments discussed in the section on memory. It is also consistent with Schaie's (1977/1978) model of intellectual development. There is, then, an entire body of literature concerned with the *process* of problem solving. This work includes analyses of concept formation and use. We will examine intelligence in two parts, one dealing with intelligence test research on structure and the other looking at the more process-oriented components of intelligence.

Intelligence Test Research

The Classic Aging Pattern: Early research with the Wechsler Adult Scales of Intelligence (WAIS) indicated that performance on the test declined as people aged (Wechsler, 1939). Indeed, the picture seemed rather bleak, as abilities seemed to peak in the twenties and then fall off. Even this early work, however, indicated that the decline was not the same for all measured abilities. In other words, the decrements were larger and earlier for some subtests of the WAIS than for others. Performance tests, especially those requiring speed, showed greater losses than verbal tasks.

This early research was questioned on several grounds. For one thing, it was predominantly cross-sectional, and age and cohort were confounded (see Schaie, 1979). Education differences, for example, were mixed up with age. Such education differences would consistently favor the younger cohorts (Willis, 1990). This is no small issue, because education level is strongly related to intelligence test performance. Second, there were complaints that the tests used, such as the WAIS, were too general to specify the changes. As we have already seen in Tables 4–4 and 13–2, factor analytic work has identified numerous mental abilities. Even the early work suggested that they might be differentially affected by aging.

The factor analytic researchers, led by John Horn (Horn & Donaldson, 1976; Horn, 1982) eventually identified what has come to be known as the *classic pattern of aging.* They have concluded that there are real, reliable, meaningful declines in intellectual functioning as people age. Such declines typically become evident during middle age. However, and this is crucial, not all abilities follow the same pattern of decline. Crystallized intelligence (Gc) is not as affected by aging as fluid intelligence (Gf) is. Indeed, crystallized intelligence may actually *increase* through much of adulthood. Vocabulary tests in particular commonly showed increases. It is noteworthy that the definition for Gf is similar to the Performance IQ of the WAIS, while Gc is comparable to the Verbal IQ.

Looking at the definitions of Gc and Gf also provides clues to why they might show differential aging patterns. Gc reflects what Horn (1982, p. 853) has called "acculturation learning." These are the skills that are systematically taught in schools and are viewed as necessities for survival in a society. It is likely that people develop these skills to close to their maximum potential. It is also likely that these skills are routinely exercised in daily activities. Think, for example, of vocabulary skills or understanding social conventions. Abilities that are used routinely seem to retain higher levels of functioning. Indeed, "lost" abilities can be improved by practice and use (see Denney, 1982; Willis, 1990).

Gf, on the other hand, represents abilities that are not directly trained (Horn, 1982). These concepts are extracted by the individual from perceptions of the environment, so certain concepts may be better developed in some people. Some are used frequently by a particular individual, but since they are not viewed as sufficiently critical to be part of systematic education, they are not typically required for daily living. Think, for example, of being able to figure out what letter comes next in a sequence.

Such differential use of Gc and Gf skills may well be a significant factor in their variant developmental patterns (Denney, 1982; Horn, 1982). However, even use of Gf skills does not erase their decline (Salthouse & Mitchell, 1990; Salthouse et al., 1990); and Gc skills show some decline too. Therefore, use cannot be the sole determinant. Horn has suggested that brain changes may be involved. He argues that Gc and Gf are mediated through different brain structures. The neurological structures associated with Gf are seen as more susceptible to age-related decline. Of course, evidence for this argument is sparse. Indeed, as we saw in Chapter 12, there is no strong evidence of significant brain losses in the absence of pathology. Nonetheless, it is apparent that different parts of the brain age at varying rates, so the hypothesis remains plausible.

Questions about the Classical Pattern: Not surprisingly, some researchers disagree with Horn's portrayal of intellectual aging. One question is whether the age-related decline is as marked as Horn's work indicates. Another is whether the pattern of intellectual functioning in old age is best described in terms of fluid versus crystallized intelligence.

Schaie and his colleagues presented data throughout the 1970s that seemed to question the impact of age on the primary mental abilities (see Schaie, 1979, for a summary of this research). Indeed, their findings seemed to indicate that cohort was more responsible for the so-called aging patterns than was age alone (Schaie & Labouvie-Vief, 1974). In other words, the education, work experience, and technological demands of daily living seemed more responsible for the relatively better performance of the young than did age. This is not to say that Schaie and his colleagues did not find age-related decline in IQ performance; they did. Rather, they found that the decline associated with age alone was small.

Furthermore, they argued, the decline began later than Horn and his colleagues suggested. Schaie's (1979) estimates for the beginning of "significant" decline on the subtests of the Primary Mental Abilities test (PMA) are shown in Table 13–3. He further suggested that decline could not be documented for all abilities or all individuals until very old age (the late eighties) (Schaie, 1979). The Duke Longitudinal Study findings similarly suggested maintenance of intellectual functioning into the eighties (Busse & Maddox, 1985). The only people for whom Schaie predicted an early decline were those in poor health (especially victims of cardiovascular problems) or those who lived in deprived environments.

These findings were criticized on a variety of grounds, including that the design of the data set made it easier to find cohort effects than age effects (Denney, 1982; Horn & Donaldson, 1976). Many of these methodological flaws were corrected in a later report on the 21-year follow-up of the study (Schaie & Hertzog, 1983). Once again, cohort effects were reported for several of the PMA subtests. However, the cohort effects were small; in fact, they were considerably smaller than the age effects. Furthermore, although functional decrements were clearest after age 60, some statistically significant decline was noted in late middle age (53 and older) on all PMA

TABLE 13-3:   Estimates of Ages at Which Reliable Decline for PMA Subtests Occurs

Subtest	Description of Subtest	Longitudinal Population Estimate	General Population Estimate
Word fluency	Measures semantic retrieval based on a lexical rule	67	53
Number	Simple addition skills	None	None
Verbal meaning	Recognition vocabulary	None	74
Reasoning	Rule induction from alphabetic series	81	53
Space	Visualization of object rotation in two-dimensional space	None	67

Note the difference between longitudinal sample and general population estimates. All estimates were probably optimistic.

Source: Based on Schaie, K. W. (1979). The primary mental abilities in adulthood: An exploration in the development of psychometric intelligence. In P. Baltes & O. Brim (eds.), *Life-span development and behavior,* vol. 2. New York: Academic.

subtests. Indeed, declines on the space subtest were evident in the late forties.

There is, however, the issue of the significance of this decline. The declines are statistically significant—in other words, the findings do not seem to be random, unreliable, or due to chance. They are systematic, commonplace, and detectable by IQ tests. However, the losses prior to age 60 do not appear to be large enough to affect daily living substantially (Schaie & Hertzog, 1983). For example, in any research we are attempting to explain 100 percent of the variance—that is, the differences among individuals' scores on a particular behavior. In the Schaie and Hertzog study, they were trying to explain 100 percent of the variance, over time, on the PMA subtests. Prior to age 60, age did not explain more than 1 percent of the variance on any of the subtests. After age 60, however, age explained as much as 8 or 9 percent. While still not an incredibly large effect, this may be enough to be noticeable. Sex, by the way, explained as much as 23 percent of the variance on some subtests at some ages (though the percentage explained by sex was typically lower than this). This gives some idea of the relative contribution of nonpathological aging to IQ functioning.

Schaie and Hertzog's findings raise another issue. All PMA subtests showed performance declines after age 60. The losses in verbal meaning were not particularly different from those on other tests. Thus, crystallized intelligence did not seem to be "spared" in either timing or extent of decline. It is possible that this discrepancy from the classic pattern is attributable to the timed nature of the PMA. After all, one of the clearest findings concerning aging is that performance on timed tasks declines (Salthouse, 1985).

On the other hand, it is possible that the relationship between Gc and Gf changes with age. More specifically, it has been suggested that the two become less distinct as people age (Cunningham & Birren, 1980). This would suggest that the increased differentiation of intellectual skills associated with child and adolescent development (Werner, 1948) somehow reverses or at least changes in old age, resulting in a neo-integration (dedifferentiation) of the skills (Baltes, Cornelius, Spiro, Nesselroade, & Willis, 1980). Some research has been reported that supports such a shift (Baltes et al., 1980). There seems to be a collapse of the Gc and Gf factors, though memory and speed still retain some separateness.

The neo-integration hypothesis is appealing because it could help to explain why the elderly select different strategies than young adults do. They do not seem to use specific strategies for specific types of problems; instead, they adopt a more general, function-oriented approach (Labouvie-Vief, 1985; Labouvie-Vief & Schell, 1982). However, most research still supports the distinction between Gc and Gf, even into old age (Horn, 1982; Lachman, 1983). More research will be needed to resolve this question.

Influences on IQ Decline: There are substantial individual differences in both the rate and extent of decline in intellectual functioning during aging (Willis, 1990). For example, as we have noted several times, older participants in longitudinal studies seem to fare better on IQ tests than those in cross-sectional studies. Research has indicated that longitudinal subjects are better educated, healthier, and more involved in community and professional activities than either those in cross-sectional studies or in random samples of the elderly. In other words, they are a "select" group.

In terms of maintenance of intellectual functioning, these data may be interpreted in two ways. First, we might argue that better health, higher education, and more involvement mediate IQ declines. There is research that supports this position. Architects, for example, show higher levels of visual spatial skills as they age than do people without extensive experience using these abilities (Salthouse et al., 1990; Salthouse & Mitchell, 1990). Schaie and his colleagues also reported that relative disengagement was related to lower IQ scores (Schaie, 1979). Inasmuch as involvement is an indicator of depression, a common problem for the elderly, we would expect it to be correlated with IQ performance. People suffering from severe hypertension or cardiovascular disease seem to experience greater than average IQ losses (Busse & Maddox, 1985; Schaie, 1979). And controlling education level seems to result in virtual elimination of the IQ decline, at least in some studies (see Labouvie-Vief, 1985).

On the other hand, we must consider the baseline performance when evaluating these findings. It is probable that the longitudinal studies' participants start out at a higher than average level of IQ functioning. They may continue to be higher than the young adult average even once their abilities have begun to decline. Thus, it is imperative that the amount of decline within the longitudinal sample itself be evaluated, rather than simply comparing their performance to that of young adults. This type of analysis tends to indicate decline occurring later and less dramatically than in cross-

Skills may be better maintained through use, and experience may easily compensate for physical declines.

sectional samples. But the decline does still occur and is apparently quite substantial after about age 60 (Schaie & Hertzog, 1983; Willis, 1990).

Another health issue may be related to age-related IQ declines. Since the early 1970s, there has been evidence that closeness to death might be related to IQ. It was hypothesized that IQ functioning declines more dramatically as a person moves closer to death. This decline, known as the *terminal drop,* supposedly begins to become evident about five years before death (Riegel & Riegel, 1972). Research has supported the value of considering distance-from-death in evaluating IQ changes (Busse & Maddox, 1985). As people get closer to death, their intellectual capabilities do seem to diminish. This may be due to physiological changes, medical treatment, disengagement from activities due to illness, or any number of other factors. More recent research, however, tends to suggest that the effect of terminal drop may not begin until about two years before death. Furthermore, it is not clear that all intellectual abilities are equally affected. It may be that terminal drop affects only certain skills, perhaps those verbal skills which are relatively unscathed by age until late in life (White & Cunningham, 1988).

Problem-Solving Research: It is important to define the processes involved in problem solving, for it is possible that age differences could occur at any point. In this sense, problem solving is similar to memory.

The first step in problem solving is to define the problem. To do this, one must assess the present situation and decide how it differs from some desired state. This is where the elderly and the young adult may begin to differ. In fact, motivation to address problems seems to influence how well the elderly perform (Denney, 1982; Labouvie-Vief, 1985). Relatively meaningless tasks, like those often used in laboratory experiments, for example, do not challenge the older adult. A young person may like solving such problems for the sheer joy of the process; the older person may want to know why he or she should bother (Schaie, 1977/78).

Similarly, old and young adults may disagree as to what the most desirable outcome is. Take, for example, a task in which people are asked to arrange houses so that there is the least area of lawn to mow. Young adults may act upon the "facts" and arrange the houses such that there is the least amount of *area* to mow. Older adults, however, may settle on a different solution, one that is technically "incorrect." There may be more area to mow but they expect that it will take less *time* to mow it because there are fewer angles and turns to negotiate. Thus, the elderly respondents' most desired outcome was one large, easy-to-mow area, whereas the younger ones tried to lessen the total area even if it resulted in scattered patches of grass (Newman-Hornblum, Attig, & Kramer, 1980).

Once the difference between present and desired situation is evaluated, the person must generate hypotheses as to how to get from the actual to the preferred state. In other words, problem solving involves selecting the "best" way to transform some existing state to something else (Reese & Rodeheaver, 1985). Once again, the older adult is more likely to focus on functional solutions (Labouvie-Vief, 1985). For example, the elderly may ignore the price of an item in determining which brand is a better buy and emphasize their own experience with the quality of the brands (Capon & Kuhn, 1979). There are always several possible solutions to a problem. The decision about the best choice apparently varies with the age of the respondent.

The research, in fact, indicates that older people differ from young adults in their definition of the problem and in their approach to solving it. In general, the older person's performance more closely approximates that of children than of younger adults. The elderly, like young children, tend to be less efficient in selecting a strategy and tend to opt for more practical approaches in their solutions (Labouvie-Vief, 1985). This has frequently been interpreted as indicative of deterioration in cognitive functioning (Reese & Rodeheaver, 1985). On the other hand, greater emphasis on real-life solutions to real-life problems has sometimes been viewed as an indicator of wisdom. Indeed, wisdom is colloquially viewed as a positive outcome of aging. It is a difficult concept to measure. Recently, however, Paul Baltes and his associates have attempted to build an empirical definition of wisdom (Smith & Baltes, 1990). This definition does focus on expertise in the "pragmatics of life" (Smith & Baltes, 1990, p. 494). Table 13–4 shows some of the specific criteria used in evaluating this expertise. While research in this area is still in its infancy, Smith and Baltes report no age or cohort differences in wisdom. While this is inconsistent with beliefs that wisdom increases in old age, it does suggest that this form of intelligence

TABLE 13-4:   Specific Dimensions of Wisdom

1. *Rich factual knowledge:* General and specific knowledge about the conditions of life and its variations

2. *Rich procedural knowledge:* General and specific knowledge about strategies of judgment and advice concerning life matters

3. *Life-span contextualism:* Knowledge about the multiple contexts of life and their interrelationships over the life span

4. *Relativism:* Knowledge about differences in values, goals, and priorities

5. *Uncertainty:* Knowledge about the relative indeterminancy and unpredictability of life and ways to manage uncertainty

Source: Smith, J., & Baltes, P. (1990). Wisdom-related knowledge: Age/cohort differences in response to life-planning problems. *Developmental Psychology, 26,* 494–505.

is at least maintained in the elderly. This distinguishes wisdom from, for example, fluid intelligence.

Examples of Age Differences: A few examples may help to clarify age differences in performance. A variety of tasks are used to test concept attainment, but the point of all of them is to identify what process is used to ascertain the rules for dividing objects or events into subsets. Thus, 20 questions, a task in which a subset of one (a single object) must be identified from an array, is a concept attainment task. Independently of what type of task is used, research consistently indicates that older people are slower at solving concept attainment problems than young adults are (Reese & Rodeheaver, 1985).

The basic mechanism involved in this age difference seems to be strategy efficiency. For example, the elderly appear to be less efficient hypothesis testers. In tasks where feedback is provided for hypotheses, the elderly do not use it well. For example, they are as likely to modify as maintain their hypothesis even when feedback indicates that they are on the right track (Offenbach, 1974). Similarly, they are more likely to ask redundant questions in a 20 questions task (Denney & Denney, 1974). They also tend to focus on perceptual rather than abstract characteristics. For example, an older person might be more likely to ask "Does it have fur?" rather than "Is it alive?" as a first question. This means it takes them longer to "narrow" the field of possibilities.

Piagetian tasks such as conservation have also been widely used to assess cognitive functioning in adults. Some people (Reese & Rodeheaver, 1985) have questioned the validity of using such measures, since the application of Piagetian theory to adulthood is poorly defined. After all, the theory stops at adolescence. Nonetheless, there is a large body of research using these tasks, and in general the findings indicate a pattern of age-related decline reversing the order of the acquisition of cognitive operations (Denney, 1982; Reese & Rodeheaver, 1985). So older people are likely to fail at least some conservation measures. This means that they appear to be functioning at a preoperational level. Most young adults would perform at the concrete operational level, with at least some exhibiting formal operations. However, the research on conservation performance is inconsistent in several ways (Reese & Rodeheaver, 1985). For one thing, not all studies show conservation in all tasks. In addition, the percentage of elderly people failing any given task differs considerably from study to study. Some studies find virtually no decline. Finally, there is the issue of whether or not the tasks actually assess the competence of the respondents or whether performance factors are masking true abilities.

Competence versus Performance: Evidence that the elderly and children perform similarly on various problem solving tasks has been interpreted to mean that there are cognitive losses in old age. This conclusion rests on the assumption that the performance reflects the same underlying abilities in both groups. How correct is this assumption?

Training studies suggest that the underlying competence of the elderly exceeds that of children (Denney, 1982; Labouvie-Vief, 1985; Reese & Rodeheaver, 1985). Performance on a variety of problem-solving tasks can be quickly and dramatically improved by several different training techniques. Direct practice alone will improve performance on conservation tasks. Feedback will improve 20 questions performance; instruction will increase the speed and efficiency of concept attainment. In general, the training improvements are too marked and rapid to argue that the concepts are actually being *learned;* rather, it appears that the strategies, concepts, and so on are being *activated.* Indeed, Piaget argued against the possibility of training conservation.

Training studies have been undertaken on a wide range of cognitive tasks, including measures of conservation, fluid intelligence, and memory. Success has been reported in many realms (Kleigl et al., 1990; Willis & Nesselroade, 1990). Recent data suggest that the effects of training may "carry over" even two years after the training and that even the very old may benefit (Willis & Nesselroade, 1990).

These studies, then, indicate that older people may simply not use strategies that are available to them. This could be because the strategies have generally not proved useful in daily living and so are not among the first tried (Labouvie-Vief, 1985; Reese & Rodeheaver, 1985). For example, the elderly are more likely to use complementarity than similarity between objects as the basis for associating words, objects, and so on. They *can* use similarity, but they usually do not. It has been argued that, in real-life situations, complementarity is generally a more useful approach. Think about it—hammer and nail, knife and fork, pen and paper, can opener and can. Certainly, occasionally we need to recognize similarity in order to "make do" when we are missing an appropriate tool. But in general, complementarity dominates.

Piagetian theorists have listed numerous factors that might cause a gap between competence and performance (see Neimark, DeLisi, & Newman, 1985, for examples). Some of these seem particularly relevant to the performance of the elderly (Reese & Rodeheaver, 1985). Declines in the capacity of working memory may be important. So might decreased motivation to solve irrelevant or meaningless tasks (Davidson & Sternberg, 1985; Schaie, 1977/78).

Increased caution, or decreased willingness to take risks, may also be a factor. Perhaps the elderly are less willing to have their intellectual capabilities evaluated (Reese & Rodeheaver, 1985). This makes sense, given the impact of intellectual performance on self-perception of one's abilities (Lachman, 1983). Remember, the elderly seem more aware of and concerned about their mistakes than young adults are. Perhaps they simply do not want evidence of their declining abilities.

Difference or Decline: Once more we are faced with the issue of whether these age differences represent real decline (Labouvie-Vief, 1985; Reese & Rodeheaver, 1985). Following Schaie's model, it is possible to suggest that the changes represent a *reintegration,* in which there is a simplification of the cognitive structures. This, of course, is also consistent with work indicating a collapse of the crystallized/fluid factor structure in IQ (Baltes et al., 1980; Cunningham & Birren, 1980). Schaie proposed that, by late in life, cognitive complexity has achieved an overload level, requiring some simplification. Concurrently, there is a decline in social role requirements (retirement and the reduction in parenting). These combine to produce greater selectivity in what types of problems the individual chooses to address and which strategies he or she selects to solve them.

More specifically, Schaie argued that the elderly are motivated by the significance or the importance of the problem to be solved. As he says, this stage " . . . completes the transition from the 'what should I know.' through the 'how should I use what I know.' to the 'why should I know' phase. . . . " (Schaie, 1977/78, p. 135). This conceptualization points out the extensive difference between the young adult approach—in which knowledge for knowledge's sake is paramount—and the elderly perspective of using what one has wisely, and in situations where it is important. This difference was demonstrated in the opening example of this chapter.

How important is this distinction? Schaie (1977/78), Labouvie-Vief (1985), and others argue that it is crucial. If it is correct, we have underestimated the abilities of older adults. Furthermore, our measures of intelligence are inappropriate. To assess intelligence accurately in old age we would need measures rooted in personal relevance. First, of course, we would have to define the parameters of personal relevance. This is a major task, like developing the tasks to test Piaget's theory or the IQ tests themselves.

LANGUAGE

You might think that linguistic functioning during adulthood would have received considerable research attention. After all, few skills are so necessary to daily success as language. It is our main channel of communicating our needs to others, of gaining information, and of engaging in social interaction. It would seem to be an ideal skill for assessing whether or not daily practice prevents all or most decline. Yet there is relatively little research concerning language during adulthood generally or among the normal elderly in particular.

Language in Normal Adults

Most areas of research have suffered from our early emphasis on childhood as the primary, and perhaps sole, period of "development." Nowhere is this more evident than in the realm of language development. People routinely think of language as being acquired during the first two or three years. There is some refinement until the early school years, then almost nothing. We recognize that there may be some vocabulary growth and some improved ability to consider others' perspectives during conversation. But by and large, most of us think there are few major changes in linguistic functioning after early childhood. A quick glance at most lifespan development textbooks will confirm the bias.

Yet there is language development during adulthood. For example, adults probably learn a variety of new *language registers* (Obler, 1985). They learn the specific vocabulary, syntactic structures, and other features associated with language use in a particular setting or situation. A gerontologist may speak differently to a group of relatives of Alzheimer's victims than to a graduate seminar in gerontological neuropsychology. The ability to recognize and acquire a new register can affect success in a new job or a new social situation. Think, for example, of a worker transferred from one part of the country to another. Continuing to use Mississippi phrases and accents in Detroit (or vice versa) may mark the person as an outsider. Simi-

Problem-solving skills are not lost in old age.

larly, many education experts have argued that speakers of Black English need to learn Standard English if they are to succeed in the job market.

As people age, we see changes in some areas of language but not others. Discourse appears to become more elaborate with age (Obler, 1985; Obler & Albert, 1985). This means that more words are used to express a thought. An older person is more likely to describe an item than simply name it on a vocabulary task. This may represent memory problems. Perhaps the older person has more difficulty accessing the most appropriate word to name the item. It may also again demonstrate the elderly person's greatest emphasis on functionality so that the use of the item is more accessible than its proper name.

This elaboration is also evident in daily discourse (Obler & Albert, 1985). Where a middle-aged person might use an incomplete sentence or a brief phrase, an older adult is more likely to produce a complex sentence with embedded clauses, redundancy and repetition, personalization, and various other features that lengthen the sentence. When asked to describe a picture, middle-aged subjects might say "Boy standing on stool. Mother washing dishes." An elderly subject, however, might respond "The boy is standing on the stool while the mother is carefully drying dishes, unaware that the water is running over" (Obler, 1985, p. 293). Many of us might assume that such elaboration is undesirable. After all, we are all taught to be concise in writing and speaking. While brevity may indeed be valuable in composition and in professional speech, typically repetition and redundancy will be useful in daily speech. They help to clarify or reinforce a point, for example. And they help to establish certain rhythms and patterns in speech which help to make it more recognizable as well as pleasant to hear.

It is difficult to ascertain whether there are changes in language comprehension as people age (Obler & Albert, 1985). Many older people have hearing impairments that affect their ability to understand. When researchers control for such problems, there is little evidence of comprehension differences. For example, older adults do not appear to rely more on facial expression, lip reading, or linguistic context in interpreting a word than young adults do. Both young and older adults are more likely to correctly identify the word "thorn" in the sentence "a rose bush has prickly thorns" than in the statement "the boy can't talk about the thorns" (Obler & Albert, 1985, p. 467).

On the other hand, there is some evidence to suggest that the elderly may be more automatic in their language processing than children and young adults are (Warren & Warren, 1966). In tasks where one word is presented repeatedly, all people eventually report hearing a different word. Older people, however, report hearing fewer new words than younger ones do. Furthermore, young adults and children report hearing words that could be English words (given their phonological structure) but are not. The elderly rarely report such patterns. This may suggest greater efficiency and less distractability on the part of the elderly.

It would appear, then, that there are few significant losses in linguistic functioning during aging. If an individual does seem to suffer major vocabulary losses, an inability to comprehend speech, difficulty in producing comprehensible speech (either because of phonological, syntactic, or semantic structuring), or any other noticeable linguistic impairment, some form of hearing loss or organic brain syndrome should be suspected. Strokes frequently affect language abilities. Alzheimer's disease can result in complete loss of language. And any of the drugs cited in Chapter 12 that produce confusion may result in altered language patterns.

SUMMARY

What are we to conclude about cognitive functioning in old age? First, it is clear that there are differences between young adults and the elderly in most areas. In memory, short-term and working memory seem to be less efficient in the elderly. On the other hand, long-term memory seems to be left more or less intact. In terms of IQ performance, tests of crystallized intelligence seem to demonstrate some declines. Fluid intelligence, on the other hand, seems less affected. Studies of problem solving indicate that the elderly define both problems and the optimal solutions differently. Language seems minimally affected by aging, although the elderly do produce more elaborate discourse and lexical definitions.

Listing these age-related changes raises a second point. Even within cognitive areas (memory, IQ, language), losses are not universal. Not every aspect of memory declines, for example. Similarly, there is uneven loss across areas, so that IQ seems more affected than language. Of course, the losses are not independent of each other; it may be that part of the reason that the elderly use more elaborate speech lies in their memory problems. Similarly, slowdown in speed of behavior probably affects performance on many tasks.

There is no doubt that the elderly do not perform the same way that young adults do. There is some question, though, as to whether the elderly person's performance is *deficient* or *different*. Keep in mind that many of the theories used to develop tests of memory, intelligence, problem solving, and so on defined peak performance as "what occurs during adolescence or young adulthood." This is particularly evident in the case of Piagetian theories and tasks. Such definitions are arbitrary and may simply reflect a bias that development is confined to childhood and adolescence.

This argument is strengthened by the rather consistent finding that age differences are primarily attributable to strategy differences. Older adults seem to use a more realistic, function-based approach to most problems. Indeed, they may even refuse to work on irrelevant tasks. They may opt for a pragmatic approach even when it is inconsistent with "logic." While this counts against them in psychological research, it may actually make them better adapted for daily living than the 21-year-old who is long on abstract thinking but short on practical experience.

The question of whether the elderly are deficient or different from young adults cannot currently be resolved. We will first need more information about *daily* tasks and what skills and abilities are necessary to cope with them. Then we will need to ascertain whether the elderly are more or less efficient in such areas. In other words, we will need to develop new measures and approaches before the question can be answered.

14 Personality

In considering functioning in the physical and cognitive arenas, we have been able to make several generalizations. First, there is indeed decline. The body becomes more susceptible to disease and injury. It becomes less efficient. The memory starts to lose some of its edge. Speed of information processing slows.

We have also, however, seen considerable stability. Language skills, for example, do not show substantial decline. Nor do many reasoning abilities, assuming they are still used routinely. Individual differences are also evident. Better educated people tend to maintain their cognitive skills longer. Those who did not smoke and were physically active experience better health. Genetic endowment too has a role to play in health, longevity, and cognitive functioning.

How generalizable are these principles to other realms? More specifically, what might we expect to see in terms of personality functioning? Do we expect decline? Certainly, the stereotype of the elderly suggests a certain amount of helplessness and unhappiness. This may be especially true of the very old. Take as an example this appraisal by Lehmann (1982, p. 29):

> Aging may be regarded as a . . . continuous chain of losses. Since depression is the normal reaction to any significant loss, the aging individual seems to be prone, in a tragic existential scenario, to become easy prey to depression.

On the other hand, the data we reviewed in Chapter 9 indicated considerable stability in personality functioning. Certainly there was some room for change. Areas such as sex role functioning and, perhaps, interiority seemed particularly malleable. But we began to argue that those who had developed effective, efficient coping mechanisms by early adulthood would do well in middle age and, by implication, into old age. So maybe we should expect stability.

There is one more possibility—perhaps there is growth. Perhaps people become *more* integrated with age. This optimistic view, which is struggling to find a place in the cognitive realm, has been institutionalized in personality theory by Erik Erikson's work. It is a view shared by some of the older people interviewed by Joan and Erik Erikson:

> ... patience is one thing you know better when you're old than when you were young. . . .

> ... Old people are slower to anger ... with people who don't understand their point of view. They are able to take the viscissitudes of life in a calmer manner.

> ... If you're going to keep on living, you better keep on growing. . . . (Erikson, Erikson, & Kivnick, 1986, pp. 60–62)

Three broad areas of personality functioning might display patterns of growth, stability, or decline. The first is the self-system itself, including self-constructs, basic personality characteristics, and self-esteem. The second is ability to cope with stress. Do people become more or less adaptable with age? Finally, we need to consider the possibility of more extreme decline. How much of a problem is mental illness for the elderly? And how does mental illness differ for adults as a function of age?

SELF-DEVELOPMENT IN OLD AGE

Several aspects of self might be of interest to gerontologists. The first is self-esteem. How positively do you feel about yourself? The other is self-concept. Who are you? What do you like and value? What are your abilities? In many ways, *self-concept* is synonymous with the term *identity*. Indeed, identity throughout the life cycle is the focus of Erikson's theory of self-development.

A Growth Perspective: Erikson's Theory

It has been nearly half a century since Erik Erikson challenged the notion that development ended in childhood. He postulated eight stages of development (see Chapter 1) that *culminate* in the old age "crisis" of integrity versus despair. We cannot overemphasize that Erikson views this as the peak of personal development:

> Only he who in some way has taken care of things and people and has adapted himself to the triumphs and disappointments of being, by necessity, the originator of others and the generators of things and ideas—only he may gradually grow the fruit of the seven stages. I know no better word for it than *integrity*. (Erikson, 1980, p. 104)

Each of Erikson's stages has a *syntonic* and a *dystonic* aspect that must be brought into balance for healthy personality functioning. In old age, the syntonic component is integrity. It has been an elusive term to define, even for Erikson. He has described it as an acceptance of one's life cycle, a realization that one did what one could. Integrity also includes an appreciation for the others in our lives, especially our parents and spouses, who helped us and who also did the best they could. There is a sense of connectedness with other people, living and dead. This would explain, for example, why men and women become more similar as they age. It also represents a broader attempt to define one's place in history as both a descendant and an ancestor. People who are able to achieve integrity would be expected to have positive morale, low death anxiety, and yet an acceptance that their lives were coming to an end (Wlaskay, Whitbourne, & Nehrke, 1983–1984).

The dystonic component is despair. As is true of each of Erikson's crises, despair will constitute some portion of the healthy resolution. A common example of this "healthy" despair is concern over the next generation's difficulties. Oldsters will often lament "I'm glad I won't have to live in the world the children are inheriting," or "I don't know if the future will be as good as the past" (Erikson et al., 1987, p. 67). Such feelings of despair can reflect a certain amount of happiness about one's own life as it was lived, as well as some sympathy for what others face. It is even conceivable that it would spur some people into volunteering for organizations that might effect change.

Too much despair will result in what Erikson calls a "malignant disdain." Such people will focus on what has been wrong in their own lives as well as with humanity generally. They will often be bitter people who feel they have been cheated out of opportunities and time. Instead of becoming more peaceful and less anxious about death, they become angrier (Erikson, 1980).

One can also resolve the crisis on the side of too little despair. In this case, a maladaptive presumptiveness will reign (Erikson et al., 1986). These people will "overtrust" and will be unable to acknowledge and work with the negative aspects of life. They might ignore physical limitations or health problems. They may be unable to accept and deal with problems in their children's marriages. They expect things to turn out well but are often disappointed and do little to help ensure success.

The ideal outcome is a preponderance of integrity tinged with realistic despair. This leads to *wisdom* (Erikson et al., 1986). Wisdom enables the elder to maintain dignity and an integrated self in the face of physical deterioration and even death. The limitedness of one person's influence is understood, but so is the connectedness among all people. Thus, the wise oldster sees the future continuing in grandchildren and beyond. Again, tolerance becomes a hallmark as the relationship among peoples of different values, cultures, races, and genders is understood in a clear, unequivocal way.

Much of Erikson's description of old age sounds almost mystical. And it has never been easy to translate any of Erikson's concepts into operational definitions and measurement scales. Nonetheless, Erikson does present a framework for how personality *development* may continue until the end of life. Given that substantial numbers of elderly adults (especially those

Most elderly people believe they have something to contribute to younger generations. They do not feel useless.

under 80 or so) seem quite satisfied with their lives and optimistic about the future (Bengston et al., 1985; Campbell et al., 1976; Erikson et al., 1986), his description would appear to have at least some potential.

Stability as the Norm

Erikson's theory may be the most optimistic, growth-oriented view of personality and aging, but it is not the only "non-decrement" perspective. In fact, stability models of personality are almost as old. Many of these are not full-scale, life-span models. There are, however, numerous classification systems of types of people and how they age. These types incorporate both basic personality characteristics and commonly played social roles.

One of the earliest categorization systems was developed by Bernice Neugarten and her colleagues (Neugarten et al., 1968, 1965). These categories, shown in Table 14–1, were derived from longitudinal observations of the Kansas City Study (see Chapter 2). They were intended to describe people in their seventies. Given the selectiveness of any longitudinal sample, the descriptions may, of course, be optimistic. Perhaps the most maladaptive patterns have died off. Furthermore, maladaptive patterns might have been more evident had the people experienced greater problems with health or living situation.

Neugarten and her colleagues examined the integrity of personality, activity level (in terms of role involvements), and morale or life satisfaction among their sample. What they claim is that all of these things generally represent a continuation of long-established patterns. The highest functioning group, the "integrated," have always been well-adapted, while the

TABLE 14-1: **Personality Type in Relation to Activity and Life Satisfaction (Age 70–79)**

Personality Type	Role Activity	LIFE SATISFACTION		
		High	Medium	Low
Integrated	High	9 A	2	
	Medium	5 B		
	Low	3 C		
Armored-defended	High	5 D		
	Medium	6	1	
	Low	2	1 E	1
Passive-dependent	High		1	
	Medium	1	4 F	
	Low	2	3	2 G
Unintegrated	High		2	1
	Medium	1		
	Low		2	5 H
	Total	34	16	9

Name of pattern: A—Reorganizer E—Constricted
B—Focused F—Succorance-seeker
C—Disengaged G—Apathetic
D—Holding on H—Disorganized

Source: Neugarten, B., Havighurst, R., & Tobin, S. (1968). Personality and patterns of aging. In B. Neugarten (ed.), *Middle age and aging.* Chicago: University of Chicago Press, © University of Chicago.

"armored-defended" have always built walls to protect themselves. If anything, consistency becomes greater with age as one has more control over how one's energy, time, and resources will be invested (Neugarten et al., 1968, 1965). Such a view is consonant with current developmental genetic models which suggest that the influence of heredity may become greater because of increasingly close matches between one's predispositions and one's environment. The match improves because one is able to select friends, spouses, activities, and so on that the infant and young child have to accept more passively (Plomin, 1987; Scarr & McCartney, 1983). The environment reinforces the genetic predispositions, which in turn select increasingly supportive (to the genetic characteristic) environments (Atchley, 1989; Lerner, 1990).

Consistency in activity and social interaction levels is exemplified by the elderly residents of single-room occupancy hotels (Antonucci, 1985). The stereotype of these people is that they are isolated, with little contact with family or friends. While they probably have more social interaction than most of us assume, they have considerably less than the average older person does. This has been true throughout their lives. Most of them have lived alone for at least 25 years. Many were never married. Those who were typically had only brief marriages. They have always limited their family interactions. Indeed, they have long limited all their social interactions, tending to compartmentalize them to serve one specific purpose or function. Their intimacy needs seem minimal. It is not surprising, then, to find that most of their social interactions are instrumental (task-oriented) rather than affective (emotion-based). But, the instrumental interactions that they have tend to be consistent across their lives.

Other data from both the Duke Longitudinal Study and the Baltimore Longitudinal Study of aging also show considerable stability in personality characteristics or types. Maddox (1968), for example, reported that only 12.5 percent of the men and 27.3 percent of the women in the Duke sample failed to show a predominant pattern of activity level during a seven-year period. In other words, those who had the most social contacts early in the study also tended to be those with the most contacts at the end of the study. Other reports from the Duke data also demonstrate considerable stability in certain personality traits, at least until about age 70 (Siegler et al., 1979). Among these traits were relaxed versus tense and reserved versus outgoing patterns. These finds overlap with those of Costa and McCrae from the Baltimore Study (Costa & McCrae, 1984; Costa et al., 1983; Costa et al., 1981). Their argument that the traits of neuroticism, extraversion, and openness are substantially stable throughout the life span was outlined in Chapter 9. Indeed, there is broad-based acceptance of considerable stability on at least these types of traits (Bengston et al., 1985).

However, there is also room for caution. First, to reiterate the point made in Chapter 9, one person's stability is another person's change. None of these studies report absolute consistency in functioning. This was exemplified in one study, where the authors remarked on the " . . . impressive stability in personality functioning . . . " even when the differences between the number of subjects showing no category change was not *statistically* significantly different from those showing code shifts (Leon, Gillum, Gillum, & Gouze, 1979, pp. 520–521). Some people do change from one category to another.

Furthermore, most people show at least some absolute change. In fact, when researchers compare average scores across ages, they report considerably less stability than when they correlate people's positions within a group (Bengston et al., 1985). Thus, for example, in Maddox's (1968) study, most people showed some decline in number of activities. His argument was that the *relative* amount of activity was stable; active people stayed active, and less involved people did not tend to pick up more activities.

We also have evidence that some characteristics, notably those associated with sex roles, may change throughout adulthood (see Chapter 9; Bengston et al., 1985). There are also reported changes in energy levels, self-confidence, and sense of autonomy after middle age. It is especially interesting that subjective evaluations show people view themselves as changing (Bengston et al., 1985). They are likely to believe that changes in social or living circumstances, for example, change their attitudes or outlook. Such findings will need to be reconciled with the more "objective" questionnaire data before an assessment of the stability hypothesis can be completed.

There are still more problems to be resolved. First, although samples from several different longitudinal studies have shown similar patterns, we cannot tell how much of the similarity is due to methodological constraints. Many of these studies used the Cattell 16PF Scale (see Chapter 9). Certainly replicability is important; but it is equally critical that wider measures be used to tap other possible characteristics as well as different facets of traits already studied. More important, even broader data bases must be examined before definitive statements are possible. The currently available data are from samples made up overwhelmingly of white, middle-class Americans. We have only clues as to what old age might be like for other groups. There is some evidence, for example, that elderly, lower-class, urban Puerto Rican women maintain their social and familial roles in patterns consistent with a stability model of aging (Sanchez-Ayendez, 1989). Nonetheless, we know that participants in longitudinal studies tend to have better health, finances, and resources than many (perhaps most) elderly do. The special stresses faced by the poor, infirm, and isolated may cause more change not only in their level of adaptation, but also in their self-structure. Losing competence may cause a deterioration of identity (Erikson et al., 1986).

In the same vein, we do not know much about the very old, those in their eighties and beyond. Risks increase at this point. Health and cognitive declines are more widespread. Widowhood and other forms of bereavement (including the death of children) become more likely. In other words, roles and values may be changed by uncontrollable circumstances. New opportunities may be few and far between. It is plausible, then, that self-structure may begin to deteriorate. Neither existing models nor data provide an answer to this question.

MORALE IN OLD AGE

Assume for the moment that the current models are correct; assume there is no significant deterioration in the basic self-structure. Personality characteristics remain similar across adulthood; perhaps there is even some growth, some broadening of personality. Does this imply that, at worst, the elderly have self-esteem as high as young adults do? Are older people as happy with themselves and their lives as they once were? Maybe they are even happier and more satisfied as time goes on.

These questions have been addressed in a variety of ways. There is research concerning mood and affect among the elderly (Schulz, 1985). We can point out, first, that such research suggests the elderly show more depressed affect than young adults do. Indeed, as we have already seen, the rates of depression are fairly high among the elderly, although the peak is probably in middle age (Gaylord & Zung, 1987; LaRue et al., 1985; Schulz, 1985). However, nonclinical levels of depressive affect may also be more common among the elderly (Leon et al., 1979). We need to be cautious in interpreting findings of elevated scores on depression scales that are not accompanied by clinical depression. Many of these scales contain items that evaluate health complaints. In healthy young adults, somatic complaints may be indicative of depression. But among the elderly, they are more likely to be realistic appraisals (Costa & McCrae, 1985; Leon et al., 1979). In fact, acceptance of physical limitations may be part of healthy adjustment to aging (Erikson et al., 1986). Other negative emotions, such as anger or fear, do not seem to be particularly more prominent among the elderly than among other age groups (Schulz, 1985).

Several studies of life satisfaction and morale have also been reported. Participants in these studies are asked how happy they are and how satisfied with their lives. Generally, satisfaction with life is either steady or improves with age (Andrews & Withey, 1976; Campbell et al., 1976). This is more true of people who are relatively healthy and who are able to maintain the types and amount of activity they prefer (Busse & Maddox, 1985; Neugarten et al., 1968). Similarly, the more the environment meets the individual's needs for social interaction, health care, intellectual stimulation, and so on, the more likely he or she is to be satisfied (Antonucci, 1985; Lawton, 1987). Some people may therefore be quite satisfied living in a nursing home.

Although life satisfaction does not appear to differ across age, the basis of life satisfaction may change. In a recent study, Lucille Bearon (1989) reported that older women (average age about 70) were more likely than middle-aged women (average age about 45) to mention material well-being and health as sources of satisfaction in their lives. Middle-aged women were more likely to note the opportunities they saw as available to them as well as their work as sources of satisfaction. Both groups of women, however, noted that families, including marriage, are a primary source of satisfaction. Table 14–2 shows the similarities and differences in sources of life satisfaction for the two groups of women.

As Table 14–2 also demonstrates, older and middle-aged women also differed on sources of dissatisfaction. Not surprisingly, the older women mentioned health as a source of dissatisfaction more frequently; the middle-aged noted family, work, and their own personal inadequacies. It is interesting to note that 4 (of 30) older women, but none of the middle-aged ones, claimed no dissatisfaction.

Satisfaction is not the same thing as happiness. Some studies have found that the elderly may be less happy, though more satisfied, than younger adults (Campbell et al., 1976). This is not a universal finding (Andrews & Withey, 1976; Schulz, 1985). But it is possible that the elderly have lower expectations of what life will offer and so are able to be satisfied without being extremely happy. Indeed, this is Bearon's conclusion from her study of life satisfaction. She argued that the middle-aged women expected to advance and improve their family and work situations. The elderly women, on the other hand, seemed mainly to hope to maintain the

TABLE 14-2:   Sources of Satisfaction and Dissatisfaction in the Lives
of Middle-Aged and Elderly Women

	SOURCES OF SATISFACTION (percent)		SOURCES OF DISSATISFACTION (percent)	
	Older Women	Younger Women	Older Women	Younger Women
Material well-being	77	43	30	27
Family	67	80	37	60
Activities/options	33	27	17	20
Health	30	10	37	3
Work	17	47	3	17
Self	7	40	10	27
None			13	

Source: Based on Bearon, L. (1989). No great expectations: The underpinnings of life satisfaction for older women. *The Gerontologist, 29,* 772–776.

status quo, particularly in terms of health and financial well-being. The
older women, then, seemed to have more limited expectations (Bearon,
1989). Nonetheless, the elderly do not report themselves as "unhappy." Furthermore, like other groups, they tend to believe they are better off than
their peers are (Andrews & Withey, 1976).

There is also research concerning self-esteem in which the affective or
evaluative components of self are evaluated. People's sense of competence
and self-liking are at issue. Research in this area is seriously limited by lack
of longitudinal data (Bengston et al., 1985). The available data indicate
either a neutral or a positive relationship between age and self-esteem
among whites. African-Americans also show increases in self-esteem with
age. This raises the possibility that the self-esteem gap between African-
Americans and whites in adolescence and young adulthood may be reduced
by old age (Jackson, Antonucci, & Gibson, 1990). There may be some decline in self-esteem among the very old (Bengston et al., 1985). The variables
that influence self-esteem in young adults influence old age functioning.
Not surprisingly, then, people who are isolated, sickly, and perceive themselves as a burden to others have lower self-esteem (Kahana, 1982). At least
one additional issue may play a role. People who have negative attitudes
toward old people may suffer from declining self-esteem as they age (Bengston et al., 1985). This seems to be a reciprocal relationship; people who
have long had higher levels of self-esteem are less likely to endorse negative
stereotypes of aging (Kahana, 1982).

STRESS AND COPING

Although there are many models of stress and coping, several elements cut
across them. First, there is the issue of stress itself. In Chapter 9, for example, we made a distinction between major life events and daily hassles. Sec-

ond is the question of resources, which can range from individual characteristics to government agencies. Stress and resources are not unrelated, of
course. Someone who is well-adjusted may be less likely to experience many
events as stressful and may also be more apt to have friends to help weather
the stresses that do occur. Nonetheless, stress and resources do make some
independent contributions to how well a person can adapt. In other words,
both affect an individual's well-being. And both may change with age. Thus,
if level or type of adaptation changes with age, it may be attributable to
changes in stressors or resources. The perspective that age-related changes
in coping are attributable primarily to age-related changes in stressors is a
form of the contextual hypothesis we have seen in other realms of functioning (Folkman, Lazarus, Pimley, & Novacek, 1987; Lerner, 1990).

Stressors and Age

Major Stressors: Richard Lazarus and his colleagues (Folkman & Lazarus, 1980; Lazarus & Launier, 1978) have suggested that some major life
events constitute "entrances." Although individual appraisal of such events
will vary, they will generally be perceived as (and so are termed) *challenges.*
They are stressful, perhaps, but positive. Marrying, having a baby, or getting
a promotion might be included here. Other life events are "exits." These
fall into two subcategories: *threats* and *losses.* The threatening exits are those
that seem imminent or probable. The danger may be immediate but the
effect has not been felt. A diagnosis of a heart problem that could be limiting or fatal eventually might be a threatening exit. Something is likely to
be lost in terms of activity, diet, or even life, but it is not yet clear what that
is. A loss event, on the other hand, is one that has occurred and now
requires adaptation. The death of a spouse or child is an example. The
survivor is faced with getting on with life without the support of the
deceased.

Challenges, threats, and losses can and do occur at any point in the
life span. But old age has long been associated with a disproportionate
number of threats and losses. Loss of job, spouse, health, home—all of these
have been considered hallmarks of aging in the United States (Holt & Datan, 1984). Indeed, one of the early models of "successful aging" argued
that disengagement from roles was expected, encouraged, and accepted by
both society and the individual elderly (Cumming & Henry, 1961). Loss was
not only expected, it was good!

The data suggest that challenges do decrease with age (McCrae, 1982).
The elderly get fewer opportunities to play new roles. Threats, particularly
in terms of health, increase. Losses, however, do not seem to show dramatic
age differences. It may be that the losses experienced by the elderly are
more serious. They may pose more potential damage to self (Erikson et al.,
1986). They may remove core components of identity such as "John Smith's
wife" or "college professor." They may also represent more permanent or
far-reaching changes than the losses in early adulthood. There may also be
differences in how much of the loss was voluntary. Compare, for example,

divorce (which is more common among younger adults) and widowhood. Such questions have yet to be investigated.

Daily Hassles: Major life events are not the only source of stress—they may not even be the main source. Rather, daily frustrations, inconveniences, and irritations may constitute the steadiest, and even the greatest, stressors for most of us (Lazarus & Folkman, 1984). Some of these hassles will be more central, more distressing and important, than others (Gruen, Folkman, & Lazarus, 1988). People are more likely to report hassles with their children as being central than problems cooking a meal. But there are considerable individual differences in which hassles are reported as central. Furthermore, hassles that involve personal needs and expectations are more likely to be considered central (Gruen et al., 1988).

Both findings suggest age-related changes in the perception of hassles. Research has demonstrated that middle-aged adults report different hassles than college students do (Kanner, Coyne, Schaefer, & Lazarus, 1981). Age-related differences in hassles have also been reported in a study comparing older (about 68 years) to middle-aged adults (about 40 years) (Folkman et al., 1987). The older adults reported relatively fewer hassles related to work. The younger men were especially likely to report work-related hassles. The older group reported relatively more hassles related to health, home maintenance, and environmental/social issues. This last finding is particularly interesting, because it suggests that the elderly may indeed take a broader world view, as theorists such as Erikson have predicted.

Lawton (1987) has suggested five basic competency areas (see Figure 14–1). Health refers to actual physical status, including illness. Functional or applied health concerns the ability to perform daily living tasks ranging from self-feeding to holding a job. Cognitive skills include memory, intellectual, and learning abilities. Time use and social behaviors are more complex domains which acknowledge that, for most of us, most of our time is spent doing "nonessential" things. In other words, we are not just doing what we need to do to survive. Inasmuch as our abilities in each or any of these areas declines, we will become more vulnerable. We will increasingly rely on the environment to fill those needs in specific ways. A person with good mobility skills can drive, walk, take any bus or taxi, ride in any car, or use the subway to get to the bank. Someone using a walker or a wheelchair will be limited to transportation provided by others. A bus stop three blocks away is of little use. Furthermore, the vehicle must be able to accommodate the entrance and storage of the walker or wheelchair.

There may, then, be new types of hassles and they may occupy a more central portion of the person's life. Furthermore, the hassles may be less controllable, especially as the deterioration of very old age sets in. These questions will be answered by future research.

Of course, Lazarus and his colleagues have emphasized that stress is in the eye of the beholder (Lazarus & DeLongis, 1983; Lazarus & Folkman, 1984). Both major life events and daily hassles are interpreted by the individual (Gruen et al., 1988). So, for example, in one study, 2.7 percent of the participants said that "having enough money for extras" was the *most* cen-

FIGURE 14-1: **Hierarchy of Behavioral Competence.**

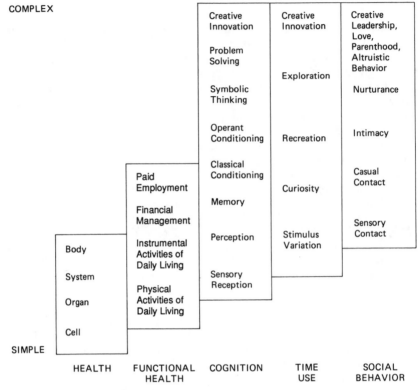

Source: Lawton, M. P. (1987). Environment and the need satisfaction of the aging. In L. Carstensen & B. Edelstein (eds.), *Handbook of clinical gerontology.* New York: Pergamon. Copyright © The Gerontological Society of America.

tral hassle in their lives; another 2.7 percent said it was the *least* central hassle in their daily lives (Gruen et al., 1988).

It is likely that the elderly often do not find aging and its hassles to be as bad as young adults think they will be (Erikson et al., 1986). After all, much of the change is gradual and relative. You do not lose *all* your physical stamina on your 65th birthday. Furthermore, some of the changes are anticipated—we expect to become less healthy. Some changes are even anticipated with joy. Think of the people who have been waiting for years to retire to Florida! (Kahana, 1982).

How much of a hassle aging is also seems to be a function of one's comparison group. Older people who compare themselves to their youth experience more stress than those who compare themselves to their peers (Schulz, 1985). A 70-year-old who compares herself to what she could do at 25 is virtually guaranteed to find a sharp discrepancy. But in comparing herself to other 70-year-olds, she may find she fares very well. This seems especially likely given Americans' tendency to rate themselves as "better off" than their contemporaries (Campbell et al., 1976). Similarly, elders may look to their parents or grandparents for models of aging (Erikson et al., 1986). This approach may provide not only inspiration, but also a sense of continuity between generations (a part of integrity).

Resources

Social Support: Models of stress and coping have long argued that social support is an important mediator of reactions to stress (Antonucci & Jackson, 1987; Holt & Datan, 1984; Whitbourne, 1985). Research has consistently indicated that older people with strong social supports have a higher quality of life (Antonucci, 1985; Antonucci & Jackson, 1987; Kahana, 1982; LaRue et al., 1985; Phifer & Murrell, 1986: Rozzini, Bianchetti, Carabellese, Inzoli, & Trabucchi, 1988). For example, morale is stronger among elderly people living with a spouse than among those living alone. Participation in organizations is positively associated with higher levels of life satisfaction. Good social support is also associated with lower rates of coronary disease, hospitalization, mental illness, and need for social services. In other words, people with strong social support are generally physically and mentally healthier than people who are more isolated. Those with better social networks even show lower mortality rates!

Most of the research linking social support and positive outcomes is correlational. This means that the direction of causality within the relationship is unclear. It is possible that being healthier, for example, allows you to continue social contacts and hence have better social support. Furthermore, the characteristics of social networks that provide the most effective forms of social support have not been identified (Bowling & Browne, 1991). But it is possible that, for many elderly, social support wanes (Holt & Datan, 1984). After all, old age is a time of role loss. Spouses and friends die. Retirement takes away work contacts. Physical decline may make it difficult to visit or even keep in telephone contact with friends and family. And institutionalization in a nursing home may move one away from all the people and places one has ever known.

Luckily, the picture is not really as bleak as this for most people. First, research indicates that the size of social networks does not appear to decline markedly with age (Kahn & Antonucci, 1983). Even housebound, very old (85+) community dwellers seem to have substantial social networks (Bowling & Browne, 1991). Furthermore, the types of support provided by the members of a social network does not seem to differ much across ages. This does not mean that there are no differences between the elderly's social networks and those of younger adults (Antonucci, 1985). For one thing, the elderly's networks tend to have a higher proportion of family members. The elderly with large social networks, however, are likely to have both family and friends in their networks (Bowling & Browne, 1991). Second, the elderly are less likely to *provide* support to network members.

The elderly are also more likely than young adults to be satisfied with their networks (Antonucci, 1985). They are satisfied with both friends and families. They enjoy both the type and level of interactions in which they participate. Most of them do not view themselves as isolated or very lonely. It is not clear whether these differences in network satisfaction are attributable to age or to cohort. An age effect is possible in that one's expectations of others may change (Erikson et al., 1986; Whitbourne, 1985). On the other hand, it may be that today's young adults expect more social support than the Depression-era generation ever did. There is some evidence for both age and cohort effects, so only further research can answer this question (Antonucci, 1985).

Numerous factors affect the types and availability of social networks for the elderly. As at any phase of life, women tend to have more extensive social networks than men (Antonucci, 1985; see Chapter 10). However, there may not be any sex differences among the very old (Bowling & Browne, 1991). Women are also more likely to be satisfied with their relationships with their friends, though men and women seem to be equally satisfied with family relationships. In fact, men tend to report higher marital satisfaction than women do. This gender difference in social networks may put older men at some risk (Antonucci, 1985). Often men have only one real confidante—their wives. If something happens to the wife, they are left alone. The social networks women have spent a lifetime developing may be particularly valuable in old age, when more help is needed but some supporters (like a spouse) are likely to die.

Friends may be particularly valuable as sources of emotional support (Sanchez-Ayendez, 1989). They may act as confidants and sounding boards. Friends will also do things together, such as watch television or go shopping. They "check in" with each other, often through daily phone calls. Such contact helps to ensure the safety of both friends. And it most cer-

Social support from family and friends helps older people cope more effectively.

tainly is a comfort to those who live alone. Typically, women have only other women as close friends. Aside from family members, men are rarely part of their close social networks (Antonucci, 1985; Sanchez-Ayendez, 1989). This is especially true of widows.

One major source of support for the elderly is their children (Antonucci, 1985). Women seem to expect more of their children, especially their daughters, than men do. Family may be a particularly strong source of support among Latino-Americans and African-Americans (Jackson et al., 1990). The extended family network can provide a variety of forms of assistance, even in the face of limited financial resources. One older Puerto Rican woman expressed it this way:

> Of course I go to my children when I have a problem! To whom would I turn? I raised them and worked very hard to give them the little I could. Now that I am old, they try to help me in whatever way they can.... Good offspring should help their aged parents as much as they are able to. (Sanchez-Ayendez, 1989, p. 176)

Daughters are indeed likely to provide social support to their elderly parents (see Chapter 10). Having a daughter increases the likelihood that the elder will receive phone calls, visits, and help with tasks of daily living. Sons are not as likely to offer these supports, even when there is no daughter. Sons and daughters are, however, equally likely to have parents living with them (Spitze & Logan, 1990).

The church may also serve as an important source of social support. This seems to be particularly common among elderly African-Americans, for example (Jackson et al., 1990). The church as a form of social support is not necessarily synonymous with deep religiosity. Rather, social support is a potentially separate function of the church within the community, an alternative to family and friends.

Living arrangements also affect social networks and the availability of social support. Elderly people who live around other old people tend to have more social interactions than those who live in more mixed neighborhoods (Antonucci, 1985; Kahana, 1982). That's one of the attractions of retirement communities. They tend to be full of upper-income, healthy, better-educated elderly who are looking for other people to share various activities. Older people usually think that younger people will not want to do things with them. They may also prefer the company of agemates. These communities provide safe, convenient ways of meeting people and interacting. Given the crime victimization fears of many urban elderly, this can be an important advantage (Kahana, 1982).

Institutionalized elderly may have a more difficult time feeling socially supported. After all, they often are placed in a nursing home because their social network is not able to care for them at home (Antonucci, 1985). Their familiar social networks become less available to them (Kahana, 1982). Institutionalized elderly who have regular "outside" visitors tend to fare better, as do those who feel supported by the nursing home staff. We should also note that for some people, institutional living may represent an *improvement* in social interactions (Kahana, 1982). This is especially true for people who were homebound and living alone.

Social support does not always have its intended positive effect (Antonucci, 1985; Antonucci & Jackson, 1987). Sometimes the support can actually make the situation worse. It can make the recipient feel old or useless, thereby contributing to lower self-esteem. Or it can make the recipient dependent when some degree of autonomy could have been maintained. Such artificial dependency may be a particular problem in institutional settings, including nursing homes and hospitals.

What determines whether social support is effective? What influences whether a person finds a support network adequate? These are complex questions that we are only beginning to answer. But it seems likely that one contributing factor for the elderly is the duration of the network or relationship (Antonucci, 1985; Antonucci & Jackson, 1987). This is because social support is most effective within reciprocal relationships. Yet the elderly are less able to provide services to others. They can be comfortable accepting assistance, however, if they have provided it to the giver in the past. This is probably why older people are so willing to accept help from their children or from old friends but less likely to turn to more casual or newer acquaintances in times of crisis (Antonucci & Jackson, 1987; Sanchez-Ayendez, 1989).

Thus, throughout our lives, we develop a *convoy* of social supporters (Antonucci, 1985). Some members of the convoy will drop out temporarily or permanently; others will be added. But gradually we will form a core group for whom we have done much and from whom we expect much. Note, however, that there will be wide individual differences in how large and how deep our convoy is. This is a lifelong process, and people who are relatively isolated early in life will tend to remain so later on. Once again we see the effects of a life-span pattern being played out in old age.

Size of the convoy is probably a relevant factor in how supported the individual feels (Antonucci & Jackson, 1987). A convoy that is too large may lack the close reciprocal ties necessary to yield a sense of support. One that is too small, on the other hand, might place impossible expectations upon its members. The strain of filling the needs of the elderly person may be more than the small number of members can stand. This may be why a convoy of one person may actually be worse than no available support. In such a situation, the elderly recipient may feel disappointed that the "supporter" is not coming through. Furthermore, when a convoy is larger, the elder's problems are more likely to be noticed more quickly (Bowling & Browne, 1991).

Another critical factor is the individual's appraisal of the support and the supporter (Antonucci & Jackson, 1987). If the recipient perceives the supporter's behavior as appropriate and well-intentioned, the results of the support are more likely to be positive. Again, reciprocity is an important component of this appraisal. People expect those for whom they have done things, including their children, to help them when they need it. They are uncomfortable accepting help from people who "owe them nothing." This may be one reason why assistance from community volunteers meets with only limited success among the elderly. Recipients will also try to ascertain why the supporter is helping. If they believe help is offered for the wrong reason, such as trying to secure a place in the person's will, the support will be less effective. As we will see later, increased paranoid behavior among some elderly may foster such interpretations (Post, 1987). In a similar vein, older people are more likely to interpret support positively if they feel that they are in control of their environment (Antonucci & Jackson, 1987). Again, this may be especially difficult to achieve in an institutional setting.

The informal support given by family and friends is crucial to the well-being of many elderly Americans. Indeed, policymakers are relying on these informal systems to provide for many of the needs of the growing elderly population (Antonucci & Jackson, 1987). However, there are some formal supports available, from Social Security to Meals on Wheels. Often the noninstitutionalized elderly will need family or friends to assist them in order to take advantage of these services (Kahana, 1982). They may need transportation or help filling out the necessary forms. Unfortunately, many frail elderly do not take advantage of the available services (Antonucci, 1985); instead, they rely exclusively on their families. Indeed, it is unusual for a frail older person to have both informal and formal social supports. Such a combination would be much more efficient for both the individual and the family. It might also enable some older people to continue independent community living.

Physical Environment: In Chapter 12, we suggested that there are ways to arrange the physical environment so that it is a support rather than a stressor to the elderly. This is particularly important for people whose abilities have started to decline, because they may be particularly susceptible to the effects of an environment deficit (Lawton, 1987).

Lawton (1987) has suggested that a good environment has four characteristics. First, it is safe. This would include safety from falls, burns, and other physical injury. Second, it is secure. This refers to psychological as well as physical security. There is a sense that one's needs for food, shelter, social interaction, and so on will be met. Third, the ideal environment is accessible. People can get in and out of buildings, rooms, furniture, and so on. Finally, the environment should be legible or comprehensible. It should be arranged in a manner that is sensible to the person using it.

Aside from these basic requirements, an environment may be more or less adequate for meeting intellectual and social needs. These issues are particularly salient in institutions (Kahana, 1982; Lawton, 1987). It is important, for example, to provide a balance of privacy and social interactions; lack of either one could create stress. It also appears important for residents to have some sense of control in their lives (Antonucci, 1985; Kahana, 1982; Lawton, 1987). This could involve making some of their own decisions about time use, room decor, or activity participation. As always, different individuals will want varying degrees of privacy, social interaction, and autonomy. It is therefore essential that the match between institutional structure and individual needs be carefully considered.

Personal Resources: All things being equal, some people will always seem to cope more effectively than others. There are, apparently, lifelong personality characteristics that contribute to adaptive capability. Recall, for example, Lowenthal's typology of people who felt challenged by life events versus those who felt overwhelmed (see Chapter 9). Some people who had actually had relatively few stressful events felt more stressed than those who had had many.

The personality dimension of neuroticism is particularly relevant here (Costa & McCrae, 1985; Costa, McCrae, & Norris, 1981). This has been shown to be a fairly stable dimension of personality. Research has indicated that it is negatively related to life satisfaction in old age (Costa et al., 1981; Costa & McCrae, 1984). It is also associated with higher levels of hypochondriasis and generalized somatic complaints (Costa & McCrae, 1980, 1985). Such people seem ill-prepared to deal with daily life, much less with unexpected or major stressors. People high on neuroticism are more likely to view midlife as a crisis. They are more distressed at retirement; they find it frustrating and disappointing. They are also more prone to depression. These effects can be somewhat offset if the person is high in extraversion. Extraverts are more positively oriented in their emotional reactions and tend to find life exciting (Costa & McCrae, 1984). Of course, the best combination would be high on extraversion and low on neuroticism. Such people tend to really enjoy life well into old age.

One reason that personality affects coping abilities is because it affects social networks (Antonucci, 1985). As we have seen, establishing the reciprocal ties of a social network is a lifelong endeavor. Given that several personality traits related to social behavior, notably extraversion and neuroticism, appear to be stable (Costa & McCrae, 1984), it is not surprising that personality affects the size and depth of one's convoy. People who have been relatively isolated or guarded in social relationships are less likely to have established the informal networks that can provide help in times of crisis. If such people face a health crisis, they are much more likely to end up institutionalized. This is particularly true if they have never married or had children (Antonucci, 1985; Antonucci & Jackson, 1987).

Other personal resources will also play a role in how well an older person adapts to stress. As we saw in Chapter 12, finances are certainly an issue. People with better incomes are more likely to get appropriate medical help. They are more likely to live in adequate homes and eat adequate diets. They are less likely to get sick in the first place. Lower-class people may, however, have stronger family ties, which may partially offset this effect (Antonucci, 1985; Sanchez-Ayendez, 1989). But by and large the social networks of the lower class are smaller and less adequate than those of the middle class. Thus, lower-class people may report greater loneliness. They also have a greater need for formal social services (Antonucci, 1985).

Adaptation

It is possible that adaptive mechanisms break down so completely in old age that mental illness becomes an overwhelming problem. This possibility will be dealt with later in the chapter. Short of such a breakdown, there are at least two hypothesized declines in adaptive functioning. One is that people become more rigid with age (Erikson et al., 1986; McCrae, 1982). The stereotype is that the elderly are more "set in their ways," less able to change or compromise as the situation demands. This, supposedly, makes the elderly more difficult to deal with and less efficient in their choices.

The second decline hypothesis deals with defense mechanism use. Gutmann (1974) has argued that as men age, they become less mature in their use of ego defense mechanisms. They switch from active mastery styles of coping to more passive mechanisms. Later still they move into "magical mastery." The "magical" defense mechanisms involve wishing away problems instead of coping with them. In some sense, this is the ultimate passive response. Thus, old people are assumed to rely primarily on defense mechanisms like denial, projection, or withdrawal rather than sublimation or humor in coping with stress (Pfeiffer, 1977).

On the other hand, Valliant (1977) found that the use of more mature defense mechanisms actually increased during adulthood. However, his sample was quite select and was followed only into middle age (see Chapter 9). It is possible that deterioration begins later in life or would be more prominent in a more representative group. Nonetheless, we have already seen considerable personality data that indicate more stability than change in basic characteristics. This might lead us to predict no change in adaptive capability with age. In fact, if Erikson's or Valliant's position is correct, we might actually expect increasingly mature defense mechanism use as we age (McCrae, 1982).

Research directly addressing coping mechanisms in old age is somewhat limited. Cross-sectional data have generally indicated substantial stability (Costa & McCrae, 1984; Erikson et al., 1986; Kahana, 1982; McCrae, 1982). However, there has been some indication of improved coping, too. McCrae (1982) reported a decline in the use of wishful thinking and escapist fantasy in response to stress as people age. Data have also indicated that the elderly use less confrontational coping (Folkman et al., 1987; McCrae, 1989). Confrontation is often an ineffective coping technique (at least according to those who used it), so this too seems like an "improvement" (McCrae, 1989). On the other hand, the elderly in cross-sectional studies do seem to be more passive, and the declining use of confrontation is one indicator. So is their greater use of positive reappraisal and distancing as techniques (Folkman et al., 1987). It is not clear that this represents a decline in functioning. The elderly seem to have less control over the causes of their hassles. Their relative passivity may allow them to be more accepting of what cannot be changed, and they may therefore actually face less stress than do younger, more action-oriented adults (Folkman et al., 1987).

Aside from Valliant's (1977) data, there is little longitudinal data on coping mechanisms. A recent study by Robert McCrae (1989) using the Augmented Baltimore Longitudinal Study of Aging participants does report limited longitudinal data. McCrae was able to report cross-sectional, longitudinal, and sequential data on coping mechanisms. He concluded that there was very little age-related change in coping. Indeed, not one of the 31 coping mechanisms examined showed age-related changes in all five types of analysis he performed. Even in the cross-sectional data, age seems to account for only a small (< 5 percent) percentage of the individual differences in the use of defense mechanisms (McCrae, 1982). This, in combination with the longitudinal findings, suggests that personality patterns appear to be an important determinant of coping with the stresses of old age (McCrae, 1982; Kahana, 1982). Even problem behaviors among the elderly frequently predate old age. So, for example, about two-thirds of all elderly alcoholics had a drinking problem earlier in adulthood (Zimberg, 1987).

Certainly, personality dispositions will interact with the resources available from the environment (Kahana, 1982). Researchers are increasingly recognizing the importance of person-environment fit (Lawton, 1982, 1987) in determining adaptation. Matching privacy and socialization opportunities to levels of extroversion, for example, can help make a person's adjustment to a nursing home much easier.

Some Methodological Warnings: There are at least two major perspectives on age-related changes in coping. One is the contextual hypothesis. The other might generally be called the developmental perspective, although within this model some theorists call for improvements and others for decline. Distinguishing which model is more accurate in portraying age-related changes in coping (if there are any) is a challenging task. Both major stressors and hassles change with age. Hence, to make the comparisons most appropriate to the developmental model, we need to equate the stressors of different age groups. Several investigators have tried to do this (Folkman et al., 1987; McCrae, 1982), but this is not a completely satisfactory solution. After all, appraisal of the stressor is probably more important than the objective characteristics of the stressor, and events may have different meanings at different ages.

Similarly, true longitudinal data are hard to come by. Ideally, the measures are identical at the various times of measurement in a longitudinal study. But it is virtually impossible to replicate stressors and therefore demands on coping at two or more points in time (McCrae, 1989). Again, the researcher must try to equate disparate stressors in order to ascertain whether someone's coping style has changed.

MENTAL ILLNESS AND ITS TREATMENT

There are age-related trends in the types of mental disorders that bring people to treatment. Organic brain syndromes increase dramatically, especially after age 75. In fact, after 75, brain syndromes account for about 85 percent of all first admissions to psychiatric hospitals/wards (LaRue et al., 1985). Schizophrenia and mania, on the other hand, rarely begin after 40. Only about 10 percent of elderly schizophrenics first experienced symptoms after age 40. Those cases that do onset late in life virtually always include paranoid symptoms (LaRue et al., 1985; Post, 1987). Indeed, paranoid disorders appear to increase with age. This is so marked that one para-noid disorder, late-onset paraphrenia, is considered exclusively an old-age problem (LaRue et al., 1985; Post, 1987). Finally, depression appears to be a major problem among the elderly, although there is considerable debate as to its prevalence (Gaylord & Zung, 1987; LaRue et al., 1985). Overall, more than 10 percent of all Americans over 65 suffer cognitive or emo-tional impairment that needs professional treatment (LaRue et al., 1985). As is true at any point in the life span, not all those needing help get it.

Despite these age-related trends, there is little or no distinction be-tween old age and young adulthood in the Diagnostic and Statistical Man-ual of the American Psychiatric Association (DSM-IIIR; APA, 1987) except in terms of dementias. Thus, in the APA's estimation, the disorders suffered by the elderly are fundamentally the same ones experienced by younger adults. This too is an area of some debate (LaRue et al., 1985). The DSM-IIIR does, however, indicate that there may be differences in the symptoms most commonly exhibited by old and young adults suffering from some disorders, including depression.

Depression

Prevalence: Aside from organic brain syndromes, depression is prob-ably the most common mental health problem among the elderly. Indeed, some researchers have argued that the over-65 population is the most at risk for depression, though most put the peak in the 40–50 age group (Gay-lord & Zung, 1987; Phifer & Murrell, 1986). Perhaps 30 to 65 percent of community-dwelling elderly show at least some symptoms of depression (LaRue et al., 1985). Probably more than a third of older patients at ambula-tory care centers are clinically depressed. And about half of the acute psy-chiatric care admissions among the elderly are for depression. About half of these are first-time psychiatric hospital admissions. Overall, probably 2 to 6 percent of the elderly suffer from what DSM-IIIR terms "Major Depres-sion" (see Table 3–5) and a total of 10 to 15 percent benefit from some intervention for depressive symptoms (LaRue et al., 1985).

As is true throughout the life span, women tend to be more prone to develop depression (Holt & Datan, 1984; LaRue et al., 1985). There may be a reversal of this trend in very old age, however; after 80, men may be more likely to develop depression (LaRue et al., 1985). Elderly Hispanics appear to have higher rates of depression than either African-American or white elderly do (Santos, Hubbard, & McIntosh, 1983). The differences in depres-sion rates for African-American versus white elderly are unclear, with some studies showing higher rates among African-American while others indicate lower rates (Santos et al., 1983). However, information about rates in the African-American and Latino-American communities should be viewed with caution. It is possible that cultural differences concerning emotional expression may increase the likelihood that Hispanic but decrease the like-lihood that African-American elderly will be diagnosed as depressed (Mc-Gadney, Goldberg-Glen, & Pinkston, 1987; Santos et al., 1983).

Similarly, suicide rates among African-American elderly are only

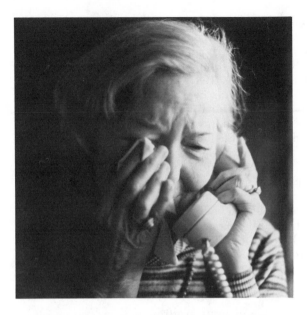

Depression and loneliness can be problems for the elderly, especially for those with serious infirmities.

about one-third of the white rate (McGadney et al., 1987). It is easy to attribute this to the resilience of the African-American elderly, who have survived so much hardship. While it is certainly true that African-Americans have had to be adaptable in order to survive, they can also experience difficulties in old age, including depression. Indeed, if one considers more "indirect" forms of self-destruction, such as alcoholism, drug abuse, and self-imposed isolation, it is evident that many older African-American people are unhappy and suffering the effects of deprivation (McGadney et al., 1987). Furthermore, suicide rates among very old "nonwhite" (the Census Bureau category) men may be higher than for other groups (Manton et al., 1987).

Suicide rates vary considerably from culture to culture (see Table 14–3). Cross-cultural statistics indicate that suicide does tend to be more common among the elderly, especially the very old. Those above age 85 may be at particular risk, at least in the United States (Manton et al., 1987). This suggests that old age may generally be a risk period for depression. However, this trend is not universal; ageism plays a big role in the hopelessness of many elderly.

Symptoms and Diagnosis: The same diagnostic criteria used with young adults are applied to older adults (see Table 3–5). Research to date has supported using the same criteria. The elderly may display apathy rather than highly emotional behaviors more frequently than young adults

TABLE 14-3:   Suicide Rates (per 100,000 population) in Selected Countries

Sex and Age	Australia (1984)	Canada (1984)	Denmark (1984)	Japan (1985)	Poland (1984)	Sweden (1984)	West Germany (1985)	United States (1985)
Male								
15–24	18.8	26.9	16.1	13.0	18.2	16.4	19.8	21.4
25–34	23.9	27.8	37.7	23.4	36.3	36.5	29.5	24.5
35–44	20.1	25.3	53.2	30.5	37.0	36.5	31.8	22.3
45–54	22.7	28.6	57.1	49.6	39.0	42.2	40.3	23.5
55–64	24.3	28.8	65.5	41.4	31.2	30.5	36.2	26.8
65–74	24.7	25.1	48.8	42.6	29.1	37.9	50.2	33.3
75+	30.4	33.0	67.3	74.8	29.7	47.5	79.4	54.3
Female								
15–24	4.4	4.3	4.1	5.9	3.8	6.2	5.3	4.4
25–34	6.5	7.0	12.9	9.8	5.7	15.3	8.9	5.9
35–44	6.7	9.2	28.3	11.9	6.6	15.3	8.9	7.1
45–54	10.6	10.5	41.1	17.3	8.3	20.1	16.5	8.3
55–64	8.2	10.7	38.1	18.6	8.0	15.0	18.3	7.7
65–74	6.5	8.4	37.7	29.7	7.5	17.9	24.7	6.9
75+	5.7	5.8	32.2	54.3	6.4	11.7	24.6	5.7

Source: *Statistical Abstract of the United States, 1988,* pp. 803 and 78. Washington, D.C.: Government Printing Office.

do. But, in general, depression appears to be displayed quite similarly across the adult years (Gaylord & Zung, 1987; LaRue et al., 1985).

There are two major problems involved in diagnosing depression among the elderly. First, some of the commonly employed diagnostic instruments have not been validated with older adults (Gaylord & Zung, 1987). This can create a problem in gathering prevalence data, though it is probably less central in making an individual clinical assessment. Problems arise because many of the scales focus heavily on physical symptoms. This is reasonable because, even among the elderly, depressed people will report a variety of nonspecific physical problems. Nonetheless, older people also report more physical symptoms generally than young adults do. For example, Leon et al. (1979) believed that the age differences they found in the MMPI Depression subscale were primarily attributable to real physical or health problem differences, not to shifts in depressive symptomology.

On an individual assessment level, the more crucial problem is differentiating depression from the early stages of dementia. Both groups may complain of memory losses and other cognitive impairment. Both groups may be apathetic and have low energy, or may show depressed affect (Rubin & Kinscherf, 1989). Indeed, depression in older adults can so resemble the early stages of OBS that some clinicians have proposed the diagnostic category of "depressive pseudodementia." Unfortunately, this category is so poorly defined that it is impossible to say whether it really is a unique form of depression (LaRue et al., 1985). It is probably more useful as a descriptive than a diagnostic category (Teri & Riefler, 1987). On the other hand, it does underscore how difficult it can be to distinguish depression and early dementia.

The problem is compounded by the fact that some elderly people are suffering from both depression and dementia (Teri & Reifler, 1987). Perhaps 20 to 30 percent of all dementia victims are also suffering depression. This translates to roughly 1 to 4 percent of the general elderly population. Depression is particularly likely to accompany the early stages of dementia, when the victim is still aware of declining cognitive abilities. The presence of depression will exacerbate the dementia symptoms. Thus, relieving the depression will often reduce the cognitive impairment, at least temporarily (Teri & Reifler, 1987).

One way to ascertain whether an individual is suffering from dementia or depression is to see what happens with treatment. Depression, of course, will respond to certain drug therapies, whereas dementia will not. When in doubt, many clinicians will follow this route. However, it is not without its risks. Many of the drugs commonly prescribed for depression may produce side effects that can increase the likelihood of injury or illness. Therefore, it is always preferable to be able to distinguish between dementia and depression (LaRue et al., 1985).

There is some evidence that depressed elderly will respond differently to standardized testing than dementia patients will. The depressed will still use organizational and semantic properties in encoding or retrieving an event (LaRue et al., 1985). They may perform markedly better on a task where categories are used to organize a list than on a random word list memory task. The OBS victim would perform similarly on both tasks. The depressed may also be more cautious in their approach to the testing, frequently making errors of omission, whereas the demented will make more random errors (LaRue et al., 1985). The depressed are also likely to underestimate their cognitive abilities. Their reports of memory loss, etc., are not borne out by the testing. OBS patients' tests, on the other hand, tend to show at least the level of decline they (or their families) report (LaRue et al., 1985; Teri & Riefler, 1987). Finally, the depressed are more likely to be concerned about, and even preoccupied with, negative feedback from the tester. However, all these differences have been documented only in post hoc evaluations. In other words, they are demonstrated by people who are already known to be demented not depressed (LaRue et al., 1985).

Etiology: Beginning with Freud, theorists have often argued that loss is a major factor in the development of depression (Gaylord & Zung, 1987; Holt & Datan, 1984). The loss could be real or imagined, but it needs to constitute some threat to sense of self. Certainly the elderly routinely experience substantial real and self-threatening loss (Erikson et al., 1986; Holt & Datan, 1984). They may lose their homes and familiar surroundings through relocation. Group status may be lost through retirement. Retirement also threatens financial well-being so that a particular standard of living may be lost. Health declines may force someone to limit or abandon hobbies or activities. Illness may even require them to give up favorite foods. And of course there is bereavement. Friends and family members die. It is common for old people to lose their spouses, the loss that is generally considered the most stressful experience most people endure (Holt & Datan, 1984; Gaylord & Zung, 1987; Holmes & Rahe, 1967). If loss truly is instrumental in depression, it would not be surprising to find high levels of the disorder among the elderly.

Yet the data show fairly weak relationships between these forms of losses and clinical depression (LaRue et al., 1985). Retirement is not correlated with depression. Bereavement does not appear to be strongly related. There is a period of normal mourning, but this is distinguishable from clinical depression (DSM-IIIR calls it uncomplicated bereavement). The link between relocation and depression is unclear, partially because there can be many reasons for relocation (LaRue et al., 1985). Furthermore, the match between the person's new environment and needs can vary considerably and may also influence depressive reactions (Lawton, 1987). The data on retirement, relocation, and bereavement in the elderly are consistent with the more general finding that major life events seem to be of relatively little importance in the onset of depression (Phifer & Murrell, 1986). There will be individual differences in adjustment, however. So, for example, retirement will be more traumatic for people who do not have pension plans or savings (McGadney et al., 1987).

On the other hand, health and social support do appear to play a role. Loss of friends or family members would not usually, in and of itself, trigger severe depression (LaRue et al., 1985). However, if the person's main or sole confidante was lost, depression might follow (Antonucci & Jackson, 1987). Loss of friends may be associated with milder forms of depression (LaRue et al., 1985). Furthermore, social support does seem to be important in mediating the effects of other influences. For example, strong social support can reduce the negative effects of health problems (Phifer & Murrell, 1986).

Health seems to be a particularly strong factor in the development of depression (LaRue et al., 1985; Phifer & Murrell, 1986). The detrimental effects of poor health are evident both in studies of life satisfaction and in studies of depression. Research indicates that health is more important than social support in determining emotional well-being among the very old (Bowling & Browne, 1991). Certain illnesses seem particularly likely to trigger depression: cerebral cancers, tuberculosis, congestive heart failure, thyroid disorders, various forms of anemia, Parkinson's disease, Huntington's disease, and diabetes (LaRue et al., 1985).

We need to be cautious in assuming that all physical problems cause depression. It is likely that some complaints are rooted in the depression (LaRue et al., 1985; Rozzini et al., 1988). Indeed, a cycle of depression and illness may develop in some individuals. Furthermore, various prescription drugs may have side effects that mimic depression. Thus, a depressive episode that seems attributable to an illness may actually be caused by the drug treatment (see Chapter 12).

Other biological factors may also play a role in depression among the elderly. Central nervous system dysfunctions have been linked to certain types of depression. And there are CNS changes with aging. This has led some to hypothesize that the age-related CNS shifts, especially in neurotransmitters, may cause depression (LaRue et al., 1985; Phifer & Murrell, 1986). Currently, there is no empirical evidence that this is the case. Genetics also seems important in some cases of depression. However, the influence of genetics seems to be greater in early onset (before age 50) than late onset cases (Gaylord & Zung, 1987).

Treatment: Depression in the elderly is quite amenable to treatment. All forms of treatment for depression that work with young adults also appear to work with the elderly. This includes electroconvulsive therapy (ECT), colloquially known as shock treatment. There is no known upper age limit for ECT. Most of the drug treatments are useful at all ages (Gaylord & Zung, 1987). However, as we noted in Chapter 12, the body's ability to metabolize drugs changes with age. Therefore, precautions are needed in prescribing any drug, but particularly psychoactive drugs, to the elderly. Furthermore, the elderly will typically be taking medications for other health problems. Drug interaction effects are a real threat, so careful monitoring is necessary.

Virtually all of the various forms of group and individual therapy developed to treat depression can be successful with a motivated elderly client (Gaylord & Zung, 1987). Among these are insight therapy, group supportive therapy, cognitive therapy, and behavioral therapy.

Paranoid Disorders

In ancient Greek law, the term *paranoia* referred to the mental disturbance that frequently developed in old men. The deterioration was so great that sons were permitted to take over their father's affairs once paranoia set in. Although the term is no longer age-associated by definition, it remains true that paranoid behavior is particularly common among the elderly (LaRue et al., 1985; Post, 1987).

Prevalence: There are problems with classification categories for paranoid disorders (LaRue et al., 1985). And paranoid symptoms often accompany other disorders (Post, 1987). This makes it difficult to estimate the prevalence of paranoid symptomology and disorders among the elderly. Nonetheless, it is generally acknowledged that symptoms are common, and full-blown disorders are more frequent among the elderly than among young adults (LaRue et al., 1985; Post, 1987). Furthermore, the disorders are more common among elderly women than men.

Post (1987) has identified three forms of paranoid disorders occurring in people over 60: simple paranoid symptom patterns, schizophreniform pictures, and paranoid schizophrenic states. Their central features are described in Table 14–4. Generally, they are similar to the paranoid symptoms that might occur at any age. In fact, paranoid schizophrenic states are virtually identical at all ages and typically begin prior to old age. Probably 90 percent of schizophrenics first exhibit symptoms during early or middle adulthood (LaRue et al., 1985). The delusions that occur in young adults, however, tend to be more varied than those seen in the elderly. The elderly's

TABLE 14-4: Types of Paranoid Disorders

Type	Major Symptoms
Simple paranoid symptom patterns	One or two symptoms usually present. Domestically-oriented delusions or hallucinations. Often the family can handle the victim.
Schizophreniform pictures	Pervasive symptoms. Agitated, aggressive, distressed, makes accusations; often looks disheveled. Multifaceted delusions and hallucinations.
Paranoid schizophrenic states	Symptoms leading to diagnosis of schizophrenia. Paranoid delusions/hallucinations.

Source: Based on Post, F. (1987). Paranoid and schizophrenic disorders among the aging. In L. Carstensen & B. Edelstein (eds.), *Handbook of clinical gerontology.* New York: Pergamon.

delusions are nearly always persecutory in nature and usually center on the domestic situation. One woman might suspect, for example, that noxious substances are being pumped into her home; another might think that relatives are conspiring to take her house from her because they are jealous (Post, 1987).

In addition to these syndromes, paranoid symptoms may also appear in conjunction with other psychiatric disorders (Post, 1987). They frequently accompany both acute and chronic organic brain syndromes. They are particularly common in the early stages of Alzheimer's disease (see Chapter 12). This is understandable. At least in the early stages of the disease, the Alzheimer's victim seeks an explanation for memory failures. What happened to his keys? How could he have forgotten that doctor's appointment? One answer is that others are out to make him look bad or are somehow responsible. His wife took the keys and hid them. She changed the doctor's appointment without telling him. She wants to control everything. To some extent, the Alzheimer patient's delusions will gradually come true. As the disease worsens, loved ones may hide keys (so the victim won't drive off and get lost) or in other ways try to limit his activities. This, however, is not the basis of the paranoid fears. In fact, as the disease worsens and the family exercises more control, the paranoid elements of the person's behavior will gradually lessen.

Paranoid behaviors may also accompany severe depression (Post, 1987). This is especially likely if the victim is a rigid or suspicious person to begin with. Usually any paranoid symptoms that do occur are clearly secondary to the depressive mood.

Senile seclusion is a rare problem that also has paranoid components (Post, 1987). This condition probably occurs in less than 0.5 persons per 1000 over 60 years old. Yet cases will frequently make headlines. These people are typically found dead or dying in terrible living conditions, in places infested with vermin and with inadequate food, heat, and clothing. As far as others in the neighborhood know, they have no friends, no family,

no social contacts of any sort. Investigation often turns up not only a middle class or above family, but also substantial personal savings. For some
reason, these people want so much to be isolated from others that they
establish this bizarre, self-destructive, reclusive life style. The behavior does
not emerge in old age; rather, it is a culmination of a lifelong tendency to
mistrust others and fear social interactions.

Finally, there is a disorder known as senile paraphrenia, which appears to be related to schizophrenia (LaRue et al., 1985; Post, 1987). Indeed,
it may be a late-appearing form of schizophrenia and may affect as many
as 2 percent of the elderly, although it has not been formally recognized as
a diagnostic category by the American Psychiatric Association (LaRue et al.,
1985; Post, 1987). Victims of the disorder have serious, chronic paranoid
delusions, but do not exhibit the severe thought deterioration typical of
schizophrenia. In other words, they maintain better contact with reality
than would be expected with schizophrenia. Their paranoid delusions, however, are sufficiently damaging to keep many of them permanently hospitalized (Post, 1987).

Etiology: Paranoid behavior rarely appears in people under 30 and
becomes increasingly common after 40 (Post, 1987). This age pattern has
led to the suggestion that aging may "cause" paranoid symptoms. What
component of aging might be implicated is unclear; perhaps CNS or sensory changes contribute. Or perhaps the entrenchment and exacerbation
of early personality characteristics is the key. Some young adults who seem
to have difficulty trusting others and establishing social relationships may
eventually exhibit full-blown paranoid symptoms. Or maybe some of the
changes that commonly accompany aging—relocation, retirement, bereavement—result in social isolation that contributes to paranoid reactions
(Post, 1987).

Probably 70 to 90 percent of the late paraphrenics demonstrated earlier personality problems (Post, 1987). The problems typically were not severe enough to require hospitalization. In fact, these people often have stable work histories. They do not usually show prior delinquency, neurosis,
or alcoholism. But other people have always found them difficult. Their
interpersonal inadequacies may take several forms. Some are jealous and
suspicious; others are quarrelsome and hostile; still others are shy and withdrawn. The common thread is that they all have characteristics that tend to
limit social contact and drive others away. One can imagine a cycle in which
these people become increasingly isolated and suspicious of others.

Chronic deafness is also associated with paranoid behaviors. This is
not the deafness that typically begins in old age; it is longstanding conduction deafness. These people have relatively few personality problems prior
to their paranoid symptoms. It seems plausible that the social isolation accompanying the handicap contributes to personality changes (feelings of
persecution) that culminate in paranoid thought patterns (Post, 1987).

In keeping with their basis in longstanding characteristics, paranoid
syndromes and behaviors usually show a gradual onset. People begin with
some mistrust and a few accusations and eventually demonstrate elaborate,

pervasive delusional thought. If the onset is very sudden, so that the personality change seems abrupt and dramatic, organic brain syndrome should be suspected (Post, 1987).

Treatment: Inasmuch as a paranoid symptom is a result of another problem, treatment of the primary problem will relieve the paranoid behaviors (Post, 1987). In the cases of acute OBS, removal of the toxin will stop the paranoid behavior. Relieving depression will end the paranoid behaviors associated with it. The exception to this, of course, is dementia. Dementia cannot be effectively treated. As degeneration progresses, paranoid symptoms will automatically abate.

In cases where the paranoid behaviors are the primary problem, relocation will often result in a spontaneous and permanent remission of the problem (Post, 1987). This is only true, however, for those exhibiting simple paranoid symptom patterns and schizophreniform patterns. If schizophrenia is present, relocation will not work. Since paraphrenia seems to be related to schizophrenia, simple relocation will also fail. In fact, in tracking over 90 late-onset paraphrenics, Post (1987) reports only once case of spontaneous remission.

In cases where relocation is not sufficient, major tranquilizers and antipsychotics are the treatments of choice (Post, 1987). Over 90 percent of all cases can be helped, at least to some degree, by these drugs. However, treatment will only be successful on a long-term basis if the drug therapy is continued uninterrupted. Drug treatment with paranoids is extremely difficult. Their mistrust and suspiciousness makes them unlikely to comply with prescriptions. This may be one reason why the prognosis is slightly better for people who are married or who have some close relationships (Post, 1987). Their social network may help ensure compliance with the drug therapy.

SPECIAL PROBLEMS OF THERAPY WITH THE ELDERLY

There is little reason to believe that the elderly cannot benefit from most available forms of psychological therapy (Gatz, Popkin, Pino, & VandenBos, 1985; Klerman, 1983; McGadney et al., 1987). It is a myth that they are "too set in their ways" or "too far gone" to benefit from anything other than drug intervention. Nevertheless, drug therapy is disproportionately used in treating mentally ill elderly, and "talking" therapies are underutilized (Gatz et al., 1985; Klerman, 1983).

The elderly are also less likely to receive any kind of treatment. Gatz and her colleagues (1985) estimated that less than 3 percent of all clinical psychological services are delivered to the elderly, though they constitute 11.3 percent of the general population. Poor and minority elderly are even less likely to receive treatment (McGadney et al., 1987). Older adults are also more likely to drop out of therapy prematurely (Gatz et al., 1985; Klerman, 1983). Again, this is even more true of minority elderly (McGadney et al., 1987; Santos et al., 1983).

There are many reasons why the elderly do not receive more adequate mental health care, and they range from ageism among therapists to payment difficulties. Gatz et al. (1985) have suggested the problems fall into three categories: client, therapist, and system variables.

Problems in Obtaining Care

Client Variables: People, including therapists, routinely believe that the elderly simply do not want to visit psychologists (Gatz et al., 1985). They think the elderly are superstitious about mental illness; or that they find it shameful to admit mental problems; or that they are suspicious about the effectiveness of treatment. The elderly are also viewed as wanting to maintain their independence and self-reliance at all costs. Certainly there are elderly people who hold these beliefs. There are many young adults who think the same way. This is probably a major reason why only a fraction of all adults who could benefit from treatment receive it. The difference between these attitudes in the elderly and young adults is how they are perceived by social service and mental health workers. When a younger adult is involved, professionals are likely to try to overcome the resistance; with older adults, the resistance is seen as an explanation for failed treatment (Gatz et al., 1985).

There is also the issue of the age difference between therapist and client (Gatz et al., 1985; McGadney et al., 1987). It certainly would not be surprising to find that the elderly did not have much confidence in young therapists. However, this does not actually seem to be much of a problem as long as the therapist respects the elderly client. The therapist should not, for example, presume to call the client by his or her first name. Little signs of respect like these may be particularly important in working with cultures in which the elderly are held in high esteem, including both the African-American and Hispanic subcultures (McGadney et al., 1987; Santos et al., 1983).

Therapist Variables: It is clear that the medical profession generally is not enthusiastic about treating elderly clients. This is repeatedly reflected in surveys of both students and practitioners (Kuhn, 1987). The mental health profession is also less than enthusiastic about working with old people. Practitioners think it is not the optimum use of their time or the resources of the mental health system generally (Gatz et al., 1985). It would make more sense, some of them argue, to spend their time treating younger patients who have more of a future and have more to give to society.

In the same vein, therapists often think that the likelihood of successfully counseling an older person is slim. This idea probably finds its roots in Freudian psychoanalysis (McGadney et al., 1987). Freud argued that people became less able to change as they aged. As we have already seen, this does not seem to be the case. But it is still a widely held myth, even among psychologists.

Clinicians do not routinely receive training in gerontology. They may therefore harbor misconceptions about the aged (Gatz et al., 1985). Perhaps they believe that withdrawal is a normal part of aging rather than a potential symptom of depression. Or perhaps they think that most behavioral problems in old age stem from "senility."

Probably the most dangerous myth, however, is that old people are incapable of benefitting from therapy. They are viewed as rigid; as lacking the verbal and intellectual skills necessary to participate in some forms of therapy; as not having the educational and cultural background that bodes well for therapy (Gatz et al., 1985; McGadney et al., 1987). Such myths tend to be even more entrenched when the client is poor or a member of a minority group. These attitudes may prevent a therapist from taking on gerontological cases or from handling them successfully.

Mental Health System Variables: Pragmatic concerns keep some elderly people out of the mental health system. There is no doubt that psychological services are expensive. Many elderly people simply cannot afford to pay for them (Gatz et al., 1985; McGadney et al., 1987). And many health insurance programs, including Medicare, have large deductibles or low ceilings on how much care they will cover (especially on an outpatient basis). Again, the poor are particularly affected. In fact, insurance structures may be part of the reason why African-American elderly are overrepresented in institutional settings but underrepresented in outpatient and community mental health facilities (McGadney et al., 1987). Furthermore, travel to the psychologist's office may be difficult and expensive. For some, it will be impossible.

Referral systems may also be less than adequate (Gatz et al., 1985; McGadney et al., 1987). Physicians, for example, seem less apt to refer older adults for psychiatric treatment. Again, minority people may be especially unlikely to receive appropriate referrals. Furthermore, many people have never used the mental health system and so are unaware of what services might be available. They need someone to guide them through the system and help them take full advantage of it.

Toward a More Effective System

First and foremost there is a need to educate mental health professionals. There should be a gerontological component in their education that emphasizes the needs and abilities of the elderly. The prejudices commonly found among therapists need to be directly challenged and overcome.

Those therapists working with minority people face additional concerns. They need to learn about, and develop respect for, the culture of the people with whom they are working (McGadney et al., 1987; Santos et al., 1983). Bilingual therapists must become more available. Therapists also need to understand what the family means and how it operates in the Latino-American and African-American communities. Of course, there is no such thing as one African-American or Hispanic "family." But particularly among poor African-Americans and Latino-Americans certain traditional patterns are evident. Multigenerational households are more common. Extended families, including people not related by blood, are also more common. These families can be a substantial source of help and support to the person. And the therapist should be prepared to work with the family.

There is also a need for more available, better integrated systems (McGadney et al., 1987). These might include assigning aides to escort the elderly through the social service system, coordinating physical and mental health care, making transportation available, or bringing some of the services to the elderly. For example, many poor elderly African-Americans are active in their churches. And traditionally black churches have provided many of the services the white government has failed to provide. These include day help, running errands, hot meals, and even financial assistance. The knowledgeable therapist can work with church groups to ensure appropriate care for clients.

SUMMARY

The history of theorizing about personality and aging is dramatically different from that of other behavioral realms. From the beginning, personality theorists typically hypothesized either growth or stability. Yet there was always room for the pessimists, who considered old age to be a time of unparalleled loss and unequaled depression and withdrawal.

The research clearly indicates that much of what we see in old age was begun and established in early and middle adulthood. This is true of several personality characteristics, including neuroticism, openness, and extraversion. It is true of self-definitions and self-esteem. It is true of activity and social interaction patterns. It is true of alcohol abuse, schizophrenia, and often of depression.

On the other hand, old age can be stressful. Losses are many; new and interesting challenges are fewer. Health losses, in particular, seem to take a heavy toll. They can undermine ability to control daily life and perform daily activities. They can make it difficult to get out and socialize. They can cause pain. They can raise fears about death.

Social support networks may shrink as friends and relatives die or as the person relocates. The loss of social support may exacerbate the effects of other losses. Conversely, a strong social network can lessen the negative effects, and may even help to prevent depression. Family members, particularly children, are especially effective as supporters.

Most elderly people have adequate support networks. In fact, they are more satisfied with their networks than young adults are. The elderly also do not typically feel buffeted by stressors; most are quite happy and satisfied with their lives. They feel they have grown, are more tolerant and understanding than they used to be, are wiser and more accepting. They look forward to the future, though they know their time is drawing to a close. They have achieved what Erikson calls integrity.

Not all elderly fare this well. At any stage of the life span, there are people who experience serious emotional and behavioral problems. Aside from organic brain syndrome, the most common disorders facing the elderly are depression and paranoid behaviors. Depression is readily treat-able in most cases. Paranoid behaviors, however, are often more difficult and may require long-term hospitalization.

Stability has been the dominant theme of this chapter. We have already seen that this stability extends to social networks. Let us now see if it is reflected in family and social relationships.

15 Family and Social Relationships

We have many stereotypes of family relationships during old age. We believe, for example, that most of the elderly are no longer married, usually because of widowhood. We picture them as living alone or with one of their children. Think of the number of elderly who live with their children in television shows, especially situation comedies. The older person may be portrayed as a fount of wisdom on these shows—or, more likely, as a meddlesome but lovable nuisance.

Our image of the elderly who live alone is even worse. We picture them as isolated, neglected by families and without friends. Multiple infirmities keep them from getting around, so they rely on others to visit them. But their families are too busy to take care of them or even to visit. Of course, it used to be different, before so many women went to work. Then at least daughters had time to call or stop by. But now there is no one.

If you simply review the preceding three chapters, you should start to question these images of the elderly. We have seen that most elderly people are not seriously incapacitated, mentally or physically. They are certainly able to get out of their homes and to participate in social life. Most of them, in fact, seem to have broad social support networks. Add to this the fact that many of them are comfortable financially, and you start to get a more accurate picture of what their lives are probably like. Again, however, we must acknowledge that there are wide individual differences in living needs and situations.

LIVING ARRANGEMENTS

There is always a relationship between home and family. Indeed, for most of us, family is part of our definition of home. Home and family are even more intertwined for the elderly. Widowhood, physical or mental declines, and geographical mobility can all affect both family relationships and living arrangements. Furthermore, family relationships can determine living arrangements. For example, never-married elderly are more likely to end up in nursing or residential care homes (Mor, Sherwood, & Gutkin, 1986). On the other hand, the burden of caring for an ill or disabled older person may strain a spousal or parent-child relationship (Brody, Kleban, Johnsen, Hoffman, & Schoonover, 1987; Moritz, Kasl, & Berkman, 1989; Noelker & Bass, 1989; Quayhagen & Quayhagen, 1988).

Demographics

The common stereotypes of living arrangements among older Americans are of the elderly widow living with her children or the senile resident of the nursing home. Neither one of these describes most (or even many) oldsters' living situation. As Table 15–1 indicates, most elderly people live with their spouses in their own houses or apartments. This is particularly true of the young-old and of men. Even those with no spouse, are more likely to live alone than with someone else (see Table 15–2). With increasing age and infirmity, however, it is more common for people to live with their children. Disabled widows are especially likely to live with their children, particularly their daughters (Spitze & Logan, 1989).

Throughout the twentieth century, the percentage of elderly people living with their children has decreased dramatically, from more than 60 percent to less than 15 percent, (Aizenberg & Treas, 1985). Similarly, the percentage of people over 65 who live by themselves has increased sharply. This should not, however, be interpreted as evidence of the erosion of the American family. First, it has always been the case that the children tend to live in the elder's home rather than the parent moving in with the children. This is still true today (see Chapter 6). As more people live to be older, it becomes more acceptable and easier for them not to live with their children. Widowhood does not occur as early as it once did. And there are more social services than there used to be. Changes in government policy (especially Social Security and Medicare) have improved the economic lot

TABLE 15–1: Percentage of Elderly in Various Living Arrangements by Age and Gender

Age		Living Alone	Living with Nonrelative	Living with Spouse	Living with Other Relative
65–69	M	12.6%	0.9%	82.0%	4.6%
	F	31.4	0.8	55.0	12.8
70–74	M	14.3	1.0	78.1	6.7
	F	40.3	1.3	42.1	16.3
75+	M	20.2	0.8	69.2	9.9
	F	53.0	1.8	22.5	22.7

Source: Spitze, G., & Logan, J. (1989). Gender differences in family support: Is there a payoff? *The Gerontologist, 29*(1), 108–113. © The Gerontological Society of America.

TABLE 15-2:   Percentage of Unmarried Elderly in Various Living Arrangements by Age and Gender

Age		Living Alone	Living with Nonrelative	Living with Other Relative
65–69	M	70.0%	4.4%	25.6%
	F	70.0	1.8	28.4
70–74	M	65.3	4.6	30.6
	F	69.6	2.2	28.2
75+	M	65.6	2.6	32.1
	F	68.4	2.3	29.3

Based on a national sample (N = 4884)

Source: Spitze, G, & Logan, J. (1989). Gender differences in family support: Is there a payoff? *The Gerontologist, 29*(1), 108–113. © The Gerontological Society of America.

of the elderly so that more of them can afford to live alone (Aizenberg & Treas, 1985).

Women, as a group, outlive men (see Chapter 1). Therefore, more of them are widowed in old age. About half of all women over 65 are widows, compared, to about 14 percent of older men (Aizenberg & Treas, 1985). This difference is not exclusively attributable to longevity. As was true post-divorce (see Chapter 6), widowed men are more likely to remarry than are widowed women—about five times more likely (Aizenberg & Treas, 1985). To some extent, this simply reflects the greater availability of potential partners for men. After 65, there are about 68 men for every 100 women, and after 85 there are more than twice as many women as men. Furthermore, it is more acceptable for men to marry younger women (thereby increasing their pool of potential spouses even further) than it is for women to marry younger men (Aizenberg & Treas, 1985).

Over 80 percent of older people have living children. About 10 percent of these "children" are over 65 themselves, a statistic which has important implications for the ability of children to care for aging parents (Giordano & Beckman, 1985; Mor et al., 1986). Grandparenthood is also a typical family role; over 90 percent of those with surviving children having grandchildren; nearly half are great-grandparents (Giordano & Beckman, 1985).

About 5 percent (or 1 million) of today's elderly have never married (Rubinstein, 1987). However, this does not mean that they are without family or that they have always lived alone. Indeed, many of them never married because of family obligations; they supported or cared for parents or siblings instead (Allen & Pickett, 1987; Rubenstein, 1987). Many have nieces, nephews, cousins, or siblings to whom they can turn for family interaction and support. Furthermore, although they are more at risk for institutionalization due to lack of available family care, the majority of them live independently in the community.

The Meaning of Home

There is little doubt that older people prefer to live in their own houses or apartments, even if this means living alone. They do not want to move in with children or grandchildren. In fact, the elderly are more likely to say such intergenerational housing is inappropriate than their children or grandchildren are. The elderly are likely to give only conditional support to the idea that they should live with their children. In other words, they want to (and, in fact, to some extent expect to) live with their children if they become ill or disabled, but not before. Younger adults, especially those under 30, are more likely to give unconditional support to the concept of intergenerational living arrangement. This is yet more evidence that the willingness of American families to help each other is not declining. The percentage of people of all ages endorsing intergenerational households has actually *increased* since the early 1970s (Okaraku, 1987).

Why do the elderly want to maintain their own homes, even if it means living alone? First, home can fill both utilitarian and emotional needs for a person (R. Patterson, 1987; Rubenstein, 1989). They may, for example, be able to arrange the physical layout of the home to suit their personal tastes and needs. Take the case of a 68-year-old man who was a double amputee. He lived only on the first floor of his house because he needed a wheelchair to get around. Although he had lots of possessions, he tended not to keep them in a very organized or particular order. There was an exception to his messiness, however. A central corridor—a passage for his wheelchair—ran through the clutter. In fact, everything appeared to be arranged around the passage (Rubenstein, 1989).

As a person loses mobility, it is not unusual to set up a "control center" in the home. The "center" might consist of a comfortable chair, snacks, view of a television, reading or writing materials, a telephone, medications, and any other objects needed to make it through a normal day. This arrangement limits the number of times the person has to get up and down and also decreases the likelihood of forgetting or losing something important (R. Patterson, 1987; Rubenstein, 1989). These idiosyncratic arrangements can be difficult to establish in someone else's home.

A home also may hold special meaning for people. Perhaps they raised a family in that house. There may be repairs or improvements of which they are proud. They may be strongly attached to the house. Mrs. Stein, a 76-year-old widow who lived most of her years (as both a child and an adult) in the same house, provides a dramatic example of such attachment:

> It's a crazy thing to say, but I love it here. I love the feel of the house. I love being in it. And, I think if I had to be put away somewhere . . . I think I'd want to die . . . I feel all the presences of all the things that ever happened to me. . . . A lot of things have happened in my lifetime and . . . I did my own praying . . . in my home. Maybe that's what makes my home so close to me. I feel all my thoughts and all prayers and all my wishes and all my trials and tribulations were settled right here in this house. (Rubenstein, 1989, p. S50)

The most typical living situation for elderly Americans is with their spouse in their own home where they enjoy doing things like tending a garden together.

Older people also want to avoid being a burden to their children. They do not wish to invade their children's privacy or interfere with their daily lives or put them into financial difficulties (Blieszner & Mancini, 1987; Brody, Johnsen, & Fulcomer, 1984). They want to ask their children for help only if they absolutely need it. Married elders, especially, are reluctant to ask too much of their children; they expect that most of their needs will be fulfilled by spouses (Blieszner & Mancini, 1987; Spitze & Logan, 1989).

Living Alone

Living alone is not always easy for an older person. It may be difficult for them to clean their homes, get groceries, keep medical appointments, maintain good financial records, and perform other activities necessary for daily living. Yet at least for now, it is important that so many elderly do live in their own homes. There is not enough space in nursing homes, residential care homes, or public housing for the elderly, or any other form of specialized residence to accommodate them. Thus, the question of what enables the elderly to live alone in the community has important social policy implications.

Health is probably the single greatest determinant of whether people can live alone (Soldo, Sharma, & Campbell, 1984; Stone, Cafferata, & Sangl, 1987). People who are healthy enough to get around (at least within their own homes) and perform daily activities (such as meal preparation and self-care) are much more likely to live alone than those who need assistance with basic routines. For example, in one study, women who did not need much help with such activities were more than seven times more likely to live alone than those who needed considerable aid (Soldo et al., 1984). Even among women who do live alone, those who are in poor health receive more informal assistance from their families (Spitze & Logan, 1989). Poor health even affects expectations concerning family help; people of all ages believe it is more appropriate to give help (including intergenerational residence) when an elderly person's health is failing (Brody et al., 1984). Indeed, middle-aged and younger adults may expect that parents will need help as their health fails. This expectation may actually reduce some of the stress we would expect to accompany caring for a frail parent (Deimling & Bass, 1986).

Large-scale surveys consistently indicate that the vast majority of people over 65—perhaps 80 percent or more—do not need significant help in performing daily activities (Soldo et al., 1984; Spitze & Logan, 1989). Even when help is needed, it is often of a low enough level to be provided by children who "visit" rather than reside with the elder (Matthews, Werkner, & Delaney, 1989; Soldo et al., 1984; Stone et al., 1987).

Certain groups of elderly are more likely than others to suffer from poor health. These include women and the very old (Soldo et al., 1984; Spitze & Logan, 1989). Age itself, independent of health status, predicts whether or not people live at home (Soldo et al., 1984). This may be because families become more worried and more protective as people age. On the other hand, although research sometimes seems to suggest that women are at risk for living alone, this effect is mainly due to gender differences in marital status, health, and finances. All things being equal, women are no more likely to live alone than men (Spitze & Logan, 1989).

Income also affects whether or not elderly people live alone (Krivo & Mutchler, 1989; Soldo et al., 1984). Poorer people are more likely to live with relatives in their old age. This is especially true if available social services are limited (Krivo & Mutchler, 1989). Minority elderly people are also less likely to live alone, partly due to the greater likelihood that they will have relatively low incomes. However, income differentials do not fully explain why minority elderly people are more likely to live with relatives. Apparently, cultural and familial norms also contribute (Krivo & Mutchler, 1989).

Income is not the only financial factor affecting living alone. Many elderly own their homes free and clear. Such people are more likely to be able to afford to live alone, even on a modest income (Krivo & Mutchler, 1989). Children's income can also play a part. If the middle-aged children have sufficient resources to contribute regularly to their parent's resources, the parent may be able to continue to live independently (Soldo et al., 1984). The elderly prefer *not* to take money from their children; however, they do expect that their children will help to the best of their ability if the need arises (Brody et al., 1984).

Nonindependent Living

There are at least three categories of nonindependent living to be considered. Some elderly—fewer than 10 percent—live with their children because they can no longer care for themselves. This is probably the largest single group of dependent elderly, aside from those being cared for by spouses in their own homes (Stone et al., 1987). A second group, consisting of at least 600,000 people, live in the community in residential care homes (Mor et al., 1986). Finally, there are the people who are probably the most disabled, those living in nursing homes. This group probably accounts for about 5 percent of those over 65 (Shanas & Maddox, 1985).

Study after study has demonstrated that family members are most likely to care for the frail elderly (Gatz, Bengston, & Blum, 1990; Stone et al., 1987). This is true even when the person needs considerable care. Those who are ill may require more than 50 hours a week in care, so that the caregiver's role is equivalent to a full-time job (Birkel & Jones, 1989). Nonetheless, care is most likely to be provided by a family member (usually a spouse, daughter, or daughter-in-law) without assistance from formal service agencies (Noelker & Bass, 1989). However, as impairment becomes more severe, the use of formal services (nursing help) increases. The professionals usually perform services the family member cannot (monitoring blood pressure) in addition to helping the caregiver with tasks like bathing or dressing (Noelker & Bass, 1989).

Residential care homes (RCH) can be divided into two groups: small facilities with fewer than 25 beds and larger facilities (Mor et al., 1986). Over 90 percent of the available RCH beds are in the larger facilities. RCHs routinely provide elderly residents with assistance in securing medical care, social services, and transportation. Most also help with personal care. Although they are supposed to provide clients with greater autonomy than a nursing home would, they routinely have rules limiting (or forbidding) alcohol and tobacco use, as well as locking the door on one's room (Mor et al., 1986). RCHs have policies that define how impaired a person can be and still live at the home. This should guarantee that residents will not be as sick as those using nursing homes and thus not need the specialized care nursing homes provide. However, smaller RCHs sometimes bend these admissions rules and then struggle to provide care for clients whose needs they cannot meet. In general, though, both residents and professional observers rate most client-RCH matches as being at least adequate (Mor et al., 1986).

Family members are also often satisfied with care in nursing homes (Aizenberg & Treas, 1985; Bowers, 1988). However, they are more likely to be satisfied with the technical care provided by the staff than with the "preservative" or "protective" care (Bowers, 1988). *Preservative* or *protective care* refers to efforts to ensure the dignity and self-esteem of the elderly resident. Family members typically see themselves as responsible for providing some continued sense of family connection as part of this effort. They also try to inform the staff, often in subtle and indirect ways, about the person's preferences and needs. So, for example, they encourage the staff to respect the client's needs for privacy during bathing or toileting, preferences regarding food or clothing, and the "right" to select the timing of various events (meals, movement from one room to another, extra-institutional appointments). Families often feel that the staff is only minimally responsive to such attempts. Indeed, they blame the patient's depression or negative affect on the staff's failure to provide sensitive care. Staff, on the other hand, often believe that the families are interfering and do not know what is best for clients (Bowers, 1988). So, whereas the staff might believe that realistic openness with the patient is important, the family might view maintenance of hope for recovery as critical. The two perspectives often come into direct conflict.

In all three types of dependent living, the aged are more likely to be very old (over 75), female, and in poor health. These characteristics, especially age and health, also predict level of dependent living, so that the oldest and sickest clients tend to be in nursing homes. They are also likely to be without spouses. Never-married people are overrepresented in RCH and nursing home populations (Mor et al., 1986). It is possible that those suffering from mental impairment are more likely to be institutionalized than those suffering from only physical problems, since mental impairment appears to generate greater caregiver stress (Birkel & Jones, 1989).

FAMILY RELATIONSHIPS

Marital Relationships

We have already seen that at virtually any age, men are more likely to be married than single. Women, on the other hand, become more likely to be single somewhere between 65 and 75 years of age. After 75, less than a quarter of all women have a husband who lives with them (Aldous, 1987). Some of this gender difference is attributable to longevity. Since women tend to outlive men, they are more likely to be widows. Some of the difference, however, is due to the increased likelihood of men remarrying following widowhood or divorce.

In any case, many of today's elderly are married. In fact, many of them are still married to their first spouse. Keep in mind that many of today's elderly did not find divorce to be an option, even when their marriages were very troubled.

Marital Satisfaction: Older couples report higher levels of companionship, emotional satisfaction, and marital satisfaction than do young marrieds (Giordano & Beckman, 1985). Some of this increase is attributable to a building up of shared experiences (Hagestad, 1987). The couple will have been together for a variety of "events"—major and minor, good and bad. As these accumulate, the couple is likely to find their goals and attitudes moving closer and closer together (Hagestad, 1987).

Changes in expectations may also play a role in increased marital satisfaction (Erikson et al., 1986; Hagestad, 1987; Giordano & Beckman, 1985).

As we noted in Chapter 14, there appear to be changes in sex role expectations that enable men to become more attentive and nurturant. This is likely to affect women's relationship satisfaction. Indeed, late in life men seem to become more interested in family issues and may even be more committed to the marital relationship than women (Guttman, 1987). People also become more tolerant of others' faults and idiosyncrasies as they gain perspective from experience. And retirement will enable the couple to spend more time together. This, combined with decreasing family demands, allows a freedom the couple probably never had before.

However, several caveats are in order. First, the marriages that have survived the longest are likely to include those that were happiest from the beginning. This is indicated by the positive correlation between earlier and present coping within marital relationships (Giordano & Beckman, 1985). The most unhappy will have divorced, separated, or at the very least may be reluctant to volunteer for research concerning marital satisfaction.

Similarly, research volunteers tend to be middle-class, healthy, well-adjusted people. They do not face many of the strains—especially the financial ones—that may undermine a marriage in old age (or at any time). Indeed, many studies report a positive correlation between marital satisfaction and socioeconomic status (Giordano & Beckman, 1985).

Overall, then, the limited available research suggests that older married couples are very happy. They know each other well and are comfortable in their relationships. As we will see, they are extremely dedicated when illness strikes. But before we accept this rosy picture, it is important to remember the potential sample biases in the available research.

Parents and Children

Throughout the life span, relationships between parents and their children are reciprocal. This reciprocity becomes particularly clear when the children are adults. Young adults can influence their parents' social, political, career, and even familial attitudes and behaviors. Yet the parents clearly continue the parental role, providing monetary and other forms of assistance as well as advice and guidance.

What happens in old age? Do the parents continue to act as parents? Or do the infirmities and financial declines of aging cause a role reversal in which the parents become psychologically, physically, and socially dependent on the children? And what about the children's feelings toward their parents? Do the children become resentful? Or do they willingly move in to help as needed? Do they try to spend even more time with their parents as they recognize that their parents' time is limited? In sum, how do parent-child roles, including affective status, change as the parents become elderly?

Parenting: We have already seen that most older adults prefer to live independently of their children. On the other hand, they clearly expect that their children will demonstrate filial responsibility, and maintain regular contact and provide help as needed. These findings demonstrate the focus of much of the extant research on family in old age—namely, expectations of and aid from the children. There has been considerably less interest in what the parents do for the children and how they view their parental role. The evidence that is available, however, clearly indicates that older parents are a continuing resource for their children.

Of course, most elderly Americans have living children. But, while they still define themselves as parents, they do not view the parental role as central to their identities (Blieszner & Mancini, 1987). If both parents are still living, their lives are apt to be maritally rather than parentally focused. They will allocate their time and energy to limit their contact and involvement with their children's (and grandchildren's) lives (Aldous, 1987). Nonetheless, they are in frequent contact with their children. Most elderly parents see their children at least once a week. If we add phone calls and letters to visits, contact between the elderly and their children is substantial (Aizenberg & Treas, 1985; Aldous, 1987; Greenberg & Becker, 1988). Older widows who live alone are somewhat more likely to live closer to at least one of their children, see them slightly more often, and perhaps receive more phone calls from them (Spitze & Logan, 1989).

Parents see certain continuities in their role even as their children grow up (Blieszner & Mancini, 1987). Biological and emotional ties, for example, are strong no matter how old your children are. Parents still love, worry about, and are interested in their children. Parents (especially mothers) whose children are undergoing a crisis report higher levels of stress themselves as they worry about their children. And a mother's stress level affects the father's well-being. Hence, both parents are negatively affected by high levels of stress in their children's lives (Greenberg & Becker, 1988).

Parents also still offer advice. In fact, in one study, all 29 of the healthy married elderly couples interviewed reported that their children regularly sought their advice (Greenberg & Becker, 1988). Parents are particularly likely to assist single children, especially those who have children of their own (Aldous, 1987). Children asked their parents' advice on a variety of topics ranging from household repairs to marital problems. Parents try to offer advice and emotional support only when asked for it because they do not want to be perceived as interfering in their children's lives. They think that if their children perceive them as interfering, the children will be alienated (Greenberg & Becker, 1988).

In some families, especially middle- and upper-class families, the parents provide financial assistance (Giordano & Beckman, 1985; Greenberg & Becker, 1988). Indeed, although intergenerational aid and assistance tends to be bidirectional, more monetary aid goes from parent to child than vice versa (Aldous, 1987). It is only in families where poor health dominates the relationship that the children provide unilateral aid. As we have seen, such families are a minority. When parents are healthy, on the other hand, they may provide money to help children purchase a house, take a vacation, start a business, or clear up debts (Greenberg & Becker, 1988). Again, parents are especially likely to help children who are single parents (Aldous, 1987). In families where the elderly parents are unable to help financially, they may provide tangible aid in the form of babysitting, temporary housing, or moral support. This is especially likely in the extended family structure of African-Americans and Latino-Americans (Jackson et al., 1990).

Parents try to limit how much they help but seem to be readily available when an emergency arises (Aldous, 1987; Greenberg & Becker, 1988). When a problem develops—be it financial, marital, or health-related—they let their children know they will help. And their children do call on them. They may provide emotional support to a divorcing child. They may also provide temporary housing, loans, and childcare, especially if the child involved is a daughter who has custody of her own children (Greenberg & Becker, 1988). If an adult child develops a drug or alcohol problem, parents are likely to help pay rehabilitation bills (Greenberg & Becker, 1988). The forms of help offered by parents are almost limitless.

Parents also see some discontinuities in their role. While they still feel some responsibility for their children's welfare, the extent and nature of the commitment changes (Blieszner & Mancini, 1987). The children are expected to take care of themselves. This gives the parents greater freedom with their time, money, and other resources.

Strong parent-child relationships are associated with higher life satisfaction among the elderly (Giordano & Beckman, 1985). Expressive support from children (feeling loved by your children) is associated with lower rates of depression (Dean, Kolody, Wood, & Ensel, 1989). It is the quality of the relationship, rather than the sheer amount of contact, that is important here. The quality of the parent-child relationship depends on levels of affection, communication, and consensus concerning values and attitudes. Of course, a strong relationship does not develop overnight. Therefore, it is not surprising that earlier strength of the parent-child relationship is predictive of its level in old age (Giordano & Beckman, 1985).

The shared values in question include beliefs about filial responsibility (Brody et al., 1984). Although groups of parents and children agree about sharing households, financial support, and so on, there is some evidence suggesting that older women may have somewhat higher expectations than men or young adults (Brody et al., 1984; Spitze & Logan, 1989). Older women are more likely than younger to believe that children should adjust their work schedules to provide help to their elderly parents (Brody et al., 1984). Such differences in expectations could increase the likelihood that older women will be disappointed with family relationships.

The importance of shared values is evident in what parents say individual children mean to them (Aldous, Klaus, & Klein, 1985). In some families, parents are able to identify one particular child who provides them with more care and comfort than the others do. Such children are likely to be daughters who live close by, agree with their parents about filial responsibility, and visit frequently. In identifying the child who serves as their "confidant," mothers are most likely to name a daughter who shares their interests. On the other hand, "disappointing" children do not share their parents interests or values about filial responsibility (Aldous et al., 1985).

Parents, especially fathers, often report feeling closer to their children after the children marry and become parents themselves (Aldous et al., 1985). This is probably because it gives the parents and children one more thing in common, another set of shared experiences (Aizenberg & Treas, 1985). Older adults sympathize with the problems their children face in their parental duties. Indeed, they frequently say that their children's parenting tasks are much more difficult than their own were because of the rise in divorce, single parenting, crime, and drug use (Blieszner & Mancini, 1987; Erikson et al., 1986).

Demographic trends are increasing the likelihood that parents and children will have shared experiences (Hagestad, 1987). As people live longer, parents and children will all experience marriage, childbearing and rearing, nest emptying, work, retirement, and widowhood and other forms of bereavement. The current educational gap between parents and their children (and grandchildren) will diminish. Similarly, women's work experience will probably become more similar across generations. All these changes should make parents and children even closer in the future than they are today (Hagestad, 1987).

Overall, however, today's elderly parents are quite satisfied with their relationships with their children (Aldous, 1987). There are numerous ways to assess the quality of parent-child interaction (Bengston, Cutler, Mangen, & Marshall, 1985). One could look at availability, contact, interactional quality, consensus on values and attitudes, levels of assistance, and expectations of roles and relationships (Bengston et al., 1985). No matter which relational aspect is examined, however, most elderly parents report being happy in their relationships with their children (Aldous, 1987). They do not feel neglected or forgotten. They do not think their children are ungrateful. They do not feel they have failed as parents. If anything, they feel more respected and loved than they have at earlier points in their children's lives. As one woman in her late sixties said: "I love being my age! It's the first time in my life that all my children liked me!" (Hagestad, 1987, p. 419).

Filial Responsibility: There is no empirical basis for the stereotype that adult children are distant, uncaring, disinterested, or even too busy for their parents (Brody & Schoonover, 1986). Indeed, much of the contact that occurs is because of the child's effort. Especially among the very elderly or the infirm, children are more likely to visit their parents' home than to receive visits from them (Aizenberg & Treas, 1985).

Women tend to be in charge of familial relationships. Therefore, intergenerational closeness tends to be along maternal, rather than paternal, lines (Aizenberg & Treas, 1985). Daughters report feeling closer to their mothers than to their fathers. They also report greater emotional closeness and less autonomy than sons do (Frank, Avery, & Laman, 1988). This is consistent with Gilligan's (1982a,b) argument that women's development is centered more around intimacy and interpersonal relationships, while men are directed toward independence and separateness.

Given the greater closeness between daughters and their parents (especially their mothers), it is not surprising that daughters are more likely than sons to provide direct assistance to their parents. Indeed, having a daughter seems to be the key to parents' receipt of aid from children (Spitze & Logan, 1990). Daughters are about twice as likely as sons to assume primary responsibility for the care of a seriously ill parent (Stone et al., 1987). Women of all ages expect daughters to provide more help, including re-arranging their work schedules and sharing their homes (Brody et al., 1984). But in recent years, women have flooded into the workforce. This has led to substantial concern as to whether daughters can or will continue to pro-vide this high level of care, assistance, and support. Without female rela-tives to care for the elderly, our social service agencies and old age institu-tions would quickly become dramatically overburdened.

Working Daughters: When an elderly parent's health is relatively good, working and nonworking daughters provide comparable services (Brody et al., 1987; Brody & Schoonover, 1986; Matthews et al., 1989). Work-ing and nonworking daughters all provide assistance with transportation, managing money, making phone calls, and providing emotional support (Brody & Schoonover, 1986). Working daughters are, however, more likely to hire someone to help an elderly parent with housework, laundry, cook-ing, and personal care. The parent still receives the same amount of help; however, it comes from a hired aide (paid for by the daughter) rather than from the daughter herself. Furthermore, such hired assistance is rarely ob-tained from government or social service agencies. Families prefer to han-dle these needs privately (Brody & Schoonover, 1986; Noelker & Bass, 1989).

What happens when the parent needs more intensive, prolonged as-sistance? There is no simple answer to this question. No doubt some women quit working to care for their parents (Brody et al., 1987). This is an espe-cially likely choice when the parent becomes very sick and the daughter is not very committed to her job (she viewed it more as "just a job" than as a "career"). Such jobs also may not pay enough to justify or allow hiring someone to care for the parent while the daughter works. Nevertheless, the daughter's family income will fall substantially, creating additional stress for her and her family. Furthermore, such women may be unable to buy respite aid. It is not surprising, then, that the women who quit work experi-ence considerable health declines (Brody et al., 1987).

It is not clear how severe the parent's disability has to become before a daughter will quit working. There is probably some interaction among the daughter's income (is it high enough to hire someone to help the par-ent?), job commitment, sense of filial obligation, and parental need. Atti-tudes concerning women's roles may also be influential (Brody et al., 1987). Many women who have high job commitment and infirm parents feel con-flicted and wrestle with the decision of whether to quit work.

The decision will be affected by the availability of alternate caregivers. In a study of the caregiving efforts of employed versus nonemployed sisters, Sarah Matthews and her colleagues (1989) found that few of the employed sisters considered quitting work, even when their parents were ill. Instead, both employed and nonemployed sisters assumed that the latter would per-form more of the daily caregiving activities. Consider these statements from some of the nonemployed sisters:

> She was working and I wasn't while Mother was so ill. I assumed responsibility for my parents then. My sister might feel some guilt because she didn't do as

The elderly expect—and typically receive—help from their children if health declines necessitate it.

much as I did. I said I'd take care of driving to the clinic since I was free and I'd call her if I needed her.

She (the Mother) spent the first weekend (following surgery) with my sister, but she and my other sister were working, so then my mother came here until she could go home. (Matthews et al., 1989, p. S42)

When their parents became ill, the nonemployed sisters provided more personal service, did more household chores, dealt more with social service or medical agencies, and provided more emotional and moral support to their parents (Matthews et al., 1989). Some things virtually have to be done by the nonemployed sister. Doctor's and agency appointments, for example, are routinely scheduled during normal business hours. Most full-time employees could not themselves help their parents with these needs. The differences in assistance provided by employed versus nonemployed sisters is clearly evident only when the parents' health is poor (Matthews et al., 1989). There may be differences in the specific types of assistance they provide. Employed sisters are most likely to perform tasks like grocery shopping that can be done after work. Nonemployed sisters are more likely to be called on when an emergency develops. Overall, however, the sisters believe they make comparable efforts on their parents' behalf.

What about the effects of working on the daughter who is trying to provide some aid to her parents? If the parents are well, there appears to be relatively little work-family conflict. In other words, the women do not feel serious role conflict (Brody & Schoonover, 1986; Brody et al., 1987; Matthews et al., 1989), for several reasons. First, many of the women have jobs that make it relatively easy for them to help out. They can get time off to take a parent to a doctor's appointment or help with some task, as evidenced by these women's situations:

> If something is necessary, the job would not get in the way. I'm manager of the store and I would just go. I don't have to ask permission from anybody.

> If my parents need me for something I can switch days. My mother had to go to the doctor on Thursday and I just changed days with another girl in order to take her. (Matthews et al., 1989, p. S42)

Second, many women have jobs—particularly nursing and social work—that may be helpful to an aging parent (Matthews et al., 1989). These women have contacts and information that may facilitate obtaining medical and social services.

Of course, some women who work feel guilty that they don't have more time to spend with their parents. However, this is also true of nonemployed women. Look at the similarity of sentiments expressed by first an employed and then a nonemployed daughter:

> I know she'd love to go to lunch, to outings, and shopping together, but working five days a week, I have only one day to catch up on my own things and keeping up with people in my own life.

> I don't think I spend more time with her because I'm not working and sometimes I feel guilty about that. I don't think I'm giving her any more attention than when I was working. (Matthews et al., 1989, p. S42)

Apparently, then, work–elderly parent conflicts are minimal until the parent becomes seriously disabled, mentally or physically (Matthews et al., 1989). If there is no one else readily available to provide appropriate care, women start to consider whether or not they should quit their jobs (Brody et al., 1987). Those who do seem to suffer more mental and physical problems from caring for their parents than those who don't quit. This is partially because work can provide a needed respite from caring for the parent. However, the financial burdens caused by leaving work may also play a role. And it may be that the parents of those who quit are so much worse off than parents whose daughters have not yet left the workforce that the demands on the daughters are simply greater and more stressful (Brody et al., 1987).

Grandparenting

As we saw in Chapter 10, most Americans become grandparents while they are middle-aged. By old age, most grandparents have had considerable time to adapt to and define the role. Furthermore, given that grandparenting is *not* typically a central role for middle-aged people and that parenting is *not* the focal role for the elderly, it should not be surprising to find that most elderly do not consider the grandparent role crucial to their identity. In fact, elderly grandparents may be even less actively involved in their grandchildren's lives than middle-aged grandparents (Johnson, 1988). Finally, we must note that for many elderly, most of their grandchildren will be adults. When grandchildren are young, their parents may determine how often and in what contexts they see their grandparents. This is one reason why divorce can pose such a threat to the grandparent-grandchild relationship. As the grandchild becomes an adult, however, he or she can take the initiative in seeing grandparents. And an adult grandchild may have more in common with grandparents and may seek different kinds of support from them than young grandchildren would (Hagestad, 1987).

Both elderly grandparents and adult grandchildren seem to enjoy and value their relationship (Aizenberg & Treas, 1985; Hagestad, 1987; Thompson & Walker, 1987). Grandparents may provide adult grandchildren with sense of stability (Hagestad, 1987). Since they are typically retired, they are often available for consultation or consolation. Their life experience may allow them to help the younger adult put events into perspective. Just as these elders may provide aid to their children in times of crisis, they may be an important resource to their grandchildren when they are faced with life crises (Hagestad, 1987).

While grandchildren and grandparents report positive feelings towards one another, their relationship seems to be mediated by the "middle generation" (Aizenberg & Treas, 1985; Thompson & Walker, 1987). Indeed, at least one study has found that grandmothers' feelings toward their granddaughters are virtually indistinguishable from their feelings toward their own daughters (Thompson & Walker, 1987). In other words, older women have a general sense of love of their family that extends to include both daughter and granddaughter. Granddaughters have somewhat more of a tendency to distinguish their feelings for their mothers and grandmothers. Nonetheless, their mothers' feelings about their grandmothers influence the granddaughters' feelings. In fact, when granddaughters have only limited contact with their grandmothers, they tend simply to adopt their mother's attitude toward their grandmother (Thompson & Walker, 1987).

Great-grandparents: Over 40 percent of elderly Americans have great-grandchildren (Doka & Mertz, 1988). Relatively little is known about the relationship between great-grandparents and great-grandchildren. Using the grandparenting research as a basis, we might expect that great-grandparents are interested in their great-grandchildren but not involved in their lives on a regular basis. After all, the great-grandparent is likely to be older and less able (or willing) to care for young children and must negotiate seeing the young child through even more "family layers" than is necessary for visits with grandchildren (Doka & Mertz, 1988).

In general, great-grandparents are favorably disposed toward the role and attach at least some emotional significance to it (Doka & Mertz, 1988; Wentowski, 1985). They suggest that the role brings a sense of personal and family renewal, a new diversion in their lives, and a marker of longevity (Doka & Mertz, 1988). Most of them feel emotionally close to their great-

While not a central life role, great-grandparenthood can bring real satisfaction, including as a marker of longevity and intergenerational relatedness.

grandchildren but see them only on formal occasions. They do, however, usually have pictures of the children and know what they are doing. Such information is likely to be provided by their own children (the great-grandchild's grandparent). Generally close family relationships predict close great-grandparent/great-grandchild relationships (Doka & Mertz, 1988).

Great-grandparents may be afforded a special status in the family. After all, they are much less common than grandparents. Great-grandchildren who are old enough to remember and appreciate the great-grandparents are even less common (the children are usually quite young while the great-grandparents are living). The unusual nature of the relationship may result in special efforts to preserve it. For example, in one divorcing family, the ex-wife's mother facilitated the child's continued relationship with her paternal great-grandmother:

> She (the mother) said, "What you and Tom (husband) had together should not affect Lil (the great-grandmother). She's an old woman who can't be deprived of that joy. And you wouldn't want your child deprived of that relationship. How many children know their great-grandparents? (Doka & Mertz, 1988, p. 196)

CARING FOR THE INFIRM ELDERLY

Most elderly people do not require substantial assistance in their daily activities. People aged 65–74 constitute the majority of the elderly, and probably less than 10 percent of them require institutional care or daily assistance (Hagestad, 1987). As health care improves, the percentage of people who are relatively healthy during old age will probably increase. Nonetheless, age does bring with it the increased risk of mental and physical disability. When such problems arise, be they temporary or chronic, the family is the most likely source of care.

If there is a surviving spouse, she or he is the single most likely caregiver, with wives being more likely to play the role than husbands (Gatz et al., 1990; Stone et al., 1987). This means, of course, that the caregiver is likely to be elderly and may have health problems too. Furthermore, the frailest elderly tend to be older, so their children are typically at least in late middle-age. Some of the daughters who provide assistance to their parents are elderly themselves. Estimates suggest that fully a quarter of the women born during the 1930s will have living mothers when they reach age 60 (Gatz et al., 1990). This means the potential caregiver daughter may be facing illness and other problems of aging herself. Furthermore, she may be faced with both a sick spouse and sick parents. It is not surprising, then, that a national survey found that the average age of a caregiver was slightly over 57 years. Fully 25 percent of those providing care to the frail elderly were 65 to 74 and 10 percent were over 75 (Stone et al., 1987).

Caring for the infirm older person may present familial or work conflicts. Overall, about 20 percent of the caregivers have minor children still living with them, and nearly a third of them are still employed (Stone et al., 1987). Of those who work, about 20 percent experience work-caregiving conflicts that lead them to quit their jobs, take time off, cut their hours, or rearrange their schedules (Stone et al., 1987). Spouses and daughters are more likely than sons to make such work accommodations (Stone et al., 1987).

As we saw earlier, familial caregivers devote large amounts of time to the task. The vast majority provide unpaid caregiving every day. Of course, virtually all spouses help daily. And almost three-quarters of the caregiving children provide daily aid (Stone et al., 1987). They put in several hours daily, averaging four hours per day. They help with shopping, transportation, housekeeping, personal hygiene, and indoor mobility (Stone et al., 1987).

It would seem that family members who serve as caregivers to the infirm elderly are placing themselves at considerable risk for familial, physical, and mental health problems. We assume that the stress of providing such care would be considerable. In the face of such stress, the caregiver may become resentful or even abusive. Thus, familial relationships and support of the elderly person would be undermined. On the other hand, people who help are strong believers in the extended family and would feel it inappropriate to institutionalize a loved one (Stone et al., 1987). Perhaps this attitude reduces the stress of a difficult task. Caregiver stress, then, is a multidetermined phenomenon. There are a variety of potential sources of stress, as well as numerous possible mediating factors. Figure 15-1 presents one model of caregiver stress and coping.

Sources of Stress

The stress of providing care to an infirm elderly person depends to some extent on the symptoms of the victim. As physical symptoms worsen and functional impairment increases, families rely increasingly on outside assistance (Noelker & Bass, 1989). This suggests that these families may be feeling more stress than they had when the elder person was healthier, though still in need of assistance.

Mental symptoms too can generate considerable stress. Not all symptoms are equally stressful. Simple cognitive incapacity, marked, for example, by memory loss, does not appear to have strong negative effects. This may be because many people expect a certain amount of cognitive decline to accompany advancing age (Deimling & Bass, 1986). On the other hand, disruptive behavior and loss of ability to function in a social situation may have more dramatic effects (Deimling & Bass, 1986; Quayhagen & Quayhagen, 1988). As the elder person requires more and more supervision, and as the behavior becomes more potentially embarrassing, the caregiver may find decreasing opportunities for respite. The caregiver's own social and leisure patterns will change. As the caregivers' recreational outlets disap-

FIGURE 15-1: Conceptual Model of Caregiver Stress and Coping

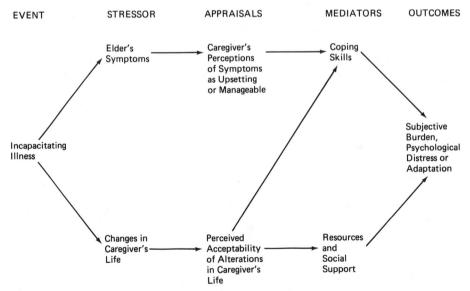

Source: Gatz, M., Bengston, V., & Blum, M. (1990). Caregiving families. In J. Birren & K. W. Schaie (eds.), *Handbook of the psychology of aging,* 3rd ed., pp. 407–426. San Diego: Academic Press.

pear, their own health may begin to deteriorate. They may even experience depression (Deimling & Bass, 1986; Moritz et al., 1989). Thus, the amount of distress and burden experienced by a caregiver is a function of the ill person's impairment and available social support. The caregiver's own health and attitudes, including coping style, also play a role (Vitaliano et al., 1991).

Of course, caregivers of physically impaired but mentally lucid elderly parents face similar isolation. They too face the risk of physical and emotional decline. Yet the physically impaired seem to have a larger caregiving network (Birkel & Jones, 1989). This means that caregiver respite is more available. Furthermore, the networks of the physically impaired often include nonfamily members. Family members can go out together, and the impaired elder has contact with a variety of people. This is probably a positive situation for both the caregivers and the impaired (Birkel & Jones, 1989). On the other hand, although demented elders seem to do best in multiple-caregiver households, these arrangements are not usually available (Birkel & Jones, 1989).

It is interesting to note that wives often report more caregiver stress than husbands, although some studies find the differences are small (Miller, 1990). While there are probably many contributing factors to this difference, Pruchno and Resch (1989) suggest that the sex role changes seen in old age may play a role. Men, moving toward a greater family orientation, may actually be more interested in providing such care than women, who may feel they have already spent most of their lives looking after their families. It is also possible, however, that the differences in caregiver strain that emerge are methodological artifacts. Women may be more willing to admit health problems, for example, than men are (Miller, 1990).

Caregivers may be so dedicated to their task that, despite complaints about time demands, they are generally satisfied with the situation and willing to make whatever sacrifices it demands. Indeed, spousal caregivers report considerable gratification from their tasks (Motenko, 1989). Many of them provide the care because they believe their spouse has given much to them during their life together. Others simply think that they can provide more tender loving care than a nursing home could. (Family members frequently complain about nursing homes' failures in this regard.) Still others provide the care out of a sense of responsibility. Those who are caregivers for the first two reasons are likely to feel more gratified with the role. Higher levels of gratification, in turn, are associated with higher caregiver well-being (Motenko, 1989).

Furthermore, caregiver frustration does not necessarily increase as the spouse's illness drags on (Motenko, 1989). In fact, as adjustments are made, frustrations may actually decrease. This is especially likely if the original level of closeness between spouses is maintained throughout the illness. The continuity of the relationship, even if it was not close to begin with, combined with the long-term acceptance of a caregiving routine, underscores the importance of continuity in the morale and adjustment of the elderly (Atchley, 1989; Motenko, 1989).

We do not want to paint too optimistic a picture, however. Caregiving can be stressful and may have detrimental effects. For example, spousal caregivers of Alzheimer's victims have poorer immune functioning and hence more illnesses than is typical. This was especially true of those with poor social support (Kiecolt-Glaser, Dura, Speicher, Trask, & Glaser, 1991). Their mental health may also be affected. In one recent study, 34 percent of adult children who were caregivers suffered from a depressive or anxiety disorder, compared to 8 percent of a noncaregiver control group (Dura, Stukenberg, & Kiecolt-Glaser, 1991). Spousal caregivers also showed higher rates of depression (Kiecolt-Glaser et al., 1991).

We see once again, then, that family members do not "desert" the infirm elderly and are indeed very committed to their care. This is true even once the elder has been placed in a nursing home (Bowers, 1988). This sense of love and loyalty also helps us to understand why so many infirm elderly are maintained in the community with little or no aid from social service agencies. Future research needs to examine the types of respite and aid that will be most useful within the context of families who want to provide most of the care themselves. It may be, for example, that families are more interested in learning techniques for dealing with disruptive or embarrassing behaviors than in procuring regular respite (R. Patterson, 1987).

ELDER ABUSE

In the late 1970s, Americans "discovered" elder abuse (Callahan, 1988). To their astonishment and dismay, they heard repeatedly about old people who were neglected, belittled, and mistreated. Given the attention "granny bashing" received on the evening news, most Americans came to believe that elder abuse is a widespread problem. Indeed, early estimates indicated that there were over 1,000,000 cases of elder abuse annually, with estimates ranging from 0.5 to 2.5 million (Callahan, 1988; Salend, Kane, Satz, & Pynoos, 1984).

Most of these estimates were based on social service case reports or on small, nonrandom samples of elderly. Such data can hardly be viewed as conclusive. On the one hand, they may represent serious underestimates of the problem (Kosberg, 1988). It has been suggested that only about 1 of 6 cases of elder abuse is ever brought to the attention of social service agencies. The abuse may be hidden because of the sanctity of the family, which is the site of most cases of maltreatment. Americans are generally reluctant to intrude in other people's family business. Furthermore, the relative isolation of each family makes it difficult for an "outsider" to know what is actually going on in the home. And the older person may be unwilling to substantiate, much less initiate, a report of abuse (Salend et al., 1984). After all, they may view the alternative of a nursing home as worse than the abuse they currently face. Or they may fear getting a child or spouse in trouble (Callahan, 1988; Kosberg, 1988; Pillemer & Finkelhor, 1988; Salend et al., 1984).

On the other hand, these data may overestimate the rate of abuse. Statutory definitions, which would bring cases into the social services system, tend to be vague. Some states consider self-neglect to be a form of elder abuse and lump it with abuse by others (Salend et al., 1984). Many states define financial exploitation as a form of elder abuse (Salend et al., 1984). While financial exploitation is certainly undesirable and ought to be illegal, it is not what most people understand when they hear the term "elder abuse." Furthermore, friends and neighbors may be uncertain about what constitutes abuse. This may partially explain why the evidence on substantiation of reports indicates that only about half of the complaints can be legally proved (Salend et al., 1984).

Karl Pillemer and David Finkelhor (1988) recently published the first large-scale, random sample survey of elderly people to assess rates of elder abuse in the community. Their survey covered physical abuse, chronic verbal abuse, and neglect. After surveying more than 2000 older people, they concluded that the rate of these three types of elder abuse was approximately 32 cases/1000 (with a range of 25–39 cases/1000). Their sample was based in Boston but if their results are extrapolated to the entire country, somewhere between 701,000 and 1,093,560 elderly people are neglected or physically or verbally abused every year (Pillemer & Finkelhor, 1988).

Pillemer and Finkelhor found physical violence to be the most common of the three types. It occurred at a rate of approximately 20 per 1000. Of the victims, 63 percent had been shoved or grabbed, 45 percent had had something thrown at them, 42 percent were slapped, and 10 percent had been bitten, kicked, or punched. Chronic verbal abuse was reported at a rate of 11 per 1000 and neglect at a rate of 4 per 1000.

Social service agencies report higher rates of neglect than physical abuse. This is probably mainly attributable to cases of self-abuse, which constitute the largest percentage of neglect cases (Salend et al., 1984). Self-neglect was not part of Pillemer and Finklherhor's definition of neglect. Furthermore, it is widely believed that exploitation is very common and may actually be the most frequent form of elder abuse (Finkelhor & Pillemer, 1988; Giordano & Beckman, 1985; Salend et al., 1984).

Victim Characteristics

Social service reports indicate that women are more likely to be victims of elder abuse than men (Giordano & Beckman, 1985; Kosberg, 1988). However, Pillemer and Finkelhor's (1988) survey found that men are actually slightly more likely to be abused. This is probably partially attributable to the fact that the most likely perpetrator of elder abuse is someone who lives with the victim. Older women are much less likely to share a house than older men are (Pillemer & Finkelhor, 1988; Spitze & Logan, 1989). Women may be more likely to be brought to the attention of social service agencies because their injuries tend to be more serious than men's (Pillemer & Finkelhor, 1988).

Social service and small sample reports also suggest that very old people (those over 75) were more likely to be victimized (Callahan, 1988; Giordano & Beckman, 1985; Kosberg, 1988). Pillemer and Finkelhor, on the other hand, reported no age differences in abuse rates. This may be an artifact of their failure to include institutionalized elderly. This group, which is older than community dwellers, is probably more at risk. Furthermore, Pillemer and Finkelhor did not examine financial exploitation as a form of abuse. This too may be more common among the old-old, especially those suffering from mental disabilities.

Indeed, it is the connection between poor health and age that has led many to postulate that the old-old would be more frequent victims than the young-old. Those in poor health (physically or mentally) are at greater risk for abuse (Giordano & Beckman, 1988; Kosberg, 1988; Pillemer & Finkelhor, 1988). In fact, elders in poor health are probably three to four times more likely to be abused (Pillemer & Finkelhor, 1988). There are probably a number of reasons for this: They may be less able to defend themselves (Kosberg, 1988). Their needs may be greater than family or friends can fill. This may explain why the ill elderly are particularly likely to be neglected (as opposed to physically abused) (Pillemer & Finkelhor, 1988). Caring for an ill elderly person may create inordinate stress, resulting in abuse (Kosberg, 1988).

Certain personality or interpersonal characteristics may also affect the risk of abuse (Kosberg, 1988). Elderly people who are loyal to or dependent on a caregiver may be reluctant to report abuse. People who stoically accept adversity or blame themselves for everything may tolerate abuse. This may be particularly true in situations where the older person is a long-time victim of abuse (as in cases of spouse abuse, for example). Finally, some elderly may be particularly difficult to live with because they are demanding, complainers, or otherwise unpleasant. Saying that an elder's characteristics may contribute to abuse is not intended as a justification for the abuser's behavior.

Abuser Characteristics

Elderly people who live alone have about a quarter of the chance of being abused that those who live with someone do (Pillemer & Finkelhor, 1988). As we have already seen, elders who share a household with someone are most likely to be living with a spouse. It should not therefore be surprising to learn that the most common perpetrator of elder abuse is the victim's spouse (Pillemer & Finkelhor, 1988).

But the stereotype is that an overburdened, angry child-turned-caregiver is most likely to be the abuser (Giordano & Beckman, 1985). Can the stereotype and the data be reconciled? Raw numbers show spouses to be the most frequent abusers, perhaps because more elderly live with their spouses than with their children (Spitze & Logan, 1989). When one corrects for this difference and compares the rate for elderly living with spouses versus that for elders living with their children, a different picture emerges. The rate of elder abuse among those living with a spouse is 41 per 1000, whereas that for those living with their children is 44 per 1000 (Pillemer & Finkelhor, 1988).

Spouse abuse does appear to be fairly common among elderly couples, yet it has received relatively little attention. Perhaps this is because people believe that such abuse is not as likely to be serious as abuse by a younger adult (Pillemer & Finkelhor, 1988). In fact, however, spousal and child elder abuse are equally serious in terms of how great the injuries are and how much the victim is upset by the episode (Pillemer & Finkelhor, 1988).

Caregivers who are economically dependent on the older person may be more likely to abuse (Callahan, 1988; Kosberg, 1988). This may involve financial exploitation, motivated, perhaps, by greed or resentment. Resentment may be vented in the form of physical violence or verbal aggression (Pillemer & Finkelhor, 1988). This link between caregiver dependency and abuse may also help explain why wives are more likely than husbands to be abusers (although, as noted earlier, much of this difference may be due to the fact that more women live alone than men do).

In addition, caregivers who drink, use drugs (including some prescribed medications), or are mentally incompetent may be more likely to be abusive (Kosberg, 1988). This may take the form of passive neglect, where a caregiver "forgets" to do something for the elder. This may also help us to understand the relatively high rate of spousal abuse reported earlier. If the caregiver has developed a form of dementia, he or she may be unable to be a reasonable, effective care provider. Furthermore, if a spouse or child has a longstanding problem with mental illness (schizophrenia or depression), the elder may be particularly reluctant to "turn them in" for fear of institutionalization of the relative. There are, for example, approximately 400,000 schizophrenics who live with an elderly parent(s) (Callahan, 1988). While the majority of these children are not violent, they may not be capable of providing dependable care to their parents.

"Stress" is often cited as a cause of elder abuse. It is always difficult to ascertain whether the stress is a cause or an effect of the abuse (Kosberg, 1988). However, it is evident that certain kinds of "stress" contribute. Economic problems may be a particularly powerful predictor. Again, these problems may predate the necessity of caring for a sick old person or they may arise partly because of the person's needs (Kosberg, 1988). In either case, the risk for elder abuse rises.

Some cases of abuse, particularly neglect, are due simply to ignorance. Some people do not understand what an ill old person needs. Others are inexperienced in providing care, especially on a long-term, intensive basis. Recall that most family caregivers for ill elderly provide about four hours of care seven days a week (Stone et al., 1987). This can be a significant drain on time, energy, and family life, especially if the investment was unexpected.

Family Dynamics

Longstanding conflict or violence between spouses or parent and child is a powerful predictor of elder abuse (Kosberg, 1988). Furthermore, conflict between the child and his or her spouse increases the risk of elder abuse (Kosberg, 1988). This may be particularly important when a daughter-in-law is asked to care for the parent(s) of a husband she is fighting with.

There is also the question of the caregiver's perspective about providing assistance to the elderly infirm relative (Kosberg, 1988). Sometimes social workers, in their zeal to keep an older person out of an institutional setting, push relatives to care for him or her. This is a mistake. If the caregiver is reluctant to assume the role, he or she is more likely to become frustrated, resentful, angry, and perhaps abusive. Similarly, an appointed relative who feels the person is too much to handle and should be institutionalized is a poor risk as a caregiver. Furthermore, if the rest of the family is unable or unwilling to provide relief support or if they disagree with the way the primary caregiver does things, trouble may develop.

Preventing Elder Abuse

One of the best ways of preventing elder abuse is to screen caregiving individuals (Kosberg, 1988). Social workers can interview the prospective care provider, assess the needs of the elderly client, and then evaluate the match between them. The social worker can also help by providing relief help, educational classes or materials, contact with other agencies (such as Social Security), or other forms of aid.

However, we must remember that many family caregivers have little or no contact with social service agencies (Noelker & Bass, 1989). Therefore, the social worker will not have any opportunity to evaluate either the caregiver or the elderly adult. Social service agencies can only react to reports of abuse in such situations. It is important for states to clearly define responsibilities and channels for reporting elder abuse. Public education concerning the signs and risk factors is also important.

In fact, Jordan Kosberg (1988) has argued that societal attitudes are a major factor in elder abuse. He suggests that as long as the United States is a violent, ageist society, we will have elder abuse. Other societal values, such as discrimination against the disabled and women, also play a role. And factors that increase the likelihood of familial dysfunction—including poverty, unemployment, lack of community resources, and cyclic violence—will all need to be addressed before elder abuse can be eliminated (Kosberg, 1988).

FRIENDSHIPS

The focus on families in this chapter is not meant to suggest that elderly people do not have friends. Indeed, many of them have extensive nonfamilial social networks (Antonucci, 1985). This may be especially true for women, who place more emphasis on intimate friendships across the life span (Rubin, 1985). It may also be more true of middle-class than lower-class families (Giordano & Beckman, 1985; Sanchez-Ayendez, 1989). But lower-class families tend to be more neighborhood-oriented, so they too have multiple nonfamilial contacts. Healthy elders may also have more contact with their friends. And those who are healthy and financially able may move to a retirement community to increase interactions with peers (Kahana, 1982; Litwak & Longino, 1987).

Friends can be an important source of support in a crisis (see Chapter 14). Even neighbors and acquaintances may help with errands or supervision of infirm elderly (Aizenberg & Treas, 1985; Birkel & Jones, 1989; Sanchez-Ayendez, 1989). Nonetheless, friends are not treated in the same way as family members. They are less likely, for example, to be asked to perform intimate personal care. Most people would not turn to friends for financial assistance. Nor would they expect a friend to make a long-term, time-consuming care commitment of the sort families routinely make (Aizenberg & Treas, 1985; Brody et al., 1984; Sanchez-Ayendez, 1989).

As we saw in Chapter 14, there is typically a positive relationship between life satisfaction and friendships. Furthermore, we might expect that some of these friendships would be very close and special. After all, the friends may have known each other for many years and, like married couples, may have experienced a great deal together. They may also have built up a reciprocal exchange of favors, goods, and services that provides a strong basis for asking for help in old age (Antonnuci & Jackson, 1987). The data describing the initiation, maintenance, and function of friendship in old age are sparse, however (Aizenberg & Treas, 1985). It is therefore difficult to ascertain whether friendships fulfill their potential, especially during emergencies.

SUMMARY

We can make several "factual" statements about family life in old age. The research has been extremely consistent, often for two or more decades, on these issues.

First, most elderly live with spouses or alone. They live with children only when health or finances require. In fact, it is often the *children's* financial situation that creates the need. It is commonly more accurate to say that adult children are living with their parents than that parents are living with their adult children. The parent is typically the head of household, and the home is his or hers. Furthermore, particularly in middle-class families, parents are probably more likely to be resources for their children than vice versa. This is especially true of financial assistance.

Second, the elderly prefer *not* to live with their children. They prefer to maintain their own independence. This is partially because they do not wish to interfere with their children's lives or become a burden to them. However, they also want to maintain their own privacy. Like the middle-aged parent who expresses some relief and excitement at nest-emptying, elderly parents often want to limit their interactions with their children so that they can pursue their own interests.

Nonetheless, parents and children are typically quite close. They see each other frequently. When phone calls and letters are considered, the norm is for parents to be in contact with at least one of their children at least once a week. Even when children work or live some distance from their parents, the contact tends to be frequent and warm.

Of course, parent-child relationships are not the whole story of family in old age. Significant numbers of the elderly, especially old men, are still married. Spousal relations tend to be better in old age than they were during the years when children and jobs competed for the couple's attention. However, research biases must temper our assessment of the strength of this finding.

When the elderly need help because of illness, finances, or other problems, they usually get it from a family member. The most common provider is the spouse, with children (especially daughters) running a close second. The care is voluntary and requires considerable time commitment. Yet even when spouses or children work, they seem willing to make such commitments. One of the policy challenges of the coming years is to find ways to get families to allow agency intervention or assistance (including respite) when the situation requires it.

Indeed, unwillingness to seek outside help may be one reason why elder abuse occurs. Elder abuse is probably not as common as was once believed. However, it is a significant problem, particularly in the areas of neglect and financial exploitation. The relative isolation of the infirm elder and her/his caregiver make it particularly difficult to identify cases of abuse.

The face of family relationships in old age is influenced by changes in work and financial status. The elderly have more time for themselves and their families. Social security and other government programs have helped to reduce the risk of poverty and dependence on children in old age. These issues are the focus of the next chapter.

16 Work

The word "retirement" conjures up different images for each of us. Some of us envision living in a sunny, warm climate where we can fish or play golf all year. Others imagine time with grandchildren and families. Still others look toward retirement with fear, fear of boredom and too much free time. We might also fear poverty, for many of us cannot imagine living on the reduced income Social Security offers. Indeed, we worry that Social Security, inadequate though it may be, will not even be available by the time we retire.

The fact that we *have* diverse images of retirement underscores two points. First, most of us expect to retire. In other words, retirement has become a normative event. This has ramifications for both the timing and rationales for retirement. Second, adjustment to retirement is affected by what comes before it. Thus, our investment in work as well as our lifetime earnings (and savings!) are among the factors affecting retirement satisfaction.

Of course, not everyone retires at the same age. Some people retire early, both in terms of when they had expected to retire and compared to when others retire. Other people retire late, or perhaps not at all. Pension fund managers, including the Social Security Administration, are very interested in the bases for such decisions. Social scientists are also concerned with these decisions, since they have implications for adjustment.

Assuming that people do retire, they are then faced with more leisure. The question is, how do they use it? Not as they did as younger adults? Or is leisure an area in which there is considerable continuity so that it does not look very different at various points in development?

Methodological Issues: Employment and retirement of the elderly has considerable social policy implications. There is, for example, the issue of "opening up" slots in the workplace so that younger workers can enter the

455

market and move up the ladder. Social Security and its companion programs are a major component of the federal budget. Americans have come to depend upon the availability of these programs. It is critical that strong databases for studying employment and retirement late in life be generated.

It is not surprising, then, that there are several large-scale, longitudinal data series about work patterns (Parnes, 1988). One of the best known of these is the Retirement History Survey (RHS) conducted by the Social Security Administration. The original sample consisted of about 11,000 men and unmarried women. They were first interviewed in 1969 and reinterviewed every other year through 1979. Questions covered work status and history, attitudes toward retirement, retirement plans, pension availability, and health (Anderson et al., 1986; Parnes, 1988).

Another widely used data set was collected by the University of Michigan Institute for Survey Research. This is the Panel Study of Income Dynamics (PSID), in which the sample overrepresented poverty-level families. The PSID started with 5,000 families and, because of marriages and divorces, now includes more than 7,000 families with over 20,000 members. The families were first interviewed in 1968 and will be followed at least into the 1990s (Parnes, 1988).

Other large data sources are the Census Bureau, the Department of Labor, and the Social Security Administration, all of which conduct periodic surveys of wealth, retirement, and employment (see Radner, 1989; Rones, 1988). Other smaller or less representative longitudinal samples are also available (see Ekerdt et al., 1989). All in all, one might expect that we have more representative data on retirement and related issues than on most other topics. However, we must be cautious in interpreting the results of studies using these data. Often the researcher defines a subsample of the RHS, PSID, or other survey data. In doing so, representativeness may be lost. For example, those who died during the course of the study might be omitted from an analysis (Anderson et al., 1986), which might eliminate workers who were in poor health early in the study. This, in turn, might bias findings concerning the relationship between health and retirement. Many studies opt to examine only the men's data (Anderson et al., 1986; Bazzoli, 1985). Given the difference between the typical work histories of men and women, we probably cannot assume that the factors which influence men's retirement are the principal predictors of women's workforce decisions. Indeed, research has shown that women and men do not weigh factors in the same way in deciding to retire (Shaw, 1988).

Furthermore, the women included in some of these surveys could hardly be considered representative. The RHS sample included only *unmarried* women—who, of course, are a minority until age 70 or so. In addition, the dramatic shifts in women's labor force participation since the early 1970s will require new data on their work decisions. Such data are only now becoming available for middle-aged women (Shaw, 1988). It will be several more years before retirement information for these women can be gathered and analyzed.

In general, then, we do have strong information on retirement patterns. This is especially true for white, married men. However, there are also strong data concerning minority retirement (the National Longitudinal Study, or NLS; Parnes, 1988). The data for women are weaker, partially because of changes in their work lives. Furthermore, one must always evaluate the constraints a researcher puts on subsamples of these surveys for a particular analysis.

There is another warning to be made about retirement studies: These studies have tended to categorize people as "retired" and "nonretired." This can be misleading, since a sizable portion of the elderly continue to work part-time, especially the self-employed elderly (Quinn & Burkhauser, 1990). Their work patterns are markedly different from what they were during young and middle adulthood, yet these people are not really retired. The common dichotomy of retired versus nonretired, therefore, may be misleading.

RETIREMENT

Americans clearly view work as a crucial component of their identity. Indeed, we consider the ability to support oneself by working a criterion for adulthood. Even Freud viewed work as one of the core components of normal adult functioning. In earlier chapters, we spent considerable time discussing how careers are chosen and developed, balanced with family life, and integral to life satisfaction and health.

Yet most of us will not work for our entire lives. Instead, we will retire. In fact, retirement is so common that it might be viewed as a rite of passage between middle and old age (Robinson, Coberly, & Paul, 1985). Many social scientists have painted it as a potentially difficult transition, precisely because it ends our work life and thereby takes away a piece of our identity.

Is retirement traumatic? Do retirees feel useless? Or do they feel that retirement is the reward for having worked hard for many years? If they would rather continue working, why do they quit? Is it voluntary, or do businesses (and, perhaps, unions and government) virtually force people into retirement? It should not surprise us to find that the circumstances surrounding retirement will affect the individual's adjustment.

Demographics

Less than 3 percent of the American labor force is over 65. In 1988, only 16.5 percent of the men and 7.9 percent of the women over 65 were still working (*Statistical Abstracts of the United States*, 1990). These represent declines in labor force participation for older workers, especially men. For example, during the early portion of this century, 65 percent of men 65 and older were in the labor force. By the 1950s, this had declined to just under 50 percent, and by 1986 only about 16 percent of men in this age group were still working. A smaller percentage of men aged 55–64 are now in the labor force than in the 1950s (about 67 percent in 1986 versus 87 percent in 1950) (Parnes, 1988). Furthermore, most of the people receiving Social Security benefits are receiving reduced benefits because of early retirement. Taken together, these statistics indicate that early retirement—especially between the ages of 62 and 64—is more common now than in the 1950s (Robinson et al., 1985).

The trend toward early retirement is stronger for men than for women (Robinson et al., 1985; Shaw, 1988). In fact, women aged 55–64 are more likely to be in the labor force today than they were in the 1950s (Robinson et al., 1985). There are several possible explanations for men's greater likelihood of earlier retirement. In recent cohorts, women may have only recently entered the workplace and so may be uninterested in leaving or may not yet have enough work time to collect pensions (including Social Security). Women also tend to be healthier than men and so are less likely to leave due to illness or disability. Single women (especially, perhaps, those who are divorced) may simply be financially unable to retire.

Older African-American men are less likely to be in the labor force than are white men (Robinson et al., 1985; Rones, 1988). Some of this differential is due to consistent racial differences in employment (Smith & Welch, 1989); for example, African-Americans are more likely than whites to be affected by unemployment (Dressel, 1988). For many elderly, unemployment may be the first step to retirement; the person may simply opt out of the job market. Unemployment may be a factor in the retirement decisions of up to 20 percent of American men (Robinson et al., 1985). In addition, elderly African-American men are more likely to have health problems. Health is probably the largest single variable in accounting for the differen-

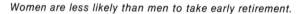

Women are less likely than men to take early retirement.

tial labor force participation of older African-American and white men (Robinson et al., 1985; Rones, 1988). Furthermore, African-American men are more likely to be in lower-paying, blue-collar jobs. Blue-collar workers are generally more likely to retire early than white-collar workers (Mitchell, Levine, & Pozzebon, 1988). When low pay is combined with poor health, the availability of Social Security Supplements or Disability may make retirement especially attractive (Rones, 1988).

Older African-American women, on the other hand, are more likely than older white women to be in the labor force (Robinson et al., 1985). This is probably partly due to the African-American women's greater responsibility for familial financial well-being across their lifetimes. African-American women also have lower-paying jobs than white women or any men (Dressel, 1988). They are less likely to be covered by pension plans. So it may not be financially feasible for them to retire, especially early.

Men in dangerous, strenuous jobs, such as mining and construction, retire earlier than those in professional or service positions. This is partly because blue-collar workers are more likely to suffer some limitations in their work. In other words, they have more health problems that interfere with their productivity. This probably contributes to another reason blue-collar workers retire earlier—namely, they feel they are not advancing at work while white-collar workers still report "progress" in their work status. These variables do not, however, completely account for the retirement patterns of blue- and white-collar employees (Mitchell et al., 1988).

Finally, we should note that the decision to retire is usually a permanent one (Parnes, 1988; Rones, 1988; Shaw, 1988). Only about a third of all retirees have any significant "postretirement" work experience. Those that do tend to have "marginal" jobs, working part-time or part of the year. Especially among men, finding *new* employment (as opposed to continuing with one's preretirement position, albeit in a reduced capacity) typically means downward mobility in terms of salary and status. This is less true for women, probably because they are generally in low-status positions to begin with (Rones, 1988; Shaw, 1988).

It is not necessarily the case that retirees prefer to not work at all. Indeed, many of them would like to work part-time or seasonally. Elderly men are about eight times more likely to work part-time than younger men, while elderly women work part-time nearly three times more frequently than younger women (Quinn & Burkhauser, 1990). The older workers would especially like to continue in their previous position at comparable salary levels (Quinn & Burkhauser, 1990; Rones, 1988). However, such opportunities are rare. The older part-time worker typically suffers a substantial decrease in wage rate after leaving full-time work. Furthermore, there are often disincentives to even part-time work. For example, in 1989, people under 65 could make $6480 while those over 65 could make $8880 before experiencing a reduction in their Social Security benefit such that $1 of Social Security is lost for every $2 made over the limit (Social Security Administration, 1988). Concerns about the solvency of Social Security have led to shifts in some of these policies (as of 1990, $1 will be lost for every $3 earned over the limit). Nonetheless, many private pension plans encourage early and complete retirement (Parnes, 1988; Rones, 1988). If meaningful, well-paying part-time work were available, probably even more people over 65 would continue some labor force participation (Quinn & Burkhauser, 1990).

The Decision to Retire

Both individual and institutional factors play a role in an individual's "decision" to retire. Some of the more important ones are shown in Table 16-1. These variables are likely to be weighed in some form of cost-benefit analysis. For example, the worker may weigh the value of the money to be made from continued employment against the amount of time left to enjoy the money (Robinson et al., 1985). It is not surprising, then, that factors which affect financial status, such as pension availability and progress in salary, are related to the timing of retirement. Similarly, we would expect that factors which influence ability to use accumulated wealth, especially health, would predict retirement. Indeed, studies have found that health and economic factors are the most powerful predictors of the decision to retire (Anderson, Burkhauser, & Quinn, 1986; Anderson & Burkhauser, 1985; Bazzoli, 1985; Mitchell et al., 1988; Parnes, 1988; Quinn & Burkhauser, 1990).

Economists have suggested that at least the economic variables are weighed over long time periods. In this life cycle approach, the worker is seen as evaluating the "best" time for retirement based on currently available information about pensions, Social Security, and work income (Fields & Mitchell, 1984; Anderson et al., 1986). This suggests that the timing of retirement is a well-thought-out decision. We might expect that it is made considerably in advance of retirement. Indeed, this assumption is one of the reasons that changes in Social Security eligibility are being phased in very slowly (Anderson et al., 1986). For example, the 1983 Social Security Amendment raised the "full" retirement age from 65 to 67—but this will not take effect until 2022 (Sammartino, 1987).

There is some evidence that people do plan when they will retire. For example, men aged 58–63 in the Retirement History Study (conducted by the Social Security Administration) were asked in 1969 when they planned to retire (Anderson et al., 1986). Not surprisingly, most of them said at 65, the standard age for receipt of full benefits under Social Security and most

TABLE 16-1: Factors in the Decision to Retire

Individual	Institutional
Financial resources	Workplace conditions and employee policies
Health status	Public policy regulations
Attitudes toward work and retirement	Economic conditions
Social support pressures	Societal events and values

Source: Robinson, R., Coberly, S., & Paul, C. (1985). Work and retirement. In R. Binstock & E. Shanas (eds.), *Handbook of aging and the social sciences,* 2nd ed., pp. 503–527. New York: Van Nostrand.

private pension plans. However, men selected a variety of different ages. When interviewed again in 1979, 57 percent were found to have retired "on time"; that is, within one year of their plans. As Table 16–2 shows, older men were more likely to match their plans and actual retirement behavior. But even men in their late fifties were likely to carry out their plans most of the time. This study may have underestimated "early" retirements, however, since people who died between 1969 and 1979 were omitted from the analysis (Anderson et al., 1986). Many of these people were probably sufficiently ill long enough to take early retirement before their deaths.

When short-term, prospective plans for retirement are examined, people seem to be quite likely to leave work as planned. Thus, almost two-thirds of the men in the Veterans' Normative Aging Study who said they would retire within two years did so (within one year of their planned date). However, when retrospective reports were taken from retirees, a third said their retirement was completely unexpected, while another 25 percent retired either earlier or later than they had planned (Ekerdt et al., 1989). Thus, while people do make plans for retirement, there is some flexibility. And when they do change their minds, it is most likely due to economic or health factors.

Health and Retirement

The argument that poor health leads to retirement is intuitively appealing. After all, the two co-occur with some frequency. Careers with high rates of early retirement also often have high rates of injury and mortality among workers. These include mining, construction, heavy labor, and farming. Professionals tend to enjoy better than average health and relatively low rates of early retirement (Burtless, 1987). Furthermore, it certainly is sensible for someone whose health is failing to miss work and even to leave it altogether.

There is a substantial amount of research connecting poor health and

TABLE 16–2: **Retirement Behavior Relative to Retirement Plans, Male Workers in 1969 (Percentages)**

Age in 1969	Early	On Time*	Late	Number
58	32	47	20	343
59	25	55	20	295
60	29	54	17	297
61	17	62	21	250
62	18	64	18	257
63	9	76	15	138
Total	24	57	19	1580

*The category *On Time* refers to those who retired within one year of when they said they would.

Source: Anderson, K., Burkhauser, R., & Quinn, J. (1986). Do retirement dreams come true? The effect of unanticipated events on retirement plans. *Industrial and Labor Relations Review, 39,* 518–526. © Cornell University.

retirement (Anderson et al., 1986; Anderson & Burkhauser, 1985; Bazzoli, 1985; Burtless,1987; Packard & Reno, 1989; Sammartino, 1987; Social Security Administration, 1986). It appears that health is a more important variable in early than on time retirement (Anderson et al., 1986; Sammartino, 1987; Social Security Administration, 1986). More specifically, ill health tends to play a role in retirement between the ages of 62 and 64. At younger ages, pensions are not readily available. Even partial Social Security is not available until 62. Thus, people who *can* work will usually try to stay on the job until they become eligible for benefits.

Certainly some people have such serious health problems that they retire prior to age 62; this is more true of men than women (Packard & Reno, 1989). However, many of these people, especially the married men, have the financial assets to allow the retirement. Furthermore, many men who have to retire early do so because of unemployment or job-specific mandatory retirement requirements, rather than for health reasons. Some of the men who retire early, especially those who are almost 62, do so voluntarily simply because they want the leisure. Women, too, also often retire early to gain leisure (Packard & Reno, 1989). Keep in mind the flip side of the poor health issue; many elderly (or near elderly) want to retire while they still have their health and can enjoy traveling, sports, family, and so on.

Once pensions become available, people who have been "holding on" will retire. There are several mitigating factors, however. First, those in poorer health who are most likely to retire are those whose jobs are physically demanding (Sammartino, 1987; Social Security Administration, 1986). There is an important interaction between job requirements and health. While this may seem obvious, the interaction is worth mentioning because it has created serious methodological problems. It means, for example, that objective measures of health, such as symptom checklists, may be inadequate because symptoms that may force one person to retire may be almost meaningless for another (Sammartino, 1987; Social Security Administration, 1986). Consider, for example, the meaning of a back injury for a dockworker and a lawyer.

Second, people who retire early due to health are more likely to be in lower-paying jobs (Social Security Administration, 1986). There are probably several reasons for the earlier retirement of the ill, lower-income worker. In some cases, the disability is likely to be work-related. This may be true of miners, for example. Many lower-paying jobs are also the more physically demanding—like custodian, farmer, and construction worker (Social Security Administration, 1986). Health problems may be more debilitating, in terms of continuing work, for these people. Finally, lower-paid workers may have less to gain financially from staying on the job, particularly if they are also eligible for disability payments.

People who retire "on time" rarely cite health as a reason, perhaps because retirement has become so acceptable that no explanation is needed. This argument is supported by findings that those who retire as planned are less likely to cite health as a reason. Furthermore, health is cited as a reason for retirement more frequently in retrospective than in prospective studies of retirement (Anderson et al., 1986; Bazzoli, 1985). This has led many researchers to conclude that health is often rationalization for an early retirement decision.

There is little agreement as to how much of a factor ill health is in retirement decisions. While passing the 1983 Social Security Amendments, Congress even requested an evaluation of the role of health to ascertain whether or not the decrease in early retirement benefits (from 80 percent of full benefits to 70 percent) and the increase in age for receiving full benefits (from 65 to 67) would unduly burden some part of the population (Social Security Administration, 1986). The study concluded that one segment of elderly workers would be adversely affected; lower-paid, ill workers would suffer, partly because they are more likely than other retirees to rely heavily on Social Security as their main source of income. As Table 16–3 shows, this was especially true of unmarried workers. The table also shows the percent reduction in income suffered by these people as a result of the changes in Social Security. Early retirees in the lowest fifth of income distribution would suffer about a 10 percent loss in total postretirement income, whereas those in the highest quintile would lose only about 3 percent. Thus, retirees in ill health, who are more likely to retire early, will be more affected.

How much of a problem will this be? The Social Security Administration (1986) estimates that by the year 2020, when the benefit changes are fully in place, about 7–9 percent of older workers will be in jobs with heavy strength requirements, the jobs from which people in poor health are most likely to retire early. This is a lower percentage than in the current workforce, where just over 11 percent of the older workers are in physically demanding jobs. This trend should reduce the effect of health on early retirement such that those who retire earlier will do so because they want to and can afford to. In such cases, the reduction of benefits is not as much of an issue.

Of course, this argument assumes that older workers of the future will

TABLE 16-3: The Effects of Decreasing Social Security Early Retirement Benefits as a Function of Health and Marital Status*

	Social Security Benefits as Percent of Income	Percent Reduction in Income
New retirees (total)	52%	6.4%
New retirees (not disabled)	50	6.3
New retirees (disabled)[†]	58	7.1
Unmarried disabled retirees	67	8.0
Married disabled retirees	55	6.8

*Calculated as if 1983 legislation changes had been in effect in 1982.
[†]*Disabled* includes those unable to work or having partial work limitations who had held jobs with heavy strength requirements.

Source: Social Security Administration (1986). Increasing the Social Security retirement age: Older workers in physically demanding occupations or ill health. *Social Security Bulletin, 49,* 5–23.

be at least as healthy as those of today. This is not an automatic assumption. There has been a dramatic increase in life expectancy and a decrease in mortality rates for every age group. Health professionals have been particularly successful at reducing deaths from cardiovascular disease. But lower mortality rates do not necessarily translate into less disability (Baily, 1987; Poterba & Summers, 1987; Social Security Administration, 1986; Sammartino, 1987). People who would have died from heart attacks, strokes, and cancer now survive, but not without ill effects. Many of them are partially or completely disabled. Table 16–4 shows the amount of activity restriction for older persons from the early 1960s to the early 1980s. These statistics indicate little progress, especially for those in the 64–74 range. Some cautions are needed in interpreting these numbers, however. The availability of disability programs, especially Social Security disability, may have increased the number of people reporting disabilities (Baily, 1987). Indeed, this argument seems especially plausible when the effects of our ability to "save" extremely ill people is considered. Martin Baily estimated that even if everyone who now survives formerly fatal illnesses is assumed to be disabled, the percentage of 45- to 64-year-old male workers reporting disability would have increased by 1.25 percent. Instead, it rose from 4.4 percent in 1960 to 10.8 percent in 1980. It is not only potentially fatal diseases, however, that can result in disability. Many nonfatal diseases, notably arthritis,

TABLE 16–4: Average Days per Person of Restricted Activity and Bed Disability among Aged, Selected Years, 1961–1980

Health Indicator and Year	AGE AND SEX			
	65–74		75 AND OVER	
	Men	Women	Men	Women
Restricted Activity Days				
1961	31.9	34.8	36.1	46.2
1963	31.3	36.3	41.4	49.6
1965	30.9	30.7	36.0	41.9
1968	31.2	30.3	35.0	47.6
1971	26.6	30.6	38.8	44.9
1975	31.1	36.2	40.7	49.4
1980	34.2	39.2	36.0	46.6
Bed Disability Days				
1961	11.4	12.5	14.6	23.6
1963	10.8	11.3	17.6	20.0
1965	11.5	11.1	14.5	16.0
1968	12.0	11.6	16.3	20.9
1971	9.0	10.9	17.9	18.9
1975	9.8	10.6	17.0	17.7
1980	10.9	12.9	13.4	19.1

Source: Poterba, J., & Summers, L. (1987). Public policy implications of declining old-age mortality. In G. Burtless (ed.), *Work, health, and income among the elderly.* Washington, D.C.: Brookings Institution.

may limit work ability. Mortality figures tell us nothing about these diseases. In fact, the available data suggest they are increasing, perhaps because more people are living longer.

Furthermore, it is not clear that there will be changes in medical treatment that will significantly improve the health of the older worker. Nor is it obvious that there will be enough changes in work and living environments, life style, or availability of medical care to improve their lot (Social Security Administration, 1986). Thus, neither the current trends in the health of the elderly nor the changes in future environments and health care guarantee better health for older workers.

Pensions and Retirement

About one-third of all elderly households receive income from private pensions. About two-thirds have assets, such as certificates of deposit or rental property, that pay them some income. Less than a fourth are earning money from a job. These income sources may be sufficient for some households, especially in the upper socioeconomic levels, but the more typical case is that the family relies heavily on Social Security. Over 90 percent of all American elderly households receive Social Security (Fields & Mitchell, 1984). Those who retire early due to ill health and unmarried retirees rely heavily on Social Security (Fields & Mitchell, 1984; Social Security Administration, 1986).

The dominance of Social Security as retirement income provides some interesting research possibilities because changes in Social Security benefits can dramatically affect potential retirement income. Researchers can evaluate the effect of available levels of retirement income on the decision to retire just by looking at Social Security. Certainly this approach has its limitations, especially in generalizing to upper-income professionals' retirement decisions. Nonetheless, since the government provides consistent information on all Social Security beneficiaries and since most people participate in the program, there is much valuable information to be gained about retirement decisions from looking at the program.

Throughout the 1960s, Social Security benefits did not grow in real terms. In other words, the growth in benefits did not even always keep pace with inflation. Beginning in 1969, however, the benefit increases in most years exceeded the inflation rate, resulting in real growth. This effectively means that those who retired during the late 1970s were able to maintain a substantially better standard of living from their Social Security benefits. This was not a benefit increase that older workers had expected. Researchers have thus been able to evaluate how an unexpected increase in Social Security benefits affected retirement decisions. The results indicate that these benefit increases changed the probability of retirement (Anderson et al., 1986). More specifically, the likelihood of retiring earlier than planned increased, while the probability of delaying retirement declined. As we noted earlier, most retirees left the workforce as planned and so apparently did not consider the increases in benefits in their decision (Anderson et al., 1986).

How dramatic are these effects? Bazzoli (1985) reported that a 10 percent increase in Social Security benefits increased the likelihood of early retirement by 1.3 percentage points. On the other hand, she found that if a private pension was available only if the worker waited until age 65 to retire, workers were 18 percentage points less likely to retire early than those without any private pension. It appears, then, that people who have private pensions take them into account in making their retirement decisions. However, we must be cautious in our assumptions as to precisely how such financial issues are figured into the retirement decision. Certainly, economists like Bazzoli (1985) who use group data find that pension availability is a powerful predictor. However, other data (GAO, 1987) indicate that a substantial number of workers do not know the details of their retirement plans. For example, 41 percent of the workers covered by early retirement options either knew nothing or had erroneous information about the plans. Younger workers (those more than five years from retirement) were especially unlikely to know when they would be eligible for early retirement benefits; over 75 percent did not know. Even more amazing, 65 percent of the pension-eligible workers over age 55 did not know when they would be eligible for normal benefits. Women are less likely than men to know about their benefits (GAO, 1987), perhaps because they are less likely to be eligible or because they are more likely to look at their husband's potential income and retirement timing in making their own retirement decision (Parnes, 1988; Shaw, 1988).

The data, then, suggest that changes in Social Security benefits do not dramatically alter retirement decisions, though the effect is statistically significant. Similarly, inflation seems to have limited impact (Parnes, 1988). Many workers do not seem to know enough about their pension plans to argue that such resources are the major influence on the retirement decision.

Does this mean that economic variables are unimportant? Of course not. People apparently make some assumptions, often mistaken ones, about retirement benefits. Perhaps with better information, they would make different decisions. However, two points need to be made. First, people are unlikely to retire without assurances of some sort of income, typically from Social Security and private pensions. Second, the financial issues form a basis for the timing of retirement insomuch as people generally will not retire without them. Many people also reach a point where continuing to work may cost them more than they make; the loss in retirement income is greater than the work-generated income (Quinn & Burkhauser, 1990). Nonetheless, the details of the decision seem to rely much more heavily on attitudes toward retirement than on economics. Indeed, fully 40 percent of new retirees give no other reason for the decision than wanting to retire (Parnes, 1988). As we noted earlier, some portion of those who cite health as a reason probably could continue working but would rather not.

Job and Retirement Attitudes

It is clear that neither health nor economic variables can completely explain the decision to retire or its timing. Clearly, much of the variance is due simply to a desire to retire, and this is indeed the most commonly cited reason for retirement (Parnes, 1988).

People who do not like their jobs are more likely to retire early (Parnes, 1988). Professionals and executives tend to be particularly satisfied with their jobs (Mitchell et al., 1988), and these are among the least likely groups to take early retirement. Indeed, they tend to continue working even past age 65 (Rones, 1988). Laborers and machine operatives report much lower job satisfaction and tend to retire early, although this is partly due to the physical demands of their jobs (Mitchell et al., 1988). In general, blue-collar workers are less satisfied than white-collar employees and are also more likely to opt for early retirement (Mitchell et al., 1988).

There can be little doubt that retirement has become increasingly acceptable in American society (Parnes, 1988; Robinson et al., 1985). Recent cohorts may be more oriented toward early retirement than workers of even thirty years ago. This does not mean that Americans have lost their work ethic (Burrus-Bammel & Bammel, 1985). However, they do increasingly recognize the tradeoff between making money and having the time to spend it. They may also be aware of the effect of continued work on their health. Especially among higher-income people, leisure has a strong appeal (Burrus-Bammel & Bammel, 1985). Such attitudes, which have been institutionalized in Social Security, probably make it easier for people to retire. On the other hand, some people, especially Type A men, may be extremely reluctant to retire voluntarily (Swan, Dame, & Carnelli, 1991).

We should note that, especially among women, the conflict between family responsibilities and career continues even into old age. Women are more likely than men to retire or switch to part-time work in order to care for an ailing family member (Parnes, 1987; Rones, 1988). Among those 65 and over who worked part-time, nearly 25 percent of the women, but only 3 percent of the men, said they did so because of home obligations (Rones, 1988). Similarly, research indicates that married couples tend to retire at about the same time (Parnes, 1988). Since the husband is typically the older member of the couple, this means that wives are likely to take early retirement.

Adjustment to Retirement

Retirement has often been viewed as a negative event, a stressor (Rosenmayer, 1985). Insomuch as work is viewed as part of an adult's identity, it was thought that retirement undermined the self-system. Not being part of the workforce supposedly made the person marginal in society, so it seemed appropriate to compare the status of the elderly to that of children or adolescents. Furthermore, it was supposed that the elderly, forced to retire, felt as useless as an old shoe tossed out in the trash. Indeed, retirement was seen as part of a mutual disengagement process in which the person withdrew from society and vice versa (Cumming & Henry, 1961). Retirement was actually a component of a process that removed the older person from society.

At least two assumptions underlie this perspective. One is that most people are forced to retire by law or lack of opportunity. The other is that the elderly do not have the financial resources, health, or desire to enjoy leisure time. Neither assumption appears to be strongly supported by the data. It would not be surprising, then, to find that the negative outcomes postulated by these theorists also receive little empirical support.

As might be expected, there are wide individual differences in adjustment to retirement (Atchley, 1975, 1989; Robinson et al., 1985). Some of these differences are accounted for by personality variables. Some people are more flexible and adaptable than others; they are less likely to interpret events as stressful and can modify their plans and life styles to accommodate change. People who are flexible are likely to adjust to retirement fairly easily; those who are more rigid are likely to encounter difficulties, just as they probably have at every other life transition (Atchley, 1989).

People who are heavily invested in their work are likely to find it hard to leave. Those who derive their identity, or at least a major component of it, from work will be lost. Atchley (1975, p. 92) provides an example. Imagine a man who has the following set of personal goals, ranked in order of importance:

> Being a decent, moral person
> Being a good husband
> Having a comfortable, well-furnished home ·
> Being a good golfer
> Being a good neighbor
> Being a successful insurance salesman
> Keeping a lid on my temper
> Improving myself through reading
> Being a dutiful son-in-law to my wife's mother

and a second man with the following goals:

> Being a successful corporation president
> •
> •
> •
> •
> Being a good husband
> (*The dots indicate distance.*)

The second man is much more likely to find it difficult to retire, especially if his goals have not been achieved (Atchley, 1975). To use Erikson's concept of despair, the man is apt to feel that time is running out and that he is being robbed of his opportunities.

Retirees who have financial difficulties are also likely to be unhappy (Atchley, 1975; Bossé, Aldwin, Levenson, & Workman-Daniels, 1991; Robinson et al., 1985). In fact, this is the most common reason given for dissatisfaction. Some of these people will seek employment after retirement; others may turn to their families for help and may even live with their children. As we saw in Chapter 15, the elderly really do not want to live with their children. They do not want to give up their independence. Any circumstance that increases dependence on the family is likely to generate dissatisfaction.

Health is also a major factor in postretirement adjustment (Atchley, 1975; Bossé et al., 1991; Robinson et al., 1985). Those who are in poor health will have more trouble adjusting. There are probably several factors operating here. First, when people have to retire unexpectedly, poor health is the most common reason (Anderson et al., 1986; Ekerdt et al., 1989). They may not be as prepared financially or psychologically as those who plan retirement. Indeed, involuntary retirees show poorer adjustment, including symptoms of depression, than do people who retire voluntarily (Swan et al., 1991). In addition, their families may not be as supportive as those whose retirement occurs at the "agreed upon" time. After all, the family's expectations have been violated too, and they will need time to adjust (Atchley, 1989). Inasmuch as retirement is a family decision and the family's attitude mediates the retiree's adjustment, this can be a critical factor (Giordano & Beckman, 1985).

Furthermore, health may cause financial burdens in terms of direct care costs and in income reductions. It may also limit ability to participate in leisure activities (Burrus-Bammel & Bammel, 1985). All these relationships help explain why health is the most significant single predictor of morale among the aged, whether or not they are retired (Burrus-Bammel & Bammel, 1985). In those cases where the retiree is ill, it is most probably poor health rather than retirement that accounts for the dissatisfaction (Atchley, 1975; Robinson et al., 1985). Furthermore, retirement does not, in and of itself, typically cause a decline in physical health. Indeed, in some cases retirement may preserve or even improve health. Think of the coal miner with black lung disease or the mover with a back problem.

Despite the complexity of the factors influencing retirement adjustment, most retirees report being happy with their lives. In a recent study (Bossé et al., 1991), less than a third found retirement stressful. Indeed, retirement and spouse's retirement were rated as the least stressful on a list of 31 possible events. Marital problems, difficulties with children, parental health problems, and even changes in volunteer work were all rated as more stressful. However, two points need to be made about the nature of the "positive adjustment."

First, positive adjustment does not always happen overnight. It may take as long as two years to complete the transition (Giordano & Beckman, 1985). Atchley (1976) has suggested that retirees move through five stages in adjusting to retirement. The first is the *honeymoon* phase: retirees may feel they are on a vacation. They are getting to do all those projects and activities they'd been putting off. They can sleep late and go where they wish. Retirement seems like a great idea.

Most of us have had the experience of being glad to get back to work or school after a vacation. There's a certain amount of comfort in the routine, as well as intellectual stimulation and social interaction. In the *disenchantment* phase, retirees may begin to miss work, or at least enjoyable components of it such as challenge or companionship. They may find that working children or friends don't have any more time to get together than they used to, but the retirees do. Money problems may begin to emerge.

At this point, retirees need to identify the specific difficulties being experienced and make adjustments. This is called the *reorientation* phase. How much reorientation is necessary depends on a number of factors, including how crucial work was to the retiree's identity (Atchley, 1975). It also depends on whether or not the individual is able to pursue hobbies or interests. For example, many people plan to travel or do things with their spouses after retiring. If the spouse dies, the retirement period can become very lonely, and substantial reorientation may be necessary (Atchley, 1975). Reorientation can take many forms, ranging from spending more time with the family (Giordano & Beckman, 1985) to starting an entirely new career (Havighurst, 1980).

Once reorientation has occurred, the retiree enters a period of *stability*. This does not mean that there are no further adjustments or changes in the individual's life. Keep in mind that Atchley is a continuity theorist (Atchley, 1989; see Chapter 1). He argues that a structure for valuing and interpreting is redefined (by some people) with retirement, and after the reorientation phase, that general structure remains constant. The final stage is *termination* of the retirement role. Of course, this could be caused by death, but it can also be caused by serious illness or disability. In such situations, the person's primary role becomes invalid rather than retiree.

Thus, adjustment is a gradual process. Furthermore, not everyone adjusts in the same way. Just as there are individual differences in adjustment to marriage, divorce, birth, departure of children, and every other major life transition, there will be different approaches to retirement. Chances are that these approaches will reflect lifelong personality dispositions, values, interests, and goals (Atchley, 1989). For example, in a study of male, upper-level college administrators, Havighurst (1980) found four patterns of retirement. The "maintainers" continued their professional activity by assuming a variety of part-time obligations and assignments. The "reducers" moved out of virtually all professional activities. The "reorganizers" channeled their administrative and leadership capabilities into other endeavors, sometimes in the education field, but sometimes in a new field or in government or community service. The "transformers" moved into a whole new area, but did not serve as leaders or administrators. One ex-college president, for example, began painting.

Retirement, then, appears to be similar to other life transitions. Most people adjust well, just as they have all their lives. Since attitudes toward retirement are positively correlated with adjustment (Robinson et al., 1985), we might expect that people will do even better in future cohorts. After all, retirement has become not only acceptable, but a normative life experience. This implies that the "on-time" retiree will enjoy the support of a peer group. Furthermore, the anticipation of retirement should facilitate better financial planning.

THE OLDER WORKER

Not all older people are retired. About 20 percent of the men and 10 percent of the women aged 70 to 74 are still working (Rones, 1988). Certainly, most people do retire. In fact, as we have seen, there is a trend toward earlier retirement, especially among men. But who are the people who choose to continue working?

Between 62 and 64, about two-thirds of the men and nearly half of the women workers are employed full-time, year round (Rones, 1988). Although many of these people are eligible to retire at age 62, many are either unaware of their options or unwilling to accept the lower benefits that often accompany early retirement (as in Social Security, for example). After age 65, however, those who stay in the workforce are much less likely to work full-time. Among men, about a third are full-time employees, while only 22 percent of the women workers over 65 work full-time. This appears to be by choice. Only about 10 percent of the over-65s who are working part-time cite lack of employment opportunities as the explanation (Rones, 1988).

The older worker is not likely to have started a second career after retiring (Rones, 1988); less than 2 percent of the older workers switched occupations during the two-month period of one study. This can be compared to career switches by about 7 percent of the 35- to 45-year-old men, 8 percent of the 35- to 45-year-old women, and 5 percent of the 45- to 54-year-olds (Rones, 1988). As Table 16–5 shows, most older workers had been with their current employer for a while. On the other hand, it is fairly common for the older part-time worker to have left a "career job" of earlier adulthood because it permitted only full-time work (Quinn & Burkhauser, 1990).

The over-65-year-olds who continue to work are likely to be better educated (Rones, 1988). This is true for both men and women. They are also more likely to be self-employed (Quinn & Burkhauser, 1990). Self-employment is about three times more common among workers over 65 than in the general population. Given these trends, it is not surprising that

TABLE 16–5:   Percent of Workers with Current Employer Three Years or Less, by Sex and Age, January 1983

Age	MEN		WOMEN	
	1 Year or Less	3 Years or Less	1 Year or Less	3 Years or Less
35–44 years	16.7%	31.7%	24.2%	45.4%
45–54 years	11.2	21.0	15.5	31.0
55–59 years	9.6	17.7	10.5	22.5
60–64 years	7.7	15.4	11.3	23.2
65–69 years	10.5	23.1	9.6	21.1
70 years and over	9.5	18.0	11.6	21.1

Source: Rones, P. (1988). Employment, earnings, and unemployment characteristics of older workers. In M. Borus, H. Parnes, S. Sandall, & B. Seidman (eds.), *The older worker.* Madison, WI: Industrial Relations Research Association.

older male workers are overrepresented as executives. They are also over-represented in farming, sales, and service work, as are older women. Older men are underrepresented as laborers and technicians; older women are underrepresented in technical, labor, executive, and professional jobs (Rones,1988). The underrepresentation of women in these fields may, how-ever, be indicative of lifelong patterns, especially in the cohorts for whom data are currently available.

We have already seen several explanations for these trends. For exam-ple, people who work in blue-collar jobs are more likely to retire early if they have health problems, since health is more likely to interfere with their jobs. In addition, it is likely that some jobs offer more psychological incen-tive to work at least part-time (Rones, 1988). The intellectual stimulation of continuing to teach might make an older professor want to keep at it. It seems unlikely that a janitor would offer a similar reason for continuing to work. Furthermore, many professions, including teaching, may offer more opportunities for part-time work. Indeed, *retention rates* (rates of continued employment) are probably highest among self-employed doctors, lawyers, and other professionals. This is at least partially attributable to the greater scheduling flexibility enjoyed by these workers (Rones, 1988). We have seen that continued employment would probably be even higher among the el-derly if part-time scheduling were more widely available.

We need to be cautious about "glamorizing" continued work in old age. Many elderly people work in order to survive. Private household work-ers have the highest rated of continued employment among women, prob-ably because they have a long history of low pay (and hence little or no savings), low or no pension, and high availability of part-time work (Shaw, 1988).

Creative Contributions and the Older Worker

Much of what was said in Chapter 12 about the productivity of the middle-aged worker can be generalized to the older worker, with the recog-nition that physical deterioration plays an increasing role. However, the discussion in Chapter 12 focused on how much work was produced and how efficiently and safely the production occurred. Questions of creativity and leadership were not addressed.

The question of when people make their most significant career con-tributions has been an issue of investigation for over a century. The data seem fairly clear: For most fields, both the number and quality of contribu-tions rises to a single age peak and then falls off (Simonton, 1988). This is true whether the unit of analysis is scientific theory or research, musical compositions, poetry, or novels. The rate of increase and decrease as well as the peak age of creativity vary from field to field. For example, the peak tends to be quite early—in the late twenties or early thirties—for poets. In fields where training and experience are more important, such as philoso-phy or medicine, the peak tends to be later—in the late forties or beyond. The decline in creativity tends to be greatest (and steepest) for fields that peak early. In fields with later peaks, the dropoff is much more gradual and may even approximate a plateau. There are, of course, many fields that fall in between. These fields tend to have a peak around 40, with a decline of about 50 percent in creativity by the career's end (Mumford, 1984; Simonton, 1988).

Research on leadership is more sparse and not easily summarized. There appears to be no relationship between age at inauguration and U.S. presidents' performance (Simonton, 1988). On the other hand, a study of hereditary monarchs showed that leadership capability tended to peak in the middle years (Simonton, 1988). Of course, it is not clear how generalizable either of these situations is to leadership in a community group or the workplace. Indeed, one of the problems in both the creativity and the leadership literature is their limited relationship to daily life and the average elderly American. Nonetheless, there are situations in which a person's creative or leadership potential may be relevant to employment decisions. This might be true, for example, of decisions to offer training programs or leadership roles or specific work assignments to an older versus a younger worker. Furthermore, it might be argued that the declines in creative potential are attributable to some form of cognitive shift that would also influence other performance variables. Thus, the research on creativity and leadership may hold clues to other aspects of aging and work ability.

Unfortunately, the age patterns in creativity and leadership remain largely unexplained. It has been suggested that extrinsic factors, including age discrimination, might play a role (Simonton, 1988). Perhaps declining health or increasing family obligations make it difficult for the older professional to produce as much work. The amount of work produced may be related to the quality of the work, inasmuch as the likelihood of a highly influential discovery improves with enhanced output. On the other hand, it may be that there are changes in motivation or intellectual ability that account for the age curve (Simonton, 1988). The young adult, for example, may be more adaptive and accommodating in cognitive style. He or she may be more open to new ideas and approaches than the older worker, who adopts a more realistic, task-specific orientation (Mumford, 1984).

In any case, there are wide individual differences in productivity curves. Those who produce the most tend to be the most creative (Simonton, 1988). Furthermore, it is clearly possible for someone to produce his or her greatest work—in terms of creativity or leadership—quite late in life (Mumford, 1984). This is one of the lessons from the study of U.S. presidents, for age is not an important predictor of performance for them.

FINANCIAL WELL-BEING

While there is considerable debate about the effects of retirement, one outcome is clear: retirement is virtually always accompanied by a drop in income. Pension plans do not pay the same monthly rate that the last salary does. And even the addition of disability (if the retiree is qualified) will not raise the monthly "take home" to preretirement level. Even the combination of Social Security and private pension is not enough. For example, the median income of 45- to 54-year-olds' households was $28,570 in a 1984 survey; that of older households was $12,250 (Radner, 1989).

Does this mean that most elderly are poor or struggling financially? Or have they been able to prepare for the drop in income by investing in pension plans, savings accounts, and other assets while reducing their amount of indebtedness (by paying off mortgages, for example)? Large-scale surveys suggest that net worth actually rises with age, peaking during the immediate preretirement years of 55–64 (Radner, 1989) (see Table 16–6). The median net worth for the 18,700 households in the Survey of Income and Program Participation (conducted by Social Security) was $32,600. For older households, median net worth was $59,680. More specifically, those aged 65–74 had a median worth of $62,060, and those households with heads over 75 had a median worth of $54,620 (Radner, 1989).

We might conclude that the average elderly household is quite comfortable. After all, net worth is noticeably higher than that of young adults. Furthermore, we might expect that expenses will be lower. The house is paid for, and there are no children to support. However, we need to be cautious about drawing such conclusions.

First, it is not clear that elderly people's expenses are low enough to allow them to live comfortably despite the drop in income. Certainly, there are many people whose expenses are lower than those of young adults (Habib, 1985). But the costs of one older person living alone are higher than those associated with a child in a two-parent family (Habib, 1985), yet more government dollars are spent helping to support the child. Other groups, particularly the ill elderly, may also find that expenses clearly exceed income and savings. The research needed to answer these questions has not yet been done.

Second, some of the assets included in the net worth calculation are not very liquid. It may be difficult to convert a car or house to cash in an emergency. It is important to examine just the financial assets of households, such as savings accounts or mutual funds, which are more liquid and therefore more accessible. Table 16–7 shows the financial assets of households by age of the head (Radner, 1989). Again, the median level for the aged is higher than that of younger adults. Unlike net worth, the liquid assets of the elderly are even higher than those of preretirees. However, an examination of Tables 16–6 and 16–7 indicates a wide dispersion of levels of net worth and financial assets among the elderly (Radner, 1989). Such diversity is not surprising, because financial status in old age is the outcome of a lifetime of career, family, spending, and savings choices and opportunities. While 30 percent of the aged have net worths of at least $100,000, 20 percent have less than $20,000. When we consider that this figure includes all assets (such as house, savings, car), it is evident that the households in the lower ranges are in a precarious situation. This is underscored by the fact that a quarter of the aged have less than $1000 in financial assets (Radner, 1989).

Who Is at Risk for Poverty?

Overall, about 12 to 13 percent of elderly Americans live below the poverty line (Ford Foundation, 1989). This is a lower poverty rate than

TABLE 16-6: Percentage Distribution of Households, by Net Worth and Age of Householder, 1984

Net Worth*	All Ages	AGE					AGED 65 OR OLDER		
		Under 25	25–34	35–44	45–54	55–64	Total	65–74	75 or older
Total number of households (in millions)	86.9	5.7	20.1	17.4	12.6	12.9	18.2	10.7	7.5
Total percent	100	100	100	100	100	100	100	100	100
Negative or $0	11	26	17	10	8	5	7	7	6
$1–9,999	21	55	35	18	12	11	13	11	15
$10,000–24,999	12	12	18	13	11	8	9	9	10
$25,000–49,999	15	4	14	18	14	14	16	15	17
$50,000–99,999	20	2	10	21	25	26	26	26	25
$100,000–$249,999	16	1	4	15	22	27	24	25	23
$250,000 or more	4	*	1	4	7	10	6	7	4
Median	$32,600	$2,160	$8,100	$35,500	$56,500	$72,460	$59,680	$62,060	$54,620

*Less than 0.5 percent.

TABLE 16-7: Percentage Distribution of Households, by Financial Assets and Age of Householder, 1984

Financial Assets	All Ages	AGE					AGED 65 OR OLDER		
		Under 25	25–34	35–44	45–54	55–64	Total	65–74	75 or older
Total	100	100	100	100	100	100	100	100	100
$0	15	26	19	13	13	12	12	13	11
$1–$999	24	46	34	26	19	14	13	13	13
$1,000–$9,999	30	25	34	34	32	23	23	21	26
$10,000–$24,999	13	3	8	13	14	17	15	16	14
$25,000–$49,999	8	1	3	7	10	14	14	15	13
$50,000–$99,999	7	*	1	4	7	11	15	14	16
$100,000 or more	4	*	1	2	4	8	8	8	7
Median†	$2,600	$350	$800	$2,160	$4,150	$10,000	$11,000	$11,900	$10,100

*Less than 0.5 percent. †For all households in the group.

Source: Radner, D. (1989). Net worth and financial assets of age groups in 1984. *Social Security Bulletin, 52,* 2–15.

Many elderly people have the physical and financial resources to enjoy their retirement.

among young adults, but it masks the situation of some subgroups. Single older people are much more likely to be poor than are the married (Radner, 1989). Minority members are more likely to be poor (Dressel, 1988; Jackson, 1985); for example, 27 percent of the Hispanic elderly are poor (Ford Foundation, 1989). Women are more likely than men to be poor. Among single elderly white women, over 25 percent live in poverty. And those suffering the discrimination of being both female and a minority are particularly likely to be poor; over 60 percent of single African-American elderly women are impoverished (Ford Foundation, 1989).

There are many reasons why some elderly are more likely to be poor. Many of them are captured in the generalization that those who have higher-status, higher-paying jobs throughout their lives are more likely to be financially comfortable in their retirement. Since white men make more money than women or minorities (see Chapter 7) throughout their lives, it is not surprising that they have more money in retirement. White men are more likely to be in high-status jobs, such as executive or professional positions, which carry private pensions. Women are less likely to hold jobs that offer pensions and are less likely to be vested in pension plans, even when plans are available, partly because women are less likely to have uninterrupted work histories (Shaw, 1988). We might expect, then, that the influx of women into the workplace might mean that future cohorts of women will be better off than today's elderly females.

There are two arguments against too much optimism. First, most of today's young women still interrupt their work lives to raise children. Mott and Shapiro (1982) looked at the work patterns of women aged 24–34 in 1978 for the first seven years after having their first child. They found that only 12 percent of the women worked at least 6 months in each of the seven years, while 30 percent had not worked at all during any of the time. Women's workforce participation is increasing, but it is still commonly interrupted. Such interruptions may have negative ramifications for pension investments (Shaw, 1988).

Second, we can examine the experiences of African-American workers. Beginning in the 1960s, significant legal advances were made in ending discrimination. African-Americans began to move into better jobs and to get more education. Since education is probably the single greatest predictor of salary and retirement status (Rones, 1988; Taylor & Chatters, 1988), this shift boded well for future generations of African-Americans (Jackson, 1985). Certainly some advances have been made, but it is clearly true that even among younger cohorts, African-Americans are concentrated in blue-collar occupations and are underrepresented in the white-collar careers (Rones, 1988). This means, among other things, that they are less likely to have private pension funds available. African-Americans are more likely to suffer periods of unemployment during their work lives, and this too affects the availability of pensions (Jackson, 1985; Rones, 1988). Finally, and most discouragingly, limited evidence indicates that more education does not translate into a higher standard of living for African-Americans to the same extent it does for whites (Dressel, 1988; Jackson, 1985; Klein & Rones, 1989).

Surely, racial discrimination is a major reason that blacks and other minorities have lower lifetime and retirement incomes than white men (Dressel, 1988). It is equally clear that lifelong sex discrimination has affected the financial status of elderly women (Shaw, 1988). When the two "devalued" statuses of female and minority intersect, the result can be devastating (Taylor & Chatters, 1988). African-American women are probably the greatest single risk group for poverty. And as always, being single increases the risk of poverty (Radner, 1989; Taylor & Chatters, 1988).

Other factors also influence the likelihood of poverty in old age. In general, people with more education have higher levels of wealth (Rones, 1988; Taylor & Chatters, 1988). They are less likely to retire early, suffer ill health, or rely exclusively on Social Security for retirement income. People who get divorced are less likely to be prepared for retirement (Fethke, 1989). This may be because of a loss of assets at the time of the divorce, the drain of paying child support while maintaining a separate household, interruptions in savings due to the expense of starting a new household, or any of the other financial burdens associated with divorce (Fethke, 1989).

Getting Out of Poverty

We have seen that poverty rates among the elderly are generally lower than those for young adults. Nonetheless, there often seems to be more sympathy and compassion for the elderly poor. After all, they have worked hard all their lives. Furthermore, we do not believe they have the same options available to them to end their poverty as younger adults do (Coe, 1988).

In fact, the elderly poor are almost as likely as young poor people to escape poverty during the first three years of poverty (Coe, 1988). More than half of the elderly poor are poor for less than three years. However, once an elderly person has been poor for more than three years, the chances of getting out are very small. Most of the young adults who are poor for three years will escape within a decade, but most of the elderly will be chronically poor. Using survey data from the Michigan Panel Study of Income Dynamics, Coe (1988) reported that the elderly who had been poor more than three years had less than a 5 percent chance of exiting poverty. Women were particularly unlikely to escape. Approximately 25 percent of the women, but only about 10 percent of the elderly men, who are ever poor can expect it to be a permanent (15 or more years) status (Coe, 1988).

LEISURE

Leisure can serve a variety of functions at any stage of life. It can provide relaxation and regeneration, needed exercise, skill maintenance and development, and a basis for social interaction. Leisure activities may take on a new dimension in old age; they may make a person feel more active, involved, and vital. For the elderly who have experienced a recent life transition, such as retirement or widowhood, leisure activities may provide an important form of continuity (Heinemann, Colorez, Frank, & Taylor, 1988).

It is somewhat surprising, then, to find that leisure activities do not

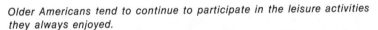

Older Americans tend to continue to participate in the leisure activities they always enjoyed.

increase with age (Burrus-Bammel & Bammel, 1985; Heinemann et al., 1988). Indeed, researchers often report an age-related decline in general participation, especially after age 75. This is not true in every activity, of course. For example, rates of relaxing, watching television, gardening, and solitary activities may increase with age. Physical activities, on the other hand, tend to decline. Older Americans are less likely to participate in sports or physical exercise (Burrus-Bammel & Bammel, 1985; Heinemann et al., 1988). In fact, only a minority of elderly have an organized, regular exercise program, despite the potential benefits. Nearly half of the elderly list no hobby or sports participation (Burrus-Bammel & Bammel, 1985).

But is it age alone that accounts for the low to moderate rates of participation in leisure activities by the elderly? Does the declining rate indicate "disengagement" or "withdrawal" from society? The research indicates that two factors seem more important than age itself in leisure patterns. First is earlier participation patterns (Atchley, 1988; Burrus-Bammel & Bammel, 1985; Heinemann et al., 1988). Most young adults, for example, do not participate in regular fitness programs. Americans, especially men, are very work-oriented; they may so enjoy their work that they have difficulty distinguishing work from leisure (Burrus-Bammel & Bammel, 1985). This may be one reason why so many professional men continue to work at least part-time after retirement (Havighurst, 1980). As people age, they do not become more likely to pick up new activities; rather they will tend to spend their leisure as they always have or engage in undemanding activities, such as TV viewing. Heinemann and his associates (1988) reported that participation in active crafts (gardening and auto maintenance), sports, and social activities (church or clubs) were predicted by earlier participation levels.

Heinemann and associates' data also demonstrate the other factor—namely, health. In their visually impaired elderly sample, duration of low vision was negatively related to participation in sedentary crafts, such as sewing or knitting. Overall, the better the elderly perceive their health to be, the more likely they are to participate in leisure activity (Burrus-Bammel & Bammel, 1985). Over half of the visually impaired elderly in Heinemann's study reported giving up at least one favored activity because of sight losses. It may also be that health problems generate other difficulties, with transportation or finances for example, that preclude participation (Burrus-Bammel & Bammel, 1985). Other factors may also influence participation. Those with low incomes are less likely to participate in hobbies and recreation. Apartment dwellers spend less time on hobbies than do homeowners (Burrus-Bammel & Bammel, 1985). But the critical variables appear to be previous patterns and health. In fact, it may be these factors, rather than age itself, which account for the decline in certain activities (Heinemann et al., 1988).

SUMMARY

For many years, retirement has been viewed as a negative event. Indeed, it was this perception that led to changes in the mandatory retirement age for many business and government employees. Certainly some elderly people wish to continue to work. Anti-ageism legal protection needs to be developed to ensure that these people have the opportunity to continue working.

However, most people want to retire. Many would be willing to continue to work part-time, but given the choice between full-time work and retirement, they opt for the latter. The most common reason they give for retiring is simply that they want to. Certainly income availability affects retirement; people are not very likely to retire before they are eligible for their pensions (including Social Security). But the majority of elderly Americans are now eligible for at least Social Security, including early retirement benefits, and so pension availability seems to be less of a constraint than it once was. In fact, not only are more people retiring now than early in the century, but increasing numbers, especially among men, are choosing early retirement.

Health may also play a role in the decision to retire. This is particularly true of decisions to retire earlier than planned. Health problems that directly interfere with work are especially likely to increase the likelihood of retirement. It is not surprising, therefore, that people engaged in physically demanding jobs are more apt to take early retirement. It is important to recognize, however, that health may sometimes be given as a reason more to rationalize an earlier decision than because it really was an important determinant. Some people probably still think it is lazy or somehow wrong to retire, especially early. As attitudes toward retirement continue to become more favorable, we should see a decline in such rationalizations and should be better able to assess health's true role in the retirement decision.

Most people adjust quite well to retirement. Those who don't have higher rates of health and financial problems. Poor adjustment is also associated with high levels of investment in work (as a part of identity) and negative attitudes toward retirement. As with any other transition, adaptation may take time. The among of adaptation needed will vary according to individual value systems, availability of social support, and anticipation of retirement.

One of the major reasons people thought retirement was stressful was that it brings a sizable drop in income. Theorists and policymakers assumed that this translated into poverty for many elderly people. The image of the impoverished old person is a common one. It is not, however, an accurate one for the majority of people. Those who are poor are likely to have been poor throughout their lives. In other words, they tend to have had frequent unemployment or have worked in low-paying jobs that offer little or no pension. Given this, it is not startling to learn that women and minority members are most likely to be poor. Almost two-thirds of single black elderly women are poor. Policymakers need to recognize that the problem is not necessarily being old; most poverty problems are established well before age 65.

Some of the elderly poor continue to work. Among women, domestic workers are the most likely group to continue working into old age. Such people work primarily for the money. Other elderly, especially self-employed professionals like doctors and lawyers, also frequently continue to work. This is partly because they can easily limit their hours and yet continue to work. This option would be exercised by more people if it were more widely available.

This underscores the point that Americans enjoy working. American men in particular may be so identified with their work that they have difficulty distinguishing work and leisure. They do not establish any real hobbies or leisure interests. These patterns persist into old age; old people do not typically establish new leisure activities. In fact, health may force them to abandon or spend less time on some forms of recreation.

If health is maintained into old age and more people retire early, we might expect to see changes in leisure patterns among retirees. Communities and services that make leisure more accessible to the elderly would make such developments easier.

Overall, then, the retired elderly are satisfied and active. Retirement policies probably do not need to be modified to further delay retirement. Indeed, when such policies are implemented, as in the 1983 Social Security Amendment, care must be taken not to penalize those who benefit by retiring early (the ill elderly). Policies encouraging more equitable employment, salary, and benefits throughout the life span will do much to reduce old-age poverty on a long-term basis. In the short run, more needs to be done to ensure that the poor elderly, who consist mainly of single women, are receiving adequate care and attention.

17 Death and Dying

Acceptance ... is almost void of feeling. It is as if the pain had gone, the struggle is over, and there comes a time for "the final rest before the long journey" as one patient phrased it ... the dying patient has found some peace and acceptance.... We should be aware of the monumental task which is required to achieve this stage of acceptance.... We have found two ways of achieving this goal more easily.... (Kübler-Ross, 1969, pp. 100–105)

Do not go gentle into that good night,
Old age should burn and rave at close of day;
Rage, rage against the dying of the light

Though wise men at their end know dark is right,
Because their words had forked no lightning they
Do not go gentle into that good night ...

And you, my father, there on the sad height,
Curse, bless, me now with your fierce tears, I pray.
Do not go gentle into that good night.
Rage, rage against the dying of the light.
(Dylan Thomas)*

The first passage here is from the work of Elisabeth Kübler-Ross, renowned researcher and counselor. She is describing what she terms the "final stage" of the dying process, acceptance. While not universally achieved, it is, in her opinion, the most desirable outcome of the psychological process of coping with a terminal illness. Certainly, as she notes, one does not want a person to accept death too early. Premature acceptance could lead the person to "give up" too soon, thereby hindering therapeutic interventions.

*Dylan Thomas, *Poems of Dylan Thomas.* Copyright 1952 by Dylan Thomas. Reprinted by permission of New Directions Publishing Corporation.

Nonetheless, she is so convinced that acceptance is the appropriate goal that she offers counselors suggestions on how to help patients reach this point (Kübler-Ross, 1969).

The second quotation is from Dylan Thomas's famous poem, "Do not go gentle into that good night." In it, Thomas implores his father to fight vigorously against death. He does not want his father to give up and suggests that both good and wise men fight death. In other words, his advice to his father is diametrically opposed to what we might expect Kübler-Ross to offer.

We may have a tendency to put more stock in Kübler-Ross's appraisal because we think of her approach as being more "scientific." But both Thomas and Kübler-Ross are observers of the human condition. And certainly neither stands alone in their view of how people do and should deal with dying. Furthermore, Kübler-Ross's work has been criticized for not being methodologically rigorous and for lack of empirical support (Kalish, 1985; Kastenbaum, 1985, 1986).

There is no doubt that people will go to great lengths to elude death. For example, in one study of over 600 cancer patients, only 8 percent had restricted themselves to "conventional" treatment methods (Cassileth, Lusk, Strouse, & Bodenheimer, 1984). The rest had pursued unorthodox treatments, including two (metabolic therapy and mental imagery) which have been directly criticized by the American Cancer Society. Such findings are especially powerful given that the data collection postdated the well-publicized laetrile hoax (Cassem, 1988).

Death is a universal phenomenon and may, in some sense, be the most common "normative life crisis" (Kastenbaum, 1986). And since it is another life event, we might expect to see considerable individual differences in adaptation to the news of impending death or the loss of a loved one. On the other hand, given that it is a truly universal event, we might anticipate certain similarities in reactions, even across cultures. And inasmuch as deaths vary in terms of suddenness, painfulness, and even "appropriateness," we might predict that the responses will be situationally variable. Clearly, we have a myriad of issues to confront in explaining how people cope with death.

WHAT IS DEATH?

Most of the time, it is easy to decide if someone is dead. There is no pulse, no respiration. The individual's body does not appear to be functioning in any way. The person is not conscious and does not respond to the environment. The situation seems unambiguous. Yet death means different things to different people in different situations. If someone is comatose for a long time or if functioning has been substantially below a pre-illness level, we might think of the person as already "dead" in some ways. Certainly this is no longer the person we knew. So at least a part of that person, and our relationship to him, has died even before physical functions end (Kastenbaum, 1986). Indeed, this may be part of what we mourn during the pre-death period in the anticipatory grief process (Rando, 1986).

Other people believe that no one ever really dies, that there is an afterlife. In some ways, these differences in attitudes are irrelevant. After all, they do not change the legal, objective fact of death. However, attitudes can affect both the treatment of the dying and the adjustment of the survivors (Cassem, 1988; Edelstein, 1984; Kastenbaum, 1985; Rando, 1986). For example, those who believe in an afterlife may see little need to extend life (with medical technology) beyond what seems "comfortable," since the true life comes after death (Kastenbaum, 1985).

Legal Issues

We tend to think that it is only the advent of medical technology that has raised legal issues in defining death. This is simply not true. There have long been coroners to verify and certify death. There have long been inquests in cases of suspicious or difficult to explain deaths. And Mark Twain (cited in Kastenbaum, 1986, p. 7) reported that the nineteenth-century Germans sent their dead to "dead houses" before burial. The bodies lay there under careful observation in order to ensure that the deceased actually were dead. The Germans thus anticipated part of our current standards (see Table 17–1) in requiring that the "symptoms" of death be demonstrated over some period of time.

What *has* changed with the advances in medicine are the "symptoms" of death. Table 17–1 lists the Harvard criteria for defining death. They have been widely used as a foundation for legal definitions. These criteria in-

TABLE 17-1:   The Harvard Criteria for Determination of a Permanently Nonfunctioning (or Dead) Brain

1. *Unreceptive and unresponsive.* No awareness is shown for external stimuli or inner need. The unresponsiveness is complete even under the application of stimuli that ordinarily would be extremely painful.

2. *No movements and no breathing.* There is a complete absence of spontaneous respiration and all other spontaneous muscular movement.

3. *No reflexes.* The usual reflexes that can be elicited in a neurophysiological examination are absent (when a light is shined in the eye, the pupil does not constrict).

4. *A flat EEG.* Electrodes attached to the scalp elicit a printout of electrical activity from the living brain. These are popularly known as brain waves. The respirator brain does not provide the usual pattern of peaks and valleys. Instead, the moving automatic stylus records essentially a flat line. This is taken to demonstrate the lack of electrophysiological activity.

5. *No circulation to or within the brain.* Without the oxygen and nutrition provided to the brain by its blood supply, functioning will soon terminate. (Precisely how long the brain can retain its viability, the ability to survive, without circulation is a matter of much current investigation and varies somewhat with conditions.)

Source: Kastenbaum, R. (1986). *Death, society, and human experience,* p. 9. Reprinted with permission of Merrill, an imprint of Macmillan Publishing Company. Copyright © 1986 by Bell & Howell Company.

clude a flat EEG and cessation of blood flow to and throughout the brain. Although they seem straightforward and irrefutable, these criteria do not really resolve all the issues (Kastenbaum, 1986). For example, does functioning and blood flow have to be absent in *all* areas of the brain for the person to be considered dead? Or is the cessation of activity in the cerebral cortex sufficient?

Such criteria are not invoked in every death; they are reserved for situations where there is some debate (Kastenbaum, 1986). They are used when doctors and families are trying to decide whether to turn off respirators and other life support systems. Ever since 1976, when Karen Ann Quinlan's case came to court, the judicial and legislative systems have been trying to define who has the right to make such decisions and under what circumstances life supports can be terminated (Robbins, 1986).

Who Decides?

The term "life support systems" makes it sound as if the person has no possibility of surviving without the machinery. Furthermore, it leaves the impression that the patients all have the same hopeless prognosis. Neither is true. Before a decision is made to discontinue a treatment, it must first be established that the person is already dead (usually brain dead) so that the machines are actually functioning *for* the person. Furthermore, there must be no reasonable likelihood of recovery.

Assuming that the preliminary criteria are met, there is still the question of who decides. How hopeless does one have to feel? What if the doctor says there is no chance for recovery, but the family believes in miracles? Or, what if the family says they do not want the patient to suffer but the doctor

Defining death is not always easy in this era of rapidly improving medical technology.

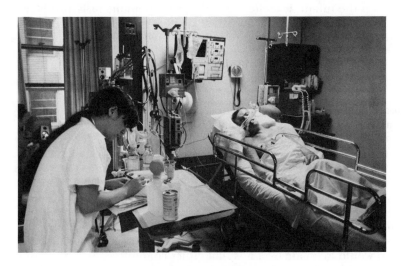

believes that life can be prolonged, though not saved, by a particular treatment?

The first possibility is that the person who is ill decides. Perhaps the person is still cognizant enough to make a decision. Such a person might refuse chemotherapy, surgery, or other treatments. Typically, neither medical nor legal personnel would intervene. Again, this assumes the patient is of "sound mind." At least some courts have held that a competent patient may refuse treatment, even if it would save his or her life (the case of *Lane v. Candura* in Massachusetts; see Robbins, 1986). Furthermore, people have always been permitted to refuse medical treatment for themselves on the basis of religious beliefs.

The patient's wishes may rule even if he or she is no longer able to make a decision. More and more states are recognizing the Living Will as a guide to a patient's wishes. An example of a Living Will is shown in Figure 17–1. The document outlines the circumstances under which the signatory wishes medical intervention to be limited. Of course, for such a document to be effective, the medical team must be aware of it. A less formal statement can also serve to limit treatment, but again, it must somehow be brought to the doctor's attention.

When the patient's wishes are not known, the situation becomes more complex. In many cases, the family (especially parents or spouse) meet with the doctor and arrive at a mutual agreement. Sometimes, however, there is disagreement. For example, Sylvie Le Clezio, wife of Australian producer David Roe, gave birth to a very premature baby (23.5 weeks gestational age) in a major California medical center (Halpern, 1989). The doctors informed the parents of the poor, indeed almost nonexistent, chance the baby had for survival. Furthermore, the doctors believed that during whatever time the baby did live, painful, expensive, intrusive medical care would be necessary. Therefore, while Ms. Le Clezio was in labor, the parents and doctors agreed not to use "heroic" measures to save the infant.

But when the infant, Isabelle, was born, she spontaneously produced a strong cry. This and other behaviors led doctors to believe that Isabelle had a better chance than they had initially expected. Without the parents' permission, the doctors began extensive medical intervention. When they requested parental permission, it was denied. The parents did not want their baby to suffer. The doctors persisted without the permission (Halpern, 1989).

Whose wishes reign in such a situation? Do the parents have any recourse? Can the doctors enforce their decision? The specifics of any "right to die" procedure vary from state to state (Robbins, 1986). However, it is fairly common for hospitals to have Ethics Boards that weigh medical opinion and family wishes. Such committees were first legally established in the Karen Quinlan case (Robbins, 1986). In 1976, Quinlan was a comatose young New Jersey woman maintained on a respirator and given no hope for recovery. Her father wanted to be declared guardian of her person (as opposed to property) so that he could request the respirator be turned off. His request was denied by the New Jersey courts. They instead decided that the decision would be made by a hospital ethics committee. A similar committee was available to David Roe and Sylvie Le Clezio, although they never

LIVING WILL

DIRECTIVE MADE this _____ day of _____ , 19 _____ , to my physicians, my attorneys, my clergyman, my family or others responsible for my health, welfare or affairs.

BE IT KNOWN, that I, _____ , of _____ State of _____ , being of sound mind, willfully and voluntarily make known my desire that my life shall not be artificially prolonged under the circumstances set forth below and do hereby declare that, if at any time I should have an incurable injury, disease or illness certified to be a terminal condition by two physicians and where the application of life-sustaining procedures would serve only to artificially prolong the moment of my death and where my physician determines that my death is imminent or needlessly prolonged whether or not life-sustaining procedures are utilized, I direct that such procedures be withheld or withdrawn and that I be permitted to die naturally with only the merciful administration of medication to eliminate or reduce pain to my mind and body or the performance of any medical procedure deemed necessary to provide me with comfort care. In the absence of my ability to give directions regarding the use of such life-sustaining procedures, it is my intention that this directive shall be honored by my family and physician(s) as the final expression of my legal right to refuse medical or surgical treatment and I accept the consequences from such refusal. If I have bequeathed organs, I ask that I be kept alive for a sufficient time to enable the proper withdrawal and transplant of said organs.

Special provisions:

_____

As a witness to this act I state the declarer has been personally known to me and I believe said declarer to be of sound mind.

Signed in the presence of:

_____   _____
Witness   Address

_____   _____
Witness   Address

State of _____

County of _____   SS .   , 19 _____

Be it known, that the above named _____ , personally known to me as the same person described in and who executed the within Living Will acknowledged to me that said instrument was freely and voluntarily executed for the purposes therein expressed, and that said Living Will was duly executed in my presence.

_____
Notary Public

My Commission Expires: _____

FIGURE 17-1: An Example of a Living Will

Source: E-Z Legal Forms, 1991.

exercised their right to go to the committee to try to override Isabelle's doctors' decision.

There are situations where someone tries to override all the involved parties' decisions and goes to court. This route is also available to the doctor or the family if they are dissatisfied with the situation. Perhaps the most dramatic example of this was the "Baby Boy Doe" case (Halpern, 1989). In 1982 a baby boy was born in Indiana. He had Down syndrome and various physical birth defects. His parents believed he was destined for a life filled with pain and suffering. They therefore decided to refuse the surgery to repair the most immediately life-threatening birth defect, a procedure that would have prolonged his life.

Two doctors disagreed; they wanted to require the surgery. Later two prosecutors tried to gain state guardianship for the baby on the basis that the parents were negligent. The state, then, would have been able to consent to the surgery and other medical procedures. The baby died before the case could be heard by the Supreme Court, but the case did lead to a clause in the Child Abuse and Neglect Prevention and Treatment Act that defines the withholding of medical treatment as a reportable form of child abuse and neglect (Halpern, 1989). This ensures that the courts can continue to be a forum in cases where parents decide against medical treatment for their children. Furthermore, it has created an atmosphere in which doctors go to extreme lengths to keep premature infants alive, regardless of the child's prognosis or the parents' wishes (Kolata, 1991).

How will the courts decide these and similar cases? At least two types of criteria have been established (Robbins, 1986). The first, cited in the Quinlan case, is the "cognitive and sapient life" criterion. Under this measure, the question is whether or not the patient is likely to recover the ability to think as a human being (though not necessarily at the pre-illness level). The other criterion, established by Massachusetts courts, is "substituted judgement." The question here is what the patient would have wanted. This criterion was cited in the case of an elderly, severely retarded cancer patient. His guardian argued that the man should not be subjected to chemotherapy to prolong (but not save) his life because he would not understand the rationale for the pain and discomfort involved in the treatment. The court then tried to decide whether the man would want the treatment if he could take all factors (including his retardation) into account (Robbins, 1986).

BEREAVEMENT, GRIEF, AND MOURNING

We have spent a substantial amount of space considering how to define death. But as we noted earlier, the death will eventually be "certifiable" and the survivors will be left to carry on. Most of us use terms such as *bereavement, grieving,* and *mourning* interchangeably. Indeed, even in the professional literature there is some intermixing of the terms. However, they technically refer to different components of the survivor process and role. To fully appreciate this role and process, we need to distinguish among them.

Bereavement

Bereavement refers to the actual, objective loss of another person through death (Stroebe & Stroebe, 1987). This may be a highly emotional experience, or it may elicit almost no emotional reaction. In one study of widows under 65, 70 percent experienced "high" distress at the time of their husband's death. This means that 30 percent experienced "low" or no distress (Vachon, 1986). Similarly, the loss may or may not be fully cognitively appreciated at the time it occurs. Reactions will depend, among other things, on the circumstances of the death (sudden versus expected), characteristics of the deceased (a beloved spouse versus a stranger, a child versus an elderly person), and characteristics of the survivor (previous experience with loss).

Is the "shock" of bereavement different from any other major stressor? Research suggests that it is, at least if a spouse or a child is lost. For example, Vachon (1986) compared distress in a group of women who had just been told they had breast cancer to a group whose husbands had just died. The cancer victims reported considerably lower levels of distress, with only 40 percent experiencing "high" distress, whereas 70 percent of the widows indicated high distress. Life stress researchers (Holmes & Rahe, 1967) have also typically identified loss of a spouse as more stressful than other events such as job loss, illness, and financial difficulties.

Grief

Grief is one possible reaction to bereavement. It is an emotional reaction marked by despair, sadness, and even depression. The "symptoms" may be affective, cognitive, or behavioral (see Table 17–2). At times, the symptoms may seem contradictory. The bereaved may have no energy and yet be unable to sleep. There will be strong individual differences. Some will try to suppress memories of the deceased; others will dwell on them. Some will overeat and gain weight; others have no appetite.

Nonetheless, there are some similarities in grief, at least in the acute stages (Cassem, 1988; Edelstein, 1984; Stroebe & Stroebe, 1987). Survivors feel waves of somatic distress. They may feel, for example, as if they cannot get their breath. They sigh a good deal. There may also be guilt feelings. They are likely to feel anger toward others. The widows in one study reported being angered by people who said nothing about their loss as well as by people who said how well the widow seemed to be doing (Morgan, 1989). Abnormal activity patterns are also common, although these may take a variety of forms.

Grief resembles depression in many ways. The grief-stricken and the depressed report sadness, tearfulness, and somatic distress (especially appetite and sleep problems, breathing difficulty) (Breckenridge, Gallagher, Thompson, & Peterson, 1986; Clayton, 1982). However, the two are distinguishable, as the DSM-IIIR (APA, 1988) classification system indicates (see Table 17–3). Part of the difference, of course, is the precipitating event. In addition, grieving people are also less likely to report self-deprecatory thought patterns such as feelings of worthlessness or pervasive guilt, and

TABLE 17-2: Symptoms of Grief

Symptom	Description
A. Affective	
Depression	Feelings of sadness, mournfulness, and dysphoria, accompanied by intense subjective distress and "mental pain": feelings of despair, lamentation, sorrow, and dejection
Anxiety	Fear, dread, and forebodings such as fear of breaking down, of losing one's mind, or of being unable to cope
Guilt	Self-blame and self-accusation about events in the past, notably about events leading up to the death
Anger and hostility	Irritability toward family and with friends; anger about fate, toward the deceased, and toward medical personnel
Anhedonia	Feeling that nothing can be pleasurable
Loneliness	Feeling alone, even in the presence of others
B. Behavioral Manifestations	
Agitation	Tenseness, restlessness, overactivity, often without completing task
Fatigue	Reduction in general activity level (sometimes interrupted by bouts of agitation)
Crying	
C. Attitudes Toward Self, the Deceased, and Environment	
Helplessness, hopelessness	Pessimism about present circumstances and future, loss of purpose in life
Sense of unreality	Feeling of "not being there" or "watching from outside"
Suspiciousness	Doubting the motives of those who offer help or advice
Interpersonal problems	Difficulty in maintaining social relationships
Attitudes toward the deceased	*Yearning* and longing for deceased
	Imitation of deceased's behavior, interests
	Idealization of deceased, tendency to ignore deceased's faults and exaggerate positive characteristics
	Ambivalence
	Images of the deceased in an almost hallucinatory manner
	Preoccupation with memory of the deceased and need to talk, sometimes incessantly, about deceased
D. Cognitive Impairment	

TABLE 17-2:   (continued)

Symptom	Description
E. Physiological Changes and Bodily Complaints	
Loss of appetite	(Occasionally, overeating) accompanied by changes in body weight
Sleep disturbances	Mostly insomnia, occasionally oversleeping; disturbances of day/night rhythm
Bodily complaints	Headaches, neckache, back pain, muscle cramp, nausea, vomiting, lump in throat, dry mouth, blurred vision, tremors, palpitations, shortness of breath, indigestion, constipation
Physical complaints of the deceased	Appearance of symptoms similar to those of the deceased, particularly those symptoms of the terminal illness
Changes in drug taking	Increase in use of mood-altering drugs, including alcohol and tobacco
Susceptibility to illness and disease	Particularly infections and illnesses related to lack of health care and illnesses related to stress

Source: Adapted from Stroebe, W., & Stroebe, M. (1987). *Bereavement and health: The psychological and physical consequences of partner loss.* New York: Cambridge.

TABLE 17-3:   Differences in Diagnostic Criteria for Uncomplicated Bereavement

This category can be used when the focus of attention or treatment is a normal reaction to the death of a loved one (bereavement).

A full depressive syndrome frequently is a normal reaction to such a loss, with feelings of depression and such associated symptoms as poor appetite, weight loss, and insomnia. However, morbid preoccupation with worthlessness, prolonged and marked functional impairment, and marked psychomotor retardation are uncommon and suggest that the bereavement is complicated by the development of a Major Depression.

In Uncomplicated Bereavement, guilt, if present, is chiefly about things done or not done by the survivor at the time of the death; thoughts of death are usually limited to the person's thinking that he or she would be better off dead or that he or she should have died with the deceased person. The person with Uncomplicated Bereavement generally regards the feeling of depressed mood as "normal," although he or she may seek professional help for relief of such associated symptoms as insomnia or anorexia.

The reaction to the loss may not be immediate, but rarely occurs after the first two or three months. The duration of "normal" bereavement varies considerably among different cultural groups.

Source: Reprinted with permission from the *Diagnostic and statistical manual of mental disorders, Third Edition, Revised.* Copyright 1987 American Psychiatric Association.

they experience less suicidal ideation (Breckenridge et al., 1986; Clayton, 1982).

Stages of Grief: Grief "symptoms" will change over time. In this sense, grief is a process rather than a status (Parkes, 1970). Several researchers have proposed various stages of the grieving process (see Table 17–4). Typically, these stages begin with a sense of numbness or shock, when the death is not fully real to the survivor. These are particularly common reactions when the death is sudden or unexpected (Glick, Weiss, & Parkes, 1974). Sometimes the numbness is preceded by great distress, as in the case of one of the widows in the Parkes (1970) study:

> "I suddenly burst. I was aware of a horrible wailing and knew it was me. I was saying I loved him. . . . " She went into the bathroom and retched. Then the feeling of numbness set in. "I felt numb and cold for a week. It's a blessing. . . . Everything goes hard inside you. . . . " She felt that the numbness enabled her to cope without weeping. (Parkes, 1970, p. 448)

The sense of numbness is not usually very long-lived. Parkes and his colleagues (Glick et al., 1974; Parkes, 1970), for example, report that it usu-

TABLE 17–4: Examples of Models of the Grieving Process

Stage	Major Dynamics
Edelstein (1984, p. 15)	
Disorganization (early days)	Disruption in equilibrium due to trauma (acclimating period)
Holding on/letting go	Struggle to relinquish the deceased while retaining memories and identification
Reorganization	Modified equilibrium; loss is integrated into life
Glick et al. (1974)	
Early reactions	
Disbelief, shock	
Emotional expressions of grief	
Disorganization	
Grieving	
Public mourning	
Obsessional review and search for meaning	
Solitary mourning	
Recovery	
Kübler-Ross (1969)	
Denial and isolation	
Anger	
Bargaining	
Depression	
Acceptance	

ally lasts a week or less. This is enough time to allow the bereaved to "get through" the wake and initial post-death procedures. It probably also provides a respite or moratorium from the pain of the loss until the bereaved is better able to cope with it (Glick et al., 1974). Thus, like the woman quoted above, many view numbness as a blessing.

The sense of numbness is often accompanied by disbelief that the death has occurred (Edelstein, 1984; Glick et al., 1974; Parkes, 1970). As with numbness, disbelief is more common when the death is unexpected but also can occur when the death is expected. Consider the reaction of a woman whose husband died following a lengthy illness:

> He was just like he was when he was sleeping, you know. He was still warm, although he was very pale. I didn't want to believe it, yet I saw it right there. So it was as though I were torn between what I wanted to believe and what was really there. (Glick et al., 1974, p. 54)

Furthermore, the disbelief may last longer than the numbness, with some survivors reporting at least occasional difficulty believing that their loved one was dead even a year later (Parkes, 1970).

The period of numbness is followed by yearning and searching for the deceased. It is as if the survivor is experiencing the loss step by step, missing the deceased in a variety of circumstances and situations. This may at least partly be a means of gradually letting go of or separating from the deceased (Edelstein, 1984). As it becomes devastatingly clear that the deceased will not be found anywhere and that life must proceed, a sense of despair or depression may set in. The bereaved may find themselves crying suddenly or uncontrollably; they may stare at things or places associated with the deceased, such as a favorite chair; they may find it difficult to get on with daily activities; they may need social support, counseling, or medication (Edelstein, 1984; Morgan, 1989; Parkes, 1970; Stroebe & Stroebe, 1987).

Finally, grieving ends with recovery and restitution (Edelstein, 1984; Stroebe & Stroebe, 1987). The days when the bereaved feels "normal" and happy outnumber the bad ones. This is not always an easily won state; survivors may feel guilty about getting on with their lives, as if it were some betrayal of the deceased. They may worry that happiness without the deceased makes it seem as if that person was unimportant (Edelstein, 1984). Thus, the recovery process is often uneven, and marked by temporary setbacks and reversals (Cassem, 1988).

Furthermore, there may still be moments or days when the sense of loss dominates again. The anniversary of the death, the deceased's birthday, or holidays (Christmas, wedding anniversary) may be painful (Cassem, 1988; Stroebe & Stroebe, 1987). One mother who had lost a child noted how difficult it was when her younger child reached the age at which the other one had died. It reminded her that her younger child had "caught up" to the older one, an unnatural occurrence. It also reminded her that her older child would never experience any of the things that routinely happen beyond that age (Edelstein, 1984).

It is important to emphasize that there is much individuality in how people cope with and express their grief. The stages are meant as a descriptive guide, not a prescription for how people should react. Similarly, different people will need more or less time to adjust to a loss. It is not uncommon for the process to take one or two years when a spouse or child has died. Finally, grief is not the only possible reaction to death, even when the deceased was someone close to the survivor. The death of an abusive parent or spouse may be greeted with a sense of relief or at least ambivalence.

Mourning

Mourning refers to the behaviors that express or demonstrate bereavement and grief (Kalish, 1985; Stroebe & Stroebe, 1987). These are culturally determined, although some cultures have much more stringent or clear rules than others. Some of the behaviors, such as dressing in black, are traditions and are not really required in the United States. Others, such as disposal of the body, are actually regulated by law.

In the United States, the funeral is the primary ritual of mourning (Kalish, 1985). It involves five steps. First, the body is removed from areas where the living are; we take the deceased to a morgue or funeral home. There is some visitation (a wake, shiva), during which community members can express their condolences. This is also a time when the family can

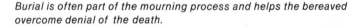

Burial is often part of the mourning process and helps the bereaved overcome denial of the death.

grieve openly and even dramatically with full support from the community. Neighbors may bring food or provide childcare so that even the activities of daily life need not burden the bereaved family. The third step is the funeral rite itself. This is typically a religious ceremony, although it may also be more informal and take place at the funeral home, for example. Then there is a procession from the funeral to the burial place, followed by interment.

The funeral serves several functions (Cassem, 1988; Kalish, 1985). It provides a forum for community support to the bereaved as well as an opportunity for the community to grieve with the family. It also helps the bereaved to recognize the finality of the death as others offer their condolences and as the body is viewed and then laid to rest. The funeral also provides a framework for getting through those first few days. The funeral puts some limits on grieving while still sanctioning expressions of sorrow. It may be a final way to honor the deceased or at least portray the importance and individuality of that person. A woman whose child had died said of the funeral plans:

> We wanted "Fire and Rain" to be played at the memorial service, and the minister . . . wasn't all that thrilled about it. He said the organist said "I don't think we have the sheet music," and we said "We'll get it." So we were trying . . . I remember that was a big deal. We had to get it. (Edelstein, 1984, p. 53)

Not all societies follow the same mourning procedures (Stroebe & Stroebe, 1987). The Japanese, for example, may build a small altar within the household to routinely honor their dead. The Hopi Indians, on the other hand, never mention the deceased after the burial. The Samoans seem to have a very limited period of mourning, whereas the Kota (of South India) have one funeral at the time of the death and another some time later (this one is held once a year) so that the mourning period is very extended. It is noteworthy that despite differences in mourning patterns, crying, or at least the urge to cry, appears to be universal as a sign of grief (Stroebe & Stroebe, 1987).

REACTIONS TO DEATH

We have already described the general grieving process in reaction to death. However, grieving is not all there is to coping with a death.

Psychological problems, especially depression, are a real risk (Stroebe & Stroebe, 1987). The widowed are more likely to suffer from depression than are the still married, and depression is especially common shortly after the bereavement.

Interestingly, following an initial adjustment period, this is more true of men than of women. In other words, the difference between widowed and married men is greater than that between widowed and married women. Certainly, some of this is due to the higher baseline rate of depression among married women. Nonetheless, it appears that men are at greater risk for postbereavement depression, perhaps because they relied more on their wives for social support and interaction (see Rubin, 1985). Or it may be that social support is less available to men (Stroebe & Stroebe, 1987). In line with this contention, recently bereaved mothers report they feel they received more direct sympathy and support than their husbands did (Edelstein, 1984).

The increased risk of depression may also be associated with alcohol abuse (Stroebe & Stroebe, 1987). Spouses are more likely than other family members to abuse alcohol following the death of a loved one (Mor, McHorney, & Sherwood, 1986). Again, men are more likely to show such difficulties (Mor et al., 1986; Stroebe & Stroebe, 1987).

Physical health may also be affected (Stroebe & Stroebe, 1987). This effect is less well documented than the depression-bereavement link. There is evidence that the recently bereaved visit their doctors more frequently than matched comparison groups (Mor et al., 1986). These visits are particularly common among those who were primary caretakers of the deceased during a terminal illness. So the visits may represent routine care that was neglected during the caregiving period. This interpretation is supported by the finding that hospitalization rates are not higher among the recently bereaved (Mor et al., 1986).

Furthermore, depression may mediate the effect; the physical symptoms and physician visits may be more linked to the depression than any other single factor (Mor et al., 1986). This is evident from Table 17–5 which shows some of the somatic complaints in widows versus a control group.

TABLE 17–5:   Physical Complaints of Widows (Bereaved 13 Months Earlier) Compared to Matched, Married Controls

Symptom or Complaint	Total Widows (N = 375) (%)	Total Control (N = 199) (%)
Psychological symptoms		
General nervousness	41.3	16.1
Depression	22.7	5.5
Requiring medical treatment	12.8	1.0
Requiring hospitalization	1.3	0
"Fear of nervous breakdown"	13.1	2.0
Feelings of panic	12.0	2.5
Persistent fears	12.0	3.0
Repeated peculiar thoughts	8.5	2.0
Nightmares	8.8	1.0
Insomnia	40.8	12.6
Trembling	10.4	1.0
Neurological		
"Migraine"	4.8	3.0
Headache	17.6	9.0
Dizziness	9.1	4.5
Fainting spells	1.3	0
Blurred vision	13.7	7.5
Facial pain	1.9	0.5

TABLE 17-5: (continued)

Symptom or Complaint	Total Widows (N = 375) (%)	Total Control (N = 199) (%)
Dermatological		
Skin rashes	6.1	2.5
Excessive sweating	9.3	5.0
Gastrointestinal		
Indigestion	9.9	4.5
Difficulty in swallowing	4.8	1.5
Peptic ulceration	2.1	2.0
Colitis	0.5	0
Vomiting	2.7	0
Excessive appetite	5.4	0.5
Anorexia	13.1	1.0
Weight gain	8.5	9.0
Weight loss	13.6	2.0
Genitourinary		
Menorrhagia	3.4	0.5
Cardiovascular		
Palpitations	12.5	4.0
Chest pain	10.1	4.5
Respiratory		
Dyspnea	12.0	4.5
Asthma	2.4	1.5
General		
Frequent infections	2.1	0
General aching	8.4	4.0
Reduced work capacity	46.7	26.1
Gross fatigue	29.6	11.6
Neoplastic growth	0.8	0
Diabetes mellitus	0.8	0.5

Source: Stroebe, W., & Stroebe, M. (1987). *Bereavement and health: The psychological and physical consequences of partner loss.* New York: Cambridge.

The symptoms showing differences between the groups tend to be those that commonly occur with depression (insomnia, weight loss, general aching).

But we must be cautious and avoid overstating the effect of depression on postbereavement physical health. At the very least, we must acknowledge the severity of the postbereavement symptoms. There may be an increased risk of death among the recently widowed, although the data addressing this link are inconsistent (Clayton, 1982; Stroebe & Stroebe, 1987). The risk is probably greater among men than women. Mortality is highest in the first few months after a spouse's death. In any case, it is not usual for a bereaved person to die shortly after the death of a loved one.

But does this prove that someone can in fact die of a broken heart? Perhaps. Both cardiovascular disease and suicide are particularly likely causes of death in the recently widowed (Stroebe & Stroebe, 1987). Researchers tend to compare widowed to married without regard for the fact that some of the latter have been widowed at some time. It may be that younger widowed people who are unhealthy are less likely to remarry, and this would confound the effect of widowhood itself. Furthermore, the spouses shared an environment. Any element of the environment that contributed to the death of the first spouse might also be fatal to the second (Stroebe & Stroebe, 1987). This is certainly different than dying from a broken heart.

There are several methodological problems with findings concerning postbereavement illness and death rates (Stroebe & Stroebe, 1987). The failure to account for previous marital status of the controls is one. So is the common failure to account for the physical or psychological health of the bereaved earlier in their lives. This is important, since prior health is the best predictor of later health (Mor et al., 1986). Furthermore, samples are often small. This is a problem because the death rate among widowed people is still typically less than 5 percent (Stroebe & Stroebe, 1987).

INDIVIDUAL DIFFERENCES IN REACTIONS

Many factors may influence an individual's reaction to his or her own dying or the death of a loved one. These can be broadly categorized into characteristics of the death itself, characteristics of the deceased (including relationship to the survivor), and characteristics of the survivor.

Characteristics of the Death

It has long been common wisdom that a sudden death is harder to accept than an expected one. But almost as soon as someone offers those words of comfort—"Well at least you knew it was coming"—they qualify their belief in the advantages of "knowing" with some statement that all losses are hard. Indeed, when we think of the financial, psychological, and physical strain that may be involved in caring for a terminally ill person, we might wonder whether a fast, sudden (and preferably painless) death is not easier.

There is some evidence that a very sudden death—as in an automobile accident—is more difficult to accept, at least in the early stages of mourning (Edelstein, 1984; Rando, 1986). When the death is completely unexpected, the shock, numbness, and disbelief may be more intense and prolonged. Initial distress may be greater (Parkes, 1970; Vachon, 1986). Indeed, some have argued that the entire grieving process will be more intense and prolonged (Edelstein, 1984; Rando, 1986). This may be one reason the loss of a child is so difficult; it frequently is unexpected and it always violates our cultural expectation that only old people die (Edelstein, 1984; Kalish, 1985). Suicides may be similarly difficult to accept and may generate considerable self-blame and confusion (Stroebe & Stroebe, 1987). Life is more likely to be disrupted by a sudden death because there could be no preparation for the death. All the changes must be made afterward.

In fact, unexpected death may result in an abnormal form of grieving known as the *unexpected-grief syndrome* (Stroebe & Stroebe, 1987). In this form, the bereaved have a persistent sense of the deceased's presence. They may hear voices or footsteps. They blame themselves for the death; they think they might have been able to do something that would have prevented it. This sense may be especially strong when a child, whom the parent was supposed to "protect," dies:

> I said, "Somehow I didn't do a good enough job," and they said "You did the best you could." I said "But it wasn't good enough." . . . That's what's so hard to accept. (Edelstein, 1984, pp. 38–39)

This self-blame may also lead to a continued sense of obligation to the deceased (Stroebe & Stroebe, 1987).

Some authors (Lindemann, 1944; Rando, 1986) suggest that the knowledge that death is coming gives the dying person and the survivors-to-be the opportunity to go through *anticipatory grief,* a phase of grieving that begins after the terminal diagnosis is made but before the actual death. This period is sometimes called the *living-dying interval* (Rando, 1986). It is a time when both the dying person and the family can make certain adjustments. Financial issues can be handled. Funeral arrangements might be made. There may be an opportunity to resolve a family conflict, to express love and concern, or to see people who have meant a great deal.

Such adjustments will not eliminate postdeath grieving; the survivors will still need to cope with the loneliness and other losses associated with the death. The finality of the death will still need to be absorbed. In fact, there is little reason to believe that postdeath grief is lessened by anticipatory grief (Rando, 1986). But the effects of the death are less overwhelming, because some plans and adjustments have been made; coping with the grief may be improved. Anticipatory grief cannot replace the postdeath grieving process and does not guarantee a better long-term adjustment to the loss (Cassem, 1988; Vachon, 1986).

Not all researchers believe that anticipatory grief is a positive process under all circumstances (Kalish, 1985). It is possible that a survivor-to-be will separate too thoroughly from the dying person before the death. This will interfere with the survivor-to-be's ability to provide support, comfort, and care to the patient. It would be particularly devastating if the patient did not die. Complete detachment prior to the death is rare, however, and should be considered an abnormal adjustment (Rando, 1986). Indeed, it is more common for family to take the opportunity to provide more care and spend more time with the dying member because they know death is coming. The continued attachment to the dying person is one reason postdeath grief is a reality (Rando, 1986).

There also appears to be an optimal living-dying interval (Rando, 1986). If the illness lasts less than 6 months, the time is insufficient to allow any significant anticipatory grieving. On the other hand, if the illness lasts more than 18 months, the strain of caring for the person outweighs the value of preparing for the death (Rando, 1983). The experience may be so emotionally exhausting that normal postdeath grieving is delayed (Rando, 1986). Furthermore, when an illness is prolonged, the survivor may become convinced that the terminally ill person will not really die, that he or she has "beaten the odds." The death may then be *more* shocking than a sudden death (Edelstein, 1984; Rando,1986).

The exhaustion associated with caring for the dying person may explain why some researchers have found that older women may not be as well served by an anticipatory period as younger widows are (Marshall, 1980). The younger widows may benefit from the psychological rehearsal for widowhood; the older widows are more prepared for their husbands to die and perhaps need less rehearsal (Kalish, 1985).

Characteristics of the Deceased

We have just implied one important characteristic of the deceased— namely, age. There are several reasons why we routinely believe that it is appropriate for only older people to die (Kalish, 1985; Kastenbaum, 1985). Medical technology has greatly reduced infant and child mortality; we are usually stunned when a child dies. Our ancestors expected to lose children to diseases such as typhus, measles, whooping cough, pneumonia, and polio. Furthermore, we generally associate growth with the early years and decline with the later ones (Kastenbaum, 1985). We have seen that there are wide individual differences in the rate and extent of physical and psychological losses in middle and old age. Nonetheless, they are certainly more common among older people than young adults or children. This belief is also reflected in our societal norms, which limit an elderly person's participation in the community, especially in the workplace. We seem to expect that these people have no future (Kalish, 1985). Thus, at least in the United States, the death of an elderly person is typically easier to accept. This tends to be true both for the dying person and for the family (Kalish, 1985).

Our relationship to the deceased is also important. Loss of a spouse, for example, is routinely considered one of the most stressful events in an adult's life (see, for example, Holmes & Rahe's Life Events Scale). Reactions will vary, of course, with the quality of the marital relationship (Stroebe & Stroebe, 1987). If the relationship was plagued with problems that were left unresolved, the survivor may suffer from abnormal grieving. The person may experience an *ambivalent-grief-syndrome* (Stroebe & Stroebe, 1987). In this form of abnormal grief, the bereaved loses hope in all kinds of relationships and is likely to engage in a great deal of self-punishment, blaming him or herself for old failures and wishing for a chance to rectify old wrongs.

The reactions of the person who is dying also affect the survivor. This is true both during the anticipatory grief period and in mourning itself (Rando, 1986). So, for example, if neither the dying person nor the survivor-to-be will acknowledge the terminal nature of the disease, the two will be unable to discuss both practical and psychological issues (Kalish, 1985). Funeral arrangements are left undiscussed; old wrongs do not get rectified; frustration and even anger over the impending death are left unresolved. All of this can complicate grieving.

Characteristics of the Bereaved

Age: The age and developmental level of the bereaved are critical in determining grieving patterns and outcomes. Young children may understand death differently. Very young children, of course, cannot differentiate it from any other separation, and they therefore display the separation reaction described by Bowlby (1973) and others. The child is first angry and cries for the lost attachment figure. Many parents have seen this reaction when they first leave their child at a daycare center. The child may cry off and on for a long time. The child may also stand at a door or a window and watch for the parents to return. In daycare, of course, the child comes to anticipate the parent's return and so eventually is less distressed. But with a death, the loved one does not return. The child continues the separation protest for a while (perhaps several days) and then gives up. What might be termed depression in an adult sets in as the child becomes apathetic and withdrawn.

In some ways, this reaction is similar to the grieving process commonly described in adults (see Table 17-5). There is anger, searching, and despair. The difference is that the young child does not understand that this separation is different; it is permanent and irreversible. In the same way, the child does not understand that death is universal.

Throughout the preschool years, children seem unable to fathom the irreversibility of death; they tend instead to think that the deceased is not fully alive. Robert Kastenbaum (1986, p. 17) tells of a 3-year-old girl who was saving her comic books for her grandmother though she was concerned that grandma may not have taken her glasses with her when she was buried. Given their failure to understand that life has completely ceased, it is not surprising that children often view death as temporary (Kastenbaum, 1986). It is as if the deceased is away or on a trip, perhaps to heaven or the cemetery, and could or will someday return.

During the early school years, children come to understand that death is final (Kastenbaum, 1986). They tend to believe that death is caused by some external agent and may even personify death (for example, in the form of the bogeyman or as a skeleton). Young children may also think that death can somehow be escaped or avoided if you can stay away from the external force. It is not until age 9 or 10 that children understand death as universal and permanent. In other words, they then understand that everyone, including themselves, will die someday (Kastenbaum, 1986).

It has been demonstrated (Koocher, 1973) that children's conceptions of death are related to their level of cognitive development. Some theorists (Flavell, 1985) have argued that level of cognitive development in any specific knowledge area is related to experience. In other words, the more experience and knowledge a child has of any particular content area, the more advanced the child's thinking will be on that subject. Many young children have little or no contact with death in modern American society, and this may partly explain their lack of sophistication in reasoning about death. Indeed, some research (Bluebond Langer, 1977) indicates that terminally ill children have a more accurate understanding of death than their peers do.

Developmental stage may affect more than simply understanding the "facts" of death. It may also influence attitudes toward, and therefore reactions to, death. For example, death may seem especially remote to teenagers and they may be especially distraught at its unexpected appearance. Elderly people have faced death many times. Although it never becomes easy to lose a loved one, older people are less surprised by it and probably better able to accept it. This may explain why there is a negative correlation between age and postbereavement health deterioration (Stroebe & Stroebe, 1987).

Gender: We have already seen that men tend to fare somewhat less well than women in the face of loss of a spouse. Few other sex differences have been documented. Women may cry more than men do after a death (Stroebe & Stroebe, 1987). Women may also be more willing to admit fears about death, at least from adolescence through middle age (Stillion, 1985). These differences appear to be consistent with sex role expectations of social behavior, rather than fundamentally different approaches to the grieving process.

Social Support: Models of stress and coping frequently note the value of strong social supports in successfully negotiating life crises. Indeed, one of the explanations for men's poorer adjustment to widowhood is their narrower, smaller, and less intimate social networks. We might expect, then, that strong social support is helpful in dealing with bereavement.

However, studies of widows indicate that not all social support is equally helpful (Bankoff, 1986; Morgan, 1989). In one study, about 40 percent of the comments made by widows about postbereavement social relationships were negative (Morgan, 1989). Support from peers, especially those who have also experienced spousal loss, seems more helpful than family support. In Morgan's study, 45 percent of the comments about family relationships were negative, compared to 37 percent of the comments about nonfamily relationships. This may be because widows perceive family obligations as a drain rather than a support. Parents were viewed as particularly nonsupportive, typically due to illness. This is exemplified by the experience of a younger widow:

> I thought I'd go back to Indiana, where my parents are, to get some help with the children, and a little comfort for myself. . . . But my mother had a heart attack so I had to end up taking care of her and the children and my father. . . . I didn't get to grieve then because I was too busy taking care of everybody else. (Morgan, 1989, p. 103)

Friends who are widows seem more helpful than those who are not. Bankoff (1986), for example, reported that widows with stronger peer support had more widowed friends than those with weaker support. There was

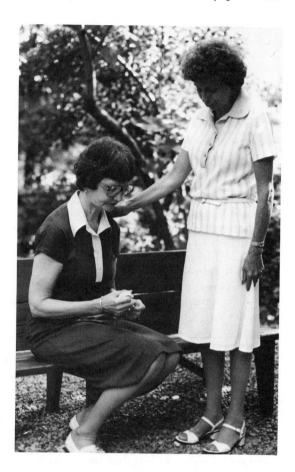

Some forms of social support are more effective than others in helping the bereaved cope and adjust.

no difference between the two groups, however, in the availability of family or married friends. This helps to explain why young widows, who are unlikely to find many agemates in the same situation, tend to adjust less well than older widows. Even new friends who are widows may be more helpful than old friends who are not (Lopata, 1987). Morgan (1989) found that almost 85 percent of the comments about a widowhood support group were positive, but only about 56 percent of those pertaining to friends were. Parents who have lost a child often find contact with others whose children have died particularly comforting (Edelstein, 1984).

Why would widows be particularly helpful to other widows? One reason is that they are probably more comfortable with the distress, confusion, anger, and other emotions displayed by the newly bereaved. The widow's demands for comfort, attention, sympathy, and assistance may begin to feel one-sided to other friends, who feel they are giving more than the widow is giving (Lopata, 1975). People may lose patience with the grieving and pressure the widow to "adjust":

My [sons] would say, "Oh Mom, you're sitting down there having a pity party." They're right, I was. They had no sensitivity for me whatsoever and I really thought I was losing my mind.

I had a lady friend just put the kibosh on me and I'll never forget her, forget that. Boy! Because I was talking too much about my dead husband. (Morgan, 1989, pp. 104–105)

These quotes exemplify both the desire of the non-widowed to avoid the grieving and the anger of the widowed over being treated badly.

It is not surprising, then, that widows and recently bereaved mothers look for people who understand. These are people who have suffered similar experiences. In some cases, lasting friendships are formed; it is not unusual for older widows to become part of a "society of widows" who do things together (Cumming & Henry, 1961; Lopata, 1975). They may meet for lunch, travel together, or get together for social events. In other cases, the friendship may last only while the bereaved needs special comfort and support (Edelstein, 1984). After that, the bereaved may rejoin his or her old social network.

A variety of factors seem to influence how much peer support is available. Women of higher social classes and with more education tend to have more friends. However, many of these friendships may be couple-oriented. Working-class couples tend to do less together, and hence the women are likely to have their own friends. This implies that working-class women's friendships may be less disrupted by their husbands' deaths (Bankoff, 1986).

The more couple-oriented a married woman's social life is, the more likely she is to lack peer support when widowed. Women who relied on their husbands for social contacts are less likely to have the skills and interests to develop their own support networks (Bankoff, 1986). Their social lives are apt to be disorganized without the husbands. They may wish to make social contacts, but they don't know how to do such things as join a club or get a job (Lopata, 1975). Women who have been socialized into passivity are particularly likely to find it difficult to build a social life for themselves. Such women cannot take advantage of the opportunities available to them (Lopata, 1975).

Widows with low self-esteem or limited coping abilities also seem to have less peer support (Bankoff, 1986). One reason for this is that they may lean too heavily for too long on friends. People seek balance and equity in their relationships. While people are willing to tolerate—and indeed expect—some "taking" by their friends, they are not willing to endure it indefinitely. The widow who still seems very needy a year or more after the death is likely to find her friends turning away (Bankoff, 1986; Lopata, 1975).

DYING

The focus thus far has been on the reactions of the survivors. We have looked at both short- and long-term reactions to the news that a loved one is dying or dead. It is also important, however, to examine the process of dying itself. For many people, it is an identifiable stage of development, and as in other stages, there are challenges and supports, moments of growth and times of decline. This can be true whether the dying person is a child or an octogenarian. Of course, it differs from other stages in that not everyone has the time and conscious awareness to identify and deal with the challenges. And like other stages, some people will be unable to negotiate them.

Fears about Death

We have already seen that older people are less afraid of death than younger ones are. For example, Kalish and Reynolds (1976) reported that about 40 percent of their young adult respondents were afraid of death; among their middle-aged participants, only about 25 percent say they are afraid, and over half claim not to be. This is, as we noted earlier, at least partly attributable to the expectation that older people do deteriorate and die. The middle-aged and elderly themselves often adopt this view. Furthermore, they have had more experience with death and dying.

Not all older people, of course, are ready to die. Certainly some are (Erikson et al., 1987; Kalish, 1981), but there are substantial individual differences among the elderly in terms of anxiety about death (Stillion, 1985). Some older people, coping with Erikson's crisis of ego integrity versus despair, will end up with a preponderance of the latter. They are likely to feel cheated, as if there is not enough time. They may feel they did not have enough opportunities or did not make good choices. They may wish they could start over again. Of course, they cannot. Erikson (1963) suggested that this type of despair might translate into great anxiety concerning death. Such people may be terrified at the prospect of no more time and may be desperate to delay their deaths.

Inasmuch as older adults have family or job obligations, their fears concerning death may be similar to those of younger adults. So, for example, the grandmother who is responsible for raising her grandchildren may worry about her survivors the same way a young mother does. Who will raise the children? How will their financial needs be met? Will they be loved? Dying young adults also worry about their spouse's ability to go on. In addition, they may simply not want to leave their spouse and children. They know they will not see their children's graduations, marriages, and other accomplishments. They will never reach their career goals. In other words, the young adult has a lot to lose and knows it. All this certainly contributes to their greater fear of death (Kalish, 1981; Kastenbaum, 1985, 1986; Shneidman, 1980). The sense of frustration and anger this may cause is captured in the words of a 22-year-old man dying of leukemia:

> ... They told me I had a really good chance. And they've tried everything. Now a perfectly good person with an awful lot to give is going to die. A young person is going to die. The death is going to be absolutely senseless. (Shneidman, 1980, p. 108)

People are also afraid of the process of dying (Cassem, 1988; Kastenbaum, 1986). They are afraid of the pain and the other physical problems, especially shortness of breath. Thus, when asked what they would like the last three days of their life to be like, hospice patients say they want to be physically able to do things and have no pain (Kastenbaum, 1986).

Pain is not the only aspect of dying people fear. They are also afraid of being alone. They worry that family and friends will abandon them and fail to provide the love and support they need (Cassem, 1988; Kastenbaum, 1986). They worry that they will become too ugly or too disgusting or too needy for others to tolerate. This is not an unrealistic fear; our own death anxiety often keeps us from being able to face physical deterioration in others. We may find it too distressing to watch a loved one die. Or we may simply feel incompetent to help, not knowing what to say or do. Medical personnel are often not very helpful in such situations. After all, their job is to *save* lives, and they tend to focus on those who can be helped. The terminally ill patient may well find that medical staff are less attentive and friendly (Hillier, 1983; Kastenbaum, 1986). Indeed, concern for relieving the dying person's abandonment fears was one of the motivating forces in the establishment of hospices.

All these fears can influence how a person adapts to the news that he or she is dying. These fears also affect how we react to various components of the process, including how we make decisions about medical treatment, legal issues (such as wills), and plans for the future.

Initial Reactions

Before someone can react to the fact of dying, he or she must first recognize it. This seems like an obvious statement. Yet many serious illnesses are potentially, as opposed to definitely, fatal (Kastenbaum, 1986). People may live for months or even years with the possibility that a treatment will fail and they will die. On the other hand, the treatment may be successful, and they may live a relatively normal life for an extended period of time. Sometimes the situation is so ambiguous that the individual does not know whether to begin the psychological process of dying.

In addition, some people are unprepared to hear the news that they are dying. Some deny that they are dying, even when the news has been clearly communicated to them by a physician (Cassem, 1988; Kastenbaum, 1986). In one study, for example, 20 percent of cancer patients denied they had the disease despite being told explicitly that they did (Gilbertsen & Wangensteen, 1962). Similar results have been reported for heart attack victims (Croog, Shapiro, & Levine, 1971). Such denial is also evident in the public endorsement and personal use of unproved, ineffective, and often dangerous treatments, such as laetrile for cancer (Moertel et al., 1982; Relman, 1982).

Most people, however, want to know the truth about their illness. Studies routinely indicate that 80 percent or more want to know their diagnosis (see Cassem, 1988, for a review). This is true both before and after they know the test outcomes; it is also true whether the news turns out to be good or bad. Less than 10 percent typically report great unhappiness with the physician's honesty. Not surprisingly, many terminally ill people already know they are dying:

A housewife of 57 with metastatic breast cancer, now far advanced, was seen. . . . She reported . . . nervous tension. . . . "I am nervous because I have lost 60 pounds in a year, the priest comes to see me twice a week, which he never did before, and my mother-in-law is nicer to me even though I am meaner to her. Wouldn't this make you nervous?" The physician replied, "You mean you think you're dying." "That's right, I do," she answered. He . . . said quietly, "You are." She smiled and said, "Well, I've finally broken the . . . barrier; someone's finally told me the truth." (Hackett & Weisman, 1962, quoted in Cassem, 1988, p. 737)

This example does not mean that everyone wants to be told bluntly that they are dying (Cassem, 1988). People often want to know that they have cancer, heart disease, and so on, but they may not want to be told the situation is hopeless. Indeed, they will often ask if they have a particular disease. It is less common for them to ask if they are dying, unless death is imminent (Cassem, 1988). People often need time to absorb the news. This may mean telling them over the course of several conversations, allowing them to ask questions, and permitting at least temporary denial of the prognosis (Cassem, 1988; Kastenbaum, 1986). Ned Cassem tells of a patient with severe bone cancer who:

On the first day . . . said he did not know what he had and did not like to ask questions; on the second, that he was "riddled with cancer"; on the third, that he did not really know what ailed him; and on the fourth, that even though nobody likes to die, that was now the lot that fell to him. (Cassem, 1988, p. 737)

Those readers familiar with Kübler-Ross's stages of death and dying (summarized in Table 17-4) recall that she proposes denial as the first phase in the adjustment to dying. The evidence clearly indicates that this is not universally true. Indeed, there is no universal reaction to the news of impending death. Rather, a wide range of factors, including age, gender, life situation, nature of the disease (length of dying interval), and social support, influence reactions at all phases of the dying process.

Individual Differences

Religion: It seems logical that religion, particularly belief in an afterlife, might provide support and comfort to a dying person. Belief in an afterlife could be adaptive in a variety of ways (Kastenbaum, 1985). It might, for example, remove the necessity of trying unreasonable treatments to prolong life, since a "better place" awaits. Furthermore, information from the National Hospice Study indicates that over half of hospice clients believed in an afterlife. Yet when asked to rate their greatest source of strength, less than 4 percent mentioned belief in an afterlife (Kastenbaum, 1985).

Empirical data concerning the role of religion as a comfort are plagued by methodological inconsistencies (Cassem, 1988). Some evidence suggests that a religious commitment can provide comfort and strength; it can also be a source of stability and continuity. On the other hand, religion that is practiced for the "status" or "safety" of it rather than from deeply held belief appears to provide little relief to the dying (Cassem, 1988).

Social Support: When asked what they want their last three days to be like, hospice patients first mention that they want certain people around them (Kastenbaum, 1986). Over half of the clients in the National Hospice Demonstration Study cited family and friends as the most important source of strength. Similarly, a prospective study of breast cancer patients found that women who lived alone were more likely to die within eight years than those who lived with someone (Vachon, 1986). Of the women who were widowed and living alone, 83 percent died. About two-thirds of those who were widowed but lived with someone died; less than half of those who were not widowed and lived with someone died. Among married women, higher anxiety in the husband and sexual problems were both related to higher death rates. It is worth noting that neither age nor type of surgery used to treat the cancer (lumpectomy versus mastectomy) predicted death rates (Vachon, 1986).

We have already noted that many people find it difficult to provide support. They may worry about upsetting the dying person by saying the wrong thing. They may worry that they do not have the patience to provide love and care. The diary of a dying young doctor addresses this issue of "protecting" the patient and maintaining "normal" social relationships:

> The relationship between me and my wife was also exceedingly important at this time ... she was able to express some of the deeper feelings concerning me and my illness. ... Since then we have been able to share feelings, more openly than ... before. ... People wrongly assume that a sick person should be "protected" from strong, and particularly negative, feelings. The truth is that there is probably no more crucial time in a person's life when he needs to know what's going on with those who are important to him. (Shneidman, 1980, p. 132)

Cause of Death: People die for a variety of different reasons. In the United States, most people die of a disease (as opposed to accidents, war, or natural calamity). The most common killers are heart disease and cancer. The cause of death is part of the context or ecology of the dying process and can influence the experience. A sudden death can be a shock and a tremendous disruption because of lack of preparedness. A death that is too prolonged, however, can be a drain on the psychological and material resources of the survivors.

Similarly, the length of time a person knows about the terminal nature of the illness can influence his or her reaction to dying. Glaser and Straus (1968) have described several different "trajectories" of the dying process. Some people follow a *lingering trajectory*. Death is expected but not imminent. The situation is not a crisis. There are no noble lifesaving efforts going on most of the time. Many of these people can feel they are in control of the situation, can make decisions about their daily lives and their medical treatment (Kastenbaum, 1986). Such a sense of control usually facilitates adjustment. Furthermore, there is time to prepare, to do things that one wants to do or feels need to be done. Wills can be written, loved ones can be contacted, funeral arrangements can be made.

The disadvantage is that the process may go on too long (Kastenbaum, 1986). The person may be too ill to work or in too much pain to enjoy life, yet there is no end. People may not know how to treat the dying person and may even question whether he or she is really dying. At the very least, they may be reluctant to acknowledge that the person is terminally ill. Consider the situation of a healthy-looking, still-functioning college student who probably had about two years to live before his leukemia killed him:

> ... My old buddies just felt awfully uncomfortable around me.... If I wanted to make things easier for everybody, I could have just shut up about my condition.... But I didn't think I had to. I mean, you talk about important things with your best friends, don't you.... When something new happened, or I started feeling shaky about it, I would say something. Oh, man—they just couldn't handle it. (Kastenbaum, 1986, p. 88)

Clearly, such reactions influence the social support available to the dying person.

Some people die in a *quick trajectory*, which may be expected or unexpected (Glaser & Strauss, 1968). One issue, of course, if whether people have enough time to prepare what needs to be prepared. Since some of us are always partly prepared (we have wills, cemetery plots, and so on), the amount of time needed varies. With insufficient time, there may be a sense of panic, which may be heightened by the reactions of the survivors. In addition, there is a real risk of losing control over medical intervention in these cases (Kastenbaum, 1986). The medical staff, especially in the emergency room, may be so anxious to try to prolong the person's life that they lose sight of the individual's wishes.

Causes of death differ in more than just their dying trajectories. Some diseases are more disfiguring than others. Some are more painful. And some are likely to produce especially frightening symptoms. It should not be a surprise that such diseases tend to be especially feared and may even carry a stigma. Think, for example, of cancer. Until recently, there was so much fear associated with the disease that even victims were often not told the diagnosis (G. J. Patterson, 1987). When Babe Ruth developed cancer in 1947, the press announcements did not mention the disease. Even as his condition deteriorated over the next year and a half, the word cancer was not used. His illness was attributed to "bad weather." Ruth himself was never told he had the disease. Ten years later, Humphrey Bogart's cancer was initially described in the media as "nerve root pressure" (G. J. Patterson, 1987).

Of course, we are much more open nowadays, following the very public cancers of Betty Ford and Nancy and Ronald Reagan. But there still are stigmatized, dreaded diseases. AIDS is probably the most frightening one. Even hospice workers, who are accustomed to dealing with death and contagious diseases, are frightened by AIDS (Geis & Fuller, 1986). They are confused and frightened about the possibility of contracting the disease, a sense heightened by the current lack of knowledge about the likelihood of one-time, small blood transfers (through, for example, a cut on the hand of a lab worker) transmitting the disease. They wonder about their obligation to their own families, not only in terms of their own health but also in transmitting the disease to their spouses and children. Hospital workers are similarly concerned (Lessor & Jurich, 1986).

There is concern not only about physical illness in the case of AIDS, but also about "social contamination" (Lessor & Jurich, 1986). It is still the case that AIDS is commonly associated with homosexuality and that many people do not wish to be labeled as gay. Indeed, plumbers at one hospital wanted to be reassured that they could not contract the disease by working on the pipes: "It's not really being afraid of getting AIDS, but if you got it everybody would know you were gay" (Lessor & Jurich, 1986, p. 255). Again, such attitudes increase the isolation of the sick and deprive them of important social support. In the case of AIDS, the situation may be even worse because some hospices and hospital wards may refuse to treat AIDS patients (Geis & Fuller, 1986; Lessor & Jurich, 1986).

Caring for the Dying

Many factors contribute to the comfort and well-being of the dying patient. Some of them, including the amount of pain, control, and social support perceived by the patient, are at least partially within the control of the environment. They may sometimes conflict, as when painkillers limit a person's awareness and ability to make decisions. But overall the environment within which the dying process is played out exerts a powerful influence on the quality of the experience.

Medical Care: Medical technology has the potential not only to prolong life (compared to earlier this century and even compared to twenty years ago), but also to improve the quality of life, even for the terminally ill. Analgesics can ease pain, antinauseants and fluid drainage techniques can improve comfort, tranquilizers can reduce anxiety and fear. As this list and Table 17–6 indicate, care of the terminally ill is a complex endeavor. There are often a variety of symptoms and problems, both physical and psychological, to be addressed. Often a complex treatment plan is required. This plan may be made more complicated by procedures designed to prolong life and even attempts to cure the disease. Some patients wish that everything possible be done to extend their lives. Others wish only to have their pain ameliorated and to die peacefully.

These features—competence, concern, comfort, communication, family integration, children, cheerfulness, and consistency—are all valuable components of good care for the terminally ill. However, many practitioners have argued that hospital care does not routinely include these features. They claim that technology can go too far and emphasize curing over the needs of the dying patient (Hillier, 1983; Kastenbaum, 1986; Munley, 1983). This orientation may lead to unspoken assumptions concerning

TABLE 17-6:   Some Common Physical and Psychiatric Symptoms in Terminal Illness

Physical
Pain
Nausea and vomiting
Loss of appetite
Gastrointestinal problems (including incontinence, constipation, diarrhea)
Mouth problems (e.g., dry mouth)
Respiratory problems (e.g., "death rattle")
Urinary tract problems (including incontinence, renal failure)
Skin problems (e.g., pressure sores)
Fluid accumulation (e.g., edema)
Dehydration

Psychiatric
Depression
Delirium
Weakness
Treatment-resistant pain
Anticipatory nausea (in anticipation of going to the hospital, treatment, etc.)

Source: Reprinted by permission of the publishers from Cassem, N. (1988). The person confronting death. In A. M. Nicholi, Jr., M.D. (ed.), *The new Harvard guide to psychiatry.* Cambridge, MA: Harvard University Press. Copyright © 1988 by the President and Fellows of Harvard College.

the care of the dying. For example, focusing on the patient's physical needs may be seen as paramount, even if it involves invasive techniques that patient or family may prefer to avoid. The cases concerning "legal" death certainly make this possibility dramatically real. Add to this the assumption that people should die quietly and without disrupting routines and you have a formula for social isolation (Kastenbaum, 1986). These concerns caused some people, led by Dame Cicely Saunders, to begin the hospice movement.

Hospice: The goal of a hospice is to provide care to the dying patient in such a manner that the person's dignity is preserved (Geis & Fuller, 1986; Kastenbaum, 1986; Munley, 1983). Since the emphasis is on care rather than cure, medical intervention tends to be limited to symptom, especially pain, control. The patient's family is heavily involved in providing the care. Indeed, many hospice programs are home-based. In other words, the hospice staff provides support and training for the people caring for the patient at home. This is a common approach, since most people prefer to die at home or to at least stay at home as long as possible (Hillier, 1983).

Hospice care is provided by an interdisciplinary team, including doctors, nurses, nutritionists, home health care workers, and social workers. Volunteers are usually an important facet of the team. All aspects of a patient's needs are considered. The wishes of the patient and the family are carefully evaluated and are the primary guide in developing the treatment plan. The hospice program may be based in a hospital or it may be independent; it may provide beds for dying patients or it may be exclusively targeted at home care.

There is some evidence (from the National Hospice Demonstration Study) that hospice care may be less expensive than standard hospital care in many cases (Kastenbaum, 1986). This is partly attributable to the use of fewer medical tests and interventions in hospice settings. However, when the person becomes very debilitated and requires constant professional care, hospital costs may actually be lower than repeated home visits by professionals (Kastenbaum, 1986).

It is difficult to say how well hospices achieve their goal of "death with dignity"; data are simply too limited to draw strong conclusions (Kastenbaum, 1986). Certainly the goals of hospice care are in line with people's concerns about dying (especially concerning pain control and isolation). Anecdotal data tend to indicate that both pain control and social quality of life are good, and perhaps better than in hospitals (Hillier, 1983; Munley, 1983). But systematic data are less conclusive. So, for example, in the National Hospice Demonstration Study, family members, but not the patients themselves, reported decreased pain while in the hospice program (Kastenbaum, 1986). Furthermore, most of the available research deals with cancer patients. It remains to be seen how well hospices will serve other clients, including victims of AIDS (Geis & Fuller, 1986).

Hospice, then, seems like a humane approach to dying. Given the individual differences in people's desires about how to die, however, it would be startling to find that everyone found hospice programs valuable. Future research must delineate the circumstances under which hospice programs are maximally effective.

SUMMARY

The placement of this chapter at the end of a text on adult development is a largely arbitrary decision. As we have been reminded, people can die at any age. Furthermore, we are likely to experience the death of a loved one at almost any point during our adult years. Nevertheless, we associate death with old age. Indeed, violation of that expectation is one of the factors that can make adjusting to a death particularly difficult.

Other factors can also influence adjustment to bereavement. Some of these are associated with the nature of the death; for example, initial adjustment tends to be best if the terminal illness was long enough to allow some arrangements to be made but not so drawn out as to become a draining, exhausting experience. Other factors are related to the deceased. Death of a spouse or a child tends to require the greatest levels of adaptation. Finally, some of the factors reflect the bereaved's characteristics. Previous experience with death, as well as preexisting coping style, affect adjustment.

Similar variables determine how well we deal with our own impending death. The dying process does not follow one universal path. Instead, it reflects the individual differences that affect all life crises. Some of us cope better than others. Some of us want honesty, others want a little deception.

There are, however, some commonalities in our approaches to death. Most of us want relief from pain and wish to be near family or friends. Even these are not universally true, of course. Some people, for example, do without painkillers in order to be more mentally alert. In any case, family members and professionals caring for the terminally ill need to consider the wishes of the dying person. Commitment to providing sensitive, individualized care was the basis for the hospice movement, which is devoted to the care of the terminally ill.

References

ABEL, E. (1984). *Fetal alcohol syndrome and fetal alcohol effects.* New York: Plenum Press.

ABPLANALP, J. (1983). Premenstrual syndrome: A selective review. *Women and Health, 8,* 107–123.

ABRAHAMS, B., FELDMAN, S., & NASH, S. (1978). Sex role self-concept and sex-role attitudes: Enduring personality characteristics or adaptations to changing life situations? *Developmental Psychology, 14,* 393–400.

ADAMS, G., & FITCH, S. (1982). Ego state and identity status development: A cross-sequential analysis. *Journal of Personality and Social Psychology, 43,* 574–583.

AHRONS, C. (1983). Divorce: Before, during, and after. In H. McCubbin & C. Figley (eds.), *Stress and the family* (Vol. I). New York: Brunner/Mazel.

AIZENBERG, R., & TREAS, J. (1985). The family in late life: Psychosocial and demographic considerations. In J. Birren & K. Schaie (eds.), *The handbook of psychology of aging* (2d ed.) (pp. 169–189). New York: Van Nostrand Reinhold.

ALDOUS, J. (1985). Parent-adult child relations as affected by the grandparent status. In V. Bengston & J. Robertson (eds.), *Grandparenthood* (pp. 117–132). Beverly Hills: Sage.

ALDOUS, J. (1987). New views on the family life of the elderly and the near-elderly. *Journal of Marriage and the Family, 49,* 227–234.

ALDOUS, J., KLAUS E., & KLEIN, D. (1985). The understanding heart: Aging parents and their favorite children. *Child Development, 56,* 303–316.

ALLEN, K., & PICKETT, R. (1987). Forgotten streams in the family life course: Utilization of qualitative retrospective interviews in the analysis of lifelong single women's family careers. *Journal of Marriage and the Family, 49,* 517–526.

ALLPORT, G. (1961). *Pattern and growth in personality.* New York: Holt, Rinehart & Winston.

ALPERT, J. & RICHARDSON, M. (1980). Parenting. In L. Poon (ed.), *Aging in the 1980s* (pp. 441–454). Washington, DC: American Psychological Association.

AMERICAN PSYCHIATRIC ASSOCIATION (1987). *Diagnostic and statistical manual of mental disorders.* (3rd ed., revised). Washington, D.C.: American Psychiatric Association.

AMERICAN PSYCHOLOGICAL ASSOCIATION (1973). *Ethical principles in the conduct of research with human participants.* Washington, DC: APA.

ANDERSON, K., & BURKHAUSER, R. (1985). The retirement-health nexus: A new measure of an old puzzle. *The Journal of Human Resources, 20,* 315–330.

ANDERSON, K., BURKHAUSER, R., & QUINN, J. (1986). Do retirement dreams come true: The effect of unanticipated events on retirement plans. *Industrial and Labor Relations Review, 39,* 518–526.

ANDREWS, B., & WITHEY, S. (1976). *Social indicators of well-being.* New York: Plenum Press.

ANTONUCCI, T. (1985). Personal characteristics, social support, and social behavior. In R. Binstock & E. Shanas (eds.), *Handbook of aging and the social sciences* (2d ed.) (pp. 94–128). New York: Van Nostrand Reinhold.

ANTONUCCI, T., & JACKSON, J. (1987). Social support, interpersonal efficacy, and health: A life course perspective. In L. Carstensen & B. Edelstein (eds.), *Handbook of clinical gerontology* (pp. 291–311). New York: Pergamon Press.

AQUILINO, W. S. (1990). The likelihood of parent-adult child coresidence: Effects of family structure and parental and characteristics. *Journal of Marriage and the Family, 52,* 405–419.

ARLIN, P. (1975). Cognitive development in adulthood: A fifth stage? *Developmental Psychology, 11,* 602–606.

ASSO, D. (1983). *The real menstrual cycle.* Chicester, Eng.: Wiley.

ATCHLEY, R. (1975). Adjustment to loss of job at retirement. *International Journal of Aging and Human Development, 6,* 17–27.

ATCHLEY, R. (1989). A continuity theory of normal aging. *The Gerontologist, 29,* 183–190.

ATKINSON, A., & RICKEL, A. (1984). Depression in women: The postpartum experience. In A. Rickel, M. Gerrard, & I. Iscoe (eds.), *Social and psychological problems of women* (pp. 197–215). Washington, DC: Hemisphere.

AUSUBEL, D., MONTEMAYOR, R., & SVAJIAN, P. (1977). *Theory and problems of adolescent development.* New York: Grune & Stratton.

AVERILL, J. (1984). The acquisition of emotions during adulthood. In C. Malatesta & C. Izard (eds.), *Emotion in adult development.* Beverly Hills: Sage.

BAILY, M. (1987). Aging and the ability to work: Policy issues and recent trends. In G. Burtless (ed.), *Work, health, and income among the elderly* (pp. 59–97). Washington, DC: Brookings Institution.

BALDESSARINI, R. (1985). Drugs and the treatment of psychiatric disorders. In A. Gilman, L. Goodman, T. Rall, & F. Murad (eds.), *Gilman and Goodman's The pharmacological basis of therapeutics* (7th ed.). New York: Macmillan.

BALTES, M., & BALTES, P. (1982). Microanalytical research on environmental factors and plasticity in the psychology of aging. In T. Field, A. Huston, H. Quay, L. Troll, & G. Finley (eds.), *Review of human development* (pp. 524–539). New York: Wiley.

BALTES, P. (1968). Longitudinal and cross-sectional sequences in the study of age and generation effects. *Human Development, 11,* 145–171.

BALTES, P. B. (1987). Theoretical propositions of life-span developmental psychology: On the dynamics between growth and decline. *Developmental Psychology, 23,* 611–626.

BALTES, P., CORNELIUS, S., SPIRO, A., NESSELROADE, J., & WILLIS, S. (1980). Integration versus differentiation of fluid/crystallized intelligence in old age. *Developmental Psychology, 16,* 625–635.

BALTES, P., & GOULET, L. (1970). Status and issues of a life-span developmental psychology. In L. Goulet & P. Baltes (eds.), *Life-span developmental psychology: Research and theory* (pp. 3–21). New York: Academic Press.

BALTES, P., & SCHAIE, K. (1974). The myth of the twilight years. *Psychology Today,* 35–40.

BALTES, P., & SCHAIE, K. (1976). On the plasticity of intelligence in adulthood: Where Horn and Donaldson fail. *American Psychologist, 31,* 720–725.

BALTES, P., & WILLIS, S. (1977). Toward psychological theories of aging and development. In J. Birren & K. Schaie (eds.), *Handbook of the psychology of aging* (pp. 128–154). New York: Van Nostrand Reinhold.

BALTES, P., & WILLIS, S. (1982). Plasticity and enhancement of intellectual functioning in old age: Penn State's adult development and enrichment project (ADEPT). In F. Craik & S. Trehub (eds.), *Aging and cognitive processes* (pp. 353–389). New York: Plenum Press.

BANKOFF, E. (1986). Peer support for widows: Personal and structural characteristics related to its provision. In S. Hobfoll (ed.), *Stress, social support, and women* (pp. 207–222). Washington, DC: Hemisphere.

BARASH, D. (1979). *The whisperings within.* New York: Penguin.

BARDWICK, J. (1971). *Psychology of women.* New York: Harper & Row.

BARNETT, R., & BARUCH, G. (1987a). Determinants of fathers' participation in family work. *Journal of Marriage and the Family, 49,* 29–40.

BARNETT, R., & BARUCH, G. (1987b). Social roles, gender & psychological distress. In R. Barnett, L. Biener, & G. Baruch (eds.), *Gender and stress* (pp. 122–143). New York: Free Press.

BART, P. (1971). Depression in middle-aged women. In V. Gornick & B. Moran (eds.), *Women in sexist society.* New York: Basic Books.

BARTOSHUK, L., & WEIFFENBACH, J. (1990). Chemical senses and aging. In E. Schneider & J. Rowe (eds.), *Handbook of the biology of aging* (pp. 429–444). San Diego: Academic Press.

BAUMRIND, D. (1971). Current patterns of parental authority. *Developmental Psychology Monographs, 4.*

BAUMRIND, D. (1986). Sex differences in moral reasoning: Response to Walker's (1984) conclusion that there are none. *Child Development, 57,* 511–521.

BARUCH, G., & BARNETT, R. (1986). Role quality, multiple rule involvement, and psychological well-being in midlife women. *Journal of Personality and Social Psychology, 51,* 578–585.

BARUCH, G., BIENER, L., & BARNETT, R. (1987). Women and gender in research on work and family stress. *American Psychologist, 42,* 130–136.

BAZZOLI, G. (1985). The early retirement decision: New empirical evidence on the influence of health. *The Journal of Human Resources, 20,* 214–234.

BEARON, L. (1989). No great expectations: The underpinnings of life satisfaction for older women. *The Gerontologist, 29,* 772–776.

BECK, A., & YOUNG, J. (1978). College blues. *Psychology Today, 12,* 80–92.

BEHRMAN, D. (1982). *Family and/or career: Plans of first-time mothers.* Ann Arbor: University of Michigan: Research Press.

BELL, A., & WEINBERG, M. (1978). *Homosexualities.* New York: Simon & Schuster.

BELLE, D. (1982). The stress of caring: Women as providers of social support. In L. Goldberger & S. Breznitz (eds.), *Handbook of stress: Theoretical and clinical aspects.* New York: Free Press.

BELSKY, J., LERNER, R., & SPANIER , G. (1984). *The child in the family.* Reading, MA: Addison-Wesley.

BELSKY, J., & ROVINE, M. (1990). Patterns of marital change across the transition to parenthood: Pregnancy to three years postpartum. *Journal of Marriage and the Family, 52,* 5–19.

BELSKY, J., STEINBERG, L. & DRAPER, P. (1991). Childhood experience, interpersonal development, and reproductive strategy: An evolutionary theory of socialization. *Child Development, 62,* 647–670.

BEM, S. (1975). Sex role adaptability: One consequence of psychological androgyny. *Journal of Personality and Social Psychology, 31,* 634–643.

BEM, S. (1985). Androgyny and gender schema theory: A conceptual and empirical integration. In T. Sonderegger (ed.), *Nebraska Symposium on Motivation: Psychology and gender* (pp. 179–226). Lincoln, Nebraska: University of Nebraska Press.

BENGSTON, V. (1985). Diversity and symbolism in grandparental roles. In V. Bengston & J. Robertson (eds.), *Grandparenthood* (pp. 11–26). Beverly Hills: Sage.

BENGSTON, V., CUTLER, N., MANGEN, D., & MARSHALL, V. (1985). Generations, cohorts, and relations between age groups. In R. Binstock & E. Shanas (eds.), *Handbook of aging and the social sciences* (2d ed.) (pp. 304–338). New York: Van Nostrand.

BENGSTON, V., REEDY, M., & GORDON, C. (1985). Aging and self-conceptions: Personality processes and social contexts. In J. Birren & K. Schaie (eds.), *Handbook of the psychology of aging* (2d ed.). New York: Van Nostrand Reinhold.

BENSHOFF, J., & ROBERTO, K. (1987). Alcoholism in the elderly: Clinical issues. *Clinical Gerontologist, 7,* 3–14.

BERARDO, D., SHEEHAN, C., & LESLIE, G. (1987). A residue of tradition: Jobs, careers, and spouses time in housework. *Journal of Marriage and the Family, 49,* 381–390.

BERGMANN, B. (1981). The economic risks of being a housewife. *The American Economic Review, 71,* 81–86.

BERGMANN, B. (1986). *The economic emergence of women.* New York: Basic Books.

BERNARD, J. (1981). The good provider role: Its rise and fall. *American Psychologist, 36,* 1–12.

BERNSTEIN, R. (1983). Evaluation and treatment of obesity. In E. Feldman (ed.), *Nutrition in the Middle and Later Years* (pp. 71–92). Boston: John Wright.

BIELBY, W., & BARON, J. (1986). Sex segregation within occupations. *American Economic Review, 76,* 43–47.

BIERMAN, E. (1985). Arteriosclerosis and aging. In C. Finch & E. Schneider (eds.), *Handbook of the biology of aging* (2d ed.) (pp. 842–868). New York: Van Nostrand.

BIRKEL, R., & JONES, C. (1989). A comparison of the caregiving networks of dependent elderly individuals who are lucid and those who are demented. *The Gerontologist, 29,* 114–119.

BIRREN, J., & CLAYTON, V. (1975). History of gerontology. In D. Woodruff & J. Birren (eds.), *Aging* (pp. 15–27). New York: Van Nostrand.

BIRREN, J., WOODS, A., & WILLIAMS, M. (1980). Behavioral slowing with age: Causes, organization, and consequences. In L. Poon (ed.), *Aging in the 1980s* (pp. 293–308). Washington, DC: American Psychological Association.

BLANCHARD, K., & CHESKA, A. (1985). *The anthropology of sport.* Westport, CT: Bergin & Garvey.

BLANCK, W., & BLANCK, G. (1968). *Marriage and personal development.* New York: Columbia University Press.

BLANKENHORN, D., NESSIM, S., JOHNSON, R., SANMARCO, M., AZEN, S., & CASHIN-HEMPHILL, L. (1987). Beneficial effects of combined colestipol-niacin therapy on coronary atherosclerosis and coronary venous bypass grafts. *Journal of the American Medical Association, 257:* 3233–40.

BLASI, A. (1980). Bridging moral cognition and moral action: A critical review of the literature. *Psychological Bulletin, 88,* 1–45.

BLAU, F., & FERBER, M. (1986). *The economics of women, men, and work.* Englewood Cliffs, NJ: Prentice-Hall.

BLAU, Z., ROGERS, P., & STEPHENS, R. (1978). School bells and work whistles: Sounds that echo a better life for women in later years. In *Women in Midlife-Security and fulfillment* (pp. 61–85). Washington, DC: Government Printing Office.

BLENKER, M. (1965). Social work and family relationships in later life with some thoughts on filial maturity. In E. Shanas & G. Streib (eds.), *Social structure and the family: Generational relations.* Englewood Cliffs, NJ: Prentice Hall.

BLIESZNER, R., & MANCINI, J. (1987). Enduring ties: Older adults' parental role and responsibilities. *Family Relations, 36,* 176–180.

BLUEBOND-LANGER, M. (1977). Meanings of death to children. In H. Feifel (ed.), *New meanings of death* (pp. 47–66). New York: McGraw-Hill.

BLUMSTEIN, P., & SCHWARTZ, P. (1983). *American couples.* New York: William Morrow.

BOLTE, G., & FOWLER, D. (1991). Where do they go from here? *Time, 137,* 66.

BONDAREFF, W. (1985). The neural basis of aging. In J. Birren & K. Schaie (eds.), *The handbook of the psychology of aging* (2d ed.) (pp. 95–112). New York: Van Nostrand.

BOOTH-KEWLEY, S., & FRIEDMAN, H. (1987). Psychological predictors of heart disease: A quantitative review. *Psychological Bulletin, 101,* 343–362.

BOSS, P. (1983). The marital relationship: Boundaries and ambiguities. In H. McCubbin & C. Figley (eds.), *Stress and the family* (Vol. 1). New York: Brunner/Mazel.

BOSSÉ, R., ALDWIN, C., LEVINSON, M. & WORKMAN-DANIELS, C. (1991). How stressful is retirement? Findings from the Normative Aging Study. *Journal of Gerontology, 46,* 9–14.

BOSTON WOMEN'S HEALTH COLLECTIVE. (1984). *The new our bodies, ourselves.* New York: Simon & Schuster.

BOTWINICK, J. (1978). *Aging and behavior.* New York: Springer.

BOUVIER, L. (1980). America's baby boom generation: The fateful bulge. *Population Bulletin, 35,* 1–35.

BOWERS, B. (1988). Family perceptions of care in a nursing home. *The Gerontologist, 28,* 361–368.

BOWLBY, J. (1973). *Attachment and loss.* (Vol. 2). New York: Basic Books.

BOWLING, A., & BROWNE, P. (1991). Social networks, health, and emotional well-being among the oldest old in London. *Journal of Gerontology, 46,* S20–32.

BRACKEN, M., KLERMAN, L., & BRACKEN, M. (1978). Abortion, adoption, or motherhood: An empirical study of decision-making during pregnancy. *American Journal of Obstetrics and Gynecology, 130,* 251–262.

BRAY, D., & HOWARD, A. (1980). Career success and life satisfactions of middle-aged managers. In A. Bond & J. Rosen (eds.), *Competence and coping during adulthood.* Hanover, NH: University Press of New England.

BRAY, D., & HOWARD, A. (1983). The AT&T longitudinal studies of managers. In K. Schaie (ed.), *Longitudinal studies of adult psychological development.* (pp. 266–312). New York: Guilford.

BRECKENRIDGE, J., GALLAGHER, D., THOMPSON, L., & PETERSON, J. (1986). Characteristic depressive symptoms of bereaved elders. *Journal of Gerontology, 41,* 163–168.

BRIM, O. (1968). Adult socialization. In J. Clausen (ed.) *Socialization and society.* Boston: Little, Brown.

BRITANNICA WORLD DATA (1986). See Daume & Davis.

BRODY, E. (1981). Women in the middle and family help to older people. *The Gerontologist, 21,* 471–480.

BRODY, E., KLEBAN, M., JOHNSEN, P., HOFFMAN, C., & SCHOONOVER, C. (1987). Work status and parent care: A comparison of four groups of women. *The Gerontologist, 27,* 201–208.

BRODY, E., JOHNSEN, P., & FULCOMER, M. (1984). What should adult children do for elderly parents? Opinions and preferences of three generations of women. *Journal of Gerontology, 39,* 736–746.

BRODY, E., & SCHOONOVER, C. (1986). Patterns of parent-care when adult daughters work and when they do not. *The Gerontologist, 26,* 372–381.

BRODZINSKY, D. (1985). On the relationship between cognitive styles and cognitive structures. In E. Neimark, R. DeLisi, & J. Newman (eds.), *Moderators of competence* (pp. 147–174). Hillsdale, NJ: Erlbaum.

BROVERMAN, I., VOGEL, S., BROVERMAN, D., CLARKSON, F., & ROSENBERG, P. (1972). Sex role stereotypes: A current appraisal. *Journal of Social Issues, 28,* 59–78.

BROWN, G., HARRIS, T., & BIFULCO, A. (1986). Long-term effects of early loss of parent. In M. Rutter, C. Izard, & P. Read (eds.), *Depression in young people.* New York: Guilford.

BROWN, T. (1979). Three who aren't making it. In R. Kanter & B. Stein (eds.), *Life in organizations.* New York: Basic Books.

BUHLER, C. (1935). The curve of life as studied in biographies. *Journal of Applied Psychology, 19,* 405–409.

BUHLER, C., & MASSARIK, F. (eds.) (1968). *The course of human life.* New York: Springer.

BURKE, R., & WEIR, T. (1976). Relationship of wives' employment status to husband, wife and pair satisfaction and performance. *Journal of Marriage and the Family, 38,* 279–287.

BURRUS-BAMMEL, L. & BAMMEL, G. (1985). Leisure and recreation. In J. Birren & K. Schaie (eds.), *Handbook of the psychology of aging* (2d ed.) (pp. 848–863). New York: Van Nostrand.

BURTLESS, G. (1987). Occupational effects of the health and work capacity of older men. In G. Burtless (ed.), *Work, health, and income among the elderly.* Washington, DC: Brookings Institution.

BURTON, L., & BENGSTON, V. (1985). Black grandmothers: Issues of timing and continuity of roles. In V. Bengston & J. Robertson (eds.), *Grandparenthood* (pp. 61–78). Beverly Hills: Sage.

BUSS, A., & PLOMIN, R. (1984). *Temperament: Early developing personality traits.* Hillsdale, NJ: Erlbaum.

BUSSE, E. (1978). Duke Longitudinal study I: Senescence and senility. In R. Kateman, R. Terry, & K. Beck (eds.), *Alzheimer's disease: Senile dementia and related disorders.* New York: Raven Press.

BUSSE, E. & BLAZER, D. (1980). Disorders related to biological functioning. In E. Busse & D. Blazer (eds.) *Handbook of geriatric psychiatry* (pp. 390–416). New York: Van Nostrand Reinhold.

BUSSE, E., & MADDOX, G. (1985). *The Duke longitudinal studies of normal aging.* New York: Springer.

CALDWELL, R., BLOOM, B., & HODGES, W. (1984). Sex differences in separation and divorce: A longitudinal perspective. In A. Rickel, M. Gerrard, & I. Iscoe (eds.), *Social and psychological problems of women* (pp. 103–119). Washington, DC: Hemisphere.

CALLAHAN, J. (1988). Elder abuse: Some questions for policymakers. *The Gerontologist, 28,* 453–458.

CAMPBELL, A., CONVERSE, P., & RODGERS, W. (1976). *The quality of American life.* New York: Russell Sage Foundation.

CAMPBELL, J., & CHARNESS, N. (1990). Age-related declines in working-memory skills: Evidence from a complex calculation task. *Developmental Psychology, 26,* 879–888.

CAPON, N., & KUHN, D. (1979). Logical reasoning in the supermarket: Adult females' use of a proportional reasoning strategy in an everyday context. *Developmental Psychology, 15,* 450–452.

CARROLL, J., & REST, J. (1982). Moral development. In B. Wolman (ed.), *Handbook of developmental psychology* (pp. 434–451). Englewood Cliffs, NJ: Prentice-Hall.

CARVER, C., & HUMPHRIES, C. (1982). Social psychology of the Type A coronary-prone behavior pattern. In G. Sanders & J. Suls (eds.), *Social psychology of health and illness.* Hillsdale, NJ: Erlbaum.

CASSEM, N. (1988). The person confronting death. In A. Nicholi (ed.), *The new Harvard guide to psychiatry* (pp. 728–758). Cambridge, MA: The Belknap Press.

CASSILETH, B., LUSK, E., STROUSE, T., & BODENHEIMER, B. (1984). Contemporary unorthodox treatments in cancer medicine. *Annals of Internal Medicine, 101,* 105–112.

CATTELL, R. (1941). Some theoretical issues in adult intelligence testing. *Psychological Bulletin, 38,* 592.

CATTELL, R. (1963). Theory of fluid and crystallized intelligence: A critical experiment. *Journal of Educational Psychology, 54,* 1–22.

CAVANAUGH, J., GRADY, J., & PERLMUTTER, M. (1983). Forgetting and use of memory aids in 20- and 70-year-olds' everyday life. *International Journal of Aging and Human Development, 17,* 113–122.

CHERLIN, A., & FURSTENBERG, G. (1985). Styles and strategies of grandparenting. In V. Bengston & J. Robertson (eds.), *Grandparenthood* (pp. 97–116). Beverly Hills: Sage.

CHESTER, N. (1979). *Pregnancy and new parenthood: Twin experiences of change.* Paper presented at the meeting of the Eastern Psychological Association, Philadelphia.

CHILMAN, C. (1982). Adolescent childbearing in the United States: Apparent causes and consequences. In T. Field, A. Huston, H. Quay, L. Troll, & G. Finley (eds.), *Review of human development* (pp. 418–431). New York: Wiley.

CHIRIBOGA, D., & CUTLER, L. (1980). Stress and adaptation: Life span perspectives. In L. Poon (ed.), *Aging in the 1980s.* Washington, DC: American Psychological Association.

CHRISTMAN, J., & THOMPSON, D. (1980). *Everywoman's health guide to body and mind.* Garden City, NY: Doubleday.

CICIRELLI, V. (1980). Sibling relationships in adulthood: A life-span perspective. In L. Poon (ed.), *Aging in the 1980s* (pp. 455–462). Washington, DC: American Psychological Association.

CICIRELLI, V. (1985). Sibling relationships throughout the life cycle. In L. L'Abate (ed.), *The handbook of family psychology and relations* (Vol. 1) (pp. 180–210). Homewood, IL: Dorsey.

CLAYTON, P. (1982). Bereavement. In E. Paykel

(ed.), *Handbook of affective disorders* (pp. 403–415). New York: Guilford.

CLINGEEMPL, G., & SEGAL, S. (1986). Stepparent-stepchild relationships and the psychological adjustment of children in stepmother and stepfather families. *Child Development, 57,* 474–484.

COCKBURN, J., & SMITH, P. (1991). The relative influence of intelligence and age on everyday memory. *Journal of Gerontology, 46,* P. 31–36.

COE, R. (1988). A longitudinal examination of poverty in the elderly years. *The Gerontologist, 28,* 540–544.

COHEN, C., TERESI, J., & HOLMES, D. (1988). The physical well-being of old homeless men. *Journal of Gerontology, 43,* S121–126.

COHEN, G. (1979). Language comprehension in old age. *Cognitive Psychology, 11,* 412–429.

COHLER, B., & BOXER, A. (1984). Personal adjustment, well-being, and life events. In C. Malatesta & C. Izard (eds.), *Emotion in adult development.* Beverly Hills: Sage.

COLARUSSO, C., & NEMIROFF, R. (1981). *Adult development.* New York: Plenum Press.

COLBY, A., KOHLBERG, L., GIBBS, J., CANDEE, D., SPEICHER-DUBIA, B., HEWER, A., & POWER, C. (1983). *The measurement of moral development: Standard issue scoring manual.* New York: Cambridge University Press.

COLBY, A., KOHLBERG, L., GIBBS, J., & LIEBERMAN, M. (1983). A longitudinal study of moral judgement. *Monographs of the Society for Research in Child Development, 48,* Ser. No. 200.

COLEMAN, J., BUTCHER, J., & CARSON, R. (1984). *Abnormal psychology and modern life* (7th ed.). Glenview, IL: Scott, Foresman.

Columbus Dispatch, July 12, 1985, p. 3.

COMFORT, A. (1980). Sexuality in later life. In J. Birren and R. Sloane (eds.), *Handbook of mental health and aging.* (pp. 885–892). Englewood Cliffs, NJ: Prentice-Hall.

COMMONS, M., RICHARDS, F., & KUHN, D. (1982). Systematic and metasystematic reasoning: A case for levels of reasoning beyond Piaget's stage of formal operations. *Child Development, 53,* 1058–1069.

COONEY, T., SCHAIE, K., & WILLIS, S. (1988). The relationship between prior functioning on cognitive and personality dimensions and subject attrition in longitudinal research. *Journal of Gerontology, 43,* P12–17.

COOPER, K., & GUTTMAN, D. (1987). Gender identity and ego mastery style in middle-aged, pre- and post-empty nest women. *The Gerontologist, 27,* 347–352.

COOPER, T., DETRE, T., & WEISS, S. (1981). Coronary prone behavior and coronary heart disease: A critical review. *Circulation, 63,* 1199–1215.

CORSO, J. (1977). Auditory perception and communication. In J. Birren & K. Schaie (eds.), *Handbook of the psychology of aging* (pp. 535–553). New York: Van Nostrand Reinhold.

CORTESE, A. (1989). The interpersonal approach to morality. *The Journal of Social Psychology, 129,* 429–441.

COSTA, P., FLEG, J., MCCRAE, R., & LAKATTA, E. (1982). Neuroticism, coronary artery disease, and chest pain complaints: Cross-sectional and longitudinal studies. *Experimental Aging Research, 8,* 37–44.

COSTA, P., & MCCRAE, R. (1980). Still stable after all these years: Personality as a key to some issues in adulthood and old age. In P. Baltes & O. P. Brim (eds.), *Life-span development and behavior* (Vol. 3). New York: Academic Press.

COSTA, P., & MCCRAE, R. (1982). An approach to the attribution of aging, period, and cohort effects. *Psychological Bulletin, 92,* 238–250.

COSTA, P., & MCCRAE, R. (1984). Personality as a lifelong determinant of well-being. In C. Malatesta & C. Izard (eds.), *Affective processes in adult development and aging.* Beverly Hills: Sage.

COSTA, P., & MCCRAE, R. (1985). Hypochondriasis, neuroticism, and aging: When are somatic complaints unfounded? *American Psychologist, 40,* 19–28.

COSTA, P., MCCRAE, R., ANDRES, R., & TOBIN, J. (1980). Hypertension, somatic complaints, and personality. In M. Elias & D. Streeten (eds.), *Hypertension and cognitive processes* (pp. 95–110). Mt. Desert, ME: Beech-Hill.

COSTA, P., MCCRAE, R., & ARENBERG, D. (1980). Enduring dispositions in adult males. *Journal of Personality and Social Psychology, 38,* 793–800.

COSTA, P., MCCRAE, R., & ARENBERG, D. (1983). Recent longitudinal research on personality and aging. In K. Schaie (ed.), *Longitudinal studies of adult psychological development.* (pp. 222–265). New York: Guilford.

COSTA, P., MCCRAE, R., & NORRIS, A. (1981). Personal adjustment to aging: Longitudinal prediction from neuroticism and extraversion. *Journal of Gerontology, 36,* 78–85.

COUNCIL OF ECONOMIC ADVISORS. (1987). *The economic report of the President.* Washington, DC: Government Printing Office.

COUNCIL OF ECONOMIC ADVISORS. (1990). *The economic report of the President.* Washington, DC: Government Printing Office.

COWAN, R. (1983). *More work for mother.* New York: Basic Books.

CRAIK, F. (1977). Age differences in human memory. In J. Birren & K. Schaie (eds.), *Handbook of the psychology of aging* (pp. 384–420). New York: Van Nostrand.

CRAIK, F., & LOCKHART, R. (1972). Levels of processing: A framework for memory research. *Journal of Verbal Learning and Verbal Behavior, 11,* 671–684.

CRAIK, F., & SIMON, E. (1980). Age differences in memory: The roles of attention and depth of processing. In L. Poon, J. Fozard, L. Cermak, D. Arenberg, & L.Thompson (eds.), *New directions in memory and aging: Proceedings of the George A. Talland Memorial Conference.* Hillsdale, NJ: Erlbaum.

CROCKENBERG, S. (1981). Infant irritability, mother responsiveness, and social support influences on the security of infant-mother attachment. *Child Development, 52,* 857–862.

CROOG, S., SHAPIRO, D., & LEVINE, S. (1971). Denial among male heart patients. *Psychosomatic Medicine, 33,* 385–397.

CROPPER, D., MECK, D., & ASH, M. (1977). The relation between formal operations and a possible fifth stage of cognitive development. *Developmental Psychology, 13,* 517–518.

CUBER, J., & HARROFF, P. (1965/1986). Five types of marriage. In A. Skolnick & J. Skolnick (eds.), *Family in transition* (pp. 263–274). Boston: Little, Brown.

CUMMING, E., & HENRY, W. (1961). *Growing old: The process of disengagement.* New York: Basic Books.

CUNNINGHAM, J., & ANTILL, J. (1984). Changes in masculinity and femininity across the family life cycle: A reexamination. *Developmental Psychology, 20,* 1135–1141.

CUNNINGHAM, W. & BIRREN, J. (1980). Age changes in the factor structure of intellectual abilities in adulthood and old age. *Educational and Psychological Measurement, 40,* 271–290.

CUTRONA, C. (1990). Stress and social support—In search of optimal matching. *Journal of Social and Clinical Psychology, 9,* 3–14.

CUTRONA, C. & TROUTMAN, B. (1986). Social support, infant temperament, and parenting self-efficacy: A mediational model of postpartum depression. *Child Development, 57,* 1507–1518.

CVEJIC, H. et al. (1977). Follow-up of 50 adolescent girls two years after abortion. *Canadian Medical Association Journal, 116,* 44–46.

CYTRYNBAUM, S., BLUM, L., PATRICK, R., STEIN, J., WADNER, D., & WILK, C. (1980). Midlife development: A personality and social systems perspective. In L. Poon (ed.), *Aging in the 1980s* (pp. 463–474). Washington, DC: American Psychological Association.

DALSKY, G., STOCKE, K., EHSANI, A., SLATOPOLSKY, E., LEE, W., & BIRGE, S. (1988). Weight-bearing exercise training and lumbar bone mineral content in postmenopausal women. *Annals of Internal Medicine, 108,* 824–828.

DALTON, K. (1980). Cyclical criminal acts in premenstrual syndrome. *Lancet,* 1070–1071.

DANIELS, P. & WEINGARTEN, K. (1982). *Sooner or later: The timing of parenthood in adult lives.* New York: Norton.

DAUME, D., & DAVIS, J. (1986). *The Britannica book of the year: 1986.* Chicago: Encyclopaedia Britannica.

DAVIDSON, J., & STERNBERG, R. (1985). Competence and performance in intellectual development. In E. Neimark, R. DeLisi, & J. Newman (eds.), *Moderators of competence* (pp. 43–76). Hillsdale, NJ: Erlbaum.

DAWKINS, R. (1976). *The selfish gene.* London: Oxford University Press.

DEAN, A., KOLODY, B., WOOD, P., & ENSEL, W. (1989). Measuring the communication of social support from adult children. *Journal of Gerontology, 44,* 571–579.

DEIMLING, G., & BASS, D. (1986). Symptoms of mental impairment among elderly adults and their effects on family caregivers. *Journal of Gerontology, 41,* 778–784.

DEMEIS, D., HOCK, E., & MCBRIDE, S. (1986). The balance of employment and motherhood: A longitudinal study of mothers' feelings about separation from their firstborn. *Developmental Psychology, 22,* 627–633.

DENNEY, M. (1982). Aging and cognitive changes. In B. Wolman (ed.), *Handbook of developmental psychology* (pp. 807–827). Englewood Cliffs, NJ: Prentice-Hall.

DENNEY, N., & DENNEY, D. (1974). Modelling effects on the questioning strategies of the elderly. *Developmental Psychology, 10,* 458.

DEUTSCHER, I. (1968/1964). The quality of postparental life. In B. Neugarten (ed.), *Middle age and aging* (pp. 263–268). Chicago: University of Chicago Press.

DEVRIES, H. (1975). Physiology of exercise and aging. In D. Woodruff & J. Birren (eds.), *Aging: Scientific perspectives and social issues* (pp. 257–278). New York: Van Nostrand.

DOHERTY, W., & JACOBSON, W. (1982). Marriage and the family. In B. Wolman (ed.), *Handbook of developmental psychology.* Englewood Cliffs, NJ: Prentice-Hall.

DOKA, K., & MERTZ, M. (1988). The meaning and significance of great-grandparenthood. *The Gerontologist, 28,* 192–197.

DOLLARD, J., DOOB, L., MILLER, N., MOWER, O., & SEARS, R. (1939). *Frustration and aggression.* New Haven, CT: Yale University Press.

DONOVAN, R. (1984). Bringing America into the 1980s. *American Psychologist, 39,* 429–431.

DOUGLAS, K., & ARENBERG, D. (1978). Age changes, cohort differences, and cultural change on the Guilford-Zimmerman Temperament Survey. *Journal of Gerontology, 33,* 737–747.

DRESSEL, P. (1988). Gender, race, and class: Beyond the feminization of poverty in later life. *The Gerontologist, 28,* 177–180.

DUBRIN, A. (1978). Psychological factors: Reentry and mid-career crises. In *Women in midlife—Security and fulfillment.* Washington, DC: Government Printing Office.

DUCK, S. (1983). *Friends, for life: The psychology of close relationships.* Brighton, Eng.: Harvester Press.

DUNN, J. (1983). Sibling relationships in early childhood. *Child Development, 54,* 787–811.

DUNN, J. (1984). Sibling studies and the development impact of critical incidents. In P. Baltes & O. Brim (eds.), *Life-span development and behavior* (Vol. 6) (pp. 335–353). Orlando, FL: Academic Press.

DURA, J. STUKENBERG, K., & KIELCOLT-GLASER, J. (1991). Anxiety and depressive disorders in adult children caring for demented parents. *Psychology and Aging, 6,* 467–473.

DWECK, C., & ELLIOTT, E. (1983). Achievement motivation. In P. Mussen (ed.), *Carmichael's manual of child psychology* (Vol. 3). New York: Wiley.

DYER, E. (1963). Parenthood as crisis: A restudy. *Marriage and Family Living, 25,* 196–201.

EDELSTEIN, L. (1984). *Maternal bereavement.* New York: Praeger.

EDWARDS, C. (1981). The comparative study of the development of moral judgment and reasoning. In R. Munroe, R. Munroe, & B. Whiting (eds.), *Handbook of cross-cultural human development* (pp. 501–527). New York: Garland.

EDWARDS, S. (1983). Nutrition and lifestyle. In E. Feldman (ed.), *Nutrition in the middle and later years.* Boston: John Wright.

EKERDT, D., VINICK, B., & BOSSE, R. (1989). Orderly endings: Do men know when they will retire? *Journal of Gerontology, 44,* S28–35.

ELDER, L., CASPI, A., & BURTON, L. (1988). Adolescent transition in developmental perspective: Sociological and historical insights. In M. Gunnar & W. Collins (eds.), *Minnesota symposia on child development* (Vol. 21): *Development during the transition to adolescence* (pp. 151–179). Hillsdale, NJ: Erlbaum.

ELLWOOD, D. & CRANE, J. (1990). Family change among black Americans: What do we know? *Journal of Economic Perspectives, 4,* 65–84.

ENGEN, T. (1977). Taste and smell. In J. Birren & K. Schaie (eds.), *Handbook of the psychology of aging* (pp. 554–561). New York: Van Nostrand.

ENTWISLE, D. (1985). Becoming a parent. In L. L'Abate (ed.): *The handbook of family psychology and therapy* (Vol. 1) (pp. 560–578). Homewood, IL: Dorsey.

ERIKSON, E. (1963). *Childhood and society.* New York: Norton.

ERIKSON, E. (1968). *Identity: Youth and crisis.* New York: Norton.

ERIKSON, E. (1980). *Identity and the life cycle.* New York: Norton (orig. pub. 1959.)

ERIKSON, E. (1982). *The life cycle completed.* New York: Norton.

ERIKSON, E., ERIKSON, J., & KIVNICK, H. (1986). *Vital involvement in old age.* New York: Norton.

EVANS, D., FUNKENSTEIN, H., ALBERT, M. SCHERR, P., COOK, N., CHOWN, M., HEBERT, L., HENNEKENS, C., & TAYLOR, O. (1989). Prevalence of Alzheimer's disease in a community population of older persons. *Journal of the American Medical Association, 262,* 2551–2556.

EVANS, P. (1990). Type A behavior and coronary heart disease: When will the jury return? *British Journal of Psychology, 81,* 147–157.

EVE, S. (1988). A longitudinal study of use of health care services among older women. *Journal of Gerontology, 43,* M31–M39.

EWEN, R. (1980). *An introduction to theories of personality.* New York: Academic Press.

EXTON-SMITH, A. (1985). Mineral metabolism. In C. Finch & E. Schneider, (eds.), *Handbook of the biology of aging* (2d ed.) (pp. 511–539). New York: VanNostrand.

EYSENCK, H. (1975). *The inequality of man.* San Diego: Edits Publishers.

FAKOURI, M. (1976). "Cognitive development in adulthood: A fifth stage?": A critique. *Developmental Psychology, 12,* 472.

FAVER, C. (1984). *Women in transition.* New York: Praeger.

FEIN, R. (1976). Men's entrance to parenthood. *The Family Coordinator, 25,* 341–348.

FEINBERG, I., FEIN, G., PRICE, L., JERNIGAN, T., & FLOYD, T. (1980). Methodological and conceptual issues in the study of brain-behavior relations in the elderly. In L. Poon (ed.), *Aging in the 1980s* (pp. 71–77). Washington DC: American Psychological Association.

FELDMAN, E. (1983). Nutritional factors in cardiovascular disease. In E. Feldman (ed.). *Nutrition in the middle and later years* (pp. 107–126). Boston: John Wright.

FELDMAN, H., & FELDMAN, M. (1984). The filial crisis: Research and social policy implications. In V. Rogers (ed.), *Adult development through relationships* (pp. 70–87). New York: Praeger.

FELDMAN, S., & ASCHENBRENNER, B. (1983). Impact of parenthood on various aspects of masculinity and feminity: A short-term longitudinal study. *Developmental Psychology, 19,* 278–289.

FELDMAN, S., BIRINGEN, Z., & NASH, S. (1981). Fluctuations of sex-related self-attributions as a function of stage of family life cycle. *Developmental Psychology, 17,* 24–35.

FERBER, M., GREEN, C., & SPAETH, J. (1986). Work power and earnings of women and men. *American Economic Review, 76,* 53–56.

FETHKE, C. (1989). Life-cycle models of saving and the effect of the timing of divorce on retirement economic well-being. *Journal of Gerontology, 44,* S121–128.

FIELDS, G., & MITCHELL, O. (1984). *Retirement, pensions, and Social Security.* Cambridge, MA: MIT Press.

FINCHAM, F., & BRADBURY, T. (1990). Social support in marriage: The role of social cognition. *Journal of Social and Clinical Psychology, 9,* 31–42.

FINKELHOR, D. (1984). *Child sexual abuse.* New York: Free Press.

FISCHMAN, J. (1987). Getting tough. *Psychology Today, 21,* 26–28.

FISKE, M. (1982). Challenge and defeat: Stability and change in adulthood. In L. Goldberger & S. Breznitz (eds.), *Handbook of stress.* New York: Free Press.

FLANAGAN, J. (1980). Quality of life. In L. Bond & J. Rosen (eds.), *Competence and coping during adulthood.* Hanover, NH: University Press of New England.

FLAVELL, J. (1985). *Cognitive development* (2d ed.). Englewood Cliffs, NJ: Prentice-Hall.

FLOWERS, R., MONCADA, S., & VANE, J. (1985). Analgesic-antipyretics and anti-inflammatory agents; Drugs employed in the treatment of gout. In A. Gilman, L. Goodman, T. Rall, & F. Murad (eds.), *Goodman and Gilman's The pharmacological basis of therapeutics* (7th ed.) (pp. 674–715). New York: Macmillan.

FOLKMAN, S., & LAZARUS, R. (1980). An analysis of coping in a middle-aged community sample. *Journal of Health and Social Behavior, 21,* 219–239.

FOLKMAN, S., LAZARUS, R., PIMLEY, S. & NOVACEK, J. (1987). Age differences in stress and coping processes. *Psychology and Aging, 2,* 171–184.

FORD FOUNDATION PROJECT ON SOCIAL WELFARE AND THE AMERICAN FUTURE. (1989). *The common good: Social welfare and the American future.* New York: The Ford Foundation.

FORSSTROM-COHEN, B., & ROSENBAUM, A. (1985). The effects of parental marital violence on young adults: An exploratory investigation. *Journal of Marriage and the Family, 47,* 467–472.

FOZARD, J. (1980). The time for remembering. In L. Poon (ed.), *Aging in the 1980s* (pp. 273–290). Washington, DC: American Psychological Association.

FOZARD, J. (1990). Vision and hearing in aging. In J. Birren & K. Schaie (eds.), *Handbook of the psychology of aging* (3rd ed.) (pp. 150–171). San Diego: Academic Press.

FOZARD, J., WOLF, E., BELL, B., MCFARLAND, R., & PODOLSKY, S. (1977). Visual perception and communication. In J. Birren & K. Schaie (eds.), *Handbook of the psychology of aging* (pp. 497–534). New York: Van Nostrand.

FRANK, S., AVERY, C., & LAMAN, M. (1988). Young adults' perceptions of their relationships with their parents: Individual differences in connectedness, competence, and emotional autonomy. *Developmental Psychology, 24,* 729–737.

FREI, E. (1982). The national cancer chemotherapy program. *Science, 217,* 600–606.

FREUD, S. (1961/1930). *Civilization and its discontents.* New York: Norton.

FRIEDLANDER, D., SCHELLEKENS, J., BENMOSHE, E., & KEYSER, A. (1985). Socio-economic characteristics and life expectancies in nineteenth-century England: A district analysis. *Population Studies, 39,* 137–151.

FRIEDLANDER, M., & SIEGEL, S. (1990). Separation-individuation difficulties and cognitive-behavior indicators of eating disorders among college women. *Journal of Counseling Psychology, 37,* 74–78.

FRIEDMAN, W., ROBINSON, A., & FRIEDMAN, B. (1987). Sex differences in moral judgments? A test of Gilligan's theory. *Psychology of Women Quarterly, 11,* 37–46.

FRIEDMANN, E., & HAVIGHURST, R. (1954). *The meaning of work and retirement.* Chicago: University of Chicago Press.

GAIL, S. (1985). The housewife. In C. Littler (ed.), *The experience of work* (pp. 183–189). New York: St. Martin's Press.

GARFINKEL, R. (1982). By the sweat of your brow. In T. Field, A. Huston, H. Quay, L. Troll, & G. Finley (eds.), *Review of human development* (pp. 500–510). New York: Wiley.

GATZ, M., BENGSTON, V., & BLUM, M. (1990). Caregiving families. In J. Birren & K. Schaie (eds.), *Handbook of the psychology of aging* (3rd ed.) (pp. 405–426). San Diego: Academic Press.

GATZ, M., POPKIN, S., PINO, C., & VANDENBOS, G. (1985). Psychological interventions with older adults. In J. Birren & K. Schaie (eds.), *Handbook of the psychology of aging* (2d ed.) (pp. 755–785). New York: Van Nostrand Reinhold.

GAYLORD, S., & ZUNG, W. (1987). Affective disorders among the aging. In L. Carstensen & B. Edelstein (eds.), *Handbook of clinical gerontology* (pp. 76–95). New York: Pergamon.

GEIS, B., & GERRARD, M. (1984). Predicting male and female contraceptive behavior: A discriminative analysis of groups high, moderate, and low in contraceptive effectiveness. *Journal of Personality and Social Psychology, 46,* 669–680.

GEIS, S., & FULLER, R. (1986). Hospice staff response to fear of AIDS. In D. Feldman & T. Johnson (eds.), *The social dimensions of AIDS: Method and theory.* New York: Praeger.

GENERAL ACCOUNTING OFFICE (1987). *Pension plans: Many workers don't know when they can retire.* Washington, DC: Government Printing Office.

GERRARD, M. (1987). Sex, sex guilt, and contraceptive use revisited: The 1980s. *Journal of Personality and Social Psychology, 52,* 975–980.

GERSON, M. (1980). The lure of motherhood. *Psychology of Women Quarterly, 5,* 207–218.

GIELE, J. (1982a). Women in adulthood: Unanswered questions. In J. Giele (ed.), *Women in the middle years.* New York: Wiley.

GIELE, J. (1982b). Women's work and family roles. In J. Giele (ed.), *Women in the middle years.* New York: Wiley.

GILBERTSEN, V., & WANGENSTEEN, O. (1962). Should the doctor tell the patient that the disease is cancer? In *The physician and the total care of the cancer patient.* New York: American Cancer Society.

GILLIGAN, C. (1982a). Adult development and women's development: Arrangements for a marriage. In J. Giele (ed.), *Women in the middle years.* New York: Wiley.

GILLIGAN, C. (1982b). *In a different voice.* Cambridge, MA: Harvard University Press.

GILLIGAN, C., & ATTANUCCI, J. (1988). Two moral orientations: Gender differences and similarities. *Merrill-Palmer Quarterly, 34,* 223–237.

GILMAN, A., GOODMAN, L., RALL, T., & MURAD, F. (eds.). (1985). *Goodman and Gilman's the pharmacological basis of therapeutics* (7th ed.). New York: Macmillan.

GIORDANO, J., & BECKMAN, K. (1985). The aged within a family context: Relationship, roles, and events. In L. L'Abate (ed.), *Handbook of family psychology and therapy* (Vol. 1) (pp. 284–320). Homewood, IL: Dorsey.

GLASER, B., & STRAUSS, A. (1968). *Time for dying.* Chicago: Aldine.

GLICK, I., WEISS, R., & PARKES, C. (1974). *The first year of bereavement.* New York: Wiley.

GLICK, P. (1984). Marriage, divorce, and living arrangements: Prospective changes. *Journal of Family Issues, 5,* 7–26.

GLICK, P., & LIN, S. (1986). More young adults are living with their parents: Who are they? *Journal of Marriage and the Family, 48,* 107–112.

GOETTING, A. (1982). The six stations of remarriage: Developmental tasks of remarriage after divorce. *Family Relations, 31,* 213–222.

GOETTING, A. (1986). The developmental tasks of siblingship over the life cycle. *Journal of Marriage and the Family, 48,* 703–714.

GOLDSMITH, H. (1983). Genetic influences on personality from infancy to adulthood. *Child Development, 54,* 331–355.

GOODEN, W., & TOYE, R. (1984). Occupational dream, relations to parents and depression in the early adult transition. *Journal of Clinical Psychology, 40,* 945–954.

GOODMAN, M. (1980). Toward a biology of menopause. In C. Stimpson & E. Person (eds.), *Women: Sex and sexuality.* Chicago: University of Chicago Press.

GOODSTEIN, R., & PAGE, A. (1981). Battered wife syndrome: Overview of dynamics and treatment. *American Journal of Psychiatry, 138,* 1036–1044.

GORDON, C., GAITZ, C., & SCOTT, J. (1976). Leisure and lives. In R. Binstock & E. Shanas (eds.), *Handbook of aging and the social sciences.* New York: Van Nostrand.

GOTLIB, I. (1984). Depression and general psychopathology in university students. *Journal of Abnormal Psychology, 93,* 19–30.

GOULD, R. (1972). The phases of adult life: A study in developmental psychology. *American Journal of Psychiatry, 129,* 521–531.

GRAY, W. (1990). Formal operational thought. In W. Overton (Ed.), *Reasoning, necessity and logic: Developmental perspectives* (pp. 227–254). Hillsdale, NJ: Erlbaum.

GREENBERG, J., & BECKER, M. (1988). Aging parents as family resources. *The Gerontologist, 28,* 786–791.

GREENBERG, M., & MORRIS, N. (1974). Engrossment: The newborn's impact upon the father. *American Journal of Orthopsychiatry, 44,* 520–531.

GREENE, J., & MCADAM (1983). Nutritional requirements and the appropriate use of supplements. In E. Feldman (ed.), *Nutrition in the middle and later years.* Boston: John Wright.

GREENGLASS, E., & DEVINS, R. (1982). Factors related to marriage and career plans in unmarried women. *Sex Roles, 8,* 57–70.

GRIFFEN, J. (1977). A cross-cultural investigation of behavioral changes at menopause. *Social Science Journal, 14.*

GROSSMAN, M., & BART, P. (1970). Taking the men out of menopause. In R. Hubbard, M. Henifin, & B. Fried (eds.), *Women look at biology looking at women.* Boston: G. K. Hall.

GROTEVANT, H., & COOPER, C. (1985). Patterns of interaction in family relationships and the development of identity exploration in adolescence. *Child Development, 56,* 415–428.

GRUEN, R., FOLKMAN, S., & LAZARUS, R. (1988). Centrality and individual differences in the meaning of daily hassles. *Journal of Personality, 56,* 743–762.

GUNTER, B., & LEVY, M. (1987). Social contexts of video use. *American Behavioral Scientist, 30,* 486–494.

GURIN, P. & BRIM, O. (1984). Change in self in adulthood: The example of sense of control. In P. Baltes & O. Brim (eds.), *Life-span behavior and development* (Vol. 6) (pp. 281–334). New York: Academic Press.

GUTTENTAG, R., & HUNT, R. (1988). Adult age differences in memory for imagined and performed actions. *Journal of Gerontology, 43,* P107–108.

GUTMANN, D. (1974). The country of old men: Cross-cultural studies in the psychology of later life. In R. LeVine (ed.), *Culture and personality: Contemporary readings* (pp. 95–121). Chicago: Aldine.

GUTMANN, D. (1975). Parenthood: A key to comparative study of the life cycle. In N. Datan & L. Ginsberg (eds.), *Life-span developmental psychology: Normative life crises.* New York: Academic Press.

GUTMANN, D. (1987). Reclaimed powers. *Toward a new psychology of men and women in later life.* New York: Basic Books.

GWARTNEY-GIBBS, P. (1986). The institutionalization of premarital cohabitation: Estimates from marriage license applications, 1970 and 1980. *Journal of Marriage and the Family, 48,* 423–434.

HABIB, J. (1985). The economy and the aged. In R. Binstock & E. Shanas (eds.), *The handbook of aging and the social sciences* (2d ed.) (pp. 479–502). New York: Van Nostrand.

HACKMAN, J., & OLDHAM, G. (1976). Motivation through the design of work: Test of a theory. *Organizational Behavior and Human Performance, 16,* 250–279.

HAGESTAD, G. (1985). Continuity and connectedness. In V. Bengston & J. Robertson (eds.), *Grandparenthood* (pp. 31–48). Beverly Hills: Sage.

HAGESTAD, G. (1987). Able elderly in the family context: Changes, chances, and challenges. *The Gerontologist, 27,* 417–422.

HALBREICH, U. & ENDICOTT, J. (1985). The biology of premenstrual changes: What do we really know? In H. Osofsky & B. Blumenthal (eds.), *Premenstrual syndrome: Current findings and future directions* (pp. 13–24). Washington, DC: American Psychiatric Press.

HALL, D. (1984). *The biomedical basis of gerontology.* Bristol, England: Wright.

HALL, G. S. (1922). *Senescence, the second half of life.* New York: Appleton.

HALPERN, S. (1989). Miracle baby. *Ms. 18,* 56–64.

HAMILTON, E. (1942). *Mythology.* New York: Mentor.

HARMAN, D. (1956). Aging: A theory based on free radical and radiation chemistry. *Journal of Gerontology, 11,* 298–300.

HARRIS, R., ELLICOTT, A., & HOLMES, D. (1986). The timing of psychosocial transitions and changes in women's lives: An examination of women aged 45 to 60. *Jour-*

nal of Personality and Social Psychology, 51, 409–416.

HARRISON, A., WILSON, M., PINE, C., CHAN, S., & BURIEL, R. (1990). Family ecologies of ethnic minority children. Child Development, 61, 347–362.

HARVEY, S. (1985). Gastric antacids, miscellaneous drugs for the treatment of peptic ulcers, digestants, and bile acids. In A. Gilman, L. Goodman, T. Rall, & F. Murad (eds.), Goodman and Gilman's The pharmacological basis of therapeutics (7th ed.) (pp. 980–993). New York: Macmillan.

HASHER, L., STOLTZFUS, E., ZACKS, R., & RYPMAN, B. (1991). Age and inhibition. Journal of Experimental Psychology: Learning Memory, and Cognition, 17, 163–169.

HASHER, L., & ZACKS, R. (1988). Working, memory, comprehension, and aging: A review and a new view. In G. H. Bower (ed.), The psychology of learning and motivation, vol. 22 (pp. 193–225). San Diego, CA: Academic Press.

HAUSMAN, P., & WEKSLER, M. (1985). Changes in the immune response with age. In C. Finch & E. Schneider (eds.), Handbook of the biology of aging (2d ed.), (pp. 414–432). New York: Van Nostrand.

HAVIGHURST, R. (1972). Developmental tasks and education (2d ed.). New York: McKay.

HAVIGHURST, R. J. (1980). The life course of college professors and administrators. In K. Back (ed.), Life course: Integrative theories and exemplary populations. Boulder, CO: Westview Press.

HAVIGHURST, R. (1982). The world of work. In B. Wolman (ed.), Handbook of developmental psychology (pp. 771–787). Englewood Cliffs, NJ: Prentice-Hall.

HAVIGHURST, R., & FEIGENBAUM, K. (1968/1959). Leisure and life style. In B. Neugarten (ed.), Middle age and aging (pp. 347–353). Chicago: University of Chicago Press.

HAVIGHURST, R., MCDONALD, W., PERUN, P., & SNOW, R. (1976). Social scientists and educators: Lives after sixty. Chicago: University of Chicago Press.

HAYFLICK, L., & MOORHEAD, P. (1961). The serial cultivation of human diploid cell strains. Experimental Cell Research, 25, 585–621.

HEGELSON, V. (1991). The effects of masculinity and social support on recovery from myocardial infarction. Psychosomatic Medicine, 53, 621–633.

HEINEMANN, A., COLOREZ, A., FRANK, S., & TAYLOR, D. (1988). Leisure ativity partici-

pation of elderly individuals with low vision. The Gerontologist, 28, 181–184.

HELSON, R., & PICANO, J. (1990). Is the traditional role bad for women? Journal of Personality and Social Psychology, 59, 311–320.

HERTZ, R. (1986). More equal than others: Women and men in dual-career marriages. Berkeley: University of California Press.

HETHERINGTON, E. M. (1989). Coping with family transitions: Winners, losers, and survivors. Child Development, 60, 1–14.

HETHERINGTON, E., & BALTES, P. (1988). Child psychology and life-span development. In E. Hetherington, R. Lerner, & M. Perlmutter (eds.), Child development in life-span perspective (pp. 1–20). Hillsdale, NJ: Erlbaum.

HEWLETT, S. (1984). A lesser life: The myth of women's liberation in America. New York: Warner Books.

HILL, R., FOOTE, N., ALDOUS, J., CARLSON, R., & MACDONALD, R. (1970). Family development in three generations. Cambridge, MA: Schenkman.

HILLIER, E. (1983). Terminal care in the United Kingdom. In C. Corr & D. Corr (eds.), Hospice care: Principles and practice (pp. 319–335). New York: Springer.

HOBBS, D. (1965). Parenthood as crisis: A third study. Journal of Marriage and the Family, 27, 367–372.

HOBBS, D., & COLE, S. (1976). Transition to parenthood: A decade of replication. Journal of Marriage and the Family, 38, 723–731.

HOCHSCHILD, A. (1989). The second shift. New York: Avon Books.

HOCK, E., MORGAN, C., & HOCK, M. (1985). Employment decisions made by mothers of infants. Psychology of Women Quarterly, 9, 383–402.

HODGSON, J., & FISCHER, J. (1979). Sex differences in identity and intimacy development in college youth. Journal of Youth and Adolescence, 8, 37–50.

HODGSON, J., & FISCHER, J. (1981). Pathways of identity development in college women. Sex Roles, 7, 681–690.

HOFFMAN, B., & BIGGER, J. (1985). Digitalis and allied cardiac glycosides. In A. Gilman, L. Goodman, T. Rall, & F. Murad (eds.), Goodman and Gilman's The pharmacological basis of therapeutics (7th ed.) (pp. 716–747). New York: Macmillan.

HOFFMAN, J. (1984). Psychological separation of late adolescents from their parents. Journal of Counseling Psychology, 31, 170–178.

HOFFMAN, L. (1979). Maternal employment: 1979. American Psychologist, 34, 859–865.

HOFFMAN, L. (1989). Effects of maternal employment in the two-parent family. *American Psychologist, 44,* 283–292.

HOLLAND, J. (1973). *Making vocational choices: a theory of careers.* Englewood Cliffs, NJ: Prentice-Hall.

HOLMES, T., & RAHE, R. (1967). The social readjustment rating scale. *Journal of Psychosomatic Research, 11,* 213–218.

HOLSTEIN, C. (1976). Development of moral judgment: A longitudinal study of males and females. *Child Development, 47,* 51–61.

HOLT, L., & DATAN, N. (1984). Senescence, sex roles, and stress: Shepherding resources into old age. In C. Widom (ed.), *Sex roles and psychopathology.* New York: Plenum Press.

HOLT, R. (1982). Occupational stress. In L. Goldberger & S. Breznitz (eds.), *The handbook of stress: Theoretical and clinical aspects.* (pp. 419–444). New York: Macmillan.

HORN, J. (1970). Organization of data on life-span development of human abilities. In L. Goulet & P. Baltes (eds.), *Life-span developmental psychology: Research and theory.* New York: Academic Press.

HORN, J. (1982). The aging of human abilities. In B. Wolman (ed.), *Handbook of developmental psychology.* Englewood Cliffs, NJ: Prentice-Hall.

HORN, J., & CATTELL, R. (1966). Refinement and test of the theory of fluid and crystallized general intelligences. *Journal of Educational Psychology, 57,* 253–270.

HORN, J., & DONALDSON, G. (1976). On the myth of intellectual decline in adulthood. *American Psychologist, 31,* 701–719.

HORN, J., & DONALDSON, G. (1977). Faith is not enough: A response to the Baltes-Schaie claim that intelligence will not wane. *American Psychologist, 32,* 369–373.

HORNBLUM, J., & OVERTON, W. (1976). Area and volume conservation among the elderly: Assessment and training. *Developmental Psychology, 12,* 68–74.

HOROWITZ, A. (1985). Family caregiving to the frail elderly. In C. Eisdorfer (ed.), *Annual review of gerontology and geriatrics* (pp. 194–246). New York: Springer.

HOROWITZ, M., & WILNER, N. (1980). Life events, stress, and coping. In L. Poon (ed.), *Aging in the 1980s.* Washington, DC: American Psychological Association.

HOUSEKNECHT, S. (1977). Reference group support for voluntary childlessness: Evidence for conformity. *Journal of Marriage and the Family, 39,* 285–292.

HOUSEKNECHT, S. (1982). Voluntary childlessness: Toward a theoretical integration. *Journal of Family Issues, 3,* 459–471.

HOUSEKNECHT, S., VAUGHAN, S., & STATHAM, A. (1987). The impact of singlehood on the career patterns of professional women. *Journal of Marriage and the Family, 49,* 353–366.

HULTSCH, D., MASSON, M., & SMALL, B. (1991). Adult age differences in direct and indirect tests of memory. *Journal of Gerontology, 46,* P22–30.

HUNT, J., & HUNT, L. (1982). The dualities of careers and families: New integrations or new polarizations. *Social Problems, 29,* 499–510.

HUNT, M. (1974). *Sexual behavior in the 1970s.* Chicago, IL: Playboy Press.

HUNTER, F. (1985). Adolescents' perception of discussions with parents and friends. *Developmental Psychology, 21,* 433–440.

HYDE, J. S. (1985). *Half the human experience: The psychology of women.* Lexington, MA: D. C. Heath.

HYDE, J. S. (1986). *Understanding human sexuality* (3rd ed.). New York: McGraw-Hill.

HYDE, J. S., KRAJNIK, M., & SKULDT-NIEDERBERGER, K. (1991). Androgeny across the life-span: A replication and longitudinal followup. *Developmental Psychology, 27,* 516–519.

HYLAND, D., & ACKERMAN, A. (1988). Reminiscence and autobiographical memory in the study of the personal past. *Journal of Gerontology, 43,* P35–39.

ILFELD, F. (1982). Marital stressors, coping styles, and symptoms of depression. In L. Goldberger & S. Breznitz (eds.), *Handbook of stress* (pp. 482–495). New York: Free Press.

IZARD, C. (1977). *Human emotions.* New York: Plenum Press.

JACKLIN, C. N. (1989). Female and male: Issues of gender. *American Psychologist, 44,* 127–133.

JACKSON, H., & MINDELL, M. (1980). Motivating the new breed. *Personnel, 57,* 53–61.

JACKSON, J. (1985). Race, national origin, ethnicity, and aging. In R. Binstock & E. Shanas (eds.), *Handbook of aging and the social sciences* (2d ed.) (pp. 264–303). New York: Van Nostrand.

JACKSON, J., ANTONUCCI, T., & GIBSON, R. (1990). Cultural, racial, and ethnic minority influences on aging. In J. Birren & K. Schaie (eds.), *Handbook of the psychology of aging* (3rd ed.) (pp. 103–123). San Diego: Academic Press.

JAYNES, G. (1990). The labor market status of black Americans: 1939–1985. *The Journal of Economic Perspectives, 4,* 9–24.

JERNIGAN, T., ZATZ, L., FEINBERG, J. & FEIN, G.

(1980). The measurement of cerebral atrophy in the aged by computed tomography. In L. Poon (ed.), *Aging in the 1980s* (pp. 86–94). Washington, DC: American Psychological Association.

JOHNSON, C. (1985). Grandparenting options in divorcing families: An anthropological perspective. In V. Bengston & J. Robertson (eds.), *Grandparenthood* (pp. 81–96). Beverly Hills: Sage.

JOHNSON, C. (1988). Active and latent functions of grandparenting during the divorce process. *The Gerontologist, 28* 185–191.

JOHNSON, T. (1988). Minireview: Genetic specification of the lifespan: Processes, problems, and potentials. *Journal of Gerontology, 43,* B87–92.

JONES, H., & JONES, H. (1977). *Sensual drugs.* New York: Cambridge University Press.

JOSEPH, G. (1983). *Women at work: The British experience.* Oxford, England: Philip Allan Publishers.

JUNG, C. G. (1931/1960). The stages of life. In H. Read, M. Fordham, & G. Adler (eds.), *The collected works of C. G. Jung* (Vol. 8). New York: Pantheon.

JURKOVIC, G., & ULRICI, D. (1985). Empirical perspectives on adolescents and their families. In L. L'Abate (ed.), *The handbook of family psychology and family therapy.* Homewood, IL: Dorsey.

KAHANA, B. (1982). Social behavior and aging. In B. Wolman (ed.), *Handbook of developmental psychology* (pp. 871–889). Englewood Cliffs, NJ: Prentice-Hall.

KALISH, R. (1985). The social context of death and dying. In R. Binstock & E. Shanas (eds.), *Handbook of aging and the social sciences* (pp. 149–170). New York: Van Nostrand.

KALISH, R., & REYNOLDS, D. (1976). *Death and ethnicity: A psychocultural study.* Los Angeles: University of Southern California Press.

KALLEBERG, A., & ROSENFELD, R. (1990). Work in the family and in the labor market: A cross-national, reciprocal analysis. *Journal of Marriage and the Family, 52,* 331–346.

KAMERMAN, S., KAHN, A. & KINGSTON, P. (1983). *Maternity policies and working women.* New York: Columbia University Press.

KANNEL, W. (1985). Hypertension and aging. In C. Finch & E. Schneider (eds.), *Handbook of the biology of aging* (2d ed.) (pp. 859–877). New York: Van Nostrand.

KANNER, A., COYNE, J., SCHAEFER, C., & LAZARUS, R. (1981). Comparison of two modes of stress measurement: Daily hassles and uplifts versus major life events. *Journal of Behavioral Medicine, 4,* 1–39.

KANTER, R. M. (1977). *Men and women of the corporation.* New York: Basic Books.

KAPLAN, B. (1986). A psychobiological review of depression during pregnancy. *Psychology of Women Quarterly, 10,* 35–48.

KAPLAN, G., BARELL, V., & LUSKY, A. (1988). Subjective state of health and survival in elderly adults. *Journal of Gerontology, 43,* S114–1120.

KART, C., METRESS, E., & METRESS, J. (1978). *Aging and health.* Menlo Park, CA: Addison-Wesley.

KASL, S., & COBB, S. (1982). Variability of stress effects among men experiencing job loss. In L. Goldberger & S. Breznitz (eds.), *The handbook of stress: Theoretical and clinical aspects.* (pp. 445–465) New York: Macmillan.

KASTENBAUM, R. (1985). Dying and death: A life-span approach. In J. Birren & K. Schaie (eds.), *The handbook of the psychology of aging* (2d ed.) (pp. 619–643). New York: Van Nostrand.

KASTENBAUM, R. (1986). *Death, society and human experience.* Columbus, OH: Merrill.

KELLEY, H. H. (1983). Love and commitment. In H. Kelley, E. Berscheid, A. Christensen, J. Harvey, T. Huston, G. Levinger, E. McClintok, L. Peplau, & D. Peterson, *Close relationships.* New York: Freeman.

KELLY, J. B. (1982). Divorce: The adult perspective. In B. Wolman (ed.), *Handbook of developmental psychology* (pp. 734–750). Englewood Cliffs, NJ: Prentice-Hall.

KELVIN, P., & JARRETT, J. (1985). *Unemployment: Its social psychological effects.* Cambridge, Eng.: Cambridge University Press.

KEMPE, R., & KEMPE, H. (1984). *The common secret.* New York: Freeman.

KESSLER, R., & MCRAE, J. (1982). The effect of wives' employment on the mental health of married men and women. *American Sociological Review, 47,* 216–227.

KIDWELL, J., FISCHER, J., DUNHAM, R., & BARANOWSKI, M. (1983). Parents and adolescents: Push and pull of change. In H. McCubbin & C. Figley (eds.), *Stress and the family* (Vol. 1). New York: Brunner/Mazel.

KIELCOLT-GLASER, J. DURA, J. SPEICHER, C., TRASK, J., & GLASER, R. (1991). Spousal caregivers of dementia victims: Longitudinal changes in immunity and health. *Psychosomatic Medicine, 53,* 345–362.

KIRKWOOD, T. (1985). Comparative and evolutionary aspects of longevity. In C. Finch & E. Schneider (eds.), *Handbook of the biology of aging* (2d ed.) (pp. 27–44). New York: Van Nostrand.

KITSON, G. & SUSSMAN, M. (1982). Marital complaints, demographic characteristics, and symptoms of mental distress in divorce. *Journal of Marriage and the Family, 44,* 87–101.

KIVNICK, H. (1985). Grandparenthood and mental health: Meaning, behavior, and satisfaction. In V. Bengston & J. Robertson (eds.), *Grandparenthood,* (pp. 151–158). Beverly Hills: Sage.

KLAGSBRUN, F. (1985). *Married people.* Toronto: Bantam Books.

KLEIGL, R., SMITH, J., & BALTES, P. (1990). On the locus and process of magnification of age differences during mnemonic training. *Developmental Psychology, 26,* 894–904.

KLEIN, B. & RONES, P. (1989). A profile of the working poor. *Monthly Labor Review,* 3–13.

KLERMAN, G. (1983). Problems in the definition and diagnosis of depression in the elderly. In L. Breslau & M. Haug (eds.), *Depression and aging: Causes, care, and consequences.* New York: Springer.

KLINE, D., & SCHIEBER, F. (1985). Vision and aging. In J. Birren & K. Schaie (eds.), *The handbook of the psychology of aging* (2d ed. (pp. 296–331). New York: Van Nostrand.

KOBASA, S. (1979). Stressful life events, personality, and health: An inquiry into hardiness. *Journal of Personality and Social Psychology, 37,* 1–11.

KOBASA, S., MADDI, S., & KAHN, S. (1982). Hardiness and health: A prospective study. *Journal of Personality and Social Psychology, 42,* 168–177.

KOHLBERG, L. (1966). A cognitive-developmental analysis of children's sex-role concepts and attitudes. In E. Maccoby (ed.), *The development of sex differences.* Stanford, CA: Stanford University Press.

KOHLBERG, L. (1969). Stage and sequences: The cognitive-developmental approach to socialization. In D. Goslin (ed.), *Handbook of socialization theory and research.* Skokie, IL: Rand McNally.

KOHLBERG, L. (1976). Moral stages and moralization: The cognitive-developmental approach. In T. Lickona (ed.). *Moral development and behavior: Theory, research, and social issues* (pp. 31–53). New York: Holt, Rinehart, & Winston.

KOLATA, G. (1991). Parents of tiny infants find care choices are not theirs. *New York Times,* Sept. 30, 1991, p. A1.

KOMAROVSKY, M. (1982). Female freshmen view their future: Career salience and its correlates. *Sex Roles, 8,* 299–314.

KOOCHER, G. (1973). Childhood, death, and cognitive development. *Developmental Psychology, 9,* 369–375.

KOSBERG, J. (1988). Preventing elder abuse: Identification of high risk factors prior to placement decisions. *The Gerontologist, 28,* 43–50.

KOSNIK, W., WINSLOW, L., KLINE, D., RASINSKI, K., & SEKULER, R. (1988). Visual changes in daily life throughout adulthood. *Journal of Gerontology, 43,* P63–70.

KRIVO, L., & MUTCHLER, J. (1989). Elderly persons living alone: The effect of community context on living arrangements. *Journal of Gerontology, 44,* S54–S62.

KÜBLER-ROSS, E. (1969). *On death and dying.* New York: Macmillan.

KUHN, D., LANGER, J., KOHLBERG, L., & HAAN, N. (1977). The development of formal operations in logical and moral judgment. *Genetic Psychology Monographs, 95,* 97–188.

KUHN, M. (1987). Politics and aging: The Gray Panthers. In L. Carstensen & B. Edelstein (eds.), *Handbook of clinical gerontology.* New York: Pergamon Press.

KURDEK, L. (1991). Predictors of increases in marital distress in newlywed couples: A 3-year prospective longitudinal study. *Developmental Psychology, 27,* 627–636.

KURDEK, L., & SCHMITT, J. P. (1986). Early development of relationship quality in heterosexual married, heterosexual cohabiting, gay, and lesbian couples. *Developmental Psychology, 48,* 305–309.

LABOUVIE, E. (1982). Issues in life-span development. In B. Wolman (ed.), *Handbook of developmental psychology* (pp. 54–62). Englewood Cliffs, NJ: Prentice-Hall.

LABOUVIE-VIEF, G. (1985). Intelligence and cognition. In J. Birren & K. Schaie (eds.), *Handbook of the psychology of aging* (2d ed.) (pp. 500–530). New York: Van Nostrand.

LABOUVIE-VIEF, G., & SCHELL, D. (1982). Learning and memory in later life. In B. Wolman (ed.), *Handbook of developmental psychology.* Englewood Cliffs, NJ: Prentice-Hall.

LACEY, W. (1968). *The family in classical Greece.* Ithaca, NY: Cornell University Press.

LACHMAN, M. (1983). Perceptions of intellectual aging: Antecedent or consequence of intellectual functioning? *Developmental Psychology, 19,* 482–498.

LAKATTA, E. (1985). Heart and circulation. In C. Finch & E. Schneider (eds.), *Handbook of the biology of aging* (2d ed.) (pp. 377–413). New York: Van Nostrand.

LAMBRINOS, J., & JOHNSON, W. (1984). Robots

to reduce the high cost of illness and in-jury. *Harvard Business Review, 62,* 24–28.

LANG, A., & BRODY, E. (1983). Characteristics of middle-aged daughters and help to their elderly mothers. *Journal of Marriage and the Family, 45,* 193–202.

LAPSLEY, D., RICE, K., & SHADID, G. (1989). Psychological separation and adjustment to college. *Journal of Counseling Psychology, 36,* 286–294.

LAROSSA, R. (1983). The transition to parent-hood and the social reality of time. *Journal of Marriage and the Family,* 579–589.

LARSON, L., & HEPPNER, P. (1985). The rela-tionship of problem-solving appraisal to career decision and indecision. *Journal of Vocational Behavior, 26,* 55–65.

LARUE, A., DESSONVILLE, C., & JARVIK, L. (1985). Aging and mental disorders. In J. Birren & K. Schaie (eds.), *Handbook of the psychology of aging* (2d ed.) (pp. 664–702). New York: Van Nostrand Reinhold.

LARUE, A., & JARVIK, L. (1982). Old age and biobehavioral changes. In B. Wolman (ed.), *Handbook of developmental psychology* (pp. 791–806). Englewood Cliffs, NJ: Pren-tice-Hall.

LAWTON, M. P. (1982). Competence, environ-mental press, and the adaptation of older people. In M. Lawton, P. Windley, & T. By-erts (eds.), *Aging and the environment: Theo-retical approaches.* New York: Springer.

LAWTON, M. P. (1987). Environment and the need satisfaction of the aging. In L. Cars-tensen & B. Edelstein (eds.), *Handbook of clinical gerontology* (pp. 33–40). New York: Pergamon Press.

LAZARUS, R., & FOLKMAN, S. (1984). *Stress, ap-praisal, and coping.* New York: Springer.

LAZARUS, R., & DELONGIS, A. (1983). Psycho-logical stress and coping in aging. *Ameri-can Psychologist, 38,* 245–254.

LAZARUS, R., & LAUNIER, R. (1978). Stress-re-lated transactions between person and en-vironment. In L. Pervin & M. Lewis (eds.), *Perspectives in interactional psychology.* New York: Plenum Press.

LEARY, M., & DOBBINS, S. (1983). Social anx-iety, sexual behavior, and contraceptive use. *Journal of Personality and Social Psychol-ogy, 45,* 1347–1354.

LEE, T., MANCINI, J., & MAXWELL, J. (1990). Sib-ling relationships in adulthood: Contact patterns and motivations. *Journal of Mar-riage and the Family, 52,* 431–440.

LEHMAN, D., & NISBETT, R. (1990). A longitudi-nal study of the effects of undergraduate training on reasoning. *Developmental Psy-chology, 26,* 952–960.

LEHMANN, E. (1982). Affective disorders in the aged. In L. Jarvik & G. Small (eds.), *The psychiatric clinics of North America* (pp. 27–44). Philadelphia: Saunders.

LEMASTERS, E. (1957). Parenthood as crisis. *Marriage and Family Living, 19,* 352–355.

LEON, G., GILLUM, B., GILLUM, R., & GOUZE, M. (1979). Personality stability and change over a 30-year period—middle age to old age. *Journal of Consulting and Clinical Psy-chology, 47,* 517–524.

LERNER, R. (1990). Plasticity, person-context relations, and cognitive training in the aged years: A developmental contextual perspective. *Developmental Psychology, 26,* 911–915.

LESSOR, R., & JURICH, K. (1986). Ideology and politics in the control of contagion: The social organization of AIDS care. In D. Feldman & T. Johnson (eds.), *The social di-mensions of AIDS: Method and theory* (pp. 245–259). New York: Praeger.

LEVINSON, D. (1978). *The seasons of a man's life.* New York: Knopf.

LEVINSON, D. (1986). A conception of adult development. *American Psychologist, 41,* 3–13.

LEVINSON, D. (1990). The seasons of a wom-an's life: Implications for women and men. Presented at the 98th Annual Con-vention of the *American Psychological Associ-ation,* Boston.

LEVINSON, H. (1983). A second career: The possible dream. *Harvard Business Review, 61,* 122–129.

LINDEMANN, E. (1944). Symptomatology and management of acute grief. *American Jour-nal of Psychiatry, 101,* 141–148.

LIPKOWSKI, Z. (1983). Transient cognitive dis-orders (delirium, acute confusional states) in the elderly. *American Journal of Psychiatry, 140,* 1426–1436.

LITWAK, E., & LONGINO, C. (1987). Migration patterns among the elderly: A develop-mental perspective. *The Gerontologist, 27,* 266–272.

LLOYD, S., CATE, R., & HENTON, J. (1984). Pre-dicting premarital relationship stability: A methodological refinement. *Journal of Mar-riage and the Family, 46,* 71–76.

LONG, B. (1983). Evaluations and intentions concerning marriage among unmarried female undergraduates. *The Journal of So-cial Psychology, 119,* 235–242.

LOPATA, H. (1975). Widowhood: Societal fac-tors in life-span disruptions and alterna-tives. In N. Datan & L. Ginsberg (eds.), *Life-span developmental psychology: Normative life crises.* New York: Academic Press.

LOPATA, H. (1987). Widowhood. In G. Maddox (ed.), *The encyclopedia of aging*. New York: Springer.

LOPER, R., KAMMEIER, M., & HOFFMAN, H. (1973). MMPI characteristics of college freshmen males who later became alcoholics. *Journal of Abnormal Psychology, 82,* 159–162.

LOWENTHAL, M. (1975). Psychosocial variations across the adult life course: Frontiers for research and policy. *Gerontologist, 15,* 6–12.

LOWENTHAL, M., & CHIRIBOGA, D. (1972/1982). Transition to the empty nest. In L. Allman & D. Jaffe (eds.), *Readings in adult psychology* (pp. 334–340). New York: Harper & Row.

LOWENTHAL, M., THURNHER, M., & CHIRIBOGA, D. (1975). *Four stages of life.* San Francisco: Jossey-Bass.

MACCORQUODALE, P. (1984). Gender roles and premarital contraception. *Journal of Marriage and the Family, 46,* 57–63.

MACDERMID, S., HUSTON, T., & MCHALE, S. (1990). Changes in marriage associated with the transition to parenthood: Individual differences as a function of sex-role attitudes and changes in the division of household labor. *Journal of Marriage and the Family, 52,* 475–486.

MACKLIN, E. (1978). Nonmarital heterosexual cohabitation. *Marriage and Family Review, 1,* 1–12.

MADDI, S., BARTONE, P., & PUCCETTI, M. (1987). Stressful events are indeed a factor in physical illness: Reply to Schroeder and Costa (1984). *Journal of Personality and Social Psychology, 52,* 833–843.

MADDOX, G. (1968/1966). Persistence of life style among the elderly: A longitudinal study of patterns of social activity in relation to life satisfaction. In B. Neugarten (ed.), *Middle age and aging* (pp. 181–183). Chicago: University of Chicago Press.

MAGNUSSON, E. (1990). *Newsweek 116,* 22.

MAHLER, M., PINE, F., & BERGMAN, A. (1975). *The psychological birth of the human infant.* New York: Basic Books.

MALATESTA, C., & CULVER, L. (1984). Thematic and affective content in the lives of adult women. In C. Malatesta & C. Izard (eds.), *Emotion in adult development*. Beverly Hills: Sage.

MALATESTA, C., & HAVILAND, J. (1985). Signals, symbols, and socialization: The modification of emotional expression in human development. In M. Lewis & C. Saarni (eds.), *The socialization of emotions* (pp. 89–116). New York: Plenum Press.

MALATESTA, C., & IZARD, C. (1984). Introduction: Conceptualizing emotional development in adults. In C. Malatesta & C. Izard (eds.), *Emotion in adult development*. Beverly Hills: Sage.

MANTON, K., BLAZER, D., & WOODBURY, M. (1987). Suicide in middle age and later life: Sex and race specific life table and cohort analyses. *Journal of Gerontology, 42,* 219–227.

MARCIA, J. (1976). Identity six years after: A follow-up study. *Journal of Youth and Adolescence, 5,* 145–160.

MARCIA, J. (1980). Identity in adolescence. In J. Adelson (ed.), *Handbook of adolescent psychology*. New York: Wiley.

MARCIA, J., & FRIEDMAN, M. (1970). Ego identity status in college women. *Journal of Personality, 38,* 249–263.

MARKHAM, E. (1979). Realizing that you don't understand: Elementary school children's awareness of inconsistencies. *Child Development, 50,* 643–655.

MARSHALL, V. (1980). *Last chapters: A sociology of aging and dying.* Monterey, CA: Brooks/Cole.

MARTARANO, S. (1977). A developmental analysis of performance on Piaget's formal operations tasks. *Developmental Psychology, 13,* 666–672.

MARTIN, G., & TURKER, M. (1988). Model systems for the genetic analysis of mechanisms of aging. *Journal of Gerontology, 43,* B33–39.

MASLOW, A. (1971). *The farther reaches of human nature.* New York: Viking.

MASTERS, W., & JOHNSON, V. (1970). *Human sexual inadequacy.* Boston: Little, Brown.

MATLIN, M. (1987). *The psychology of women.* New York: Holt, Rinehart & Winston.

MATTHEWS, K., & RODIN, J. (1989). Women's changing work roles: Impact on health, family and public policy. *American Psychologist, 44,* 1389–1393.

MATTHEWS, K., & SIEGEL, J. (1982). Type A behaviors by children, social comparison, and standard for self-evaluation. *Developmental Psychology, 19,* 135–140.

MATTHEWS, S., WERKNER, J., & DELANEY, P. (1989). Relative contributions of help by employed and nonemployed sisters to their elderly parents. *Journal of Gerontology, 44,* S36–S44.

MAXWELL, N., & D'AMICO, R. (1986). Employment and wage effects of involuntary job separation: Male-female differences. *American Economic Review, 76,* 373–377.

MCBRIDE, A. (1990). Mental health effects of

women's multiple roles. *American Psychologist, 45,* 381–384.

MCCANDLESS, B., & COOP, R. (1979). *Adolescents: Behavior and development.* New York: Holt, Rinehart & Winston.

MCCLEARN, G., & FOCH, T. (1985). Behavioral genetics. In J. Birren & K. Schaie (eds.), *The handbook of the psychology of aging* (2d ed.) (pp. 113–143). New York: Van Nostrand.

MCCRAE, R., (1982). Age differences in the use of coping mechanisms. *Journal of Gerontology, 37,* 454–460.

MCCRAE, R. (1989). Age differences and changes in the use of coping mechanisms. *Journal of Gerontology, 44,* P161–169.

MCCRAE, R., & COSTA, P. (1982). Self-concept and the stability of personality: Cross-sectional comparisons of self-reports and ratings. *Journal of Personality and Social Psychology, 43,* 1282–1292.

MCCRAE, R., & COSTA, P. (1986). Personality, coping, and coping effectiveness in an adult sample. *Journal of Personality, 54,* 385–405.

MCFALLS, J., JONES, B., GALLAGHER, B., & RIVERA, J. (1985). Political orientation and occupational values of college youth, 1969 and 1981: A shift toward uniformity. *Adolescence, 20,* 697–713.

MCGADNEY, B., GOLDBERG-GLEN, R., & PINKSTON, E. (1987). Clinical issues for assessment and intervention with the black elderly. In L. Carstensen & B. Edelstein (eds.), *Handbook of clinical gerontology.* New York: Pergamon Press.

MCWHIRTER, D., & MATTISON, A. (1984). *The male couple: How relationships develop.* Englewood Cliffs, NJ: Prentice-Hall.

MELLINGER, J., & ERDWINS, C. (1985). Personality correlates of age and life roles in adult women. *Psychology of Women Quarterly, 9,* 503–514.

MEREDITH, N. (1984). The gay dilemma. *Psychology Today, 18,* 56–62.

MILARDO, R., & LEWIS, R. (1985). Social networks, families, and mate selection: A transactional analysis. In L. L'Abate (ed.), *The handbook of family psychology and therapy* (Vol. 1). Homewood, IL: Dorsey.

MILLER, A. (1957). *Death of a salesman.* In *Arthur Miller's Collected Plays* (Vol. 1) (pp. 130–224). New York: Viking.

MILLER, B. (1990). Gender differences in spouse caregiver strain: Socialization and role explanations. *Journal of Marriage and the Family, 52,* 311–321.

MILLER, B., & MYERS-WALL, J. (1983). Parent-

hood: Stresses and coping strategies. In H. McCubbin & C. Figley (eds.), *Stress and the family* (Vol. 1). New York: Brunner/Mazel.

MILLER, I. (1988). Human taste bud density across adult age groups. *Journal of Gerontology, 43,* B26–30.

MITCHELL, O., LEVINE, P., & POZZEBON, S. (1988). Retirement differences by industry and occupation. *The Gerontologist, 28,* 545–551.

MITTENTHAL, S. (1985). New sexual attitudes: More choice, less pressure. *Glamour, 83,* 338–339+.

MOERTEL, C., FLEMING, T., RUBIN, J., KVOLS, L., SARNA, G., KOCH, R., CURRIE, V., YOUNG, C., JONES, S., & DAVIGNON, J. (1982). A clinical trial of amygdalin (laetrile) in the treatment of human cancer. *The New England Journal of Medicine, 306,* 201–206.

MOKROS, J., ERKUT, S., & SPICHIGER, L. (1981). Mentoring and being mentored: Sex-related patterns among college professors. Working Paper No. 68 *Wellesley College Center for Research on Women.*

MONROE, S. (1987). Brothers. *Newsweek, 109,* 18–21.

MOORE, D. (1987). Parent-adolescent separation: The construction of adulthood by late adolescents. *Developmental Psychology, 23,* 298–307.

MOR, V., MCHORNEY, C., & SHERWOOD, S. (1986). Secondary morbidity among the recently bereaved. *American Journal of Psychiatry, 143,* 158–163.

MOR, V., SHERWOOD, S., & GUTKIN, C. (1986). A national study of residential care for the aged. *The Gerontologist, 26,* 405–417.

MORAN, J. & JONIAK, A. (1979). Effect of language on preference for responses to a moral dilemma. *Developmental Psychology, 15,* 337–338.

MORGAN, D. (1989). Adjusting to widowhood: Do social networks really make it easier? *The Gerontologist, 29,* 101–107.

MORITZ, D., KASL, S., & BERKMAN, L. (1989). The health impact of living with a cognitively impaired elderly spouse: Depressive symptoms and social functioning. *Journal of Gerontology, 44,* S17–27.

MOSHER, D., & VONDERHEIDE, S. (1985). Contributions of sex guilt and masturbation guilt to women's contraceptive attitudes and use. *The Journal of Sex Research, 21,* 24–39.

MOSHMAN, D. (1990). The development of metalogical understanding. In W. Overton (ed.), *Reasoning, necessity, and logic: Develop-*

mental perspectives (pp. 205–226). Hillsdale, NJ: Erlbaum.

MOSHMAN, D. & NEIMARK, E. (1982). Four aspects of adolescent cognitive development. In T. Field, A. Huston, H. Quay, L. Troll, & G. Finley (eds.), *Review of human development*. New York: Wiley.

MOSS, H. & SUSSMAN, E. (1980). Longitudinal study of personality development. In O. Brim & J. Kagan (ed.) *Constancy and change in human development*. Cambridge, MA: Harvard University Press.

MOSSEY, J., & SHAPIRO, E. (1982). Self-rated health: A predictor of mortality among the elderly. *American Journal of Public Health, 72,* 800–808.

MOTENKO, A. (1989). The frustrations, gratifications, and well-being of dementia caregivers. *The Gerontologist, 29,* 166–172.

MOTT, F. & SHAPIRO, D. (1982). Continuity of work attachment among young mothers. In F. Mott (ed.), *The employment revolution*. Cambridge, MA: MIT Press.

MUELLER, K. (1954). *Educating women for a changing world*. Minneapolis: University of Minnesota Press.

MULVEY, A., & DOHRENWEND, B. (1984). The relation of stressful life events to gender. In A. Rickel, M. Gerrard, & I. Iscoe (eds.), *Social and psychological problems of women*. Washington, DC: Hemisphere.

MUMFORD, M. (1984). Age and outstanding occupational achievement: Lehman revisited. *Journal of Vocational Behavior, 25,* 225–244.

MUNLEY, A. (1983). *The hospice alternative: A new context for death and dying*. New York: Basic Books.

MUNRO, G., & ADAMS, G. (1977). Ego-identity formation in college students and working youth. *Developmental Psychology, 13,* 523–524.

MURRAY, H., et al. (1938). *Explorations in personality*. New York: Oxford University Press.

MURSTEIN, B. (1976). *Who will marry whom? Theories and research in marital choice*. New York: Springer.

MURSTEIN, B. (1982). Marital choice. In B. Wolman (ed.), *Handbook of developmental psychology* (pp. 652–666). Englewood Cliffs, NJ: Prentice-Hall.

NASH, J., & WILWERTH, J. (1991). A puzzling plague. *Time, 137*(2), 48–52.

NATHANSON, C., & LORENZ, G. (1982). Women and health: The social dimensions of biomedical data. In J. Giele (ed.), *Women in the middle years*. New York: Wiley.

NEIMARK, E. (1979). Current status of formal operations research. *Human Development, 22,* 60–67.

NEIMARK, E. (1981). Explanation for the apparent nonuniversal incidence of formal operations. In I. Sigel, D. Brodzinsky, & R. Golinkoff (eds.), *New directions in Piagetian theory and practice*. Hillsdale, NJ: Erlbaum.

NEIMARK, E. (1982). Adolescent thought: Transition to formal operations. In B. Wolman (ed.), *Handbook of developmental psychology* (pp. 486–502). Englewood Cliffs, NJ: Prentice-Hall.

NEIMARK, E. (1985). Moderators of competence: Challenges to the universality of Piagetian theory. In E. Neimark, R. DeLisi, & J. Newman (eds.), *Moderators of competence* (pp. 1–14). Hillsdale, NJ: Erlbaum.

NEIMARK, E., DELISI, R., & NEWMAN, J. (1985). *Moderators of competence*. Hillsdale, NJ: Erlbaum.

NESTEL, G., MERCIER, J., & SHAW, L. (1983). Economic consequences of midlife change in marital status. In L. B. Shaw (ed.) *Unplanned careers: The working lives of middle-aged women*. Lexington, MA: Lexington Books.

NEUGARTEN, B. (1966). Adult personality: A developmental view. *Human Development, 9,* 61–73.

NEUGARTEN, B. (1968). The awareness of middle age. In B. Neugarten (ed.), *Middle age and aging* (pp. 93–98). Chicago: University of Chicago Press.

NEUGARTEN, B. (1979). Time, age, and the life cycle. *American Journal of Psychiatry, 136,* 887–894.

NEUGARTEN, B. and ASSOCIATES (1964). *Personality in middle and later life*. New York: Atherton Press.

NEUGARTEN, B., & GUTMANN, D. (1958/1968). Age-sex roles and personality in middle age: A thematic apperception study. In B. Neugarten (ed.), *Middle age and aging* (pp. 58–71). Chicago: University of Chicago Press.

NEUGARTEN, B., HAVIGHURST, R., & TOBIN, S. (1965/1968). Personality and patterns of aging. In B. Neugarten (ed.), *Middle age and aging* (pp. 173–177). Chicago: University of Chicago Press.

NEUGARTEN, B., MOORE, J., & LOWE, J. (1968/1965). Age norms, age constraints, and adult socialization. In B. Neugarten (ed.), *Middle age and aging* (pp. 22–28). Chicago: University of Chicago Press.

NEUGARTEN, B., & WEINSTEIN, K. (1964/1968). The changing American grandparent. In B. Neugarten (ed.), *Middle age and aging* (pp. 280–285). Chicago: University of Chicago Press.

NEUGARTEN, B., WOOD, V., KRAINES, R., & LOOMIS, B. (1968/1963). Women's attitudes toward the menopause. In B. Neugarten (ed.), *Middle age and aging.* Chicago: University of Chicago Press.

NEWMAN, B. (1982). Mid-life development. In B. Wolman (ed.), *Handbook of developmental psychology* (pp. 617–635). Englewood Cliffs, NJ: Prentice-Hall.

NEWMAN, P. (1982). The peer group. In B. Wolman (ed.), *Handbook of developmental psychology* (pp. 526–536). Englewood Cliffs, NJ: Prentice-Hall.

NEWMAN-HORNBLUM, J., ATTIG, M., & KRAMER, D. (1980). The use of sex-relevant Piagetian tasks in assessing cognitive competence among the elderly. Paper presented at the Conference of the American Psychological Association, Toronto.

NOCK, S. (1982). The life-cycle approach to family analysis. In B. Wolman (ed.), *Handbook of developmental psychology* (pp. 636–651). Englewood Cliffs, NJ: Prentice-Hall.

NOELKER, L., & BASS, D. (1989). Home care for elderly persons: Linkages between formal and informal caregivers. *Journal of Gerontology, 44,* S63–S70.

NORRIS, F. (1985). Characteristics of older nonrespondents over five waves of a panel study. *Journal of Gerontology, 40,* 627–636.

NORTH CENTRAL INSTITUTE (nd). Do you have PMS? Columbus, OH: North Central Institute.

NORTON, A. (1983). Family life cycle: 1980. *Journal of Marriage and the Family, 45,* 267–275.

OAKLEY, A. (1974). *Woman's work: The housewife, past and present.* New York: Vintage.

OBLER, L. (1985). Language through the lifespan. In J. Gleason (ed.), *The development of language.* Columbus, OH: Merrill.

OBLER, L., & ALBERT, M. (1985). Language skills across the life-span. In J. Birren & K. Schaie (eds.), *Handbook of the psychology of aging* (2d ed.) (pp. 463–473). New York: Van Nostrand.

OCHS, A., NEWBERRY, J., LENHARDT, M., & HARKINS, S. (1985). Neural and vestibular aging associated with falls. In J. Birren & K. Schaie (eds.), *The handbook of the psychology of aging* (2d ed.). New York: Van Nostrand.

O'CONNELL, A. (1976). The relationship between life style and identity synthesis and resynthesis in traditional, neotraditional, and nontraditional women. *Journal of Personality, 44,* 675–688.

OFFENBACH, S. (1974). A developmental study of hypothesis testing and cue selection strategies. *Developmental Psychology, 10,* 484–490.

OFFER, D., & OFFER, J. (1975). *From teenage to young manhood: A psychological study.* New York: Basic Books.

OFFER, D., OSTROV, E., & HOWARD, K. (1984). The self-image of normal adolescents. In D. Offer, E. Ostrov, & K. Howard (eds.), *Patterns of adolescent self-image* (pp. 5–18). San Francisco: Jossey-Bass.

O'HARA, M., ZEKOSKI, E., PHILIPPS, L., & WRIGHT, E. (1990). Controlled prospective study of postpartum mood disorders: Comparison of childbearing and non-childbearing women. *Journal of Abnormal Psychology, 99,* 3–15.

O'HERON, C., & ORLOFSKY, J. (1990). Stereotypic and nonstereotypic sex role traits and behavior orientations, gender identity, and psychological adjustment. *Journal of Personality and Social Psychology, 58,* 134–143.

OKARAKU, I. (1987). Age and attitudes toward multigenerational residence, 1973 to 1983. *Journal of Gerontology, 42,* 280–287.

OLSHO, L., HARKINS, S., & LENHARDT, M. (1985). Aging and the auditory system. In J. Birren & K. Schaie (eds.), *Handbook of the psychology of aging* (2d ed.) (pp. 332–377). New York: Van Nostrand.

O'NEILL, J. (1990). The role of human capital in earning differences between black and white men. *Journal of Economic Perspectives, 4,* 25–46.

O'NEIL, J., HELMS, B., GABLE, R., DAVID, L., & WRIGHTSMAN, L. (1986). Gender-role conflict scale: College men's fear of femininity. *Sex Roles, 14,* 335–350.

ORGEL, L. (1970). The maintenance of the accuracy of protein synthesis and its relevance to aging: A correction. *Proceedings of the National Academy of Science, 67,* 1476.

ORLOFSKY, J. (1977). Sex role orientation, identity formation, and self-esteem in college men and women. *Sex Roles, 3,* 561–575.

ORLOFSKY, J. (1978). Identity formation, achievement and fear of success in college men and women. *Journal of Youth and Adolescence, 7,* 49–62.

ORLOFSKY, J., MARCIA, J., & LESSER, I. (1973). Ego identity status and the intimacy versus isolation crisis of young adulthood. *Journal of Personality and Social Psychology, 21,* 211–219.

OSHERON, S., & DILL, D. (1983). Varying work

and family choices: Their impact on men's work satisfaction. *Journal of Marriage and the Family, 45,* 339–346.

OSOFSKY, H., & KEPPEL, W. (1985). Psychiatric and gynecological evaluation and management of premenstrual symptoms. In H. Osofsky & S. Blumenthal (eds.), *Premenstrual syndrome: Current findings and future directions.* Washington, DC: American Psychiatric Association.

OVERTON, W. (1985). Scientific methodologies and the competence-moderator-performance issue. In E. Neimark, R. DeLisi, & J. Newman (eds.), *Moderators of competence* (pp. 15–41). Hillsdale, NJ: Erlbaum.

OVERTON, W., & REESE, H. (1973). Models of development: Methodological implications. In J. Nesselroade & H. Reese (eds.), *Life-span developmental psychology: Methodological issues* (pp. 65–86). New York: Academic Press.

OWLSLEY, C., BALL, K., SLOANE, M., ROENKER, D., & BRUNI, J. (1991). Visual/cognitive correlates of vehicle accidents in older drivers. *Psychology and Aging, 6,* 403–415.

PACKARD, M., & RENO, V. (1989). A look at very early retirees. *Social Security Bulletin, 52,* 16–29.

PALKOVITZ, R. (1985). Fathers' birth attendance, early contact, and extended contact with their newborns: A critical review. *Child Development, 56,* 392–406.

PAMUK, E. (1985). Social class inequality in mortality from 1921 to 1972 in England and Wales. *Population Studies, 39,* 17–31.

PARKE, R., & SAWIN, D. (1980). Father-infant interaction in the newborn period: A reevaluation of some current myths. In E. Hetherington & R. Parke (eds.), *Contemporary readings in child psychology.* New York: McGraw-Hill. (Originally presented at the American Psychological Association, 1975.)

PARKES, C. (1970). The first year of bereavement. *Psychiatry, 33,* 444–467.

PARKES, C. (1972). *Bereavement: Studies of grief in adult life.* New York: International Universities Press.

PARLEE, M. B. (1978). Psychological aspects of menstruation, childbirth, and menopause. In J. Sherman & F. Denmark (eds.), *The psychology of women: Future directions in research.* New York: Psychological Dimensions.

PARNES, H. (1988). The retirement decision. In M. Borus, H. Parnes, S. Sandell, & B. Seidman (eds.), *The older worker.* Madison, WI: Industrial Relations Research Association.

PARR, J. (1980). The interaction of person and living environments. In L. Poon (ed.), *Aging in the 1980s* (pp. 393–406). Washington, DC: American Psychological Association.

PATTERSON, G. R. (1980). Mothers: The unacknowledged victim. *Monographs of the Society for Research in Child Development, 45,* Ser #186.

PATTERSON, J. T. (1987). *The dread disease: Cancer and modern American culture.* Cambridge, MA: Harvard University Press.

PATTERSON, R. (1987). Family management of the elderly. In L. Carstensen & B. Edelstein (eds.), *Handbook of clinical gerontology* (pp. 267–276). New York: Pergamon.

PEARLMAN, R., & UHLMANN, R. (1988). Quality of life in chronic diseases: Perceptions of elderly patients. *Journal of Gerontology, 43,* M25–30.

PERRY, W. (1970). *Forms of intellectual and ethical development in the college years.* New York: Holt, Rinehart & Winston.

PETERSON, A. (1987). The nature of biological-psychosocial interaction. In R. Lerner & T. Foch (eds.), *Biological-psychosocial interactions in early adolescence.* Hillsdale, NJ: Erlbaum.

PETERSON, K., & ROSCOE, B. (1984). Factors influencing selection of major by college females. *College Student Journal, 29–34.*

PETIT, T. (1982). Neuroanatomical and clinical neuropsychological changes in aging and senile dementia. In F. Craik & S. Trehub (eds.), *Aging and cognitive processes.* New York: Plenum Press.

PEYSER, H. (1982). Stress and alcohol. In L. Goldberger & S. Breznitz (eds.), *Handbook of stress* (pp. 585–598). New York: Free Press.

PFEIFFER, E. (1977). Psychopathology and social pathology. In J. Birren & K. Schaie (eds.), *Handbook of the psychology of aging* (pp. 650–671). New York: Van Nostrand Reinhold.

PFEIFFER, E., & DAVIS, G. (1971). The use of leisure time in middle life. *Gerontologist, 11,* 187–195.

PFEIFFER, E., & DAVIS, G. (1972). Determinants of sexual behavior in middle and old age. *Journal of American Geriatrics Society, 20,* 4.

PHIFER, J., & MURRELL, S. (1986). Etiological factors in the onset of depressive symptoms in older adults. *Journal of Abnormal Psychology, 95,* 282–291.

PHILLIS, D., & GROMKO, M. (1985). Sex differences in sexual activity: Reality or illusion? *The Journal of Sex Research, 21,* 437–448.

PIAGET, J. (1972). Intellectual evolution from adolescence to adulthood. *Human Development, 15,* 1–12.

PIERCE, R., & CHIRIBOGA, D. (1979). Dimensions of adult self-concept. *Journal of Gerontology, 34,* 80–85.

PILLEMER, K., & FINKELHOR, D. (1988). The prevalence of elder abuse: A random sample survey. *The Gerontologist, 28,* 51–57.

PIOTROWSKI, C. (1982). Women's work and personal relations in the family. In P. Berman & E. Ramey (eds.), *Women: A developmental perspective* (pp. 221–235). Washington, DC: National Institutes of Health.

PITT, B. (1982). Depression and childbirth. In E. Paykel (ed.), *Handbook of affective disorders.* New York: Guilford.

PLECK, J. (1977). The work-family role system. *Social Problems, 24,* 417–427.

PLOMIN, R. (1987). Developmental behavioral genetics and infancy. In J. Osofsky (ed.), *Handbook of infant development* (2d ed.). New York: Wiley.

PMS ACTION. (1983). What is PMS? *The PMS Connection, 1,* 1.

POGUE-GEILE, M., & ROSE, M. (1985). Developmental genetic studies of adult personality. *Developmental Psychology, 21,* 547–557.

POLIT, D. (1978). Stereotypes relating to family size status. *Journal of Marriage and the Family, 40,* 105–116.

PONDS, R., BROUWER, W., & VAN WOLFFELAAR, P. (1988). Age differences in divided attention in a simulated driving task. *Journal of Gerontology, 43,* P151–156.

POON, L. (1985). Differences in human memory with aging: Nature, causes, and clinical implications. In J. Birren & K. Schaie (eds.), *The handbook of the psychology of aging* (2d ed.) (pp. 427–462). New York: Van Nostrand.

POPE, H. & HUDSON, J. (1984). *New hope for binge eaters.* New York: Harper & Row.

POST, F. (1987). Paranoid and schizophrenic disorders among the aging. In L. Carstensen & B. Edelstein (eds.), *Handbook of clinical gerontology* (pp. 43–56). New York: Pergamon Press.

POTERBA, J., & SUMMERS, L. (1987). Public policy implications of declining old-age mortality. In G. Burtless (ed.), *Work, health, and income among the elderly.* Washington, DC: Brookings Institution.

PRATT, M., GOULDING, G., HUNTER, W., & SAMPSON, R. (1988). Sex differences in adult moral orientations. *Journal of Personality, 56,* 373–391.

PREVITE, J. (1983). *Human physiology.* New York: McGraw-Hill.

PRICE-WILLIAMS, D. (1981). Concrete and formal operations. In R. Munroe, R. Munroe, & B. Whiting (eds.), *Handbook of cross-cultural human development* (pp. 403–422). New York: Garland.

PRUCHNO, R., & RESCH, N. (1989). Husbands and wives as caregivers: Antecedents of depression and burden. *The Gerontologist, 29,* 159–165.

PRUSINER, S., & BENHEIM, P. (1984). Creutzfeldt-Jakob disease: A related disorder. *ADRDA Newsletter, 4,* 3.

PUGILISI, J., PARK, D., SMITH, A., & DUDLEY, W. (1988). Age differences in encoding specificity. *Journal of Gerontology, 43,* P145–150.

QUAYHAGEN, M., & QUAYHAGEN, M. (1988). Alzheimer's stress: Coping with the caregiving role. *The Gerontologist, 28,* 391–396.

QUINN, J., & BURKHAUSER, R. (1990). Work and retirement. In R. Binstock & L. George (eds.), *Handbook of aging and the social sciences* (3rd ed.) (pp. 308–327). San Diego: Academic Press.

RADIN, N. (1981). Role-sharing fathers and preschoolers. In M. Lamb (ed.), *Nontraditional families: Parenting and child development.* Hillsdale, NJ: Erlbaum.

RADNER, D. (1989). Net worth and financial assets of age groups in 1984. *Social Security Bulletin, 52,* 2–15.

RANDO, T. (1983). An investigation of grief and adaptation in parents whose children have died. *Journal of Pediatric Psychology, 8,* 3–20.

RANDO, T. (1986). A comprehensive analysis of anticipatory grief: Perspectives, processes, promises, and problems. In T. Rando (ed.), *Loss and anticipatory grief.* Lexington, MA: Lexington Books.

RATNER, H., PADGETT, R., & BUSHEY, N. (1988). Old and young adults' recall of events. *Developmental Psychology, 24,* 664–671.

REBOK, G., MONTAGLIONE, C., & BENDLIN, G. (1988). Effects of age and training on memory for pragmatic implications in advertising. *Journal of Geronotology, 43,* P75–78.

REDER, L., WIBLE, C., & MARTIN, J. (1988). Differential memory changes with age: Exact retrieval versus plausible inferences. *Journal of Experimental Psychology: Learning, Memory, & Cognition, 12,* 72–81.

REESE, H., & OVERTON, W. (1970). Models of development and theories of development. In L. Goulet & P. Baltes (eds.), *Lifespan developmental psychology: Research and theory* (pp. 116–149). New York: Academic Press.

REESE, H., & RODEHEAVER, D. (1985). Problem solving and complex decision making. In J. Birren & K. Schaie (eds.), *The handbook of the psychology of aging* (2d ed.) (pp. 474–499). New York: Van Nostrand.

REFF, M. (1985). RNA and protein metabolism. In C. Finch & E. Schneider (eds.), *Handbook of the biology of aging* (pp. 225–254). New York: Van Nostrand Reinhold.

REISBERG, B. (1983). *Alzheimer's disease.* New York: Free Press.

RELMAN, A. (1982). Closing the books on laetrile. *The New England Journal of Medicine, 306,* 236.

REPETTI, R., MATTHEWS, K., & WALDRON, I. (1989). Employment and women's health: Effects of paid employment on women's mental and physical health. *American Psychologist, 44,* 1394–1401.

REST, J., DAVISON, M., & ROBBINS, S. (1978). Age trends in judging moral issues: A review of cross-sectional, longitudinal, and sequential studies of the Defining Issues Test. *Child Development, 49,* 263–279.

REST, J., & THOMA, S. (1985). Relation of moral judgment development to formal education. *Developmental Psychology, 21,* 709–714.

RHODES, S. (1983). Age-related differences in work attitudes and behavior: A review and conceptual analysis. *Psychological Bulletin, 93,* 328–367.

RHODEWALT, F. & AGUSTSDOTTIR, S. (1984). On the relationship of hardiness to the Type A behavior pattern: Perception of life events versus coping with life events. *Journal of Research in Personality, 18,* 212–223.

RICE, G., & MEYER, B. (1986). Prose recall: Effects of aging, verbal ability, and reading behavior. *Journal of Gerontology, 41,* 469–480.

RIEGEL, K. (1973). Dialectic operations: The final period of cognitive development. *Human Development, 16,* 346–370.

RIEGEL, K. (1976). The dialectics of human development. *American Psychologist, 31,* 689–701.

RIEGEL, K. (1977). History of psychological gerontology. In J. Birren & K. Schaie (eds.), *Handbook of the psychology of aging* (pp. 70–102). New York: Van Nostrand.

RIEGEL, K., & RIEGEL, R. (1972). Development, drop and death. *Developmental Psychology, 6,* 306–319.

ROBBINS, D. (1986). Legal and ethical issues in terminal illness care for patients, families, caregivers, and institutions. In T. Rando (ed.), *Loss and anticipatory grief* (pp. 215–228). Lexington, MA: Lexington Books.

ROBINSON, R., COBERLY, S., & PAUL, C. (1985). Work and retirement. In R. Binstock & E. Shanas (eds.), *Handbook of aging and the social sciences* (2d ed.) (pp. 503–527). New York: Van Nostrand.

ROCHE, A. (1979). Secular trends in stature, weight, and maturation. In A. Roche (ed.), Secular trends in human growth, maturation, and development. *Monographs of the Society for Research in Child Development* (pp. 3–27). Serial No. 179.

ROCHE, A., & DAVILIA, G. (1972). Late adolescent growth in stature. *Pediatrics, 50,* 874–880.

RODIN, J., & ICKOVICS, J. (1990). Women's health: Review and research agenda as we approach the 21st century. *American Psychologist, 45,* 1018–1034.

RODIN, J., SILBERSTEIN, L., & STRIEGEL-MOORE, R. (1985). Women and weight: A normative discontent. In T. Sonderegger (ed.), *Nebraska symposium on motivation 1984: Psychology and gender* (pp. 267–307). Lincoln: University of Nebraska Press.

ROGERS, J., & BLOOM, F. (1985). Neurotransmitter metabolism and function in the aging central nervous system. In C. Finch & E. Schneider (eds.), *Handbook of the biology of aging* (2d ed.) (pp. 645–691). New York: Van Nostrand.

RONES, P. (1988). Employment, earnings, and unemployment characteristics of older workers. In M. Borus, H. Parnes, S. Sandall, & B. Seidman (eds.), *The older worker.* Madison, WI: Industrial Relations Research Association.

ROOSA, M., FITZGERALD, H., & CRAWFORD, M. (1985). Teenage parenting, delayed parenting, and childlessness. In L. L'Abate (ed.), *Handbook of family psychology and therapy* (pp. 623–659). Homewood, IL: Dorsey.

ROSE, R., & ABPLANALP, J. (1983). The premenstrual syndrome. *Hospital Practice,* 129–141.

ROSE, R., & DITTO, W. (1983). Developmental-genetic analysis of common fears from early adolescence to early adulthood. *Child Development, 54,* 361–368.

ROSENMAN, R., & CHESNEY, M. (1982). Stress, Type A behavior and coronary disease. In L. Goldberger & S. Breznitz (eds.), *The handbook of stress: Theoretical and clinical aspects* (pp. 547–565). New York: Macmillan.

ROSENMAYER, L. (1985). Changing values and positions of aging in Western culture. In J. Birren & K. Schaie (eds.), *Handbook of the psychology of aging* (2d ed.) (pp. 190–215). New York: Van Nostrand.

ROSENZWEIG, M. (1984). Experience, memory, and the brain. *American Psychologist, 39*, 365–379.

ROSS, M. (1983). *The married homosexual man.* London: Routledge & Kegan Paul.

ROSSMAN, I. (1980). Bodily changes with aging. In E. Busse & D. Blazer (eds.), *Handbook of geriatric psychiatry.* New York: Van Nostrand Reinhold.

ROTHBART, M., & DERRYBERRY, D. (1981). Development of individual differences in temperament. In M. Lamb & A. Brown (eds.), *Advances in developmental psychology.* Hillsdale, NJ: Erlbaum.

ROTHSTEIN, M. (1982). *Biochemical approaches to aging.* New York: Academic Press.

ROWE, J., ANDRES, R., TOBIN, J., NORRIS, A., & SHOCK, N. (1976). The effect of age on creatinine clearance in men: A cross-sectional and longitudinal study. *Journal of Gerontology, 31*, 155–163.

ROWE, I., & MARCIA, J. (1980). Ego identity status, formal operations, and moral development. *Journal of Youth and Adolescence, 9*, 87–99.

ROZZINI, R., BIANCHETTI, A., CARABELLESE, C., INZOLI, M., & TRABUCCHI, M. (1988). Depression, life events and somatic symptoms. *The Gerontologist, 28*, 229–232.

RUBIN, E., & KINSCHERF, D. (1989). Psychopathology of very mild dementia of the Alzheimer type. *American Journal of Psychiatry, 146*, 1017–1021.

RUBIN, L. (1976). *Worlds of pain: Life in the working-class family.* New York: Basic Books.

RUBIN, L. (1980). The empty nest: Beginning or end? In L. Bond & J. Rosen (eds.), *Competence and coping during adulthood* (pp. 309–321). Hanover, NH: University Press of New England.

RUBIN, L. (1985). *Just friends: The role of friendship in our lives.* New York: Harper & Row.

RUBINOW, D., ROY-BYRNE, P., HOBAN, M., GROVER, G., & POST, R. (1985). Menstrually related mood disorders. In H. Osofsky & S. Blumenthal (eds.), *Premenstrual syndrome: Current findings and future directions.* Washington, DC: American Psychiatric Association.

RUBINSTEIN, R. (1987). Never married elderly as a social type: Reevaluating some images. *The Gerontologist, 27*, 108–113.

RUBINSTEIN, R. (1989). The home environments of older people: A description of the psychosocial processes linking person to place. *Journal of Gerontology, 44*, S45–53.

RUBLE, D. (1977). Premenstrual symptoms: A reinterpretation. *Science, 197*, 291–292.

RUDD, P., & BLASCHKE, T. (1982). Antihypertensive agents and the drug therapy of hypertension. In A. Gilman, L. Goodman, T. Rall, & F. Murad (eds.), *Goodman and Gilman's The phamacological basis of therapeutics* (7th ed.) (pp. 784–805). New York: Macmillan.

RUSBULT, C., JOHNSON, D., & MORROW, G. (1986). Determinants and consequences of exit, voice, loyalty, and neglect: Responses to dissatisfaction in adult romantic involvements. *Human Relations, 39*, 45–63.

RUSSELL, C. (1974). Transition to parenthood: Problems and gratifications. *Journal of Marriage and the Family, 36*, 294–301.

RUSSELL, G. F. M. (1979). Bulimia nervosa: An ominous variant of anorexia nervosa. *Psychological Medicine, 9*, 429–448.

RYFF, C. (1984). Personality development from the inside: The subjective experience of change in adulthood and aging. In P. Baltes and O. Brim (eds), *Life-span development and behavior* (Vol. 6) (pp. 243–279). New York: Academic Press.

SALEND, E., KANE, R., SATZ, M., & PYNOOS, J. (1984). Elder abuse reporting: Limitations of statutes. *The Gerontologist, 24*, 61–69.

SALTHOUSE, T. (1984). Effects of age and skill in typing. *Journal of Experimental Psychology: General, 113*, 345–371.

SALTHOUSE, T. (1985). *A theory of cognitive aging.* Amsterdam: North Holland Press.

SALTHOUSE, T. (1990). Cognitive competence and expertise in aging. In J. Birren & K. Schaie (eds.), *Handbook of psychology and aging* (3rd ed.) (pp. 311–319). San Diego: Academic Press.

SALTHOUSE, T., BABCOCK, R., SKOVRONEK, E., MITCHELL, D., & PALMON, R. (1990). Age and experience effects in spatial visualization. *Developmental Psychology, 26*, 128–136.

SALTHOUSE, T., & MITCHELL, D. (1990). Effects of age and naturally occurring experience on spatial visualization performance. *Developmental Psychology, 26*, 845–854.

SALZMAN, C. (1982). A primer on geriatric psychopharmacology. *American Journal of Psychiatry, 139*, 667–74.

SAMMARTINO, F. (1987). The effect of health on retirement. *Social Security Bulletin, 50*, 31–47.

SANCHEZ-AYENDEZ, M. (1989). Puerto Rican elderly women: Shared meanings and informal supportive networks. In L. Richardson & V. Taylor (eds.), *Feminist Frontiers II* (pp. 174–182). New York: Random House.

SANDE, M., & MANDELL, G. (1985). Antimicrobial agents: General considerations. In A. Gilman, L. Goodman, T. Rall, & F. Murad (eds.), *Gilman and Goodman's The pharmacological basis of therapeutics* (7th ed.) (pp. 1066–1094). New York: Macmillan.

SANTOS, J., HUBBARD, R., & MCINTOSH, J. (1983). Mental health and the minority elderly. In L. Breslau & M. Haug (eds.), *Depression and aging: Causes, care, and consequences.* New York: Springer.

SCARR, S., & MCCARTNEY, K. (1983). How people make their own environments: A theory of genotype/environmental effects. *Child Development, 54,* 424–435.

SCARR, S., PHILLIPS, D. & MCCARTNEY, K. (1989). Working mothers and their families. *American Psychologist, 44,* 1402–1409.

SCHAIE, K. W. (1970). A reinterpretation of age-related changes in cognitive structure and functioning. In L. Goulet & P. Baltes (eds.), *Life-span developmental psychology: Research and theory* (pp. 486–507). New York: Academic Press.

SCHAIE, K. W. (1973). Methodological problems in descriptive developmental research on adulthood and aging. In J. Nesselroade & H. Reese (eds.), *Life-span developmental psychology: Methodological issues* (pp. 253–280). New York: Academic Press.

SCHAIE, K. W. (1977/1978). Toward a stage theory of adult cognitive development. *Journal of Aging and Human Development, 8,* 129–138.

SCHAIE, K. W. (1979). The Primary Mental Abilities in adulthood: An exploration in the development of psychometric intelligence. In P. Baltes & O. Brim (eds.), *Life-span development and behavior* (Vol. 2). New York: Academic Press.

SCHAIE, K. (1990). Intellectual development in adulthood. In J. Birren & K. Schaie (eds.), *Handbook of the psychology of aging* (3rd ed.) (pp. 291–310). San Diego: Academic Press.

SCHAIE, K. W., & BALTES, P. (1975). On sequential strategies in developmental research: Description or explanation. *Human Development, 18,* 384–390.

SCHAIE, K. W. & HERTZOG, C. (1982). Longitudinal methods. In B. Wolman (ed.), *Handbook of developmental psychology* (pp. 91–115). Englewood Cliffs, NJ: Prentice-Hall.

SCHAIE, K. W., & HERTZOG, C. (1983). Fourteen-year cohort-sequential analyses of adult intellectual development. *Developmental Psychology, 19,* 531–543.

SCHAIE, K. W., & LABOUVIE, G. (1974). Generational versus ontogenetic components of change in adult cognitive behavior: A fourteen-year cross-sequential study. *Developmental Psychology, 10,* 305–320.

SCHAIE, K. W., & PARHAM, I. (1976). Stability of adult personality traits: Fact or fable. *Journal of Personality and Social Psychology, 34,* 146–158.

SCHAIE, K. W., & STROTHER, C. (1968). A cross-sequential study of age changes in cognitive behavior. *Psychological Bulletin, 70,* 671–680.

SCHAIE, K. W., & WILLIS, S. (1986). Can decline in adult intellectual functioning be reversed? *Developmental Psychology, 22,* 223–232.

SCHIEDEL, D., & MARCIA, J. (1985). Ego identity, intimacy, sex role orientation, and gender. *Developmental Psychology, 21,* 149–160.

SCHMITZ-SCHERZER, R. & THOMAE, H. (1983). Constancy and change of behavior in old age: Findings from the Bonn longitudinal study on aging. In K. Schaie (ed.), *Longitudinal studies of adult psychological development,* (pp.191–221). New York: Guilford.

SCHNECK, M., REISBERG, B., & FERRIS, S. (1982). An overview of current concepts of Alzheimer's disease. *American Journal of Psychiatry, 139,* 165–173.

SCHNEIDER, E. (1985). Cytogenetics of aging. In C. Finch & E. Schneider (eds.), *Handbook of the biology of aging* (pp. 357–376). New York: Van Nostrand Reinhold.

SCHULTZ, D., & SCHULTZ, S. (1986). *Psychology and industry today.* New York: Macmillan.

SCHULZ, R. (1985). Emotion and affect. In J. Birren & K. Schaie (eds.), *Handbook of the psychology of aging* (2d ed.) (pp. 531–543). New York: Van Nostrand Reinhold.

SCHWARTZ, J., & ZUROFF, D. (1979). Family structure and depression in female college students: Effects of parental conflict, decision-making power, and inconsistency of love. *Journal of Abnormal Psychology, 88,* 398–406.

SEARS, P., & BARBEE, A. (1977). Career and life satisfaction among Terman's gifted women. In J. Stanley, W. George, & C. Solano (eds.), *The gifted and creative: Fifty year perspective* (pp. 28–65). Baltimore: Johns Hopkins University Press.

SELIGMAN, M. (1975). *Helplessness: On depression, development, and death.* San Francisco: Freeman.

SELTZER, B. (1988). Organic mental disorders. In A. Nicholi (ed.), *The new Harvard guide to psychiatry* (pp. 358–386). Cambridge, MA: Belknap Press.

SHANAS, E., & MADDOX, G. (1985). Health, health resources and the utilization of care. In R. Binstock & E. Shanas (eds.), *Handbook of aging and the social sciences* (2d ed.) (pp. 697–726). New York: Van Nostrand.

SHAPIRO, J. (1987). The expectant father. *Psychology Today, 21,* 36–42.

SHARPS, M., & GOLLIN, E. (1988). Aging and free recall for objects located in space. *Journal of Gerontology, 43,* P8–11.

SHAW, L. (1983). Problems of labor-market reentry. In L. B. Shaw (ed.), *Unplanned careers: The working lives of middle-aged women.* Lexington, MA: Lexington Books.

SHAW, L. (1988). Special problems of older women workers. In M. Borus, H. Parnes, S. Sandell, & B. Seidman (eds.), *The older worker.* Madison WI: Industrial Relations Research Association.

SHAW, L., & O'BRIEN, T. (1983). Introduction. In L. B. Shaw (ed.), *Unplanned careers: The working lives of middle-aged women.* Lexington, MA: Lexington Books.

SHEHAN, C., BOCK, E., & LEE, G. (1990). Religious heterogamy, religiosity, and marital happiness: The case of Catholics. *Journal of Marriage and the Family, 52,* 73–79.

SHEPARD, R., & MONTELPARE M. (1988). Geriatric benefits of exercise as an adult. *Journal of Gerontology, 43,* 86–90.

SHEPARD, B., & SHEPARD, C. (1982). *The complete guide to women's health.* Tampa: Mariner Publishing.

SHERWIN, R., & CORBETT, S. (1985). Campus sexual norms and dating relationships: A trend analysis. *The Journal of Sex Research, 21,* 258–274.

SHNEIDMAN, E. (1980). *Voices of death.* New York: Harper & Row.

SHOCK, N. (1972). Energy metabolism, caloric intake and physical activity of the aging. In L. Carson (ed.), *Nutrition in old age, X Symposium Swedish Nutrition Foundation.* Uppsala: Almqvist & Wiksell. (Reprinted in N. Shock et al. (1984). *Normal human aging: The Baltimore Longitudinal Study of Aging* (pp. 372–383). Washington, DC: Government Printing Office.)

SHOCK, N., GREULICH, R., COSTA, P., ANDRES, R., LAKATTA, E., ARENBERG, D., & TOBIN, J. (1984). *Normal human aging: The Baltimore longitudinal study of aging.* Washington, DC: National Institutes of Health.

SIEGLER, I., & COSTA, P. (1985). Health behavior relationships. In J. Birren & K. Schaie (eds.), *Handbook of the psychology of aging* (2d ed.) (pp. 144–166). New York: Van Nostrand.

SIEGLER, I., GEORGE, L., & OKUN, M. (1979). Cross-sequential analysis of adult personality. *Developmental Psychology, 15,* 350–351.

SILVERBERG, S., & STEINBERG, L. (1990). Psychological well-being of parents with early adolescent children. *Developmental Psychology, 26,* 658–666.

SIMONTON, D. (1988). Age and outstanding achievement: What do we know after a century of research? *Psychological Bulletin, 104,* 251–267.

SIMPSON, E. (1974). Moral development research. *Human Development, 17,* 81–106.

SINFELD, A. (1985). Being out of work. In C. Littler (ed.), *The experience of work* (pp. 190–208). New York: St. Martin's Press.

SKINNER, B. F. (1971). *Beyond freedom and dignity.* New York: Knopf.

SKINNER, B. F. (1983). Intellectual self-management in old age. *American Psychologist, 38,* 239–244.

SKINNER, D. (1983). Dual career families. In H. McCubbin & C. Figley (eds.), *Stress and the family* (Vol. 1). New York: Brunner/Mazel.

SLANEY, R. (1980). Expressed vocational choice and vocational indecision. *Journal of Counseling Psychology, 27,* 122–129.

SLANEY, R., & BROWN, M. (1983). Effects of race and socioeconomic status on career choice variables among college men. *Journal of Vocational Behavior, 23,* 257–269.

SMETANA, J. (1988). Concepts of self and social convention: Adolescents' and parents' reasoning about hypothetical and actual family conflicts. In M. Gunnar & W. A. Collins (eds.), *Minnesota symposia on child development (Vol. 21): Development during the transition to adolescence* (pp. 79–122). Hillsdale NJ: Erlbaum.

SMITH, J., & BALTES, P. (1990). Wisdom-related knowledge: Age/cohort differences in response to life-planning problems. *Developmental Psychology, 26,* 494–505.

SMITH, D. & BRUBAKER, L. (1983). Nutrition and cancer. In E. Feldman (ed.) *Nutrition in the middle and later years* (pp. 127–150). Boston, MA: John Wright.

SMITH & WELCH (1989). Black economic progress after Myrdal. *Journal of Economic Literature, 27,* 519–564.

SMOLAK, L. (1986). *Infancy.* Englewood Cliffs, NJ: Prentice-Hall.

SNAREY, J., REIMER, J., & KOHLBERG, L. (1985). Development of social-moral reasoning among Kibbutz adolescents: A longitudinal cross-cultural study. *Developmental Psychology, 17,* 3–17.

SNAREY, J., SON, L., KUEHEN, V., HAUSER, S., & VALLIANT, G. (1987). The role of parenting in men's psychosocial development: A longitudinal study of early adulthood infertility and midlife generativity. *Developmental Psychology, 23,* 593–603.

SOCIAL SECURITY ADMINISTRATION. (1986). Increasing the Social Security retirement age: Older workers in physically demanding occupations or ill health. *Social Security Bulletin, 49,* 5–23.

SOLDO, B., SHARMA, M., & CAMPBELL, R. (1984). Determinants of the community living arrangements of older unmarried women. *Journal of Gerontology, 39,* 492–498.

SOMMERS, T., & SHIELDS, L. (1978). Problems of the displaced homemaker. In *Women in midlife—security and fulfillment.* Washington, DC: Government Printing Office.

SPANIER, G. (1983). Married and unmarried cohabitation in the United States. *Journal of Marriage and the Family, 45,* 277–288.

SPENCER, M. (1985). *Foundations of modern society.* Englewood Cliffs, NJ: Prentice-Hall.

SPITZE, G., & LOGAN, J. (1989). Gender differences in family support: Is there a payoff? *The Gerontologist, 29,* 108–113.

SPITZE, G., & LOGAN, J. (1990). Sons, daughters, and intergenerational social support. *Journal of Marriage and the Family, 52,* 420–430.

SPITZER, M. (1988). Taste acuity in institutionalized and noninstitutionalized elderly men. *Journal of Gerontology, 43,* P71–74.

STAGNER, R. (1985). Aging in industry. In J. Birren & K. Schaie (eds.), *The handbook of the psychology of aging* (2d ed.) (pp. 789–817). New York: Van Nostrand.

STAINES, G., POTTICK, K., & FUDGE, D. (1986). Wives' employment and husbands' attitudes toward work and life. *Journal of Applied Psychology, 71,* 118–128.

STAPP, J., FULCHER, R., NELSON, S., PALLAK, M., & WICHERSKI, M. (1981). The employment of recent doctorate recipients in psychology: 1975–1978. *American Psychologist, 36,* 1211–1254.

STATTIN, H., & MAGNUSSON, D. (1990). *Pubertal maturation in female development.* Hillsdale, NJ: Erlbaum.

STEFFENSMEIER, R. (1982). A role model of the transition to parenthood. *Journal of Marriage and the Family, 42,* 319–334.

STEINBERG, L. (1987). Bound to bicker. *Psychology Today, 21* (9), 36–39.

STEINER-ADAIR, C. (1991). New maps of development, new models of therapy: The psychology of women and the treatment of eating disorders. In C. Johnson (ed.), *Psychodynamic treatment of anorexia nervosa and bulimia* (pp. 225–244). New York: Guilford.

STERNBERG, R. (1986). A triangular theory of love. *Psychological Review, 93,* 119–135.

STERNS, H., BARRETT, G., & ALEXANDER, R. (1985). Accidents and the aging individual. In J. Birren & K. Schaie (eds.), *Handbook of the psychology of aging* (2d ed.) (pp. 706–724). New York: Van Nostrand.

STEWART, A. (1978). A longitudinal study of coping styles in self-defining and socially defined women. *Journal of Consulting and Clinical Psychology, 46,* 1079–1084.

STEWART, A., & SALT, P. (1981). Life stress, lifestyles, depression, and illness in adult women. *Journal of Personality and Social Psychology, 40,* 1063–1069.

STEVENS, D., & TRUSS, C. (1985). Stability and change in adult personality. *Developmental Psychology, 21,* 568–584.

STILLER, N., & FOREST, L. (1990). An extension of Gilligan and Lyons's investigation of morality: Gender differences in college students. *Journal of College Student Development, 31,* 54–63.

STILLION, J. (1985). *Death and the sexes: An examination of differential longevity, attitudes, behaviors, and coping styles.* Washington, DC: Hemisphere Publishing.

STOCKTON, N., BERRY, J., SHEPSON, J. & UTZ, P. (1980). Sex-role and innovative major choice among college students. *Journal of Vocational Behavior, 16,* 360–367.

STONE, R., CAFFERATA, G., & SANGL, J. (1987). Caregivers of the frail elderly: A national survey. *The Gerontologist, 27,* 616–626.

STRAITS, B. (1985). Factors influencing college women's responses to fertility decision-making vignettes. *Journal of Marriage and the Family, 49,* 585–596.

STRANGE, C., & REA, J. (1983). Career-choice considerations and sex role self-concept of male and female undergraduates in nontraditional majors. *Journal of Vocational Behavior, 23,* 219–226.

STRAUMANIS, J. (1986). The case against human sociobiology. Unpublished manuscript.

STROEBE, W., & STROEBE, M. (1987). *Bereavement and health: The psychological and physical consequences of partner loss.* New York: Cambridge University Press.

SUAREZ, E., WILLIAMS, R., KUHN, C., ZIMMERMAN, E., & SCHANBERG, S. (1991). Biobehavioral basis of coronary-prone behavior in middle-aged men. Part II: serum cholesterol, the Type A behavior pattern, and hostility as interactive modulators of physiological reactivity. *Psychosomatic Medicine, 53,* 528–537.

SUGGS, D. (1987). Female status and role transition in the Tswana life cycle. *Ethnology, 26,* 107–120.

SULLIVAN, K., & SULLIVAN, A. (1980). Adolescent-parent separation. *Developmental Psychology, 16,* 93–99.

SUPER, D. (1953). A theory of vocational development. *American Psychologist, 8,* 185–190.

SUPER, D. (1957). *The psychology of careers: An introduction to vocational development.* New York: Harper & Row.

SUPER, D. (1985). Coming of age in Middletown: Careers in the making. *American Psychologist, 40,* 405–414.

SUPER, D., STARISHEVSKY, R., MATLIN, N., & JORDAN, J. (1963). *Career development: Self-concept theory.* New York: College Entrance Examination Board.

SUSSMAN, M. (1985). The family life of old people. In R. Binstock & E. Shanas (eds.), *Handbook of aging and the social sciences* (2d ed.) (pp. 415–449). New York: Van Nostrand.

SUTKER, P. (1982). Adolescent drug and alcohol behaviors. In T. Field, A. Huston, H. Quay, L. Troll, & G. Finley (eds.), *Review of human development research* (pp. 356–380). New York: Wiley.

SUTTON-SMITH, B., & ROSENBERG, B. (1970). *The sibling.* New York: Holt, Rinehart & Winston.

SWAM, G., DAME, A. & CARMELLI, D. (1991). Involuntary retirement, Type A behavior, and current functioning in elderly men: 27-year follow-up on the Western Collaborative Group Study. *Psychology and Aging, 6,* 384–391.

SWANSON, J., & HANSEN, J. (1985). The relationship of the construct of academic comfort to educational level, performance, aspirations, and prediction of college major choices. *Journal of Vocational Behavior, 26,* 1–12.

SWIFT, W., ANDREWS, D., & BARKLAGE, N. (1986). The relationship between affective disorder and eating disorders: A review of the literature. *The American Journal of Psychiatry, 143,* 290–299.

TAYLOR, R., & CHATTERS, L. (1988). Correlates of education, income, and poverty among aged blacks. *The Gerontologist, 28,* 435–441.

TERI, L., & REIFLER, B. (1987). Depression and dementia. In L. Carstensen & B. Edelstein (eds.), *Handbook of clinical gerontology.* New York: Pergamon Press.

TESCH, S., & WHITBOURNE, S. (1982). Intimacy and identity status in young adults. *Journal of Personality and Social Psychology, 43,* 1041–1051.

THOMAS, A., & CHESS, S. (1980). *Dynamics of psychological development.* New York: Brunner/Mazel.

THOMPSON, L., & WALKER, A. (1987). Mothers as mediators of intimacy between grandmothers and their young adult granddaughters. *Family Relations, 36,* 72–77.

TICE, R., & SETLOW, R. (1985). DNA repair and replication in aging organisms and cells. In C. Finch & E. Schneider (eds.), *Handbook of the biology of aging* (2d ed.) (pp. 173–224). New York: Van Nostrand.

TIEDJE, L., WORTMAN, C., DOWNEY, G., EMMONS, C., BIERNAT, M., & LANG, E. (1990). Women with multiple roles: Role-compatibility perceptions, satisfaction, and mental health. *Journal of Marriage and the Family, 52,* 63–72.

TIMERAS, P. (1972). *Developmental physiology and aging.* New York: Macmillan.

TISCHLER, H., WHITTEN, P., & HUNTER, D. (1983). *Introduction to sociology.* New York: Holt, Rinehart & Winston.

TODD, M., DAVIS, K., & CAFFERTY, T. (1983/1984). Who volunteers for adult development research? Research findings and practical steps to reach low volunteering groups. *International Journal of Aging and Human Development, 18,* 177–184.

TOMLINSON-KEASEY, C. (1972). Formal operations in females from eleven to fifty-six years of age. *Developmental Psychology, 6,* 364.

TROLL, L. (1980). Grandparenting. In L. Poon (ed.), *Aging in the 1980s* (pp. 475–481). Washington, DC: American Psychological Association.

TROLL, L. (1982). *Continuations: Adult development and Aging.* Monterey, CA: Brooks/Cole.

TROLL, L. (1985). The contingencies of grandparenting. In V. Bengston & J. Robertson (eds.), *Grandparenthood* (pp. 135–150). Beverly Hills: Sage.

TROST, C. (1986). The new majorities: The pink-collar ghettos. *Wall Street Journal,* March 24, 1986, p.15D.

TURRINI, P. (1980). Psychological crises in normal pregnancy. In B. Blum (ed.), *Psychological aspects of pregnancy, birthing, and bonding.* New York: Human Sciences Press.

U.S. DEPARTMENT OF COMMERCE. (1987). *The statistical abstract of the U.S.: 1987.* Washington, DC: Government Printing Office.

U.S. DEPARTMENT OF COMMERCE. (1990). *The*

statistical abstract of the U.S.: 1990. Washington, DC: Government Printing Office.

U.S. DEPARTMENT OF HEALTH AND HUMAN SERVICES. (1986). *Drug use among American high school students, college students, and other young adults.* Washington, DC.

VACHON, M. (1986). A comparison of the impact of breast cancer and bereavement: Personality, social support, and adaptation. In S. Hobfoll (ed.), *Stress, social support, and women.* Washington, DC: Hemisphere.

VALLIANT, G. (1977). *Adaptation to life.* Boston: Little, Brown.

VESTAL, R., & DAWSON, G. (1985). Pharmacology and aging. In C. Finch & E. Schneider (eds.), *Handbook of the biology of aging* (2d ed.) (pp. 744-819). New York: Van Nostrand.

VISHER, E., & VISHER, J. (1983). Stepparenting: Blending families. In H. McCubbin & C. Figley (eds.), *Stress and the family* (Vol. 1). New York: Brunner/Mazel.

VITALIANO, P., RUSSO, J., YOUNG, H., TERI, L., & MAIURO. R. (1991). Predictors of burden in spouse caregivers of individuals with Alzheimer's disease. *Psychology and Aging, 6,* 392-402.

WALASKAY, M., WHITBOURNE, S., & NEHRKE, M. (1983-1984). Construction and validation of an ego status integrity interview. *International Journal of Aging and Human Development, 18,* 61-72.

WALDMAN, D., & AVOLIO, B. (1986). A meta-analysis of age differences in job performance. *Journal of Applied Psychology, 71,* 33-38.

WALKER, L. J. (1984). Sex differences in the development of moral reasoning: A critical review. *Child Development, 55,* 677-691.

WALKER, L. J. (1986). Sex differences in the development of moral reasoning.: A rejoinder to Baumrind. *Child Development, 57,* 522-526.

WALKER, L., & WALLSTON, B. (1985). Social adaptation: A review of dual earner family literature. In L. L'Abate (ed.), *Handbook of family psychology and therapy* (pp. 698-740). Homewood, IL: Dorsey.

Wall Street Journal, February 14, 1989, p. A16.

WALLACE, P., & GOTLIB, I. (1990). Marital adjustment during the transition to parenthood: Stability and predictors of change. *Journal of Marriage and the Family, 52,* 21-29.

WALLACE, R., & WALLACE, W. (1985). *Sociology.* Boston: Allyn & Bacon.

WALLERSTEIN, J. (1983). Children of divorce: Stress and developmental tasks. In N. Garmezy & M. Rutter (eds.), *Stress, coping, and development in children.* New York: McGraw-Hill.

WALLERSTEIN, J., & BLAKESLEE, S. (1989). *Second chances: Men, women, and children a decade after divorce.* New York: Ticknor & Fields.

WARE, N., & STECKLER, N. (1983). Choosing a science major: The experience of women and men. *Women's Studies Quarterly, 11,* 12-15.

WARREN, R. M., & WARREN, R. P. (1966). A comparison of speech perception in childhood, maturity, and old age by means of the verbal transformation effect. *Journal of Verbal Learning and Verbal Behavior, 5,* 142-146.

WATERMAN, A. (1982). Identity development from adolescence to adulthood; An extension of theory and a review of research. *Developmental Psychology, 18,* 341-358.

WATERMAN, A., & GOLDMAN, J. (1976). A longitudinal study of ego identity development at a liberal arts college. *Journal of Youth and Adolescence, 5,* 361-370.

WATERMAN, A., GEARY, P., & WATERMAN, C. (1974). A longitudinal study of changes in ego identity status from the freshman to the senior year at college. *Developmental Psychology, 10,* 387-392.

WATERMAN, A., & WATERMAN, C. (1971). A longitudinal study of changes in ego identity status during the freshman year at college. *Developmental Psychology, 5,* 167-173.

WECHSLER, D. (1939). *The measurement of adult intelligence* Baltimore: Williams & Wilkins.

WEG, R. (1975). Changing physiology of aging: Normal and pathological. In D. Woodruff & J. Birren (eds.), *Aging: Scientific perspectives and social issues* (pp. 229-256). New York: Van Nostrand.

WEIDEGER, P. (1976). *Menstruation and menopause.* New York: Knopf.

WEINER, I., & MUDGE, G. (1985). Diuretics and other agents employed in the mobilization of edema fluid. In A. Gilman, L. Goodman, T. Rall, & F. Murad (eds.), *Goodman and Gilman's The pharmacological basis of therapeutics* (7th ed.) (pp. 887-907). New York: Macmillan.

WEINER, N., (1985). Drugs that inhibit andrenergic nerves and block adrenergic receptors. In A. Gilman, L. Goodman, T. Rall, & F. Murad (eds.), *Goodman and Gilman's The pharmacological basis of therapeutics* (7th ed.) (pp. 181-214). New York: Macmillan.

WEISSMAN, M., & MYERS, J. (1978). Affective disorders in a U.S. urban community. *Archives of General Psychiatry, 35,* 1304-1311.

WEITZMAN, L. (1984). *The divorce revolution.* New York: Free Press.

WELFORD, A. (1977). Motor performance. In J. Birren & K. Schaie (eds.), *Handbook of the psychology of aging* (pp. 450–496). New York: Van Nostrand.

WENTOWSKI, G. (1985). Older women's perceptions of great-grandparenthood: A research note. *The Gerontologist, 28,* 593–596.

WERNER, H. (1948). *Comparative psychology of mental development.* New York: International Universities Press.

WHITBOURNE, S. (1985). The psychological construction of the life span. In J. Birren & K. Schaie (eds.), *Handbook of the psychology of aging* (2d ed.) (pp. 594–618). New York: Van Nostrand Reinhold.

WHITE, N., & CUNNINGHAM, W. (1988). Is terminal drop pervasive or specific? *Journal of Gerontology, 43,* 141–144.

WILLAMS, R., SUAREZ, E., KUHN, C., ZIMMERMAN, E., & SCHANBERG, S. (1991). Biobehavioral basis of coronary-prone behavior in middle-aged men. Part I: Evidence for chronic SNS activation in Type As. *Psychosomatic Medicine, 53,* 517–527.

WILLIS, S. (1985). Towards an educational psychology of the older adult learner: Intellectual and cognitive bases. In J. Birren & K. Schaie (eds.), *Handbook of the psychology of aging* (2d ed.) (pp. 818–847). New York: Van Nostrand Reinhold.

WILLIS, S. (1990). Introduction to the special section on cognitive training in later adulthood. *Developmental Psychology, 26,* 875–878.

WILLIS, S., & NESSELROADE, C. (1990). Long-term effects of fluid ability training in old-old age. *Developmental Psychology, 26,* 905–910.

WILSON, E. O. (1975). *Sociobiology: The new synthesis.* Cambridge, MA: Harvard University Press.

WINDLEY, P., & SCHEIDT, R. (1980). Person-environment dialectics: Implications for competent functioning in old age. In L. Poon (ed.), *Aging in the 1980s* (pp. 407–423). Washington, DC: American Psychological Association.

WINICH, R. (1958). *Mate selection.* New York: Harper & Bros.

WOODRUFF, D. (1978). Brain electrical activity and behavior relationships over the life span. In P. Baltes (ed.), *Life-span development and behavior.* New York: Academic Press.

WOODRUFF, D. (1985). Arousal, sleep, and aging. In J. Birren & K. Schaie (eds.), *Handbook of the psychology of aging* (2d ed.), (pp. 262–295). New York: Van Nostrand.

WOODRUFF, D., & BIRREN, J. (1972). Age changes and cohort differences in personality. *Developmental Psychology, 6,* 252–259.

World Almanac. (1981). *The Hammond Almanac: 1980.* Maplewood, NJ: Hammond Almanac Inc.

WURTMAN, R. (1985). Alzheimer's disease. *Scientific American, 252,* 62–75.

YALOM, M., ESTLER, S., & BREWSTER, W. (1982). Changes in female sexuality: A study of mother/daughter communication and generational differences. *Psychology of Women Quarterly, 7,* 141–154.

YANKLELOVICH, D. (1974). *The new morality: A profile of American youth in the 70's.* New York: McGraw-Hill.

ZARIT, S., EILER, J., & HASSINGER, M. (1985). Clinical assessment. In J. Birren & K. Schaie (eds.), *Handbook of the psychology of aging* (2d ed.) (pp. 725–754). New York: Van Nostrand.

ZASLOW, M., PEDERSEN, F., KRAMER, E., CAIN, R., SUWALSKY, J., & FIVEL, M. (1981). Depressed mood in new fathers: Interview and behavioral correlates. Presented at the Society for Research in Child Development, Boston.

ZIMBERG, S. (1987). Alcohol abuse among the elderly. In L. Carstensen & B. Edelstein (eds.), *Handbook of clinical gerontology* (pp. 57–65). New York: Pergamon.

ZUCKERMAN, D. (1980). Self-esteem, personal traits, and college women's life goals. *Journal of Vocational Behavior, 17,* 310–319.

ZUENGLER, K., & NEUBECK, G. (1983). Sexuality: Developing togetherness. In H. McCubbin & C. Figley (eds.), *Stress and the family* (Vol. 1). New York: Brunner/Mazel.

Photo Credits

Index

AUTHOR INDEX

SUBJECT INDEX